ICELAND

Hvalfjördhur

20°

10°

FAEROE ISLANDS

D1599360

Londonderry

IRELAND

Liverpool

ENGLAND

FRANCE

PORTUGAL

SPAIN

AZORES

MR.
ROOSEVELT'S
NAVY

PATRICK ABBAZIA

MR. ROOSEVELT'S NAVY

THE PRIVATE WAR OF THE

U. S. ATLANTIC FLEET, 1939-1942

NAVAL INSTITUTE PRESS   ANNAPOLIS, MARYLAND

For My Parents, Who Believed

An ill-favoured thing, sir, but mine own.

Shakespeare, As You Like It

Before you judge this or that officer harshly . . . imagine yourself on the bridge of a little ship, in pitch black night, with the wind howling and spray drenching you continually, and in close proximity to a hundred other ships that you can feel but not see. Then imagine an emergency of some sort—a collision, a submarine attack, an engine breakdown—and decide whether you could make a quick and correct decision!

John W. Schmidt, U. S. Navy

Oh, they've got no time for glory in the Infantry . . . .

Frank Loesser, The Ballad of Rodger Young

40°   20°   0°   20°

GREENLAND

DENMARK STRAIT

ICELAND

Reykjavik

Trondheim

Faeroe Is.

Scapa Flow

EUROPE

Cape Farewell

Hamburg

London

Bremen

Wilhelmshaven

Londonderry

Liverpool

Plymouth

Portsmouth

St. Nazaire

Lorient

La Rochelle

Bay of Biscay

Rochefort

40°

Valladolid

AZORES

Corvo

Horta

Lisbon

Flores

Terceira

Fayal

Strait of Gibraltar

Ponta Delgada

San Miguel

Canary Islands

20°

Cape Verde Islands

Dakar

Lagos

0°

Natal

Recife

Bahia (Salvador)

Ascension Is.

Contents

Preface

CURIOSITY IS THE BEST PROD OF RESEARCH, and this book has its origins in curiosity. As student and historian, I have long had an interest in strategic studies and the study of battle; and when reading the history of World War II, I sometimes came upon brief, cryptic, tantalizing references to American combat operations at sea months before the Japanese attack at Pearl Harbor. For the U.S. Navy was at war in the Atlantic long before 7 December 1941: the first American warship to sustain damage and loss of life in battle in World War II was the destroyer USS *Kearny*, torpedoed in the North Atlantic more than seven weeks before Pearl Harbor; the first American warship sunk in combat in World War II was the destroyer USS *Reuben James*, torpedoed in the North Atlantic more than five weeks before Pearl Harbor. Surely such combat reflected wider operations, and suggested an undeclared naval war in the Atlantic. What were those operations? What exactly was the U.S. Navy's role in the Battle of the Atlantic prior to American entry into the war? To what extent was the Navy escorting Allied convoys? Were there many contacts and battles with German U-boats? Were there many casualties? Were there morale problems, as there often are in limited, undeclared wars? What were the problems, hardships, and lessons of early naval operations in the Atlantic? Numerous tactical questions suggested themselves. And the tactical questions suggested strategic questions. To what extent was the classic American strategy of sea power still valid in the age of the airplane and submarine? What was the U.S. Navy's state of readiness to conduct modern operations of sea warfare at the outset of World War II? How did Franklin Roosevelt manage and control "his" Navy's limited, undeclared war? The numbers of my questions increased, but I found scant answers in published sources; most historians of naval operations were primarily concerned with post-1941 events and the great battles of the Pacific War.

Then necessity prodded curiosity. Wanting a topic for scholarly research, I was determined to work in some area of the operational history of World War II; much of that area having been amply written about (although not always adequately researched), I sought a virgin corner of the field. The merger of curiosity and necessity produced a decision to write a study of the U.S. Atlantic Fleet and its role in the undeclared war and after.

The result of my research is this book. It is the story of a fleet, the U.S. Atlantic Fleet, its education at war, and its impact upon strategy.

And perhaps the best reason why the story of the Atlantic Fleet needs to be told can be summed up in a personal anecdote. Recently, I was sitting in my college office, passing time in a pleasant discussion of historical topics with several colleagues. The subject turned to the high quality of American military and naval leadership at the time of World War II, and I contributed a few sea stories about the redoubtable Admiral Ernest J. King; then while making a point about pre-war planning, I happened to mention the sinking of the *Reuben James* with heavy loss of life on Halloween morning, 1941. Surprised, one of my colleagues, a capable professor who has taught American history at the college level for seven years, interrupted, saying, "Wait a minute. That was before Pearl Harbor! What was the Navy doing at war in the Atlantic at that time?"

I told him to read this book.

Prologue

The President
Defines
the Problem

IT WAS ONLY EIGHT DAYS before Christmas, 1937, but none of the men
seated at the long table in the Cabinet Room took note of the season.
Five days earlier, Japanese aircraft had bombed and sunk the U.S.
gunboat *Panay* in the shallows of the Yangtze River. And now, the
Secretary of the Navy, Claude A. Swanson, was telling his colleagues
and President Franklin Roosevelt what should be done about this
latest crisis in the Far East. Swanson was a stiff, gaunt man; seriously
ill, he could not stand up unsupported. White-haired and sallow, he
spoke earnestly, a long, full, gray moustache rising and falling with
the movement of his lips. He spoke in a thick, gravelly voice which
made it difficult for his listeners to understand what he was saying.
Sometimes his words gargled together, and only harsh rasps, scratchy
and phlegmy, could be heard above the small, restless noises that men
make when they are listening to another speak. Secretary Swanson
spoke of the need for force; at the least, the U.S. Fleet should be
moved from the West Coast to Hawaii.

In a dreamy, distracted way, the crotchety Secretary of the Interior,
Harold L. Ickes, evaluated the proposals of his infirm colleague. He
sensed in Swanson's urgency something of the shiny-eyed tenacity of
the half-dead man who wants to precipitate grand events to mark his
passing. Ickes had absorbed much of the strident, ingenuous pacifism
of the liberalism of his generation; indeed, he had once deemed it
virtually immoral for the President to allocate WPA funds to the

3

construction of warships. Yet, increasingly, he was coming to believe that he who turns the other cheek gets slapped with the other hand; he feared that only force might restrain the totalitarian regimes. So, almost despite himself, Ickes wondered if the Secretary of the Navy might not be right. If we had to fight, he told himself, perhaps it was a case of better now than later.

Henry Morgenthau, the balding, sad-eyed Secretary of the Treasury, knew that the old man was saying things that needed to be said. Morgenthau had moved through this dismal week with an ache of rage and shame stabbing at him with the remorseless insistence of an abscessed tooth. Outraged by the Japanese attack, he was appalled and then ashamed at the number of people in the government who preferred to ignore the fate of the *Panay*. To Morgenthau, this was not only bad policy, but also bad morality; a nation had to protect its own. His Department was studying the feasibility of seizing Japanese assets in the United States, and he hoped that the President would announce measures of firmness. Three days ago, Franklin Roosevelt had told him that in the old days the sinking of an American vessel would have automatically been considered an act of war.

But the President had known all week that neither the state of the nation's arms nor the temper of its people was equal to the task of restraining Japan. The Japanese seemed willing to make reparation for the "incident," and the President wanted a quick and discreet settlement. Now, the President interrupted Swanson to remark that he wanted to achieve the same ends in the Pacific—but without risking war. He then turned the discussion toward vaguer and safer ground, the possibility of economic sanctions and a "quarantine" of the aggressor states.

But Franklin Roosevelt knew that there were likely to be other such galling episodes, and it profoundly annoyed him that the totalitarian powers were able to achieve diplomatic victories and territorial conquests without formally making war. They achieved their ambitions in a world technically at peace through "civil wars," "undeclared wars," and "incidents," lulling other nations by an avoidance of full-scale, overt war. The President felt that the United States might have to develop a similar technique. And so he told his Cabinet, "If Italy and Japan have evolved a technique of fighting without declaring war, why can't we develop a similar one?"

Thus, on 17 December 1937, President Franklin Roosevelt defined the problem.[1]

A few days later, Captain Royal E. Ingersoll, head of the War Plans Division of the Office of Naval Operations, was invited to the White House. Ingersoll was a "rumpled," scholarly officer with a bent for staff work and a distaste for publicity. The President ordered him to Britain to discuss the possibility of Anglo-American naval cooperation, but he was to make "no commitments" on behalf of the United States. Ingersoll understood. As he explained, "We had to make preliminary arrangements to explore what could be done—for communicating with each other, for establishing liaison, intelligence, and other things, so if war did come we would not be floundering around for months until we got together."[2]

The President had taken his first step toward a policy of "fighting without declaring war." It was merely a small, tentative step, but in due time, his pace would quicken, and ships yet unbuilt would steam away on business in great waters.

I:

Early Days in the Atlantic

1.

Bending the Pencil

THE MAJOR FUNCTION OF THE NAVY of the thirties was training.

The service enjoyed high-quality personnel because the Great Depression allowed its recruiters to exercise an unprecedented selectivity. For example, between July 1938 and June 1939, 159,409 volunteers were examined, but only 14,512—9 percent—were accepted. The average recruit had 2.9 years of high school education. Reenlistment rates were extremely high: 72.2 percent in 1938, 80.8 percent in 1939, and 73.0 percent to the middle of 1941; desertions were negligible, averaging only about sixty a year. The result was an experienced, thoroughly professional service.[1]

Because of the stability of personnel and economies necessitated by the Depression, the rate of promotion was very slow. Men were occasionally sent home on payless "furloughs," Naval Academy classes were cut back, and in 1933, only part of the graduating class was commissioned. Nevertheless,

> While reduced appropriations forced the Navy to cut down on personnel, the lack of civilian jobs . . . increased the desirability of getting into the Navy and staying in.
>
> Economically, the naval officer . . . was very well off compared to his civilian contemporaries. In many of the principal "home ports" . . . the average lieutenant lived in a rented two or three bedroom house and employed a full-time maid . . . . At the same time civilian graduates of good colleges were manning the pumps at gas stations . . . .[2]

The slow tempo of promotion kept men in grade for a long time, giving them ample experience at their job and resulting in highly efficient crews. But the desire of men to stand out in order to qualify for promotion thus intensified the significance of competitive training exercises.

The Navy was able to use a large proportion of its funds for training, unlike the Army, which had to spend excessive amounts on maintaining obsolete posts and bases due to Congressional pressure. And it was generally understood that the Navy would have to fight immediately in event of war, perhaps before it called up its reserves, digested masses of recruits, or acquired more modern equipment. Hence, training was conducted with greater flavor of urgency in the Navy[3] than the Army.*

There were various competitions to measure the performance of men and ships.

In the engineering competition, each ship was assigned an annual fuel allowance; her "score" was the ratio between the amount of fuel allocated and the amount consumed. But ships that did well found their allowances lowered each year until even prodigies of economy could not produce a low enough ratio of consumption to win an efficiency pennant. In certain vessels, use of fresh water, light, and heat was restricted. In one ship, a young officer suggested that the running lights be turned off at night, thus risking collision in order to save an amount of fuel so small that the engineers could not even measure it. Captains gave prizes to those watches during which the least quantity of oil was burned; others toured the ship, unscrewed all standard light bulbs, and replaced them with bulbs of lower wattage.[4] Arrivals and departures, alterations of course and speed, and other routine activities were often governed by a desire to raise engineering scores.

> Engineering officers not only worked hard at engineering efficiency but also at ways to "beat the competition" without breaking the rules. They became the corporate tax lawyers of their day—it was called "bending the pencil."[5]

But the mandate to save fuel restricted innovative exercises and useful steaming—in practices, battleships were usually limited to a

---

*In the Air Corps in the 1930's ". . . we were operating under the old Army principle: you never fight the outfits which you have in peace. You're actually just a holding operation, to develop new tactics perhaps — new equipment, new training measures and aids. But when war comes . . . you will need to form your outfits from the Reserves, and build them up. Then, eventually, you . . . fight."

speed of 15 knots and other warships to 24 knots: thus, savings and material upkeep were often purchased in another coin and at too high a price, tactical creativity.

The most important of the competitions were the gunnery exercises. The reputations of men and ships were at stake in these contests, and feelings of rivalry were intense; but the activity was inherently pleasing, and a holiday atmosphere attended these occasions. Practices were held in good weather in a southerly clime, the idea being that a crew could learn more from a successful "shoot" than a poor one, although many felt such training limited the quality of naval gunnery under more realistic battle conditions. Still, eccentricities of wind or sea, or a busy operating schedule that precluded preliminary range-taking, might serve to hamper an unlucky vessel and impair her crew's chance for recognition and promotion.

Short-range gunnery was highly accurate, but as distance increased, precision declined dramatically. The major problem was inability to judge fall of shot accurately. To spotters, most shell splashes appeared to fall "just over the [target] raft"; so they called for minor adjustments in range instead of trying to cross and recross the target systematically. Constant personnel shifts also reduced gunnery efficiency. The annual turnover on most ships was about 85 percent; in one cruiser, for almost a year, "no two successive practices were fired with the same crew." The vessels were undermanned by about 15 percent in order to keep as many as possible in operation; the result was an admirable versatility, but such specialized endeavors as gunnery suffered from the diffusion of talent. The system of frequent transfers had evolved prior to World War I when the Navy was small and its few ships were dispersed throughout the world; it helped to standardize practices amongst far-flung ships and stations and helped morale, as well, by limiting a sailor's tour of duty on an undesirable station.[6] But the policy was out of place in the large and concentrated fleet of the 1930s:

> One of our ships fires a long-range battle practice in the spring and attains the highest score ever made. The officers and men participating are jubilant; the rest of the Navy rejoices because it proves we can shoot. What happens? Three months later probably half the officers and crew of that very efficient vessel are scattered to the four winds. [7]

For example, in the summer of 1938, the destroyer *Simpson* led her flotilla in short-range fire, with twenty-two hits in twenty-eight shots; in the spring of 1939, the *Simpson* was last in her flotilla in a long-range battle practice, scoring not a single hit in forty-five shots. The destroyer *Tucker* went from the worst gunnery score in her division to the best in the entire flotilla in fourteen months.[8]

In 1937 and 1938, in the highly successful short-range practices, the battleships averaged 87.7 percent hits; only once in the decade of the thirties did the percentage of hits drop below 80. But at more realistic ranges, the scores fell. In the summer of 1938, heavy cruisers fired 669 rounds of 8-inch at target sleds an average of 5,249 yards away, still reasonably close range; but only sixteen hits (2.4 percent) were scored.[9]

In July 1938, the results of an excellent cruiser "shoot" were:[10]

	Shots	Hits		Shots	Hits
Northampton	89	0	Chester	90	5
Pensacola	97	5	New Orleans	89	1
Salt Lake City	100	5	Houston	87	0
Indianapolis	89	3	Tuscaloosa	89	8
Chicago	86	3	Quincy	90	4

In March 1938, the battleships held a gunnery practice. *Arizona* suffered from poor spotting and worse luck; a powder charge misfired, causing five casualties. *California* lost sight of her sled in the haze of blue-gray gunsmoke and ignominiously bombarded the wrong target. *Colorado* displayed a rapid rate of fire and neat, tightly bunched patterns; four minutes of her fire would have disabled any ship. *Idaho* also sustained a rapid rate of fire, but her accuracy suffered as a result. *Maryland* spotted methodically and so had a slow rate of fire; a deflection error further lowered her score. *Mississippi* was unwilling to shoot while making a turn and had a slow rate of fire. *Nevada*'s first salvos were extremely wild due to a deflection error, but her gunners retained their poise under pressure and turned in a better-than-average performance despite the bad start. *New Mexico* straddled the sled with her first salvo, but poor spotting then lowered her score. *Oklahoma* took too much time spotting and thus had a low volume of fire. *Pennsylvania* fired rapidly, but poor spotting marred her accuracy. *Tennessee* was "unsatisfactory" because she had mediocre spotting and a low volume of fire; her third salvo straddled the target, but the next eleven salvos all fell well short. *West Virginia* shot wildly at times, but maintained a rapid rate of fire and showed some good deflection shooting. The report on the exercise noted: "Improper spotting is the outstanding cause of the majority of poor performances." Admiral Claude Bloch, commander of Battle Force, penciled on the report the acid comment: "Isn't it possible to insure more spotting training by demanding attendance of spotters at firings of *all other divisions*? Or would the ship's service and the basketball team suffer too much?"[11]

In combat, it was expected that warships would average about two hits for each hundred rounds fired.

Surface torpedo practices were somewhat artificial, especially after 1921 when Commander William F. Halsey's destroyers in a clever close-range attack scored twenty-two dummy-warhead torpedo hits on four battleships, which cost over $1½ million to repair. Torpedo firings were done at excessive range versus vessels operating at moderate speeds, and computed scores indicated an improbably high level of accuracy; it was thought that a torpedo salvo from a destroyer would get a hit on a major target (a light cruiser or larger warship) in a ratio of about thirty-two out of seventy chances.[12] The Fleet did not know that its torpedoes were defective, a result of peacetime parsimony and the stupid complacency of bureaucrats and technicians in precluding effective testing.

Exercises were important in the development of tactics, ship-handling, and a feel for the chaos of combat. For example, in February 1938, three groups of destroyers learned a lesson when they essayed a coordinated torpedo attack on the battleline. As they approached, the searchlight-simulated fire of the battleships forced the destroyers to take evasive action which resulted in crowding, producing confusion and the need to slow speed to 10 knots to avoid collision. In the attack, one division of ships did not bother to compute a base torpedo course, relying on the division leader's signals to release their "fish" at the proper time. However, they misread a course signal from the flagship, fired at the wrong moment, and all eight torpedoes passed well ahead of the battleships, some as much as 7,000 yards ahead! One commander seethed: "Steps will . . . be taken to prevent the occurrence of any future incidents of this nature."[13]

Most naval officers of the thirties sensed that the shape of their professional lives would be altered by the airplane; yet at the same time, many were repelled by the oversimplified claims of the advocates of air power, who promised "to sink all surface craft like tin cans under a shower of destruction from the skies." It was understood that the airplane, because of its range, would be used first in major sea battles, and that the advantage in war would be on the side of the fleet that had command of the air, even if only for improved gunnery spotting. However, as the planes lacked speed and sufficient bomb capacity, many of them would be lost and they would be unable to halt the advance of the two battle lines.[14]   In exercises, when the contending air contingents were expended, the "preliminary round" would be over and "the championship bout between the heavyweight craft" could proceed, "or else money refunded."[15]

Training exercises seemed to bear out the conventional analysis; generally, the airplane was not a decisive weapon in the mock naval battles. The planes were used too conservatively, partly to prevent accidents. Built for stability and durability in order to survive the operational hardships of carrier duty, naval aircraft were relatively slow and undergunned, with various performance limitations: Grumman biplane and Brewster monoplane fighters were slow and inadequately armed; the Vought dive bomber was acknowledgedly "obsolescent"; and the standard torpedo bomber, the Douglas Devastator, was slow and so vulnerable to modern land-based fighters that the fliers considered it "unfit for combat service." The pilots were well trained and versatile, for the vicissitudes of carrier operations bred skill and lack of appropriations and the inherent limitations of the biplane configuration, which militated against aircraft specialization, forced the use of planes in every role, so that fliers became skilled in bomber and fighter tactics. However, since they had similar equipment and employed similar tactics, and practice odds were relatively even numerically, the normal result of the training problems was the mutual attrition of the participating air arms.[16]

The Fleet's major defense against air attack was the antiaircraft gun. The new 5-inch dual-purpose gun offered excellent protection against high-altitude, horizontal bombing, a form of attack that was correctly thought to be wildly inaccurate against maneuvering warships anyway. But the ships were defenseless against dive bombers and torpedo planes. The old, reliable .50-caliber machine gun was adapted for shipboard use as an antiaircraft weapon; unfortunately, it could not hit anything at ranges beyond 600 yards. For example, in the summer of 1938, eleven heavy cruisers fired 5,824 rounds at target sleeves, but scored only three hits (0.055 percent). Few gunners could qualify for the cash awards offered for good shooting, and faith in the weapon declined as frustration mounted. About all that could be hoped for was that a heavy volume of fire might force attacking planes to release their bombs prematurely. The vaunted 1.1-inch pom-pom, introduced with such high hopes, increased the rate of fire, but was not much more accurate than the "50" and lacked the reliability of the older gun, jamming frequently. In one practice in March of 1939, five destroyers fired 623 rounds and scored no hits. Eventually, two foreign-made weapons, the Bofors 40 mm. and Oerlikon 20 mm., solved the problem prior to World War II.[17]

But some in the Navy understood that in defending against the airplane the ancient prescription for catching a thief was relevant: it took an airplane to intercept an airplane.

In the summer of 1938, Vice Admiral Ernest J. King, Commander Aircraft, Battle Force, decided to test the ability of fighters to defend ships against land-based bombers; many felt that the defensive firepower of modern bombers made them virtually immune to successful interception. Three squadrons of patrol bombers were ordered to attack the target ship *Utah*, defended by two fighter squadrons. Relying on visual contact, the stubby fighters were able to locate and attack the lumbering PBYs before they reached their release point; according to the evidence of gun cameras, the fighters scored about seven hits for every one they sustained.* Despite artificiality in the test, King felt that "fighting planes may engage large bombers . . . with a reasonable expectancy of a favorable outcome."[18]

The results of offensive bombing strikes by naval aircraft were misleading, because of the absence of defending fighters or hostile antiaircraft fire. For instance, attacks by torpedo planes on maneuvering ships indicated that a 30 percent hit factor could be attained, even at release ranges of 3,000 yards and beyond. This was recognized as being much too optimistic, and torpedo planes were urged to close to shorter ranges.[19]

In May 1938, planes from the carriers *Lexington*, *Saratoga*, and *Ranger* conducted bombing exercises. The scout bombers made horizontal attacks from an average height of 13,700 feet and scored 16 hits with 90 bombs, 17.8 percent. The dive bombers released at an average of 3,000 feet, hitting on 51 of 101 bombs, 50.5 percent. One squadron scored heavily with a formation dive, but it was recognized that this type of attack would be too vulnerable to AA fire to be

---

*The bombers sustained about 80 .50-caliber hits per plane, the fighters 12.

used in combat. The *Ranger*'s deck hands did very well, recovering seventy-two planes in 37½ minutes, rearming seventy in 82 minutes and relaunching them in less than 24 minutes. By 1940, a squadron of planes could be launched from a carrier in 4 minutes and 57 seconds; recovery took 9 minutes and 53 seconds; speed in launching and recovering aircraft was vital, as carriers were most vulnerable during these operations. Carrier operations were the most dangerous activity of the peacetime Navy; aircraft were damaged at a rate of 5.79 per 1,000 flights.[20]

It was thought that the patrol bombers would play an important offensive role in wartime, * utilizing tenders to mount surprise attacks from advanced bases.[21] However, later experience showed that the PBYs, while possessing excellent endurance characteristics which made them ideal all-weather, high-altitude reconnaissance aircraft, lacked the speed to survive for long at altitudes at which effective bombing was feasible.

Thus, the Navy's use of the airplane in the thirties was both limited and promising. In the operating forces, practical considerations outweighed conservative theory. The airplane was, and therefore it had to be thought about, lest an officer jeopardize his career by failing in a training problem that involved aircraft. And so, tough and astute men like Admiral King were able to shape the tactics and refine the techniques needed to bring about victories under enemy skies in the distant days of more and better planes.

A major failing of the peacetime Navy was antisubmarine warfare.

Most Navies in the thirties assumed that sonar and the convoy system had ended the menace of the submarine. But technology and tactics do not long remain stagnant; the range, speed, and durability of the submarine increased, and the night surface attack replaced the daylight submerged attack, restoring to underwater craft their former superiority.[22]

American naval strategy was based on the concept of command of the seas: to destroy the main fleet of the enemy in battle, so as to secure the Western Hemisphere from attack and permit offensive operations elsewhere. A trade war seemed superfluous and timid. Hence, in peacetime exercises, submarines were employed as part of

---

*Lieutenant Commander A.B. Vosseller was one of those who believed in a significant offensive role for the PBY. In 1941, he would command a Patrol Squadron in the North Atlantic and discover that sometimes theory and practice are unfriendly companions.

the main fleet, and considered, like the airplane, a tool for whittling down the enemy battleline before it could confront the American heavy ships. American submarine tactics developed for attacking fast and well-defended warships were too cautious, relying on submerged and even futile, "blind" sonar attacks. Escort tactics suffered, too; shepherding destroyers, trained to defend fast warships, whose high speeds were nearly proof against successful attack under normal conditions and whose turbulent wakes fouled sonar equipment, became complacent and inefficient in escort technique. Without slow, unruly merchant convoys to escort in peacetime, there could be little useful antisubmarine warfare and escort doctrine, for doctrine must be built on experience. Hence, there was no agreement on such basic matters as the most effective escort formation, the optimum distance between the screening ships and the convoy, whether the escorts should patrol station, when to leave the convoy unprotected in order to dog a contact, the efficacy of illumination, precise search and attack procedures, and many other significant points of escort technique.[23]

Small escorts such as subchasers had been improvised during World War I, and many, including President Roosevelt, felt that the experience could be easily repeated, if necessary. Once Admiral King warned the President,"Nothing remains static in war or in military weapons, and it is consequently often dangerous to rely on courses suggested by apparent similarities in the past." Admiral King was right. The World War I U-boat had been forced by its limitations to operate in the immediate approaches to the United Kingdom, where interception was easiest. Hence, escorts operated out of Queenstown on relatively short trips, not having to cross the ocean, and the strain on men and ships was small. In World War II, however, escorts had to have the size and endurance to fight in mid-ocean.

The General Board of the Navy rejected various escort prototypes in the prewar years because they were almost as expensive to build as destroyers, yet nowhere as efficient or versatile. Corvettes were too slow; "Treasury"-class cutters and destroyer-escort types lacked the speed, ruggedness, versatility, and firepower of modern destroyers, and specialized escorts were not always economical—one modern destroyer could be built for less money, for example, than two proposed 875-ton antisubmarine warfare vessels. Hence, the Navy preferred to invest in the better ship, but lacked a cheap, easily produced, specialized antisubmarine type at the outbreak of war.[24]

Also, antisubmarine warfare was dependent upon World War I weapons. Depth charges had rarely been lethal in individual patterns, most submarines having been sunk by accumulated damage over long periods of attack; evidence of World War I showed that 1,000 depth charges had been expended for each U-boat sunk. Experience indicated that about 2½ hours of persistent attack were required to kill a submarine, and that it would require a pattern of forty depth charges to ensure the destruction of a located submarine. But of course, lack of means to drop depth charges as fast as that or to carry a sufficient number on ships made such huge patterns impossible.

Not only was sonar gear affected by the salinity and temperature of the water, ships' wakes, currents, fish, and debris, but the beam broke contact in the crucial attack run because the angle of the sound cone passed above the target as it was neared. Furthermore, the echo increased as the target was closed, causing the operator to believe he was on target when actually the submarine might be edging to the outer limits of the sonar beam.[25] But, as one officer noted:

> Given a true contact and a skilled sound operator the problem is still only half solved. The conning officer of the destroyer must make an accurate "landing" on an object which he cannot see and which is attempting to evade him. He must "lead" the submarine about 15 degrees as he closes to 500 yards, then order flank speed, and decrease the lead as his speed increases. Conning and timing an accurate attack requires excellent teamwork between sound operator and conning officer, which can only be developed by practice against a submarine.[26]

But destroyer practices with "live"submarines were rare; and the Key West Sound School could not adequately prepare men for the dismal water and weather conditions of the North Atlantic. As late as 1938, some destroyers had not been fitted with depth-charge racks, indicating the casual, complacent approach to antisubmarine warfare.[27] The CO of one destroyer division, noting that only two of his ships had depth charges and racks, observed, "The use of depth charges in time of war may assume great importance. . . . The theory of making depth charge attacks is well known . . . but until the practice is actually carried out, the details are usually not known and study of the problem is usually not attempted due to other more pressing work."[28]

Depth-charge battle practices usually ended with the destruction of the submarine, but these successes were artificial. They were based on certain "knowledge that a submarine was actually present in the near vicinity," and often pitted a team of five destroyers, unhampered by an array of slow, vulnerable merchant vessels, against a single submarine. It was noted that in problems where surprise was possible, the destroyers "have not shown corresponding proficiency."[29] In one practice, an attacking destroyer failed to measure the changing relative speed and bearing of the target and dropped depth charges well away from the submarine. Her companion destroyers dropped depth charges "apparently at random," with one charge, the official report caustically noted, "accidentally dropped . . . on the submarine."[30]

One prewar tactical exercise will illustrate the problems of anti-submarine warfare. In the spring of 1939, seven destroyer divisions exercised off Guantanamo Bay with "live" submarines.

The ships of Destroyer Division 2 failed to locate the *S-42*. They searched at too high speeds and thus did not hear the submarine. After slowing down, the *Dale* passed only 900 yards to port of the submarine, but was echo-ranging in the opposite direction at the time and did not detect her quarry.

DesDiv 3 located the *Perch*, but the submarine increased speed after the sonar gear lost contact, and the destroyers made their attacks too far astern; one destroyer attacked too soon and steamed into a predecessor's dummy barrage. Then the submarine turned away to starboard, creating wake-turbulence under water; the destroyermen echo-ranged on the wake, the *Perch* soon passed beyond the sound beam, and the destroyers lost contact.

DesDiv 4 picked up the *Seal* quickly and pressed home successful attacks. This was an excellent division, consistently scoring well in gunnery, too; the good ships were the *Smith*, *Cushing*, *Perkins*, and *Preston*.

DesDiv 7 found *Skipjack* quickly, but the submarine reduced speed, and *Blue* passed ahead of her; the next destroyer attacked *Blue*'s wake. The *Fanning*'s pattern was closer, and the *Blue* then attacked on target; the *Mugford*'s pattern missed astern, and *Patterson* could not get an attack off in time.

DesDiv 8 turned in an average performance. The *Cummings* found *S-43*, and the *Dunlap* and *Gridley* made competent attacks, but the *Bagley* depth-charged *Gridley*'s wake.

DesDiv 11 found the *Stingray*, but the submarine increased speed, sending out "knuckles" of water turbulence, which two of the destroyers attacked. The *Henley* underestimated the target's speed, and attacked astern; *McCall* failed to "lead" the target sufficiently, neglecting to allow for the time it took the depth charges to sink.

DesDiv 17 did not locate *S-43* at all, because of excessive speed, sporadic echo-ranging, and deteriorating water conditions.[31]

But such valuable practices were too rare, and fear of accident and personnel losses precluded realistic night destroyer-submarine training. When in January 1941 five old, slow, and cranky "S" boats "sank" three destroyers in an exercise off Panama, it was partly because none of the destroyers had ever worked with submarines before.[32] After another practice, the CO of a destroyer squadron reported that because of lack of training with "live" submarines and the newness of his skippers to their ships, his destroyers

> had not received . . . the very considerable experience apparently necessary to enable them to detect, maintain contact and attack a submerged submarine with a high degree of precision. . . . Inability of sound operators to distinguish between authentic and false contacts was an outstanding feature of the practice. . . . The procedure to be followed after the initial sound contact is made . . . appears to be highly important. Evaluation, authentication and maintenance of the contact, designation of the first vessel to attack, time of first attack and operations in connection with subsequent attacks are subjects regarding which more information and experience than now available are needed.[33]

So, too much relating to antisubmarine warfare was left undone in the thirties. Such operations were difficult with the technology available, seemed unnecessary in light of World War I experience, and lacked glamour. As one destroyerman grimly remembered, "It was the Battle of Jutland. We spent too much time fighting the Battle of Jutland."[34]

In general, then, the training cycles of the thirties reflected the expectation that naval wars of the future would be decided primarily by clashes between opposing battlelines. Technical limitations, inexperience, and conservatism hampered greater stress on aviation and submarine warfare, but the importance of the airplane was increasingly accepted, and it was understood that it was vital to achieve command of the air over the battle fleet. Gunnery was adequate, although all ships could have used more practice; antiaircraft gunnery was impaired by lack of effective short-range weapons. Results of carrier operations were impressive, but bomb and torpedo effectiveness was exaggerated by the fliers. Engineering and shiphandling were excellent. Tactics were deficient because of reluctance to train intensively at night and inexperience; the Navy had seen very little combat in World War I, and this lack of experience made it difficult to plan realistically for future war.[35]

Then, too, the promotion lag generated intense pressures in the various competitions and exercises, and the need to demonstrate efficiency sometimes took precedence over sound procedures. For instance, too many junior officers were assigned to battleships to help gun crews squeeze out a few extra hits for the ship, depriving enlisted gunners, who would have to do the job in wartime, of vital supervisory experience under pressure.[36]

Once, a ship lost her gunnery efficiency pennant because sailors from another ship, acting as umpires at a "shoot," chose to interpret the rules with unusual stringency. To balance accounts, a contingent of men off the aggrieved vessel ambushed their judges ashore and administered to them a rather severe lesson in the wisdom of tempering justice with mercy.[37]

On another occasion, a senior officer made the skipper of a sister ship run an irregular course during firing practice, so that his own destroyer might compile a better comparative score.[38]

The pressures produced two kinds of sailors: men who sought longevity in the avoidance of mistakes; and men who realized that their only security lay in maintaining a high level of professional competence, best fostered by pride and dedication. But peacetime training was only sufficiently rigorous to undermine the careless and patently unfit; it took active operations to distinguish between good shiphandlers and great captains.[39]

If not always realistic, the peacetime competitions bred alertness, willingness, and a faculty for what Hemingway called grace under pressure. More than the careful statistics of technical accomplishment recorded by the Fleet Training Division, these intangibles of the professional were the legacy that the regular sailors of the thirties left for the young volunteers of the forties.

2.

A Destroyer for
Sadie Hawkins Day

THE FIRST ATLANTIC FLEET was born in January 1906, evolving out of the old North Atlantic Station, then North Atlantic Fleet. But ironically, as a harbinger of the future, its first important mission was in the Pacific as part of Theodore Roosevelt's "Great White Fleet." In World War I, its heavy ships maintained ocean patrols, but it was the humble destroyers and subchasers that saw combat against the U-boats and won the victory at sea.

After the war, despite fears over dispersing the Navy, Secretary Josephus Daniels overruled his assistant, Franklin Roosevelt, and determined to transfer ships to the Pacific to deter Imperial Japan, which during the war had improved her strategic position by capturing Germany's Pacific islands. Thus, on 30 June 1919, half of the Atlantic forces were detached to make up the new Pacific Fleet; the latter received the more modern vessels. The shift was announced as a means of stirring a healthy spirit of rivalry in the service by creating competing fleets.

Then, in 1922, the Navy was divided into four components: Battle Force, the major task force, which comprised most of the heavy ships and was shaped to fight the main fleet engagement of the future; Scouting Force, which was organized to conduct reconnaissance in strength and thus was strong in cruisers; Control Force, which consisted of the light forces, mainly older cruisers, destroyers, and small craft, needed to defend advanced bases and lines of communication against raiders; Base Force, which conducted training and provided logistical support. The Atlantic Fleet, as such, was abolished by General Order No. 94, of 6 December 1922. Its ships were distributed between Scouting Force and Control Force. One-third of the battleships—about six—were retained with Scouting Force in the Atlantic, so that the East Coast was still well defended against all but the strongest attack.

But the task force organization, so excellent in wartime, showed weaknesses in peacetime. The ships evolved different procedures and doctrines as a result of different missions in different oceans. Since the entire Fleet would have to be concentrated in the event of war, standardized training was vital to cohesion in battle. Thus, in December 1930, type commands were set up within each task force to ensure adequate maintenance and common training. Then, in April 1931, Control Force was abolished in order to free ships for other duties; only Scouting Force remained assigned to the Atlantic.

Early in 1932, as a result of the Japanese invasion of Manchuria, Scouting Force was sent to the Pacific to join Battle Force for the annual Fleet Problem, after which it did not return to the Atlantic. Although East Coast politicians complained at the fait accompli, the transfer was a warning to Japan. Less than a score of ships, most of them old, remained in the Atlantic. These were known collectively as Training Squadron, for their major duty was to conduct the annual training cruises for midshipmen and reservists. The force consisted of the old battleships *Arkansas* and *Wyoming* and the nine four-stack destroyers of Destroyer Squadron 10. In the Canal Zone, the Special Service Squadron, or "Banana Fleet," mustered an ancient light cruiser or two, several gunboats, and in flush times, a few old four-stackers; its function was to protect Americans during the periodic revolutions of the Caribbean states. Its last significant sortie was made in August 1933, during Fulgencio Batista's "Sergeant's Revolt" in Cuba, when the light cruiser *Richmond* and several four-stackers dashed for Havana, but there proved no need for intervention. In the fall of 1936, Squadron 40-T was established to evacuate and assist American nationals in Spain during the Spanish Civil War and "keep an eye on things" in European waters. Usually consisting of an old light cruiser and a pair of four-stackers, the Squadron, basing for the most part at the French Mediterranean ports, remained on duty until October 1940. Once in the early going, off Bilbao, a Nationalist bomber mistakenly attacked the *Kane*, dropping six bombs in the water nearby; the destroyer fired two 3-inch antiaircraft rounds at the plane, but missed. Both the Forty Tares and the Banana sailors generally enjoyed cushy duty, but the former, amid the European glitter, were expected to maintain a spit-and-polish image.

In July 1937, Training Squadron became Training Detachment, and the force received reinforcement. The battleships *Texas* and *New York* joined the *Arkansas* and *Wyoming*, and the number of four-stackers was increased to seventeen: Flagship *Decatur* and Destroyer Division 28 (the *Roper, Dickerson, Leary, Herbert,* and *Schenck*), DesDiv 29 (the *Tattnall, Badger, Jacob Jones, Tillman,* and *J. Fred Talbott*), and DesDiv 30 (the *Manley, Fairfax, Taylor, Babbitt, Claxton,* and *Hamilton*).[1]

From May through September, the ships carried out midshipmen's practice cruises, ROTC cruises, merchant marine training cruises, and Reserve cruises; from January through March, they conducted the annual Fleet Landing Exercises, known as Flex, in the Caribbean. The rest of the time, the ships carried out individual battle practices, participated in division and squadron tactical exercises, went into the yards for upkeep and refitting, and showed the flag in East Coast and Caribbean ports.

Rear Admiral Alfred W. Johnson commanded Training Detachment. He was a solid, able officer, but somewhat lacking in dynamism. His force's connection with the Flex problems convinced him of the usefulness of amphibious warfare, and he was one of the few naval officers of the thirties who gave much thought to the complexities of landing assault troops on hostile beaches and supporting them with gunfire and supplies. He worked to expand the scope of the Flex practices and helped to secure patrol planes and submarines for them. The Flex landings off Puerto Rico did much to demonstrate the feasibility of the amphibious theories being developed by the Marines, but lack of suitable assault craft, vital transports, tankers, and auxiliaries, necessary communications equipment, and other important gear meant that the state of the art still lagged well behind the hopes of the Marines.

In the Flex 4 exercises of 1938, lack of transports resulted in the assault troops being crowded into the battleships, cramping the infantrymen and hampering the ships in their delivery of effective gunfire support. The shortage of cargo ships hampered the landing of artillery and other heavy equipment. Ship-to-shore communications were inadequate to permit necessary control and coordination of the battle. The lack of landing craft meant that the assault troops had to use ships' boats, which were fragile, exposed, difficult to handle in the surf, and too small to accommodate sufficient men to allow a rapid buildup of firepower and momentum on the beaches; because less than two battalions could be landed simultaneously, assaults were not formidable, and invariably the piecemeal commitment of troops caused dispersion and confusion ashore. Although in shore bombardment practices against bunkers and other beach-defense targets, the Training Detachment battleships and destroyers scored a hit factor of 31 percent, some observers felt that conventional naval gunfire produced imposing explosions and deep craters but did little real damage to soundly built installations. Nevertheless, little was done to provide the necessary ships, equipment, and research to master amphibious techniques, as only the Marines and the Training Detachment were seriously interested in the problem.[2] This inertia later cost the lives of riflemen on bloody beaches, and was perhaps the darkest sin of the peacetime Navy.

The training cruises succeeded in giving useful, if cursory, shipboard experience to greenhorns, but more important, they helped to instill in the youngsters who joined the Fleet in more parlous times a sense of accomplishment and a feeling of responsibility assumed and mastered. The sailors of the forties proved well satisfied with the reservists who fought in the Atlantic, and it would be kind to think that the humble steaming of the old battleships and destroyers of Training Detachment in peaceful days had a little to do with it.[3]

Then there were the port visits, called Flower Shows ever since a Florida senator requested that a "battleship or other suitable vessel" visit his state in connection with a flower show. New Orleans needed a destroyer to make its Mardi Gras complete; Brunswick, Georgia, could count on a destroyer for local ceremonies. One California congressman futilely but insistently demanded that the annual Fleet Problem be cancelled so that large ships could be provided for the opening of the Golden Gate Bridge. Sometimes the nature of the event did not warrant the attendance of a warship; for instance, the four-stacker Bernadou was sent in July 1940 to the Cambridge (Maryland) Regatta, but it turned out that only nine members of a private yacht club visited the ship, to the chagrin of the skipper. In July 1939, the old Leary was sent on a highly successful visit to seafaring New Bedford because the local Democratic organization needed a popular diversion to blunt the impact of the mayor having been indicted for corruption in the grand manner. The bigger cities got the battleships.*

The port visits made planning of operating schedules difficult, and for the sailors they entailed a spit-and-polish performance, but usually also a compensating liberty. The crews enjoyed the functions in proportion to the number and interest of the visitors to their ship. Few men were so lost to tradition as not to accept as obvious the superiority of their ship over all others of similar type.[4]

For old and undermanned vessels, the Detachment's operating schedule was murderous; the midshipmen's cruise alone entailed a voyage of ten thousand miles. The busy schedule did not leave time for adequate upkeep. The deck- and side-plating of the destroyers became badly rusted, and their old power plants required more and more attention. As Admiral Johnson suggested, ". . . the material condition of these old ships brings up the problem of balancing their usefulness as against the usefulness of the new ships which might be bought with the money now expended on vessels that are obsolescent." The destroyers lacked torpedoes and antiaircraft machine guns, and Johnson warned that they were "practically defenseless" against air attack. The old battleships lacked modern guns and antiaircraft weapons.[5] In February 1939, the *Arkansas'* skipper was surprised to find his ship scheduled for a practice with .50-caliber AA machine guns during the midshipmen's cruise; he wrote the Navy Department that if he was to comply "it is felt that .50 caliber anti-aircraft machine guns should be installed."[6]

Serving prosaically in an ocean devoid of a tradition of romance and without a formidable potential enemy, Training Detachment was regarded as a noncombatant command, "out of Fleet," and outside the mainstream of promotion. The Bureau of Navigation considered it a seagoing replacement center to be bled for special drafts of manpower, and considered its personnel assigned on a temporary basis while awaiting reassignment to other commands; in 1938, the personnel turnover in the Detachment was 700 percent! The turnover made complicated tactical training impossible, for as the crews became sufficiently well trained to carry out tactical

---

*New Bedford's seafarers turned out 5,000 strong one day to see the *Leary*; in comparison, New York City had produced a maximum crowd of 3,000 to see the *Texas* a few weeks before.

exercises with other ships they were decimated by transfers, and the training process had to start all over again at a simpler level.[7] It seems likely that Johnson was given more than his share of hard cases and mediocre people; good officers developed a tendency to deem Atlantic commands second-rate or even injurious to their careers, and they longed for the major fleet units and "sunny, starched-white pageantry" of the Pacific. Some felt that the Atlantic received the capable administrators, the competent plodders, while the most dynamic officers were assigned to the Pacific.[8]

Because of the turnover, material defects, and its rigorous operating schedule, which deprived it of important tactical exercises, the Detachment was not ready to carry out major offensive combat operations. Nevertheless, perhaps because it acquired the stubborn, you-be-damned pride of the subtly despised, it performed its mechanical tasks well. Its gunnery compared favorably with that of better-endowed ships, and engineering performance, despite the limitations of the equipment, was "satisfactory." In the face of reduced personnel levels, its damage-control practices remained "very satisfactory" and communications were "excellent." Indeed, after Flex 4, the ships of Destroyer Squadron 10 were rated excellent in maneuvering and gunnery, and one inspecting officer reported, "I consider these vessels to be in a high state of readiness for battle." The ships and men were hardened to steaming great distances without the support of fleet auxiliaries. There were few morale problems, and discipline was "uniformly good." The venereal disease rate was high, about 120 cases per 1,000 men, roughly double the Pacific norm, due to frequent visits to West Indian ports. On balance, and allowing for the difficult conditions in which they served, Admiral Johnson was pleased with his men, observing, "The morale and efficiency of the bluejackets. . . is of the highest quality and is satisfactory in every way."[9]

In the thirties, Congress carefully watched over the Navy, making certain that new installations were located in appropriate districts and repair work was evenly shared by Depression-ridden cities.* The East Coast wanted the extra income that a large fleet could provide, and in 1937 the Adequate Coast Defense Association was founded in Norfolk under the motto, "A Battle Fleet for the Atlantic

*Congressman Donald O'Toole thought the Brooklyn Navy Yard should get more repair work because New York City contributed "more financially to the support of the Navy in the way of taxation" than other coastal regions.

Coast." It was argued that it would take three weeks for the Fleet to reach the East Coast from the Pacific in a sudden emergency, more than forty days if the Panama Canal could not be used. The movement gained converts because of the Navy's obvious weakness in the Atlantic as international affairs in Europe grew more ominous. That winter H.R. 8819 was introduced in Congress; it directed the President to establish a "permanent" fleet that should "in all peacetime be maintained on the Atlantic Coast." The bill also prescribed a minimum strength for the fleet in each category of ships and aircraft.[10] Clearly unconstitutional because it infringed the President's prerogative as Commander-in-Chief to dispose the nation's armed forces, H.R. 8819 did not pass; but it placed Franklin Roosevelt in the happy position of being prodded and pressed to do what he had planned to do anyway.

American naval planning in the thirties was not unduly complex. As a result of a decade and a half of isolationist and pacifist sentiment, the planners shunned alliances and expeditionary forces as unthinkable, lending an artificial quality to their efforts. They were chiefly concerned with the danger of a Pacific War with Japan, a formidable naval power, and neglected Europe and the Atlantic. America's basic war plan envisaged a conflict in one ocean against a single power, an uncomplicated contingency requiring a simple response, a long naval thrust across the Pacific to secure bases from which to defeat the Japanese main fleet in a decisive engagement in the central Pacific. However, by the late thirties, these inchoate arrangements were soon rendered obsolete by a forced march of untoward events; the increasing aggressiveness of Germany raised the spectre of a war in Europe, which in turn would pose grave problems of hemispheric defense. In Latin America, endemic poverty and an unstable political tradition offered favorable conditions for a German-nurtured military putsch, and the events of the Spanish Civil War seemed to underscore Hitler's willingness to forcibly export Fascism. The United States required a more flexible strategy, one that provided for the possibility of a complex, two-ocean war against a coalition of hostile powers; and in the winter of 1937-1938, the Army-Navy Joint Board began to plan for "readiness for action in both oceans."

American strategic planning in the next two years took increasing account of the possibility of simultaneous Japanese and Axis aggression in both oceans, and the nation's basic war plan, Plan Orange, was modified and then replaced by five contingency plans, Rainbows I-V. Since American strategic interests in Europe—primarily, control over the Atlantic approaches to the Americas—seemed adequately safeguarded by the Royal Navy and the French Army, much of the Rainbow planning was focused on the Pacific and on problems of hemispheric defense. Although Rainbow V did provide for a strategic defensive in the Pacific and an offensive in the Atlantic in concert with the Allies, service planners devoted much of their time and attention to the details of Rainbow II, which seemed most relevant to existing world conditions. Rainbow II provided for the projection of American forces into the western Pacific, with but "limited participation of U.S. forces in Continental Europe and the Atlantic"; Britain and France would handle most of the European-Atlantic operations.[11]

Meanwhile, in the spring of 1938, in order to test the implications of the new Atlantic ingredient in American strategy, President Roosevelt had decided that the U.S. Fleet should visit the East Coast the following winter and that the annual Fleet Problem, which had invariably taken place in the Pacific, should be conducted in the Caribbean early in 1939. The Fleet's presence in the Atlantic could be ascribed to ceremonies related to the opening of the New York World's Fair. For once, a Flower Show proved useful.[12]

That fall, 1938, in anticipation of the Munich Agreement, which Roosevelt thought shameful,* the President directed Admiral William D. Leahy, Chief of Naval Operations, to speed up the reconditioning of the World War I destroyers reposing in "red lead" rows at Philadelphia and San Diego. After inquiring into the status of new construction on the East Coast, the President then ordered the formation of a temporary squadron of new cruisers in the Atlantic. He made it clear that these ships were to function independently of Training Detachment; they were to constitute a separate task force reserved for operational use. The task force was to be given an identity of its own: the Atlantic Squadron.[13]

The Atlantic Squadron was born on 6 September 1938. It was allotted fourteen new ships, and its mission was to serve as a task force strong enough to "discover and to turn back a sudden raid into the Caribbean" pending reinforcements from the Pacific. Three of its cruisers were to be held in readiness to show the flag in Latin America. The Squadron consisted of Cruiser Division 9 (the light cruisers *Boise*,

---

*At the time of Munich, FDR was prepared to impound German ships in U.S. ports for Allied use.

Honolulu, and *Phoenix*), Cruiser Division 8 (the quick-firing, 10,000-ton light cruisers *Philadelphia*, *Savannah*, *Brooklyn*, and *Nashville*, which were favorites of the President), and the destroyers *Sampson*, *Somers*, *Warrington*, *Ralph Talbot*, *Mugford*, *Helm*, and *Shaw*.[14] Since 1932 all new construction ships had been sent to the Pacific as a matter of routine, so Rear Admiral Sherwoode A. Taffinder, Director of the Ship Movements Division, wrote one of the cruiser commanders to explain his surprising assignment and perhaps to assure him that a command in the Atlantic was not evidence of official disfavor: " . . . the function of the Atlantic Squadron . . . is evidently a gesture aimed at political conditions abroad. The President personally directed the formation of the Squadron."[15]

But Rear Admiral Johnson was vexed to discover the sudden appearance of an independent task force in his domain, especially as command of the Squadron, now the key post in the Atlantic, had been given to an officer junior to him, Rear Admiral Ford A. Todd, of CruDiv 8. Admiral Leahy coolly, if untruthfully, had to explain that the oversight was due to the speedy nature of the President's decision. Roosevelt then agreed to honor the mandate of seniority, and on 10 October, the old battleships and destroyers of Training Detachment became part of the Atlantic Squadron commanded by Rear Admiral Alfred W. Johnson. While Johnson lacked the youth and fire that the President relished, he knew his ships and was not indifferent to progressive techniques of naval warfare.[16] He would do.

Fleet Problem XX was slated for the Caribbean, and the Squadron was to participate. The ugly ducklings of Training Detachment had become part of a fighting command at last. It was a good feeling.

3.

A Mirror
to War:
Fleet Problem XX

IN KEEPING WITH THE NEW TREND of strategic thought, Fleet Problem
XX was to be a comparatively realistic exercise in hemispheric
defense. Its basic assumptions were these: A Fascist-led revolt had
taken place in a friendly South American nation, Green (Brazil).
While the United States (Black) tried to rally support for the
legitimate government of Green, the rebels, fearing American
intervention, requested the protection of a powerful European Fascist
nation, White (Germany). Anxious to secure a base in the Americas
from which to menace the Panama Canal and extend its influence in
Latin America, the White government decided to assist the revolt
with military advisers, aircraft, and modern arms. The White fleet
sortied, escorting a supply convoy to the New World. In response,
Black transferred part of its split main fleet from the Pacific to the
Atlantic to reinforce the Atlantic Squadron and intercept White's force.

The Black fleet was commanded by Vice Admiral Adolphus
Andrews, 59 years old, somewhat pompous, intelligent and flexible,
but perhaps too long a staff officer. His force consisted of 6
battleships, 8 heavy cruisers, 6 light cruisers, 32 destroyers, and 15
auxiliaries, mostly aviation tenders. The backbone of his air power
was the carrier *Ranger* with 54 light bombers and 18 fighters; for
long-range scouting and strikes he had 102 shore-based patrol bombers; 62 land-based Marine scout bombers and fighters rounded out
his air force.

The Black fleet steamed at sea off Puerto Rico, as Admiral Andrews did not have a large anchorage to accommodate his force and was reluctant to disperse ships in several harbors or in a close blockade of Green lest the separate elements be defeated in detail by the concentrated enemy force.* Andrews reasoned that the White fleet, not the convoy, was his proper objective, for even if the White supplies allowed the rebels to gain control of Green, the permanence of their rule must depend on the ability of White sea power to keep open the lines of communication to Germany. Andrews' decision, while technically sound, was politically flawed, for it meant that the rebels would be given time to solidify their position in Green, blurring the distinction between internal revolution and external aggression, thus making it more difficult for the United States to justify intervention.

However, Admiral Andrews had scant choice. Lacking air bases in the southern Caribbean, he had to use ships, not planes, to scout for the enemy convoy. Hence, the radius and effectiveness of his search must be limited. He sent a scouting line of 7 cruisers, backed by the *Ranger*, out to seek the White convoy and hopefully direct the *Ranger*'s planes to it; but the *Ranger* could not be risked in too close support of the cruisers because of the uncertain whereabouts of the White fleet's three aircraft carriers.

Lack of sea and air bases in the Caribbean limited Admiral Andrews to a defensive strategy. He kept his fleet off Puerto Rico, protected by his shore-based aviation. His plan was to engage the White fleet in a decisive, daylight surface battle when the enemy passed within range of his land-based air power.

The White fleet was commanded by Admiral Edward C. Kalbfus, an experienced, conventional battleship officer. He had a force of 6 battleships, more modern than those of his adversary, 6 heavy cruisers, 6 light cruisers, 31 destroyers, 13 submarines, and the auxiliary *Utah*, which simulated the White convoy. His air power consisted of the carriers *Enterprise*, *Lexington*, and *Yorktown*, with 72 light bombers, 54 torpedo planes, 36 torpedo-bombers, and 54 fighters.

Admiral Kalbfus' intention was to escort the convoy to Green while keeping his main battle fleet well beyond a 600-mile circle out from the Black air bases on Puerto Rico and Haiti. The convoy and

*In order to avoid diplomatic complications, Trinidad served as the coast of Brazil.

its escort were protected by one carrier in close support and by a second carrier astern; farther back were the battleships and main fleet; the third carrier screened the flank of the fleet. Kalbfus' formation was designed to allow the battle line to protect the convoy from surface attack but keep the battleships safe from surprise air attack. Admiral Kalbfus' plan was to protect the convoy's passage to Green, then use his carrier aviation to erode Black air power before seeking to close for the decisive surface battle.

Thus, each admiral made air power the cornerstone of his strategy. Admiral Andrews intended to fight at sea only within range of his air support and Admiral Kalbfus intended to destroy his foe's air power before confronting him at sea.

Fleet Problem XX commenced at 0600, 20 February 1939.

No contacts were made on the 20th.

The 21st was a gray day, and the wind blew sprinkling black squalls across a choppy, slate-colored sea. Despite the bad weather, Admiral Andrews' scout cruisers managed to launch float planes, and several of the reconnaissance aircraft located the lead White ships and got off contact reports before being shot down by an angry swarm of chunky fighters from the *Lexington*. The Black cruisers sped eastward to try to regain contact with the enemy.

Meanwhile, throughout the morning, White planes from the *Enterprise* and *Yorktown* flew strike missions in search of the *Ranger*, the Black fleet's only carrier, disdaining the cruiser targets scouting below. As Vice Admiral King, unhappy at the tight leash thus far held on his carriers by Admiral Kalbfus, gladly ordered his fliers: "Black carrier will be the primary objective for all attacks." But King's men could not find the *Ranger*, which was lurking to the west and north.

Soon three of the Black scout cruisers, the *Northampton, Salt Lake City,* and *Pensacola*, sighted the White convoy at long range. They were promptly taken under fire by three matching White heavy cruisers of the escort, the *San Francisco, Quincy,* and *Tuscaloosa*, and a running battle developed, with the Black ships firing at long range while dodging in and out of rain squalls. Then seventy-two *Yorktown* planes, returning in dark humor from the futile search for the *Ranger*, found the *Northampton* and *Pensacola* and bombed the twisting, firing cruisers, sinking both. The *Salt Lake City*, damaged in the gun battles, ran out of the dripping shelter of a squall in an attempt to circle the White cruisers and get in some distant shots at the convoy; but the *San Francisco* headed her off, and *Salt Lake City* was sunk by gunfire. The remainder of the scout cruisers also fared badly. *Enterprise* and *Lexington* planes sank the *Philadelphia* and *Savannah* and heavily damaged the *Brooklyn* and *Nashville.*

Admiral Andrews, learning of the massacre of his scouts, decided to send the *Ranger* after the White convoy, then reconsidered. He could not send one carrier against three. The *Ranger* was directed to come north, and the White convoy reached Green unharmed. The cost of overturning the Monroe Doctrine was three White heavy cruisers damaged and 39 carrier aircraft lost.

The ordeal of the picket cruisers showed that the airplane had deprived the modern cruiser of its traditional functions in naval warfare, scouting and quick thrusts against the enemy's line of communications; more than the battleship, whose guns could still prove useful for shore bombardment and antiaircraft defense, the cruiser was obsolescent.

Despite his early successes, Admiral Kalbfus understood that in order to secure Green he must defeat the Black fleet and establish an advanced base in the Puerto Rico-Virgin Islands region from which to support future operations in the Western Hemisphere. But he knew that he could not achieve either objective until his forces destroyed Black shore-based aviation. Thus, on the 22nd, White submarines poked about the bays and inlets of the Puerto Rican coast, looking for the Black aircraft tenders. A landing party from the submarine *Salmon* discovered that with the Black fleet out at sea the tenders and patrol planes were vulnerable. The White force destroyermen then conceived of a series of hit-and-run raids designed to reduce Black air strength.

Four ships of Destroyer Division 3 running close offshore of the Leeward Islands were nearly overlooked by Black patrol bombers searching for larger ships in deeper waters; when they were sighted, lowering clouds and slow pilot reactions prevented successful attacks. At 0256 on the morning of the 23rd, *Drayton* and *Flusser* sneaked into Culebra harbor past the somnolent picket destroyer *Hopkins.* Inside, the two destroyers sank the small tenders *Sandpiper* and *Lapwing* with torpedoes and gunfire and shot up four of the moored PBYs. The *Hopkins* tried to intervene, but the four-stacker was no match for the modern ships and she went down in an unlucky thirteen minutes.

The two destroyers went on to San Juan, *Flusser* to attack, *Drayton* to cover her. Two Black guardships were patrolling outside the en-

Fleet Problem XX — the *Lexington, Ranger, Yorktown,* and *Enterprise*

trance to the harbor; the *Flusser* steamed boldly for the channel and tried to slide between the split defenders, but in the increasing daylight, one of the ships sighted her and winked out a challenge. *Flusser* cleverly flashed the same challenge to the second enemy ship, got the correct response in return, then flashed it out to her own inquisitor. But daylight meant planes. Soon, the *Flusser* was attacked by a patrol of Marine scout bombers and fighters and was damaged. In the harbor, she attacked a tender and an oiler, but hit neither. She then wandered into a minefield and was ruled sunk. Outside, the *Drayton*, wearing a false bow number, deceived one Black ship, but was attacked by the second picket ship, *Elliot*, damaged in a running fight, and finally finished off by the Marine dive bombers and stubby fighters.

The other two destroyers of DesDiv 3, *Lamson* and *Mahan*, found no tenders at St. Thomas, so went on to San Juan to see if the hunting was better there; it was, but the quarry was now alert and snarling as a result of the earlier attacks and the coming of daylight. Both destroyers were sunk off San Juan by the Marine planes and the two picket ships.

The destroyers had fought well, doing some damage and creating much confusion in the enemy camp; but all four were sunk, and they had wrecked but four of the patrol planes. Such dramatic sorties were too dangerous in the age of the airplane. Although some of the destroyermen insisted that the surprise factor would make hit-and-run tactics valuable in war, there could be no surprise in waters dominated by enemy planes.

On the morning of the 23rd, Admiral Kalbfus told Ernie King what his fliers were waiting to hear: it was up to them to take out the Black air force. So the *Lexington* and *Enterprise* and their plane-guard destroyers formed up in an independent task force with three heavy cruisers and seven destroyers and steamed toward "Indian country."

To help the impending air strikes, two destroyers were detached from the carrier task force on the 24th to try another raid on the Black seaplanes and tenders. One of the raiders, the *Cushing*, entered San Juan harbor at 0220 on the 25th, and discovered six ships and thirty-six patrol bombers asleep. The *Cushing* found too much cold meat on her table, tried to devour everything, and in eating indiscriminately deprived herself of the choicest fare. She fired torpedoes at three of the ships and brought five others and the planes under fire in a wild half-hour of reckless fighting; then she bumped a dummy mine and sank. The *Cushing* had damaged several of the ships, but she did not get any of the vital patrol planes. The *Preston* searched St. Thomas and Culebra vainly, then investigated off San Juan, where she was caught unawares by the *Elliot*, torpedoed, then finished off by gunfire.

Meanwhile, several of the White submarines scouting off Puerto Rico were damaged in attacks by the now more vigilant Black PBYs, and one was sunk. But off San Juan, the *Perch* torpedoed and sank the *Reuben James*, which was listlessly patrolling the harbor entrance. Thereafter, Black destroyers were ordered to maintain speed and zigzag when on patrol.

Admiral King meanwhile decided to strike the Black patrol plane bases with aircraft off the *Enterprise*, while planes from the *Lexington* searched for the Black fleet's lone carrier, the *Ranger*. But his plan necessitated shifting a *Lexington* scout bomber squadron to the *Enterprise* in exchange for the *Enterprise* fighter squadron; the plane trade would increase the power and scope of the *Enterprise*'s raid on the Black bases and strengthen the *Lexington*'s defenses against air strikes from the *Ranger*. Hence, King's pilots were much surprised at being told when they were briefed for launching that some of them should take along their toothbrushes and pajamas! King's interesting improvisation was a foreshadowing of the mixed carrier air groups sometimes used in the Pacific in World War II for greater flexibility.

But in the forenoon of the 24th, a Black PBY, one of defunct *Sandpiper*'s brood, located the White carrier task force as it approached Puerto Rico from the north. In the afternoon, patrol bombers from San Juan and Samana Bay made three uncoordinated attacks on Admiral King's task force. The planes attacked out of the sun at too high altitudes, about 13,500 feet, and the bombing was poor, a total of 76 bombs being dropped to no avail; the White ships monitored the radio frequencies used by the planes and maneuvered accordingly to avoid the bombs.

Then two other squadrons of patrol bombers, having left their base at 1300, reached the scene and began to cruise in the bright sky about twenty-five miles from the ships, waiting until a fuzzy mass of clouds drifted between the planes and the ships. At nearly 1700, with the sun behind them and the clouds masking the vision of the ships, the PBYs swept in in a horizontal attack from 13,500 feet. The lead squadron was supposed to attack the *Lexington* and the trailing squadron the *Enterprise*, but the planes became confused in the assault and more struck at "Lady Lex" than at the "Big E."

The 30 planes dropped 116 500-pound bombs; the fliers believed that about 41 percent would have hit the carriers in actual combat, which was, of course, wildly optimistic. The umpires ruled both carriers moderately damaged, and Admiral King detached the worse-hurt *Lexington*. Although antiaircraft fire shot down a dozen attacking bombers during the day, essentially the carriers lacked sufficient fighters to maintain an effective combat air patrol over the task force, and this was the major reason why the lumbering PBYs were able to inflict crucial damage. It would be necessary in future to increase the strength of carrier fighter contingents.

At 0630 on the 25th, just south of 20N, about one hundred and twenty miles north of San Juan, the *Enterprise* launched her white, shiny planes into the brightening tropical sky; the buzzing planes climbed into squadron clusters and swarmed south toward Culebra, Samana Bay, Rincon Bay, and San Juan.

En route to Samana Bay, six Devastators of Torpedo Squadron 6 sighted the Black fleet for the first time. Admiral King ordered the planes to quit their assigned mission and try to find the *Ranger*, which he hoped might be in the vicinity of the Black main body. But the *Ranger* was 100 miles north of the main Black fleet in a separate task force for greater mobility and concealment, waiting to learn where the *Enterprise* was.

Scouting Squadron 3 off the *Enterprise* attacked a large tender and tanker in San Juan harbor and strafed ships, moored planes, and the airfield. Scouting 6, finding nothing at Culebra or Rincon Bay, finished the job at San Juan, sinking the tender *Wright* and tanker *Neches.* Then the planes strafed the moored seaplanes. Bombing Squadron 6 struck at Samana Bay, sinking the tender *Langley* and tanker *Kanawha* with steep, whistling dives; then the dive bombers strafed three small tenders and destroyed five planes on the sparkling, blue-green water. Out at sea, Torpedo 6 continued to search for the *Ranger*.

But the *Ranger* hit first. One of her scout bombers found the *Enterprise* at 0710, and between 0845 and 1040, the "Big E" was attacked by large formations of green-tailed *Ranger* planes. After a long fight, the fighter-poor *Enterprise* went down.

At 0915, the Torpedo 6 planes discovered Black carrier bombers on a northerly course, obviously returning from a strike. The TBDs trailed the scout bombers and at last found the *Ranger*. But it was too late. The *Enterprise* would launch no more planes, and the *Lexington* was far away and crippled.

King's carrier raid had cost the Black forces two large tenders, two tankers, and 14 patrol bombers. Damage to facilities made it difficult to repair the 47 remaining bombers, and quantities of gas and bombs had been destroyed, severely curtailing the offensive potential of the surviving planes.

On their way home, the *Enterprise*'s plane-guard destroyers, *Conyngham* and *Reid*, ran into two White heavy cruisers, but saved themselves with a desperate torpedo attack, and although heavily damaged, escaped. The cruisers had not been alert, then made the mistake of closing too near the badly outgunned destroyers instead of smashing them with long-range fire.

Hoping that the *Enterprise* had done her job, Admiral Kalbfus for the first time ordered his fleet into range of Black air power; he had decided to close for the decisive surface action. The White fleet moved west; Admiral Andrews' fleet steamed eastward to meet it.

White fleet had better battleships and two carriers, one still undamaged; Andrews had the PBYs for distant reconnaissance, which meant that he might find his foe first and gain the initiative with strikes by the undiscovered *Ranger*. It had the look of an even fight.

On the afternoon of the 25th, a PBY sighted the White fleet northeast of Puerto Rico. At 1527, a patrol bomber damaged the *San Francisco* in a high-altitude attack. At 1605, three seaplanes tried to bomb the *Lexington* from 12,000 feet, but all were shot down by the combat air patrol and AA fire. A minute later, three more planes attacked the carrier while the fighters were busy with the first group of attackers, but the shrewd ploy was wasted because the bombing was inaccurate and no damage was done to "Lady Lex."

On the morning of the 26th, the high-flying PBYs kept the White force under steady scrutiny, mostly watching, sometimes attacking separately and ineffectively. The combat air patrol shot down seven of the snoopers during their long vigil. In the afternoon, the last bombs were loaded onto 22 PBYs at San Juan for the seaplanes' final strike; it was only possible because the tender *Williamson* had sped to Trinidad and returned with 21,000 gallons of aviation gasoline swishing in her belly.

Meanwhile, White submarines formed an advance patrol line for Admiral Kalbfus' force. The submarine *Seal* found the *Ranger*, but her skipper unwisely delayed sending off a contact report for an hour and a quarter while he stalked the carrier. At 1030, the *Seal* fired three torpedoes in a submerged attack from 2,500 yards, inflicting minor damage. Destroyer *Patterson* located the submarine and sank her with depth charges. Then at 1235, while the *Salmon* was cruising on the surface, her lookouts sighted against the horizon the dark, oblong bulk of *Ranger*; the submarine submerged for an approach, but her underwater speed was too slow, and the *Ranger* pulled away. *Salmon* fired four torpedoes at long range, but all missed.

But then, before the White carrier planes could hunt down the *Ranger*, before the Black seaplanes could try a final strike at the *Lexington* and *Yorktown*, the Problem abruptly and anticlimactically ended. It had run on long, and only one day remained in which to stage the battleship action which traditionally concluded Fleet Problems. It was time to fight the Battle of Jutland.

The battle commenced at 0600 on the 27th, the two forces stationed 120 miles apart on an axis running southeast-northwest, off the north shore of the Greater Antilles; no attacks were permitted for four hours to prevent the planes from inflicting damage while the battle fleets closed. The two sides used similar formations: heavy cruisers and destroyers in the van, then the battleships, with light cruisers and destroyers bringing up the rear. Planes from each fleet tracked the other, but because the fliers had much to learn of the nuances of over-water navigation and ship identification, the copious reports were sometimes confused or contradictory. White submarines scouted to the southwest, trying to stay on the surface to add range to the search; sometimes approaching Black planes forced them to dive, but they usually found that they could sight the aircraft long before they themselves were sighted and so could submerge to safety in ample time.

When the submarines found the Black ships, they essayed submerged attacks. However, the high-speed warships were difficult targets, and the submarines were able to do very little damage. The *Snapper* made an utterly impractical attack, using sound bearings alone. The battle line was hardly aware that it had been attacked. The destroyers screening the heavy ships were ineffective in discovering the submarines due to the high-speed operations and deficient sonar training.

At 1100, the opposing battle fleets made visual contact at a range of twenty miles. At 1121, at a range of 30,000 yards, the White battleships commenced firing, aided by spotting aircraft; five minutes later, the Black battleships began to return the fire. In the meantime, many lesser duels flared. Overhead, 70 Black patrol bombers and 12 torpedo planes, escorted by 36 Marine fighters, swept in on the White ships; nine White fighters attacked the rear squadron of seaplanes, but their interception was too late and too weak. The patrol bombers struck from high altitude with 152 1,000-pound bombs; the slow, stubby torpedo planes slashed in in a low-level attack off the bow of the White van, but they were badly shot up by antiaircraft fire from three White heavy cruisers. Meanwhile, three other White heavy cruisers and a formation of destroyers attacked the light cruisers and destroyers at the rear of the Black column, causing considerable damage. Then six Black heavy cruisers seized the moment and attacked the three remaining heavy cruisers at the head of the White formation, sinking them all.

With the opening provided by the victory of the heavy cruisers, a Black destroyer squadron launched a torpedo attack against the White battle fleet from off the starboard beam. Admiral Kalbfus ordered his White battleships to make a right-about maneuver to avoid the torpedo attack; his lead battleship, the *Tennessee*, was hit by fire from the Black battleships and suddenly slowed to 8 knots. The five trailing White battleships then also reduced speed, so that it took them too long to complete the reversal of course and redeploy; for several minutes in the long turn, the three lead battleships masked the fire of the rear three. During this crucial interval, the White battleships suffered costly damage.

The exercise ended at 1236. The Black fleet could claim a victory. Its cruisers had kept heavy pressure on the White light forces, preventing them from attacking the Black battleships, while its own destroyers attacked the White battleships. Black losses were one battleship, four heavy cruisers, one light cruiser, and six destroyers. White losses were one battleship, three heavy cruisers, five light cruisers, and eleven destroyers. The White battleships were more heavily damaged than the Black.[1]

At the conclusion of the Fleet Problem, the Atlantic Squadron's old battleships of Battle Division 5 and destroyers of Destroyer Squadron 10 were called upon to participate in Fleet Landing Exercise 5, to test the amphibious capability of Admiral Johnson's command.

The warships fired gunfire support practices off eastern Vieques. The naval fire blasted deep craters on the island, and the din and rumble of the earth seemed demoralizing, but a very disappointing amount of substantive damage was done to the mock-up target defenses. Reconnaissance flights were flown over the island, and a Marine Reconnaissance and Intelligence team went ashore to reconnoiter, a luxury not usually available in combat operations because of the limited time ships might spend in waters patrolled by enemy planes and fear of compromising tactical surprise.

The landing exercises took place on 10 and 11 March. The assault troops, 1st Battalion, Fifth Marines, were as usual carried in the cramped old battleships *Wyoming, Texas,* and *New York* due to lack of transports. The Marines' supplies and heavy equipment were carried in the venerable cargo ship *Capella;* to a force long bereft of auxiliaries, the vessel, recently refitted after nineteen years out of commission, seemed the "most useful vessel in the expedition." The main assault landings were carried out despite rising seas and shoals off the beaches. Defending planes simulated strafing attacks on the naked boats, inflicting "appalling" losses. The Marines then quickly established a beachhead, as the troops of the defending battalion, thinly stretched over an impossible 25-mile frontage, pulled back in order to concentrate their dispersed forces.[2]

Thus ended Fleet Problem XX and Flex 5. The mock warfare campaign illuminated significant trends in naval strategy and tactics, although some lessons remained shadowy.

Generally, the Problem exemplified the psychological advantages of the offensive in warfare. White ships and planes for the most part fought daringly, cleverly, and vigorously; Black ships and planes, leashed in a necessary but seemingly sterile defensive role, were less alert, more careless and lethargic.

Concretely, the Problem illustrated that it would be difficult to fight a major naval foe in the Atlantic while much of the Fleet had to be based in the Pacific. The lack of adequate bases in the Caribbean was particularly ominous. Admiral Andrews commented:

> . . . secure and well equipped bases at Port of Spain and beyond will be essential if our fleet be called upon to uphold the Monroe Doctrine by operations against an aggressive enemy in central or south Atlantic.
>
> To project the fleet into such an area against a strong foe without the facilities for maintaining it there or without a secure line of communications would be contrary to any sound concept of strategy and so hazardous to our own control of vital sea areas that it is unlikely ever to be attempted unless suitable bases are provided.[3]

Sailors in the *Pennsylvania* line the rail to honor President Roosevelt after
Fleet Problem XX

He warned,

> A fleet on which the country may depend for its existence should never be placed in the position of operating in the face of an aggressive enemy without first having established a base in its lee. . . . In view of the present world conditions, the importance of the West Indian area to our national defense, and the maintenance of our national policies, and the lack of bases therein, it is high time that corrective measures be taken.[4]

Andrews believed that a base on the Gulf of Paria was indispensable, and the fliers thought Samana Bay could be made into an excellent base for patrol planes. The latter also felt that both San Juan and Trinidad had excellent potential as patrol-plane bases, although they believed Culebra's Great Harbor was misnamed; it was too small to be a PBY base. Andrews' recommendations included building up the inadequate existing American bases in the Caribbean and leasing bases in the area from foreign governments. His report was seen by the President, for whom the absence of bases in the Caribbean was a pressing matter.[5]

Significantly, while both Admiral Andrews and Admiral Kalbfus were orthodox, veteran officers, both had made air power the determinant of his strategy. Neither force had attempted to close for the decisive surface action that each desired until the enemy's air forces had been decimated. The battleships had not fired a single round from their main batteries in all the six days of the Problem.

However, had the battle lasted another day, the planes would no longer have been able to function decisively. The remaining forty PBYs were down to their last bombs, and the *Ranger* had but 57 planes of all types left; the White carriers had only 86 planes still operational. The mutual air attacks scheduled for the 26th would have exhausted the offensive potential of the aircraft, and it would have been left to the battleships to determine the victor. The peacetime practices and exercises generally suggested the same trend: the efforts of the air forces ended in mutual extinction through attrition. Yet, as long as the planes remained formidable, no surface engagement was feasible. The trend was toward longer and longer postponement of the fleet action as aircraft performance improved until, finally, in World War II, the decisive surface action could not take place at all.

Technically, both sides handled their naval air power well, and the carrier commanders appeared to be thoroughly familiar with correct doctrines and tactics of carrier warfare: both fleets made the carrier, not the vaunted battleship, the target of their air strikes; and both tended to deploy the carrier as the core of an independent task force, for greater mobility and concealment, rather than to keep the flattop leashed to the battle line (although this deprived the carrier of the concentrated AA protection of a more central position). And Admiral King's strike against concentrations of Black shore-based aviation was a sure harbinger of the fast carrier strikes of the Pacific War.

It should have been clear from the Problem that carriers needed more fighter planes aboard to protect them from enemy bombers and torpedo planes, but this lesson had to be learned again at high tuition early in the Pacific War. The Problem indicated that high-level, horizontal bombing was an ineffective technique against firing ships maneuvering on the open sea, but that dive bombers and torpedo planes were the mortal nemeses of modern warships.

The pivotal role of naval air power and carrier aviation in Fleet Problem XX strongly suggests that the peacetime Navy was far from indifferent to the uses of aircraft, as is too often alleged. Airplanes and carriers existed, and like it or not, officers had to take account of them and use them, or risk failure in a highly competitive profession; most did, and thus carrier task forces were used offensively and imaginatively in the training operations of the thirties and crews of all types of ships gained precious experience in working with carriers and a better understanding of the virtues and limitations of aircraft. Consequently, some of the early, crucial carrier battles of the Pacific War, such as Midway, were managed successfully by men who were not aviators. The efficient carrier operations of the early Pacific War were not mere frantic improvisations following upon the defeat of the battle fleet at Pearl Harbor; they were the merited legacy of the doctrines and techniques of carrier warfare generated by the training exercises of the thirties*

Throughout the exercise, the battleships had been tucked away in the positions of greatest security; hence, their antiaircraft potential

---

*I suspect that a study of administrative history would support the operational evidence that the fliers were hardly a scorned and oppressed minority in the peacetime Navy, their visions ruthlessly dissipated by reactionary gunners in high places. Aside from the fact that the distinction between aviators and sailors with experience in or with aviation became increasingly blurred as many officers underwent flight training, or served in carrier crews, or served in ships operating with carriers, the Navy's cumbersome, decentralized system of administration did not permit any one faction, even the Gun Club, completely to dominate the decision-making process. Amid the numerous independent fiefdoms of the Department, consensus was essential to get anything done. The decentralized machine of administration required much "grease"—personal pacts, compromises, horse trades—to function; as did the political system of the nation it existed to

was wasted. The airplane by ruling out long-range scouting by ships, was making the cruiser obsolete. The increasing size and augmented fighting power of destroyers was working toward the same end, as the minor action of the *Conyngham* and *Reid* against two heavy cruisers suggested. As the battles off the Solomons in the Pacific War showed, the cruiser was vulnerable to aircraft in daytime and not a match for destroyers at night or in confined waters.

Submarines lacked the speed to function effectively against major warships in the open sea; they were rarely able to achieve a favorable attack position. And as a result of training against large fleets of warships, submarine tactics grew too cautious, and since the submariners got no experience in attacking slow, vulnerable merchant convoys, they were largely untrained for their natural role in combat, a war on commerce; tactically, emphasis was on concealing the periscope and generally avoiding discovery rather than on attack tactics. Night surface tactics were unknown. These deficiencies, perhaps almost as much as the well-known inadequacies of torpedo performance, were responsible for the spotty record of the submarine service in the early period of the Pacific War, when the submariners struggled to create doctrine in a combat different from their training.

The destroyers were at their best in daring operations, such as the hit-and-run raids on the Black harbors, or the torpedo attack on the White battle line on the 27th. In more prosaic work, such as picket

---

defend, it responded to internal pressures, lobbies, and interest groups. The fliers received recognition and appropriations commensurate with their ability to use political leverage inside the system; and since their ability was not inconsiderable, they did not have to resort to the unseemly publicity that marred the Army-Air Corps relationship. Such a system of administration by "genial conspiracy" rather than by executive fiat involved duplication of effort on the part of separate commands and bureaus, delay in reaching decisions, and then more delay in making certain that decisions attained were faithfully implemented by those who felt that the inevitable compromise had been achieved too much at their expense. Yet it also permitted factions to ride their own hobby horses and carry out projects of interest to no one else, to experiment, sometimes wastefully, sometimes creatively, without fear of interference from doubting superiors.

Today, of course, the system of naval administration under the Defense Department is more centralized, resulting in speedier decision-making, less friction in implementing decisions, and elimination of some waste and duplication of effort, but also in the power to bring both obstructionists and creative dissenters into the fold of orthodoxy. In the past, men like Admiral William S. Sims and his gunners, John H. Towers and his fliers, and Hyman G. Rickover and his submariners were able to prevail over the orthodoxies of their times. They triumphed mostly because they were right, but partly because the orthodox lacked the power to overwhelm them without producing administrative chaos. Today, administrators have such power, and while it is often beneficial to Navy and nation that they do, it will not prove so in the long run unless they remember that, the proverb to the contrary notwithstanding, often in unity there is weakness.

duty, they sometimes performed indifferently; the loss of the *Reuben James* was inexcusable. The antisubmarine escorts were ineffective not only because the high-speed operations with heavy warships both fouled the sonar gear with noise and made submarine attack less likely, but also because of the inexperience of the sonar men. As the *Babbitt's* skipper observed, "Right now the sonic material is probably far in advance of the experience of the average listening personnel on destroyers."[6]

Both the Problem and Flex 5 indicated the dire need for fleet auxiliaries. There being no tankers, destroyers had constantly to scurry to and from San Juan and St. Thomas, carrying oil to the ships at sea. The lack of cargo ships, transports, and specialized amphibious command vessels marred the Flex practices.

Flex 5 exposed other old weaknesses, such as the need for modern assault craft, tank lighters, and efficient ship-to-shore communications. It also illustrated the lack of killing power of current naval gunfire techniques. But what Admiral Johnson remembered best was the fighters strafing low over the vulnerable boats of the assault Marines. He wrote, "It is in fact doubtful if any beach landing, other than a night surprise, can succeed in the face of enemy air control."[7] Flex 5 reinforced the lessons of the Fleet Problem as to the need for bases in the Caribbean and the importance of aviation as the first defense against hostile landings on the southern approaches to the United States.

Thus, Fleet Problem XX, besides starting President Roosevelt down the long, winding road leading to the Destroyers-for-Bases transaction with Great Britain, symbolized the increasing significance of the Atlantic and Caribbean in American defense planning, and held a mirror to war to help thoughtful sailors better prepare their service for the uncertain future.

After remaining in the Caribbean for a time, the fleet settled into East Coast ports preparatory to concentrating for a majestic review in New York Harbor on 29 April 1939. The Pacific sailors looked forward to an imposing liberty in New York City.

Meanwhile, Admiral Johnson was writing a plea for more modern ships for the Atlantic Squadron, one soon to be heeded by the President:

Over and above the shore based aircraft which can be relied upon to turn back a hostile raid at the beaches, there is the larger problem of our naval power in the Atlantic. Even though we plan to guard against no more than a temporary raid, our Atlantic defenses must include naval ships numerous and fast enough to locate the raiders. A ready squadron sufficient to scout the passes into the Caribbean and sea areas adjacent thereto is the minimum force necessary to implement the oldest and most fundamental of our foreign policies, the defense of the Western Hemisphere under the Monroe Doctrine.[8]

But the State Department, worried about Japanese intentions in the Far East during the fleet's sojourn in the Atlantic, prevailed upon the President to order the abrupt return of Battle Force and Scouting Force to the Pacific. The news "surprised officers and men alike." On the 26th and 27th of April, most of the Pacific ships, except those refitting and resupplying, steamed grimly out to sea. The fleet review of the 29th was thus of much diminished grandeur. Nevertheless, the *Texas*, the old battleships of Battle Division 5 and the four-stackers of Destroyer Squadron 10 looked bright and trim as they proudly led the other ships past the Battery into the green swells of the Hudson.

Probably as a result of Fleet Problem XX and Admiral Johnson's report, the President decided to retain a carrier, the *Ranger*, in the Atlantic, along with the heavy cruisers of Cruiser Division 7 (the *San Francisco, Quincy, Vincennes, Tuscaloosa*) and four modern destroyers, but to send the light cruisers of CruDiv 9 and CruDiv 8 to the Pacific; and two squadrons of patrol bombers from the Pacific were added to Patrol Wing 5 in the Atlantic. Thus, the Atlantic Squadron was substantially strengthened in the year of the outbreak of war in Europe.[9]

In ensuing days, the remainder of the Pacific ships steamed away, while the vessels of the Atlantic Squadron stayed behind to work at what seemed lesser tasks in safer waters. It was an old story to the Atlantic sailors. And it endured until they shaped a tradition of prideful legends out of the muted battles of their own rough, chill ocean.

4.

Germany: Ships and Strategy

BERLIN WAS ALWAYS WELL AWARE of the hostility of the United States, even in the thirties when few substantive issues arose to mar relations between the two powers. The problems that did evolve were not of a critical politico-strategic nature but peripheral matters involving German attempts to undercut U.S. markets in Latin America as part of the general economic nationalism of a Depression decade or, more importantly, German persecution of Jews. But ideological animosity engendered bitterness, and consequently, despite the lack of pivotal grievances, German-American relations were cold and mutually distrustful.[1]

German statesmen well understood that American isolationism was "an unreal utopianism" that would soon vanish once "values which concern the United States are at stake." Ambassador Hans H. Dieckhoff warned from Washington that "neither the indifference of the rank and file toward foreign affairs" nor "the dogmatism of the pacifists" would preserve American neutrality if the survival of Britain were at stake. He reported so frequently on the transient nature of American isolationism that he was moved to apologize for his tenacity:

> I am perhaps becoming a bore in Berlin, because I repeatedly point out . . . we can no longer count on America's isolation, and that, on the contrary, we must certainly be prepared, in case of a world conflict, to see the Americans throw their weight into the British scale.[2]

In Berlin, both the political and naval leadership assumed at the outset of World War II that American intervention was inevitable,

51

merely "a question of time and opportunity." Hitler sought to avert American entry into the war in two ways: first, by driving America's natural allies out of the war quickly through blitzkrieg techniques of warfare; second, by keeping German warships out of the western Atlantic and by forbidding U-boats to attack American shipping anywhere on the high seas, thereby avoiding "incidents" with the United States.[3] A Wehrmacht command memorandum issued on the eve of war best expressed the Fuehrer's policy:

> The American Neutrality Law is a shackle for the most war-loving of American Presidents, one which presumably cannot be shaken off so long as we do not provide him with the excuse to breach this shackle. . . . Even if we are convinced that, should the war be of long duration, the USA will enter it in any case . . . it must be our object to delay this event so long that American help would come too late.[4]

Yet Hitler soon found that "the American danger was the one against which he could do nothing directly in advance." The Germans lacked the sea power and bases to project their ample military strength to the approaches to the New World. For their part, the Americans lacked the Army and Air Force necessary to intervene in Europe, and their youth were "little inclined to war service." Both sides needed time: the Americans to repair their weak defenses and refurbish their spirit; the Germans to deter American intervention by defeating the Allies. Thus, the Fuehrer's policy was prudent and sensible. But it possessed two great drawbacks: first, German military successes, far from intimidating the Americans, only spurred them to a more combative position; second, Hitler's reticence left the initiative in the Atlantic to the American President.[5]

Adolf Hitler once said that he was a hero on land, but a coward at sea. A continentalist, he eschewed colonies and large ships as hostages to his enemies' fleets. He believed that modern improvements in military transportation and communications made it possible at last for land powers to hold their own in warfare against the traditionally more mobile sea powers.

Germany's geographical position between France and Russia has bred in her statesmen an obsession with national security and a desire to gain strategic depth by encroaching on the domains of weaker neighbors. To this traditional thrust of policy, the Fuehrer added the intense nationalism of an Austrian outlander and the fever of an ideology half-revolutionary, half-atavistic. The new states of central and eastern Europe were weak, allowing Nazi expansionism to march along the path of least resistance. This course had the additional advantage of leading to Hitler's ultimate foe, Russia, which, because of shared origins and characteristics, both repelled and fascinated Hitler's Germany in, as H.R. Trevor-Roper has said, the same way a snake repels and fascinates a bird. But another impulse moved the Germans east. Although the Fuehrer often ridiculed large warships, he never quite evaded the nagging ghost of Mahan. Thus, he found the teachings of the geopoliticians attractive. In the vast Eurasian heartland, immune to the assaults of the sea powers, he saw the ultimate haven of his Reich. Psychology was perfectly wedded to strategy, for years of constant strife gave the Fuehrer the harried weariness of the inveterate outlaw; in the Urals heartland, he might rest at last, finally secure from foes both real and imagined. The escapism inherent in high places and dark forests appealed to him; it was more than the good infantryman's respect for tenable ground that impelled him to seek recreation or conduct business in mountain or forest regions. He sought an impregnable redoubt and built one in his mind.

A creative soldier, he complained often—as did his great adversaries, Roosevelt and Churchill—that his military advisers were too conservative. "The technicians," he asserted, "know only one word: No." A shrewd tactician, he saw better than his generals that tanks, trucks, aircraft, and mobile artillery had restored mobility to modern warfare and that the positional tactics and trench-fortress cast of thought from World War I were passé. But restless and impulsive, he lacked the patience and method to plan an effective long-range strategy for Germany. He built a powerful modern Army, the best in the world, and a largely tactical Air Force to support the tanks and infantry. But his continental outlook and impulsiveness, German industry's sluggishness in making a thorough transition to wartime production requirements, and Germany's insufficiency of vital natural resources, including metal ores and oil, all limited the growth of the Navy, which had a small submarine fleet and no aircraft at all.* Without a formidable Navy and a strategic Air Force, the Germans lacked the best weaponry to defeat Great Britain in time to deter the

*In addition to other priorities, Goering's insistence that all that flew belonged to the Luftwaffe dealt a fatal blow to German naval aviation. The Luftwaffe had efficient, if slow, dive bombers for use against shipping, but it lacked the other vital components of air-sea operations, effective torpedo armament and specialized torpedo aircraft. Goering dreamed of developing a bomber with the range to attack America, but did little to implement his reverie.

intervention of the rearmed United States, and lacked the realistic strategic planning efficiently to wage a protracted war once American intervention occurred.[6]

Frustration had long been the companion of the German Navy, which had played an insignificant part in the nineteenth century wars of unification; unlike the U.S. Navy, its traditions were not inextricably linked with the birth of the nation. The service fared better in the era of rapid industrialization and colonial expansion, and by World War I disposed a formidable array of modern vessels, outnumbered by but qualitatively superior to those of the Royal Navy. But geography and inexperience at sea doomed the Germans. They expected the British to mount a close blockade of the German coast, dispersing their forces in order to keep the German High Seas Fleet penned up in its ports. The Germans planned to whittle down the British blockading units spread out by weather, need to refuel, and tactical imperatives with quick, hit-and-run attacks by superior forces. Eventually, with British strength sapped by these tactics, the High Seas Fleet might be able at last to steam boldly into the North Sea and challenge the Grand Fleet in equal and decisive battle for command of the seas and victory.

But geography, the speed of radio communications, and the mine, submarine, and airplane impelled the British to forego the traditional close blockade; they found that they could intercept the High Seas Fleet from home waters. The British Isles served as a cork wedged deep into the neck of the North Sea bottle; and in home ports, the Grand Fleet might remain concentrated instead of dispersed.

The Germans, their prewar strategy foiled, sent their ships to conduct minor nuisance raids against the British coast and spent two years trying to maneuver the High Seas Fleet so as to force a battle against only a part of the stronger Grand Fleet. One such attempt resulted in the Battle of Jutland, in which the Germans fought well but were outnumbered and perhaps spared a crippling defeat only by the great caution of the British leadership. But, thereafter, the German heavy ships remained in port, their sailors disheartened by the contrast between hopes and achievement, while the Army bled copiously into the gray mud of the Western Front. There were rumors that cowardice, not strategic adversity, was responsible for the Navy's failure to fight harder. But morale amongst the submariners, who sustained increasingly high losses as the United States entered the war and the convoy system was introduced, remained sound. It was on the big ships, amongst men who had fought too little, not too much, that the soul of the Imperial Navy decayed. Then in 1919 came the Navy's ultimate humiliation; the surrendered High Seas Fleet was scuttled in Scapa Flow to keep it out of Allied hands.[7]

In the twenties, a small cadre of professionals kept a torpedo-boat Navy alive and clandestinely planned for future growth. In 1928, Erich Raeder became Commander-in-Chief of the Navy. Raeder, then fifty-two, came from a middle-class background. A dedicated, somewhat rigid and austere man, he deplored the glamour and hedonism of the times and strove to instill in the service his own reserve and commitment to cool professionalism. He was respected for his integrity, knowledge, and decisiveness; his staff had few strong wills or independent minds, as he preferred men who did not embarrass his shyness with unseemly controversy. Raeder detested the Nazis as ruffians, but hoped Hitler's nationalism might mean a larger Navy. He intended to keep faith with the dead by providing Germany with another battle fleet. A fine scholar and administrator, as well as an experienced sailor, yet never having commanded a ship in battle, Raeder sought for both his Navy and himself the glory both had missed in the past. However, Hitler did not intend to repeat the Kaiser's error of provoking the British with a significant naval building program; he also remembered that the Navy had played a major part in the nation's spiritual collapse in 1918. So, in the thirties, the service replaced superannuated ships, but did not grow appreciably. Besides, the geographic problem still seemed insoluble: a large surface fleet would be useless because the British once again would block its access to the Atlantic.

However, in the late thirties, the German naval staff became convinced that conquest of Norway or certainly of the French Channel ports would give the fleet safe access to the Atlantic and so restore the Navy's long-dormant offensive capability. At the same time, the Fuehrer was coming to see that the British would not indefinitely underwrite his advance toward the heartland. Prior to Munich, his foreign policy successes had resulted from the alleged superiority of the Luftwaffe; realizing this, Britain was improving her Air Force, and the Fuehrer felt the need of an additional weapon of intimidation. Thus, interest in a new High Seas Fleet was reawakened in Germany.[8]

In 1938, the Navy prepared two plans envisaging eventual war with Great Britain. The first supposed that time was the crucial factor, that the Navy would unexpectedly find itself at war with a much stronger British Navy, and thus, it would not be able seriously to contend for command of the seas. Therefore, this plan provided for a war on commerce, with the construction emphasis on submarines, the mobile, long-range pocket battleships, and merchant cruisers. The second—or "Z"—plan supposed that war would not come for at least a half-dozen years and that the Navy would have time to construct a large, balanced fleet of modern, high-speed, long-range ships; by 1945, the Germans hoped to possess 25 battleships, 4 aircraft carriers, nearly 50 cruisers, and 68 destroyers, all incorporating the latest design refinements. Operating in mobile task forces, they would ravage the merchant convoys and batter a Royal Navy dispersed in protection of commerce; the U-boats and Luftwaffe would besiege the British Isles and destroy the enemy war economy. Then the main fleet would wrest command of the seas from the weary, beset Royal Navy, paving the way for invasion and victory. It was an exhilarating concept, especially for a service whose tradition was one of defeat and unwarranted humiliation.

Raeder presented the alternate plans to the Fuehrer, explaining that the modest, quickly built force was necessary if there was likelihood of war soon; the formidable, balanced fleet could not be completed for seven or eight years, and in the meantime, if war came unexpectedly, the German Navy would be too weak and unbalanced to influence the outcome. Hitler replied that he would not require such a fleet until 1946; in January 1939, he formally approved the Navy's Z Plan.[9] But Hitler promised the Navy a peace he could not deliver; Britain was forced, as she had been historically, to uphold a European balance of power in the interest of her own security. Raeder, a reflective man and an historian, must have sensed this; but he repressed the knowledge, anxious for another chance at the foe who had bested his proud surface ships in a different war. Like Ahab, Erich Raeder sailed after glory and revenge, and his vanity and ambition killed too many of his shipmates.

The Z Plan was the triumph of the Navy's older officers. Raeder and his staff were comic figures to the submariners, led by Karl Doenitz, a fair, sharp-featured officer whose admiral's greatcoat hung baggily on his rangy frame. The conflict was as much one of generations as of naval strategy. Doenitz was a fitting product of the instability of his times. Unlike Raeder, he deprecated his middle-class origins and scorned the verities and platitudes of olden days. Dynamic and opportunistic, he adjusted well to the Nazi creed, whose emotionalism, vitality, and activism appealed to him. To Doenitz, Raeder reflected the stuffiness and complacency of a securer age. He detested the battleship outlook of the Naval Staff and deemed it madness to once again squander precious steel on ships that would never fight. With three hundred submarines, he promised, he could defeat Great Britain; in September 1939, he had fifty-seven.

Doenitz was unquestionably a great tactician of submarine warfare.* He was the pioneer of the night surface and "wolf pack" submarine tactics of World War II. He thought to employ submarines on the surface in the manner of oceangoing motor torpedo boats to counter the development of sonar; he evolved the *Rudeltaktic* of coordinated search and attack by several U-boats to counter the augmented defenses of the convoy system. And Doenitz was immensely popular with the submariners, whose morale he buoyed with hard training and fulsome praise. He pelted the naval hierarchy with prophecies of calamity. Raeder was annoyed by the unseemly pushiness of the younger man, but he was too dedicated to the service to replace so able, if obnoxious, an officer on personal grounds. He promoted conciliation by promising that U-boats would receive the highest construction priorities under the Z Plan. But the recriminations continued. Doenitz argued that the Z Plan would leave the Navy "unequipped for a war with Britain" and that the battleships would once again be prevented from moving into the Atlantic, this time by air power if not geography. The older officers, who regarded the Nazi apparatus with contempt, called the submariner "Hitler-Youth Doenitz." They pointed out that the narrow

---

*Yet in his absorption with the war on commerce he lacked strategic insight. He was preoccupied with the ratio between tonnage sunk and U-boat losses, the so-called "integral tonnage theory." But to those who thought of naval warfare in terms of command of the sea, there seemed a quantity-over-quality theme to Doenitz' tonnage war; they could not make themselves believe that an empty 10,000-ton tanker was necessarily a more valuable target than an 8,000-ton freighter carrying tanks that might help decide control of the Mediterranean if they reached North Africa.

Also, Doenitz' unwillingness to accept high losses meant that U-boats were shifted from vital, but dangerous, operating areas to low-risk patrol areas where sinkings could be maintained at low cost. To his critics, of course, all cargoes were not equal; to Doenitz, it was the ships, not the cargoes or destinations, that mattered, for if enough shipping were destroyed the enemy could not sustain his war effort.

The conflict was an expression of the classic confrontation in naval thought between war on commerce and strategic warfare for command of the sea. The submarine was a weapon to inhibit use of the sea; but it could not gain command of the sea.

wunderkind, despite his mastery of submarine tactics, knew little of the operations of great fleets and less of grand strategy.[10] The submariners retorted that the Naval Staff preferred battleships because they "couldn't put a band on the . . . deck" of a U-boat.[11]

In the end, of course, Doenitz was right. Upon the outbreak of war, one of Raeder's first acts was to suspend the Z Plan and abandon the construction of heavy ships. On 3 September 1939, he wrote an epitaph for his Navy: ". . . the submarine arm is still much too weak . . . to have any decisive effect on the war. The surface forces, moreover, are so inferior in number and strength to those of the British Fleet that, even at full strength, they can do no more than show that they know how to die gallantly. . . ."[12]

For Erich Raeder, the war came a half-dozen years too soon, and he abandoned himself to self-pity and memoranda of pessimism. The proud surface fleet was never built, and his smug rival, Doenitz, had charge of the only naval operations that mattered—the U-boat campaign. Eventually, the Fuehrer tired of Raeder's brusqueness and condescension and replaced him with a man of deeper enthusiasm for his flagging crusade, Karl Doenitz. Raeder, who had striven successfully to keep Nazi influence from corrupting the Navy, suspected that the Party might have a long memory; he carried a pistol on his person. If the thugs came for him, he, like his navy, would know how to die.

II:
The
Neutrality
Patrol

5.

The Long, Bad Days Ahead

On the eve of World War II, Admiral Johnson assessed his refurbished command. He felt that his old battleships were "not well fitted for the battle line" in wartime because of age, old guns, and lack of speed; hence, he thought that their best use would be for screening convoys against surface raiders. In his opinion, only the *Ranger*, his newly arrived heavy cruisers, and the PBYs and submarines seemed

> to have a logical place in an Atlantic Squadron in time of war, granted it is conceived as an instrument adequate to . . . turn back a sudden raid into the Caribbean pending the arrival of reinforcements from our West Coast. In fact, the Atlantic Squadron as now organized is not a logical task force. Rather it is a remnant of the former Training Detachment plus a division of heavy cruisers and a carrier, these latter ships the nucleus of a proper Atlantic Squadron.

After noting the continuance of such old problems as shortage of personnel, especially radiomen and signalmen, and lack of torpedoes for the destroyers and modern fire control for the old battleships, he added: "The real difficulty encountered in connection with enlisted personnel is the extensive turnover. The Squadron is used as a reservoir from which personnel is drawn for the entire Navy and is a repository for men awaiting transfer to newly commissioned units. This transiency is a serious bar to contentment. . . ."[1]

Meanwhile, the President was contemplating work for Admiral Johnson's small command. The idea of an Atlantic Patrol was a favorite of the President. On 20 April 1939, he told the Cabinet that he intended to establish "a patrol from Newfoundland down to South America and if some submarines are laying there and try to interrupt an American flag and our Navy sinks them it's just too bad. . . ." To the Secretary of the Treasury, this meant: "In other words, he is going to play the game the way they are doing it now. If we fire and sink an Italian or German . . . we will say it the way the Japs do, 'so sorry.' 'Never happen again.' Tomorrow we sink two. We simply say, 'so sorry,' and next day we go ahead and do it over again."[2]

That summer, after two months of negotiation, the President prevailed upon the British to lease seaplane-base sites at Trinidad and Bermuda to Pan American Airways, which would develop the bases for use by the American Navy. In the thirties, the British Caribbean islands were racked by sporadic paroxysms of violence, bred by the vicissitudes of the Great Depression and racial animosities of long standing. The Colonial Office feared that the Yankees, with their recklessly high wages and unsettling notions of democracy, would subvert the authority of the Crown and pave the way for American annexation. But the Foreign Office, anxious to make powerful friends in parlous times, was more realistic, and the President's overtures were accepted. However, the outbreak of war in September caused the plan to be dropped; to build bases on belligerent islands might involve the nation in war by accident.[3]

Shortly after the war began, on the morning of 6 September, the President's press secretary announced that the Navy would establish a patrol two or three hundred miles off the East Coast to report the presence of belligerent ships. Designed to keep the war away from the Western Hemisphere, the project allowed the nation a sense of participation in grand events without committing it to grave burdens or risks. The President hoped to prevent German submarines and German merchant vessels refitted as auxiliary cruisers and submarine tenders from operating in the western Atlantic, for it was feared that the first wolves would come forth in the raiment of lambs. A line was installed between the White House and the desk of the Director of the Ship Movements Division, and a large wall chart was set up in the President's office so that he could keep a plot of the Atlantic Squadron's divided forces. Admiral Johnson's old battleships and destroyers were still conducting summer training cruises, and the "order from the White House came as something of a shock" to the Navy.[4]

Immediately, the ships of Destroyer Squadron 10 rushed back from training cruises and were hastened out of upkeep status in the yards; the destroyers loaded fuel and provisions to capacity, took aboard live ammunition allowances, and, as the President's press secretary, Steve Early, was announcing the Patrol, took up their stations along the major trade routes off the coast. The four-stackers were undermanned, having crews of 56, instead of their full peacetime strength of 106; 13 of the 17 destroyers had no torpedoes or warheads, nine had no AA machine guns, and one had no depth charges. On 6 September, about a hundred miles east of Nantucket, the British merchantman *Aquitania* was looked over by a four-stacker of DesDiv 21, thus opening the store for the Neutrality Patrol.[5]

A few destroyers and seaplanes operated out of Boston-Newport, Norfolk, Charleston, Key West, Guantanamo Bay, and San Juan, with two cruisers in local reserve at Guantanamo; the *Ranger*, three heavy cruisers, the old battleships, and several destroyers were based at Hampton Roads as a reserve striking force.[6]

The Navy Department issued only "broad and general" instructions to the patrol commanders, who were somewhat perplexed by the nature of their duties. Commander Bill Greenman, skipper of DesRon 10, told his men, "It is my opinion, lacking advice to the contrary, that our patrol mission . . . is to make every effort to contact, diligently trail and report fully on the acts of all belligerent and suspicious vessels within our areas."[7]

Admiral Johnson limited the role of his ships to observation and reconnaissance. No one knew what action would be authorized if belligerent ships attempted to conduct active operations in the patrol zones, which were far outside the limits of American territorial waters. Franklin Roosevelt would decide that when the time came. Meanwhile, all that the Chief of Naval Operations could tell Admiral Johnson was, ". . . in all such matters obviously individual good judgment and common sense has to be exercised by the man on the spot."[8] With orders as flexible as these, the destroyer skippers feared that, in case of sudden trouble, they were indeed going to be "on the spot."[9]

The Patrol was slow in getting under way because of lack of support facilities. Two of Greenman's destroyers were sent to the Caribbean on one day's notice and sustained themselves there for over a month without tender support. At Key West, the fliers had no messing facilities, no small boats, no gasoline-storage tanks, nor even moorings for their planes; there were no tractors, and the aircraft were manhandled ashore to be refueled from pump trucks which brought the gas in from Fort Lauderdale where it was purchased from private sources.[10]

Another problem was the shortage of ships. It took a long time for the reconditioned World War I destroyers to join the Squadron; in the expectation that they would not be needed again, the ships had been laid up in too thorough a manner.

At San Diego, Commander W.W. Bradley took command of Destroyer Squadron 31 on 4 September, hoping to have the four-stackers ready for sea in about a month. But the ships needed substantial repairs, as they had been decommissioned after hard service and at that time it had seemed prodigal to expend precious funds to overhaul them. A lot of machinery had been dismantled and spare parts and tools removed, and it took time to get replacement parts and such necessary items as ships' boats and sonar gear from elsewhere in the country. Because ships' papers could not be found, defects had to be discovered by the tedious process of trial and error. Dock space and facilities were limited. Then there was the eternal problem of too few people. The first enlisted men to report were just out of boot camp; their unfamiliarity with the innards of a destroyer did not fit them for the surgery at hand. The reservists called to active duty appeared in driblets, and some of them were physically unfit and had to be sent to the base hospital instead of to the ships, causing Commander Bradley to recommend that higher physical standards be set for the Naval Reserve. Inexperience lengthened the time required to perform tasks. Help came from "broken service" men—those who reenlisted after brief stints as civilians—but their numbers were small; other men were drawn from cushy billets in the Naval Districts. But these sources supplied only little over half of the eight hundred men required, and it was necessary to apply the leech to the forces afloat, evoking much lamentation from commands already anemic. It took seven weeks to man all the old destroyers.

The thin crews, assisted by destroyermen from the base and off ships in port, worked in pools on those ships scheduled to leave earliest; thus, some ships received scarcely any attention at all, and as the supply of labor was diminished by sailings, their crews had to ready them without help. Working long hours at oil-clogged machinery and old guns, swapping esoteric parts, and tracing unfamiliar pipes to their source, the sailors tried to make up in tenacity for what they lacked in knowledge. Though he distrusted their inexperience and polyglot backgrounds, Commander Bradley could not help but grow fond of his hard-working crews. They were learning early that things were never easy in the destroyer service.[11]

At Philadelphia, Destroyer Squadron 30 was suffering similar adversity. Personnel was slow to report, hand tools were scarce, there were no check-off lists, and there had been excessive use of preservatives on equipment and machinery; for years, the Philadelphia yard had been a building yard, not a repair yard, and the workers were not skilled at reconditioning the four-stackers. But ample dry-dock space and good equipment and facilities were available, and the proximity of other East Coast yards made it possible to obtain essential equipment without frustrating delays. The first ships were recommissioned with crews of between 45 and 70 men. But the destroyers were not all in prime condition when they left the yard. The *Ellis* left for duty with her starboard shaft out of line, leaky heating coils on fuel tanks, dented hull plating, some corrosion on surfaces, and without some of her .50-caliber AA guns and her sonar gear.[12]

It was hoped that the best of the scheduled thirty-six recommissioned ships would be available for duty at about the end of the first week in October. However, the first of the Philadelphia ships did not report for duty with the Atlantic Squadron until the third week in October, and the last of the destroyers did not arrive until 22 November. The first of the San Diego vessels reported on 24 November; the last did not arrive until 15 December.[13]

At first, the Neutrality Patrol was fairly named. Admiral Johnson warned his ships:

. . . do not make report of foreign men-of-war or suspicious craft sighted immediately on making contact or while in their vicinity. This is for the purpose of avoiding performing unneutral service. . . . Do not give belligerents the opportunity of utilizing their interception of your radio transmissions for obtaining information useful to them.[14]

The patrolling ships were to report all belligerent warships, except convoy escorts, by radio. In the event of a submarine contact, "the movements of the submarine shall be observed and a surveillance patrol maintained in the general area . . . ."[15]

As there were no German warships in the western Atlantic, the Patrol was routine work; sea and air patrols were limited in bad weather to avoid needless risks. Nevertheless, Captain Louis E. Denfeld's division of new destroyers took some scars from the elements in its Grand Banks sweeps. Heavy seas wrecked boats and damaged bulwarks and lockers; it proved "almost impossible" for the men, who slept aft, to reach forward stations in rough weather. The *Benham* and *Ellet* sustained cracked plating and minor equipment failures; the gun ports in their forward turrets were not watertight, so tarpaulins were lashed across the turrets, restricting the guns. Both ships were docked for repairs, but the *Davis* and *Jouett* hung on.[16]

The patrol craft encountered many ships and a variety of temperaments. Some masters willingly provided their ship's name and destination when hailed, and sometimes a little information about vessels seen during the passage. Often, ships poor at reading signals had to be chased and harried at close quarters to make them respond. Some merchant skippers observed the traditional independence of their calling and refused to cooperate; if the destroyermen were unable to make out a flag or read a bow name, a PBY was called to buzz the hardhead. Sometimes distance or weather precluded identification. In October, 1,072 vessels were identified; 136 were sighted, but not identified. In November, 1,924 were identified and 178 remained unidentified. In December, 2,648 ships were identified, and 241 were not identified. In the three months, about fifty PBYs from Patrol Wing 5 flew 7,070 hours, 740,000 miles, and scanned 15¼ million square miles of sea; and their commanding officer reported that planes and men were in better condition than before the start of the Patrol. The destroyers kept a few rounds of ammunition in their ready racks, but no shot was fired across the bows of an unidentified ship.[17]

Nevertheless, the President was not satisfied with the scope or intensity of the Patrol. He had recently appointed his old friend, Admiral Harold R. "Betty" Stark, as Chief of Naval Operations. Stark's white hair, blue eyes, pink cheeks, and rimless spectacles softened his solid, bulldog features and betokened both toughness and gentleness. A calm, reserved man, his honesty and fairness were respected in the service, although some felt that he lacked decisiveness and fire. A careful and thoughtful planner, he had a sound grasp of strategy. But, because he had little aptitude for playing on the fears and ambitions of subordinates to make his purposes their own, he was not always able to coordinate in common effort the sundry independent fiefdoms of the vast naval bureaucracy; embarrassed by petty bickering, he sometimes tended to back away from sticky issues, and so was not always a sufficiently forceful administrator. And, despite their friendship, he and the President did not always understand each other.

Stark was restrained and logical; he never confused what was desirable with what was possible, and he trusted in methodical planning and precise thinking. The President, however, was glib, impulsive, and optimistic; he left it to others to work out the contradictions and impracticalities of his sudden inspirations. He distrusted the restraint imposed by fixed plans, and complained that his military advisers were "always conservative," ever ready to provide myriad technical reasons why something could not be done. Stark's reticence in argument, sense of propriety, suspicion of the President's grandiose schemes, and awe of the politician's flair for words, limited communication between the two men. The President mistook Stark's thoughtful silences for approbation of his sweeping designs.[18]

Late in September, when Stark and Roosevelt were discussing the ubiquitous problem of bases, the President abruptly turned to his wall chart of the Atlantic, took up a pencil, and made a sweeping boundary mark along the meridian of 60 degrees west longitude. The line began between Newfoundland and Nova Scotia and ran south all the way to the tip of British Guiana, passing 270 miles east of Bermuda. Roosevelt jubilantly asked Stark, "How would the Navy like to patrol such a neutrality zone?" The line extended a thousand miles east off Charleston; the Navy already had all it could do to maintain a token 200-mile patrol. Stark answered that such a patrol would require a very large number of ships and planes. The President seemed satisfied with the cautious rejoinder and turned to other matters.

Then, on 27 September, Assistant Secretary of State Adolf A. Berle asked the Navy for the details of its plans for the expanded security zone and of its method of dealing with the German merchantships stranded in hemisphere ports. Department spokesmen said they did not know anything specific about the zone, to which Berle replied that he thought Admiral Stark and the President "had thoroughly discussed the question." When Berle referred to an immense patrol of the scope that the President had seemingly hypothetically marked on his office chart for the bewildered Admiral Stark, the shocked sailors denounced the concept as "fantastic and impossible." They warned that the plan was not logistically feasible because of the lack of adequate bases in the Caribbean, and, even if it were, to carry it out effectively would require 290 ships and from 3,000 to 4,000 planes— virtually the entire surface fleet and some three times as many planes as the Navy possessed. Berle reassured them that, for the time being, the President would settle for a "token" patrol; there was no use exposing weakness by trying to do too much. The sailors, not appreciably cheered to learn that they were pregnant with merely a "token" white elephant, unhappily accepted the idea in principle, as the President flayed the Navy Department with critical memoranda. But they remained fearful of what would occur if and when the President ordered the full-blown patrol; since the vast majority of contacts were made close to shore, the sailors continued to believe the extended patrol wasteful and superfluous.[19]

But on 9 October, the President exploded again, writing:

I have been disturbed by:
(a) The slowness of getting the East Coast, Caribbean and Gulf Patrol under way.
(b) The lag between the making of contacts and the follow-up of contacts.
(c) The weakness of liasion between Navy, Coast Guard and State Department.
It is, therefore, necessary to make the following orders clear:
(1) The patrol operations will be rushed to completion. . . .
(2) When any aircraft or surface ship sights a submarine a report thereof will be rushed to the Navy Department for immediate action. The plane or surface ship . . . will remain in contact for as long as possible. On the disappearance of the submarine, immediate steps will be taken . . . to try to pick up the submarine again at dawn . . . and during the night endeavor to patrol such area as the submarine might use for a refueling operation from a tanker.
(3) On establishing contact with any suspicious surface craft of any nationality which might conceivably be carrying oil or supplies for a submarine, such surface craft will be followed day and night. . . .
(4) Planes or Navy or Coast Guard ships may report the sighting of any submarine or suspicious surface ships in plain English to Force Commander or Department. In this whole patrol business, time is of the essence and loss of contact with surface ships cannot be tolerated.

FDR [20]

Accordingly, a Galveston patrol was set up in November, although in the absence of naval facilities, a private firm, Todd Shipyards Corporation, had to service the destroyers. The Gulf Patrol was a response to the large number of German merchant ships hiding in Mexican ports preparatory to making a dash for home. The President's "plain language" dictum was aimed at the German vessels, for it was they who behaved suspiciously by steaming evasively, showing no lights, and altering prominent design features. Allied merchantmen, far removed from the presence of their foes, had no need for subterfuge.[21]

On 30 September, in a routine transfer, Rear Admiral Hayne Ellis replaced Admiral Johnson as commander of the Atlantic Squadron. Ellis was a competent older officer, pleasant, forbearing, and settled in his ways; like Johnson, he ran a sensible, efficient command, but lacked fire. He commanded, but did not lead.[22]

Meanwhile, "submarine" sightings were coming in. They had begun on the very first day of war and continued thereafter. U-boats were reported being refueled off Cuba, and empty gasoline drums washed ashore on the Haitian coast spurred rumors of similar activity there; a German submarine was said to have refueled from a merchant ship in the Gulf of Mexico and transferred demolitions to be used for sabotage. Although Admiral Raeder as early as 1937 had considered the possibility of Germany sustaining naval operations against the United States from bases in Mexico and South America, it soon became obvious that this was impossible. Germany lacked the naval power, and Hitler lacked the inclination to challenge the U.S. Navy in the western Atlantic. There were no German submarine operations in the American patrol zone. Nevertheless, the sighting reports were usually lucid, quite detailed, and the work of sober, responsible individuals; but they were all false.[23]

Early in October, the four-stacker *Borie* investigated several eyewitness "sightings" at various ports in the Virgin Islands. She made an extensive, thorough search, but found no U-boats. As a cruiser officer caustically told the *Borrie's* skipper: "The local inhabitants are very accommodating about furnishing rumors of submarines if that is what you want . . . If there are German submarines in these waters they are making no attempt to sink British and French shipping, and it would therefore appear to be a very wasteful employment of German forces."[24]

In December, the four-stacker *Twiggs* shadowed the British destroyer *Hereward* in Yucatán Channel, discreetly observing as the British ship refueled from a "G"-class cruiser. In the same month, the *Twiggs* and *Evans* and the heavy cruiser *Vincennes* trailed the Royal Australian cruiser *Perth* in Yucatán Channel, repeatedly asking her to identify herself; but the *Perth* persistently refused, responding vaguely, "British warship." Her skipper, Captain H.B. "Fighting Freddie" Farncomb, searching for a German merchant ship, was annoyed at the presence of the Americans. Angrily he roared, "Queer ideas of 'neutrality' these Americans have!"[25]

The British were not pleased with the Neutrality Patrol because they feared it might protect German vessels in the western Atlantic from attack, and more importantly, because it symbolized America's desire to remain aloof from the war. As the neutrality zone was too vast to be effectively patrolled, the British reserved the right to pursue German ships inside the zone. Thus, in December, three British cruisers chased the *Graf Spee* into Montevideo, where the luckless pocket battleship was scuttled. The State Department's half-hearted protests were, the British felt, made strictly for the record.[26]

At the outbreak of the war, there were about eighty-five German merchant ships in hemisphere waters; approximately thirty-two eventually made it back to Germany. On a worldwide basis, however, the Germans were more successful; by 1940, about a hundred ships had reached Germany safely, while about twenty-six were lost as they attempted to return. The British were preoccupied with the hunt for important raiders like the *Graf Spee* and German auxiliary cruisers, allowing many of the German merchant ships to escape.[27]

The liner *Bremen* was in New York, and the President directed that State Department personnel make a thorough search of the ship for concealed ordnance; the investigation took three days, and included a one-by-one count of all the life jackets aboard! The President hoped that the *Perth* and HMS *Berwick* would be able to intercept the liner, thanks to the delay. But the *Bremen*, aided by fog off Newfoundland and a wise choice of route, reached Germany safely.[28]

In the fall, the tanker *Emmy Friedrich* was taken by British naval units shortly after leaving Tampico; *Ranger* planes also searched briefly for her. Transmission of contact reports by the destroyer *Truxtun* helped French ships in the pursuit of fleeing German merchantmen *Wangoni* and *LaPlata*. In January, the freighter *Konsul Horn*, although sighted by a PBY out of San Juan, evaded the British picket ships and made it back to Germany. In the same month, the *Bahia* fled Brazil and thanks to a tricky route made it safely home. In March, the tanker, *Hannover* was captured in Mona Channel by a British cruiser and Canadian destroyer after an attempt to scuttle failed dismally.[29]

The Navy tried to keep a close watch on the Mexican ports, because the patrol was much less effective in the open Atlantic than in the cul-de-sac of the Gulf; most contacts were made within two hundred miles of the coast. The ten PBYs at Guantanamo and San Juan flew 8,000 miles daily, but admitted that the flights were "efficient only for vessels passing from the Atlantic into the Caribbean."[30]

Occasionally, the Atlantic Squadron's prosaic duties resulted in memorable events, such as the pursuit of the North German Lloyd liner *Columbus*. The 32,500-ton ship left New York on 15 August for a tourist cruise in the West Indies. The crew sensed the probability of war and speculated worriedly over their uncertain prospects. At Barbados, the ship received news of the deteriorating diplomatic situation and Captain Wilhelm Daehne decided to top off his fuel bunkers at Curaçao. En route, the *Columbus* met the British light cruiser *Orion*; her crew did not regard the encounter as a matter of chance. At Curaçao, the Dutch officials were casually rude; the German flag was not an esteemed one amongst men who lived beyond the range of the Wehrmacht's arms. The Dutchmen refused Daehne's request for oil and threatened to search the liner for clandestine arms. The ship went on to Havana to put ashore complaining passengers, angered by the interruption of vacations. But the *Columbus*' reception in Cuba was not cordial and, desperate for oil, Daehne decided to make for Mexico. The *Columbus* skulked out past Morro Castle on a dark night, running close along the Cuban coast. On 4 September, she arrived safely at Vera Cruz. Although the war was only a day old, Captain Daehne understood that it was already over for him.

But at the end of October, the German consul in Vera Cruz told Daehne that the *Columbus* had been ordered by Berlin to run the blockade. Daehne protested, arguing that he had been fortunate to reach Mexico. He advised that the liner be sold, even for the pittance in Mexican currency that she would bring under the lamentable circumstances. The diplomat told him that the order was irrevocable; a successful escape would have a salutary effect on the Latin neutrals, encouraging them to withstand the diplomatic and economic pressure of the Allies. Besides, the consul said, there was no danger; the British would not attack inside the American neutrality zone. The *Columbus* would have to sail. "Sie muessen fahren," he insisted. "Sie muessen!"

Heartsick, Daehne felt that the loss of his ship was inevitable; but he was determined to preserve the lives of his men and keep the liner from being captured by the British. He took a long time to get the *Columbus* ready for sea. The ship was painted over and slightly modified to alter her appearance, the crew moved amidships, lifeboats and safety gear were checked, "abandon ship" drills were held;

salons once redolent of perfume and liquor smelled of paint and sweat; bandages and dressings were arrayed incongruously on polished dance floors, and men lugged sandbags and mattresses into stately cabins for splinter shields. For two full weeks, specially trained parties practiced the swift destruction of the liner; buckets of gasoline were placed so that they could quickly be emptied down ventilation shafts, and drums of oil, gas, and benzine were stored near rags and other flammable wastes. The British would not take the *Columbus.*

Despite the consul's assurances that the two American destroyers patrolling offshore would probably escort the liner safely through the security zone, Daehne was worried by them. The ships were the *Lang* and *Benham,* the latter glad to be in calm Gulf waters after her rough stint off the Grand Banks.

Columbus refueled from a Mexican tanker, and on 13 December, edged toward the channel entrance. The green sea was running high, and she began her venture under a gray sky; the expectations of the men inside her were as gloomy as the day. The *Lang* fell in behind the ship, to be relieved the first night out by two four-stackers. The weather remained dreary, and at night, the destroyers had to close to within six hundred yards of the liner's stern quarter, one on each side, in order to maintain visual contact. The American ships ran fully lighted, as always when patrolling at night, but they sometimes approached so close that Daehne reluctantly elected to keep on one of his own night lights. At times, when the destroyers were very near, his ship barely had room to turn or maneuver. He felt like a "dog on the leash."

The destroyers were replaced by a fresh pair, venerable *Cole* and *Ellis,* off Cape Canaveral. The *Columbus* cleared the dangerous Florida Strait in safety, but was consuming 450 tons of fuel per day; Daehne felt compelled to reduce speed to an economical 16 knots to save a hundred tons of fuel daily. The liner stayed close to the American coast until she was abreast of Cape Hatteras and in more crowded waters, then she swung east, out to sea, to make her break for Germany.

Cole's skipper was Lieutenant Commander Paul F. Dugan; his four-stacker was one of those recently recommissioned. She was old and short-legged, but Dugan was fond of her; he remembered that after World War I she had set a record by once making over 42½ knots. Pride is born of small things, and Dugan's men gave their best to the old *Cole* and made her a welcome friend in any melee at sea.

Now, Dugan watched the liner thrash into the moderating seas, listening sadly as the *Ellis* sent out a position report in plain language every four hours. He was sorry the *Cole* had drawn this wretched duty. Certain that the transmissions would be picked up by the Royal Navy, Dugan felt that the American vessels were giving the "kiss of death" to the liner.

About a hundred miles out, two other American destroyers appeared, swaying slightly against the horizon. Dugan told his signalman to blink out "bon voyage" to the German, and the *Columbus* sent back a similar signal. The *Cole* then swerved away from the big ship's quarter to make room for her replacement, and set course for Charleston. At sea, it was hard to think of *Columbus*' men as pawns of a vicious ideology; they seemed simply sailors working hard to save their ship, and Dugan hoped that none of them would die because of anything that he had done. It was a thoughtful trip home for the *Cole*.

Not long afterward, the heavy cruiser *Tuscaloosa* swung in behind the *Columbus*, dipping her flag politely and blinking out good wishes in bright, yellow flashes. But Captain Daehne grumbled, "What the devil does this all mean? Is he protecting us or shadowing us?"

The 19th was a mild, clear day. The British destroyer *Hyperion*, cruising about 320 miles northwest of Bermuda, picked up transmissions between the *Tuscaloosa* and another ship; *Hyperion* radioed the American cruiser, "What ship are you escorting?" Captain Harry Badt of the *Tuscaloosa* did not identify the *Columbus*, but the suspicious circumstances alerted the *Hyperion* to investigate, and Captain Badt had no orders to warn her off. An hour later, *Hyperion* sighted *Columbus* and signalled her by flag hoist to halt. The liner radioed her position and circumstances, in order to alert Berlin to her fate. Captain Daehne looked to the *Tuscaloosa* for help; his ship was about 425 miles off Cape May, and he thought her still inside the vaguely defined American security zone. He hoped to see the gun turrets of the cruiser swing to commence tracking the smaller British warship. But instead, the *Tuscaloosa* decreased speed to stand by about a mile away. The *Hyperion* fired twice in a single rumbling roar, and two high spouts of white water rose up off the liner's bow. Daehne ordered the *Columbus* stopped, and most of her crew, with a calm born of long practice, went to the lifeboats. Three officers and two score men roamed the vessel, spilling drums of petrol into the passageways, then firing Very pistols to send rivers of orange fire coursing through the insides of the liner. They opened seacocks, smashed skylights, and set fire to oil-soaked rags. Twenty-three minutes later, they went over the side.

On the bridge, Daehne watched the *Hyperion* with a numbed detachment; like all captains who have lost a ship, he suffered from a sense of guilt. It is this feeling, rather than the lure of tradition, that impels skippers to go down with their ships. Daehne flung the weighted bag containing the ship's code books and secret documents overboard. Hot flames twisted nearby metal, and it occurred to Daehne that his immolation would serve no high purpose. He swung down a rope into a launch manned by sailors off the *Tuscaloosa*, who by training and inclination did not readily concede the life of any man to fire or water.

From the scattered boats, the seamen of three nations watched the blazing *Columbus* settle into the blue swells, as spirals of brown-black smoke formed a bleak, sooty cloud over the liner. Finally, a young American sailor said to Daehne, "Isn't war awful, sir?"

With the slight accent that had charmed many a female tourist in happier times, the German answered, "It's the vorst there is!"

The scuttling cost the *Columbus* but two of her 557 men. The survivors were taken to the United States and, as "distressed mariners," were freed.[31]

The President was not inclined to have the work of the Neutrality Patrol publicized, so Admiral Stark radioed Captain Badt to give the impression that his ship had come upon the German liner by accident and, fortunately, just in time to pursue her humane role; he was to state that the British ship had not appeared ready to commence an action. As Stark noted, "we do not desire you to make public the details of the work of our . . . patrol." However, accurate accounts of the affair were soon in print, but they caused no sensation. As long as the President worked to eliminate belligerent vestiges from the hemisphere, the nation was not disposed to debate his tactics.[32]

Meanwhile, another German vessel made a break for home. On 14 December, the freighter *Arauca* left Vera Cruz to attempt the long run to Hamburg with a cargo of sisal, phosphates, hides, resin, and pepper. She was trailed by the ubiquitous American destroyers, *Truxtun*'s transmissions alerting French warships to the general whereabouts of the fleeing merchantman. The *Arauca* steamed northeast until she was about 150 miles off the mouth of the Mississippi, thence southeast toward the Dry Tortugas and along the Florida coast, only five miles offshore, making cautiously for Florida Strait. However, on the morning of the 20th, she was intercepted off

Oakland, Florida, by the British cruiser *Orion*. At 1056, the warship fired a warning cannon shell, which splashed in the water off the freighter's bow, and signalled the German to turn seaward. Instead, the *Arauca* headed toward the nearby shore, steaming into American territorial waters to be protected by the shadowing four-stackers. In the afternoon, a small party off the destroyer *Philip* boarded and checked the cargo ship; then the *Arauca* moored in Port Everglades. The *Orion* continued to patrol relentlessly offshore, a hungry cat at a mousehole. But the *Arauca* did not sail again. Occasionally, Floridians went out in small boats to the British cruiser, bringing candy, cigarettes, and good wishes, but they were soon informed by representatives of the Justice Department that such acts were in violation of the nation's neutrality laws![33]

Few German merchant ships stirred that winter and spring, and for the most part, the long vigil of the Atlantic Squadron was uneventful. In January, planes and ships on patrol contacted about 2,005 vessels; in February, the number of contacts was 1,592. As more ships joined the Squadron, and as weather improved and the Allies' war needs led to more trade with America, the number of contacts increased to 3,420 in March and to 3,647 in April.[34]

Bill Greenman observed in March:

All . . . has been accomplished under the pressure of a declared emergency, and this stimulant has boosted morale to a high degree. Now . . . the emergency has become routine, and the patrol is a matter of scheduling vessels to cover a given area day after day. The monotony of the patrol is obvious, and therefore if it is to be maintained for the day when it must demonstrate its value, (and it's sure to come if the war continues) variations must be injected. [35]

The patrol became grinding and wearying. The ships lost many experienced hands to new construction vessels; thus, as the destroyers filled out crews to their allotted 106-man complements, they were inundated with inexperienced men. Skippers, accustomed to the skilled work of veteran professionals thoroughly trained in their jobs by years of slow advancement, had to condition themselves to tolerate adequate performances and acceptable solutions from men and officers. Steady patrolling made it difficult to provide essential training for green men, and with the ships dispersed, integrated tactical exercises were impossible. In northern waters, rough seas precluded many drills, and the long-uncared-for guns on the four-stackers froze and could not be used even for simulated firing.

The *Hale's* skipper reported that "a large percentage" of his crew "had never seen a gun fired." The *Philip's* gunnery officer was untrained in that specialty and only one year out of the Naval Academy. One-third of the *MacLeish's* crew had never participated in a gunnery practice. The *Badger's* gunnery department was decimated by an "unexpected transfer of personnel." The *Claxton* and *Breckinridge*, back from frigid climes, reported worn and broken parts, green men, frozen guns, and heavy seas that made it "almost impossible for the men to stay on a target when the ship rolled even a few degrees." The *Decatur's* skipper found his men willing, indeed "outstanding in view of their lack of experience."[36]

Captains soon found the youngsters and reservists to be "damn good men," who qualified for most important duties about as quickly as Academy-trained novices. While naturally not as qualified as the veteran professionals, the newcomers quickly "developed enough confidence and judgment to know what they *did not* know, and could call for help." The good squadron officers called their key people together and gave them the word. Greenman told his men:

> It looks as though we may get into this war. You are receiving—and will continue to receive—a lot of new officers and men as a portion of your experienced people are detached to man newly constructed ships. You, and all your officers and senior petty officers, must see to it that these newcomers become proficient in the shortest possible time. The *attitude* of the older officers and men toward the reserves will be particularly important. Treat them for what they are—a selected bunch of men who have volunteered to join us and whom we are lucky to get. Give them responsibilities at every safe opportunity. Train them at every opportunity. Encourage rather than heckle them. Make it clear to your officers and chief petty officers that their ship, and perhaps their lives, may depend on these reserves becoming *good* officers and men. [37]

The skippers were determined and confident; as one recalled, "I used to think I could make a sailor out of the devil himself."[38] With demanding captains and willing youngsters, good crews developed to man the ships, all of which seemed either too old or too new.[39]

The skippers fretted because the patrol prevented most gunnery and tactical training. The skipper of DesRon 31, articulate, dynamic Captain Wilder D. Baker, reported: "Upkeep sadly needed for all vessels. . . . Tactical training is completely out." He added:

> . . . up to the present USS *MacLeish* is the only vessel having completed any gunnery exercise during the current gunnery year and she has completed only short range practice with a very unsatisfactory score.

A four-stacker—the USS *Lea*

Baker went on to stress the need for tactical exercises, so that "commanding officers of individual vessels and division commanders would thereby become accustomed to the duties required of vessels of the Fleet. At present such knowledge and training is at a minimum." Asserting that conditions made "proper training practically impossible," he requested that his Galveston-based ships join the rest of the squadron at Key West to allow integrated tactical training. He felt that U.S. consuls could keep as adequate a watch on the movements of German merchantmen in Mexican ports as could his destroyers from Galveston.[40]

Baker voiced a common complaint among destroyermen when he wrote:

> The demands of the patrol are such that practically no consistent progressive tactical and gunnery training can be accomplished. . . . If it is the intention of the Department that these vessels should be employed on active patrol to the practical elimination of satisfactory gunnery and tactical training then no comment is required. But . . . if the essential . . . training necessary to fit them for their general duties as destroyers is desired, then a radical change in the requirements of the Patrol is mandatory.[41]

The destroyer officers wanted the ships concentrated to allow unit training, with the vessels proceeding to patrol stations only in emergencies.[42]

The duties of the patrol did foster improvements in the general skills of seamanship, as the capable tracking at close quarters of belligerent ships attested, and even in certain of the specialized skills; communicators, for example, gained valuable experience. But the skills that could not be exercised, particularly gunnery and tactics, atrophied.[43]

The patrol bombers showed the same trends as the destroyers. Lack of relief crews and the transfer of trained men to new squadrons limited the PBYs to eighty hours' flying a month; with ample practice, scouting became "excellent," but tactics, bombing, and gunnery deteriorated.[44]

Mostly, the patrol "was quiet—too quiet." As the executive officer of a four-stacker put it, his ship "would go back and forth between Yucatan Peninsula and the western tip of Cuba, altering course now and then to intercept and identify ships. . . . It was all rather monotonous, but the weather was good. . . ."[45]

The Atlantic Squadron's routine operations were not without certain trials and, sometimes, cost.

Occasionally, a nervous Allied merchant crew would nearly open fire on a low-flying PBY, but no planes were harmed.[46]

The carriers were getting new planes to replace their obsolete ones, but new planes meant teething troubles; the early "bugs" of the aircraft restricted night operations and high-altitude flying. Hence, in the carriers, the price of inexperience was sometimes high. On 16 January 1940, a young *Ranger* flier stalled his fighter while pulling out over the wrong side of the ship after a fifth wave-off. The plane crashed, sinking inside of a minute, and dragged the pilot under with it. For a moment, the tail section protruded out of the water, a bulky, cross-shaped headstone.[47]

In December 1939, the *Reuben James* was driven onto a reef in Long Island Sound; her belly was ripped so badly that she required four months in dry dock. The bridge watch had not been sufficiently alert, and both the skipper and the Exec were court-martialed for negligence.[48]

The skipper of a hastily converted transport was unable to adjust to leading a green crew and had to be replaced for lack of "force and effectiveness."[49]

On the morning of 25 November 1939, the recently recommissioned four-stacker *Yarnall* was anchored placidly in Lynnhaven Roads. She had been operating for but twenty days, and the process of qualifying men for bridge watch had been slowed by the press of more compelling needs in making the old ship fit for sea. The destroyer bobbed and swung out with the sway of the tide, the water slapping against her sides with a lulling, soughing sound. It took the green watchstanders too long to sense a subtle change in the motion of the ship and take a sighting of the coastline. The destroyer was moving. The captain came to the bridge as general quarters was sounded and he gave orders to get under way, but he did not order emergency engineering procedures for fear of danger to the machinery and black gang. The lack of emergency action was academic, for the destroyer quickly drifted aground. A defective link had caused the anchor chain to part; the bridge watch had failed to provide the CO with sufficient warning to enable him to prevent the accident. But a skipper's responsibility is as broad as his authority, and the failure of personnel was held to reflect inadequacy of command. The destroyer skipper was relieved of duty.[50]

Although the sailors considered the patrol inefficient, the President insisted on retaining it. Thus, the importance of political considerations over purely technical needs was one of the Navy's first lessons in the President's new kind of war.

The President, whose self-proclaimed "map mind" had assimilated the doctrines of Mahan and applied them to the age of the airplane, was resolved to keep Axis power beyond the fringes of the outposts of the New World. *[51]

The patrol allowed the President to act, yet retain flexibility, which he liked. He once said that in the Atlantic, where the Germans were forced to play with his deck of cards (naval warfare) instead of Hitler's (land warfare), all the "jokers were wild." Deliberately, he left the scope and duties of the patrol nebulous. When asked at a press conference how far he thought American waters extended toward Europe, he answered cryptically, as far as necessary. One reporter, recalling FDR's late-lamented quip that in an age of progressive military technology the American defense frontier was on the Rhine, asked if American waters reached as far as the Rhine. The President laughed and said that he was talking only about salt water.[52]

The patrol had symbolic value, warning the Nazis of the enmity of the American people and reminding them that there were things that the Americans cherished more than peace. It served the President as a halfway house between craven idleness and dangerous boldness. It reduced German naval power in the western Atlantic to nothing, allowed Allied convoys to organize safely in American waters, and freed Allied warships for duty elsewhere,[53] yet it avoided divisive domestic antagonisms; isolationists could only applaud a scheme to bar belligerent ships from the approaches to the Western Hemisphere, and the absence of shooting and bloodshed soothed liberals of pacifist bent.

The President's temperament required activity; movement and flux inspired him, stagnation depressed his spirit and enervated his will. He *had* to act. Yet if to do nothing seemed unthinkable, the risks of diplomatic threats, as his Quarantine Speech appeared to show, outweighed their meager efficacy. Only the President's Navy could safely challenge the enemy. The Atlantic Squadron was all that Franklin Roosevelt had to fight with in the first months of World War II,[54]

*FDR said of Mahan: "He wrote that to all intents and purposes, America separated from Europe and Africa and Asia by a wide ocean, is insular in geography and that, therefore, threats of aggression can best be met at a distance from our shores rather than on the seacoast itself."

and he used it to test the purposes of the German Fuehrer. He soon discovered that his foe lacked the will to give battle at sea. That discovery proved of inestimable future value, and Mr. Roosevelt's Navy, the U.S. Atlantic Squadron, was given more formidable tasks.

Hence, the Neutrality Patrol was more than the empty, wasteful gesture that many in the Navy deemed it and less than the German Navy feared from the Americans.[55] But, by diminishing training, the patrol weakened the Atlantic ships for future tests. In naval terms, the Neutrality Patrol was not worth the massive effort that the President demanded; but in political terms, it had value. It deserved to be retained but, as the sailors wanted, much reduced in scope in order to lessen the strain on the Atlantic Squadron. The President, however, liking its symbolism, ordained that the patrol be maintained without change.

And so, the patrol continued, testing the merit of the Atlantic sailors. A careless or luckless handful failed their ships and were replaced. Most worked with skill and dedication to make old ships and new men ready for the long, bad days ahead.

6.

A Blue Flag at Ivigtut

THE COLLAPSE OF FRANCE in the desperate spring of 1940 ended the American reverie of a war without sacrifice.

On 20 May the British ambassador in Washington wrote a friend:

> The USA is at last profoundly moved and frightened. It had been dreaming on that it could keep out and that the Allies would keep the tiger away. And now the spectre has suddenly arisen that the British fleet may disappear and then what is to happen to itself? It has only one navy. Is it to keep it in the Atlantic or Pacific? If it keeps it in the Pacific, Germany and Italy will be able to take Brazil . . . and threaten the Canal. If it keeps it in the Atlantic the Japanese will take over the Pacific. If it divides its fleet it will be impotent in both oceans. [1]

Several days later, President Roosevelt ordered the preparation of emergency plans for occupation of the Allies' West Indian possessions and for an expeditionary force to support Brazil in the event of an Axis-inspired revolt, though the latter proved beyond the means of the U.S. Army. The planners warned that if the Germans acquired significant numbers of French ships, the United States would have but a six months' grace period, concluding, *"the date of the loss of the British or French fleets automatically sets the date of our mobilization."* And Admiral Ellis grimly warned: "The present composition of the [Atlantic] Squadron is quite inadequate to cope with the forces which the progress of events in Europe may soon release to operate against it."[2]

Because of the uncertain situation in Latin America, the heavy cruiser *Quincy* was ordered south from her Neutrality Patrol station at Guantanamo Bay. She spent a few days in Rio without incident, except that on 15 June a liberty party was recalled to the cruiser because of a clash between police and pro-Allied demonstrators. The American officers found the leaders of the Brazilian Navy friendly, but felt the Army was pro-German. President Getulio Vargas, who understood the vulnerable geographic position of his country in relation to Vichy-dominated northwest Africa and feared a coup by Brazilian Germans, crushed political agitation with a heavy hand; but, conscious of German power, he was reluctant to form closer ties with the United States. The *Quincy*'s skipper reported that most of Brazil's problems were economic, those of a colonial economy exchanging low-cost raw materials for high-priced manufactured goods; he recommended more liberal trade agreements with Latin America,[3] a comment that must have warmed the heart of that vehement foe of tariffs, Secretary of State Cordell Hull.

The cruiser went on to Montevideo and was well received, thousands crowding along the waterfront in welcome. Minister Edwin C. Wilson promised Uruguay assistance "in crushing all activities which arise from non-American sources."

The heavy cruiser *Wichita* visited Argentina, and the officers felt that, when the warship left, Nazi-inspired disturbances were likely as part of a plan to test U.S. reactions and "discover to what length the United States is willing to go to uphold the Monroe Doctrine."[4]

The State Department's Division of American Republics feared that "a successful revolution backed by the Nazis is becoming a more likely possibility" in Latin America. Laurence Duggan, a State Department Latin-American specialist, hoped that the *Quincy*'s visit would "put a little iron in the veins of our friends in those countries." Undersecretary Sumner Welles pressed for a task force of cruisers and destroyers to operate off South America throughout the summer.[5]

Admiral Stark was furious when he learned of these plans. His Atlantic ships were dispersed from Boston to Puerto Rico, conducting routine patrol duties that prevented vital training; reserve forces had to be maintained for emergency operations in such remote parts as Dakar and Greenland. He could not afford another diversion of ships for political reasons; besides, it would be difficult to supply so large a force as four heavy cruisers and nine destroyers from so small and distant a base as Guantanamo.

Accordingly, on 2 June, Admiral Stark wrote the President, stating that Nazism would thrive or decline in Latin America in proportion to German successes in Europe; all that visits of American ships might do was to encourage the military services to remain loyal to their governments. He opposed bringing ships from the Pacific Fleet for fear of weakening "the deterrent effect on Japan." Finally, he lamented the President's fondness for gunboat diplomacy:

> The days of the old fashioned landing party and bluff such as occurred when I was a midshipman in Caribbean and South American waters are over. If a test should come and our ships should take no physical action, the ultimate effect might be unfavorable. . . . It seems to me that interference in the internal affairs of a temperamental and suspicious people may have the opposite effect to that which is desired. . . . [6]

But Undersecretary Welles was appalled at the notion that the United States "should do nothing" when governments in the hemisphere were menaced by Nazi-nurtured revolts. The President agreed with Welles, but Stark's vehemence and fear of Japanese moves in southeast Asia restrained him. From time to time during the summer, the *Quincy* and the "Witch" showed the flag and watched developments in South America without incident.[7]

Attempts to reach tacit defense alliances with the Latin nations were uniformly unsuccessful, for the Latin Americans demanded in return shipments of arms, particularly artillery. The myth of Yankee opulence persuaded some that armaments were not provided because of penury or foolish preoccupation with European affairs. Some leaders were afraid of provoking the possibly victorious Germans, others feared domestic political opposition. Some were unwilling to invest the resources and energies of their nations in defense, since the United States, in the interest of its own security, would have to assist hemispheric countries in an emergency. Others felt that no direct threat to the hemisphere yet existed.[8]

The presence of French warships, particularly the carrier *Béarn*, in the West Indies was another source of concern in Washington. Because of pride and reluctance to antagonize their German conquerors, the French would not allow their ships to join the British. The British blockaded Martinique and Guadeloupe from their own West Indian bases. Hence, in July, the Atlantic Squadron had to furnish a cruiser and six destroyers to replace the British in watching the French islands, in order to end the British snub of the Monroe Doctrine and avoid a possible Anglo-French clash. Meanwhile, plans were prepared for the capture of the islands. In August, Rear Admiral John Greenslade was sent to Fort de France to get assurances that the French ships would not steam to Africa to join the Vichy forces. The French demurred, later arguing that they had hinted at compliance but were hardly in a position to give formal assent. The status quo continued into the fall. Intelligence reports and patrols were used to keep track of the French vessels. The American skippers assumed that, if the French warships came out, the U.S. vessels would follow and periodically broadcast position reports, allowing the British to turn back the ships, hopefully without a fight. But no one knew for certain.[9] The President kept his intentions to himself.

The Danes, fearing either German or British occupation of Greenland, requested American assistance in defending it. The State Department rejected the idea, fearing to set a precedent for occupation of the territory of defeated European powers which Japan might follow. But it was decided to send a vessel immediately to show the flag and reassure the population.

Greenland was important because a knowledge of its weather was vital to forecasting conditions in the North Atlantic and much of Europe. Early in the war, the German Navy had fitted out a weather-ship, the *Sachsen*, to operate off the east coast of Greenland, but naval fears of losing the ship to the Royal Navy and Foreign Office fears of provoking the United States by operations in the Western Hemisphere deterred its sailing. However, the Germans were believed to have set up a meteorological station on the barren northeast coast, and German patrol bombers from Norway were said to overfly the area periodically, perhaps in search of weather data, perhaps to supply clandestine parties below. Another source of Greenland's significance was the cryolite mine in the small west coast town of Ivigtut; the mineral was indispensable in the manufacture of aluminum. The Canadians seemed anxious to occupy Greenland, and the State Department feared that the Canadians were interested as much in securing exclusive use of the cryolite as in defense strategy.

It was decided to employ Coast Guard ships for the Greenland patrol operations. Coast Guardsmen were familiar with the difficult operating conditions in those waters, as a result of experience in conducting the International Ice Patrol. The presence of their cutters in northern waters was normal, and thus would attract little notice. And, finally, although the cutters mounted a 3-inch gun, several 50s, and could accommodate an SOC reconnaissance float plane, they belonged to a civilian agency, the Treasury Department, and so were technically not warships.[10]

On 10 May, Lieutenant Commander Frank Meals sailed in the *Comanche* for Greenland with civilian officials, supplies, and equipment for a radio station. At Boston, Commander Edward H. "Iceberg" Smith, an eminent oceanographer and explorer, readied other cutters for the task of prowling the east coast of Greenland for signs of German activity.

By 20 May, the *Comanche* was off Ivigtut, the crew scanning rippled, gray sea and a silent, craggy shore. The sailors watched as people came out of the mine and clustered in cheerless groups on the beach. The cutter was the first ship the Greenlanders had seen since their country had been overwhelmed by the Nazis; they were afraid to believe that it was not German. The *Comanche* anchored and broke out the blue flag of Denmark at her foremast. Soon the houses ashore were similarly arrayed, and one displayed the only American flag in town. When the Danish mine manager greeted the Americans, he did not have to explain that he was crying because he was happy. An inspection of the mine revealed it to be vulnerable; barely a half-mile inland, it was so close to tidewater that a few shells landing nearby would have flooded it.

The *Comanche* went on to Godthaab to put ashore the first foreign consul ever to serve in Greenland. Two days later, the Hudson Bay Company vessel *Nascopie* put in at Ivigtut with a party of mining engineers. It was rumored that the craft carried a small landing force of Canadian troops, so the *Comanche* hastened back to watch over the mine. However, the Canadians merely proffered some supplies and docilely departed.

The cutters *Northland, Duane, Campbell,* and *Cayuga* joined the *Comanche* and spent the summer and fall evaluating air-base sites, charting the Baffin Bay and Davis Strait areas, lugging freight and supplies to isolated coastal villages, protecting Ivigtut, and exploring the east coast for German stations. Greenland officials felt that the little ships had a salutary influence on popular morale.

In early September, *Northland*'s men heard that a party of "Norwegian" seal hunters at King Oscar's Fjord on the remote, ice-clogged northeast coast had set up a radio weather station. But the cutter could not pick up signals from the clandestine transmitter.

There were at least three German stations along the coast, manned by Norwegians working for the Abwehr's Arctic Bureau, headed by the famous German meteorologist-explorer, Dr. Paul Burckhardt. When Burckhardt tried to reinforce his enclaves, the British sent the ostensibly Norwegian gunboat *Fridtjof Nansen* to intercept the "hunters and trappers" and eliminate the stations. The British captured the German craft off Ella Island and destroyed the stations at Eskimonaes, Ella Island, and Torgilsbu. High-handedly, they also confiscated stores of gasoline and oil from natives and took several Greenlanders into custody. The State Department protested, but the President undercut Secretary of State Hull by telling Lord Lothian, the British ambassador, that the British strike was in the common interest.

Since winter icing conditions would force the American ships to leave, the Greenlanders wanted to have an American military detachment present. Instead, a 3-inch gun, 8 machine guns, and 50 rifles were provided. However, the Greenlanders proved unable to operate the cannon, so 14 of the *Campbell's* men shed their uniforms and stayed behind to protect the mine from random shelling by U-boats.

In December, the *Northland* was the last cutter to leave Iceland. The Coast Guardsmen would be back in the spring.[11]

With the defeat of France, the President had to decide whether to supply material assistance to Great Britain or husband the nation's small stock of weaponry for defense of the hemisphere; immediately, he chose the first course. He was also contemplating a shift of more warships from the Pacific to the Atlantic. But future strategy depended upon a correct estimate of Britain's chances of survival.

In June, service planners prepared a paper, "The Basis for Immediate Decisions concerning the National Defense." The staff officers stated that while "it appears reasonable to assume that the British Empire will exist in the Fall and Winter of 1940,—it appears to be doubtful that Great Britain itself will continue to be an actual combatant"; even should the Germans fail in an attempt to invade England, their bombing raids would destroy much of the British industrial potential for waging war. The entry of the United States into the conflict would not substantially influence events, for the American Army would not be capable of offensive action beyond the hemisphere for some time; and intervention in Europe might tempt Japan to strike in the Pacific. The planners, therefore, recommended a strategy of hemispheric defense, with material aid to Britain as long as her resistance seemed to bar the Axis from crossing the Atlantic.[12]

Therefore, the Army advocated that a revised Rainbow IV plan should become the basis of American strategy. Rainbow IV stressed hemispheric defense, that is, defense of the Hawaii-Alaska-Panama triangle and the South Atlantic approaches to the United States. General George C. Marshall, Army Chief of Staff, said, "Are we not forced into a question of reframing our national policy, that is, purely defensive action in the Pacific, with a main effort on the Atlantic side?"[13] But to Army planners and to Marshall himself this meant defense of the Atlantic approaches to the hemisphere, not an offensive in the Atlantic.

Since the outbreak of war, the British had made information relating to their combat experience known to the Americans; in mid-June, a committee was established under Sir Sydney Bailey to facilitate the exchange of information. While some British officers felt that the arrangement was too one-sided and resisted American requests to place observers aboard British ships, the Bailey Committee, the Admiralty, and Prime Minister Winston Churchill realized that a policy of frankness would help in obtaining American material assistance. Churchill and the Bailey Committee recommended that informal staff conversations be held between American and British planning officers, and the Committee set to work to establish general plans for Anglo-American naval cooperation in the event of American entry into the war. The Bailey Committee planners soon decided that the American Navy's role was to deter the Japanese fleet in the Pacific and, in the Atlantic, to provide destroyers for the escort of convoys and task forces of heavy ships to defend the sea lanes against German surface raiders. Meanwhile, President Roosevelt was similarly inclined toward mutual naval planning and cooperation. Both he and Admiral Stark recalled bitterly that President Woodrow Wilson had strictly forbidden such meetings in 1917, with the result that when America entered the war, months were wasted because there were no detailed plans for joint naval operations.

Yet coherent formulation of American strategy depended upon a correct estimate of Britain's moot chances of survival. Hence, the President decided to send several service representatives to London to secure reliable information. The delegation was to be headed by the Assistant CNO, Rear Admiral Robert L. Ghormley, a reserved, urbane, intelligent Virginian; Ghormley was cool and able, and his long experience as a staff officer, while causing him to lack combative drive and fire, seemed to fit him well for such a mission. He was to go to England as Special Naval Observer along with an Army and Air Corps representative.

In late July, Franklin Roosevelt met with Ghormley to brief him on his mission. Roosevelt said that he needed reliable information as a basis for planning future American defense strategy. He believed that there were three future possibilities. First, that of a German invasion of Britain, followed by a British defeat and an armistice, which might mean that the Royal Navy would be lost to the Germans. This would lead to direct or indirect German intervention in Latin America and permit the Japanese to expand in the Pacific. Secondly, there was the chance that Britain would be badly weakened by air attack or invasion, but would still be able to wage a defensive war, perhaps from the dominions. Finally, there was the chance that Britain could be successfully defended and used as an advanced base to support sufficient land and air power to make a return to the continent ultimately feasible with the help of massive material aid from the United States. Ghormley sensed that Mr. Roosevelt "was not convinced that the United States would be forced to intervene as a belligerent in the war. . . ." The President concluded by reminding Ghormley that his mission was to be presented to the British as "personal and unofficial," implying no binding commitments on the part of the United States.[14]

Admiral Ghormley and his two companions traveled incognito in the SS *Britannic*, savoring the feeling of being embarked on a secret mission of state until they were disillusioned by hearing the news of their departure routinely announced on a radio news program. The no-longer-clandestine envoys arrived in Liverpool on 15 August.

In London, Ghormley, like the naval attaché, Captain Alan Kirk, found the British determined and optimistic; morale was high, and there was an unspoken sense that America would enter the war sooner or later. The British and Americans agreed to a full exchange of information, including almost all technical secrets. Ghormley's mission became permanent, and the attaché's staff increased sixfold. Technical meetings were held on antisubmarine warfare, gunnery, naval aviation, intelligence, mine warfare, communications, tactics, liaison, and engineering.[15] As a surfeited Stark wrote Ghormley, "Get in on any and all staff conversations you can—go as far as you like in discussions—with the full understanding you are expressing only your own views on what best to do—'if and when'—but such must not be understood to commit your government in any manner or to any degree whatsoever."

The Anglo-American discussions remained on the purely technical level because the Americans as yet had no long-range strategic plans to discuss with the British; in Washington, planning had not evolved beyond three generalizations: defense of the hemisphere, discreet containment of Japan, and material aid to Britain.[16]

The fall of France thoroughly frightened the nation, for it had hoped to remain out of the war and yet safe from the Nazi frenzy by relying on the British Navy, the French Army, and American industry. Now, one of the pillars of American security had been toppled and another seemed fated soon to fall. In July, Congress passed without major opposition the 70 percent Naval Expansion Act, which provided for 257 additional ships. The skill of the German conquests led to an exaggerated awe of German arms and to a kind of jocular cynicism about the state of U.S. defenses until the two-ocean Navy should some distant day become reality. As Mayor Fiorello La Guardia lamented, it seemed that the Republic could not even guarantee the successful defense of Coney Island![17]

And as the President had told Congress in May:

> So called impregnable fortifications no longer exist. A defense which allows an enemy to consolidate his approach without hindrance will lose. A defense which makes no effective effort to destroy the lines of supplies and communications of the enemy will lose.
>
> An effective defense . . . requires the equipment to attack an aggressor on his route before he can establish strong bases within the territory of American vital interests.[18]

Meanwhile, the first request from abroad for the Navy's "surplus" World War I destroyers had come from Norway as early as January. The President had told the Norwegians that the Navy had "none to spare" because of the requirements of the Neutrality Patrol, adding that such a sale would be illegal and he preferred the American Republics to "have first call" on any U.S. ships that became available.[19] In the spring, Latin American nations sought the old ships, but there were none readily available, and in some cases the need seemed dubious; in the Uruguayan Navy, three admirals and assorted lesser brass presided over but one venerable gunboat and several tugs and dispatch boats, and were thought to pine for more imposing commands.[20]

Up until April the British Admiralty had ordered only about $2½ million worth of naval equipment—mostly torpedo boat engines and degaussing wire. In May, Prime Minister Churchill requested forty or fifty of the old destroyers, but the President replied that a transfer of warships would require an act of Congress, which did not appear politically possible. In June, despite objections in the Navy, the President did try to switch a number of motor torpedo boats and sub chasers under construction for the Navy to the British, under the dubious sanction of the general laws regarding modification of contracts. However, Congress intervened, condemned the illegality of the project and, while the President bandaged his burned fingers, added a section to a naval bill prohibiting the transfer of naval equipment unless the CNO certified it not essential to the defense of the United States.[21]

The President was reluctant to part with the destroyers until he was more sure of British survival. He told Ickes on 5 June that the four-stackers would not "be of any use" to the British because they were old and lacked firepower, especially antiaircraft weapons. He explained that he was reluctant "to enrage Hitler" to so little purpose, noting cogently: "We cannot tell the turn that the war will take, and there is no use endangering ourselves unless we can achieve some results for the Allies."[22]

However, British destroyer losses in the Dunkirk evacuation and the entry of Italy into the war, opening a Mediterranean theater, increased British need. Churchill reasoned that fright was the mother of generosity, observing to Lothian that he had "no intention of relieving the United States from any well-grounded anxieties" concerning its peril should a defeated Britain be forced to surrender its fleet into Nazi hands. But to sound too strident a note of pessimism would discourage American aid. The Prime Minister was able to adopt the appropriate tone of stern determination to carry on and pointed reminders that it might not be possible to do so without help.[23]

When the President ascertained from Admiral Ghormley and Captain Kirk in London that the British, still in possession of command of the seas and building up their air power, were hale and determined,[24] he became more amenable to the British entreaties. His only worry was the prospect of domestic opposition. As he dryly told the Cabinet, it would be difficult for Admiral Stark to certify the ships useless when over a hundred of them were either serving with the Atlantic Squadron or being reconditioned for service! Ben Cohen, an assistant to the President, argued that a transfer of destroyers would not contravene the congressional prohibition because, by helping to sustain England, it would in the long run strengthen, not weaken, American defenses. The President was unimpressed with this line of reasoning, maintaining that Congress was "in no mood . . . to allow any form of sale." He asked Secretary of the Navy Frank Knox to consider the feasibility of selling destroyers to Canada for exclusive use in the Western Hemisphere, thus releasing other warships for duty elsewhere, but no one was enamored of this obvious subterfuge.[25]

On 1 August, Knox met with Lothian and found the Englishman "almost tearful in his pleas for help and help quickly." The American Navy had long been interested in obtaining bases in the Caribbean, and during the thirties the question had become linked with that of the Allied World War I debts, so there were suggestions now that the needed bases should be seized in payment for the debts. Indeed, in late May, Lothian had recommended that his government lease base sites in Newfoundland, Bermuda, and Trinidad to the United States. The Royal Navy, wishing to reduce still further the number of its warships in the western Atlantic, was favorably inclined, but the British Cabinet rejected the suggestion because of the paucity of American aid up until then. Now, Knox raised the possibility of trading the destroyers for the bases.[26]

On 2 August, Knox broached his idea to the Cabinet. The President seemed enthusiastic, although he and Secretary of State Hull were worried about Congress. Roosevelt then sounded the British out on the proposal; he also requested "positive assurances" that the British fleet would be sent to North America and not surrendered or scuttled in the event Great Britain were to be overrun by a Nazi invasion. But the British response was discouraging. While willing to let American ships and planes use facilities at their New World bases, they did not wish to lease British territory outright. They requested 96 destroyers, 20 motor torpedo boats, and ample Navy dive bombers; also, Churchill was unwilling to give the assurances asked for by the President for fear of lowering morale by suggesting Britain's defeat and, perhaps, from a desire not to permit the Americans to feel *too* secure.

The President deemed the British response "entirely unsatisfactory." He pointed out the limited quantity of American ships and planes and argued that Churchill's remarks concerning the Royal Navy would merely involve a repetition of prior public statements. He said that he was willing to use the bases as the British thought best, but insisted on an understanding that the United States had the right to lease or purchase the territory in event of sudden necessity, such as an Axis attack on the Western Hemisphere.

The Prime Minister resented having to pawn portions of the Empire, so he decided that appearances would best be served by leasing the base sites as gifts, independent of the destroyer transfer, to avoid the sordid idea of a "deal." However, the President's needs were the reverse. How could Admiral Stark certify the ships as surplus unless they were bartered for something of greater value? On a scratchy transatlantic telephone, Churchill complained, "Empires just don't bargain." And Attorney General Robert H. Jackson responded, "Well, Republics do."

Hull thought the British were "crawfishing"; but they legitimately feared future bickering over the size of the bases if the Americans were allowed a "blank cheque." The Americans, impressed with the need for speed, could not understand the slowness of the British in coming to agreement; every moment of delay augmented the peril to both nations. The British Cabinet, save for the Colonial Secretary, favored the transaction, and a compromise was swiftly reached whereby two of the sites were given as gifts and the others handed over in exchange for the American warships. The President, fearful of entrusting the transfer to congressional debate, and impressed by the time factor, authorized the transaction by executive decree.[27]

The U.S. Navy, which felt that it could not spare so much as a "rowboat" for the British in light of its own myriad deficiencies, was presented with a fait accompli. But the bad news about the loss of the destroyers was mitigated by the acquisition of the long cherished and vitally needed Atlantic and Caribbean bases. Admiral Stark eagerly approved the transaction, and reaction in the service was generally favorable, although restrained.[28] One enthusiastic officer said, ". . . we have made a fine deal but the British Government will probably go bankrupt trying to keep those boats in oil."[29]

Critics joked that the President had the constitutional prerogative to "dispose" the fleet, not "dispose of" it, and to many people the Attorney General's legal brief on behalf of the transfer seemed strained, yet the transaction was so patently in the national interest that opposition was mild. Most Americans seemed to share Secretary of War Henry Stimson's view that the nation's safety was a more pressing consideration than the mandate of an international law that the Germans were fighting to destroy and that had failed to preserve truly neutral peoples from the Nazi menace. The Germans were not to be stopped by legal briefs, and if the President's law was bad, most Americans believed that there was nothing wrong with his head—or his heart; it had taken not a little courage to make the deal so near election time.

The President was jubilant when he announced the transfer to reporters on his campaign train, the chipper mood produced by the release of tension that follows a hard decision finally made. He compared the transfer to the Louisiana Purchase in preserving the nation's security; and, as he told one reporter, "That goes back before you and me." When he read out the list of island names, a newspaperman asked him to spell one of them, and he complied, quipping, "Now, I am not fooling on these. These are real places."[30]

And as a result of the President's efforts, a singular duty fell to the destroyermen of the Atlantic Squadron.

7.

Ceremonies Appropriate to a Neutral Nation

THE SUMMER OF 1940 was a hectic time for the Atlantic Squadron. The long absence of fleet units from the Atlantic had reduced shore facilities to the point that they could not adequately support the growing Squadron, especially south of Hampton Roads. Much essential overhaul work on the force's aged destroyers had to be accomplished by their own crews and by the overworked tender *Denebola*. The upkeep of ships and the training of men continued to be impaired by Neutrality Patrol steaming. Transfer of personnel to new construction resulted in acute shortages of radiomen and sonar operators, and Admiral Ellis lamented that many of his skippers were in their first commands and a large percentage of his gunner's mates seemed callow, "inexperienced recruits." Antiaircraft ammunition and torpedo overhaul facilities were lacking, limiting AA battle practices and torpedo exercises. Yet the Squadron desperately needed intense gunnery and tactical training if it were to be ready to "perform efficiently" in a war emergency.

Admiral Ellis set up a destroyer type-command under Rear Admiral Ferdinand L. Reichmuth, an experienced, somewhat pedestrian officer, to conduct intensive training operations on a rotational basis. Reichmuth gave his best, but the Navy was robbing Peter to pay Paul, and the need for ships to carry out ever-increasing operational duties critically hampered the training program.[1]

In early August, rumors and newspaper speculation concerning the possible transfer of destroyers to the Royal Navy impelled Atlantic Squadron staff officers to survey the readiness of all the force's destroyers and make up a list of ships in order of their fitness for transfer. The precaution proved wise, for on the morning of 20 August, Admirals Ellis and Reichmuth received telephone instructions to fly to Washington immediately; their roster of ships to be transferred was quickly approved by the Department. Two destroyer divisions were recalled from patrol, armed, and made ready for hard service. On 3 September, the order went out: "Proceed with project to turn over fifty destroyers to appropriate British authorities at Halifax . . . ."

The old *Aaron Ward, Abel P. Upshur,* and *Hale* were the first to go. On 4 September the slim four-stackers, freshly painted, and flying the American flag but shorn of their commissioning pennants, steamed out of Boston harbor, churning white creases in the blue water, as pleased motorists on a nearby bridge honked horns and flashed headlights to cheer on the destroyermen bound on a novel venture.[2]

Admiral Reichmuth was worried about "this most unneutral mission" and gave much thought to the preservation of appearances. He was "most insistent" that under no circumstances were the American destroyermen to permit themselves to be photographed in the company of British personnel. Admiral Stark, doubtless in accord with the wishes of the President, decreed a simple decommissioning ceremony "as being appropriate under the circumstances for a neutral nation."[3]

When the first eight American destroyers reached Halifax, they encountered the British transport *Duchess of Richmond,* her decks tiered with young British destroyermen; the meeting was one of the Prime Minister's whimsical touches. The destroyers docked at the north side of Pier "B," promptly took aboard British crews, and put to sea for an indoctrination cruise.

At 1000 on the morning of 9 September, the American crews lined up on the dock in front of their eight ships; the small indoctrination crews, usually consisting of one officer, normally the Exec, and eighteen of the most experienced ratings, remained out of sight below decks. There were no British personnel on the dock. Officers took station in front of their men; skippers remained on board until the colors were lowered. A bugle sounded "Attention," then "To the Colors," as the eight flags slowly dropped at the same time. The sailors felt the significance of the moment; a few of the older men shed some tears. Captains then came ashore and each took custody of his ship's ensign, jack, and pennant. Abruptly, the blue-clad American crews marched quickly across the dock to waiting trains and embarked. Then British sailors marched out on to the dock and, while the American indoctrination crews waited below, recommissioned the destroyers with suitable pomp into the Royal Navy.[4] Through one of Churchill's felicitous instincts, the destroyers were christened after towns in the United States, Great Britain, and Canada which shared common names.

As the British had difficulty providing crews for the ships, the transfer proceedings extended into the winter. Usually the American indoctrination crews remained on board the British ships, training the new crews, for about ten days. It soon became a tradition for the British, on the day of departure, to stand the Americans to rum and cocktails. The British warships in port seemed unkempt to the innocent Americans, not yet at war, and a few of the British officers showed small signs of nervous irritability born of combat fatigue. For the most part, the gregarious Americans got on well with both the British and Canadians, partly because the British preferred them to the wild and unprofessional Canadians, who in turn preferred them to the stuffy and pedantic British.

The destroyers were transferred with full wartime allowances of arms, ammunition, stores, spare parts, and equipment. The ships were shined and clean to a degree astonishing to the British. Prior to the transfer, each ship had been allocated $2,500 for provisions and was stocked with items rare in the Royal Navy that fall: cereals, fruit juice, clams, chipped beef, canned vegetables and fruits, macaroni, gelatin, and cocoa. As this was not standard fare, Royal Navy bureaucrats insisted that it be taken ashore, and most of the inexperienced commanders of the destroyers foolishly complied. The wardroom crockery on the vessels was unneutral; it bore the blue anchor and USN logo of the American Navy. The British were most impressed with the graciousness and thoroughness with which the Americans had outfitted the old ships.

However, the British crews had difficulty in adjusting to the cantankerous four-stackers, partly on account of their inexperience. While some of the new skippers were proven officers who had lost their former ships in battle, others were younger men given their first command, or older men who might have been passed over in times of lesser urgency. Many of the enlisted men were but recently removed from recruit training depots.

Also, some of the American equipment was different, and required getting used to. The American sound gear was not as good as that of the Royal Navy and lacked any range recorder; the difficult water conditions off Halifax rendered sonar operations unsuccessful, further impairing British confidence in the equipment. The British found communications on the ships slower and more awkward than their own because fuses and switches were in different locations. They were unfamiliar with the .50-caliber AA machine guns mounted on the American destroyers and needed much work with the weapon. They did not like the vulnerable glass-enclosed bridges of the old destroyers. The officers deemed the American wardrooms, with their functional steel-framed furniture, overly austere, and found their cabins smaller than in British destroyers. The enlisted men, used to hammocks, complained that the American bunks were too soft. "It's like lying on a bloody sack of jelly," one man lamented. There was a general dislike of such modern refinements as speed keys and typewriters, which were deemed suited to business offices, but not to the hardy calling of Nelson, and out of place aboard a warship. It seemed that the traditional British virtuosity at sea had imbued the Royal Navy with a perhaps unhealthy spirit of conservatism.

Then there were the eccentricities of the ships. The four-stackers were originally fast and relatively durable, but as ancient "war babies," mass produced quickly, they were not without the defects of premature birth. Their plating was thin and the watertight subdivision of their hulls was not up to modern standards, a structural problem to which advanced age contributed. They were not maneuverable; their turning circle was comparable to that of an old *Texas*-class battleship. They had been built in the days when escorts were not expected to protect convoys across the entire ocean, and so they lacked range. Long and slender ships, they rolled heavily in any kind of a sea, especially when their fuel was low. In the American Navy, it was common practice to take seawater into the empty fuel tanks as ballast, but the British feared fuel contamination and did not adopt the technique until grim experience demonstrated its necessity. Occasionally, there were condenser and generator breakdowns. The British crews found the destroyers difficult to steer in confined spaces; some thought that this was because the propellers were set too close together, while others thought it was because they were set too far apart. The Americans thought it was because of the inexperience of the British.[5]

Of the first group of eight ships, the *Churchill* (ex *Herndon*), *Clare* (ex *Abel P. Upshur*), *Chesterfield* (ex *Welborn C. Wood*), *Cameron* (ex *Welles*), *Castleton* (ex *Aaron Ward*), *Chelsea* (ex *Crowninshield*), *Caldwell* (ex *Hale*), *Campbeltown* (ex *Buchanan*), five left Halifax on schedule. Two were detained when the *Chesterfield* rammed the *Churchill*'s stern twice while maneuvering at close quarters, and the *Cameron* was briefly delayed by generator trouble. During *Campbeltown*'s voyage across the Atlantic, her officer of the deck fainted from seasickness.

Of the second octet, the *Hamilton* (ex *Kalk*), *Georgetown* (ex *Maddox*), *Brighton* (ex *Cowell*), *Roxborough* (ex *Foote*), *Bath* (ex *Hopewell*), *Charleston* (ex *Abbot*), *St. Albans* (ex *Thomas*), *St. Marys* (ex *Doran*), commissioned by the British on 23 September, only four were able to leave for England on schedule. The *Hamilton* and *Georgetown* sustained propeller damage in a collision while maneuvering to take on fuel; then, after being repaired, the unfortunate *Hamilton* ran aground on a rocky ledge, breaking her back, and she did not enter service for nine months. The *Roxborough* began the crossing with her sister ships, but excessive fuel consumption forced her to return; later she burned out a main bearing and required extensive work on her engineering plant.

The next group of six destroyers—the *Annapolis* (ex *Mackenzie*), *Columbia* (ex *Haraden*), *St. Clair* (ex *Williams*), *Niagara* (ex *Thatcher*), *St. Croix* (ex *McCook*), *St. Francis* (ex *Bancroft*)—was commissioned on the 24th of September and, since the ships were transferred to the Royal Canadian Navy, they were already at home.

The next group of eight—*Beverley* (ex *Branch*), *Broadway* (ex *Hunt*), *Broadwater* (ex *Mason*), *Belmont* (ex *Satterlee*), *Burwell* (ex *Laub*), *Burnham* (ex *Aulick*), *Buxton* (ex *Edwards*), *Bradford* (ex *McLanahan*—was commissioned on 8 October. There occurred a near tragedy during the training of this group. The *Broadwater* was pulling away from the dock one day when a British rating accidentally released a depth charge. The live drum did not explode, but lay on the bottom alongside the dock, causing what an American called "considerable consternation" until it was recovered by Canadian divers. Seven of the destroyers made it across to Britain on schedule; the *Buxton* had to return due to an outbreak of diphtheria on board.

The penultimate group was large, ten ships—*Leamington* (ex

Twiggs), *Lancaster* (ex *Philip*), *Mansfield* (ex *Evans*), *Montgomery* (ex *Wickes*), *Stanley* (ex *McCalla*), *Sherwood* (ex *Rodgers*), *Leeds* (ex *Conner*), *Lewes* (ex *Conway*), *Ludlow* (ex *Stockton*), *Lincoln* (ex *Yarnall*)—and its training was complicated because many of the ships were manned by Polish and French sailors, and instructions had to be translated. Anglo-American relations were especially good in the *Ludlow*, where Commander G.B. Sayer, RN, and Lieutenant Commander Lewis R. Miller, USN, presided. The ship had operated out of Queenstown in World War I, and after an accident, her bow had been replaced in a British yard. Hence, when Sayer first came aboard, Miller drawled, "Say, Cap'n, d'you know your ship has got a British bow!" Whenever the ship's machinery balked, Miller's favorite words of commiseration were, "That installation stinks to high heaven!" Sayer was worried that the *Ludlow*, in the event of bad weather in the Atlantic, might run out of fuel before completing the crossing; but Miller always insisted, "She's done it once and she'll do it again." The ships sailed on schedule after a late-October commissioning, and all ten made it to England on time and without incident. Shortly thereafter, Lieutenant Commander Miller received the following cable: "She stinks to high heaven, but she's done it again!"

The last group, commissioned into the Royal Navy on 26 November, was also a large one: *Reading* (ex *Bailey*), *Ramsey* (ex *Meade*), *Ripley* (ex *Shubrick*), *Rockingham* (ex *Swasey*), *Salisbury* (ex *Claxton*), *Richmond* (ex *Fairfax*), *Newmarket* (ex *Robinson*), *Newark* (ex *Ringgold*), *Newport* (ex *Sigourney*), *Wells* (ex *Tillman*). But only six of the ships sailed on time; four were detained by mechanical trouble. Then the *Newmarket*, *Newark*, and *Wells* crashed into the corner of a dock while moored together when a maneuvering valve in one of them jammed in the ahead position. The British by now were hard pressed for men, and the crews of these last vessels were very green. One skipper conceded that the training of his crew was "a chimpanzee's tea party." The *Newark* suffered damage on her crossing when two inadequately lashed depth charges were washed overboard and exploded.[6]

British naval opinion, while unhappy at the defects of the four-stackers, generally favored the transaction as a glum necessity, while those in Britain less familiar with the critical need for destroyers felt that an exorbitant price in national prestige and honor had been paid. Nevertheless, the fifty ships were equivalent to 2½ times the annual British production of destroyers; they augmented the British destroyer fleet by 29 percent after a period of very heavy losses and before an anticipated period of even higher losses.[7]

The President urged speed on the Navy in the development and use of the bases. In November, he inspected the Caribbean sites in the *Tuscaloosa* and observed the pestiferous French at Martinique. By mid-November, tender-based PBYs were operating from off St. Lucia, Trinidad, and Bermuda. Facilities were planned at Antigua, the Bahamas, British Guiana, and St. Lucia to support seaplanes and a carrier air group; Jamaica, Bermuda, Trinidad, and Newfoundland were destined for more extensive development, with facilities for destroyers and submarines, as well as patrol planes and carrier aircraft. The larger bases could also provide anchorages for task forces, and consideration was given to the possibility of building a Pearl Harbor of the Atlantic in Puerto Rico. But soon the eager Americans were confounded in their attempts to speed utilization of the bases by an unexpected obstacle—their new-found allies, the British.

President Roosevelt was most disinclined to have the United States drawn into the complex social, racial, and economic problems of the West Indian islands,[8] and insisted that American responsibilities be strictly limited to the base sites. He joked about Bermuda: ". . . we don't want it. We think too much of Bermuda! Bermuda is an American resort. Americans go there because they like to be under another flag when they travel. They wouldn't enjoy Bermuda half so much if it was under our flag. It would lose its quaintness."[9]

But the Colonial Office did not believe the President, and leaders in Bermuda and Trinidad were hostile to the Americans. The war had ruined tourism, the major business of the islands, and adversity made the locals cantankerous. Agriculture was barely viable. The islands imported food, rain was the only source of potable water, and horses were slaughtered for lack of forage.

Many of the islanders felt that the American bases would mean overcrowding, declining real-estate values, destruction of the last vestiges of the tourist trade, unemployment, and disease: unstated fears were of native blacks "spoiled" by high wages, civil strife, and eventual loss of British sovereignty over the islands.[10] The Bermudans warned:

> The attractions of Bermuda as a resort are its beauty, peacefulness, other-worldliness, facilities for outdoor recreation on land and water in pleasant surroundings, absence of mechanical transport, freedom of movement. . . . In all these respects it is clear that the character of the Colony

would be violently changed by the unsightly buildings, noise, bustle, restriction of movement. . . .[11]

The Bermudans did not want seaplanes landing in Great Sound. The Trinidadans wanted the base there placed in the middle of a swamp. At Newfoundland, squatters on the Avalon Peninsula demanded exorbitant recompense for their holdings. And everywhere local authorities insisted on the right to levy harbor dues on warships using the bases and to place duties on military and naval supplies brought in to the base sites.[12]

The Foreign Office worried lest the obstinacy of the provincials compromise passage of the Lend-Lease Act. The diplomats persuaded Churchill, himself sulking over the decline of Empire, to treat a delegation of Bermudans to syrupy prose and strong cigars. At a meeting in London with American service representatives, the Governor of Trinidad, Sir Hubert Jones, demanded that the base site be removed from a beach area to a swamp in order not to disturb bathers; one of the Americans then asked him if he knew that there was a war on. The next day, the Americans formally responded to Jones' proposal by handing him a small slip of paper with but two words on it: "No dice."

However, as even the anxious Foreign Office was not prepared to complete the transaction without carefully-worked-out arrangements to safeguard British interests, it was not until nearly spring of 1941 that many of the details relating to the extent of the sites and rights of taxation were agreed upon.[13] And even then, unfortunately, local authorities were prepared to violate the spirit of the agreements.

There was obstructionism in Trinidad, but the major contretemps occurred in Bermuda. Captain Jules James, a bright, articulate officer, was appointed CO of the Naval Operating Base, Bermuda, and because of the "delicate situation," he was briefed before his departure by Admiral Stark, Secretary Knox, and even President Roosevelt.

The base was commissioned on 7 April 1941, even though its construction was far from complete. Ominously, no one from the local government attended the commissioning ceremonies, and Captain James felt that the attitude of the populace was "distinctly cold." Soon he had graver troubles. The local wage boards struggled to keep the wages of native workers down, which tended to produce dissatisfied and apathetic toilers for the Navy; then they attempted to decrease the pay of the American construction men, too, in order to lessen the natives' dissatisfaction at the disparity of pay scales.

Local officials made persistent attempts to collect duties and taxes at the base docks, while the Americans insisted that they would pay only when using Bermudan ports and docks not leased to them. An American-financed service club soon became too expensive for sailors, but the government would not allow the Navy to close it because of the revenue it derived from a duty on the beer sold in the increasingly raffish joint. The Bermudans disliked automobiles, which they felt would impair the picturesqueness of their island and do harm to their light roads; even their governor was not permitted to drive a car. The Americans agreed to use automobiles only upon securing permission from local authorities. However, as with the customs duties, the Bermudans used the authority to harass the Navy. The Governor insisted that Captain James could drive his car only when in uniform. James retorted that the inside of his car was under the jurisdiction of the United States, and thus his driving apparel could not be a matter subject to local regulation!

Not that all of the wrongs were on one side. The constructors lived lavishly in beach-front hotels, and the officer in charge of the building program was later detached as a result of misapplied expenditures. The workers caroused, producing sporadic disorders as well as a significant prostitution problem. Such episodes were one important reason for the eventual formation of the Navy's own construction battalions, the famed Seabees. The sailors on liberty in Bermuda, worse paid and better disciplined, caused somewhat less difficulty, although they too created disturbances when intoxicated. A strengthened shore patrol improved matters in the short run, and in the long run, the fine Navy Recreation Center at Riddell's Bay solved the major problems.

Gradually, economic prosperity overcame the local resentment that accrued from too-rapid changes in ancient patterns of life, and the Navy's relations with the Bermudans grew warmer; eventually, Bermudans were borrowing American cars.

There was no difficulty on the lesser islands, where the bases were smaller and there were fewer vested interests to offend; indeed, the local people seemed quite pleased to be in the limelight of grand events. At St. Lucia, public officials gladly turned out for commissioning ceremonies at the Naval Air Station, which included a fifteen-gun salute fired by the old destroyer *Goff* and the substantial pomp of Major Max Smith's Marine detachment off aviation-tender *Curtiss*.[14]

As it turned out, the destroyer-bases transaction did not prove vital—merely helpful—to the safety of the United States and Great Britain. Victory in the Battle of Britain mitigated the need for destroyers for anti-invasion duty, and the continued security of Britain meant that the United Kingdom itself could serve as the first line of American defense until the United States entered the war and, thereafter, as an advanced base for offensive operations; the usefulness of the Western Hemisphere bases was thus reduced. There was no need to build a Pearl Harbor in the western Atlantic.

For each nation, the deal was insurance taken out against formidable but transient perils. The Prime Minister feared it would be reckoned sordid; the President feared it would lessen his popularity. But the best result of the transaction was that it became a symbol of their compact against tyranny and dramatized the tacit Anglo-American alliance.

For the Germans, the destroyers-for-bases deal was a stark, shocking warning that they could no longer ignore the growing impact of America upon the war. And so the Germans moved toward the fateful Tripartite Pact, bringing Japan into the Axis alliance.

8.

The German Response

By THE SUMMER OF 1940, the Germans had advanced as far toward Britain as their Army could take them. But the crucial weaknesses of the German Navy and Air Force prevented a cross-Channel invasion and, thus, the quick, decisive victory so vital to the Nazi cause.

In the first year of war, Germany ignored the hostility of the United States, hoping to defeat France and Britain before America was strong enough to intervene. However, the destroyers-for-bases transaction, deemed by the Germans "an openly hostile act," was followed by the defeat of the Luftwaffe in the Battle of Britain, which made possible a protracted war that Germany lacked the realistic plans to manage and increased the possibility of American intervention. These untoward events moved Germany to act more decisively in regard to the United States. Indignantly, the Fuehrer decided to chastise his upstart foe in distant parts and make use of "Japan as a club to be held over" the United States.

Thus, his response was the Tripartite Pact of September 1940, which sought to confront the United States with the menace of a two-ocean war. The Germans could not themselves strike at the United States for lack of sea power, and so had scant means of deterring American assistance to Britain. Japanese sea power would be the needed deterrent. The German Naval Staff believed that the Pact signified "for the first time a serious warning for the United States. . . ." The Pact was more than a warning to America; it was also a confession of German weakness, an admission that Britain could not be defeated in the foreseeable future and that a grim war of long duration was in the offing. Otherwise, there would have been no need for Japan's dubious help. As the Fuehrer admitted in mid-September to Benito Mussolini, "circumstances do not allow us to foresee when hostilities will cease. . . ." But the Pact portended little real trust or collaboration between Germany and Japan because of distance, Anglo-American sea power, and mutual suspicion bred by different objectives in different oceans; the Fuehrer was ever alert for "Japanese treason."* Thereafter, German diplomacy was paralyzed between alternative terrors: the Japanese might use the Pact as a pawn to bargain for American concessions in the Pacific, thus leaving Germany isolated in mortal conflict with the world's major powers; or they might strike hard in the Pacific, thus bringing about, instead of deterring, American intervention.[1]

Early in the war, German planning was largely tactical, shaped for speedy, decisive victories; now, sharp defeat and the prospect of protracted war forced the Germans to undertake systematic, long-range strategic planning. The Naval Staff came to understand that, although Britain could not be successfully invaded, she might be strangled.

At first, their small numbers and orthodox tactics hampered the U-boats. The maximum tonnage sunk early in the war was 170,000 tons in February 1940, but in some months less than half that amount was sent to the bottom. In April and May of 1940, the U-boats sank only twenty ships in the Atlantic; yet the Germans realized that, in order to win the war, they needed to sink British shipping at a rate of 750,000 tons per month for a sustained period. The submarines operated near the British Isles, where it was easiest to find targets; but these areas were the best defended.

Then in the summer of 1940, use of captured French Atlantic ports gave the submarines 22 percent greater endurance. They were then able to hunt more daringly in mid-ocean where the absence of enemy air cover permitted them to patrol at high surface speeds more frequently. Doenitz moved to coordinate the search and attack tactics of his U-boats by making great use of radio communications, risking intercepted transmissions in light of the Allies' weak ASW

---

*Japanese service attachés were soon unhappy to discover that when they inquired as to the details of German technological advances—such as radar—"the conversation always turned to something else."

technology. These improvements helped the U-boats to locate convoys far out at sea, and made the submarine an ocean-wide, rather than a largely coastal, menace for the first time. Then, the German skippers experimented with new tactics, maneuvering their small submarines on the surface like oceangoing motor torpedo boats in nighttime attacks. Invisible on the dark, night sea, they struck unseen at massed herds of convoy ships and wrought flaming destruction and terror. The Royal Navy's random collection of escorts, lacking in training and technology, were powerless to cope with the changed circumstances. In this "Golden Age," or "Happy Time," between June and October 1940, the U-boats sank 274 merchant ships, 1,392,298 tons; mine warfare, raids by surface ships, and air attack added a grim 45 percent to this toll. Yet the appalling rate of execution was maintained by a U-boat arm limited to some 20 to 25 boats operational each month, only about 6 to 8 of which were on patrol stations at a given time.[2]

Raeder advocated to the Fuehrer a comprehensive war on British lines of supply and communication "before the U.S.A. steps in"; he pressed Hitler to cut the size of the Army and allot more resources to expansion of the U-boat fleet and the Luftwaffe. He urged a Siege of Britain—land, sea, and air. The Army would be used in North Africa to gain control of the Mediterranean, jamming the "strategic pivot" of Britain's world position by preventing her ready contact with the Empire; the U-boats would strike at the convoys in decisive numbers; and the Luftwaffe would attack shipping and devastate seaports, shipyards, and other strategic naval targets. All three services would unite in a common plan and share a single strategy, the destruction of the sea communications which sustained the obdurate British.*[3] But such a strategy would require ample bases and much time.

Meanwhile, Hitler feared that the Anglo-American sea powers would strike at the periphery of his distended empire. He talked of an occupation of Iceland to shield the vulnerable Norwegian coast; he ordered plans drawn up for the capture of the Canaries, the Cape Verde Islands, and the Azores to screen southern Europe and northwest Africa. He thought, too, that the Azores would be useful as bases from which German long-range bombers might reach the United States; it would be good to keep the meddlesome Americans tending

---

*Luftwaffe and some Army elements also favored Raeder's strategy because they feared the possible alternative, a Russian campaign.

to their own weak defenses instead of sending material to Britain. Goering encouraged him to strike at Iceland, the Azores, and the Canaries "so that the United States could not use them for naval and air operations." But Raeder and the Luftwaffe's better minds convinced Hitler that, because of his enemies' power at sea,[4] the Atlantic islands could not be held, even if taken by some imaginative, lightning, sea-air stroke, such as the one that succeeded against Norway.

Thus, both Raeder's plans for a grand strategic offensive and his own concern for a defensive strategy in the West while he contemplated a thrust to the East turned the Fuehrer's thoughts toward the Atlantic isles and Africa, thence to Spain and France.

North Africa was vital in Raeder's strategy, but as British sea power made it difficult to sustain large numbers of German troops and tanks there, and the Fuehrer feared to deploy his Army over water, the Germans needed a secure land bridge to Africa—Gibraltar. Hence, the Fuehrer began to press the Spanish for a joint attack on Gibraltar, urging upon General Francisco Franco the necessity of a continental alliance of land powers against the Anglo-American sea powers. As he put it, "The European countries could maintain themselves against the American Continent only if they too conducted a European continental policy and in so doing made Africa an absolutely integral part of the Eastern Hemisphere."[5]

But Franco was no Mussolini. A dictator in the Spanish authoritarian tradition more than an ideologue of Fascism, he did not make the fatal mistake of attempting to superimpose an essentially alien cast of thought upon his people, whose temperament and institutions were ill adapted to its stern requirements. His hints of alliance with Germany were attempts to gain favor because, in the event of a Nazi victory, Spain would want to detach certain of the French African colonies. The Germans offered gasoline, grains, modern arms and technicians, even dive bombers to keep British ships from Spain's naked coasts, but the Spaniards found new excuses for delay whenever the Germans offset reasons based on material scarcity with promises of aid.* American economic and diplomatic pressure on Spain was relentless; the British Navy would take Spain's overseas possessions. Finally, in December 1940, Franco admitted that Spain could not enter the war until Britain was "about ready to collapse."[6]

---

*It appears that Hitler's intelligence chief, Admiral Wilhelm Canaris, helped thwart German plans by urging Franco to remain out of the war.

Thus, Spanish caution made it impossible to win the swift, cheap victory in the Mediterranean that the Fuehrer, with Russia on his mind, needed.

Meanwhile, the Germans sought to extort bases in West Africa from the Vichy government. At Montoire, Marshal Henri Pétain vaguely agreed to "co-operate" with the Nazis, leaving the details to future discussion. As Pétain noted privately: "It will take six months to discuss this program and another six months to forget it." Hitler, disillusioned by Spain's vacillation and preoccupied with his secret planning of the Russian campaign, did not press the French hard.[7]

Raeder prodded the Fuehrer to expand the submarine war zone westward and sanction operations off Halifax; he contended that the American Neutrality Patrol allowed the British to remove valuable warships from the western Altantic and use them against German naval forces elsewhere. Hitler invariably listened politely, then refused to take action which would yield but small battle returns and increase the chances of American intervention.[8]

Yet even while German planners worked to prepare for the southern operations—code named Felix—the Fuehrer decided to reject the Navy's strategy and attack Russia. Raeder's strategy was not feasible—there were too few U-boats—and it would take too much time to achieve decisive results; perhaps, the Army estimated, another two years, time enough for Russia to get stronger and for a rearmed America to be ready to intervene. Germany's need for Russian oil and grain grew more acute as the prospect of a protracted war grew more likely. And, of Hitler's foes, Russia was the only one in range of his landbound arms.

And so, his intense hatred of the Soviet Union, a grim sense that time was an ally of his foes, his reluctance to keep much of his formidable Army inactive, and his search for the impregnable heartland evoked Hitler's mad, epic design of a two-front war. He rationalized that a swift, decisive victory over Russia would convince the British of the hopelessness of their plight and intimidate the United States into strict neutrality. He vaguely promised his naval and military planners, who were troubled by his inconsistency and the lack of a firm strategy for protracted war, that "when the Soviet Union is defeated, then Germany must deal with the United States."[9] Despite crushing land victories in the first year of war, the Germans were but little advanced on the road to final victory, and the restless, enigmatic Fuehrer was already whistling past a graveyard.

Hence, the German attempt to organize an integrated European-African defense system failed; it failed because of the absence of a common ideology and because of the sea power of the Anglo-Americans.

If Hitler wanted a continental alliance, he first had to defeat Britain; the United States made that task harder. Yet the very measures which he took to restrain the United States only drew it closer to intervention: the American response to the Axis Pact was Lend-Lease and the creation of the U.S. Atlantic Fleet.

The Germans still could not meaningfully threaten the Americans because of the limited range of their land-based arms, but the United States made its power felt in European affairs. It menaced the Atlantic isles, West Africa, and the outposts of Festung Europa with its sea power, assisted the British with arms and material, and pressured the Spanish and French to hold fast against the Nazi tide. Because of their sea power, the Americans had less to fear from war than did the Germans. Thus, they could adopt bolder policies, and the German threats and bluffs had little deterrent effect. As always, the advantage in diplomacy went to the side that feared war less—the Americans.

9.

A Passage
to India

THE FUEHRER'S SPASM OF futile diplomacy brought consternation to his foes, who supposed that he had offered the French a lenient peace in exchange for the French Fleet. It was feared that the French warships at Martinique and Guadeloupe might try to escape to Dakar. An increase in the number of submarine "sightings" in the Caribbean lent credence to such suspicions. Rumors thrived in the climate of uncertainty, and there was public speculation that Luftwaffe pilots were being smuggled into Martinique from Colombia. Although intelligence sources did not report any unusual activity on the French islands, it was felt in Washington that the time had come to reach a specific understanding with French Admiral Georges Robert in regard to his warships.[1]

During the summer and fall, the Navy and Marines readied plans for the capture of the islands, code-named India.

At Fort de France and in its bay, the French had fourteen heavy guns, four lighter cannons, and antiaircraft weapons; elsewhere, they had four 164-mm. guns and eight 80-mm. and 95-mm. mobile pieces. The carrier *Béarn* and light cruiser *Emile Bertin* added firepower to the defenses; the old training cruiser *Jeanne d'Arc* was at Guadeloupe. There were also several armed merchant ships off the islands.

The French air defenses were weak. The *Béarn* still possessed 102 planes, but they were not operational on account of poor mainten-

113

ance facilities, lack of spare parts, aviation gasoline, and trained pilots, and general deterioration of equipment in the hot, humid climate. In effect, six twin-engine flying boats and four single-engine float planes were available at Martinique, with a dozen other obsolete types at Guadeloupe.

The French had 2,000 native troops, led by 150 white officers and NCOs, 2,000 demobilized natives with military experience in North Africa, and 3,000 sailors from the warships in port. The defenders were poorly equipped except for three hundred .30-caliber machine guns. Most of the population was not loyal to Vichy, adding a morale problem to the mediocrity of the colonial troops.

The Americans would be overwhelmingly strong in the air and at sea, but weak on the ground. Much of the strength of the Army and Marines was invested in expanded training programs; consequently, the Marines could furnish but one understrength rifle regiment and the Army one regimental combat team. Two artillery batteries from the 11th Marines and an engineer company were added to the riflemen of the 5th Marines to form a small assault brigade of about 2,900 men. The Marines were short of machine guns and mortars, were relatively inexperienced in seaborne operations, and many of the newer infantrymen were in need of physical hardening. Nevertheless, they were tough, disciplined men and seemed better prepared for the shock of combat than the 5,100 soldiers of Task Force "A," First Infantry Division, who were not slated to land until several days after the assault because of the shortage of shipping.

Admiral Ellis, who was to command the naval attack force, was worried about the lack of trained men in his ships and his weak antiaircraft defenses. Nevertheless, the Atlantic Squadron, with some hasty improvisation, managed to amass an effective striking force. Air support would be provided by the *Ranger* and the new *Wasp*, with about 150 planes, and the carriers would be screened by four new destroyers, the *Mayrant*, *Trippe*, *Rhind*, and *Sims*. The Marines and their light equipment would be carried in the transports *Henderson*, *Barnett*, and *McCawley*; the latter two ships had been recently purchased, and their conversion to naval use had been accomplished in twenty-five days; both were below service standards in material readiness and overall efficiency, but cranky auxiliaries were better than none at all. The gunfire-support and counterbattery group consisted of the battleship *Texas*, the heavy cruisers *Vincennes* and *Chester*, the light cruisers *Omaha* and *Memphis*, and the nine four-stackers of Destroyer Squadron 30—the *Ellis*, *Cole*, *Dallas*, *Bernadou*, *DuPont*, *Lea*, *Greer*, *Tarbell*, and *Upshur*. The destroyer-transport *Manley* carried a reinforced company of Marines, which was to serve as a mobile landing force employed as needed. Five old destroyers—the *MacLeish*, *Bainbridge*, *Sturtevant*, *Overton*, and *Reuben James*—and the minecraft *Seminole* were to act as a control and salvage group. Finally, the entire force was to be screened by five new destroyers, the *Moffett*, *Hughes*, *Buck*, *Russell*, and *O'Brien*, and four old ones, the four-stackers *McCormick*, *Broome*, *Simpson*, and *Truxtun*. The aircraft tender *Goldsborough* was stationed at Gros Islet Bay with a small brood of PBYs, which would fly reconnaissance and tracking missions; the small tender *Gannet* and her PBYs operated off Port of Spain, and other patrol planes were based at San Juan and Guantanamo Bay.

The plans called for Admiral Greenslade to return to Martinique in November and seek to persuade Admiral Robert that there was nothing dishonorable about compromising in the face of superior force. Since the aim was to avoid bloodshed if possible, a surprise assault was ruled out. The task force would display itself openly to lend point to Greenslade's talks; loss of surprise would mean added causalties in event of a fight, but as Admiral Ellis said, "compelling moral grounds" as well as political necessity took precedence over purely military factors.

If all efforts to reach agreement failed, the campaign would begin in mid-November. Commencing five days before L-Day, daily reconnaissance and photographic missions would be flown over the islands. Two days later, the carrier air strikes would begin, and for three days, planes from the *Ranger* and *Wasp* would strike at the French planes, ships, coastal batteries, and AA positions; on L-minus-1, the planes would attack the French positions in the landing area. On the same day, the gunfire support force led by the *Texas* would bombard shore positions and silence the remaining French batteries. On L-Day, the planes would again bomb and strafe the Fort de France infantry and gun positions north of the beaches; thirty minutes before H-Hour, the light cruisers would fire 800 rounds of 6-inch and the support destroyers 1,414 rounds of 4-inch shells at the beach defenses. Then the 2nd and 3rd Battalions of the Fifth Marines would land abreast on Beaches N1 and N2 in the Basse Terre area, near Fort de France. The reserve consisted of 1st Battalion, Fifth, embarked in the *Henderson*, less the reinforced company in the *Manley*.

Supported by air cover as practicable, the Marines would drive north to secure the Fort de France area; when the major objectives had been taken, the Army would make an administrative landing, cope with such resistance as remained, and supply an occupation force. Then, if necessary, Guadelope could be blockaded or attacked.[2]

Backed by the *Ranger*, Admiral Greenslade was able to persuade Admiral Robert to grant the United States ninety-six hours' notice of ship movements, accept American naval and air patrols within French territorial jurisdiction, and permit a naval observer at Fort de France. Robert rejected American suggestions that he transfer the French sailors off the islands, incapacitate his ships by removing vital parts, and permit regular inspection of the harbor at Fort de France by U.S. warships. Thus, the basic problems posed by the presence of the French warships in the Caribbean were not permanently solved but temporarily postponed. The Americans agreed to see that the islands were supplied with food, paid for out of blocked Vichy funds in the United States.[3]

Also that fall, plans were hastily improvised for the "protective occupation" of the islands of San Miguel, Terceira, and Fayal in the Azores in the event a German strike at the Portuguese possessions appeared imminent. Plans called for the still-building, understrength First Marine Division to make the assault landing, escorted and protected by a fast, compact naval task force built around the *Ranger*, four modern cruisers, and a squadron of new destroyers. There was little Portuguese military strength on the islands, the troops "badly armed, trained, and equipped"; it was expected that they would "offer little resistance." No assault force was assembled to strike at the Azores because shipping and equipment for such a major operation were in short supply and, anyway, the Fuehrer had abandoned Operation Felix; for as long as Gibraltar and Dakar remained out of German hands, distance (the German bases nearest the Azores were 1,200 miles away, in France) protected the weakly held central and southern Atlantic island approaches to the United States.[4]

In the fall and winter, the atmosphere of crisis dissolved. Most of the ships of the Atlantic Squadron returned to routine Neutrality Patrol duties and elements of the Fifth Marines returned from readiness at Guantanamo Bay to help shape development of the First Division. But some American ships and planes continued to patrol off the French islands.

Destroyers patrolled close off Martinique, at the three-mile limit, steaming monotonously through the blue-green sea, crews lulled by the warm golden sun and pale tropical sky. Working out of San Juan and "Gitmo" were four of the old, poorly designed *Omaha*-class light cruisers, patrolling steadily, officers and men longing for more challenging duty.[5]

But some of the fliers had their hands full. As the Caribbean base facilities were still under construction that fall and winter, tender-based PBYs operated off Bermuda, St. Lucia, and Trinidad, watching the French. High seas and gales hampered the water-based flight operations, and it was often hard to fuel and arm the planes from bowser boats; normally, it took about five hours' hard work to refuel and, perhaps, three more to arm six PBYs. It was difficult to do the necessary work on the planes because beaching and maintenance facilities were lacking. Nevertheless, the operations of the tender-based flying boats compared favorably with the record made by patrol planes using the prepared bases at San Juan and Guantanamo. The PBYs continued to overfly the French islands, sometimes landing in the bay off Fort de France to pick up reports from the naval observer. In late March, a low-flying PBY passed directly over the *Béarn*, and the French threatened to open fire if a similar incident occurred.[6] But, for the time being, the Greenslade-Robert modus vivendi worked, for neither side wanted to fight the other, save as a matter of compelling necessity.

Meanwhile, the American Navy was taking the lead in forcing the reluctant President and the preoccupied Army to reach definite conclusions concerning America's strategy in the impending war, thus advancing American strategic planning well beyond the summer's logjam of hemispheric defense, containment of Japan, and material aid to Britain. By the fall of 1940, Admiral Stark and his naval planners were prepared to revolutionize the fundamental assumptions of prewar American strategy and set the foundation of the basic American strategy of World War II.

10.

Plan Dog: Admiral Stark and the "Germany First" Decision

THAT FALL, MUSSOLINI TOLD THE GERMAN minister of foreign affairs, Joachim von Ribbentrop, that "America's intervention in the conflict on the side of England" was "to a certain extent already a fait accompli. America supported the English with materials; for any intervention by the American Army, however, it was already too late." Il Duce added that he "was not too much worried by the situation, for he asked himself what more America could really do."[1] In Washington, other men were asking the same question.

The orderly mind of Admiral Stark was distressed by the President's improvisations. Roosevelt cherished flexibility. Plans and strict agendas of policy induced in him a kind of claustrophobia; specific commitments limited the range of alternatives, and the President preferred freedom—some might have said anarchy—in making decisions. As Lincoln had observed, sometimes the best policy was to have no policy. But Admiral Stark was not a politician. Success in his technical trade often depended upon the quality of fixed plans and the precision of detailed schedules of operations. In fluidity he sensed drift and danger. He was much worried at the possibility of being called upon to carry out unexpected projects in both oceans with his one-ocean fleet; he wanted very badly to secure from the President a definite commitment as to the nation's basic strategic goals and priorities. But Roosevelt remained evasive, and the Army was preoccupied with training and hemisphere defense, so in Novem-

119

ber 1940, with the President safely reelected, Admiral Stark decided
to do the job himself.

One morning, while brooding over the thought that the nation
might suddenly be thrust into the war without plan or purpose,
Stark sought to clear his mind, "as I sometimes do, by drawing up a
paper." In that release of tension which comes from expressing one's
hopes and fears in tangible form, Stark worked on until 0200, producing a twelve-page draft. He showed the paper to his assistants
and together they "went at it, day and night, Saturdays and Sun-
days," until on 12 November, Stark's sixtieth birthday,* the draft
was ready for the President.[2]

In his paper, Stark listed four potential strategic objectives for the
United States. They were:

(a) Hemispheric defense, and a policy of exerting little influence on the
outcome of the European War.
(b) Concentration of offensive capabilities against Japan, coupled with a
purely defensive stance in the Atlantic.
(c) Attempt actively to assist Great Britain in both oceans.
(d) Build up an offensive capability in the Atlantic and maintain a defensive position in the Pacific.

Stark considered Plan Able, accompanied by maximum material
support for Britain—the course preferred by most of the Army planners, and the one being followed at the time—a temporary expedient,
not a policy. Adequate in the short run, in the long run it might not
even ensure Britain's survival, let alone help to defeat Germany and
deter Japan, the vital prerequisites of American security.

Plan Baker, to concentrate on the Pacific, was more viable, but it
did little directly to safeguard Britain, the chief potential ally of the
United States; and if Britain fell, the United States would face, virtually alone, the combined power of the Axis forces in two oceans.
Even if Japan were successfully deterred from expansion, or defeated
if it came to war in the Pacific, the United States would still have to
contend with Germany. But if America helped Britain defeat Germany
first, the combined power of the American and British fleets might
restrain Japan and render a Pacific War either unnecessary or inevitably victorious. Thus, the United States had to ensure British survival,
and that necessitated an American strategic offensive in the Atlantic.
As Admiral Stark succinctly stated, "If Britain wins decisively against

*Stark expressed the hope that "the first three score are the hardest!"

Germany, we could win everywhere; but . . . if she loses, the problems confronting us would be very great; and, while we might not
lose everywhere, we might possibly not *win anywhere*."

Plan Cast, for an offensive in both oceans, was unrealistic. The
United States lacked the power to achieve decisive results in both
oceans simultaneously, and to try to do so would disperse limited
means and risk defeat in either ocean, which would expose the hemisphere to attack.

Thus, Plan Dog, for "an eventual strong offensive in the Atlantic
as an ally of the British, and a defensive in the Pacific," offered the
best chance for decisive victory in both oceans with minimum risk to
the Americas. It was a plan to use American power, especially naval
power, to help secure the Atlantic sea lanes, preserve Britain, and
begin reducing the power of Germany. It was a plan to bring the
Fleet to the ocean where the war was—the Atlantic.

Admiral Stark then had some unpleasant truths for the perusal of
the President. "Alone," he observed, "the British Empire lacks the
man power and the material means to master Germany." When Plan
Dog was implemented, the U.S. Navy would escort convoys in the
western Atlantic; base destroyers, patrol planes, and minecraft in
Great Britain; perhaps assault the Azores and Cape Verde Islands;
and send naval task forces to the Mediterranean and Singapore. But,
Stark warned, "This purely naval assistance would not, in my
opinion, *assure* final victory for Great Britain. Victory would probably depend upon her ability ultimately to make a land offensive
against the Axis powers." Stark did not believe that the British could
accomplish this without large-scale American air and ground reinforcements, in a word, an expeditionary force.

Unlike British staffs, but like American Army planners, Stark fore-
saw the ultimate necessity for substantial ground operations on the
European continent in order to bring about the defeat of Nazi Germany. This was an assumption that, however patent it seemed to
American planners, President Roosevelt continued to shy away from.
Therefore, Admiral Stark assured the President that acceptance of
the plan "would not mean the immediate movement of the fleet into
the Atlantic. I would make no further moves until war should
become imminent," which he thought might occur by the spring. He
did, however, urge that American-British staff conversations should
be held to discuss eventual implementation of Plan Dog—on an if-
and-when basis.[3]

Several days later, Stark wrote Admiral Ghormley that he was requesting "some basic decisions" from the President, who he hoped "before long will give us some direction." Stark recognized that planning was difficult because of the fluidity of the international situation, but believed

> a theoretical plan, which can be a practical plan, can, and should in my opinion, be drawn up. I think we should be sitting around the table doing that right now. We may not be able to get the directive right now because of the political dynamite in it for the moment, but that should not deter us from going ahead on our own, with the other fellow fully understanding that it is on our own, without any backing from the State Department or the White House or anyone else. I should ask the President to let me send you our study . . . but, in line with the *no commitment* idea, it should not appear that the President has seen it.

In London, meanwhile, the Bailey Committee had devised a similar plan; but the British wanted a strong American force based at Singapore, which the Americans were coming to believe was logistically and strategically unsound. Stark suspected the British of delaying approval of the staff talks in order to extort ships for Singapore, and he tartly threatened to call off the meetings if the British restricted their representatives by a rigid insistence on this point. In the meantime, the President, Stimson, and Knox read and verbally endorsed Plan Dog, but refrained from written acceptance for political reasons and to remind the British that the United States could make no fully binding commitments.

Much depended upon the future action of Japan, especially as to what proportion of the Fleet might be safely transferred from the Pacific to the Atlantic. The nation had to wait upon events. As Admiral Stark wrote to the Commander-in-Chief, U.S. Fleet, Admiral James O. Richardson: "You know that we have no definite commitments. Perhaps none can be made. The direction which things finally take may be forced upon us."[4]

Thus, Admiral Stark in the fall of 1940 evolved the "Germany first" strategy which was to prevail as the basic American approach to World War II. His decision was pragmatic and flexible, scantly founded on prior plans or such permanent truths as Germany's superior industrial and technological potential as compared to that of Japan, but was rather a response to existing strategic realities, profoundly rooted in the exigencies of the moment: Germany was in the war and gravely menacing Britain; Japan was not. Hence, the need was to use American power to sustain America's natural ally, Britain, and to begin to sap the power of the most active of the Axis states, Germany.

Practical but fluid, sound but also amenable to future alteration forced by the power of Japan, whose carrier task forces enabled her to project her power across an ocean to strike at the roots of American power in a way that Germany could not, Plan Dog was just what Admiral Stark wanted and his Navy needed as war impended for the United States: a general guideline to future action, it was intended to bring much of the Fleet to the ocean at war—the Atlantic.

Thus, in the winter of 1940, the focus of American strategic planning shifted from the western Pacific and hemispheric defense to the eastern Atlantic. That such a shift had been sponsored by the U.S. Navy, which preferred the prospective glory of epic surface and air battles in the warm Pacific to the tedious patrols and indecisive convoy battles of the cold, wild Atlantic, was a tribute to the maturity of Admiral Stark and his naval planners.

And so the Atlantic sailors were destined for formidable help and augmented status in a future made less uncertain by the thoughtful deliberations of Admiral Stark; but in the interim, they grappled with old problems and managed prosaic responsibilities, although under a new banner.

11.

A Memento
of a
Ghostly Chase

ON 1 NOVEMBER, THE ATLANTIC SQUADRON was renamed the Patrol Force to indicate its increased size and duties; but a new name did not solve old problems. The transfer of destroyers to Britain had made 2,300 men available to the Squadron, many of them experienced petty officers. Attrition continued, however, and by year's end, the destroyers were losing petty officers to new construction ships at the rate of 1,000 each quarter. Some skippers tried not to promote their best men too rapidly lest they soon be lost to the ship. The Atlantic destroyers had an overall shortage of 920 men; they had about 80 percent of their normal complement of machinists' mates, 52 percent of fire control men, and 43 percent of gunners' mates.[1]

The President, misled by his experiences in World War I, when new construction did not make its impact felt until after much of the fighting was over, failed to see that the system of "bleeding the fleet" to man new ships was impairing the efficiency of the overall crews. He stubbornly insisted that "it is very nearly true that you can train men as fast as you can convert ships for Navy use." And he did not wish to have draftees in either the Navy or Marine Corps, partly because of tradition, partly because, as Operation India illustrated, those services would be first to fight, and it was politically inadvisable to have non-volunteers killed in action while the nation was ostensibly at peace. By spring, recruits were coming into the Navy at a rate of about 5,000 a month, about half the number that Admiral Reichmuth felt was required. Everyone understood that it was "unfeasible" to rely on volunteers any longer, but as Admiral Stark lamented, "I am struggling . . . every time I get in the White House . . . for additional men. . . . the President just has his own ideas about men."[2]

Meanwhile, the Neutrality Patrol operations continued, resulting in a mid-November action. On 31 October, the German merchantman *Rio Grande* sailed from Rio de Janeiro and, after an epic, six-week cruise, reached Bordeaux safely. This sucess and the onset of winter weather inspired several of the German vessels at Tampico to try their luck. On 15 November, lookouts on the USS *Plunkett*, on station off the Mexican port, observed the *Orinoco* and *Phrygia* making ready for sea. Several four-stackers from Galveston were ordered to the scene to watch the German ships "without approaching the Mexican coast closer than 10 miles unless special circumstances require."[3]

That night, a full yellow-white moon shone brightly in a clear sky. The Germans could not have picked a worse occasion for an enterprise of stealth, but they were determined, or perhaps too keyed up with nervous energy to tolerate postponement, and decided to come out anyway. Outside the harbor, the *McCormick* patrolled the most northerly sector, with the *Broome* and *Plunkett* stretched out to the south; the destroyers were about 13 miles off Tampico Light.

At fifteen minutes past midnight, old *McCormick* was patrolling on station when her lookouts sighted the black bulk of a darkened vessel about 6,000 yards off her port bow. The destroyer chased the steamer and challenged her for five minutes without response. Finally, at a range of 4,000 yards, *McCormick* turned on her big 24-inch searchlight, pinning the ship in a circle of white light. The vessel was black with a white superstructure; her stack markings were those of the Hamburg-Amerika Line. The ship twisted out of the glare, swinging away on a new heading; *McCormick* trailed her, maintaining a parallel course at 4,000 yards' distance. The vessel changed course again; *McCormick* stolidly followed. After futilely maneuvering to elude the destroyer, at 0115 the ship turned around and steamed back toward the harbor entrance where she was met by another vessel, and apparently passed on the news that there would be no escape this night. The *McCormick* had foiled the *Orinoco*.

The *Plunkett*, farthest south on patrol station, was alerted by *McCormick* that strangers might pass her way, and she was watchful; at 0120, a lookout said that he thought he saw a darkened ship to the southwest. *Plunkett* tried her searchlight, but the range was too great.

Steaming at 10 knots, she searched toward the coast, and the destroyermen soon sighted a ship off their port beam. When she saw the destroyer approaching, the vessel, moving south along the shoreline, reversed course and steamed back toward port. The *Plunkett* trailed on an interception course up to the 10-mile limit of her orders, then patrolled station, awaiting developments. Her acquaintance was the tanker *Phrygia*.

Meanwhile, the Germans, after being thwarted in their move to the south by the *Plunkett*, decided to scuttle the *Phrygia*, setting fires inside her and opening seacocks, as the sailors escaped in small boats. Soon, the *McCormick*'s men sighted a reddish glow to the south. Because she was watching the two German vessels at the harbor entrance, *McCormick* could not investigate the fire; so she asked the *Plunkett* to do so.

The *Plunkett* was astern and to starboard of the *Phrygia* and her men could not see that the German ship was ablaze forward; they assumed that *McCormick*'s men had buck fever and were mistaking flashes from an oil refinery ashore for a fire at sea. So "Charlie P" remained 10 miles offshore.

The men in the old *Broome* waited in the darkness, wondering what was happening to the other ships and when their turn would come. Then, at 0305, the destroyermen sighted the blazing German tanker two miles to port. The *Broome* sounded general quarters and her men broke out the live ammunition; no one was very certain what was taking place in the waters off Tampico that night, but it seemed best to be ready for the worst. Thinking that another German ship might be joining the *Orinoco* in an escape attempt, the *Broome*'s skipper took his destroyer north to assist the *McCormick*. However, the *Orinoco* and the other ship at the harbor entrance switched on running lights and docilely reentered the harbor at about 0330.

Lieutenant Commander P.G. Hale kept the *Plunkett* restively leashed to the 10-mile restraining post until 0316 when he was informed that *McCormick* and *Broome* were "investigating suspicious ships" off the channel entrance. Fearing trouble closer to shore, Hale decided to investigate; he darkened ship and took "Charlie P" in toward the orange flames now clearly visible against the dark blur of the shoreline. The lookouts reported yet another darkened ship steaming into the harbor entrance and the Americans wondered if a fourth German ship, hitherto unseen, had been turned back by the nocturnal activity at sea.

When all was quiet at the harbor entrance, the *McCormick* steamed
south to have a look at the *Phyrgia*. The fires on the tanker dimmed;
wisps of gray smoke coiled above her shadowy superstructure. Then
at 0430, orange and red flames spurted anew from the drifting ship.
The *McCormick* briefly inspected the charred tanker for signs of life
but, finding none, returned to her northern station.

The *Plunkett* then arrived, edging warily in toward the tanker.
Hale was cautious because the hydrographic charts were incomplete,
and it would not have been good form to run aground in Mexican
waters. The destroyer halted 1,000 yards from the *Phrygia*. The
tanker was burning amidships, the ruddy reflection of the flames
shimmering on the black water; the blistered, peeling paint on the
ship's sides indicated internal fires. The bridge and deckhouse, consumed by the flames, were a tangled mass of blackened wreckage.
The tanker was listing about twenty degrees to port and was down
by the stern, her lifeboats were all gone, and a Jacob's ladder was in
place on her port side. Hale anchored the destroyer, intending to
send over a boat, but the tanker began to sway in a heavy ground
swell, and he decided it would be too dangerous. The *Plunkett* then
got under way to return to her patrol station; she was 4.1 miles off
the nearest land.

The *Phrygia* drifted south the rest of the morning, still burning,
until she finally sank at noon. The Mexican Government complained
to the State Department about the destroyers' night work, and on the
19th, a biplane chugged over the American ships, taking pictures.
When the *Simpson* returned from a refueling trip to Galveston, her
men found a charred German dinghy offshore; inside was a broken
violin with the name "Robert Ockelman" on it. It was an odd me-
mento of a ghostly chase.[4]

All remained quiet on the Tampico station until the 29th, when the
German ships *Rhein* and *Idarwald* tried again. They worked south
in the darkness, hugging the coastline within Mexican territorial
waters. The *Simpson* and *Broome* trailed them from a distance, while
the old light cruiser *Memphis* and several destroyers from Key West
steamed to watch the passages into the Atlantic. The German Navy
protested these "actively hostile" movements to the U.S. Naval Attaché in Berlin.[5] It did not help the fleeing merchant ships. The long
Gulf chase went on. The skipper of the *Broome*, in a report seen by
the President, observed: "From the very beginning, the *Rhein* made
every effort to shake us off her tail and I believe we went through

every gyration of which a destroyer is capable. . . . When we finally got into the open sea . . . we felt qualified as trailers first class."[6]

The *Idarwald* was finally caught by the British cruiser *Diomede* near Yucatán Channel, and scuttled by her crew on the afternoon of 8 December, with the American four-stacker *Sturtevant* standing by.[7]

Tenacious *Rhein* lasted longer. But shortly after midnight on 11 December, she was pinned by the searchlight of the Dutch destroyer leader *Van Kingsbergen,* which fired a warning shot ahead; the Dutch, their homeland in the hands of the Nazis, probably would not have borne delay with patience, and it was well that the *Rhein* promptly halted. Three minutes later, the freighter was ablaze from the bridge aft, as the Germans scuttled her with coolness and thoroughness. The *McCormick* and *MacLeish* stood by.[8]

These were the last German sorties from American waters. The Axis ships still in American ports were seized in March. Thus, the Atlantic sailors chased the last of the foxes in December 1940. In the new year, they would be sent to hunt more dangerous game—grim, gray wolves of the sea.

III:
The Atlantic Fleet

12.

Gentlemen from the Pacific

By THE TIME THE NEW YEAR BEGAN, some German diplomatic and service leaders had come to believe that the United States could do more harm to Germany out of the war than in it; belligerency would permit the Germans to carry out naval operations in the western Atlantic and force the Americans to use their war manufactures for their own defense rather than supply them to Britain. But most remained convinced that, although America still lacked the modern arms to intervene effectively in a military sense, a state of war would arouse the American people, making possible increased defense production, and would convince neutrals that Germany could not win the war, thus wrecking German diplomacy. The Fuehrer reasoned that American material aid to Britain would be helpful but far from decisive, and he remained steadfast in his determination to avoid conflict with the United States for as long as possible. Consequently, German policy remained fundamentally unchanged, although press attacks on the United States became stronger and more bitter and German radio propaganda became more "steadily and consistently" hostile to the United States than to the nations with which Germany was already at war.[1]

Plan Dog had projected the necessity of direct American intervention in the Battle of the Atlantic, and by mid-December, most of the

President's naval and military advisers had concluded that such a step should be taken promptly; preliminary planning was undertaken by the naval War Plans Division.

On 9 January, the President met in the White House with Admiral Stark, General Marshall, and Secretaries Stimson, Knox, and Hull to clarify American planning in light of the staff conversations to be held with the British later in the month. The President was impressed by the recommendations of Plan Dog, for he told his advisers that "we would stand on the defensive in the Pacific" and that "the Navy should be prepared to convoy shipping in the Atlantic to England."

A week later, President Roosevelt again indicated his agreement with the judgments of his service planners as to the need for prompt American intervention in the Battle of the Atlantic. On 17 January, the War Plans Division informed Admiral Stark that the Atlantic forces would be able to commence escort operations by 1 April.[2]

Meanwhile, the Patrol Force got a new leader, the redoubtable Vice Admiral Ernest J. King. King was a highly intelligent, completely dedicated officer whose faith in his own abilities lent him a touch of arrogance; he had little patience with men of lesser aptitudes and lower standards. He believed that to be both wise and beloved exceeded the powers of man; he preferred to be wise. A well-rounded officer, he had seen service in submarines and carriers as well as in conventional ships. As a hard taskmaster and stern personality, he was respected but hardly beloved in the Fleet. His idea of command was succinct: "I give my men the tools, the assignment and the authority. The rest is up to them. I will tell a commander to patrol a certain area but I'll never tell him how. He should know how. If he doesn't we must get a man who does." Captain Thomas J. Hickey, Patrol Force's destroyer personnel officer, soon found that the tall, balding, efficient King was a "tough guy" who "had lots of little shore jobs for people who didn't learn fast." King made decisions rapidly, with a minimum of consultation; an austere man, he detested ostentation and sought to imbue the service with his own spartan spirit. He thrived on work and responsibility. The fliers joked that while he did not yet think that he was God, God thought that He was Admiral King. A northerner, he read Civil War history and admired Lee. Perhaps in the character of the reserved and able Vir-

Ernie King in a rare mood—laughing

ginian he sensed something of himself, or rather, of what he would have liked to be; for Lee was both wise and beloved.[3]

Admiral Stark realized that the Atlantic sailors were far from ready to carry out their wartime responsibilities under Plan Dog; therefore, King's earned reputation for firmness, efficiency, and dedication made him seem ideal for the billet of leader of the Patrol Force. As Stark wrote Admiral Husband E. Kimmel, he believed that King was "the very best possible man to handle the situation in the Atlantic, and that we can give him a free rein. He will lick things into shape. . . ." Also, kindly Admiral Stark wanted to give King another sea command before he was retired for age.[4]

On 17 December 1940, Ernie King took command of the Patrol Force. Wasting no time, three days later, in a memo called "Measures Suited to the Existence of an Emergency," he directed that ships be darkened at night, strict antisubmarine and antiaircraft precautions be maintained at sea, and fuel and stores be kept at high levels to permit rapid deployment. King wanted his crews to work harder on their old ships so as to reduce time out of service. He felt that Navy Yard delays reflected the lack of a national sense of urgency, and that there was a certain complacency and lack of initiative in the Fleet because of the psychological difficulty of maintaining vigilance and efficiency while operating in peacetime. As he told Secretary Knox, "in the Navy in general there is still too much 'business as usual' whereas we are now in an emergency . . . which bids fair to become intensified at short notice." King aimed at shaking the complacent by both admonition and hard service. He recognized that part of the problem was a legacy of the thirties, of the inclination in the days of peace and economy to achieve promotion by showing results and avoiding mistakes rather than to risk failure by assuming the initiative. In January 1941, he informed the Patrol Force:

1. I have been concerned for many years over the increasing tendency— now grown almost to "standard practice"—of flag officers and other group commanders to issue orders and instructions in which their subordinates are told "how" as well as "what" to do to such an extent and in such detail that the "Custom of the Service" has virtually become the antithesis of that essential element of command—"initiative of the subordinate."

2. We are preparing for—and are now close to—those active operations (commonly called war) which require the exercise and the utilization of the full powers and capabilities of every officer in command status. There will be neither time nor opportunity to do more than prescribe the several tasks of the several subordinates (to say "*what*," perhaps "when" and

"where," and usually, for their intelligent cooperation, "why"); leaving to them—expecting and requiring of them—the capacity to perform the assigned tasks (to do the "how").

3. If subordinates are deprived—as they now are—of that training and experience which will enable them to act "on their own"—if they do not know, by constant practice, how to exercise "initiative of the subordinates"—if they are reluctant (afraid) to act because they are accustomed to detailed orders and instructions—if they are not habituated to think, to judge, to decide and to act for themselves . . .—we shall be in sorry case when the time of "active operations" arrives.

4. The reasons for the current state of affairs—how did we get this way?—are many but among them are four which need mention; first, the "anxiety" of seniors that everything in their commands shall be conducted so correctly and go so smoothly, that none may comment unfavorably; second, those energetic activities of staffs which lead to infringement of (not to say interference with) the functions for which the lower echelons exist; third, the consequent "anxiety" of subordinates lest their exercise of initiative, even in their legitimate spheres, should result in their doing something which may prejudice their selection for promotion; fourth, the habit on the one hand and the expectation on the other of "nursing" and "being nursed" which lead respectively to that violation of command principles known as "orders to obey orders" and to that admission of incapacity or confusion evidenced by "request instructions."

King directed:

(a) adopt the premise that the echelon commanders are competent in their several command echelons unless and until they prove themselves otherwise;

(b) teach them that they are not only *expected* to be competent . . . but that it is *required* of them that they be competent;

(c) train them—by guidance and supervision—to exercise foresight, to think, to judge, to decide and to act for themselves;

(d) stop "nursing" them;

(e) finally, train ourselves to be satisfied with "acceptable solutions" even though they are not "staff solutions" or other particular solutions that we ourselves prefer.[5]

King understood that it is necessity, not exhortation, that alters rooted vices, but he wanted at the outset to create a tone of dynamism in the Patrol Force.

The Naval Academy's Class of 1941 was graduated in January instead of June to provide desperately needed officers for the expanding Fleet. The graduates understood that theirs was the first "war class," making their choice of duty particularly significant. Some, like Ensign Craig Spowers, selected destroyers, Atlantic, because they thought that war would come first in the Atlantic and believed it the obligation of a professional to be first in combat. Ensign Spowers drew the four-stacker *Reuben James* and was pleased.[6]

Admiral Stark agreed with the midshipmen. As he wrote in a letter at about the same time, "I have told the Gang here for months past that in my opinion we were heading straight for the war . . . and personally I do not see how we can avoid, either having it thrust upon us or of our deliberately going in, many months longer. And of course it may be a matter of weeks or days."[7]

And along the East Coast, veteran destroyermen were putting new construction ships into commission.

Lieutenant Commander Albert C. Murdaugh, a courtly, scholarly man, used to the ordered, scientific ken of the metallurgical engineer, was reassigned from the Naval Gun Factory to one of the building destroyers. Given a list of the ships' names, he selected the *Edison* because she was named after the inventor. The Bureau of Ships assured him that she would not be ready to be commissioned for six more months, ample time to provide a trained crew. However, at Kearny, New Jersey, Murdaugh discovered that the builders were welding rather than riveting the hull and the *Edison* would be ready in six weeks. Murdaugh scrambled to secure good men and was fortunate in drawing three experienced officers, including the Exec, and several veteran chiefs. But when he saw his crew, he underwent a trauma; the youngsters were straight from boot camp. Painfully green, they postured and tried to conceal their doubts with a facade of brashness and movie-stereotype toughness; they were cocky city youngsters from rough sections of Boston and Brooklyn. Murdaugh, used to the mature, reliable professional sailors of the thirties, thought that the Bureau of Navigation had emptied its misfit-bag on his deck. The disappointed skipper overlooked the subtler virtues of his flock. In time, the surface brashness wore off like cheap gilt, but the toughness and swagger went deeper; they were not men who quit easily, and their disdain for authority was indicative of a prideful spirit which, shaped to better ends, might someday sustain important causes in tight places.

Murdaugh went to work. The men slowly began to get the hang of their jobs; a few of the more obstreperous were tutored in propriety by tougher chiefs and ceased to give trouble. The crew got better. In April, the *Edison* steamed over to Brooklyn Navy Yard to be fitted with guns. Ashore, Murdaugh, always methodical, looked around and located a set of 5-inch guns in which he had confidence, for he had helped cast them at the Gun Factory. He promptly claimed them, but before they were installed, a British cruiser with a mangled superstructure limped into port with an emergency priority, and the *Edison* lost her skipper's guns to the British warship.

The destroyer shook down in the Caribbean without stress. Then Murdaugh lost many of his trained men to still newer construction, and training had to commence virtually all over again in addition to the normal workload in readying the ship for sea duty. Like all the Atlantic destroyers, the *Edison* was undermanned, so it was a busy time for Murdaugh's men. Then sonar equipment was installed, and the sonar operators reported fresh from the Sound School at Key West; but the gear proved cranky and did not function well at long ranges. Depth charge racks were fitted aft, but there were no forked throwers available. The ship was not given any radar equipment.

Murdaugh arranged to send his wardroom steward to Schrafft's and his mess steward to Horn & Hardart's for specialized instruction. A useful rivalry developed between the cooks, and at sea they voluntarily alternated on night duty in the galley to bake bread and prepare dessert specialties for the crew.*

The young sailors were "alert and interested," which was the prerequisite of proficiency; as they worked at their tasks, they improved, and as their skills grew, so did their pride in themselves and their ship. Thus, when the *Edison* was ordered out to work with the carrier *Wasp* in the central Atlantic, Murdaugh did not fear embarrassment in such haughty company.[8]

The Anglo-American military and naval planners met in Washington in January to consider Plan Dog. The British wanted more material assistance, major American naval units to be based at Singapore, and a clarification of the American role in the war—they wanted to know, for instance, when the United States would be prepared to implement Plan Dog, escort convoys in the western Atlantic, and assume responsibility for the defense of the Atlantic isles. President Roosevelt was not to be rushed, and so the Americans wanted at the meetings to apprise the British of the limitations as

---

*By naval custom, cooks could not be ordered to relight galley fires after the last scheduled meal of the day.

well as the extent of the American commitment in the Atlantic. For Admiral Ghormley had reported in the fall that some British leaders expected the United States to be in the war "within a few days of the reelection of the President."

The Americans feared that the British would claim strategic leadership on grounds of experience, but they believed that British military leadership was mediocre and that the United States should not "entrust our national future to British direction." The Americans also greatly feared that the British would try to use American support and aid to strengthen their postwar commercial and military prospects, in other words, to bolster colonialism.[9]

The six British representatives were put up at the Shoreham Hotel in Washington, D.C., in the guise of technical advisers to the British Purchasing Mission; Rear Admiral R.M. Bellairs headed the delegation. The American services also sent six planning officers; Admiral Ghormley and Captain Kirk represented the Navy, and Rear Admiral Richmond Kelly Turner's War Plans Division played a major role.

At the first session, on 29 January, Admiral Stark stressed that the delegates were discussing "tentative agreements . . . should the United States be compelled to engage in war against the Axis powers. . . ." President Roosevelt had helped choose Stark's words, insisting that "be compelled" be used in place of Stark's original "decide" and that the British be referred to as "associates," not "allies." State Department officials did not attend the meetings in order to stress that they were purely technical military discussions. General Marshall warned that arrangements reached would be contingent on future events and policy decisions and could not be deemed commitments.

It was reaffirmed that America's "principal military effort" was to be made in the Atlantic. The British, influenced by the heavy casualties they had sustained on the continent in World War I, by the caution of an Army leadership that was stultifyingly unimaginative and conservative, and by consciousness of their marked industrial and demographic disadvantages in relation to Germany, preferred to avoid a direct assault on the European continent in favor of attacks along the outer periphery of Axis power. They wanted to believe that Germany could be worn down and defeated largely by aerial bombardment, sea blockade, and sabotage and propaganda. The Americans, with the optimism of vast resources and historical good fortune and success, believed that a cross-Channel operation could take place as early as 1942 or 1943.

Kelly Turner assured the British that the United States would be able to accept responsibility for operations in the western Atlantic by 1 April, if America were at war by then. He promised that U.S. destroyers and patrol planes would be available for duty in the Western Approaches to the United Kingdom, as they had been in World War I.

As to Pacific strategy, it was agreed that all reasonable steps would be taken to avoid war with Japan. The Americans would not make any specific commitment to send a force to Singapore, and they became angry when the British ambassador, Lord Halifax, broached the matter to the State Department, since the military talks were supposed to remain apart from diplomacy. The President backed his service chiefs, telling Halifax that the American people would never sanction war with Japan over an attack on Singapore. He softened the refusal with the observation that to take a stronger line in the Pacific would constitute a dangerous diversion from the main Atlantic theater, which was Admiral Stark's reasoning.

The staff meetings provided for coordination of Anglo-American planning and future action, continued exchange of information, and the acceptance of a common strategy based on the necessity of British survival for command of the seas and as a base for future offensive operations against Germany, including aerial bombardment and a decisive land offensive on the European continent. The American role in the common strategy was:

1. To assure defense of the Western Hemisphere.
2. To rearm and build up an offensive capability.
3. To sustain Britain with material aid.
4. To deter Japan with the Pacific Fleet.
5. When entering the war, to concentrate on defeating Germany first, in case of a two-ocean war.

Thus, the Anglo-American staff conferences underwrote the tenets of Plan Dog, which now became the mutual policy of the United States and Great Britain.[10]

While relations at the meetings were pleasant, American naval officers tended to be leery of the British. By reason of tradition and combat experience, the Royal Navy understandably deemed itself the senior in the partnership at sea. As Captain Kirk reported from London, the British "are very jealous of their long history of successful naval leadership. They will expect to tell us what to do and where." The Americans, and most assuredly Admiral King, resented the implication of inferiority and demanded status compatible with the strength and ability of the U.S. Navy.* Each Navy thus saw the other as somewhat grasping and assertive in relation to its objective position. Probably more than disagreement over such specific issues as landing craft, proper employment of aircraft, or Pacific strategy, it was this usually repressed tension that accounted for occasional clashes between the leaders of the two navies in World War II.[11]

After the conferences, Admiral Stark wrote to his Fleet commanders:

> The question as to our entry into the war now seems to be *when* and not *whether.* . . .
>
> Public opinion, which is now slowly turning in that direction, may or may not be accelerated. My own personal view is that we may be in the war (possibly undeclared) against Germany and Italy in about two months [i.e., in April 1941], but that there is a reasonable possibility that Japan may remain out altogether.[12]

Under Plan Dog, the American Navy would have to shift units from the Pacific to the Atlantic and assume responsibility for the defense of the islands in the Atlantic and for escort operations in the Atlantic, in order to relieve British naval forces needed elsewhere and help safeguard sea communications to the United Kingdom. But as Kelly Turner observed, "If the Navy is to be ready, if required, to despatch promptly an effective force to operate from bases overseas in connection with the protection of shipping, the force must be equipped, assembled, and trained." As early as December 1940, Turner's staff had begun planning for a destroyer-patrol plane-tender force to be based in Northern Ireland and Scotland. After the Anglo-American meetings, it was decided that this "British Isles Detachment" was to be organized, trained in antisubmarine warfare at Narragansett Bay, and made ready for war service by 1 April. Turner recommended a force of 27 destroyers, 42 patrol planes, 1 destroyer tender, 3 aviation tenders, and 1 supply ship. Admiral Stark approved Turner's plans on 15 February, and the force was to be officially born

---

*The Royal Navy, while superior to the U.S. Navy in ASW operations, was inferior in all the other crucial phases of modern sea warfare: its air arm was impotent because of inferior aircraft; its amphibious capability was weakened by the decline of the Royal Marines; and its task forces lacked mobility, for it never developed the flair for refueling and resupplying at sea that endowed the U.S. Navy with such remarkable range, endurance, and striking power.

on 1 March. For security reasons, the name of the new task force was changed from Northeastern Escort Force to the more nebulous Support Force, which suggested logistics rather than combat.* Admiral Stark directed, "Since this Force may be engaged on distant service beyond the scope of normal supply and maintenance lines, it is desired that it be fully supplied and equipped . . . at the earliest practicable date. . . . This project is classified as urgent. Priority, as regards personnel, material, and logistic requirements, will be directed by the CNO as necessary." Destroyer Squadron 7 (new destroyers *Plunkett, Niblack, Benson, Gleaves, Mayo, Madison, Lansdale, Hilary P. Jones,* and *Charles F. Hughes*), DesRon 30 (four-stackers *Dallas, Ellis, Bernadou, Cole, Greer, DuPont, Tarbell, Upshur,* and *Lea*), DesRon 31 (*MacLeish, Bainbridge, Overton, Sturtevant, Reuben James, McCormick, Broome, Simpson,* and *Truxtun*), Patrol Squadrons 51, 52, 55, 56, and tenders *Denebola, Albemarle, Belknap,* and *George E. Badger* were ordered to Newport as the nucleus of the Support Force.[13]

Rear Admiral Arthur L. Bristol was summoned from his post as Commander, Aircraft, Scouting Force, at Pearl Harbor, and on 26 February, was given command of the Support Force. Admiral Bristol was an able planner and organizer; he combined a capacity for hard work with a kindly geniality. Both productive and easy to get along with, he had many friends in the service, which enabled him to secure an excellent staff that contained two future CNOs; since Admirals King and Stark reported directly to the President on the activities of the Support Force, it was assumed in the destroyers that presidential patronage had assisted Bristol to build his talented staff.

Admiral Bristol had experience in both surface ships and aircraft, had served in the Atlantic in World War I, and had been Naval Attaché at London from 1931 to 1934. These credentials seemed to fit him well for ASW operations involving destroyers and planes in the Northwest Approaches in cooperation with the Royal Navy. Nevertheless, Bristol was somewhat wary of the British and their suggestions; he did not intend to be told how to do his job. Admiral Bristol was a capable, personable officer, but like most of the senior Atlantic commanders, he perhaps lacked the combative fire and dynamism needed to "fight the U-boat on Doenitz's own terms, to imbue the fight

---

*Nevertheless, by 11 March German intelligence was aware of the composition of Support Force and, thus, of its general function.

with the spirit of the hunter." Still, Admiral Bristol's appointment conferred some of the prestige of the Pacific on the Support Force, and the Atlantic destroyermen knew that they would soon be engaged in significant operations.[14]

While the Support Force was shaking down, Captain Denfeld, of Admiral Bristol's staff, went to the United Kingdom to select base sites. The Americans chose Londonderry and Loch Erne in Northern Ireland and Gare Loch and Loch Ryan in Scotland. Two base complexes were picked in order to provide a spare in case one was put out of action by German bombing. Use of the Scottish sites was delayed by lack of existing facilities for ships, lack of transportation, changing priorities, indecision, and British red tape; they were never used by the Navy. But Londonderry served the Atlantic sailors well.

The Prime Minister of Northern Ireland was informed of the plans for construction and promised the work would be carried out secretly to avoid German attack. The number of antiaircraft guns defending Londonderry was doubled. The first construction workers arrived in June, and hastily and "unobtrusively" passed through customs. The American civilian workers tried to remain aloof from the local population and not discuss their work. The "visitors," as the Irish called them, were said to labor with "a concentration of effort not familiar to this country." They were better paid and fed than their hosts, and some found in the gray, rainy days an excuse to drink heavily, but relations with the Ulstermen were generally good. There were so many Axis agents in Dublin that the Germans were probably aware of the general nature of the projects in Northern Ireland.

While in the United Kingdom, Captain Denfeld noted that the British escorts operating in the Northwest Approaches were beginning consistently to train in antisubmarine warfare and operate as units to develop teamwork; and he secured the services of two British naval officers and one air officer to be sent to the United States to advise Admiral Bristol's staff in ASW.[15]

As if further symbolizing the importance of the Atlantic and the implications of Plan Dog, President Roosevelt promoted Ernie King to full admiral and the Patrol Force to full fleet status. On 1 February 1941, the second Atlantic Fleet was born and christened.

Then, in mid-March, the President directed that the Atlantic Fleet be brought to wartime readiness. On the 18th, Admiral Stark directed Admiral King to terminate the Neutrality Patrol, except for the watch on Martinique and the Gulf Patrol. Ships were to be sent into port for upkeep, stripped of superfluous and flammable gear, and take on their mobilization allowances of arms. All units were then to commence six weeks of intensive training. Admiral Stark told King, "This step is, in effect, a war mobilization." The Atlantic Fleet, its ships no longer widely dispersed in Neutrality Patrol duties, could at last be organized into task forces to perform the functions envisaged by Plan Dog.

By April, the Atlantic Fleet had 159 ships, including 2 carriers, 3 battleships, 8 cruisers, 78 destroyers, 29 submarines, and 39 auxiliaries of various types.

Admiral King arrayed his forces as follows:

Task Force 1. Rear Admiral David M. LeBreton. Boston and Narragansett Bay. *The Ocean Escort Force.* Three battleships, two heavy cruisers, thirteen destroyers. Mission: To provide escorts for amphibious movements.
Task Force 2. Rear Admiral Arthur B. Cook. Hampton Roads and Bermuda. *The Striking Force.* Two carriers, two heavy cruisers, four destroyers. Mission: Reserve striking force for offensive operations.
Task Force 3. Rear Admiral Jonas H. Ingram. San Juan and Guantanamo Bay. *The Scouting Force.* Four light cruisers, four destroyers. Mission: To patrol Caribbean and South Atlantic and screen northeast coast of Brazil.
Task Force 4. Rear Admiral Arthur L. Bristol. Narragansett Bay. *The Support Force.* Forty-five destroyers, fifty-one patrol planes, one destroyer tender, three aircraft tenders, ten minecraft. Mission: To provide escorts for convoys and conduct ASW operations.

The submarines, auxiliaries, patrol planes, and Fleet Marine Force, Atlantic, were also organized in appropriate task forces.[16]

Despite the appearance of formidable strength, most of the ships were old and most of the men were new. Admiral King's fleet was hampered by its birthright. Gunnery and tactical skill had deteriorated during Neutrality Patrol operations and because of the influx of inexperienced men. Lack of torpedo overhaul facilities limited the destroyers in torpedo-attack training. Techniques for ASW were primitive because there had not for a long time been much opportunity to train "with actual submarines employing evasive tactics." At Newport, classes for specialists were conducted aboard the destroyer tenders *Denebola* and *Melville;* so pressing was the need that even Admiral Bristol's flagship, *Prairie,* was not exempt from this duty. Nevertheless, about 55 percent of the Atlantic destroyermen had less than two years of service and 23 percent of the men were apprentice seamen; most destroyers were operating with only one quartermaster and about three-fifths of their prescribed complements of radiomen.[17]

In the spring, the Support Force destroyers trained hard in ASW exercises with live submarines off Newport, sometimes escorting one of the tenders. The practices gave inexperienced sonar men a chance to identify and track submerged submarines, but tactically they were of a low order, for the element of surprise was missing, there were no large, vulnerable convoys to distract the destroyers, and they involved daylight actions against submerged submarines.

Then, in May, as an experiment, the submarine *Bonita* conducted a significant series of night exercises with six modern destroyers. The first night, she made a cautious surface-attack approach on the destroyers, with her conning tower awash and only her bridge exposed above the surface of the black water. At 10,000 yards, the submarine sighted lights from the careless destroyers, and was able to close to within 800 yards before being sighted. The next night, the *Bonita* approached with deck awash, reached her attack position undetected, indicated her attack by firing a Very flare, and then retired unseen. On the third night, emboldened by success, she attacked fully surfaced, chasing the destroyers at 10 knots, no longer moving slowly to conceal her wake. Still undiscovered, the submarine turned up 12-½ knots, closing unobserved to attack range. *Bonita* fired the flare signalling her attack, and retired. The destroyers shot two search spreads of star shell into the night sky, but despite the aid of a full moon, failed to find the submarine. The last night was hazy and moonless, and the *Bonita* again closed unseen to within 1,500 yards of the surface ships and attacked. The destroyers flashed on searchlights, but the sallow beams, eerie in the drifting mist, failed to locate their attacker.[18] This exercise, little noted at the time, was an ominous harbinger of a grim destiny for the Atlantic destroyermen.

On Memorial Day, in another drill, the *Reuben James*, brought to her best days by Lieutenant Commander Heywood Lane Edwards, picked up a firm sonar contact and dropped a depth charge only 300 yards from the submerged *S-20*. When the submarine surfaced, Edwards had a message flashed across to it: "Pretty lucky. We'll get you next time." Lieutenant Commander Samuel D. Dealey, skipper of *S-20* and former Exec of the "Rube," had his signalman wink back to his friends: "Next time, I'll put a fish under your number one stack." Then the two craft headed back to Newport together, their men unaware that Sam Dealey was to prove a better prophet than "Tex" Edwards.[19]

Another recent migrant to the Atlantic was the CO of Task Force 3, Rear Admiral Jonas H. Ingram. He was a burly man with a candid and hearty manner; he had an ample paunch bulging over his belt, a tomato-shaped face, and a gold front tooth. Gruff and avuncular, he ran an efficient and happy ship; most of his experience was in battleships and destroyers. There were those who thought that his talents did not extend very far from a ship's bridge, regarding him as a slightly eccentric old salt, good with men and ships, but certainly "no mental giant." Ingram, who had played tackle at the Academy, trusted practical experience more than theories; yet in a way he was better suited for command in the fluid circumstances of modern naval warfare than ostensibly smarter men. Unpretentious and with no pet truths that had to be sheltered from the test of reality, Ingram was flexible and willing to learn from others. Although his heart belonged to the surface ships and long guns, he encouraged the fliers, used airplanes effectively, and trusted the ASW scientists when others scoffed at them.

Ingram had had command of Cruiser Division 2, which consisted of the *Omaha, Memphis, Cincinnati,* and *Milwaukee.* Lacking seaworthiness, stable secondary batteries, and effective AA weapons, these ships were assigned to the placid Caribbean, safe from northern gales and German aircraft. From San Juan and "Gitmo," they watched Martinique, putting the bored Ingram in mind of the British blockades of the French islands during the colonial wars of the eighteenth century. Ingram was supposed by his men to have told Admiral King with his customary directness, "These French and Indian wars bore the hell out of me."

When Task Force 3 was formed in the fleet realignment, Ingram was given a division of new, long-range destroyers to complement his wheezy cruisers, and his ships were ordered to patrol a vast triangle of water between Trinidad, the Cape Verdes, and Brazil to watch for German raiders and screen the Brazilian coast. When in Brazilian ports for supplies, Ingram would be responsible for diplomatic discussions with Brazilian officials concerning base sites. Sev-

eral American naval observers served in Brazil; Captain W.A. Hodgman ran an office in a vibrant section of Rio, on the Rua Bom Jesus,
which the Americans felt might more appropriately be called "Bomb
Jesus Street." The Naval Attache was flamboyant, picturesque Rear
Admiral Augustin Toutant Beauregard, whose emotional and dashing
personality was deemed simpatico with the Latin temperament. But
the efforts of these officers to secure bases on the Brazilian coast
failed. Brazilian nationalism, dislike of Britain for interrupting the
lucrative prewar trade with Germany, and fears of a German victory
prevented President Vargas from providing base sites. Now Jonas
Ingram would get a chance.

Task Force 3, small, remote from the rest of the Fleet, "less diluted
by replacements," was responsive to the personality of its chief. Its
attitudes reflected Admiral Ingram's dislike of "precedent and proto-
col," his energy, blithe spirit, and aggressiveness. When Admiral
King reminded Ingram that he might find supplies scarce along the
barren northeast coast of Brazil, Ingram replied that he would manage
to feed his men if he had to appropriate goods from passing merchant
ships. King retorted that he had always known that Ingram was an
"old pirate" at heart.

At 1800 hours on 24 April, the *Memphis* and *Cincinnati* steamed
out of Newport without destroyer escort due to the haste of their
orders, rushing to initiate the new South Atlantic Patrol, which Franklin Roosevelt first had traced for Admiral Stark a long year and a
half before. Jonas Ingram was a happy man; Ernie King was allowing
a tackle to run with the ball.[20]

As active operations loomed, Admiral King assessed his command
and tried to sound a hardy tone for it:

> In the existing emergency, we are not confronted with hazards and
> dangers (except potentially) but we are faced with difficulties and dis-
> comforts . . . . chiefly those involved in lack of trained sea-going per-
> sonnel, inadequacies of material . . . and the waiting for developments over
> which we have no control.
>
> It must be the key idea of all hands that we will make the best of what
> we have.
>
> As to personnel — we must not only train our own personnel (officers as
> well as men) to meet the current needs of our own ships but we must do our
> share in providing trained personnel to man the new ships. . . .
>
> As to material — our needs are many but there is a clear-cut distinction
> between what is necessary (urgent) and what is desirable. . . .
>
> As to operations — we must not only accept the circumstances premised
> on strategical considerations imposed by the current international situation,

but also must realize that we must do all that we can with the forces available, even though they are less in numbers and in power than appear adequate to present and prospective tasks.

As to waiting — we must make the most of the time available to perfect
the training of personnel, to improve the material condition of ships, to
better our capacity in operations, and otherwise to make ourselves ready
(physically and mentally) for the work for which the Navy exists and for
which we are in the Navy.

I expect the officers of the Atlantic Fleet to be the leaders in what may be
called the "pioneering spirit" — to lead in the determination that the dif-
ficulties and discomforts . . . shall be dealt with as "enemies" to be
overcome — by our own efforts.

We must do all that we can with what we have.[21]

It was a hard-bitten admonition to a fleet short of men and ships
to have it take pride in its adversity. The hoary service platitude "do
the best you can with what you have" had a special meaning to
King's fleet. It was what Murdaugh, his Exec, and his chiefs were
doing to make the *Edison* ready to fight; it was what "Tex" Edwards,
Craig Spowers, and the men of the four-stackers were doing to prepare old ships for a new war; it was what Bill Greenman meant when
he told his skippers that their men and ships would someday live or
die as they had trained.

Do the best you can with what you have.

Sometimes cynically, sometimes seriously, the Atlantic sailors said
the words; none denied that they were appropriate. Admiral King
had given his ill-favored fleet a motto, some words to live up to and
also to mock: good men needed to do both. The tone was right,
spare and hard, touching both pride and self-pity. The Atlantic Fleet
would do what it could.

And, so, in a new year, under a new leader, and with a new name,
the Atlantic Fleet moved closer to war, physically and psychological-
ly. Its sailors fitted out new ships and trained green men, and its
staffs organized new task forces to carry out augmented roles in the
Battle of the Atlantic, as projected by Plan Dog and confirmed by
the Anglo-American strategists. But as the Fleet worked and trained
to fight, the President continued to delay its commitment to battle.

13.

An Order
with
No Teeth

THE PRESIDENT WAS THE VICTIM of his own success. Lend-Lease, the manifestation of the nation's contradictory desires both to defeat Germany and remain out of the war, had won support as an alternative to intervention; yet the nation's defense plans were drawn on the correct assumption that Germany could not be defeated without direct American intervention.

Even before Plan Dog, Frank Knox had told Morgenthau, "The English are not going to win this war without our . . . military help. . . .We needn't talk it outdoors, but I think it is true. . . ." In December, Admiral Stark suggested extending the Patrol zone to Iceland to help goods reach England; and when the President spoke of building ships for Britain, Secretary of War Stimson told him that the thing to do with a leaky bathtub was to plug it, not put more water into it, adding, "we ought to forcibly stop the German submarines by our intervention." In the spring, the nation's leading pundit, Walter Lippmann, prodded that the "great majority of Americans know by instinct and by reason that the control of the Atlantic Ocean is vital to the defense of the United States and of the whole Western Hemisphere. They know that for their physical security, for the continuation of the free way of life, it is necessary that the other shore of the Atlantic Ocean should be held by friendly . . . powers."[1]

But the President, for political and moral reasons and because of the limited power of the Army and Air Corps, the slow pace of

151

industrial mobilization, and Japanese strength in the Pacific, was reluctant to bring the country to war unless American territory were attacked. Thus, with the policy of material assistance brought to its logical conclusion by Lend-Lease, yet unwilling to enter the war, the President groped to find an intermediate policy. In March, he told Ickes that "probably we would have to wait for a German 'incident' " before taking decisive action in the Atlantic; he seemed to be awaiting the "blunder" that Hitler was determined to avoid.[2]

The Army planners argued that it was

> highly desirable that our entry be made sufficiently soon to avoid either the loss of the British Isles or a material change in the attitude of the British Government directed toward appeasement.

At the same time, they conceded that

> in contrast to this view, it must be recognized that the Army can, at the present time, accomplish extremely limited military support to a war effort and from this point of view it is highly desirable that we withhold active participation as long as possible.

Nevertheless, most of the naval and civilian leadership felt as did Colonel Joseph T. McNarney, the Air Corps planner: ". . . it is important that we start reducing the war-making ability of Germany. We do have a Navy in being and can do something. If we wait we will end up standing alone. . . ."[3]

In the first six months of 1941, the British sustained shipping losses of 756 merchant vessels sunk and another 1,450 merchantmen damaged, a rate of loss equivalent to nearly 7,000,000 tons a year. Yet, unbeknownst to all, the seemingly desperate situation was destined to improve greatly in the second half of the year; sinkings would decline from a monthly average of 126 ships and 486,000 tons to 51 ships and 172,000 tons. The improvement was largely due to better British organization of the ASW effort. The British increasingly were learning to train the escorts together and keep them together as unified, coordinated combat groups. In addition, more British planes and escorts, the advent of radar, improved techniques for convoy routing, small numbers and dispersal of U-boats and loss of experienced German submarine personnel in battle all helped to reduce the slaughter of Allied shipping, most of which was achieved by the submarines, although important damage was also done by German aircraft and mine warfare.[4]

Aware of the grim spring statistics of the ocean struggle, Admiral Stark was too pessimistic when he wrote to another officer, "The situation is obviously critical in the Atlantic. In my opinion it is hopeless except as we take strong measures to save it. . . . Without our giving effective aid I do not believe the British can do much more than see the year through, if that." A small help was to repair British warships in American shipyards; British yards suffered from inexperienced and scarce labor and war damage, causing damaged vessels to be lost to service for long periods. Hence, eight days after the passage of Lend-Lease, American yards began repairing British warships, such as the armed merchant cruiser *Canton*, the battleship *Malaya*, and the carrier *Illustrious*.[5]

But greater succor could come only from a more active American role in the Battle of the Atlantic. By 20 March, the War Plans Division and the Atlantic Fleet staff had worked up plans for the Navy to escort convoys in the western Atlantic. Admiral Stark was worried about the shortage of destroyers and the incomplete base facilities for the Support Force in the United Kingdom. The President seemed convinced that "public opinion was not yet ready for the United States to convoy ships"; yet some such naval action appeared essential. For two weeks in April, the President writhed in uncertainty, trying out various implausible proposals on Stark and the Cabinet and, with disconcerting frequency, changing his mind as to the technical details of the naval plans. Arrangements were made to reinforce King's men by a transfer from the Pacific of powerful, modern ships—the carrier *Yorktown*, 3 battleships, 4 cruisers, and several divisions of new destroyers. Also it was agreed to investigate the possibilities of Iceland as an American escort base. The President broodingly told Stimson that he was thinking of asking Congress for the power to escort convoys, but admitted that he did not believe it would be granted. He brought out an atlas for the Secretary of War and drew a line on a map down the Atlantic midway between the bulges of Brazil and West Africa, at about 26° west longitude. He said that he was considering a new plan to "patrol the high seas west of this median line" while "the British . . . swing their convoys over westward to the west side of this line, so that they will be within our area. Then by the use of patrol planes and patrol vessels we can patrol and follow the convoys and notify them of any German raiders or German submarines that we may see and give them a chance to escape."

At the Cabinet meeting of 17 April, the President brought up his new idea. Stimson thought the extended Patrol a "clearly hostile act" and wanted the President to acknowledge it as such, instead of, in deference to "Mr. Gallup," pretending it was a purely defensive move to watch for possible aggressors approaching the Americas; as Stimson said, ". . . you are not going to report the presence of the German fleet to the Americas. You are going to report it to the British fleet." Yet the President had not fully abandoned the plan to escort convoys, for he then showed his inclination to accept a limited naval war with Germany in the Atlantic in a typically elliptical manner; recalling early American history, he observed: "we fought an undeclared naval war with the French in the Caribbean. Later our fleet was sent to fight the Corsairs. Here again we fought an undeclared war and won."[6]

But, finally, at Hyde Park that weekend, the President told Admiral King that the order to begin escort operations would not be given; instead Patrol activities would be extended to the border of the German submarine war zone or to 26° west longitude, whichever was farthest west. He consoled King, who understood that the extended Patrol was meaningless in the kind of sea warfare taking place in the Atlantic—hunting submarines, not surface raiders—and thus an order "with no teeth," with the promise of a carrier and five destroyers from the Pacific Fleet "about the first of May"; but the transfer of other warships to the Atlantic would be postponed "for the time being." Secretary of State Hull's warnings that the Russo-Japanese Nonaggression Pact would free Japan for an advance in the Pacific and Roosevelt's desire to avoid bloodshed for as long as possible, in the thin hope that something might occur to lessen the need for American intervention, led the President to turn cautious and draw back from escort operations—and war.[7]

| Admiral Stark disappointedly wrote Kimmel that the decision to escort convoys had been "agreed to, authorized and directed in its detail by the President," and then "cancelled by the President . . . for fear of the Japs. . . . What will be done about convoy and many other things, and just how much a part of our Democratic way of life will be handled by Mr. Gallup, is a pure guess." He added that the President "has on his hands . . . about as difficult a situation as ever confronted any man anywhere in public life. There are tremendous issues at stake, to which he is giving all he has got. I only wish I could be of more help to him."[8]

Meanwhile, the President wrote Churchill:

We will want in great secrecy notification of movement of convoys so our patrol units can seek out any ships or planes of aggressor nations operating west of the new line of the security zone. We will immediately make public to you position aggressor ships or planes when located in our patrol area. . . .

At the Cabinet session on 25 April, he airily asserted that escort of convoys might be obsolete, insisting that his roving patrol of screening warships was the best way of protecting merchant ships. This, of course, was not so; the technology and numbers were not yet at hand to make the hunter-killer concept of ASW effective, and besides, the President's patrol was still operating west of the major U-boat patrol areas.

"Well," the President said, "it's a step forward." And tenacious, old Henry Stimson answered, "Well, I hope you will keep on walking, Mr. President. Keep on walking." But the President soon slowed his pace. Five days later, he told Knox, "I do not think we are prepared at this time to use Iceland as a . . . base."[9]

Probably for political reasons, the President decided to order the extended patrol despite its technical limitations; he needed to buy time, to gain a respite free of pressure and demands for action, while he pondered his next moves in the Atlantic. The extended patrol provided action to appease his "hawks" while not bringing with it grave dangers to alarm Congress' "doves." It bought time for the President.

But as April passed into May, the Cabinet grew gloomy at Roosevelt's apparent lack of decisiveness. Morgenthau was not reassured when the President told him on 17 May, "I am waiting to be pushed into this situation." The Cabinet "hawks" wanted the President to essay a grand gesture, to transfer most of the Pacific Fleet to the Atlantic. Stimson reasoned that the Philippines could not be defended in any event and, without bases in the western Pacific, the Navy would be unable to strike the flank of a Japanese thrust into southeast Asia, as its Pacific war plans assumed; and he argued that the Japanese would not attack a reduced Pacific Fleet because they would not be able to reach distant Hawaii!

The Secretary of War got the idea of pressing on the President a "petition for action." On the morning of 12 May, he, Knox, Ickes, and Jackson conferred about sending a round robin to the President, stating "we are experiencing a failure of leadership that bodes ill for the country." Someone observed that Roosevelt "would probably let ships trickle thru" into the Atlantic "unannounced and very quietly to not stir things up." Knox conceded that a few ships had already passed through the Canal secretly. As Ickes then summed up, "What we want is something dramatic, something that will arrest the attention of the world and give courage, not only to our own people but to the British as well. . . ." The little group was depressed; even Knox, known for his enthusiasm and optimism, was "despondent."

But the four conspirators were not a majority of the Cabinet. Hull, worried about containing Japan, would not sign such a petition. Morgenthau, although favorable, was likely to reject it out of loyalty to the President. Secretary of Agriculture Claude R. Wickard would be wary of assuming responsibility in an area so remote from that of his competence. Propriety was apt to restrain ingenuous Frances Perkins and ambition Vice President Henry A. Wallace, who hoped to succeed Roosevelt. Even the four sponsors of the idea were not anxious to hurl so supreme an insult at the President. Besides, they had little in the way of a program of their own. As Ickes confessed, "We all felt that we were in a grave state, but what to do about it no one was quite certain."[10]

When the Cabinet met on 23 May, the President observed that "we would have to go back and found our military policy on the sea-power" theories of Mahan; he noted that the "determining" factor in the outcome of the war would be "control of the seas." Someone then asked if he were ready to use the Navy decisively in the Atlantic. He responded firmly, "I am not willing to fire the first shot."[11]

Stimson and Ickes believed that the President was waiting for an "incident" at sea, "the act of an irresponsible captain, on either side," to rally public opinion behind a stronger course of action. Although the next day was a Saturday, both men prepared notes for the President. Stimson urged him to ask Congress for permission to employ the Navy in the Battle of the Atlantic. Ickes suggested the transfer of most of the Pacific Fleet with great fanfare, thinking, "the Germans would not create an incident until Hitler was ready to move against us and that he would then do it, 'incident' or no 'incident.' "[12]

But the amateur strategists did not perceive that the Pacific Fleet served Britain well by deterring Japanese attack on Singapore and on British sea communications in the Pacific and Indian oceans; if the Japanese, emboldened by a mass transfer of the Pacific Fleet, bypassed the Philippines and struck at southeast Asia, the German design of defeating Britain without bringing America into the war might be brought perilously close to fruition.

To Stimson, if the safety of the nation required war, then it was up to the President candidly to tell the people so. But the President did not think his people wanted to hear unpleasant truths or were ready to endure hardship and suffering. It was Joseph Stalin, the supreme realist, who once noted the great difficulty of providing responsible leadership in a democratic society: when circumstances demanded sacrifice from the people, the people could simply turn out of office those who voiced the demands and replace them with those willing to offer ease and the abandonment of honorable burdens. Even resolute Henry Stimson wondered in the privacy of his mind "whether this country has it in itself to meet such an emergency. Whether we are really powerful enough and sincere enough and devoted enough to meet the Germans. . . ."[13]

The President's torment of contradictory desires perfectly reflected that of his people.

14.

The Germans: Reckoning with Mahan

To THE GERMANS, THE AMERICANS appeared to be moving toward war with great vigor, decision, and rapidity. German planning, once again looking toward a quick, ostensibly decisive victory rather than the careful evolution of a consistent, realistic long-term strategy, was focused on Russia. Reflecting the needs of the Fuehrer's kinetic temperament, it was impulsive and spontaneous; hence, Germany's great tactical victories seemed to do little but advance her further along the road of strategic defeat.

Lend-Lease and creation of the U.S. Atlantic Fleet worried the Germans and made it amply clear that the Axis alliance had not deterred the United States. The American moves stirred the Fuehrer and his planners to quixotic schemes designed to shift the American thrust from the Atlantic to the Pacific and to formulate a continental alliance. Adversity forced the impulsive Fuehrer to try to think, like the Americans, beyond the short run in terms of long-range strategic concepts.

The Germans increasingly feared diplomatic isolation. If the Americans could bluff or appease Japan into neutrality, the total power of the United States might be brought to bear against Germany. Consequently, as Hitler observed, it had become vital to prod Japan to "turn the attention of the United States toward the Pacific," even if this meant increased risk of American intervention in the war.

The Naval Staff, eager to have a fatal blow struck at British sea communications and restless at Hitler's limitations on the naval war in the Atlantic, were anxious to encourage Japan to strike, arguing that the "total advantages" of American entry into the war would "outweigh the disadvantages" for Germany.

But the Fuehrer rejected the Navy's foolish counsel and clung to his hope of keeping the United States out of the war as long as possible. The objective of German policy became to induce Japan to strike at British possessions and sea communications in Asia in order to defeat Britain and deter America.[1]

> The *aim* of the cooperation initiated by the Tri-Partite Pact must be *to bring Japan into active operations in the Far East* as soon as possible. This will tie down strong English forces and the focal point of the interests of the United States . . . will be diverted to the Pacific. . . . The quick defeat of England is to be designated as the common aim in the conduct of the war, thereby keeping the USA out of the war.[2]

This was a delicate project, for the Japanese were reluctant to move south as long as the U.S. Pacific Fleet remained poised on their eastern flank and the Americans held the Philippines. An advance in southeast Asia seemed impossible unless the Pacific Fleet and American air bases in the Philippines were neutralized. But this would mean war with the United States, precisely the eventuality which the Germans were striving to avoid, especially with their own attack on Russia impending. In order to restrain American intervention, the Germans were risking provoking it; and they hardly knew which they feared more, a Japanese attack on the Americans, or a Japanese-American rapprochement.

But despite plenty of what the Japanese took to be we'll-hold-your-coat enthusiasm, including a sand-table mockup of Singapore in the German Embassy in Tokyo, which the Germans used condescendingly to instruct their underestimated allies in the finer points of tactics, the Japanese would not strike. They were deterred by the Pacific Fleet. The Germans hoped that the American moves to strengthen the Atlantic Fleet would encourage the Japanese to attack in the Pacific, but the Japanese merely noted coyly that the American Navy must be very strong and confident thus to disperse its forces.[3]

German strategic thought reflected the official view that the airplane, submarine, and improved land mobility provided by tanks, trucks, and railroads had rendered war fleets obsolete. The traditional advantages of sea powers were concentration and mobility—the ability to move large forces great distances to strike with power and surprise at land forces dispersed along exposed coasts, and achieve a formidable buildup before the foe could concentrate his overextended, sluggish foot and horse armies. German strategists argued that airplanes and submarines could defend the coasts of land powers, destroying the ships that carried the men, supplies, and equipment needed to sustain an amphibious invasion: tanks and trucks could allow strong reserves of ground forces to concentrate rapidly at the decisive point and drive amphibious forces into the sea. Publicly, Mahan's thesis was ridiculed as a relic of Victorian times, and victorious air-sea battles, such as those in Norway and Crete, led Germany to boast, "There are no more islands."

Yet the Naval Staff feared amphibious strikes at the Atlantic isles and Dakar, and the Fuehrer spoke vaguely of withdrawing U-boats from the vital Battle of the Atlantic to defend the islands and transport troops to Iceland. In the spring, twenty precious U-boats had to be shifted to Norway to quiet Hitler's fears of an attack from the sea against Germany's northern flank.[4]

Thus, the troubled Fuehrer turned not only to the Japanese, but once again looked toward his own continent for succor from the ubiquitous sea power of his enemies.

In order to protect their Atlantic flank during the assault on Russia, the Germans sought to form a continental coalition against the sea powers. With the help of Spain and Vichy, Hitler and his Army hoped to defend Iberia, northwest Africa, and the Atlantic isles from amphibious landings. While the Navy and elements of the Luftwaffe hoped to secure sufficient domination of the Mediterranean—where the British, despite ample naval power, were being defeated from the air because they lacked first-class carrier aviation—to interdict British communications with the Empire.[5]

The Army was directed to prepare plans, code named Isabella, to send from eight to ten divisions to support Spain or Portugal against an amphibious strike. The plans called for the troops to be moved by rail across Vichy France to a plateau line between Madrid and Valladolid from which armor and infantry could strike either west and south to the Portuguese coast or south to the Spanish coast.[6]

But soon realizing that they still could neither bribe nor coerce the evasive and obdurate Spaniards into more active cooperation, the Germans turned to Vichy. In May 1941, Ribbentrop told Admiral Jean Louis Darlan, the Vichy naval commander, that "should Roosevelt enter the war, the present conflict would become a conflict between our hemisphere and the American hemisphere"; France would have to join with Germany to defend the "Atlantic Coast on behalf of the European Continent."

The French flirted with the Nazis for many reasons: dislike and envy of the British, fear that the Germans might occupy all of France, belief that Germany might win the war, desire for lower occupation costs and the release of more French prisoners of war, and an inclination to strengthen the defenses of her colonies against the Gaullists, the British, and the Germans, too. Hence, on 28 May, Darlan signed the Paris Protocols, by which the French were allowed to augment their antiaircraft and antitank defenses in North Africa in exchange for German use of the port of Bizerte to land supplies for the Afrika Korps and use of the naval and air base at Dakar to screen the Atlantic isles and northwestern Africa from amphibious attack. But in June, the Vichy government, fearing a British attack on its colonies, rebellion in Africa, and the enmity of the United States, refused to honor the Protocols, although the French were forced clandestinely to assist German forces in North Africa with their massive supply problem.[7]

The Fuehrer submitted tamely to the French recalcitrance because of German inability to project much of her formidable land power to northwest Africa. As Hitler complained to Mussolini, Spanish caution was decisive. If Franco had permitted a German thrust to Gibraltar, he would by then have had sufficient armored divisions stationed in Africa to adopt a "firm line with the French" and occupy Dakar, across the narrowest part of the Atlantic from the Americas. But to try forcibly to coerce Spain would merely drive her into the British embrace, and even to take punitive measures against hostage France would result in the "defection of the French Navy and colonies to the British side."[8]

Disappointed in the Spaniards, distrustful of the French, his dark energies preoccupied by the impending strike against Russia, the Fuehrer's interest in the Mediterranean was at a low ebb. He did not wish to create new battlegrounds to divert planes, tanks, and men from the East and he did not want to hasten the day of American intervention by basing Luftwaffe bombers at Dakar.[9]

Later, General Alfred Jodl, seeking reasons for Germany's failure to win the war in 1940 or 1941 despite smashing land victories, wrote:

> Should we have carried the war with England to a landing on a grand scale? Besides, because of the possibility of American intervention, it was necessary to take into consideration occupation of a certain number of islands in the

Atlantic, like Iceland and the Azores. With these islands, we would have been in a position to bring particularly effective blows against the English traffic and to defend the territory of Europe, exactly as Japan today defends Greater Asia from her advanced bases in the Pacific. But, very sagely, the Fuehrer spurned these objectives. Not only their conquest, but their defense and the maintenance of their sea communications would have required a naval and air force which we did not possess.

During the first period of the war, when our land superiority was total and our aerial superiority considerable, the palm of complete victory was delayed beyond our means because of our hopeless naval inferiority. [10]

The Fuehrer consoled the fatalistic Admiral Raeder, who brooded over the folly of attacking Russia while Britain grew stronger and the United States nearer intervention, with the promise that when Russia was "crushed," the strength of the Army would be reduced and the Navy and Air Force would receive priority of industrial production. The French and Spanish would then be more cooperative, and Operation Felix would "be resumed in full. . . ." Using naval and air bases in northwestern Africa and in Europe, Germany would capture the Atlantic isles and at last securely dominate the sea approaches to the Afro-European land mass. Finally, the strengthened Navy and Air Force would resume the trade war with increased ferocity and win the Battle of the Atlantic for Germany.[11]

The German Navy, shaken by Lend-Lease and the establishment of the U.S. Atlantic Fleet, was not satisfied with these promises of future glory. The Naval Staff pressed the Fuehrer for permission to conduct operations in the western Atlantic and to attack American ships in the North Atlantic. The Fuehrer was unwilling, yet he worried lest his continued indulgence of the Americans be mistaken for weakness. Such would merely encourage Franco and Pétain further to obstruct his designs and, much worse, it would persuade the Japanese that the Germans were too fearful of the Americans to make reliable partners, in which case the Axis alliance would be jeopardized and the dismal prospect of Germany's strategic isolation would be raised anew.[12]

Indeed, after passage of the Lend-Lease Act, Rear Admiral Kurt Fricke summoned the American Naval Attaché in Berlin to his office and commenced to lecture him on the iniquity of the "Help England Law." The admiral's voice grew lower and lower as he got more and more angry. Finally, he muttered curtly that it was already too late, that no earthly power could save England. The American replied briskly, "That's your opinion, admiral." Yet the American noticed that the Germans talked much and acted little; as he noted in his war diary: "It's remarkable how much these people will take until they can get Japanese assurances."[13]

The Fuehrer could ill afford to have such ideas gain widespread credence; his diplomacy was already flagging despite Germany's vast, acknowledged power and striking military victories. Also, he wished to still the Navy's persistent nagging about the limitations placed on the naval war in the Atlantic. Hence, in March, he extended the German submarine war zone west, from off Norway and the British Isles, to include the waters around Iceland, then south along 38° west longitude. But this merely confirmed existing reality; during the winter, the U-boats were forced to move northwest in search of British convoys taking advantage of the bad weather and extended darkness in the waters south-southwest of Iceland.

The Fuehrer also ordered a Naval Staff study of a "surprise U-boat attack against the American fleet in U.S. harbors. . . ." The study concluded that U.S. naval bases were too well protected to make such an attack feasible, which is doubtless what the Fuehrer intended from the outset: if the Naval Staff wanted to ride its hobbyhorse, he would provide it with a nag.

Then, in late April, Hitler agreed to permit naval operations in the South Atlantic to within 300 miles of South America (instead of 600 miles), but it was a dubious concession as the area was an unprofitable one for the submarines, which preferred to hunt nearer the African or Brazilian coasts. He again rejected the Navy's requests to station U-boats off the Grand Banks.

Hitler's reaction to President Roosevelt's extension of the American naval patrol eastward toward Germany's declared zone of unrestricted submarine warfare was mild, much to the chagrin of the frustrated and thus foolishly belligerent Naval Staff, but it befitted the harmlessness of the measure. On 25 April, a reminder was sent out to German naval forces requesting that all incidents with American ships be avoided; in the event that accidental clashes did occur, the official reports should be arranged so as to make the responsibility appear to rest upon the Americans.[14]

German diplomacy and strategy in the west had failed. The Germans knew as well as did Franklin Roosevelt that the defense of a land mass does not begin at the shoreline, but requires strong bases astride the main sea routes of approach. But Germany lacked the warships, amphibious capability, and naval air arm to seize and hold the vital Atlantic island outposts. And the Fuehrer failed to sponsor the consistent, realistic strategic planning about over-water areas needed to sustain large-scale operations in Africa. Consequently, the Germans proved unable to shield the Afro-European coast from the thrusts of their amphibious enemies or to dominate British sea communications in the Atlantic and Mediterranean. And failing to persuade the Japanese to strike the fatal blow at Britain's sea communications that they could not, the Germans were left with scant alternative to the Fuehrer's mad drive to the heartland and a disastrous two-front war.

The spectre haunting German counsels was that of Alfred Thayer Mahan.

15.

Bread and Butter for Ernie King

THE PROSPECT OF THE FRENCH PROVIDING the Germans with a base at Dakar was not viewed with complacency in Washington. Then, in late April, the French ships at Martinique became suddenly active, steaming to Guadeloupe and back on what Admiral Robert described as "testing operations" and "exercises." Even with advance notice provided by the French, the maneuvers, following a lengthy period of inactivity and coinciding with increased German-Vichy collaboration, seemed ominous; it did not appear unlikely that the French might try to send the *Béarn* to Dakar. On the 26th, the President directed intelligence units to investigate reports that twenty-five German officers were due to arrive in the French islands shortly, noting, "This is coming pretty close to home."[1]

In May, Admiral Stark told General Marshall that as British manpower was "inadequate" for "the exploitation of additional strategic areas. . . . The President may demand overseas undertakings by the armed forces on short notice." Possible objectives, he noted, included the Atlantic isles or even French West Africa—Dakar.[2]

Pursuant to these sundry perils, the Atlantic Fleet staffs refined their earlier plans for the seizure of Martinique. This time, the forces available were significantly more formidable: the Navy had a third carrier in the Atlantic; the Marines would be able to supply approximately three rifle regiments, although unevenly trained and equipped; the Army would be able to support the Marines, as shipping allowed,

167

with the developing First Infantry Division; and the Air Corps would provide units of the 7th and 19th Bombardment Groups and of the 8th Pursuit Group. The main assault, preceded by reconnaissance, air strikes, and shore bombardment, would take place along the southern beaches. Two regimental combat teams would advance from the beaches to Carraibe Hill and then to control the ridge line that extends westward from Regale Hill, thus dominating the major enemy defense positions in the Fort de France area; after clearing the high ground, the Marines would drive inland. Meanwhile, a single battalion landing team would strike farther east, below Sans Souci Point, and thrust rapidly inland to secure the Shore Road and hold a gap in the hills to protect the flank of the main drive. It was hoped that the defenders would offer but token resistance. American command of the air and sea negated the major strength of the French, their coastal fortifications; the enemy infantry, low in morale and lacking in training, was not expected to fight aggressively against first-rank troops. The main opposition ashore would come from the sailors off the French warships. The Marines would take Martinique; the only question was what the price would be. With skill and a little luck, the chances were that few men would die.[3]

The seizure of Martinique would prevent the *Béarn* from escaping eastward and would punish Vichy for its flirtation with the Nazis, but it would not provide an escort base to help protect British shipping nor would it block a German move south to Dakar or the Azores, sites from which German long-range bombers might threaten the Americas. To strike at Dakar would mean undertaking a formidable military enterprise, requiring an amphibious force of 100,000 troops, and one fraught with domestic political danger, for West Africa was clearly not a part of the Western Hemisphere. But the scope of the operation was well beyond the Army's means, and so in late May, the President, instead, asked Admiral Stark to plan for landings in the Azores requiring an amphibious force of about 25,000 troops.

The President would not launch the operation without Portuguese cooperation, but the service planners had to prepare for assault landings as a precaution. The First Marine Division, conducting routine amphibious exercises on Puerto Rico, was alerted for expeditionary service, and the men began to draw combat equipment and semi-tropical clothing. The Army's First Infantry Division, unable to join the Marines because of lack of shipping, practiced the web-footed art at Buzzard's Bay. The two divisions numbered about 28,000 men. Meanwhile, in the United Kingdom, British assault troops were also training for an invasion of the Atlantic isles.[4]

The Azores, about 900 miles west of Lisbon and 1,200 miles southeast of Newfoundland, are a chain of conical, rocky islands strategically spread over 200 miles of the central Atlantic on a diagonal northwest-southeast axis. The two northwest islands, Corvo and Flores, are separated from the central group of Fayal, Pico, San Jorge, Graciosa, and Terceira by a 120-mile channel; 75 miles southeastward lies the major island, San Miguel, and to the south, Santa Maria. The population in 1941 was 260,000, half on San Miguel. Most of the people seemed pro-Allied, although some of the powerful were Axis sympathizers. Ponta Delgada, on San Miguel, and Horta, on Fayal, were the only harbors useful to support military operations.

San Miguel would be assaulted first. The landings would take place along the southern shore at the San Roque and Populo beaches, near Ponta Delgada. Heavy surf would make landing operations hazardous, and the beaches were protected by barbed wire and trenches. San Miguel was defended by an infantry regiment and an artillery battalion; the defenders had eleven heavy guns and sixty-three machine guns. There were also 3,000 reserve militia on the island, but many of them lacked arms; the Portuguese, short of transports, would not be able rapidly to reinforce their garrisons. After San Miguel was taken, Terceira would be assaulted to provide a support base in the central islands for the attack on Fayal. The landings on Terceira would be made on the east coast, south of Praia Vittoria; the island was weakly defended by a battalion of infantry with a few mortars and machine guns. The Fayal assault would be carried out on the beaches north and south of Espalamaca Point; Fayal was defended by two battalions of infantry and supporting artillery, with ten coastal guns and thirty-one machine guns.

The planners considered several devious expedients, based on successful German operations in Norway, to knock out the shore batteries northwest of Ponta Delgada. One plan was to place an assault company and a platoon of light tanks in a common tramp steamer and have the innocuous-looking vessel dock at Ponta Delgada, thus allowing the Marines to storm the coastal guns in a surprise attack. Another was to drop from PBYs a battalion of newly trained Marine parachutists over the guns. In the end, it was wisely if prosaically decided to trust air attack and naval gunfire to wreck the batteries.

However, prior to the operation, the planners sought to introduce Marine officers in civilian guise to the islands to gain up-to-date intelligence.

A naval task force of two battleships, eight cruisers, and eighteen destroyers would escort the more than forty auxiliary ships needed to carry the troops and their equipment and supplies and to provide gunfire support for the landings. Three carriers and their planes would be available to help defend the ships and troops from air and naval opposition and provide air support for the troops. The assault landings would be carried out by the First Marine Division; the First Infantry Division, less well versed in amphibious technique, would make administrative landings. As the three islands were taken, four Marine Defense Battalions would be landed to provide antiaircraft defenses, and eight fighter squadrons and eight squadrons of scout-bombers would be based ashore to defend against counterattacks from sky or sea.[5]

At the same time, plans were prepared for operations against the Cape Verde Islands. The Cape Verdes are ten islands off the coast of northwest Africa; they range from 320 miles to 480 miles from Dakar. They would become vital if the Germans were to establish themselves at Dakar, constituting quite literally the Western Hemisphere's first line of defense. The Portuguese garrisons were small and lacked modern equipment, but heavy surf and rocky coastlines provided difficult conditions for amphibious warfare, and Dakar was only two hours' flying time away. Therefore, Admiral King's planners concluded that if the Luftwaffe proved able to stage intensive air operations out of Dakar, the Cape Verdes campaign would be "a most hazardous undertaking. Mass attack by Axis aircraft against our Naval Attack Force will probably result in disaster to our expedition."[6] Yet, partly to balance matters, the Germans would have encountered serious logistical problems in deploying aircraft in northwest Africa, the Luftwaffe was not fully trained in operations over water and in attacks on warships, and the excellent but short-range German fighters would have found it difficult to protect their undergunned bombers so far distant from Dakar. Nevertheless, the Cape Verdes operation undoubtedly did involve serious risk.

American ability to conduct a major amphibious operation was limited. The troops of the First Marine Division, although rated "the best fighting material in the US," were short of machine guns, modern equipment, and support arms; much the same was true of the greener

First Infantry Division. The troops lacked ample assault craft and were without lighters for tanks and heavy arms; there were no service and pioneer units to master movement on the beaches. Control of amphibious battles was difficult because of inadequate ship-to-shore communications, and the Navy lacked trained men for gunfire support functions. The ships were manned by too many partly trained men and their AA defenses were limited. The carrier planes were mainly old, and the new types suffered from teething problems; they lacked armor and self-sealing tanks and were not a match in speed and agility for German fighters.[7] The Atlantic Fleet was up to all three of the operations that were considered in the spring of 1941, but its limitations meant that operations in which serious German land and air resistance could be expected were risky.

The Portuguese understood that their nation survived largely by dint of British sea power, yet feared that ties with the Allies would provoke German attack. Hence, Portuguese policy was to defend their island possessions "against attack no matter from what side." In the spring, they began to augment their garrisons in the Azores.

In a nationwide radio address on 27 May, President Roosevelt stated that German occupation of the Atlantic isles would jeopardize the Western Hemisphere. Portugal, fearing an American preventive occupation, protested. Since the President was not about to move against the islands without the agreement of Portugal, his remarks seemed gratuitous; perhaps his words were meant to deter the Germans from using Dakar and warn the French and Iberians against strategic concessions to Germany.[8]

In Portugal, nationalism and fear of becoming involved in the war vexed public opinion. An American journalist, Demaree Bess, was watching a detachment of Portuguese troops board a transport at the Lisbon docks when his taxi driver asked, "Do you know where they're going?" When he replied, "No," the driver grimly said, "They're sailing to the Azores. When you Americans try to occupy the Azores . . . you will have to fight for them."[9]

The taxi driver was right. By fall, Portuguese reinforcements had pushed the number of troops on San Miguel to about 13,000, a more than fourfold increase, and the defenders possessed "a greater number of machine guns than . . . the whole 1st Marine Division." An assault on the Azores grew increasingly infeasible.[10]

The Germans did not move south that summer. The American Army was preoccupied with training, shipping was scarce, and the

Navy was concerned with protecting the North Atlantic sea lanes. The President, having grabbed bare-handed at a porcupine, let the State Department and the British deal with the Portugese thereafter. The Portugese, mindful of the contribution the sea powers had made to their independence, did not brood indefinitely over the misunderstanding, and in late 1943, decided at last that the Germans were not going to win the war. They then permitted American planes and destroyers to operate from the Azores.[11]

With amphibious operations in the Atlantic impending, the President decided to go through with the long-planned transfer of ships from the Pacific. The carrier *Yorktown*, three newer battleships (the *Idaho*, *New Mexico*, and *Mississippi*), four new light cruisers, veterans of the original Atlantic Squadron (the *Brooklyn*, *Nashville*, *Philadelphia*, and *Savannah*), and two squadrons of new destroyers to work with the heavy ships were to be brought to the Atlantic. In order to avoid comment, it was planned to stagger the transfers and make them at two-week intervals; ships would steam in small groups, darken at night, maintain radio silence, and pass through the Panama Canal after dark. Orders were secret, and crews were not to be told of the shift until the ships had put to sea on ostensibly routine duty.[12]

In early May, the *Yorktown*, conducting a training problem off Hawaii, abruptly headed southeast, escorted by the destroyers *Warrington*, *Somers*, and *Jouett*. On the night of 6/7 May, the ships passed through the Canal, the carrier wearing the *Wasp*'s hull number, and steamed on to Bermuda.[13]

The President held up the other transfers while he considered his Atlantic plans. Then in mid-May, with the Germans apparently poised to move south, he ordered that the rest of the transfers be made at once, debauching Admiral Stark's careful, staggered schedule. The move was to be accomplished on 20 May.

The *Sterett* was operating with her task force off Hawaii when fresh signals were suddenly hoisted on the big ships, and the destroyer was ordered to join the *Mississippi*, *Savannah*, and escorting destroyers *Wilson* and *Lang* on a southerly course. Her skipper, Commander Jesse G. Coward, wondering what was up, simply played follow-the-leader. The crew's imagination flourished; one delightful rumor had the force going to occupy Tahiti, but most men guessed that they were bound for the Atlantic, probably to help with the capture of Martinique. The ships arrived off Panama on the night of 2/3 June, their numbers painted over. There was a delay because an Army Coast Artillery battery understandably objected to letting darkened, unidentified ships enter the Canal; after permission had been secured, the ships made the passage in six hours. The crews were elated to come to the Atlantic; the transfer meant family reunions and lower living costs.[14]

Since the *Nashville* was scheduled to serve as gunnery training ship during exercises off Hawaii, her commanding officer, Captain Francis Craven, was puzzled when Vice Admiral Herbert F. Leary directed him to transfer all gunnery-school equipment to another ship. Then, as the cruiser started to get under way, Admiral Leary leaned over the bridge of his flagship, moored to the same buoy as the *Nashville*, and called out, "I hope you have an interesting time." As Captain Craven headed the cruiser into the channel, he thought over the "cryptic" farewell. At sea, the *Nashville* joined the *New Mexico*, *Morris*, *Roe*, and *Buck* for tactical exercises. But when Rear Admiral H. Kent Hewitt in the battleship opened his packet of sealed orders, he had new flag signals run up, and the ships steamed toward the Canal. The *Nashville*'s men were happy to break away from the tedium of routine drills in the Pacific; the Navy seemed closer to war in the Atlantic, and more meaningful duty appeared to portend there.[15]

The *Idaho* left Pearl Harbor on the same 20 May, and in company with the *Brooklyn*, *Winslow*, *Wainwright*, and *Stack*, passed through the Canal on the night of 4/5 June.[16]

Other ships followed in the migration eastward, and during the spring about 25 percent of the Pacific Fleet was brought into the Atlantic. More ships would have been transferred but for the Japanese advance into Indo-China. With new construction vessels regularly added, the Atlantic Fleet increased in strength between April and October from 159 ships to 355 ships.[17]

Meanwhile, the President's extended patrol was operating. The three old battleships—*Texas*, *New York*, and *Arkansas*—worked out of Newport alternatively on sweeps from 50° west along a northeast track to the border of the German war zone. The ships had three weeks at sea for each week in port. Every fourth week, the heavy cruisers *Tuscaloosa* and *Wichita* carried out the long ocean sweep. The ships were under orders to trail and broadcast the position of Axis craft encountered in Western Hemisphere waters (e.g., west of the German war zone, which was at 38° west south of Greenland, then slanted diagonally southeast to 20° west at the latitude of the Bay of Biscay); ordinarily, German U-boats operated to the east of the patrol, but sometimes they strayed well westward in search of convoys.[18]

As the American warships did not enter the areas of greatest submarine concentration, they had little chance to discover U-boats. Then, too, formations of heavy ships, moving at high speeds, were unsuitable instruments of antisubmarine warfare; they lacked maneuverability and their wakes fouled sonar gear. To prevent "untoward incidents," the American ships were brilliantly lit at night, and thus "easy to see and avoid"; their configuration made the U.S. battleships easily identifiable. German submarines had instructions not to attack American ships. All these factors rendered the patrol innocuous.[19] The President's extended patrol exposed men and ships to needless risk for little purpose, except to buy him time for decision.

Near-clashes at sea did take place. On 17 May, a U-boat, perhaps mistakenly, reported sighting an American battleship. Then, on 20 June, lookouts in the *U-203*, patrolling at the edge of the German war zone, sighted an American battleship and a destroyer far over the top of distant waves. The battleship was the *Texas*, nine days out of Newport, escorted by the *Rhind*, *Mayrant*, and *Trippe*. Kapitänleutnant Hermann Kottmann, skipper of the *U-203*, believed the warships to be inside the war zone and chose to disregard his instructions not to attack American vessels wherever encountered. He ordered an attack, and the *U-203* slanted toward an interception course. The seas were rough and the skies darkening. The submarine closed, but the ships were moving fast and zigzagging. Kottmann tried to lay on a long-range torpedo spread, but the ships veered sharply away; he wondered if his boat had been sighted, but later the vessels turned back to their base course. Kottmann decided to trail the vessels, in hopes that the worsening weather might force them to reduce speed. The submarine chased the ships for 140 miles. Most of the time, the Germans could not see the vessels; occasionally, the tip of a mast appeared over the sea in the far distance, luring the *U-203* on. Finally, the submarine lost contact with the warships. The American ships never saw the *U-203*.[20]

Courtesy: United Press International

The USS *Texas* on a Neutrality Patrol sweep in 1941

Meanwhile, Admiral Raeder had been trying to persuade the Fuehrer that the patrol would hamper German U-boat operations by providing the British with intelligence. He also predicted that the American Navy would soon begin to escort convoys and to operate patrol planes from Newfoundland, Greenland, and Iceland to search the North Atlantic for submarines. Yet the Fuehrer still refused to expand the war zone westward, wistfully observing that he wished it were feasible for Germany to occupy the Azores so that air strikes could be made against the United States in the event of war. He warned Raeder emphatically, "Weapons are not to be used. Even if American vessels conduct themselves in a definitely unneutral manner. . . . Weapons are to be used *only if US ships fire the first shot.*"[21]

Therefore, the Fuehrer was appalled to learn of Kapitänleutnant Kottmann's attempt to attack the *Texas*. Kottmann wryly observed that he decided to attack the battleship because for all he knew it might have been transferred to the Royal Navy! Admiral Doenitz immediately sent out orders that American ships were not to be attacked even in the war zone; attacks were to be made only on warships "definitely recognized as enemy," and attacks on destroyers and escort ships were prohibited for "the next few weeks" for fear of attacking American destroyers, which might already be secretly escorting convoys. The Fuehrer did not desire conflict with the United States at the very hour of his attack on Russia. Admiral Raeder coolly observed that the torpedoing of an American warship might be a good thing; it might convince the officious Americans that Germany meant business. But such reasoning had no appeal to the Fuehrer.[22]

Then on 3 July, there occurred another incident in the patrol area. At 1425, lookouts in the battleship *Mississippi* sighted what they took to be a periscope in the water, 600 yards away. The object trailed the battleship and her escort of three destroyers on a southerly course, apparently attempting a submerged attack approach. The *O'Brien* was detached from the formation to force the submarine down deep while the warships sped off. The contact was probably false: the *Mississippi* and her escorts were new to the Atlantic; no U-boat sent out a sighting report on a U.S. battleship in July; and the destroyers did not pick up a sonar contact. On the other hand, the odd movements of the periscope-like object suggested the presence of a submarine trying to ascertain the battleship's nationality. The President believed that a U-boat had tried to torpedo the *Mississippi* and was furious.[23]

Admiral Raeder knew that when American ships operated independently or in task forces of their own it was possible to identify them and avert incidents. However, if they began to escort merchant convoys, there would be little chance in the night fighting of the Atlantic to distinguish between American and British escorts. If this occurred, the Germans would either have to risk incidents with the United States, probably leading to war, or abandon the sea war against England. It was the inevitability of this dreadful choice that haunted the German naval leaders in the summer of 1941.

In the central Atlantic, in the long expanse of water between Bermuda and the Azores, the task groups were usually built around a carrier, whose planes could scan much more of the ocean than could surface craft, an inkling of the hunter-killer technique of ASW so successful later in the war; however, in 1941, radar technology was not sufficiently advanced, nor were the numbers of ships and planes adequate, to make such operations practicable. The sweeps sometimes went as far eastward as the line in the President's atlas, 26° west, although they usually terminated between 32° west and 37° west; as the U-boats preferred to operate off the African coast, the warships had little chance to encounter them. Between late April and the end of August, thirteen sweeps eastward were made; the ships steamed 54,568 miles, and the carrier pilots flew 12,632 hours.* The weather was fair, and the duty routine.[24]

The skippers continued to worry because "duties weren't very clearly outlined. We wondered what we would do if we did run into something. . . ." Once, the *Kearny* encountered the large French submarine *Surcouf*, and the destroyermen, not certain whether she was a Free French or a Vichy craft, did not know what to do. They did nothing, and assumed that they made the right decision because no one later reproved them.[25]

Of the three carriers, the destroyers liked least to work with the *Wasp*, because her skipper, Captain John W. Reeves, was most "exacting" in his standards. The *Sterett*'s men learned to avoid criticism by anticipating the *Wasp*'s maneuvers, acting speedily in plane-guard emergencies, and showing a willingness to steam at high speed in any kind of weather. "Black Jack" Reeves was determined that "*Wasp*

---

*Yorktown led the CVs with 4 patrols, 17,642 miles; *Wasp* had 4 and 15,982. *Quincy* led the CAs with 3 and 14,492, *Savannah* the CLs with 3 and 10,377. *Eberle* led the destroyers with 4 patrols and 17,092 miles; *Livermore* and *Kearny* both had 3 and 13,199. Ten ships steamed over 10,000 miles between 26 April and 30 September.

would not fall prey to submarines if it was humanly possible . . . to save her by any precaution."[26]

Lieutenant Commander Murdaugh brought the *Edison*, with her inexperienced crew, to Bermuda to serve with the *Wasp*. One night, the task group was running at high speed through a storm, Captain Reeves not counting on the high seas and low visibility to keep the U-boats away. The *Edison*, encountering her maiden Atlantic storm, sustained superficial damage forward from the pounding sea; because his bunk was occupied by a sailor who was sick, Murdaugh requested permission to reduce speed. Captain Reeves rejected the request. The *Edison* had gotten off to a bad start.

However, not long afterward, one of the *Wasp*'s fighters lost power during a landing approach and slammed into the sea. The *Edison* lowered a boat and had it at the site of the wreckage in quick time. As the destroyermen hauled the flier over the gunwales of the dipping gig, Murdaugh glanced across the water and noticed that the *Wasp*'s men had not yet got their launch into the water. The same fact did not go unnoticed by Captain Reeves, who congratulated Murdaugh when the ships reached Bermuda. Murdaugh explained about the ill sailor on the stormy night run, and thereafter, *Edison* and *Wasp* "got along fine." By this time, Murdaugh had to admit that his crew was getting "pretty damn good."[27]

In March, with the ice breaking up, the Coast Guard cutters returned to Greenland waters to explore the west coast for airfield sites for planes being ferried to Britain. Late in the month, there were reports of a German reconnaissance bomber flying two missions over northeast Greenland. Indeed, the Germans were beginning to study the possibility of landing bombers in Greenland or at some other mid-Atlantic staging point and refueling them from a U-boat, thus giving the Luftwaffe the range to reach American targets. The President was angered by the German overflights; he did not agree with his naval advisers who told him that the Germans lacked the sea power to become involved in Greenland in any meaningful manner. He remained adamant, insisting that ships be sent to eastern Greenland "to thoroughly search out any German or so-called Norwegian weather stations or bombing plane bases. . . . I cannot agree that Germany will not attempt to establish a military base in Northeast Greenland this year. I think Germany will probably seek to get a definite foothold even if this foothold can only defend its own location. Therefore, our own expedition should be fitted out with sufficient guns to hold the Scoresby Sound area until early September, leaving just before the ice closes in." He insisted that in the meantime one or two flights should be made from Iceland to scrutinize the northeast coast of Greenland.[28]

After appropriate diplomatic arrangements had been made, the aviation tender *Belknap* left for Iceland in mid-May escorted by four-stackers *Truxtun* and *Broome*. The ships arrived at Reykjavik, and then between 26 May and 6 June, four PBYs flew four two-plane sorties, taking photographs of Greenland's east coast and looking over the area near Angmagssalik, which the Coast Guardsmen said might prove suitable for an airfield. The fliers found "no indication of Axis activity." One pilot wrote:

> Except for the area in the immediate vicinity of Angmagssalik, there was absolutely no sign of any kind of habitation. There was no place where a possible landing site for airplanes could be imagined. Tremendous glaciers and mountains are all that formed the shore line for at least two hundred miles. . . . This entire section is by far the most barren, desolate and uninhabitable area that can be imagined. . . . The lack of any horizon, the unusual light conditions produced by snow patches on the multicolored mountain cliffs, and the green and white ice below made it necessary to fly by instruments to a great extent. All the factors combined to make this one of the most strenuous and hazardous flights and at the same time the most awe inspiring and interesting that has been experienced by this observer.

On the return trip, the American warships refueled at Halifax; it was the first time in World War II that American men-of-war refueled in a belligerent port.[29]

Meanwhile, Iceberg Smith learned of a place called Narsarssuak, which was supposed to be near the head of Julianehaab Fjord; the name meant "flat place," or "level" in Greenlandic, so he sent the Coast Guard cutter *Northland* up the fjord to investigate. Most of the party was skeptical, feeling that they were chasing a legend, but they found a gravel plain about three miles long and one mile wide that had been gouged between mountains by a retreating glacier. This was to be the site of the main airfield. The Coast Guardsmen selected sites for airfields, seaplane bases, and meteorological, radio, and direction-finder stations. In June, the *Reuben James* and *Simpson* escorted a small convoy carrying Army men and equipment to begin construction in Greenland.[30]

For the rest of the year, the cutters *Modoc, Comanche, Bear, Northland, North Star, Raritan, Bowdoin,* and sometimes *Cayuga* patrolled off the east coast. They escorted cryolite ships, broke ice, carried Army and native supplies to remote coastal settlements, maintained navigational aids, rescued survivors of submarine attacks in the waters to the southeast, and explored the hard, primitive coast, where fjords and icy mountains looked from the water like a remarkable "fairyland of jade and crystal."[31]

The Navy wanted to operate seaplanes from Greenland waters, but the Coast Guard's experience with the cutter-based float planes indicated that fog and capricious winds would hamper seaplane operations and maintenance. While conditions were somewhat better on the southwest coast than along the wild east coast, the Coast Guardsmen believed that they were not sufficiently so to justify the long and hazardous flights across the ice cap to observe the northeast coast for signs of enemy activity.[32] But the Navy decided to try anyway. A site was selected in a circular bay at the head of Tunugdliarjik Fjord, near Narsarssuak: overlooked by mountains on all but the southern side, the bay was sheltered from the wind, but offered hazardous flight approaches; there was a beach that seemed suited for a seaplane ramp. In July, the tender *Lapwing* was sent to the bay to set up a base, but there was still too much ice in the water for planes, and she had to leave. The ship and her escort returned with better weather and on 6 August three PBYs of Patrol Squadron 71 flew in from Argentia. The next day, two of the planes conducted a survey mission along the east coast; returning over the ice cap, they ran into squalls of rain and snow and twice were forced back to the coast. The seaplane men decided to remain over water, where they could land and ride out a blow in some sheltered inlet if necessary; the ground was no haven for the PBYs, especially the rugged, barren ice cap. The two planes headed down along the east coast, soon becoming separated in the squalls. One plane made it to Julianehaab Harbor and anchored there for the night. The other, also hoping to wait out the weather, made a good landing in Angmagssalik Harbor, skirting the icebergs bobbing on the slaty surface. But the water proved too deep to allow the plane to anchor, and it was too dangerous to drift all night amid the ice; taxiing the plane to keep it safe would exhaust the fuel. It was decided to fly on, and the PBY splashed across the water and curved again into the gray sky. The plane reached the south coast and turned north. Night was closing in and dense fog billowed up out of the water, but the flying and navigation were good, and the PBY was brought down on the water near the entrance to Tunugdliarjik Fjord. No one wanted to try a night landing in the bay in fog with the 3,000-foot mountain overlooking the anchorage. Both planes flew back to the *Lapwing* in the morning, and thus was completed a routine survey mission.

Wind and fog prevented flights for the next four days; after that, the survey missions were resumed as the weather allowed. On the 18th, a sudden squall struck when the air crews were aboard the moored PBYs. Hence, the *Lapwing* was unable to flee the rock-bordered bay for the safety of open sea. The wind rushed in at over 80 knots, and the tender got under way to maneuver and avoid being cast aground. In the darkness and stinging spray, it was difficult to make out other ships and, since they were dragging their anchors, it was impossible to fix position by observing their running lights. The *Lapwing* was guided by the small lights on the seaplane anchors. Thus, the moored PBYs helped keep their tender off the cold, black rocks.

The fliers crawled and huddled inside the swinging, yawing planes; wing tips dipped under water, and it looked from the *Lapwing* as if the PBYs would capsize. The pilots worked the controls, manipulating rudders and ailerons to try to keep the planes up in the water.

The storm lasted through the next day, but neither tender nor planes were damaged. On the morning of the 20th the PBYs took off in a 25-knot wind to make for the succor of the tender *Albemarle* at Argentia. The *Lapwing* departed the next day. Despite moderate weather, the fjord was covered with a crust of sludge ice caused by the wind snapping projections of ice off the interior glacier and blowing the ice chips down the fjord. In the early fall, the tender *Gannet* arrived to look the place over again and rather immodestly named it Gannet Bay.

It was decided to operate the seaplanes from Kungnat Bay, 6½ miles west of Ivigtut, on the southwest coast. The new site was 100 miles farther from the east coast patrol areas, the water in the bay was choppy, and the flight approaches were hazardous, but to the fliers any place was preferable to Gannet Bay. The *Goldsborough* and *Gannet* constructed a beaching ramp and parking area ashore in two weeks, and four PBYs flew missions along the south coast in good weather. There were two storms but nearby mountains shielded the planes from the worst of the winds. When the PBYs required maintenance they were hauled ashore by teams of thirty men working a tackle anchored to a large rock. At night, ice formed on the water, perhaps an inch thick; although most of it broke up during the day, there were some fears that it would close in permanently and lock the planes in at their moorings. Routine work on the aircraft took two to three times as long to accomplish due to the short days, the discomfort of the mechanics, and the hazards of clambering over PBYs slick with ice or glazed with frozen spray. It had been hoped that the planes might operate out over the shipping lanes to the south to help protect the convoys, but this was rarely possible on account of rain, snow, fog, icing conditions, and unpredictable gales. The few flights to the east coast were made not for offensive purposes, but to search for survivors amidst the debris of smashed ships. As the fliers wrote it, "Due to the uncertainties and violence of the weather, the proposed convoy escort patrols were not feasible. . . ."

Thus, the PBYs brought scant aid to the sailors who fought below the fog on what one of them called a cruel sea, and Admiral Bristol ordered the seaplanes back to Argentia. On 20 October, in the gray chill of morning, the *Gannet* headed past a dun headland and steamed out of Kungnat Bay for the last time.[33]

By the summer of 1941, the planes and ships of the Atlantic Fleet ranged the western ocean from the Gulf to the Azores, from Greenland to Brazil, in a patrol envisaged by Franklin Roosevelt a long time before.

Shortly after accepting command of the Atlantic Fleet, Admiral King had remarked to Roosevelt, "Mr. President, you're giving me a big slice of bread, but damn little butter." In May, after transferring strong reinforcements to the Atlantic, President Roosevelt asked King, "Well, admiral, how do you like the butter you are getting?" Mindful of his Fleet's growing burdens and far-flung commitments, Ernie King replied: "The butter is fine, Mr. President, but you keep giving me more bread."[34]

16.

When the "Nazis" Invaded the New World

IN THE SPRING, WHEN THE PRESIDENT extended the Atlantic Patrol, it became necessary to base seaplanes at Argentia, Newfoundland. There was much building going on at Argentia, and the base seemed a jumble of incomplete roads, steel girders, and "duckboards flung in the mud." Shore facilities for the PBYs were limited: flight crews had to live aboard their tender; there were no repair facilities for the planes and no ramp and parking area to beach them; the harbor was crowded, and the congestion in ships' boats made for narrow landing and takeoff lanes; the holding ground was poor, and tenders dragged anchor in high winds. Climatic conditions were also unencouraging. Fog was a problem much of the year, and drifting ice in winter; planes could not land in the harbor when the wind blew from the south, southeast, or northwest. But aside from its strategic position on the great-circle route to Europe, Argentia had one virtue: it was available.[1]

In mid-May, the *Albemarle* arrived to lay seaplane moorings and prepare meteorological data, and on the 18th, a dozen planes of Patrol Squadron 52 flew in from Quonset Point. Two days later, Admiral Bristol arrived, accompanied by the Chief of the Bureau of Aeronautics, flinty, intelligent Rear Admiral John H. Towers. The planes were checked, and then familiarization flights began. The fliers were in the midst of their training when they unexpectedly were handed the U.S. Navy's first combat mission of World War II.[2]

183

The German Navy had decided to risk sending its prize battleship, *Bismarck*, into the Atlantic. Admiral Raeder would have preferred to wait until other powerful warships, including the *Bismarck*'s sister ship, *Tirpitz*, were ready for sea in order to form a strong task force to hunt convoys in the North Atlantic, but there was not time. Intensified British air operations over the Atlantic and the loss of many German supply ships to British naval forces were making long raiding cruises by German surface ships increasingly difficult; soon they would be impossible. As Raeder observed, "the inevitable entry of the United States into the war in the near future was staring us in the face; once that occurred, our chances for successful operations in the Atlantic would drastically diminish." Indeed, Hitler did not want the battleship to sail, for fear of complicating relations with the United States before the attack on Russia and for fear of losing the great ship. When told by Raeder that the battleship had left on her mission, he asked if she could be recalled. But for once the naval view prevailed against the Fuehrer's cautious instincts, and the *Bismarck* proceeded into the North Atlantic.

The *Bismarck* passed through Denmark Strait and destroyed HMS *Hood* in a fight lasting but twenty-four minutes, a grievous blow to British naval prestige. Trailing oil, the German battleship, tenuously shadowed by two British cruisers, steamed into the cool, gray mists south of Cape Farewell, Greenland; Admiral Günther Leutjens then made the decision to head southeast for Brest. Meanwhile, the British crammed much of their Navy into the northeast corner of the Atlantic, frantic to find and sink the *Bismarck*, symbol of German sea power.

Churchill, worried over the safety of the convoy routes and anxious to bring America more overtly into the war, cabled President Roosevelt: "Should we fail to catch them going out, your Navy should surely be able to mark them down for us. . . . Give us the news and we will finish the job." And several days later, with the Royal Navy searching for the *Bismarck*'s detached consort in the ocean breakout, the heavy cruiser *Prinz Eugen*, Churchill wrote an "eyes only" memo to the First Sea Lord, Fleet Admiral Sir Dudley Pound:

> The bringing in to action of the *Prinz Eugen* and the search for her raise questions of the highest importance. It is most desirable that the United States Navy should play a part in this. It would be far better . . . that she should be located by a United States ship, as this might tempt her to fire

upon that ship, thus providing the incident for which the United States government would be so thankful.

Pray let this matter be considered from this point of view, apart from the ordinary naval aspect. If we can only create a situation where the *Prinz Eugen* is being shadowed by an American vessel, we shall have gone a long way to solve the largest problem. [3]

Meanwhile, on the morning of 24 May, some of the PBYs at Argentia were flying routine training missions; others were being serviced. Then, abruptly, the flights were recalled, and the planes were ordered readied for an extended mission. The *Albemarle* hastily began to refuel the incoming aircraft. Just before noon, the fliers were briefed for a long reconnaissance flight over the ocean, 500 miles southeast of Cape Farewell. The weather prognosis was for "indifferent to bad" conditions over the sea, and the pilots were told to return to base if the weather grew bad enough to preclude sighting surface vessels. The planes were to be brought back to Newfoundland with at least five hours of gas in their tanks in case they could not land at Argentia and had to fly south to find better weather.

At 1440, the first four planes took off from the water. At 1720, seven more of the PBYs went up in search of the *Bismarck*. The patrol area was a promising one, but the planes had gotten too late a start; it would be difficult to sight even a large warship on a black, night sea.

After a long over-water flight, the first group of planes reached their approximate search area with a little light still left. They made a coordinated search through the gauzy fog brewing up from the green sea below, but the crews saw no vessels or other aircraft, and the navigators were never completely certain of their position. After dark, the planes headed back west.

The second group of PBYs was dispersed by fog and darkness en route to the patrol area; searching independently through the mist and night and uncertain where they were, they had little chance of finding the *Bismarck*. All through the night, the planes were forced to turn back, one by one. Inside the PBYs, the huddled crews hoped the gas would hold and the fog would lift, and felt very much alone.

At Argentia, a low, thick fog lay over the water; the *Albemarle* ordered the planes with sufficient fuel to go south. The sailors could hear some of the PBYs rumbling over the ship, circling above the billowing mist, lost and lonely.

One plane flew on to Newport.

Chief P.J. Byrnes, with his PBY running short of fuel, gambled on the skills of his navigator and took his plane down into the fog, broke through just over the water, and made a gentle landing on the waves of Placentia Bay, only 14 miles south of the *Albemarle*. Byrnes taxied his plane north; in order to conserve fuel, his enterprising crew rigged a sail over the PBY's fuselage. Despite choppy water bashing against its bow, the PBY was the first to make it back to the tender.

Two planes came down in Fortune Bay; three landed and anchored in Shoal Harbor, west of Random Island; another landed in Bonavista Bay. As the fog burned off the water on the afternoon of the 25th, the six planes took off and flew back to the *Albemarle*.

Another PBY landed on the water, but the crew did not know where they were. The plane took off again when the weather cleared on the afternoon of the 25th, hoping to find a landmark to fix its position. Soon, the pilot and navigator recognized the rocky Quebec coast looming out of the water under the plane's nose. Low on fuel, they did not want to fly over land; they brought the PBY down in the water to the lee of St. Mary's Island.

Another of the lost planes precipitated a small crisis. It came down off Anticosti Island in the Gulf of St. Lawrence. Some of the fliers paddled ashore in a yellow rubber boat, looking for help. However, the people they met seemed frantic, spoke only French, and quickly ran away. The isolated peasants of Anticosti assumed that the oddly clad strangers who spoke a gutteral language could only be German. The rumor spread. The Nazis had landed on Anticosti Island. German airborne troops had struck in the Gulf of St. Lawrence! Canadian defense officials had been edgy all night because there had been persistent reports of unidentified aircraft overflying the Newfoundland-Quebec region. Hence, a precautionary air defense alert was sent out. Normally, Americans advised Canadian officials when the PBYs flew, but in the haste to seek the *Bismarck* on the 24th, perhaps because of the sensitive mission, no one had thought to do so. When the Canadians finally ascertained the nature of the night intrusion, they irately warned that, in future, unidentified aircraft would be shot at.

On the 26th, PBYs carrying extra tins of fuel found the plane off St. Mary's Island and the "Nazis" off Anticosti. Both planes refueled and returned to the *Albemarle*.

The last of the PatRon 52 planes to come home was VP 11, flown by Ensign W.T. Hardacker. The plane was anchored all of the 25th in Porteau Bay, Labrador, waiting to be sighted. During the night, the wind shifted, sweeping large chunks of ice into the bay; Hardacker moved the PBY several times to avoid the ice. Then heavy swells began to rise, and the lurching, dipping plane seemed in danger of being swamped. The icebergs crowded closer. Hardacker decided that his plane would have to be beached if it were to be saved. Groups of curious fishermen, ashore and in little boats, were willing to help. As the effort to beach the plane began, a gray-white berg smashed into the bow, punching a hole in the metal nose. One of the fliers scrambled onto the nose to check the damage, but the plane suddenly wallowed in the swell, and the man slipped down into the icy current. Fortunately, he was quickly fetched out of the water by a nearby fishing boat. Finally, the PBY was driven up onto the rough shoreline.Later in the day, a rescue force arrived, the hole in the bow was repaired, and the plane was refloated. The PBY took off, then darkness set in, and Ensign Hardacker brought the plane down in Red Bay. He took off again the following morning, but fog forced the plane down once more, this time off Botwood, Newfoundland. Finally, the weather improved, and Ensign Hardacker brought his men back to the *Albemarle*.[4]

On the long mission, the pilots proved capable, as the extended flying and numerous landings and takeoffs in uncertain conditions attested, and resourceful, as Chief Byrnes' sail and Ensign Hardacker's beaching operation demonstrated. But radio communications were too often hampered by equipment failures, perhaps partly due to the inexperience of the radiomen, and it was clear that the navigators still had much to learn of the intricacies of over-water navigation. The planes held up well. The durable, wide-ranging PBYs were slow and, to some, unlovely, but then as later, when things went badly, they brought their people home.

Also on 24 May, ships were sent out to watch for the *Bismarck* in the waters of the Western Hemisphere. For instance, the *Bainbridge* and the four-stackers of her escort group steamed in a scouting line from 57°-45' north, 40° west, to a little west of Cape Farewell. But they were too far west to have a chance of spotting the German battleship. Army Coast Artillery batteries at Argentia were also alerted to receive the *Bismarck* if she came westward. But the gunners were not given specific orders to open fire on the German battleship if she appeared, leaving them in an agony of doubt.[5]

Meanwhile, there was unexpected violence in the waters southeast of Cape Farewell. Until May, the convoys had been unescorted in the western Atlantic up to about 35° west, where they were joined by escorts from Iceland. However, as the U-boat patrol areas gradually edged westward, the British were forced to provide a western ocean escort for each convoy, thus inaugurating length-of-the-ocean escort. Convoy HX 126 was one of the last to sail without a western ocean escort. The merchant ships were ambushed by the U-boats south of Greenland, at about 40° west, and in a running battle, nine ships were sunk.

The Coast Guard cutters *Modoc* and *Northland* searched for a week for survivors from HX 126 in rough seas and high winds. At St. John's, the skipper of the cutter *General Greene* heard the radio transmissions from the two cutters and asked to join the search. Iceberg Smith had virtually abandoned hope, but he let the extra cutter come east. The cutters searched through waters black with a sheen of oil and strewn with debris; they found empty rafts and dead men propped up in the sea by their lifejackets. To avoid trouble, the cutters kept all of their lights on at night, and frequently radioed reports of their identity and mission. On the evening of the busy 24th, *Modoc's* bored sailors were startled to catch a sudden glimpse of the massive German battleship speeding south. Some of the Coast Guardsmen "from the ports and villages of New England, understood why they were there," and others "from Kansas and Milwaukee and the sunny cities of the Pacific coast" did not; but they were all "electrified" by the sight of the *Bismarck*. The experience gave them something to share, "to chew over and talk about . . . tell later to families and friends," and remember always. Suddenly eight Swordfish biplane torpedo bombers off HMS *Victorious* buzzed the *Modoc*, almost mistaking the cutter for the *Bismarck* in the declining visibility; then the British cruiser *Norfolk* rushed at *Modoc* despite frantic signals from the cutter, but HMS *Prince of Wales* identified her, and *Modoc* used up the second of her nine lives.

General Greene had beginner's luck. While searching about 260 miles southeast of Greenland, her men sighted a drifting lifeboat, well down, half full of seawater. There were twenty men in the boat, more dead than alive after six days on the stormy sea; they were from the SS *Marconi*. Then, later in the day, the cutter found nineteen more men in an open boat. As the survivors needed treatment, the *General Greene* headed for Newfoundland. A gale blew up, the seas rose, and the *Modoc* and *Northland* had to return to port without finding any live seamen.[6] But thirty-nine men were saved because one was willing to risk his ship in dangerous waters when he did not have to.

It was one of the hardy PBYs—British-flown—that ultimately found the *Bismarck*. Ensign Leonard B. Smith of the U.S. Navy was serving as pilot "adviser" aboard a Lend-Lease PBY of Squadron 209 of the RAF's Coastal Command, one of 17 U.S. naval aviators flying PBYs in three RAF squadrons. At 1030, on 26 May, about 690 miles west of Brest, the PBY, flying near 500 feet through scudding cloud cover, sighted the *Bismarck* in a gap between banks of low cloud. Smith arched the PBY up toward a safer altitude; red flashes of AA fire were silhouetted against the gray bulk of the battleship. There was a metallic, clanging sound, and the plane rocked abruptly, as shell fragments rang off its forward hull. The PBY then got off the contact report that had led British warships and other American-flown Coastal Command PBYs to the *Bismarck*. The German battleship was later shadowed by Lieutenant Jimmy Johnson's PBY from 240 Squadron, then by Ensign Carl Rinehart's PBY from 210 Squadron.[7] The fact that American aircraft had played a major role in the slaying of the *Bismarck* seemed sweet retribution to President Roosevelt, who was displeased by the German battleship's incursion into North American waters. As Secretary Ickes put it, "It is gratifying that some of our latest American airplanes played a prominent part in this great drama of the air."[8]

The President was inclined to believe that Hitler had sent the *Bismarck* west as a warning to the United States to remain out of the Battle of the Atlantic. When the battleship could not be located, the President even feared that she might be carrying a German landing force to occupy Martinique! At one point, he asked his advisers, "Suppose she does show up in the Caribbean? We have some submarines down there. Suppose we order them to attack her and attempt to sink her? Do you think the people would demand to have me impeached?"

And someone answered, "Only if the Navy misses."[9]

17.

The First Shot:
The Niblack Incident

As THE POSSIBILITY THAT THE UNITED STATES might undertake responsibility for escorting convoys in the western Atlantic and for defending the Atlantic isles became more real, Iceland became more prominent in the thinking of naval planners. Kelly Turner noted that the island was "a potential light force and air base of importance in connection with the protection of shipping," but observed that information on Iceland was "not sufficiently complete and reliable for use in planning." Therefore, it was decided to send technical experts to the island to look over the military environment; as Iceland was inside the German submarine war zone, the inspection team was to be sent in a warship. The destroyer *Niblack* was given the job and was directed to go first to Halifax to get information about convoy rout-.ings, U-boat concentrations, and weather, so that she might have a safe and uneventful paassage.[1]

The *Niblack* left Halifax on 7 April 1941. Guns were tested and torpedo stations checked; the ship was not looking for a fight, but her skipper, Lieutenant Commander Edward R. Durgin, a seasoned destroyerman, wanted his men alert in case the Germans gave them no choice in the matter. The trip was routine until 1930 hours on the night of 10 April, when the radiomen intercepted an SOS from a Dutch freighter, SS *Saleier*, which was sinking after having been torpedoed three hours before.

191

Durgin conferred with Commander Dennis L. Ryan, commander of Destroyer Division 13, along to help with the decisions if anything untoward occurred. The Dutch ship was apparently a straggler, well behind her convoy; her crew would be alone in open boats on a black and rising sea. She was at 58°-05' north, 30°-46' west, about 550 miles southwest of Iceland. Durgin and Ryan plotted the position on the charthouse map; they agreed that they would have to do what they could for the Dutchmen in the water. They worked out a course and speed to bring the destroyer to the vicinity of the sinking after daylight. It was very difficult to sight lifeboats on the sea at night, and neither man wanted the Niblack stopped in the dark in known submarine waters to pick up survivors, especially as American officers serving with the English had spread the word in the Atlantic Fleet that the U-boats liked to lurk in the vicinity of lifeboats in order to ambush well-intentioned but careless rescuers.*

The destroyer headed east at 28 knots, her sharp bow slicing white combers in the green-black sea. At 0420 on the 11th, she passed near a convoy. The men donned life jackets. The morning sky was overcast, the sea gray and choppy. Lookouts sighted floating wreckage, then at 0750, lifeboats. The Niblack slowed to 15 knots to make a sonar search of the area. The destroyer circled the three wooden boats, her sound gear pinging tinnily in the ears of the men on the bridge. At 0826, Niblack closed the boats and lay to.

The sailors brought the Dutchmen aboard quickly; the survivors, although tired and numb, had not been adrift long and were thus in good physical shape, which simplified the task. By 0840, the last of sixty Dutchmen made it up the cargo net draped along the side of the destroyer and was hauled by the bluejackets over the rail and onto the deck. At that instant, the sound man reported an unidentified contact approaching off the starboard beam; the range was 1,400 yards. Durgin ordered the destroyer under way as he and Ryan listened to the pinging and the sharp return echo, straining to determine if it had the tinny tone of a submarine contact. It was impossible to tell. The return echoes bounced back faster; whatever was out there under the water was moving toward the Niblack. Neither man spoke. Durgin looked at Ryan. Ryan nodded his head in approval,

*In reality, this was a rare ploy for an obvious reason: the rescue ships would be ASW craft, dangerous, difficult, and unrewarding (in terms of tonnage) targets.

saying, "Full speed ahead!" It seemed less dangerous to fight than to run. Ryan told Durgin to plot an intercepting course. *Niblack* swung to port to open the range, then turned on a converging course, moving slowly to listen for the submarine and watch for torpedo wakes.

The ship pitched slightly as her bow splashed into the curling rollers. Aft, the men at the depth-charge racks clung to lifelines as her stern rose and fell. At 0845, Denny Ryan gave the order to drop three depth charges; at ten-second intervals, the heavy barrels rolled down into the foamy water astern. There was a series of rumbling underwater explosions, then thick clouds of white water rose and billowed behind the ship. The sailors watched intently as the sea slowly erased the white circles. There was no wreckage in the water. Denny Ryan watched the sea with conflicting emotions. He was certain that he had acted correctly to safeguard the *Niblack*; the submarine could have had but one purpose in moving so close. He wished that the destroyer's attack had been successful. Yet, aware that just such an incident at sea might precipitate war, he also hoped that the attack had not been successful. With "a curious mixture of disappointment and relief," he ordered the *Niblack* westward at 28 knots.[2]

The next morning, near Iceland, the lookouts reported a periscope in the water 300 yards away. But moving at high speed, the destroyer easily swerved away and steamed out of range. Later in the day, the *Niblack* anchored in Reykjavik Harbor. It took eleven days to collect the necessary information in Iceland, then *Niblack* returned home, arriving in Newport on 28 April. Commander Ryan told Admiral Bristol about the sonar contact seventeen days before.

Admiral Bristol believed that the contact was not a U-boat, as false contacts were frequent at sea, and could be caused by fish, submerged objects, wakes, and various other factors, including inexperienced sonar personnel. The Germans had made no mention of an attack on a U-boat by an American warship. With the *Niblack* laying to in dangerous waters, it was natural that the crew, excited and perhaps a little edgy with buck fever, should attribute extra tinniness to the return echoes that they heard. Therefore, Admiral Bristol did not bother to pass the report on to Admiral King.[3]

The *Saleier* had been torpedoed by the *U-52*; the *U-92* and *U-94* had been in the vicinity of the sinking, too, but none of the submarines lingered in the immediate area. *U-98*, looking for the convoy that the *Niblack* met, did encounter a destroyer on the 11th, but at a position east of *Niblack's* rescue operation. *U-101* encountered what she reported as a steamer in the same general area, but she was not attacked. After accounts of the incident appeared in the American press, the German Navy investigated, but found no evidence of the encounter. Lieutenant Commander Durgin, after he had gained experience in antisubmarine warfare, came to believe that the *Niblack* had attacked a false contact, probably a large fish.[4]

Rumors of the *Niblack* incident spread throughout the Atlantic Fleet that spring, and Admiral King ordered an investigation to find out what had happened and why it had not been reported. In June the tale reached the public through a Joseph Alsop and Robert Kintner column in *The Washington Post*. The President was furious, insisting that even if the story were true, it should not have been published. The columnists argued that the President was using the Navy in the Atlantic in such a way as to provoke an incident with Germany which would serve as an excuse to permit the United States to take fuller part in the Battle of the Atlantic.*[5]

In July, Secretary Knox testified before the Senate Naval Affairs Committee, as rumors abounded of American naval battles in the Atlantic. For example, Columnist Drew Pearson published an absurd tale of a big fight off the Cape Verde Islands with British and U.S. warcraft battling German ships! Knox said of the *Niblack* incident:

> . . . the operator of the listening equipment reported to the Captain that he thought he heard a submerged submarine. The Captain immediately turned toward the direction indicated and dropped three depth charges. In doing this, he very prudently exercised the right of self-preservation, for had there been a submarine there, his destroyer might have been sunk. There was no other evidence that a submarine was there and it is quite possible no submarine was there. The listening-equipment echo might have been received from a whale or a large fish, or a cold current, instead of a submarine. . . .
>
> Now none of them knew whether there was a sub there or not, but the man in command did what any man would do who was on the verge of an attack by a submarine.

---

*The uncertainties of sea combat, particularly ASW operations and night actions, sometimes result in ambiguous incidents, which in a context of limited, undeclared war, can politically cut either way, sometimes giving cause for escalation of the conflict, at other times creating demand to further limit or end the conflict.

Asked about the Pearson story, Knox responded truthfully, if more tartly: "That is a perfect piece of fabrication. There isn't a word of truth in it of any kind."[6]

Admiral King apparently called Commander Ryan to Washington to discuss the incident. Ryan did not talk with other officers about the meeting with King, but his retention in his command was a sign that the civilian authorities were not seeking scapegoats. Because of the necessarily vague orders under which ships on patrol in the North Atlantic operated, there had been some fear in the service that when the inevitable incident occurred, some luckless captain would be replaced in order to satisfy the press. After the *Niblack* incident, the Atlantic sailors understood that a man would be protected as long as he did his duty, took legitimate action to safeguard his ship and crew, and did not "act like a damn fool."[7]

Soon another, much less decisively handled, incident occurred. On 17 June, four-stackers *Overton* and *Bainbridge* were running northeast, about 200 miles southeast of Halifax, escorting the U.S. Army transport *Alexander*, which was carrying defense and construction personnel to Argentia. Suddenly, the *Overton*'s sonar gear picked up a sharp, metallic echo; the destroyer stopped pinging, listening instead. The sonar man reported sounds like propeller noises. The *Overton*'s skipper, Lieutenant Commander J.B. Stefanac, requested instructions from the commander of DesDiv 62, who was in the *Bainbridge*. But the CO sounded an uncertain trumpet, replying that the *Overton* could attack if the U-boat appeared to be getting ready to attack her. Stefanac answered that the U-boat seemed too close to his ship to fire torpedoes and that he did not think the submarine would begin an action after having been discovered. The *Overton* tracked the contact for a time; whenever the destroyer approached, the "submarine" would stop engines and silently coast away. Eventually, the contact was lost.

Despite its seemingly firm nature, the contact was probably false, a product of inexperience and strained nerves, for at that time U-boats did not normally operate so very far west. Nevertheless, the action had been very poorly managed, with decision delayed because of the heavy responsibilities involved. As the commander of DesRon 31 noted in his critique: "It is doubtful that anyone can relieve Commanding Officers of the responsibility . . . nor can clearer and more definite directives be issued. It is hoped that the situation will clarify itself shortly and that Commanding Officers will then be free to make proper decisions unhampered by considerations of international relations."[8] Do the best you can with what you have.

While the ships and planes of the Atlantic Fleet struggled in dubious battle, the President at last made a vital decision. He authorized the Navy's next move into the Battle of the Atlantic and broke up the spring log jam of indecision and doubt.

18.

A Certain Cold Place

THE PRESSURE ON THE PRESIDENT to act decisively in the Atlantic continued to mount in the late spring and summer of 1941. Even Secretary Hull, cautious because of Japanese power, spoke feelingly of the need to strike at the Nazis. As Ickes, with his flair for malevolence, noted to Stimson, someone must have told Hull there was a war on.[1]

Admiral Stark wrote, "The British escorts . . . get thinner and thinner. The situation is not good . . . personally I give the British a longer time than do most people here. . . . But I most emphatically do not believe they can hold out indefinitely without *effective* aid from us."[2]

On 4 June, the President made up his mind to take an intermediate step between the Atlantic Patrol and the escort of convoys. He knew that the Germans were going to attack Russia, not move south. The threat to Dakar, the Azores, and the Cape Verdes was reduced; the seizure of Martinique would not help Britain to win the Battle of the Atlantic. The President decided to occupy Iceland.

The move would relieve a large British garrison for duty in the Mediterranean and bolster British morale. There was no chance of armed opposition to the occupation of Iceland, as there would have been to an attempt to occupy the Portuguese islands; and although German planes overflew the island and U-boats operated off its coasts, Germany lacked the sea power to sustain an assault.* Iceland

*Langer and Gleason, II, 523, stress the extent of the German threat to Iceland; but, on the contrary, it was probably the lack of an effective German threat that made the operation palatable to the President.

would provide a useful base for destroyers and planes, in case the President decided to begin escort operations. A move north thus gave President Roosevelt a chance to act usefully without bringing the nation to war. He probably already sensed that the need to bring supplies to the occupation force in Iceland might provide a convenient and plausible rationale for escorting Allied merchant convoys in the western Atlantic.[3]

But the military and naval planners saw Iceland from a much different aspect than did the President. While General Marshall said that Iceland's defense was second only to that of Brazil in being vital to the security of the hemisphere, he was, for several reasons, reluctant to commit numbers of American troops to its defense. Both his and the Navy's planning officers valued the island chiefly as a potential advanced base for light forces, requiring only a small garrison. In May, the Army had prepared a list of places about which it was necessary to gather information: in order of importance, Dakar was listed first, the Azores second, and Iceland, already protected by the British, sixteenth. Although the Germans had between sixty and ninety bombers in Norway capable of flying to Iceland and back and were believed to maintain as many as eight divisions in Norway, they presented no threat to the security of the island in the absence of a German amphibious capability, and in light of Anglo-American sea power in the North Atlantic.

The major reason for Marshall's diffidence was the Army's overall weakness and the imperatives of its massive training program. The Army planners were appalled at the prospect of using a high proportion of the nation's best troops in sterile garrison duty on a remote and unthreatened island, leaving the United States with a meager strategic reserve force of trained troops for emergency operations. As the Army could not use reservists and draftees overseas unless they volunteered for such duty, it would be necessary to strip cadres of regulars from the new divisions in order to muster a large force for Iceland, and that would disrupt training.

Brigadier General L.T. Gerow, of the Army's War Plans Division, said flatly and bitterly that the President's decision was entirely "political"; Iceland was not a worthwhile strategic objective. Speaking of the First Infantry Division, General Marshall said, as "this would eliminate our best trained division as an available force for a much more difficult mission, I do not concur in its use as a defense garrison for Iceland."[4] From the Army's gentlemanly Chief of Staff, these were surprisingly strong, even bitter, words.

Admiral Stark and stubborn, prickly Kelly Turner, fearful of losing the understrength First Marine Division to the President's design, were equally unenthusiastic. Turner insisted that Iceland was "strategically related" to Great Britain and "strategically unrelated" to the United States, which was not altogether so. He then concluded strongly, "Aside from the political aspects of the proposal . . . the British should be responsible on its entire Iceland garrison, and no United States troops should be stationed there."[5]

Meanwhile, in late May, when various amphibious operations seemed to be imminent in the Atlantic, it was decided at Marine Corps Headquarters to bring a reinforced regiment from San Diego to Charleston. Orders were cut for the Second Marine Division to make its best rifle regiment ready "for temporary shore duty beyond the seas." The Sixth Marines of Colonel Leo D. "Dutch" Hermle were selected; understrength, the unit was filled out with personnel from its sister regiments, the Second and Eighth Marines. To avoid getting other people's greenhorns and culls, it was stipulated that only men who had served for at least one year and possessed clean records would be accepted. The Sixth were reinforced by 2nd Battalion, Tenth Marines (artillery), and by small medical, tank, supply, and service units. On Memorial Day, the Regimental Combat Team and its gear shipped out in the transports *Fuller*, *Heywood*, and *William P. Biddle*, and four destroyer-transports.* The Marines assumed that they were going east to help the First Division take Martinique.[6]

While the Marine RCT was at sea, the President decided that it would have to be used to occupy Iceland, since neither Admirals Stark and King nor General Marshall wished to see the disruption of the growing Atlantic Amphibious Force. The unit was too small to replace the British garrison, but General Marshall said that he would have about 7,700 troops of the new Fifth Infantry Division ready to go to Iceland by late August to replace the Marines and relieve part of the British garrison. The President insisted that the Army provide at least 10,000 men.[7]

Iceland, the objective of the President's planning, is a round island situated one-third of the way east between Greenland and Norway, whose possessor, legend decreed, held "a pistol firmly pointed at England, America, and Canada." The island, 324 miles long, 223 miles wide, is the volcanic knob of an undersea ridge and consists

---

*1st Battalion in *Fuller*, 2nd Battalion in *Heywood*, 3rd Battalion in *W.P. Biddle*.

largely of bleak, treeless plains cluttered with boulders and topped
by high, jagged mountains; only 25 percent of its surface is habitable.
The population in 1941 was 120,000. Warmed by the Gulf Stream,
Iceland is not cold—thirty-one American states have lower average
winter temperatures—but the clash of Gulf Stream and chill polar
currents produces freakish storms and fog; its northern location
means scant daylight in winter. An incessant wind blows through the
valleys and fjords carved long ago by glacial erosion. The people,
reflecting bitter experience as Danish colonials, geographic isolation,
and a hardscrabble economy, were independent, highly literate, austere, and distrustful of foreigners. But, as did others, the Icelanders
found isolationism a futile defense in the twentieth century.[8]

In the 1920s and 1930s, various German expeditions explored and
surveyed the island. Scholarships to German universities were offered,
and the Nordic mythology of the Nazis was not without appeal to
the young. In the late 1930s, Dr. Paul Burckhardt and his mistress,
an Icelandic actress with larger ambitions, established espionage cells
in the country, compiling information on Iceland's resources and
airfields; many of the agents were brought back to Germany for
training. As head of the Abwehr's Arctic Office, Burckhardt's biggest
project was an attempt to establish German-controlled airlines in
Iceland. In the spring of 1940, Hitler hoped he would be able to
establish German naval and air bases in Iceland soon after his victorious campaign in Europe, in order to shield Norway from the
amphibious power of his seaborne enemies. But the British were able
to strike first, after the fall of Norway in April 1940, and by the
summer of 1941, they had about 25,000 Army troops, 500 RAF
personnel, and about 2,000 sailors stationed on the island. The British
forces included the equivalent of three brigades of infantry, three
regiments of artillery, two regiments of coast artillery, and one AA
regiment; the planes were mostly patrol bombers, Hudsons, Sunder-
lands, and a small variety of obsolescent attack aircraft and float
planes. The Royal Navy based ASW vessels and minecraft at Iceland.[9]

The Icelanders did not like the British, but feared a German invasion. In the lamentable circumstances, they preferred an American
occupation, because it would mean greater protection and better
trade agreements. However, when Prime Minister Hermann Jonasson
was told on 24 June that U.S. troops were being sent to replace the
British garrison, he shrewdly balked at the fait accompli. With the
Marines already at sea en route to Iceland, he was in a good bargain-
ing position, for the President did not want to land troops without

Icelandic permission. Thus, Jonasson was able to secure favorable commercial arrangements and, most important, an American promise to support Icelandic independence from Denmark after the war. Later, once the Marines had landed, the Althing, or Icelandic parliament, would uphold the Defense Agreement of 1941 by a vote of 39 to 3 because of the favorable terms and better protection. Even the communists approved, because of the recent German invasion of Russia, although they demanded that Russian troops be brought to participate in the occupation! The Icelanders accepted the occupation fatalistically as a "necessary evil" and, as a German diplomat in Denmark lamented, "without discernible opposition."[10]

Meanwhile, the Marines were scurrying to prepare to implement the President's decision. On 7 June, the 5th Defense Battalion was shorn of its antiaircraft guns and gunners, which were to pass to the RCT en route from San Diego. On the 10th, six Marines flew from Argentia to make a personal reconnaissance of Iceland. On the 15th, at Charleston, the men of the Sixth Marines began to suspect that they were not destined for Martinique, or even the Azores, when they were issued woolen skivvies and heavy overcoats. One Marine remembered to renew the subscription to his home-town newspaper, writing, "After July 1 send the paper to me in Iceland." Fortunately, the small newspaper did not break the story. On 16 June, the President told Admiral Stark to cut the orders sending the Marines to that "certain cold place."[11]

The composite Marine unit became officially the First Marine Brigade (Provisional); it numbered 4,095 Marines under command of Brigadier General John Marston.* The brigade was equipped with ten units of fire and carried supplies for ninety days. The Sixth Marines embarked in the same three transports that had carried them from San Diego, while the AA gunners drew the cranky transport *Orizaba*, and the guns, heavy equipment, and supplies went aboard the cargo ships *Arcturus* and *Hamul*.

The ships steamed out of Charleston on 22 June, and at sea they were joined by Task Force 19, commanded by Rear Admiral David M. LeBreton, a cocky bantam. Admiral LeBreton's force consisted of the old battleships *New York* and *Arkansas*, the light cruisers *Brooklyn* and *Nashville*, thirteen destroyers, nine modern and four four-

*The Brigade: 6th Mar Rgt; 2nd Btln, 10th Mar Rgt (FA); AA Batt, 5th Def Btln; elements of "A" Co, 2nd Tank Btln; "C" Co, 1st Engnr Btln; "A" Co, 2nd Med Btln; HQ, chemical, and service platoons, two bakery units; and a band of field musics.

stackers, the oiler *Salamonie*, and the fleet tug *Cherokee*. The modern destroyer *Buck* and four-stackers *Ellis*, *Bernadou*, *Upshur*, and *Lea* steamed 10,000 yards ahead of the main body in a scouting line, while the *Plunkett*, *Niblack*, *Benson*, *Gleaves*, *Mayo*, *Charles F. Hughes*, *Lansdale*, and *Hilary P. Jones* formed a circular inner ASW screen about the other ships.

The ships reached Argentia on the 27th and waited for three days while negotiations proceeded with the Icelanders; they departed Argentia on 1 July. Planes from Patrol Squadron 52 provided air cover out from Newfoundland. The *Orizaba*, of contrary nature and manned by a green crew, occasionally lost speed and often listed because she was improperly ballasted, but made the passage without collapse, although her crew had to drink out of the Marines' canteens when a harried engineer flooded the fresh-water lines with diesel oil while trying to trim a port list. The *Charles F. Hughes*, attracted by a red flare, picked up four Red Cross nurses and ten merchant sailors from a lifeboat off the Norwegian vessel *Vigrid*, torpedoed and sunk while straggling from an eastbound convoy on 24 June, eleven days before; no other survivors were found. Otherwise, despite sporadic rain and fog and occasional high winds, the passage to Iceland was uneventful. The auxiliary ships reached Reykjavik Harbor at 1900 on 7 July, while the warships went up the coast to the anchorage at Hvalfjördhur,[12] soon to be called "Valley Forge" by the bluejackets because of similarity of name and clime.

While the convoy was at sea, the political opposition in the United States belabored the President over imaginary combats in the Atlantic, and Senator Burton K. Wheeler, of Montana, charged the President with planning to occupy Iceland. Thus, by 4 July, the Icelanders expected the Americans in the near future, although not as soon as they actually arrived. The Germans, expecting the President to move south, were taken by surprise by news of the occupation; they regarded it as "the worst and most dangerous" failure of their intelligence system since the start of the war. The Fuehrer learned of the American move from news reports.[13]

On the morning of 8 July, the sailors and Marines had their first look at Reykjavik, or as most of them came to call it, "Rinkydink." The harbor was small with few docks and limited storage facilities. A few British steamers lolled in the green water, and some fishing smacks were tied up at jetties; the waterfront streets were cobbled and lined with fish-drying sheds. Coils of barbed wire and the sand-bags of British gun positions dotted the shoreline, and sandbagged gun sites bulked at some street intersections. The odor of fish was pervasive.

The *Arcturus* and *Hamul*, carrying the heavy equipment, were allotted Berths "A" and "B" in the inner harbor. Unloading was a problem because at low water there were only sixteen feet of water at the dock, while the draft of the *Arcturus* was twenty-three feet and that of *Hamul* twenty-two feet. Both ships went alongside at high tide and then by rapidly unloading, pumping fresh water overboard, and adjusting fuel ballast were able to reduce their draft sufficiently to continue working cargo as the tide went out. The other ships were anchored in the outer harbor, and ammunition, supplies, and equipment were unloaded into the *Cherokee*, launches from the warships, the Marines' Higgins boats and tank lighters, and two small British trawlers, then ferried to Berths "C" and "D." The Marines went ashore in their landing craft, some at the docks, most across Balbos Beach, west of the city. Because of the rapid rise and ebb of the tide at the beach, trucks were backed into the water, and the Marines climbed directly out of the boats into the vehicles. The Marines who landed at the docks were greeted by the skirling pipes of the Tyneside Scots.

There was a shortage of trucks, so the docks grew congested as supplies and equipment piled up. The British lent trucks but, since their vehicles did not have removable tops, cargo could not be loaded directly onto the trucks, but had to be dropped from the booms to the dock for later manhandling into the trucks. It became necessary for the Marines to form working parties to help with the unloading. Fortunately, there was little darkness at that season, and almost all of the work was carried out in sunlight or bright twilight, which speeded the pace of unloading. Each morning for three days, fascinated crowds gathered at the docks to watch the progress of the work. To the Americans, the unloading seemed to be going painfully slowly; to the Icelanders, it seemed amazingly speedy. Rumors spread of an American machine that could build roads simply by passing over open ground, and people talked of airplanes likely to appear in such numbers that the bird population would be menaced.

The Americans were further frustrated when a large boom on the *W.P. Biddle* broke and crashed into the sea, interrupting the unloading of the Sixth Marines' equipment. But by the evening of the

12th, all the ships were at last unloaded. Considering the limited dock facilities, refractory tide, and lack of small craft, vehicles, and service troops, the unloading had proceeded at a reasonable pace; but five days was still a long time for scantily protected ships to spend in a port vulnerable to air attack.

On the 13th, Task Force 19 and the auxiliaries sailed for home. The *Idaho* and two destroyers, which had been on patrol duty, joined the returning ships on the 15th. On the same day, the *Orizaba* broke down more seriously than usual, and the *Nashville* and three destroyers were detached to escort her at low speed while the main force steamed on at 14½ knots. The next three days were dark and foggy; there was no sign of the Germans. The force split up off the U.S. coast, some ships proceeding to Newport and others to Hampton Roads. Operation Indigo was over.[14] The U.S. Navy had carried men and equipment into the war zone for the first time. And it had proved an easy thing; a milk run.

The President explained the move to the nation in terms of protecting the outposts of the hemisphere; Germany would never be allowed to seize positions in the Atlantic that might "be used as air or naval bases for eventual attack" against the Americas. Many times previously he had spoken to the nation of the need to control the approaches to the United States, explaining his preference for a "dynamic" as opposed to a "static," or fortress, concept of national defense. His faculty for pouring new wine into old bottles, for making change seem familiar, was not the least of his talents. Most Americans wanted him to do what he could to help bring about the ruin of the Nazis— except enter the war. Consequently, the Administration had reason to be pleased with public response to the news of the occupation.[15]

But, in Germany, Admiral Raeder was furious. On 9 July, he demanded of the Fuehrer a "political decision" as to whether the American landing on Iceland could be construed by the German Navy as an act of war. Hitler said no; he was "most anxious" to delay American intervention "for another month or two" because of the Russian campaign. He hoped that a quick, striking success in Russia would help restrain the Americans. Therefore, the Navy "should continue to avoid all incidents" at sea. Raeder suggested that the Anglo-Americans would strike next in Africa, but the Fuehrer, always vexed by fears for the north, deemed Norway a likelier target. Raeder predicted that the Americans would soon be ready to start escorting convoys; the escorts, of course, should not be immune to attack. He recommended that American ships operating off Iceland should also be open to attack, since they were well inside the German war zone. But the Fuehrer replied that, while he appreciated the handicaps of the Navy, incidents with American ships should be avoided. However, he observed, "I will never call a submarine commander to account if he torpedoes an American ship by mistake. After the Eastern campaign I reserve the right to take severe action against the USA. . . ." The Fuehrer's decision to tolerate American ships in the war zone was bitter news to Admiral Raeder and his Navy.[16]

Meanwhile, the need to supply—for example, in July, the *Tarbell* and *DuPont* escorted a U.S. merchant freighter safely across to Reykjavik—and later to reinforce the Iceland garrison forced the President to clarify his instructions in regard to the increasingly likely prospect of encounters between American and German naval and air forces in the North Atlantic. All agreed that American forces must act to protect themselves from "threat of attack," but it was not easy to make precise orders of a concept. As the President wrote Admiral Stark:

> It is obviously impossible to define "threat of attack" by the presence of a German submarine or surface raider a given number of miles away from a convoyed vessel. It is necessary, under the conditions of modern sea warfare, to recognize that the words "threat of attack" may extend to reasonably long distances away from a convoyed ship or ships.
>
> It thus seems clear that the very presence of a German submarine or raider on or near the line of communications constitutes "threat of attack." Therefore the presence of any German submarine or raider should be dealt with by action looking to the elimination of such "threat of attack" on the line of communications or close to it.

Admiral King implemented the President's directions by authorizing Atlantic Fleet units to attack Axis surface ships approaching within one hundred miles of American convoys or along the Argentia-Iceland line of communications and Axis submarines "actually within sight or sound contact of" U.S.-Icelandic "shipping or of its escort."[17]

The President was anxious to have fighter aircraft sent to Iceland as soon as possible, but lack of shipping delayed the sending of the planes; the President fumed. Then someone with a flair for the unorthodox conceived the idea of using an aircraft carrier for the project. It would be risky, for a carrier was an important and prestigious ship to chance in submarine waters with the nation ostensibly at peace and Air Corps pilots were untrained in touchy carrier operations. However, the need to defend the Marine garrison and incoming ships at Iceland from air attack made the danger acceptable to the President and Admiral King. Thirty P-40s and three trainers were lifted aboard the *Wasp* at Norfolk, and 1,100 Air Corps ground support personnel boarded the transport *American Legion* at New York. The fliers carried orders authorizing them to intercept Axis planes approaching within fifty miles of Iceland. The Indigo II operation was ready.

On 28 July, the *Wasp* and her escorts joined the main body of Task Force 16 off New York. The ships were commanded by Rear Admiral Robert C. "Ike" Giffen, a colorful, likeable officer with a budding proclivity for mistaken judgments. The battleship *Mississippi* and heavy cruisers *Quincy* and *Wichita* formed a powerful triangle in the van. Then came the cargo ship *Almaack* and supply ship *Mizar*, oiler *Sangamon*, and *American Legion* in a diamond pattern, followed by the *Wasp* and heavy cruiser *Vincennes* at the rear. The modern destroyer *Sims* and five four-stackers screened the ships, *MacLeish* and *Sims* in front, *Overton* off the port bow, *Bainbridge* off the port beam, *Reuben James* off the starboard bow, *Sturtevant* off the starboard beam. The modern ships *Walke* and *O'Brien*, the carrier's plane-guard destroyers, patrolled near the *Wasp*. For so valuable a force, the destroyer screen was weak.

The ships steamed northeast at 14 knots. It was chilly, the wind brushing up spray and whitecaps; the sky was gray, and patches of mist lowered visibility. The ships rolled unsettlingly, and even on the large warships sleeping was "difficult." The *Wasp*, known to the destroyermen as "Snafu Maru" because of her propensity for mild misfortune, launched regular air patrols; but her jinx persisted, as she lost one of her planes in a crash on the 28th. The weather worsened, and by 2 August, the fog was so dense that from the *Vincennes* the other ships were "invisible except for brief intervals." The cruiser's men sighted a large bed floating past. Two distress calls were heard, but Admiral Giffen would not detach any destroyers; protecting *Wasp* came first. On the 4th, a lookout thought he saw a raft with a man on it drift past far away, but again "no action was taken." The men on "Vinnie Maru" grew unhappy at being served rice at every meal. As the ships neared Iceland, *Wasp*'s search planes mistakenly reported German surface ships off the island.

At 0400 on the morning of the 6th, when the ships were forty miles from Iceland, the Army fliers were given their chance. The weather was chill and overcast, but the seas were not rough. One by one, the shark-nosed P-40s growled across the 700-foot planked flight deck and arched into the pale sky; some seemed about to flop down into the gray-green sea, but all gained altitude and safely made it to Iceland. The 33rd Pursuit Squadron was very good that day. *Vincennes* and *Wasp* and her two destroyers headed back to Norfolk, arriving on the 14th, while the rest of the task force went on to Iceland with the convoy.

The auxiliaries reached Reykjavik Harbor at 0930 on the 6th and began unloading. The Air Corps CO refused to disembark his men until he had inspected his unit's camp to make sure that it was suitable and that progress on construction was advanced; he told the British that he did not intend to have his men live in tents for more than two weeks. The British evaded the contretemps by pointing out that the Air Corps personnel served under Marine orders, not British, and would have to do as the Marine command directed. Apart from that incident, the unloading went smoothly, if not speedily. Marines and men off the destroyers, using Marine and British trucks, helped unload the ships. The *Almaack* carried heavy roadbuilding vehicles and coal, *American Legion* Air Corps gear, and *Mizar* supplies, including 580 tons of frozen meat, 550 tons of fresh vegetables, and 800 tons of dairy products. All the unloading was completed by the 12th, and the Task Force and convoy left that night. Destroyers *Niblack* and *Hilary P. Jones*, just in from escorting an Icelandic freighter to Reykjavik, replaced four-stackers *Overton* and *Bainbridge* in the ASW screen, the two older destroyers remaining behind to escort two slow Icelandic freighters that were steaming west; the tanker *Salamonie* replaced *Sangamon* in the convoy, the latter remaining to refuel incoming warships at Hvalfjördhur.

The return trip of Task Force 16 was uneventful. However, on the 14th, *U-43* sighted *Mississippi* from afar, but the battleship and her escorts were moving too fast, and the submarine never had a chance to close; the Germans did not get near enough to see the convoy. Some of the ships passed through waters strewn with floating debris, including smashed and vacant lifeboats and sodden bales of cotton. An ensign in one of the cruisers was lonely and talked of little but "getting shore duty or out of the Navy" so that he could "be with his wife." The warships reached Newport on the 20th. After "nights of rolling and pitching" at sea, the men found it hard to sleep in bunks that remained still.[18]

In Iceland, the Marines began to dig in, hopeful that their stay would be brief. Brigade HQ was at Camp Lumley, about a dozen miles northeast of Reykjavik. The gunners of the 5th Defense Battalion mounted their 3-inch and .50-caliber AA weapons near Reykjavik to defend the port and airfield. The Sixth Marines were posted as a mobile reserve to protect the coast road between Reykjavik and the fleet anchorage at Hvalfjördhur; the regiment's mobility was "provided primarily by the feet of its well-trained infantrymen."

With usable land scarce, the Marines drew poor billets, and the infantrymen found little open ground to conduct meaningful training. The riflemen, crack assault troops, were called upon to function as labor troops. They built camps, putting up Nissen huts acquired from the British; the huts were laid out in a staggered pattern to reduce the effects of strafing attacks by enemy aircraft and dirt was heaped along their sides for added protection and also for warmth. Then additional housing was needed for incoming Air Corps personnel and for the soldiers expected to arrive in late August or September. The Marines also constructed storehouses and unloaded cargo ships, grumbling at the "continuous working party," and caustically called themselves the Sixth Labor Regiment.

Their food was mostly tinned, and there were few restaurants in Reykjavik. Candy, especially chocolate bars, were in great demand because of the bland diet and need for extra energy in the cold, thus causing the Sixth Marines to honor their derisive and hated Corps nickname, "the pogey-bait Sixth." These veteran pros also consumed large quantities of beer. Between chocolate bars and beer, the PX was able to show a surplus of $60,000. There were only two movie houses in Reykjavik, and the Icelanders were grim and remote; even the landscape, strewn with boulders and lacking the softness of trees and vegetation, seemed hard and bleak and depressing, and a few men took to "planting" metal trees and dummy fire plugs to remind them of happier places. But despite the boredom and griping, the Marines were disciplined professionals, and unpleasant incidents with the Icelanders were carefully avoided.

The British, glad to see new allies, were cordial, providing the Marines with trucks, equipment, advice, and at first even rations

The "Witch"—USS *Wichita* in a storm off Iceland

(which included a quota of rum). Their commander graciously authorized the Marines to wear the distinctive Polar Bear shoulder patch of the King's forces in Iceland.

Unidentified aircraft overflew the island seven times during July and August; no doubt several of the sightings were imaginary, but some must have been high-flying, long-range German reconnaissance bombers from Norway. Because of lack of radar and poor communications—it might take 1¾ hours for a sighting report from a remote area to reach Fighter HQ—the aircraft were not intercepted. Occasionally, the planes were fired at by the Marine AA gunners, but they were too high to hit.[19]

Men bear excruciating burdens willingly when they believe their sacrifices meaningful; but when they deem their efforts wasted, they resent even petty hardships. It was this way with the Sixth Marines in Iceland. Proud troops, they resented lonely and menial tasks and felt that lesser troops should have been assigned them. In addition, they felt a strong identification with the Pacific, where many of them had served in the past; and they missed old buddies in the Second Division. Impatiently, the Marines waited to be relieved, fearing they would be left behind, interlopers on a barren island in the wrong ocean, when old friends shipped out across the Pacific to fight for places strong in their memory. [20]

Iceland also tested other Americans that summer. In July, the aviation tender *Goldsborough* arrived at Skerjafjordhur, a narrow fjord on the island's southern coast, near Reykjavik, and laid plane moorings. In early August, six PBYs of Patrol Squadron 73* and five PBM Mariners of PatRon 74 flew in, angering the British because they had been given no prior notification of the arrival of the aircraft. The mission of the seaplanes was to scan the approaches to Iceland and Denmark Strait for German submarines and warships. But fog and sudden squalls rendered seaplane operations precarious and hazardous; high cliffs rose from the water's edge, and there were uncharted rocks in the fjörd, further complicating operations. The British warned that, in the winter, it would be very difficult to arm, fuel, and maintain the planes at their buoys. The fliers lived aboard the tender and in tents set up by the Marines.

*In a numerical shift, PatWing 5 became PatWing 7, and accordingly Squadron numerals of the Support Force planes began with a first digit of "7" instead of "5"; e.g., the former PatRon 53 was now PatRon 73, the former PatRon 54 was now PatRon 74, etc.

In August, weather conditions were not notably bad, and flight operations were carried out regularly, although fog and rain often prevented the planes from contacting incoming ships that they were supposed to protect. The pilots had trained hard in the spring and early summer, especially in use of the blind landing path, and were able to operate in the difficult circumstances without loss of life, although landings and takeoffs in darkness had to be discontinued as overly hazardous. Winter patrols would necessarily involve operations in darkness, for at those latitudes in November there are but 6½ hours of sunlight daily and in December only 4½ hours; and flights would be further hampered by frost, icing conditions, and high winds. The fliers believed that seaplane operations would not be feasible after 1 October "at the very latest," unless a suitable ramp and parking and maintenance area were provided. However, the necessary construction could not be done in time on account of other priorities, lack of indigenous material and consequent need to bring in all material from the United States, and the rapid onset of winter weather. Only one PBY and one Mariner were equipped with radar, and the early airborne sets were unreliable and subject to frequent malfunction. In addition, the PBMs were going through the teething stage usual with new aircraft; they had weight problems, engine "bugs," and other minor, but potentially dangerous, complaints. Also, as a result of the expansion of the naval air arm, the level of aircrew experience was sharply declining; the patrol planes averaged one regular officer for every two aircraft, and the pilots were qualified for flight operations after only about half the prewar flight training hours.

As a consequence of the various problems, one squadron commander reported that

> an attempt at winter patrol plane operations will not only be fruitless of results but will inevitably result in great hazard to personnel, planes, and tenders with the probable loss of some of each if operations extensive enough to be of value are attempted. . . . Actual experience to date in attempting to find and stay with convoys has been discouraging. . . . With convoys darkened and in the low visibility and low ceilings prevalent hereabouts. . . . The value of the air escort . . . is, it is submitted, very questionable.

Admiral King and Admiral Bristol were alert to the problem, but unable to deal with it. The new PBY-5A amphibians, which could operate from land fields in winter, were not yet available in the

Atlantic, although it was hard to understand how the Pacific Fleet could possibly have greater need for them. Admiral King was reluctant to turn to the Air Corps for help in obtaining suitable planes, and when he overcame his pride and did so, he found that the airfield at Reykjavik was not strong enough to support the weight of the heavy, long-range, four-engine planes required. Hence, until a better field was completed or the amphibians became available, the seaplane fliers learned that they would have to do the best they could with what they had.[21]

Late in August, the patrol planes and the warships in the fleet anchorage rallied for a coordinated search with ships of the Royal Navy when a British cruiser erroneously reported a German surface raider east of Iceland. Admiral Stark told Admiral Sir Dudley Pound, his opposite number in the Royal Navy, "We are following with keen interest the raider now loose in the Atlantic and here's hoping we get her." But the hunters returned to Hvalfjördhur with an empty bag, which did not improve dispositions aboard some of the American warships. On the battleship *New Mexico*, for example, the crew, expecting liberty after transferring from the Pacific, pined for families and friends and lamented that they had had only ten days' leave in the States in ten months; the lack of liberty and meaningful action grated on the men. Reenlistment rates dropped, and the captain fretted.[22]

Sailors, fliers, and Marines were finding that things were tough in Ernie King's ocean. And the President soon decided to slice still another loaf for Admiral King and his men.

19.

A Goodly
Company

On 24 June 1941, forty-eight hours after the German attack on Russia, Admiral Stark told the President that he assumed it was "the country's decision . . . not to let England fall" and urged that the United States "seize the psychological opportunity presented by the Russian-German clash and announce and start, escorting immediately. . . ." He conceded that such "would almost certainly involve us in the war," but believed "every day of delay in our getting into the war" was "dangerous, and that much more delay might be fatal" to Britain's survival.

Secretary Stimson and the Army planners also urged that the nation should take advantage of the German preoccupation in Russia "to push with the utmost vigor our movements in the Atlantic. . . ."[1] Frank Knox felt that his Navy could drive the U-boats out of the Atlantic in a matter of weeks. Although the improved efficiency of the Royal Navy's ASW effort was beginning to draw the fangs of the U-boats, the initiation of full-ocean escorting meant that more Allied warships would have to be deployed in the western Atlantic. According to British calculations, if the U.S. Navy expanded its role in the western part of the ocean, about twenty British and Canadian destroyers, thirteen corvettes, and nine trawlers would be released for service on other important missions. The Admiralty was coming to realize fully that the protection afforded convoys in the western Atlantic "was inadequate in size and quality," and greatly feared that the U-boats would strike hard "before the western gap in the convoy defences could be bridged." There would be an added boon in the eastern Atlantic, too; American naval operations would permit the British eastern ocean escorts to meet convoys farther east, allowing escorts to return directly to the United Kingdom without refueling in Iceland. This would result in an additional economy of escorts that would permit three escort groups to be shifted to other routes. So, at the end of June, President Roosevelt again directed the Atlantic Fleet to prepare for the escort of convoys in the Atlantic.[2]

In Germany, the Fuehrer resoundingly, if somewhat cryptically, warned:

> Let there be no mistake—whoever believes that he can help Britain must realize one thing above all: Every ship, with or without convoy, that comes within range of our torpedo tubes, will be torpedoed.

Admiral Raeder publicly stated and the Fuehrer privately hinted to a former American diplomat that "American escorts for convoys" meant "war." While Raeder was grimly serious, the Fuehrer was bluffing.[3]

Although the President tended to worry more about domestic opposition than about German threats, especially as his Atlantic Patrol had indicated that Hitler was unwilling to undertake a sea war against the United States, he was nevertheless most reluctant to take so definitive and fateful a step as escort operations. However, the occupation of Iceland offered him a perfect opportunity to discreetly initiate such operations, for, as Churchill perceptively noted, the Marines on the island would have to be supported by sea and American ships would have

> to traverse very dangerous waters and, as we have a very large traffic constantly passing through these waters, I daresay it may be found in practice mutually advantageous for the two navies involved to assist each other, so far as is convenient, in that part of the business.

Admiral Stark explained to Admiral King:

> The CNO will arrange for at least one United States or Iceland flag to depart from the vicinity of Halifax, at intervals not greater than those at which regular British convoys depart. In the same manner westbound United States or Iceland flag vessels will depart from about 26W at similar intervals. In the event that the British authorities wish so to handle their convoys that their departures from Halifax coincide with the departures of United States or Iceland flag vessels from this vicinity, the practical result would be the sailing of regular British convoys and United States . . . vessels in company.[4]

On 30 June, Senator Wheeler introduced a resolution to have the Senate Naval Affairs Committee investigate charges that American warships were escorting convoys and attacking German submarines in the Atlantic. On 2 July, Knox truthfully denied both charges. Ironically, on the same day, the President approved the Atlantic Fleet's plan for escort operations. Admiral King ordered Admiral Bristol to maintain at all times two escort groups in readiness at Argentia and Casco Bay; he also ordered a squadron of patrol planes to Iceland,* and told Admiral LeBreton to divide his force of heavy warships into three groups to be rotated between Casco Bay, Argentia, and Iceland prepared to aid the escorts if necessary by "taking offensive action against Axis surface raiders."[5]

Then, abruptly, the President for the second time in three months cancelled the escort plans. The reason was neither political opposition nor German threats, but Japanese movements in Indo-China.[6]

Throughout the summer, the Germans tried to get the Japanese to help them in the Russian campaign by striking at Siberia; but the Japanese were not interested in that barren land. They wanted to move south, into the economically and strategically important Allied colonies of southeast Asia; the Japanese hand was temporarily stayed by fear of the American Navy and the possibility of a protracted war against a nation with the vast industrial potential of the United States.

But the Japanese nibbled at Indo-China, finally occupying bases in the southern part of the French colony, moving planes and ships in closer range of their ultimate objectives in Malaysia and the Netherlands East Indies; they reasoned that the United States, bringing warships into the Atlantic from the Pacific, was unlikely to try to block a discreet move into southern Indo-China with force. However, the U.S. Pacific Fleet still restrained the Japanese from falling upon the British and Dutch possessions and severing Britain's sea communications with her Empire, thus dealing the Allied cause a perhaps fatal blow.[7]

As President Roosevelt told his Cabinet after cancelling the plans for escort operations, it was vital for the Pacific Fleet "to help keep peace in the Pacific. . . . I simply have not got enough Navy to go around. And every little episode in the Pacific means fewer ships in the Atlantic."[8]

Admiral Stark, although depressed by the President's failure to honor the decision to escort, accepted Roosevelt's reversal "without

---

*The Catalinas of PatRon 73 and Mariners of PatRon 74.

attempting to argue. . . ." Privately, he lamented that "policy seems to be something never fixed, always fluid and changing." When he went to the President with "very pointed questions, which all of us would like to have answered," Roosevelt would merely smile or reply genially "Please don't ask me that." Stark, like the civilian leaders working on various phases of industrial mobilization, was convinced that "only a war psychology . . . would speed things up the way they should be speeded up . . . it just isn't in the nature of things to get the results in peace that we would, were we at war. . . . The Iceland situation may produce an 'incident'. . . . I do not know. Only Hitler can answer."[9]

Ickes sadly worried that "many of our people don't think that democracy is worth fighting for . . . we are in an age when we are more interested in movies and the radio and baseball and automobiles than in the fundamental verities of life."[10]

Meanwhile, British planners were reaching gloomy conclusions long shared by Admiral Stark and General Marshall, conceding that they "could not see the possibility of Britain winning a clearcut victory over the Germans without the help of the United States. . . . decisive offensive action could not be taken until the United States" entered the war.[11]

The President, meantime, brooded in apparent indecision until, late in July, the atmosphere of Pacific crisis abating as it became clear that nothing short of war could be done to force the Japanese out of Indo-China, he decided to go ahead and implement the Navy's plans for escort operations in the North Atlantic.[12] It should be stressed that the decision to escort was the logical conclusion of the one great constancy in the President's prewar policy, his determination to prevent the Germans from winning the Battle of the Atlantic. It had little to do, as is sometimes said, with the need to safeguard precious Lend-Lease cargoes as such,* but rather derived from the American strategic imperative to sustain Britain and weaken Germany against the day of total American involvement in the war.

And so the Atlantic Fleet was going to war.

---

*The bulk of material carried in U.S.-escorted convoys did not consist of scarce military equipment and weaponry but of the plentiful raw resources of war — petroleum, steel, ores, meat, grains, etc.; important but not irreplaceable cargoes. The ships were as vital as the cargoes, perhaps more so; at least such was the key assumption of Doenitz's Tonnage War.

Mr. Roosevelt had long wanted to meet the Prime Minister. It being inexpedient for Churchill to visit the United States and dangerous for the President to visit Britain, it was decided that it would be appropriate for the two men to get together at a British possession in the New World. Newfoundland was chosen instead of pleasanter Bermuda because, in event a sudden emergency forced the Prime Minister to fly back home, the flight from Newfoundland would be shorter. The Admiralty wanted the meeting held in remote Loon Bay on the northern coast, but the Americans insisted on Argentia because of its defenses.

The President indulged his ample propensity for the comic-devious by evolving a ruse for the occasion. He said he was taking a long-postponed fishing trip off the Maine coast, but could not take along the usual collection of newspapermen because accommodations aboard the Coast Guard cutter *Calypso* were limited and he did not wish to take a destroyer out of service in such critical times. On Sunday, 3 August, the President's party entrained for New London where it boarded the presidential yacht *Potomac*. Roosevelt fished off Massachusetts on the 4th "to establish my location beyond a doubt"; then, that night, the yacht reversed course and made a three-hour trip to quiet Menemsha Bight at the western end of Martha's Vineyard. The destroyer *Madison* escorted the *Potomac* and *Calypso* in. Already present were the heavy cruisers *Augusta* and *Tuscaloosa*, which had carried the President's chief naval and military advisers from Long Island, where they had been brought by destroyer from New York City, and the destroyers *McDougal*, *Moffett*, *Sampson*, and *Winslow*. The President boarded the *Augusta* on the morning of the 5th, and at 0640, the seven warships headed north; *Potomac* and *Calypso* returned to Buzzard's Bay, where one of the yacht's crewmen masqueraded as the President, ostentatiously fishing. The Navy Department issued bogus announcements in Rooseveltian style: "Potomac River sailors responding to New England air after Washington summer"; and, "All members of party showing effects of sunning."

Meanwhile, the *Augusta* and her company, darkened at night, zigzagged north at 21 knots and entered Argentia on the morning of the 7th, after minesweepers had scoured the approaches. The harbor was already busy: five four-stackers, obviously Admiral Bristol's standby escort group, were in; and so was the *Arkansas* of Admiral LeBreton's striking force and several tenders and oilers destined for

Iceland. Complete radio silence was in effect, and no one was permitted to leave the base, but many of the sailors had guessed that the President was coming. That afternoon, the President really went fishing.[13]

The Prime Minister left Scapa Flow in the battleship *Prince of Wales* on the 4th, while "the Admiralty was trying to look as though nothing unusual was happening." The officers established a pool as to the nature of their mission. One unfortunate drew a slip which read "Taking Hess back to Germany"; another who was thought not to have much chance to win got one reading "Taking Winston Churchill to meet Roosevelt."

On the first night out, a gale blew up, and the three escorting "H"-class destroyers could not keep up with the battleship through the high seas even though she was steaming at the reduced speed of 18 knots; rather than further lower speed, it was decided to let the destroyers return to Scotland, for it was safer for the *Prince of Wales* to run alone at high speed. The next day, the seas calmed, and on the 6th, the ex-U.S. four-stacker *Ripley* and Canadian destroyers *Restigouche* and *Assiniboine* joined from Iceland.

Churchill spent the trip prowling the ship unobtrusively and watching such movies as *High Sierra*, with Humphrey Bogart, and *Lady Hamilton*, a dreadful film about Lord Nelson's love affair, which he unaccountably enjoyed although he was seeing it for the fifth time.

Saturday, 9 August, was cold and gray. The Prime Minister, smoking his first cigar of the day, was up early, peering through curling strands of mist; he was "anxious to be the first to greet the American Navy." As the American escort did not arrive, the battleship ran along the wavering coastline of desolate coves and hills thickly wooded with green firs; it reminded one Englishman of James Fenimore Cooper's Indian country. Two American destroyers appeared, and the delay was accounted for; the British were using Newfoundland Summer Time, while the Americans were on their own eastern time, and 0900, when the ships were supposed to enter the harbor, was only 0730 to the Americans.

Led by the *McDougal*, the ships steamed toward Argentia. The British sailors at the rails, some with telescopes, picked out the *Tuscaloosa*, then the wire-basket mast of the old *Arkansas*. Soon they could see President Roosevelt in a black suit, sitting under an awning beneath the long guns of *Augusta*'s forward turret. The cruiser's band played "God Save the King," the battleship's band played "The Star-Spangled Banner," and the sounds, intermingling, reverberated across the water. The *Prince of Wales* anchored at 0912, U.S. Navy time.

Soon the water was streaked with the wakes of small boats, as the sailors went to look over each other's ships. The battleship bore jagged lines of camouflage paint, a little tarnished from the wear of active service; the American ships were spotless gray. A boat from the "Augie" brought over 1,500 boxes, each containing a half-pound cheese, apples, an orange, a carton of cigarettes, and a card reading, "The President of the US of A sends his compliments and best wishes."

The British were entranced by the food advertisements in the American magazines—pictures of huge hams, rare roasts, and various fare long rationed in Britain. They gave freely of their gin and scotch. To one Englishman, the Americans seemed suggestive of the freshness and innocence of the prewar British, and Argentia, disheveled with construction, "a pleasing confirmation of my ideas of an Alaskan town during a gold boom."

On Sunday, the *McDougal* brought President Roosevelt over to the battleship for a stern-first "Chinese landing" made necessary by the President's infirmity. One of the destroyer's chiefs flung a line over to the battleship's stern, where a dumpy sailor in a pea jacket stood idly. The chief bluntly told the Englishman to make the line fast; Winston Churchill, with his flair for the fit gesture, made the line fast.

Church services were held on the quarterdeck of the *Prince of Wales*, about three hundred American sailors joining the British all over the forward turrets and superstructure. After prayers, the men sang "O God, Our Help in Ages Past," "Onward, Christian Soldiers," of course, and requested by the President, "Eternal Father, Strong to Save." After services, the sailors photographed the President and Prime Minister, the former with a Camel inside the cigarette holder clenched between his teeth, the latter puffing a cigar. The President and his party then enjoyed lunch.[14]

On Monday night, a dinner was held in the battleship's wardroom for about eighty British and American officers. Both groups were self-conscious; the Americans were leery of seeming too brash and outgoing and the British feared seeming too cold and reserved. Raucous entertainment, including firecrackers, screeching bagpipes, and races over obstacle courses of furniture, was designed to break the ice.

But the pleasant, if forced, camaraderie of the social relations concealed serious psychological and professional differences. The President thought of the meeting mainly as an opportunity for the Americans to get to know their British opposite numbers better in the interest of future working relationships. He wanted to relax after the harrowing decisions of summer, not make new commitments. The American approach to the meeting was so informal that no agenda had been prepared in advance!

The British, on the other hand, were expectant of bold, new decisions and hoped to secure a commitment from the President as to the time of American entry into the war. One night, before leaving the battleship to go aboard the *Augusta*, Churchill confided, "I have an idea that something really big may be happening—something really big."[15]

The conference's political deliberations produced the Atlantic Charter, reminiscent of President Wilson's Fourteen Points. The Charter reflected the President's desire to secure from the British a commitment to liberal war aims that would satisfy the numerous Americans, including himself, who were suspicious of British colonialism. The British did not dispute the ideal of political self-determination, partly because it was important in sustaining the spirit of resistance in Occupied Europe; the major political differences concerned issues relating to postwar trade policy.

On strategic questions, both groups agreed that it was necessary to warn Japan against further expansion south, but the British, weak east of Suez, wanted a strong note, while the President, hoping to avoid a clash with Japan to buy time for operations in the Atlantic, wanted and obtained agreement on a milder version.[16]

The major strategic occurrence was the announcement to the British of the President's decision to have the U.S. Navy soon commence escort operations in the western Atlantic. To the expectant Churchill, it seemed that Roosevelt "obviously was determined" that the United States should join the fight, but was still unwilling to do so officially: "The President . . . said he would wage war but not declare it. . . ."

The British sought to discuss potential land operations in North Africa, but General Marshall insisted that talks be limited to the western Atlantic and the Atlantic isles, observing that training requirements and legal restrictions on overseas service would make it difficult for the Army to provide amphibious forces for future operations, particularly, he noted pointedly, if American troops were employed to relieve the British and the U.S. Marines in Iceland. These comments were consistent with the President's wishful belief that America's immediate and primary role in support of Britain was at sea. As to long-term policy, the U.S. Army planners once again dashed British hopes of a cheap victory by stressing the ultimate need for a continental landing and large-scale ground warfare in France if the defeat of Germany was to be brought about. In addition to the strategic differences, the Army planners were somewhat unhappy with the British because they feared that the President's generosity in Lend-Lease would retard the growth of the American Army and Air Corps.

As to naval issues, the British wanted to transfer their Force "H" from Gibraltar to Singapore, but needed further American help in the western Atlantic to safely do so. Admiral Stark therefore agreed to retain the brand-new battleships *Washington* and *North Carolina* in the Atlantic and promised that, if war came, fleet units would be sent to Gibraltar, if possible. As to the details of the President's decision to undertake escort operations, it was agreed that the Support Force would be based at Newfoundland and Iceland instead of Londonderry; this simplified British escort arrangements in the eastern Atlantic and suited the President's political instincts. American naval officers rejected a British plan to use American ships to defend the Africa-United Kingdom convoy routes that ran along the west coast of Africa and secured agreement that U.S. patrol planes in the Atlantic would be used to support U.S. naval forces, not dispersed by the RAF's Coastal Command in general tasks. The Americans assured the British that U.S. forces had orders to attack Axis surface raiders approaching the North Atlantic convoy routes, which meant that the British needed to retain only a few major warships in the Atlantic west of the United Kingdom.[17]

At exactly 1657 on 12 August, HMS *Prince of Wales* stood out of Argentia Harbor, and the Atlantic Conference was over.

Four Canadian destroyers escorted the battleship toward Iceland, which the Prime Minister wanted to see. The U.S. destroyers *Mayrant* and *Rhind* steamed four miles ahead of the British-Canadian force. Ensign Franklin D. Roosevelt, Jr., served in the *Mayrant*.

Churchill, vexed by a cold and his doctor's admonitions to stop smoking for a while, watched Laurel and Hardy in *Saps at Sea* and a

Donald Duck cartoon, which he pronounced "A gay but inconsequent entertainment." He might have said the same of the meeting at Argentia.

News of the conference was broadcast on the 14th, and listeners in the *Prince of Wales* were "deflated in an atmosphere of anti-climax." One senior officer spoke for many when he said, "Well, I expect there was far more to it than just that!" Another likened the talks to an iceberg—mostly below the surface. As one disappointed Englishman recalled, "What we had all subconsciously hoped for, and not, perhaps, entirely subconsciously, was a declaration that America was coming into battle with us. . . ."[18]

The Germans, fearing the same eventuality, believed that the Americans still lacked the military capability to intervene effectively.[19]

In Iceland, the redoubtable Churchill walked the paved highway north of Reykjavik, inspecting the Sixth Marines. The tune of "The Marines' Hymn" "bit so deeply into" Churchill's memory that, as he said, "I could not get it out of my head."

When the *Prince of Wales* departed Iceland, the *Mayrant* and *Rhind* accompanied the battleship and her escort as far as 150 miles east of Iceland. On 18 August, the *Prince of Wales* safely entered Scapa Flow.

Back home, the Prime Minister stressed, as he had to, the symbolic overtones of the Atlantic Conference, saying of the last part of his trip: "And so we came back across the ocean waves uplifted in spirit. . . . Some American destroyers, which were carrying mails to the United States Marines in Iceland, happened to be going the same way, too, so we made a goodly company at sea together. . . ."[20]

In the United States, President Roosevelt pondered how best to present to his people the news of the Atlantic Fleet's entry into the Battle of the Atlantic.

20.

New Man on
an Old Ship:
The Greer Incident

IN THE NORTH ATLANTIC the morning of 4 September was sunny, although a chill breeze blew white curls across the green water. The German submarine *U-652* was cruising on the surface when her lookouts sighted a flashing glint in the southern sky. Her skipper, Oberleutnant Georg-Werner Fraatz, ordered the bridge cleared. The diving alarm rasped, and lookouts hurriedly ducked below. The *U-652* slid under, making a slender, foamy, white crease in the sea. Overhead, a twin-engine Hudson medium bomber, bearing the brightly colored roundels of the RAF on wings and fuselage, searched the empty water.

Ten miles away, at 62°-45' north, 27°-37' west, about 125 miles southwest of Reykjavik, the venerable four-stacker USS *Greer* was steaming toward Iceland at 17½ knots. Her skipper, Lieutenant Commander Laurence H. Frost, was below in the wardroom, having a cup of coffee with Commander George W. Johnson, CO of Destroyer Division 61. Also aboard, as a passenger, was Captain W.E. Brown; so Frost had plenty of rank to lean on in a crunch. The *Greer* was Frost's first command; the recommissioned destroyer had only been back in service for a year, and this was her new skipper's thirty-fifth day on board. She was on her way to Iceland carrying mail, some odds and ends of freight, and a few Army officers. The weather out of Argentia had been good, and the *Greer* was a full day ahead of schedule. At 0847, a buzzer sounded in the wardroom, and Frost went to the voice tube. The officer of the deck reported that the British patrol bomber that had passed near the ship about five minutes before had returned and was signalling the destroyer. "Something about a U-boat, sir," the OOD said. Frost and Johnson went immediately to the bridge, joined by Captain Brown; the shutters of the signal light clacked as the signalman acknowledged the message from the plane. Frost and Johnson read the message over the shoulder of the sailor with the signal pad: "Enemy U-boat observed submerging about 10 miles northwest. . . ." Frost told the OOD, "I relieve you, Lieutenant," then looked at Johnson, who nodded. Frost ordered, "All engines ahead full; make turns for twenty knots. Come left to new course two-seven-zero." The *Greer* bucked in the swells and swung to port; zigzagging, she ran west, then headed north.

Commander Johnson did not intend to attack the U-boat, but was going to trail it and broadcast its position. He felt that he lacked authority for an attack, since the *Greer* was not escorting American shipping, yet he did not think it proper to ignore the presence of the U-boat in waters through which U.S. vessels frequently passed. In making these judgments, he was scrupulously obeying standing presidential and Atlantic Fleet instructions.

General quarters were sounded and, to the clanging of the GQ gong, *Greer's* men scrambled to battle stations, tugging on yellow lifejackets and slapping on gray helmets. One by one, talkers reported action stations manned and ready. The sailors waited.

At 0915, the *Greer* reduced speed to 10 knots to begin a sonar search. Five minutes later, Radioman 2/C D.H. Shields reported a "mushy" contact 2,100 yards dead ahead. "Sound contact bearing zero-zero-zero." Larry Frost had inherited an able and alert ship.

Commander Johnson said, "Keep after it, Larry."

Frost nodded, then reminded the lookouts to watch the sea for torpedo wakes.

The *Greer* ran very slowly, hanging dead astern of the U-boat, avoiding turns in order to keep her wake from fouling the sonar contact, and presenting the smallest, bows-on, target to the U-boat.

Moving at about 4 knots, the *U-652* swerved to port, onto course three-zero-five; Radioman Shields picked up the turn, and the *Greer* swung out in slow pursuit.

At the chart table, Commander Johnson wrote out a message reporting the contact to Argentia and Iceland. He told Frost to let the British bomber know that they had found the U-boat. The blinker light clattered again.

The Hudson swung low, the co-pilot signalling with an Aldis lamp from the cockpit. A signalman called to Frost, "Wants to know if we are going to attack, sir."

Frost looked at Johnson. Many times they had discussed the possibility of something like this occurring and had agreed they would not attack first. Frost said to the signalman, "Send him a 'negative.' And make certain that both messages are in your signal bag!"

At 1032, the Hudson, short on fuel, swooped low, flew several thousand yards ahead of the destroyer, and dropped four depth charges. Not even close, thought Frost, as blossoms of white water erupted from the sea.

Below, the explosions surprised the men in the *U-652*. Using his periscope skillfully, Fraatz scanned the surface and sighted the destroyer astern; the angle was so sharp it was difficult to identify the destroyer. He was not certain whether the depth charges had been dropped by the ship or the plane, although had it been the destroyer that had attacked he almost certainly would have heard its approach on his listening gear. Another hour and a half passed. Another British plane flew over. The *Greer* hung grimly on to the stern of *U-652*, sometimes closing to within 200 yards to maintain contact, other times dropping back as much as 1,200 yards. The destroyer arched from side to side, rocking gently in the swells. Johnson and Frost sipped coffee and munched sandwiches, wondering if and when the submarine would try to break the stalemate by violent means. The *Greer* could not fight first and would not flee: the *U-652* could not flee but would fight. Shortly after noon, Oberleutnant Fraatz decided to attack.

At 1240, *U-652* swung gently to starboard, toward a parallel course with the destroyer. Fraatz was lining up an easy shot off the starboard beam of the four-stacker.

Suddenly, Radioman Shields called out that the U-boat, still off the starboard bow, was now running toward the *Greer* instead of away from her. Lieutenant Commander Frost shouted orders, and the *Greer* picked up speed and began to swing to starboard. At 150 yards, Shields lost contact because the sound cone was passing above the depth of the U-boat. The waters ahead were roiled and slightly discolored, indicating the passage of a large underwater object.

The *Greer* had picked up his turn so quickly that Fraatz had to fire before he wanted to. The *U-652* released a torpedo at the destroyer, and then Fraatz maneuvered his craft into position for a follow-up shot.

Commander Johnson, Captain Brown, and the Exec, Lieutenant T.H. Copeman, sighted a firing bubble in the water. The lookouts on the starboard wing of the bridge yelled, "Captain! Something in the water off the starboard bow. One thousand yards!" Frost shouted into the engine-room voice tube, "All ahead full speed. Right full rudder." The *Greer* shook and turned to starboard. Soon she was parallel to the torpedo wake, which passed about 100 yards away. Commander Johnson said, "Go ahead, Larry. Just make certain that this is all put down in the log."

Frost grinned back at Johnson, then ordered the depth charges readied. At 1256, the men of Ensign M.G. Evans rolled the explosive drums off the stern racks; six splashed into the sea, at 40-yard intervals. A sailor at the Y-gun tugged a lanyard, and the forked thrower blasted out two smaller depth charges on either beam. There were muted rumbles from below, the sea was ringed with a fried-egg pattern of white circles, then the ocean erupted in high geysers of white water. A lookout suddenly shouted, "Torpedo wake dead ahead!"

Oberleutnant Fraatz's second shot was arriving. The white torpedo streak was about 500 yards away, off the starboard bow. The destroyer, moving at flank speed, turned to starboard, inside the torpedo track. The shining wake streaked past, a hundred or so yards off the port beam. It was 1300. The fight had lasted twelve minutes.

Below, the depth charges had smashed out *U-652*'s light bulbs and shaken the boat, but they had not fallen close enough to do her any serious damage.

The *Greer* echo-ranged for the submarine, but the water was turbulent from the explosions and wakes, and Shields could not regain contact. The British plane reported gulls on the surface, probably pecking at dead fish, but there was no sign of wreckage. The *Greer* went through another box search. Johnson and Frost wearily discussed when the submarine might have to surface in order to recharge her batteries.

Soon the gray smear of another vessel approached over the line of the horizon. It was a British "I"-class destroyer. She signalled, asking if *Greer* wished to join her in a coordinated search. The American destroyer signalled no.

At 1416, the *Greer* started to leave the contact area, but Commander Johnson, dubious about the propriety of passing the hunt on to the British and resolved to make one more sweep of the vicinity,

The snowy plume of a depth-charge explosion

soon turned back. In the meantime, the British destroyer had found nothing. When the *Greer* returned, the British ship sulkily dropped a random depth charge and left. Doggedly, the *Greer* persisted.

At 1507, Shields reported a good contact off the starboard bow, 900 yards away. The destroyer charged in and released a full pattern of eleven depth charges, nine from the racks and two from the Y-gun. Again, the sea rumbled, the destroyer shook, and huge pillars of white seawater hissed skyward. But there was no debris on the surface.

Below, the attack had not been as close as the first one, and the *U-652* was still hale.

The *Greer* continued to search. Frost and Johnson ate on the bridge. Both men were stiff and tired, but they sensed that the *U-652* was still near, and they were resolved to keep to the hunt.

Below, the *U-652* ran quietly southwest, listening to the *Greer's* pursuit a little too far to the north. Fraatz refused to leave his patrol area. The U-boat, too, had come to stay.

But the battle of will and nerve ended at 1840; the *Greer* was ordered to give up the search and proceed to Iceland. At 15 knots, she resumed her interrupted journey. And when the destroyer disappeared over the horizon, the *U-652* surfaced, suddenly alone on a cold, darkling sea.

Larry Frost turned the duty over to the OOD and headed below for coffee and rest. Coming down the ladder from the bridge, he glanced astern. He wondered if he had done the wrong thing; an international incident might develop out of the day's grim struggle. Then he thought of the wreckage of smashed ships through which American vessels on the Iceland run so often steamed, and of men killed in flaming water; he was sorry that they had not gotten the U-boat. Larry Frost, a new man on an old ship, went below.[1]

Immediately after learning of the battle, the President directed that the U-boat be "eliminated." But Rear Admiral Giffen, Senior Officer Present Afloat, SOPA, Iceland, at first doubted the reality of the contact and took no action. When Ernie King read Giffen's report, he wrote on it the angry comment: "?!!?!? K."[2]

Tactically, in this first clash between Americans and Germans in the Battle of the Atlantic, the destroyer had been well handled; she had located the U-boat in the first five minutes of her search, then maintained contact for 3½ hours, while keeping a position that best drew the enemy's fangs. Lookouts had been alert throughout the action, with no "doping off," and, after the initial attack, the sailors, despite cold, fatigue, and alternating boredom and tension, had carried out a determined six-hour search. Radioman Shields had turned in a good day's work and, perhaps, had saved the ship when he picked up the *U-652*'s quick starboard turn. But, the attacks had been made too soon in the depth-charge run, and the charges had been set too shallow, characteristic failings of inexperience. The action showed that American destroyers would be able to master the U-boats when the battle developed in accordance with their training. It had been an individual ship fight, fought in daylight against a submerged submarine employing conventional tactics, with the *Greer* having no convoy to watch over and distract her.

The *Greer* incident provided the President with a convenient opportunity to announce what had already been decided, that the U.S. Navy would soon commence escort operations in the western Atlantic. To Roosevelt, the attack on the *Greer* symbolized the "reality of relations with Germany." On 11 September, an angry President made a fighting speech:

> To be ultimately successful in world-mastery Hitler knows that he must get control of the seas. He must first destroy the bridge of ships which we are building across the Atlantic. . . . He must wipe out our patrol. . . . He must silence the British Navy.
>
> It must be explained again and again to people who like to think of the United States Navy as an invincible protection, that this can be true only if the British Navy survives . . . .
>
> We have sought no shooting war with Hitler. We do not seek it now. But neither do we want peace so much that we are willing to pay for it by permitting him to attack our naval and merchant ships. . . . when you see a rattlesnake poised to strike, you do not wait until he has struck before you crush him.
>
> These Nazi submarines and raiders are the rattlesnakes of the Atlantic. . . . The time for active defense is now. . . .
>
> In the waters which we deem necessary for our defense, American naval vessels and American planes will no longer wait until Axis submarines lurking under the waters . . . strike their deadly blow—first. . . . That means, very simply and clearly, that our patrolling vessels and planes will protect all merchant ships—not only American ships but ships of any flag—engaged in commerce in our defensive waters. . . .
>
> But let this warning be clear. From now on, if German or Italian vessels of war enter the waters the protection of which is necessary for American defense they do so at their own peril. [3]

Partly because of passion and partly to make the larger issues stand out boldly and summon unity from his people—to avoid what he called "hair-splitting"—the President omitted the details of the *Greer*'s determined tracking of the submarine and presented the clash as an unprovoked German attack, which even members of his own Cabinet did not believe. A few days later, Admiral Stark presented the Senate with an accurate account of the action. Despite his own prissy avoidance of such words as "escorting" and "convoy," Roosevelt permitted Secretary Knox to make a strong speech heralding the beginning of American escort operations and left scant doubt that, whatever the specifics, he was embarking upon a limited, undeclared naval war in the North Atlantic.[4]

In London, Winston Churchill wrote jubilantly in a private letter:

> United States assumption of responsibility for all fast British convoys other than troop convoys between America and Iceland should enable Admiralty to withdraw perhaps forty of the fifty-two destroyers and corvettes we now keep based in Halifax. . . . This invaluable reinforcement should make killing by hunting groups other than escorts possible for the first time. Hitler will have to choose between losing the Battle of the Atlantic or coming into frequent collision with United States ships. . . .[5]

In Berlin, the German Naval Staff feared the same eventuality. Admiral Raeder told Hitler that President Roosevelt had declared war on Germany and asked that all restrictions on U-boat operations in the western Atlantic be rescinded, except for a belt twenty miles off the U.S. coast. The German Navy was frustrated because clever British routing of convoys, summer fog, and long hours of daylight in the North Atlantic were limiting the ability of U-boats to find and successfully attack merchant shipping. Between late June and early August, the submarines had sighted only two convoys in northern waters; in all of August, they sank only 90,000 tons of shipping in all operating areas, mostly small vessels in the Gibraltar convoys. The Navy tended to blame its problems on the "political" limitations imposed on operations by the Fuehrer for fear of the United States. But, despite the *Greer* incident, Hitler still refused his admirals' requests for extended operations westward, although he said that he "thoroughly approved" of Oberleutnant Fraatz's management of the *U-652* in the clash with the American destroyer.

When Admiral Raeder heard of the American escort of convoys, the news came almost "as a relief" because he felt that it would at last force Hitler's reluctant hand against the United States. As he told the Fuehrer, "There is no longer any difference between British and American ships!" But Hitler remained unwilling openly to extend the war zone, although the tendency of the U-boats was to patrol ever westward in search of their elusive prey. If it happened that U-boats accidentally attacked American ships, the Fuehrer would tolerate it, because to do otherwise would mean an end to the sea war against Britain; but he did not intend to play into the American President's hands by making belligerent pronouncements and issuing provocative orders.[6]

The President's new "shoot-on-sight" directions at last mitigated the confusion and ambiguity that had harried the Atlantic sailors for two years. A middle course, so valid and valuable in politics and diplomacy, is usually inappropriate and perilous in combat. The *Greer* should have passed on to Iceland in safety, or attacked the *U-652* immediately upon locating her. In trying to comply with existing instructions, which seemed to call for observation but not shooting unless the foe menaced shipping, Johnson and Frost might easily have lost the *Greer* to little purpose.

The Atlantic sailors heard the President's call to war and wished for the sound of a more certain trumpet and evidence of the support of a united nation. The aviation tender *Belknap*, en route from Argentia to serve the Iceland-based seaplanes, was the only ship in the U.S. Navy to keep a war diary prior to 7 December. She started it after the crew heard the President's speech on the radio; an early entry read, "United States declares war on Axis. Declaration not made in the obsolete formal exchange of diplomatic notes, but by the President's declaration of a 'shooting war' in his speech. . . ."[7]

An ensign in the *Vincennes* noted in his diary that the country should certainly enter the war, but frankly and openly, on grounds of morality and national security, not through "such a flimsy incident as that of the *Greer*. . . ."[8]

Admiral Bristol moved his flagship from Newport to Argentia, preparing to initiate escort operations. As he told one of his fliers, the Atlantic Fleet was now "playing for keeps."[9]

In a few days, the Atlantic Fleet would be at war.

21.

Buck Fever

IN AUGUST 1941, DR. BURCKHARDT selected the Norwegian scientist Hallvard Devold to head an expedition to Greenland to set up radio and weather stations; a party of twenty-seven sailed from Norway on the 29th in the 60-ton trawler *Buskoe*. However, Devold, who was not a Quisling, alerted British intelligence, and thus the Coast Guard units in Greenland were warned of visitors and began to search the east coast. Meanwhile, the trawler arrived and landed a "hunting" party in the vicinity of Franz Josef Fjord.

The Coast Guard cutters did not pick up the track of the *Buskoe* until 11 September, when two men of the native Sledge Patrol told *North Star*'s sailors of seeing a two-masted schooner flying no colors near Young Sound. The *North Star* ventured up the coast to search. Darkness and high winds made it impossible to launch the float plane for an aerial reconnaissance; then it began to snow. The cutter's CO, Lieutenant Commander Frank Meals, radioed for permission to seize the intruding ship if he found evidence of subversive action aboard, and Admiral Stark approved. At dawn, the *North Star* was able to launch her plane, and soon the pilot reported supplies strewn along a beach in Rudi Bay. Lieutenant William Hawley then led a landing party ashore and the Coast Guardsmen found food, stocks of trapping gear, and a German Minerva 415B radio, but no men.

Meanwhile, the *Buskoe* was chugging south, dropping off other trappers and agents, Devold making no attempt to conceal the movements of the ship. Then, north of Mackenzie Bay, the *Northland* encountered the trawler. The Coast Guardsmen almost let the prosaic little ship pass, but were attracted by her oversized radio rig, odd on a vessel of such ostensibly humble pursuits. The *Northland* ordered the trawler into the bay, where a boarding party investigated her. At first, the Norwegians maintained their cover story, insisting that they were on a hunting expedition and denying that they were landing men ashore, but finally they admitted dropping off two parties of "hunters" in the north.

Then the *North Star*'s men rounded up most of the northern visitors, and the *Northland* went after the landing site at Peter Bay. Commander C.C. von Paulsen, a veteran hurricane flier known as "V.P." because of his initials and his position as Iceberg Smith's second in command, ordered a landing party ashore, telling Lieutenant (JG) Leroy McCluskey the job was his: "We'll put a couple of reserves in charge. . . . We can spare them better. . . ." McCluskey easily garnered a dozen volunteers; romantic escapades were rare on the dreary Greenland Patrol.

McCluskey's dozen went ashore, nervously creeping toward a dark, quiet hunting shack. They surrounded the cabin, and then McCluskey kicked in the door and entered. There were three sleeping men inside; one of them was Jacob Bradley, a German, who was in charge of the shore stations. A new transmitter and German meteorological equipment and radio codes were discovered. Bradley admitted working for the "Gestapo" in Norway, then while heating water for coffee, tried to set fire to a list of potential station sites, but was restrained. A tenacious fellow, when taken on board the *Northland*, he tried to bribe a guard to let him escape, but the sailor told him in Coast Guard German, "Mac, du could us nicht briben. Wir are Americans." Thus, the German landing parties were broken up and their supplies and equipment captured.[1] In the clash of scientists, Iceberg Smith was one up on Paul Burckhardt.

By September, the Army at last had a brigade ready to go to Iceland; it consisted of the Tenth Infantry Regiment, 46th Field Artillery Battalion, elements of the 5th Engineers, and service and specialist troops, in all about 5,500 men. To procure even that small number produced chaos in the Fifth Infantry Division. Transfers from nineteen different units were needed to build the brigade, as but 22 percent of the drafted personnel and 82 percent of the reserve officers in the Tenth Infantry agreed to waive their legal rights and serve outside the Western Hemisphere. The President always contended that the hemispheric location of Iceland depended upon which geographer one asked, but he did not try to force his interpretation on Congress. Whenever the Army sent men to Iceland, it meant disrupting three regiments for each one sent, and the service planners grew increasingly opposed to shipping "another additional man to Iceland."[2]

The transports and cargo ships were loaded at New York, but delays in assembling the cargo and pier congestion caused by the arrival of ships at about the same time made it impossible to combat-load the vessels.* In addition, the longshoremen were lethargic; the loading time was 12½ tons per hatch per hour, a pace which the Navy deemed "intolerable" in wartime. The auxiliaries sailed northeast and, off the coast, at noon on 6 September, were met by Task Force 15, commanded by Rear Admiral William R. Munroe. The ships took station, with four-stackers *Bainbridge, Overton, Reuben James, Truxtun,* and *MacLeish* steaming 9,000 yards ahead of the main body in line abreast, 2,500 yards apart; 4,500 yards astern were the modern destroyers *Walke* and *Morris;* and 4,500 yards farther astern were three columns of ships steaming in Indian file—to port, the oiler *Cimarron* and the cargo ships *Tarazed, Alhena,* and *Hamul;* in the middle, the battleship *Idaho* followed by the heavy cruisers *Tuscaloosa* and *Vincennes;* and to starboard, the transports *W.P. Biddle, Heywood, Harry Lee,* and *Republic,* and the repair ship *Delta.* Modern destroyers *Winslow, Anderson, Mustin,* and *O'Brien* protected the port flank, and *Sampson, Benson, Hilary P. Jones,* and *Niblack* the starboard. Planes from Argentia provided air cover in good weather on the 8th and 9th.

At first, the weather was cold and clear, the seas calm. The lookouts were a little jittery and, on the morning of the 8th, the *Walke* and *Morris* searched in the vicinity of a sighting report and dropped two depth charges, but never picked up a contact. On the 9th, the *Idaho* and *Vincennes* fueled several of the destroyers, a precaution against the possibility of a long passage caused by bad weather or

---

*Loading cargo in inverse order of need, so that items likely to be required first ashore are loaded last in accessible spaces and are thus easiest to hand.

battle action. The sailors exchanged variations of a hot rumor stating that there were about twenty-five U-boats prowling between New-foundland and Iceland; the pessimistic scuttlebutt at least helped keep men alert.

The 10th was cold, damp, and foggy; the ships reduced speed from 11 knots to 8, and most of them trailed position buoys astern for other vessels to guide on, but many of the buoys were submerged by choppy seas. The *Vincennes* ran a scant 150 yards behind the *Tusca-loosa* in order to maintain visual contact. The next afternoon, the five old destroyers out ahead got a workout. At the far left of the scouting line, the *Bainbridge* made two attacks on a firm sonar contact, releasing ten depth charges; the *Winslow* and *Overton* joined the hunt, and the *Overton* quickly picked up the contact and dropped five depth charges. But the destroyers searched the area for over an hour and found nothing. The four-stackers resumed station, while the *Winslow* remained behind until dark to keep the U-boat—if the contact was a U-boat, which was unlikely—from surfacing and lo-cating the convoy again. The destroyermen were already growing conversant with the peculiar frustrations of antisubmarine warfare: "Seldom is there anything conclusive about a depth charge attack. . . . It is exasperating to fight something you cannot see. The satis-faction of victory is denied to the victor."

The next day, the 12th, fog hung over the water, thick and musty. The *Truxtun*, *MacLeish*, and *Sampson* hit a contact ahead and to starboard with more than a dozen depth charges in less than an hour, but had nothing to show for their efforts. This contact might well have been a U-boat, but the Americans lacked the experience and tenacity to find it. On the morning of the 14th, violence again flared along the starboard flank, as the *Truxtun* then *Benson* and *Hilary P. Jones* attacked two contacts with a dozen depth charges, but the rest of the day was quieter.

Shortly after 1900, the *Truxtun*, her men at evening battle stations, passed out into an open valley in the billowing hills of gray; 300 yards ahead, the fog swirled up over the green water. The ships were at 58° north, 25° west, a day's steaming southwest of Reykjavik. In the destroyer, her Exec, Lieutenant Commander G.W. Pressey, was at the secondary conning station aft when the young quartermaster striker next to him said calmly, "Mr. Pressey, what's that over there?" The officer swung his glasses ahead and to starboard, but he did not need them; for 300 yards away, a black-gray cigar-shaped object slid out from beneath the fog. It was a U-boat.

The men in the *Truxtun* and the men in the U-boat were equally stunned; they stared incredulously at each other's vessel, not thinking to act. But the Germans were more experienced men, and so they reacted first. The submarine, inside the destroyer's turning circle, began to crash dive. At last the destroyermen thought to open fire, but feared to do so lest they hit *MacLeish*, somewhere in the fog off the starboard beam. Very close—the destroyermen said only fifty yards away—the U-boat angled down into the sea in a bubbly froth of white water. The *Truxtun* turned in to attack, releasing eight depth charges, but the explosions did no harm, as the U-boat, moving at high speed at a sharp angle to the direction of her dive, went deep and then lowered speed to reduce noise. A few minutes later, a sailor on *Truxtun*'s after deckhouse reported that the submarine was surfacing, but he was seeing either shadows of first light on the water or the blur of the approaching *MacLeish*. The *MacLeish* promptly fired four rounds of star shell, illuminating a little of the darkling sea in pale light, but nothing could be seen on the shiny dark rollers. Then *Truxtun* picked up a firm echo and attacked with a too-small pattern of five depth charges, but to no avail. The *Sampson* steamed up to help, and the destroyers grimly searched the area, pinging and listening in the chill, shadowy dark. The *Sampson* and *Truxtun* made fresh attacks, and the search continued. Finally, at about 2100, the destroyers abandoned the hunt and steamed to rejoin their stations in the escort screen, conscious of a grand opportunity missed due to a "touch of buck fever."[3]

Later, when Admiral King received the *Truxtun*'s report of the surfaced U-boat, he wrote in pencil in the margin: "What a sight!!!" And Admiral Stark wrote a friend about Task Force 15, "We should have gotten at least one SS, which was attacked under favorable circumstances."[4]

Late on the night of the 15th, after a last uneventful day at sea, the ships sighted blurred harbor lights glowing in the far distant blackness. Early the next morning they reached Iceland, the auxiliaries lying off Reykjavik, the warships passing up the high, craggy coast en route to Hvalfjördhur. The journey of Task Force 15 was over.[5]

In addition to the Army troops, the ships in the convoy carried 15,800 tons of general cargo and about 25,000 tons of arms and equipment for the soldiers, including 641 trucks and vehicles. The *Hamul* and *Alhena* were unloaded at the docks in the inner harbor first; the other ships were moored in the outer harbor, and supplies and equipment were loaded into drifters and an American merchant freighter, the *Norwalk*, and ferried ashore. Troops were ferried to the docks in boats and tank lighters because the seas were so rough that only the vehicles could be unloaded directly onto Balbos Beach from the small craft. Holding ground in the harbor was poor, complicating the task of unloading, and the newly purchased *Republic* encountered stability problems which her cautious CO was reluctant to attempt to alleviate by taking in salt water as ballast. The *Norwalk* gave endless troubles, her master refusing to take cargo in a southwest swell and the crew refusing to work beyond eight hours a day without assurances of overtime pay, which the naval authorities lacked the power to grant.

Unloading operations were sorely hampered by limited dock space and facilities, lack of trucks and tank lighters, rain, rough seas, and the Army's disinclination to assign soldiers to the work. There were also errors of haste and inexperience. The cargo ships carrying the Army trucks should have been unloaded first so that they could be used to help clear the dock area of the clutter of stores and gear, but they were not. Perishable material was not always unloaded first; material loaded at Brooklyn in order of convenience, instead of in order of priority in Iceland, caused much rummaging amidst and shifting of cargo in order to get at items needed first, causing frequent delays. Tarpaulins were often inaccessible, with the result that rain-soaked cardboard packing cases collapsed, adding to the delay and clutter, and labels were washed off canned goods, a serious problem for Army cooks. The roads from the shore to the camps and supply dumps were churned into mud by the heavy traffic and rain, prolonging trips. Most of the material was gotten ashore in ten days, an intolerably slow pace in a port vulnerable to German air attack. The Marines, more experienced in seaborne operations, regarded the Army's performance as amateurish. Clearly, the most significant lesson of Indigo III was the need to combat-load cargoes destined for a war zone, but it was one sometimes forgotten or ignored in the early operations of World War II.[6]

The Tenth Infantry became the American garrison's strategic reserve, and the Marines were placed under Major General John Bonesteel, the Army commander. Bonesteel was a worrier. He felt that

60,000 men were needed to properly defend the island's long miles of exposed coastline; yet, on account of bad weather and limited facilities, Reykjavik Harbor could not accommodate supplies for much more than half that figure, a size the Anglo-American garrison had now reached. Intelligence reports indicating that the Germans were "capable of delivering an attack . . . either from the sea or from the air" nourished Bonesteel's fears.

With General Marshall and his planners adamantly opposed to sending more troops to the island and Admiral King pleading with Admiral Stark for the early return of the First Marine Brigade to augment the Atlantic Fleet's amphibious capability, the President would be unable to make good on his hope of relieving a significant number of British troops for duty elsewhere. Indeed, the Army was in little hurry to relieve the few Marines, much less the large British garrison, so the status quo prevailed on Iceland. The Marines remained and so did the British, who were able to remove only about 1,000 of their men.

The Marines and soldiers did not make boon companions, although their working relations were sound enough. The Marines considered General Marston an abler officer than General Bonesteel and thought he should have been left in charge of the American ground troops on the island. Worse, in an arrangement unique in all of World War II, the Army commander was accorded administrative as well as operational control over the Marine units (e.g., he was in a position to tell them not only what to do, but also how to do it, technically usurping indigenous Marine command arrangements). The Marines were bitter, but Admiral Stark did not want to jeopardize his fine rapport with General Marshall by bickering over so petty an issue and thus did not press the contention of the Marines in high places.

Having labored on Army accommodations and living in field conditions, without such amenities as sheets and pillows, the Marines looked askance at the affluent Army's creature comforts. When the soldiers came ashore, 3rd Battalion, Sixth Marines, was moved out of its pasture land to a stretch of dank swampland in the path of frigid winds howling down out of the mountains, and the outfit had to "button up" for the winter almost immediately.

General Bonesteel wanted entire tactical units used as working parties, while the Marines wanted to assign individuals to the tasks so that at least portions of units would be able to get in some training. The Marines felt that the Army's command system resulted in a proliferation of superfluous paperwork; as General Marston said, "The barrage of force orders coming out of staff sections is appalling." Behind the interservice woes was a conflict of psychologies; Marine psychology was combat-oriented, while Army psychology seemed garrison-oriented, as, for example, when the Army ordered a stop to the staggered layout of the Nissen huts to improve neatness and convenience at the expense of air defense needs. Doubtless, the cause of some of the Marine griping was the frustration of haughty troops given menial duty in a remote, insignificant place.

In the anchorage at Hvalfjördhur, tired sailors found little rest. The holding ground was poor, the ships sometimes dragged anchor in high winds and rising seas, and it required hard work to keep ships from grounding or smashing into one another.

Ashore, an oil tank farm, fleet air base, and sundry offices and quarters were in process of construction. Operational attrition soon reduced the 33rd Pursuit Squadron to twenty P-40s. The airfield was inadequate as to size and strength and was poorly located on a barren, "boulder-strewn field." Late in the year, the Americans secured permission to construct a new field at Keflavik strong enough to take heavy, long-range bombers needed eventually to replace the PBYs grimly hanging on at Skerjafjordhur.

Iceland's economy was prospering from the purchases of the troops and favorable trade agreements with the United States. But the prosperity made many, especially among the young, look with disfavor upon the austerity of the past and emboldened them to reject old traditions, with consequent changes in thought and demeanor. Others, especially teachers and clergymen, felt that modernity and change menaced Icelandic culture and resented the most patent symbol of change and instability, the foreign troops. Hence, relations between the troops and civilian population were virtually nonexistent.[7]

The sailors of Task Force 15 were not sad to receive orders to make ready for sea; the warships steamed down from Valley Forge on 25 September, were joined by the unloaded auxiliaries, and headed westward. The seas were running high, which diminished the danger from U-boats, but the destroyers, particularly the four-stackers, took a severe pounding in exchange. On the 28th, Admiral Munroe ordered speed reduced to 6 knots to ease the strain on the destroyers. The sailors splashed and slipped on wet decks, and got knocked down by sudden blasts of icy water; while sleeping, men tried to cling to bunk stanchions to avoid being thrown to the deck and injured, as sometimes happened. And some recalled the ancient couplets of the litany of the four-stackers:

> Pitch, pitch, goddamn your soul.
> The more you pitch the less you roll.
> Roll, roll, you mean old bitch.
> The more you roll the less you pitch.

But the wind and rain and squalls of snow cost no man his life, and no depth charges had to be dropped on the long voyage home of Task Force 15.[8]

In mid-September, Admiral Stark wrote the President:

> I have felt for some time . . . that our sweeps into the Central Atlantic from Bermuda have so far accomplished no tangible results. Our sore spirits are either well to the northward or well to the southward. . . .
> The gunnery training I have very much on my mind. I have talked to the British and they realize they are suffering from a lack of gunnery, particularly in contrast to the Germans who get trained right up to the hilt and then come out and attack. I feel we must, wherever we can, allocate more time to gunnery. . . . Whatever we do I am anxious that our first real shooting contact with the enemy be successful. Particularly would I like to get the *Tirpitz*, if opportunity comes our way. Early victory would breed confidence and be a wonderful stimulant.[9]

It was feared that the Germans might respond to the augmented American role in the Battle of the Atlantic by sending heavy warships into the western Atlantic. If the *Tirpitz* appeared, Admiral LeBreton hoped to strike the German battleship from the air before closing with his surface ships.

Thus, in late September, the carriers were brought north from Bermuda, and on 23 September, the *Wasp*, joined by the battleship *Mississippi*, heavy cruiser *Wichita*, and repair ship *Vulcan* and screened by the modern destroyers *Monssen*, *Meredith*, *Gwin*, and *Grayson*, steamed northeast from Newfoundland, bound for Hvalfjördhur. On the 26th, in the waters southwest of Iceland, a U-boat sighted several of the warships, but did not get close enough to see the *Wasp*, which was just as well. The high-speed task force was too fast for the submarines and reached Iceland safely on the 28th.[10]

From Valley Forge, the heavy warships—called the White Patrol—made sweeps in Denmark Strait. The weather was often foggy and the seas high. On a routine patrol in September, the *Vincennes* lost her escorting destroyer in the fog. Men were seasick as the waves rose to thirty feet and the lurching cruiser sustained superficial damage; one sailor suffered a broken leg when knocked against a deck railing by a blast of seawater; chairs, dishes, and food were frequently thrown about the wardroom. The ship passed huge icebergs, one about "201 feet high and 789 feet long," and a sailor noted that the Northern Lights were "very beautiful. . . . Arctic Premier rather than Hollywood." One dark winter morning, a British Wellington bomber dropped red, yellow, and white flares near the *Idaho,* and the battleship quickly fired an identification flare of her own; but the plane kept circling overhead, so the *Idaho* and her three destroyers kept zigzagging, anticipating an attack, until finally the inquisitive Wellington flew away. But the best right to be afraid belonged to the destroyermen whose little ships sometimes patrolled alone in the Strait. It was an eerie, lonely feeling, steaming through the fog, hoping not to encounter the *Tirpitz;* the seas that made life uncomfortable in the big ships, thrashed the four-stackers unmercifully. Once, when the German pocket battleship *Admiral Scheer* was believed to be at sea, SOPA Iceland put the first team, the *Idaho, Mississippi, Tuscaloosa, Wichita,* and three new destroyers, into Denmark Strait, while a British task force including the battleship *King George V,* the carrier *Victorious,* five cruisers, and nine destroyers steamed between Iceland and the United Kingdom; but no battle developed. The White Patrol was routine duty; but it was not easy duty.[11]

The *Wasp* could not remain in Iceland waters long, cooped up at Hvalfjördhur unable to conduct flight operations at sea because of the submarine danger. So, as the Germans showed no sign of responding to America's augmented role in the Battle of the Atlantic by forcing Denmark Strait with their remaining heavy ships, it was decided to send the carrier back to safer waters after only a week in Iceland. On October 6th, she, the *Vincennes,* and four new destroyers left for Newfoundland. The seas were high, and the cruiser took green water forward almost continuously. Once, a deep, sliding roll brought heavy blasts of water onto the deck of the "Vinnie Maru," striking "the fire party, and there was quite a mix-up of men, buckets, fire extinguishers, etc., washing back and forth. . . . Luckily no one was injured or lost overboard. One roll was so great that lifeboat No. 2 rested in water. . . . Few subs have been reported in this area. We must have done a pretty good job in cleaning them out. No

The USS *Mississippi* smothered in high seas in the North Atlantic

wreckage was sighted today." On the 9th, the skies cleared temporarily, although a vigorous swell continued to jostle the ships. Nevertheless, the *Wasp* conducted flight operations. Twenty-seven planes flew off the carrier's dipping deck. When they returned, the weather had worsened, and the *Wasp* was pitching about fifteen degrees. One by one, the stubby planes rumbled low out of the gray sky, feeling for the rising, slatted deck. They all landed safely, causing one sailor to observe, "The aviators certainly earned their flight pay today." The ships moored safely at Argentia on the 11th, but the crews grumbled; the men got little relaxation, for Argentia was a poor liberty port, bleak and far from a major city. It did not matter this time, because there was no liberty anyway on account of rain and high seas.[12]

And so, in port, the lack of peacetime amenities grated on the crews. A cruiser officer noted:

> The crew is very restless, as most of them have had no liberty at all since leaving Portland forty days ago. Chances of getting back to the States are pretty bleak. . . . There is certainly very little other than intense dislike of our entering the war for John Bull and Stalin. . . . I seem to be the only officer . . . who actually wants to fight for any reason. . . . The English battlewagons sit in safe harbors until there is definite work to be done. Ours cruise all over sub-infested areas trying to make another "Remember the Maine" slogan. So far our destroyers have been successful in either forcing subs to stay on the bottom . . . or in damaging them . . . we should put some of our own ships in the yard and install radars. . . .[13]

At Hvalfjördhur, the *Belknap* was forced to shift her berth frequently to accommodate incoming destroyers, and her war diary pouted: "It seems that the only berths available for assignment to escort vessels were the ones successively occupied by the *Belknap*."[14]

But at sea, where men could draw meaning from their efforts, optimism came more readily. As a *Vincennes* officer said: "It was rather peculiar this trip up that we saw no debris, after seeing so much the last trip. Maybe our patrol of these waters is making a great change."[15]

Meanwhile, with the decision to escort made, Admiral Bristol's staff began to work out the escort cycles. They calculated that at a speed of 10 knots—a somewhat optimistic assessment even for the "fast" Halifax convoys escorted b, the Americans—a convoy required seven days to steam from Cape Race to Reykjavik (in practice, the trip took a little longer due to lower speeds and bad weather). Allowing two days in Iceland to refuel, this made for a round trip of sixteen days, with some leeway needed in case of layovers at Argentia. Hence, a twenty-day cycle was devised for the American escort groups. Support Force hoped to have fifty destroyers, divided into ten escort groups, but settled for one-third less; the convoys sailed every six days. An admiral on the British Naval Staff in Washington, reported that the U-boats were now working as far west as 45° west and recommended a utopian ten to twelve escorts per convoy, as opposed to the five mandated by Support Force's limited strength. When Captain Oscar Badger, of Admiral Bristol's staff, suggested that additional destroyers be allotted to Support Force, Admiral King tersely noted on his report, "Where get them?" Admiral Bristol's destroyers were lacking in teamwork as well as in numbers, for in order to insure a blend of new and old ships in each escort group,* divisions and squadrons had to be split up to form the groups, which thus lacked continuity of training and doctrine.

The convoy system itself was a difficult balance between safety and efficient use of shipping. A fast ship sailing in convoy was limited to the speed of the slowest convoy vessel and tied to the track of the convoy instead of being able to follow a more direct route. Thus the time spent in dangerous waters was increased. But the greatest liability of the convoy system was that it was wasteful of shipping; in addition to extra time en route, time in port was increased while waiting for all ships to assemble, and port congestion was intensified by the loading and unloading of many ships at the same time. Freighters steaming independently had 10 percent lower turnaround time than freighters steaming in convoy, and tankers sailing alone had a 25 percent lower turn-around time than tankers sailing in convoy.

But convoy ships could be protected by escort vessels; ships sailing individually could not. Convoys could be intelligently controlled, routed to avoid known or suspected submarine patrol areas, based on the latest HF/DF radio intercepts of U-boat transmissions. Countless individual ships could scarcely be so managed. While some people felt that convoys were easier for U-boats to locate,

---

*So that no group should be without modern destroyers, whose larger fuel capacity in comparison to the four-stackers allowed them to remain with their convoy even in case of a protracted voyage and permitted them to patrol more aggressively.

statistics proved that there was a greater chance of submarines sighting some of many ships sailing dispersed than any ships of a compact convoy. By the end of 1940, 1,183 vessels of 4,545,000 tons had been lost while sailing independently, whereas only 687 ships of 2,937,000 tons had been lost while sailing in convoy, and it was estimated that 50 percent of the convoy vessels lost were stragglers.

Furthermore, since technology had not yet made air-sea, hunter-killer groups effective ASW instruments, escort of convoys was the best method of locating U-boats. The convoy system thus possessed an offensive and defensive value that more than offset its less efficient utilization of shipping.

The Americans derived some benefit from British experience. It was noted that kapok life jackets were too heavy and bulky to be worn as often as necessary, that masts on American warships needed to be cut down to allow AA weapons a better field of fire, and that skippers could expect scant air cover in the North Atlantic. Destroyermen were warned of the major eccentricities of the merchant convoys, straggling and poor station-keeping, breakdowns, excessive smoke, deficient signalling, showing lights at night, and masters overstating speeds in order to be assigned to a faster convoy. The Americans gleaned that escort operations in the North Atlantic were physically demanding because of stormy weather and emotionally enervating because of the need for constant vigilance in a tedious enterprise and the strain of making rapid decisions involving the fates of men and ships on the basis of incomplete information. The stress sometimes induced chronic fatigue and irritability which had to be treated by rest, lest it lead to nervous collapse. The British sought to lessen routine shipboard duties in order to allow crews more time to unwind; their ships became less "smart" but more comfortable to serve in.

In their main business, that of learning to detect and kill submarines, the Americans profited little from the experience of the British: this was partly the result of the sin of false pride—a misplaced confidence in the U.S. Navy's prowess in antisubmarine warfare—but mostly of the nature of the work, which demanded experience. They failed to grasp the ominous impact of the German night surface tactics or to eliminate typical beginner's tactical errors by paying careful attention to British procedure. However, second-hand experience and theoretical training, while helpful, tended to be of limited usefulness, for so much in ASW depended on the sensitivity of a few key men, their ability to "feel" developing circumstances. There was no way to "teach" a sonar man to distinguish between the echoes returned by a large fish and those returned by a submarine in the turbulent waters of the North Atlantic. It was difficult to tutor a conning officer to anticipate the evasive tactics of an unseen target in a variety of circumstances. And the task was inherently difficult; a 45-ship convoy presented a perimeter of more than thirty miles, while each escort ship's sonar swept an arc of a few hundred yards.

One made many trips in a destroyer, heard countless return echoes, was duped in several attack runs by crafty, veteran German submariners, saw ships burn and men die because of gaps in the escort screen, and, eventually, acquired the requisite "feel" for the art. There were shortcuts—it was possible to overcome inexperience and lack of numbers with technology, especially radar, and modern weapons, especially long-range bombers and escort-carrier aircraft able to operate in the "black pit" of mid-ocean; but both were lacking in the fall of 1941; and thus Support Force went to war bereft of the ingredients of success.

The Americans hoped to begin escort operations about 20 August, but difficulty in accumulating a backlog of American and Icelandic shipping to ensure their availability for each convoy and the President's lingering prudence delayed the undertaking for nearly a month. Mr. Roosevelt wanted to be able to cling to the dubious technicality that Support Force was not escorting British convoys as such, but was merely escorting American and Icelandic vessels which British shipping joined for mutual convenience. Not until 10 September did Admiral King send out the order to Support Force to commence escort of the Halifax convoys.[16]

On 10 August, to test the escort system, the modern destroyers *Plunkett* and *Mayo* left Argentia to escort the Icelandic steamer *Lagerfoss* to Iceland, but a thick, gray mist settled down over the ocean, and they could not find the cargo ship at the rendezvous. For three days, they searched in the fog along her projected course, but did not sight the *Lagerfoss*. Then they proceeded to Iceland alone. However, on the 19th, six hours out of Reykjavik, the destroyers encountered the wayward steamer; the Icelandic skipper explained that he had not missed the rendezvous in the fog, but simply preferred to follow his own course to Reykjavik!

But the furious escort commander, Captain J.L. "Reggie" Kauffman, was destined to suffer even more on his return trip with the freighter *Selfoss*. The Icelandic ship could make only 8 knots, so the destroyers had to steam back and forth in steady penance in order to maintain station; the *Selfoss*, carrying a small cargo, was a less desirable target than the destroyers. Later, rollers jolted two depth charges off the *Mayo*'s stern racks, and there were two loud explosions astern; fortunately, the destroyer escaped damage, and no one was hurt. In his report, Captain Kauffman recommended severe penalties for merchant skippers who disobeyed convoy instructions, and urged the necessity of employing larger, faster merchant vessels on the Iceland run. It was the need to find numbers of such ships that led to the temporary postponement of American escort operations in August.[17] All in all, Captain Kauffman's trip suggested the show-business hope that a poor rehearsal meant a successful opening performance.

Meanwhile, Support Force destroyers were escorting small groups of American and Icelandic ships carrying supplies to Iceland but not suited, because of timing or low speed, for the big Indigo convoys. In August, two four-stackers escorted one U.S. and one Icelandic cargo ship to Reykjavik; then four four-stackers took three American freighters to Iceland without incident. In early September, four destroyers escorted two American merchant ships to Iceland and, en route, the destroyer *Lansdale*, after a fruitless run of 200 miles in search of a torpedoed ship, rescued three survivors from the SS *Sessa*, a U.S. vessel of Panamanian registry that had been sunk on 17 August while carrying construction material to Iceland.[18]

On 11 September, off Newfoundland, the modern destroyers *McDougal* and *Moffett* and the four-stackers *McCormick* and *Tarbell* met three American freighters, the *City of Dallas*, *Roanoke*, and *Thomas H. Wheeler*, to begin a more eventful passage. Two days later, at 56° north, 44° west, the *McDougal* and *Tarbell* picked up a sonar contact ahead and to port. The *Tarbell* closed, lost contact at about 400 yards, but released four depth charges as a deterrent to an attack on the lead freighter. She quickly regained the contact and attacked again, but began releasing her depth charges too soon in the attack run and her pattern of a dozen depth charges achieved no results. Later, the *Tarbell* again picked up a sharp contact ahead and to port of the small convoy. She swung after the contact, but the submarine was inside her turning circle, and *Tarbell*'s attack could not succeed. She dropped seven depth charges, but the starboard rack jammed and two charges rolled off together, wasting one; it made no difference, for the depth charges were dropped well behind and to one side of the target.

On the 14th, the *McDougal* suffered dual tribulation. At 0826, her sonar man picked up a good metallic contact, then heard propeller noises off the starboard bow. The destroyer attacked prematurely because the lead freighter was near the area of the contact; largely as a deterrent, she released five depth charges, set at only 100 feet for fear of damaging the freighter. The "attack" was utterly futile. Then one of the *McDougal's* sailors, Chief Watertender Pinkney F. Cox, became seriously ill and required an emergency appendectomy, but the destroyer had on board only a pharmacist's mate. The Navy was short of medical officers; Support Force had only one doctor per escort group, and the one in this group was in the *Tarbell*. Cox could not be transferred to the four-stacker until 2140 because of the risk of submarine attack. The medical officer performed the operation on the *Tarbell's* wardroom table, completing the surgery at 0240 on the 15th. Such occurrences indicated the need for a medical officer on every escort, a necessity reinforced by the prospect of having to care for the burned, torn, or stunned survivors of torpedoed ships as wartime operations expanded in scope and intensity.

On the 15th, there were several attacks on brief contacts, and the next day, as the seas rose and the ships began to roll wildly, the cargo in the *City of Dallas* began to shift, forcing her to reduce speed; the *Tarbell* was detached to guard her. Meanwhile, a *McDougal* sailor reported a U-boat on the surface, 800 yards to starboard; but this proved a morning shadow on the sea. The destroyer investigated and picked up a sonar contact which was probably on her own wake, then dropped four depth charges set at shallow settings.

The remainder of the passage was uneventful, and the little convoy and its callow escorts reached Iceland safely on the 18th.[19]

In the meantime, on 9 September, one of the slow, Canadian-escorted Sydney (Nova Scotia) convoys, SC 42, had been discovered and attacked by a pack of eight U-boats, ravenous after the starving time of summer. The battle lasted for days, a moving red glow against sea and sky; sixteen merchant vessels were sunk, but the strengthened escort managed to kill two U-boats. At the President's direction, three American destroyers were sent southwest from Hvalfjördhur on the 13th to do what they could, but the fight was over when they reached the convoy. On the 15th, while waiting to begin

the cycle of American-escorted westbound convoys, the *Gleaves,
Madison, Lansdale,* and *Charles F. Hughes* went out on a sweep to
the southwest. The *Gleaves* attacked a contact on the 19th, but it
may have been false. The sweep was uneventful. On the 20th, the
Winslow, Overton, Truxtun, Bainbridge, and *Reuben James* went out
to scout and patrol in the vicinity of another Sydney convoy, SC 44,
which had lost five ships to submarines, but they did not run into any
U-boats.[20]

And on 22 September, Admiral Stark noted in a letter to a colleague:

> So far as the Atlantic is concerned, we are all but, if not actually, in it.
> . . . the British. . . . forces are thinly spread. . . . If Britain is to continue,
> she has to have assistance. She will now get it openly. King's forces, too,
> are thinly spread. . . . we are now escorting convoys. . . . This will be a
> boon for the British. . . . contacts are almost certain to occur. The rest
> requires little imagination.[21]

In the contacts and brief fights of September, the Atlantic Fleet
displayed the normal buck fever of first combat. There were missed
opportunities and amateurish mistakes, the *Truxtun*'s being the
worst of them. In general, attacks were too brief, due to the most
part to a laudable but misguided desire to rejoin the protective screen
and assure the convoy maximum close-in security. Yet Task Force 15
had been protected by an escort of fifteen destroyers, and the small
mid-September convoy of three freighters had been escorted by four
destroyers. If attacks were not pressed tenaciously under such
favorable circumstances, how might there be the necessary vigor
when five destroyers were charged with the defense of forty to sixty
slow merchant vessels spread out over many miles of ocean?
American escorts patrolled too close to their convoy, depriving
themselves of room to maneuver in striking at approaching U-boats
and permitting the U-boats to close to easy torpedo range. Indeed,
the *McDougal* and *Tarbell* were prevented from carrying out useful
attacks on likely contacts by the proximity of convoy vessels. Attack
tactics reflected the normal woes of inexperience: the use of futile
"embarrassing" or deterrent patterns of depth charges; the tendency
to drop depth charges too soon in the attack run, to set them too
shallow or too deep, and to use them too prodigally on weak
contacts and too niggardly on strong contacts; and the inability to
anticipate the quick, darting, evasive maneuvers of the U-boats.
Lack of numbers and of teamwork required doctrine to be defen-

sive.[22] The Atlantic Fleet needed time. But there was no more time. The Atlantic Fleet would have to fight while still learning how to fight.

At the edge of war, the Atlantic Fleet was both ready and unready; it was a weapon of much potential and limited experience. Much would depend upon how quickly it learned at war what it lacked time and foresight to learn in peace. Its crews were green; Admiral Stark worried most over its lack of gunnery training and practice against "live" submarines; its ships were deficient in some aspects of modern technology and weaponry, especially radar and modern AA guns. Its men were asked to bear the hardships of war on behalf of a nation still at peace; they were summoned to battle without the impulse of stirring events and brave slogans, as a matter of strategic necessity and professional duty; they did not resent the battle, but they sometimes felt that they were alone in it, and their eyes would automatically scan their convoys for the rare flag of their own country, seeking evidence of the support and empathy of a united people. Until their countrymen gave them a better cause, the Atlantic sailors had to fight out of duty and pride and for each other, for their nation sent them off to war without a battle cry.

Nevertheless, the Fleet had strength and character. The growing arduousness of its operations toughened it. As Admiral King well and truly said, "there have been those who found the going hard and the deprivation of certain privileges incident to operations under war conditions distasteful. These conditions have facilitated the weeding out of men of weak stamina and in the long run will prove beneficial . . . . " Despite increasing intensity of operations, it was found possible to reduce by about 40 percent regular overhaul and upkeep periods of Atlantic ships; the challenge of active operations in the war zone provided a sense of accomplishment not offered by routine training. The men, products of a victorious naval tradition, were cocky and confident; morale was high: sometimes this led to complacency and diminished the Fleet's ability to learn quickly, but it also fostered a stubborn indomitability in adversity. The Atlantic sailors were willing, steady, and tough; they did not doubt or quit.[23]

And so the Atlantic Fleet, lacking knowledge of battle, ample weaponry, and dynamism in its older leaders, but endowed with a tough hide and strong heart, went to war. It needed time. But there was no more time. And so the Atlantic Fleet went to war in September of 1941.

IV:
War

22.

Admiral Bristol
Runs the Milk

BETWEEN MID-SEPTEMBER AND THE END OF OCTOBER, Support Force destroyers brought fourteen convoys across the North Atlantic, escorting approximately 675 ships. HX 150 was first.

The fifty vessels of Convoy HX 150 sailed from Halifax on the 16th with a Canadian local escort led by HMCS *Annapolis*. The merchant ships ranged in size from a 1,500-ton freighter to a 17,000-ton liner; they carried steel, grain, petroleum products, and general cargo. Many were veterans of two years of hard service in the Atlantic, weary and infirm. During the passage, twelve ships had mechanical defects and were forced to drop out and return to port. On the 17th, 150 miles south of Argentia, the convoy was met by two modern destroyers and three four-stackers of the U.S. Navy. As the lead destroyer, the *Ericsson*, approached, the sailors of the *Annapolis* crowded the rails of their four-stacker and cheered.

Briskly, the *Ericsson* took station in the van, 1,500-2,000 yards ahead of the center of nine columns of merchant ships. The *Upshur* steamed to the port bow of the convoy and the *Dallas* took station off the port quarter; the *Ellis* and *Eberle* screened the starboard bow and quarter. Captain Morton L. Deyo assumed command of the convoy from the Canadians. His instructions, reflecting Support Force's caution in its new enterprise, urged that the first duty of his destroyers was to offer direct protection to the convoy and that they should not normally pursue a submarine contact for more than an hour. As the Canadian ships departed, the U.S. destroyers and polyglot merchant vessels steamed northeast through the choppy water, the merchantmen making a steady 9¼ knots.

At first, the Americans found it hard to accept the fact that they were at last at war; war seemed too dramatic and thunderous a concept to relate to so humble a host of vessels and so prosaic an undertaking. Officers kept prodding watchstanders to stay alert, reminding them that lives were now at stake. But the nonchalance was soon replaced by an exaggerated awe, a run of buck fever. In loading drills, gun crews tried to work too quickly and jammed guns; lookouts saw menacing shapes on the water and sonar men called out specious contacts.

HX 150 soon ran into foggy and rainy weather. Two PBYs intermittently patrolled over the ships until the convoy passed beyond 400 miles from Argentia. Every night before dark, the *Dallas* and *Eberle* roamed out five miles on each flank to make certain that no U-boats were trailing the ships. On the 19th, the vessels were diverted to a course that would take them south and east of Admiral Doenitz's clusters of U-boats between Greenland and Iceland, helping HX 150 to avoid the fate of SC 44. As the seas rose, water turbulence and the rolling of the escorts made the sonar gear unreliable. For a short time on the 20th, the *Ericsson* chased a phantom conning tower and attacked several dubious contacts; the next day, the *Eberle* dropped three depth charges near another doubtful contact. Then the first combat jitters subsided, and the destroyermen began to "steady down and become more businesslike." They worked more smoothly and there were no more false contacts. "This will teach them fast," Captain Deyo thought.

After steaming northeast to 28° west, the ships headed north into worsening weather, pounding into rolling gray crests of sea. The *Upshur's* flagstaff was snapped off and carried away by waves pouring over her stern. The *Eberle*, being a modern destroyer, had greater range and strength than the four-stackers, so she drew most of the extra assignments, such as rounding up stragglers. On the evening of the 24th, the SS *Nigaristan* reported a fire in her bunkers. Captain Deyo was reluctant to reduce the ASW screen and send a destroyer to her aid, but decided that the protection offered by the bad weather justified the risk. So the *Eberle* was given another odd job. Lieutenant Commander E.R. Gardner took his destroyer back to search in the stormy darkness for the crippled straggler, and at 2354, *Eberle's* men sighted the red glare of the *Nigaristan*, a bright beacon for U-boats.

The *Eberle* prowled the rainy blackness for men in open boats. The rescue work took 3½ hours. Once, a merchant sailor was swept out of a lifeboat; frightened, he splashed and struggled in the water as the boat crowded in, threatening to crush him against the destroyer's sheer side. Ensign L.C. Savage went into the black water to hold off the boat and fasten a line about the thrashing sailor, who was then hauled up the side of the destroyer. The *Eberle* picked up all sixty-three men of the freighter's crew. There were other stragglers in the stormy night, all but two of which were rounded up by the destroyers after daylight.

The convoy reached the mid-ocean meeting point (Momp) at 0854 on the morning of the 25th; it was only one hour late. The warships of the British eastern ocean escort were detained by the storm and did not arrive until afternoon. Then at 1338, lookouts in the American destroyers sighted three four-stackers—HMS *Churchill, Chesterfield*, and *Broadwater*, old friends in new garb—and four corvettes approaching on green distant rollers. Soon, Captain Deyo turned over thirty-three ships to the care of the Royal Navy; his destroyers were taking two vessels on to Iceland. The convoy commodore, whose well-intentioned but verbose messages provided much practice for the American signalmen, sent a gracious last signal:

> Please accept my best congratulations in the brand of work and efficiencies of all your ships in looking after us so very well, and my very grateful thanks for all your kindly advice and help. Wish you all success with best of luck and good hunting. . . .

Captain Deyo, too, in honor of a memorable moment, sent a long farewell message.

> This being our first escort job your message is doubly appreciated. As in the last war I know our people afloat will see eye-to-eye. You have my admiration for handling such a varied assortment so effectively. . . . I hope we shall meet again. Good luck.

At 1448, the American ships started north, reaching Iceland the next day; all the vessels of HX 150, including the two stragglers, reached port safely.[1]

Thus, the U.S. Navy carried out its first escort mission with an Allied merchant convoy in World War II. It was a milk run.

As Captain Deyo said, the Atlantic Fleet would learn by doing. On the afternoon of 24 September, the *Gleaves, Charles F. Hughes, Madison, Lansdale,* and *Simpson* met ten British escorts southwest of Iceland at 60° north, 26°-30′ west and assumed responsibility for the 40 to 50 ships of westbound convoy ON 18. The westbound vessels did not carry precious cargoes, hauling mainly coal, wood pulp, whiskey, chalk, clay, and like loads, and many carried no cargo at all, steaming in ballast; but the ships themselves were vital and merited protection. Originally plotted for a northern passage, ON 18 was rerouted south all the way to 55°-30′ north, 29° west, to bring it clear of the hunting grounds of the U-boats, who were now alert to the northerly routes that had served the convoys so well during the summer. The vessels steamed placidly at 7½ knots; at 55°-30′ north, they headed diagonally southwest. The weather was overcast, but not stormy. There were no submarine contacts. After a tranquil voyage, the merchantmen were dispersed south of Argentia, east of Halifax, to proceed to their sundry destinations.[2]

On the morning of the 24th, the modern destroyers *Plunkett, Livermore,* and *Kearny* and four-stackers *Decatur* and *Greer* met the forty-four vessels of HX 151 southeast of Argentia; mechanical breakdowns had forced three of the merchantmen to return to port. Ten of the convoy ships were tankers, and the rest carried steel, grain, refrigerated goods, sulphur, sugar, molasses, and general cargo. HX 151 steamed northeast, then was routed onto a more easterly heading to swing it beyond the major U-boat concentrations to the north.

On the night of the 25th, the *Kearny*'s sonar man heard intermittent propeller noises, as if a surfaced U-boat were prowling nearby in the darkness and shutting off its engines from time to time to listen for the sounds of passing ships above the slapping, soughing noises of the sea. The destroyer sounded general quarters and dropped two depth charges in the vicinity of the sounds. The sailors, straining to see evidence of damage, noted, "the water heaved upwards from the first explosion appeared to be dark in color as compared with the second." A heavy stench of fuel oil hung on the salty sea air, but it came from the bilges of passing tankers. Several minutes later, the sound man picked up the propeller noises again, a little over a mile away, and the *Kearny* rushed through the darkness and thin wisps of fog to attack, releasing three depth charges, but to no avail.

On the night of the 28th, the *Plunkett* attacked a sonar contact out ahead with eight depth charges; this was probably a large fish. The 29th was gray and windy, and the seas began to rise. The *Kearny* and *Livermore* attacked contacts, probably water turbulence. The weather grew stormy, and the four-stackers lost oil drums swept overboard. The convoy ships became badly strung out, and the destroyers were kept busy running down stragglers. On 1 October, the *Kearny* made several attacks, probably on wakes and water turbulence; the *Decatur*, far astern protecting a straggling Norwegian tanker, used eighteen depth charges in two attacks on a firmer contact. The destroyermen were not used to the sound conditions in the North Atlantic and were experiencing a little first-performance skittishness; but they were giving their merchantmen careful protection.

On the afternoon of the 1st, the convoy met the British escort of four destroyers, three corvettes, and four trawlers a few miles northwest of the Momp at about 60° north, 24°west. Despite the bad weather, all the merchant vessels were present. The American destroyers took four of the merchant ships on to Iceland; en route, the *Decatur, Greer,* and *Kearny* briefly worked over a contact without result. On the 3rd, the ships reached Iceland. And the destroyers steamed up to Valley Forge to rest as best they could for the next trip.[3]

The fifty-one ships of ON 20 made but 6 knots as they steamed southwest, screened by the *Hilary P. Jones, Benson, Niblack, Winslow,* and the venerable *Reuben James.* The trip was slow, but calm. Then, suddenly at 0314 on 2 October, a series of star shells and gun flashes flickered in the darkness like fitful summer lightning. A Canadian-escorted convoy was reported in a fight. The *Winslow* was detached to search for a torpedoed ship, but found none. Then the convoy was diverted to a more westerly heading. The signs were ominous as well as confusing; there was a feeling all day that U-boats were near, waiting until night to strike. The *Benson* impatiently worked over a contact. A Canadian corvette joined up to reinforce the escort. A fight seemed certain, and the night of 2/3 October was a long, tense one; but also a quiet one. There were no attacks.

Low speed and the route change protracted the voyage of ON 20. The destroyers grew short of fuel and two were detached on the 8th. Finally, on the 9th, the convoy vessels were safely dispersed off Newfoundland, and the weary destroyers headed for Argentia.[4]

On the afternoon of 30 September, the *Mayo* and four-stackers *Schenck, Leary, Broome,* and *Babbitt* met HX 152 off Newfoundland; with only one modern destroyer, the escorts would be in trouble if bad weather or enemy action prolonged the voyage, exhausting the fuel of the four-stackers. The convoy was a large one, sixty ships in ten columns: the freighters carried steel and scrap, ores, copper, nitrates, grain, refrigerated goods, and general cargo; the tankers carried oil, gasoline, kerosene, and benzene. One of the vessels was the Navy tanker *Salinas,* whose men were cheered by the approach of the American warships, feeling "more at home with old friends so near." As the ships steamed northeast, a PBY from Argentia reported a submarine five miles away, but no trouble developed. The next day, the route was altered to a more direct northeasterly one, as the U-boats seemed to be reacting to the recent easterly routings.

In the next few days, an intense storm struck. The ships, bucking and rolling, were rarely visible to the escorts or to each other; the destroyers scampered after the near stragglers, trying to chivvy them back on station. Then in the first few minutes of the 8th, the convoy commodore decreed a Halifax-ordered course change to starboard to swing the vessels onto a direct route to the Momp; but he should have waited until morning. In the darkness, rain, and spray, many of the wildly bucking merchant ships missed the visual signals; the vessels on the flanks did not make the turn, and in the subsequent chaos, much of the convoy was scattered. Gale winds blew at force ten.

The *Babbitt* and *Leary,* then the *Broome* and *Schenck,* low on fuel from fighting the seas, were forced to leave for Iceland. A pale gray lightness like faded wallpaper marked the change from night to morning, and visibility cleared to about 600 yards. The *Mayo* plodded on, dipping her sodden prow into the high crests, her lookouts squinting through needles of spray to see on the ship's upward surge. Her starboard bulwark was dished in and her port bulwark ripped away; lockers were smashed, hoses and life jackets swept overboard. Sailors slipped and stumbled to their watches. On the afternoon of the 8th, the *Mayo* was ordered to Iceland, and early the next morning, the scattered remnants of the convoy were directed to disperse, as the merchantmen were too far out of position to attempt to rendezvous with the British. The Redcoats tried to round up a few of the strays, but it proved impossible. HMS *Shikari* found two ships and attempted to bring them to Iceland, but soon lost both in the storm and was badly thrashed by the wild seas, taking severe damage about her bridge. A tenacious U-boat managed to torpedo one straggler, SS *Svend Foyn*, but the crippled vessel was able to stagger to Iceland.

USS *Salinas* found herself with several British stragglers, none of whom were going to Iceland. So after exchanging "Good Luck" and "Cheerio" signals, "Old Sal" bucked and butted alone into the shrill wind and mountainous seas. All her boats were smashed and her top hamper sorely battered, but she too made it safely to Iceland.

Drenched and battered, one by one, the ships of HX 152 reached their destinations. While not an artistic success, the convoy delivered the goods.[5]

Early on the 6th, the *Ericsson, Eberle, Dallas, Ellis*, and *Upshur* escorted four U.S. merchant vessels from Iceland to join the forty-eight ships of ON 22 at about 60°-25' north, 24° west. But the British, unable to get a navigational fix for three days because of bad weather, missed the rendezvous, passing fifteen miles north of the Momp. Both American and British warships were hampered by the need to protect merchantmen, which made scouting difficult.

On the 7th, Captain Deyo's task group met the British escort of four destroyers, one corvette, and one trawler, and assumed responsibility for the vessels of ON 22. The British warships then headed for Iceland, and the American destroyers took the convoy west, then south. Soon there was a route change to the east to bring the ships clear of the scattered vessels of HX 152, and then the convoy followed a southwesterly course. The destroyers made two attacks on the 8th, probably on wakes and water turbulence. As the storm intensified, the vessels of ON 22 were also badly scattered, and only a few merchantmen were with the rolling, pitching destroyers when they reached the dispersal point south of Newfoundland on the 15th. But all fifty-two ships of the convoy reached port safely.[6]

On the morning of the 7th, the *Sampson* and four-stackers *Bernadou, DuPont, Lea*, and *MacLeish* met the fifty-nine ships of HX 153 southeast of Argentia. The merchant vessels carried steel and scrap, petroleum products, trucks, grain, refrigerated goods, and general cargo. The warships and merchantmen were destined to enjoy an easy passage, with but minor problems. The vessels steamed a

direct northeasterly course to the Momp. One merchantman encountered difficulty in maintaining the convoy speed of nearly 10
knots and fell behind frequently, but always managed to catch up
again. On the afternoon of the 10th, the *Bernadou* attacked a contact
with a dozen depth charges, raising a gusher of discolored water, but
no debris. "Bernie" had two magazines flooded with 3½ feet of
seawater because her flood valves were defective, but the spaces
were quickly pumped out. The American destroyers turned the
convoy over to seven British escorts at 1600 on the 13th at 58°-27'
north, 23° west, then took three of the ships on to Iceland.[7]

    On Columbus Day, the *Plunkett, Livermore, Kearny, Decatur,* and
Greer, with two merchantmen, were steaming south from Valley
Forge, bound for ON 24. Aboard the *Decatur,* a fireman third class,
thinking that he could not endure the fear of another run through
submarine waters or the misery of a rolling four-stacker in high seas,
attempted to kill himself by slashing his wrists. However, he inflicted
only two superficial cuts, was treated, and made fit for duty. In the
destroyers, as in riding, a man thrown was expected to remount
quickly, lest his fear become permanent.
    The next morning, the destroyers met the convoy and its escort of
two destroyers, three corvettes, and four trawlers, adding their two
vessels to the fifty-four ships of ON 24. As the Redcoats headed for
Iceland, the American destroyers started southwest with the merchant
ships. Soon the convoy turned south to avoid two eastbound convoys
before returning to its southwesterly heading. On the 14th and 15th,
the *Livermore* and *Decatur* briefly attacked dubious contacts, likely
fish or wakes. There was no tangible evidence of the enemy, and the
voyage seemed to be another milk run when, abruptly, at 2137 on
the night of the 15th, the escort commander, Captain L. Hewlett
Thebaud, received orders to disperse ON 24 and take his destroyers
to assist SC 48, a slow eastbound convoy of fully-laden ships, which
was under attack by submarines about 400 miles south of Iceland,
not far distant.
    The convoy in trouble was Canadian-escorted. The Royal Canadian
Navy lacked the stability derived from long tradition. A fiftyfold
expansion from about 2,000 men and 13 ships to eventually about
100,000 men and 400 ASW vessels diluted the professional influence;
and many of the new men were from the individualistic western

provinces. The result was an informal service, impatient of discipline, boisterous, and aggressive in combat, whose major failing was a lack of mechanical aptitude. The Americans, bred to gadgetry from the cradle, excelled at repair work, amazing even the efficient British, but neither ally could understand why the Canadian ships suffered so many breakdowns. The Canadians said it was because most of their ships were too old or too new; the Americans believed that the fault lay in poor maintenance and repair. The failing sometimes cost the hard-fighting Canadians and those they protected.

With forty-nine ships in eleven columns, convoy SC 48 sailed from Sydney, escorted by only four corvettes, because its destroyer, the four-stacker HMCS *Columbia*, was delayed by mechanical problems and bad weather. The convoy's luck was all bad, as rain and fog dispersed many vessels, including that of the commodore, and then U-boats located the ships. On the morning of the 15th, in a submerged attack, the *U-553* sank two of them. The *Columbia* joined the convoy, but that night, the *U-558* and *U-568* each sank a ship in surface attacks. Alerted by the contact reports, other U-boats were closing in, and the following morning, they sighted dark smoke and slender masts against the gray sky; the submarines began to stalk SC 48 anew.

Meanwhile, Captain Thebaud dispersed ON 24 at about 53° north, 28° west, and the five American destroyers hurried through the night toward the battle ahead.[8]

23.

Sailors off the Kearny

LATE ON THE MORNING OF THE 16TH, four of Captain Thebaud's five destroyers joined the escort of SC 48. The old *Greer*, slowed by engine trouble, arrived that night, as did the British corvette *Veronica* and four-stacker *Broadwater*, and Canadian corvettes *Lobelia* and *Pictou*. For most of the long fight ahead, the convoy was defended by a massive escort of seven destroyers and seven corvettes. However, the escorts arrived at different times and were from four different navies, so it was difficult to coordinate tactics, especially in darkness and under fire. In antisubmarine warfare, unity and aggressive tactics counted for more than numbers.

The Canadians and Captain Thebaud decided to station the *Plunkett* in the van, the *Livermore* off the starboard bow, the *Columbia* off the port bow; the *Decatur* patrolled the starboard flank, *Kearny* the port; the corvettes were posted abeam and astern in pairs. Latecomers were fitted in extemporaneously. The ships of the convoy steamed at 7-7½ knots. The escorts were grouped tightly around the merchant vessels, only 1,000 to 1,500 yards distant. American escort practice stressed close defense of the convoy to deter deadly short-range attacks and minimize straggling. It was a formation that was plausible to men who had never experienced a night surface attack by U-boats. It killed many men that night.

On the *Plunkett*'s bridge, Captain Thebaud realized that he and his men were at last truly "in the war," and he permitted himself certain sardonic reflections, imagining German diplomats in Washington and American diplomats in Berlin "going out to cocktail parties and enjoying themselves as though such a thing as the Battle of the Atlantic had never been heard of!" He had to smile as he remembered something a Canadian officer had asked him at Argentia: "Suppose you sink a U-boat and pick up survivors; will you regard them as prisoners of war or rescued seamen in distress?"

At twilight, the *Kearny* went astern and dropped depth charges, hoping to keep trailing U-boats submerged, while the convoy, after steaming a north-northeast course all day, abruptly wheeled to the east. The tense evening passed slowly; it was, as one destroyerman recalled, "as black a night as I've ever seen."

Suddenly, at 2010, a Norwegian freighter in the starboard-center area of the convoy was torpedoed and sunk by the *U-553* of Kapitän-leutnant Thurmann. Several of the merchant ships fired red flares, and the escorts shot star shells up at the black night sky. The destroyermen watched the dark shadows on the suddenly palely lit sea, but saw nothing. The *Kearny* ranged out into the fringe of darkness to port and dropped a single depth charge. Soon the merchant ships, easily frightened but quickly reassured, ceased firing and calmly plodded on. The night was still again, and more than an hour passed.

Then, at 2130, a tanker on the starboard side, the *W.C. Teagle*, was hit by a torpedo from Kapitänleutnant Gunther Krech's *U-558*. A torch of red and yellow fire, three hundred feet high, seared the night sky and was followed by spirals of black-gray smoke. Less than two minutes later, another ship in the same area "exploded with a heavy dull . . . detonation." The escorts probed the darkness with clusters of star shells and dropped random depth charges, but neither saw nor intimidated the small, gray U-boats, invisible on the black surface of the night sea. Suddenly in the red-yellow glare of fire and artificial light, the *Plunkett*'s men saw a vessel low in the water, about a mile off; the destroyer swung out her torpedo tubes, but before long, the squat outline of a corvette took shape in the glasses of the destroyermen. Nerves relaxed. Soon the escorts ceased scurrying and the merchantmen stopped firing colored flares and rockets. Meanwhile, out in the darkness, several U-boats reloaded tubes and ranged after the convoy while, astern, Krech's active boat sank a Norwegian cargo ship.

Aboard the *Kearny*, Lieutenant Commander Anthony L. Danis, a short, stocky, swarthy man, lay on the bunk in his sea cabin below

The *Kearny*'s convoy—SC 48

the bridge during a lull in the fight, listening to the hum of the ship's machinery and the subdued talk of the men on duty; a thin, blue-black stubble shined on his cheeks and chin. Danis ran a well-drilled ship and, having survived the crash of the Navy dirigible *Macon* in 1935, he was not the sort of man to take alarm at phantom fears; but he was a badly worried man this night. The escorts were too close to the convoy, and thus permitted U-boats to close unmolested to short range and fire torpedo spreads with impunity at the procession of massed merchantmen; when the escorts fired star shells for illumination, it merely blinded the lookouts and helped the submarines find targets. The destroyers should be moved out, he thought, perhaps as much as 5,000 or 6,000 yards, to hunt the U-boats. Impelled by foreboding, Danis got off his bunk and ran to the bridge, just as two more ships exploded almost simultaneously on the starboard quarter of the convoy, struck by "fish" from Kapitänleutnant Schultze's *U-432*.

Again, the baffled escorts fired illumination shells and sporadically dropped depth charges. Much of the firing was directed ahead and off the bows, favorite submarine attack positions, and the *Plunkett* was brightly lit several times by the corvettes, which did not make the men of "Charlie P" fond of their allies. In the *Kearny*, the call to general quarters rasped insistently as men once again ran to battle stations, struggling with helmets and life jackets; the sailors gripped ladders and steadied themselves against bulkheads when the destroyer again veered to port to scan the edge of darkness.

At exactly midnight, the Norwegian tanker *Barfonn* was hit by a torpedo from Schultze's boat. "A colossal flash leapt from the convoy. In a moment it resolved itself into a tremendous flame which shot upwards from the water, accompanied by a roar like the passing of an express train. The great column of fire, whose diameter might have been equal to the length of the ship from whose tanks it sprang, seemed almost to reach the cloud base. The whole convoy was lit up by its brilliance. . . ." The Canadian corvette *Baddeck* rushed astern down the port side of the convoy, hoping to fetch survivors from the cold, black water. Meanwhile, the *Kearny*, having dropped a single depth charge out in the darkness to port as a gesture of deterrence, had swung back toward the convoy to return to her patrol station. Suddenly, the blunt shape of a corvette loomed ahead. On the port wing of the bridge, Lieutenant Commander Danis saw the *Baddeck* and shouted, "All engines back full, emergency." Flashing red over green identification lights, the destroyer stopped as the Canadian corvette ran past. Danis exhaled in relief. But the *Kearny*, silhouetted against sky and sea by the orange-yellow glare of the burning tanker, was marked for death by the near-collision with the corvette bound on an errand of mercy. For Kapitänleutnant Preuss' *U-568* was approaching on the surface, a little to the southeast of the *Kearny*. The U-boat fired three torpedoes at the destroyer.

Danis was about to order speed resumed when a lookout on the starboard wing shouted a warning; Danis crossed the bridge and looked out into the night. Three white wakes, iridescent against the black sea, surged through the water toward the destroyer; Danis shouted orders, then waited.

The first German torpedo passed slightly ahead of the *Kearny*'s bow. As the ship jolted into movement, another white track ran on past her fantail. Inevitably, the middle torpedo hit, striking her starboard side, a little forward of amidships, between frames 70 and 74. There was a bump, and the destroyer shuddered as the torpedo penetrated the steel plates below the waterline. Then there was the blast of an explosion. It was 0010, 17 October 1941, seven weeks before the Japanese attack on Pearl Harbor, when the first Americans died.

There were seven men on duty in the Number One fireroom: Water Tender 1/C Luther A. Curtis; WT 1/C Herman A.C. Gajeway; WT 2/C Louis Dobnikar; Fireman 1/C George A. Calvert; F 1/C Sidney G. Larriviere; F 1/C Iral W. Stoltz; F 3/C Russell B. Wade. They were the first Americans to die in combat under their own flag in World War II.

The explosion ripped out the side of the boiler room and erupted upward, smashing lines and pipes and releasing searing gusts of live steam into the mangled enclosure, scalding living and dead; torrents of icy water poured in. The blast carried upward, rupturing the starboard side of the main deck, killing four more men; the starboard wing of the bridge was shattered, the superstructure damaged, the gun director dished in, and the forward funnel knocked back. Lights and phones were out, and the siren, jammed open by the shock of the explosion, added a shrill screeching to the pandemonium of darkness, bright red glares against black sea and sky, shouted orders, and cries of pain.

On the bridge, Shipfitter 3/C Sam Kurtz, at the depth-charge release lever on the starboard wing, was knocked to the torn plating by the blast, both legs fractured. The ship rolled and Kurtz slid toward the black water below, clawing to find a grip on the bloody grating, when Chief Yeoman Henry Leenknecht, timing his lunge with the movement of the ship, grabbed him and half-dragged, half-carried him onto the bridge. Meanwhile, Lieutenant Commander Danis, with power out and communications off, was impotent to save his ship. All he could do was to rally those nearby who were deafened or in shock from the blast. The large signal rockets were wet, but a Very pistol was found, and at 0013, the destroyer fired red distress flares. Nevertheless, the *Kearny* seemed done. She could not fight or run. She lay stopped and silhouetted by the glare of a burning ship, tons of seawater gurgling into her; but her men did what they could.

The fight to save the ship was decided in her forward engine room. Wading through seawater in the darkness, Lieutenant Robert John Esslinger, Chief Machinist's Mate Aucie McDaniel, and the rest of the black gang slammed long beams of timber into place to brace the damaged bulkhead leading to the smashed fireroom, then plugged leaks along the seams of the buckled door. The *Kearny* had a re-inforced bottom to withstand explosive shock, was highly compart-mentalized to localize flooding, and had a split engineering plant, with a separate fireroom to serve each engine room. With one boiler in Number Two fireroom already lit and the other in standby readi-ness, the destroyer was able to furnish steam for the port engine minutes after the explosion. Repair parties worked, putting out elec-trical fires, fixing ruptured fuel lines, installing emergency cables, clearing away wreckage, and shifting gear to ease the strain on the starboard side. The men knew their way about the innards of the destroyer thoroughly, and the darkness did not impede the work of damage control. Seaman 1/C Harold C. Barnard insisted on leaving his safe station topside to go below, where he ranged through the dark, isolated passageways forward, checking bulkheads and water-tight fittings. No one had to remind him what would happen to him if it became necessary to flood the forward compartments in order to stabilize the destroyer. But he wanted to do what he could. Quarter-master Johnny Booth was stationed in the black, sealed cubicle aft that housed the steering mechanisms, trying to shift control to manual steering and feeling very much alone. Then he felt a breeze overhead and looked up to see his buddy, Quartermaster Muscoe Holland, unhinging the escape hatch. Holland flung down a life jacket and promised to stand by. Johnny Booth felt better.

The *Kearny*'s men: they did what they could

And so it went. The *Kearny*'s men did not give in to the fear; they did what they could and helped and cheered each other. Pharmacist's Mate Paddock healed and jollied the wounded and hurt. Sammy Kurtz ignored his own pain and told anyone who would listen that the *Kearny* was going to make it. Lieutenant Sarsfield and Ensign Perley, Chiefs Blake and Mann, led parties of willing men to do what had to be done. In a way, the dangerous posts below the waterline were the places of least tension and strain. The men there were absorbed in the performance of physical tasks and had little time for worry. Topside, all that the nervous gunners and lookouts could do was scan the black night, endlessly watching the dark water for the shadowy loom of a U-boat or the shiny, white streaks of torpedoes, and try to keep the fear out of their voices when they spoke.

The Canadians in the *Baddeck*, disappearing into the dark with the convoy, did not understand what kept the *Kearny* afloat. Within a few minutes of being hit, the destroyer was limping forward at 3 knots. Danis took her west to keep out of the way of other escorts. By 0040, radio communication had been restored. Soon, her speed kicked up to 5 knots, and she was able to zigzag. Her chronometers and gyrocompass were out, and no one wanted to switch on a flashlight to see the magnetic compass. The ship was steered by Chief Quartermaster Harold McDougal from the secondary conning station aft. He struggled to keep the destroyer out of the trough of the swells to prevent the seas from pounding through the forward fireroom against the bulkhead shored up by the engineers. So, in order to gauge the wind and run of the sea, he watched the flag flying stiffly from the mainmast overhead. A little over an hour after the explosion, the destroyer was making 8 knots through moderate northeast swells. The wounded and injured were taken below to the cabins of the officers, the stretcher cases being lowered by block and tackle. By 0721, the *Kearny* was making 10 knots, struggling north toward Valley Forge, a long way from beat.

Meanwhile, the convoy had been suffering more during the long night. The *Plunkett* did not learn of *Kearny*'s woes until nearly 0100. She started to port to go to the *Kearny*'s aid when a tanker on the port bow of the convoy exploded into an oblong mass of red, orange, and yellow flames. The glare could be seen for fifty miles. Not finding her sister ship on station, the *Plunkett* had no time to search, but returned to the head of the convoy.

On the convoy's starboard bow, the *Livermore's* men watched grimly as a torpedo coming from the port side streaked past the fiery tanker and passed two hundred yards astern. Searching, the *Livermore* at 0130 made an attack on a sonar contact, dropping eleven depth charges. Diesel oil covered the night sea, but it was probably from the punctured tankers, for no harm came to the U-boats.

The dark was fear and chaos. Red signal rockets arched from merchant ships, whistles and sirens keened, star shells burst in the black sky, casting an eerie, sallow glow over the water, and the dull underwater thumping of depth charges sounded like muted thunder. Once, the invisible foe was glimpsed. The Canadian corvette *Pictou* spotted a U-boat zigzagging away and pursued. Not wishing to submerge and perhaps lose the convoy, the submarine fired two torpedoes from her stern tubes, but they passed ahead of the *Pictou*, which was charging hard, firing whistling 4-inch shells across the dark sky at the fleeing U-boat. The *Pictou* drove in, trying to ram, but the nimbler U-boat swung inside the corvette's turning circle and crash-dived. The *Pictou* then attacked with a pattern of depth charges, but they were released too soon and exploded behind the submerged submarine.

Finally, dawn came—and surcease. The odor of gasoline was pervasive; splintered shards of wood, bales of cotton, debris drifted on the oily water. The American destroyers, with a long way to go to Argentia, were detached; the *Greer*, low on fuel, was sent to help the *Kearny* back to Iceland. No more of the merchantmen of SC 48 were lost but two of the convoy's escorts died. The British corvette *Gladiolus*, crammed with survivors, went back to look after a straggler and disappeared, torpedoed amidships and blown apart by the *U-558*. The *U-101* torpedoed HMS *Broadwater* aft and the aged four-stacker went down, consumed by fire. Thus, the defense of SC 48 cost one destroyer and one corvette sunk; ten merchant ships were lost. No U-boats were sunk; indeed, only one had even been sighted. Five submarines participated in the attacks at various times; rarely was more than one present at any one time. Fortunately, patrol planes and distance prevented more U-boats from reaching the convoy and adding to the slaughter.

The *Greer* searched many hours for the limping *Kearny*, finally taking station on her port bow at 1424; at 1622, the modern destroyer *Monssen*, out from Iceland, hove into sight, bringing a medical officer and another corpsman. She took station on the *Kearny's* starboard bow. On the 18th, in daylight, PBYs from Iceland watched over the ships. One plane dropped blood plasma and equipment for transfusions wrapped in life preservers secured to a parachute harness, but the supplies sank before recovery. Another plane was sent out, and this time the *Monssen's* men fished the package out of the water, the plasma helping to save the life of Sammy Kurtz. At 0830 on the morning of the 19th, the *Kearny* entered Reykjavik Harbor, her appearance "almost normal" despite the hole in her side. An engineer noted, "Many observers, and particularly British naval officers, were struck by her upright posture, and were amazed that she was still afloat after receiving a torpedo hit amidships." She moored in tandem with the *Monssen* and transferred the more serious of her twenty-two wounded and hurt to the British hospital ship *Avonglen*, thence to the U.S. Army hospital ashore. On the 26th, memorial services were held on board for the men who died in the battle around SC 48. Repair ship *Vulcan* pumped out much of the water from inside the *Kearny*, the hole in her side was closed over, and temporary repairs were capably effected.

In Iceland, they asked what had kept the *Kearny* afloat. An ensign explained, "Everyone just did his job—and two or three more. If I am torpedoed again I hope I have this crew with me." One escort commander observed in his report: "Except for the loss of life . . . the escort is believed to have been generally beneficial. It has given personnel confidence in their ships; has brought the war home to them with considerable realism and has strengthened their determination." The *Kearny's* men did what they could.[1]

Although the battle of SC 48 did ease prewar fears as to the stability of the large, heavily equipped, new destroyers joining the Fleet, the fight was poorly managed. Inexperience sired defeat. Conventional American escort tactics of close-in defense and illumination were useless against the small, gray U-boats, virtually invisible on the surface of the black night sea and handled daringly in the manner of oceangoing motor torpedo boats. The tragedy was that the escort commander for once had possessed sufficient warships to adopt aggressive tactics; he might have deployed his destroyers in a wide-ranging hunt while keeping his corvettes close-in. Thus the convoy would have been doubly protected and perhaps the U-boats would have taken hard and bloody blows, despite the lack of radar and unity amongst the escorts.

Where the first Americans died — the *Kearny*, October 1941

For in the Atlantic in the fall of 1941, the primary necessity was to kill U-boats. Defensive measures, especially better organization of the ASW effort, skilled evasive routing based on interception of German communications necessitated by wolf-pack tactics, more escorts and better air cover, the protection afforded by bad weather, less experienced U-boat crews as a result of combat losses, and the Fuehrer's unwise diversions of submarines to support land operations all worked to lower the rate of Allied shipping losses at the hands of U-boats to about 166,000 tons per month, about the same as the monthly building rate. Although losses from all causes, such as air attack, mine warfare, operational attrition, more than doubled the monthly toll, it still remained less than half of the 750,000 tons that the Germans needed to sink; and the declining rate of loss was achieved despite an increase in the number of U-boats from 54 to 200. U-boats were beginning to come into service at the rate of twenty per month; yet they were being sunk at the rate of but little more than three each month. With the attack technology and expertise of the escorts relatively weak, the decisive factor in the rate of loss was the ability of the U-boats to locate the convoys because, once the latter had been discovered, their escorts could not prevent successful attack by the submarines. As their numbers grew and their losses did not, the U-boats threatened to offset the gains of escorts by providing Doenitz with more and more "eyes" with which to find the convoys. If the Battle of the Atlantic was to be won by the Allies, the escorts would have to learn to kill U-boats.[2] Yet, as the battle of SC 48 showed, most of the killing at sea would be done by the U-boats. For the good shepherds of the Atlantic were hard-working and brave. But they were blind.

And thus began the Atlantic Fleet's education at war.

On Navy Day, the President responded to the torpedoing of the *Kearny* with fiery words:

> We have wished to avoid shooting. But the shooting has started. And history has recorded who fired the first shot. In the long run, however, all that will matter is who fired the last shot.
> America has been attacked. The USS *Kearny* is not just a Navy ship. She belongs to every man, woman, and child in this Nation.
> Illinois, Alabama, California, North Carolina, Ohio, Louisiana, Texas, Pennsylvania, Georgia, Arkansas, New York, and Virginia—those are the home states of the honored dead and wounded of the *Kearny*. Hitler's torpedo was directed at every American. . . . The purpose of Hitler's attack was to frighten the American people off the high seas. . . . This is not the

first time that he has misjudged the American spirit. . . .

The forward march of Hitler and Hitlerism can be stopped—and it will be stopped.

Very simply and very bluntly—we are pledged to pull our own oar in the destructionism of Hitlerism. . . .

I say that we do not propose to take this lying down.

Our determination not to take it lying down has been expressed in the orders to the American Navy to shoot on sight. Those orders stand. . . . it can never be doubted that the goods will be delivered by this Nation, whose Navy believes in the tradition of "Damn the torpedoes; full speed ahead!"[3]

One of the officers of the Canadian corvette *Baddeck* remembered,

Roosevelt said on the radio it was an unprovoked attack on a United States vessel, a neutral. Who was I to dispute that? I suppose it was a matter of definition.[4]

But in the United States, there seemed neither indignation at the Nazis for the attack, nor anger at the President, whose policy of escorting Allied merchantmen exposed American warships to attack. Most people grudgingly accepted the hard duty ahead. As *The New Republic* had put it, "if a democracy is not prepared to be militant, it is not prepared to survive."[5]

On a farm not far from Gillespie, Illinois, the parents of Fireman 1/C George A. Calvert, who had died in the *Kearny*'s forward fireroom, received an unsigned letter, which said in part, "Your dear son was sent to his death by the murdering imbecile head of our Government."[6]

In Washington, a German diplomat reported to Berlin:

The torpedoing of the US destroyer *Kearny* in the waters around Iceland will demonstrate that the American Government, in contrast with Wilson in 1917, does not make the question of war or peace dependent upon incidents on the high seas, but uses those incidents, which by its policies have become unavoidable, to dramatize its propaganda in order to break down public opposition to its present course of action.[7]

In Germany, the Naval Staff was unable to determine which U-boat had torpedoed the *Kearny* in the melee to port of SC 48. The Fuehrer told Admiral Raeder that his staff's investigation should conclude that the *Kearny* was torpedoed by another American destroyer! Hitler, still determined to postpone American intervention, reminded his naval commanders to avoid battle with American warships when possible. Publicly, he said:

> President Roosevelt has ordered his ships to shoot the moment they sight German ships. I have ordered German ships not to shoot when they sight American vessels but to defend themselves when attacked. I will have any German officer court-martialed who fails to defend himself.[8]

In the U.S. Navy, there was not much stir over the torpedoing of the *Kearny*: such an incident had been deemed more or less inevitable since the beginning of escort operations; and the ship had not been sunk. Submarine attacks were relatively rare on the Iceland run that fall, and the destroyermen worried more about bad weather, which strained ships, particularly the four-stackers, and exhausted crews, than about the possibility of attack. The *Badger*'s men watched the *Kearny* limp into port with the jagged hole in her side, then put it out of their minds. As her skipper recalled, "As for the subs, we knew they were there, but as long as they didn't attack our convoy . . . we gave them little thought."[9]

At Argentia, aboard the *Vincennes*, an ensign listened to another young officer complain about missing his wife, and thought:

> He joined the Navy to escape the draft, and is now crying because he pities himself—a type that would be run through with a sword in the old days. . . .
> I am here to do a little bit against Hitler, Mussolini, and Stalin for the United States and for what I believe. . . . There are some on board that feel that way. It is rather pitiful that we need such an incident today as the torpedoing of the *Kearny* to arouse public sentiment. . . . I wonder if wars have always been "made" in a similar manner. [10]

Admiral King wrote a friend, "I am sure that you realize that the *Kearny* incident is but the first of many that, in the nature of things, are bound to occur." He noted that the Air Corps was unready and the Navy short of ships, then added, "So—if a war status comes about—what to do?!? I am afraid the citizenry will have to learn the bitter truth that war is not waged with words or promises or vituperation but with the realities of perils, hardships, and killing." He judged that another German attack on an American warship would "likely . . . lead to an open assumption of war status."[11]

The President, despite what many believed, was not conniving to enter the war in a way satisfactory to public opinion. His concept of immediate strategic needs was "primarily 'naval,' in the sense of securing sea lanes and beach heads, rather than in the movement of massed armies on a continental scale. These concepts fitted in well with his acute political awareness of the willingness of the American people to accept naval extension, and their unwillingness to condone troop movements of any size." The President's alternating strategic boldness and caution—the Lion and Fox syndrome—produced despair in his planners, advisers, and biographers. But the enduring constancy of his policy was to prevent the Germans from winning the Battle of the Atlantic. And when he thought of his war as a "limited war" (requiring naval power, air power, and small numbers of amphibious infantry) he endorsed bold measures; but he ever became cautious when he feared that conflict might escalate into "total war" (requiring a massive commitment of ground forces). He was attempting to help the British win a decision in the Battle of the Atlantic by employing the U.S. Navy in a limited, undeclared naval war in the North Atlantic. He tried to see limited war as a substitute for, rather than a prelude to, full-scale American military intervention, at least until the American Army and Air Corps were strong enough to play an effective role in the war; hence, he did not seek to make American losses in the ocean battle reason for a declaration of war. Walter Lippmann reflected the national mood best when he wrote what the President dared to hope: "As a matter of fundamental strategy our role is on the seas and in the air and in the factory—not on the battlefields of Europe or Asia."* Both President and people put the feet of the United States toward the fire gradually.[12]

Admiral Stark had fewer illusions, and did not have the ultimate burden of making certain that when the United States entered the war, it would do so as a united nation; hence, he could be consistent and forthright in his counsel. As he wrote Secretary Hull on 8 October 1941:

> It has long been my opinion that Germany cannot be defeated unless the United States is wholeheartedly in the war and makes a strong military and naval effort wherever strategy dictates. It would be very desirable to enter the war under circumstances in which Germany were the aggressor and in which case Japan might then be able to remain neutral. However, on the whole it is my opinion that the United States should enter the war against Germany, as soon as possible, even if hostilities with Japan must be accepted. . . . I have assumed for the past two years that our country would not let Great Britain fall: that, ultimately, in order to prevent this, we would have to enter the war. . . . I have long felt and often stated that the sooner we get in the better. . . . I do not believe Germany will declare war on us until she is good and ready: that it will be a cold-blooded

*In November, of course, the President astounded General Marshall by suggesting that the Army was already too large!

decision on Hitler's part, if and when he thinks it will pay and not till then. He has every excuse to declare war on us now, if he were of a mind to. . . . When he is ready, he will strike, and not before. [13]

The torpedoing of the *Kearny* changed nothing in the Atlantic. The Americans could not abandon their efforts to sustain Britain without compromising their own safety in the long run; the Germans could not abandon their attacks on the merchant convoys without accepting a stalemate or defeat in World War II. There was war in the Atlantic, but neither nation wanted to declare it. The Germans were cautious because of the Russian campaign, fear of American industrial potential, fear that Japan would not join them in war, and the inability of their military to strike meaningful blows at the United States because of Anglo-American domination of the Atlantic approaches to the New World. The Americans were restrained by their military and industrial unpreparedness, fear of Japanese expansionism in the Pacific and a two-ocean war, and the combined idealism and selfishness of a people reluctant to go to war on the coldly realistic, unemotional grounds of national security and to accept the tragic sacrifices and weighty burdens of total war. The torpedoing of the *Kearny* changed nothing in the Atlantic. But the first Americans had died.

And the convoys continued to run.

24.

"Old Sal" at the Windy Corner

THE CONVOYS CONTINUED TO RUN.

On Columbus Day, the *Charles F. Hughes, Gleaves, Lansdale, Madison,* and *Simpson* met the fifty-one ships of HX 154 south of Argentia and took over from HMCS *Annapolis.* The convoy ships steamed northeast at nearly 10 knots; they carried petroleum products, steel, grain, lumber, paper, molasses and sugar, refrigerated goods, mail, and general cargo. HX 154 proved a model convoy, with no breakdowns or straggling. On the night of the 15/16th, the ships were routed onto a more northerly heading to hook above the U-boats closing in on SC 48. On the 16th, the *Charles F. Hughes* picked up seven wretched survivors from the British steamer SS *Hatasu;* the merchant sailors had been 14 days in a lifeboat. The next day, both the *Charles F. Hughes* and the *Gleaves* attacked sonar contacts, perhaps wakes or fish. On the 19th, the destroyers turned over the convoy to the ships of the British eastern ocean escort at 59°-25′ north, 23°-25′ west, and took five vessels, including the Navy cargo ships *Algorab, Almaack,* and *Mattole,* north toward Iceland.

After sunset on the 19th, the *Gleaves* attacked a sonar contact off her port bow with a shallow pattern of five depth charges, and twice during the night, the *Charles F. Hughes* attacked contacts, using eight depth charges. But if there was a U-boat tracking the ships, it was kept at bay easily enough; and the destroyers and their little brood reached Iceland safely on the 21st.[1]

The four-stacker *Badger* was ordered to carry mail to Iceland. At Argentia, the crew secured the Number One fireroom and "filled it to the main deck hatches with mail bags." But that night, a strong wind began to blow, and in the poor holding ground, the destroyer dragged anchor, "the hook bouncing merrily over the rocks on the bottom." Lieutenant Commander John W. Schmidt disgustedly got the *Badger* under way "and dragged that anchor out of there," his crew learning early that there was little rest for destroyermen in the North Atlantic. The *Badger* made a quiet passage to Iceland with the mails; then she took aboard new mail and a passenger, Chaplain Brady. Brady, a naval chaplain during World War I, was a Brooklyn priest who had returned to the service to wander "around the North Atlantic to see what he could do for military personnel in outlandish places."

Because of the attack on SC 48, the *Badger* was assigned to join the modern destroyer *Mayo* and four-stackers *Babbitt*, *Broome*, *Leary*, and *Schenck* at sea in the escort of westbound ON 26. The *Badger* joining late, did not have the convoy signals, so the escort CO, Commander W.K. "Sol" Phillips, gave her a roving station astern of the convoy of thirty-three ships. The ships took a northerly route along 58°-10' north to keep them clear of the U-boats hunting SC 48; then, off Greenland, they turned southwest and at 50° west headed almost due south.

There were rain and fog and moderately high seas on the passage, which was a long one because of the wide diversion and bad weather, and there were three stragglers. John Schmidt was glad to have Father Brady aboard the *Badger* to help pass the time with choice stories about his duty with the Marines in the First World War; although the priest did not ask, Schmidt thought that he was anxious to celebrate Mass aboard the destroyer and so, after casually ignoring the matter, he surprised the quietly disappointed Brady on the first Sunday out of Reykjavik by asking him to say Mass. The trip was uneventful save for a *Mayo* attack on a sonar contact, perhaps water turbulence, on the 26th. Most of the ships were dispersed southeast of Argentia on the 29th. It was a tedious passage, but a safe one.[2]

On 18 October, the new destroyer *Roe* and four-stackers *Bainbridge*, *Overton*, *Truxtun*, and *Sturtevant* met HX 155 off Argentia. There were fifty-nine ships in the convoy, one vessel with a green crew having turned back after proving unable to maintain speed. At 9+ knots, the convoy steamed northeast, then east. Then, on the 23rd, because of U-boat movements to the southeast and the difficulty of diverting HX 155 to the north on account of the presence of other convoys, seven corvettes were detached from ON 27 to form a striking force to steam 20 miles ahead of the fully laden, American-escorted convoy in order to try to clear its path. But the U-boats had exhausted torpedoes in earlier fights and new boats had not yet reached their patrol areas, so the passage of HX 155 remained an easy one despite the grim precaution. The only casualty of the trip occurred on the 25th when a *Sturtevant* sailor spilled hot coffee on himself as the destroyer pitched in moderately high seas. The convoy was turned over to the British on the 25th at 58°-50′ north, 22°-40′ west, and the American destroyers took four vessels, including the naval auxiliaries *Tarazed* and *Hamul*, safely on to Iceland.[3]

Down from Iceland, the *Sampson* and four-stackers *DuPont, Bernadou, Lea,* and *MacLeish,* escorting the venerable naval tanker *Salinas* and four merchantmen, met the British escorts and forty merchant vessels of ON 28 at 59°-55′ north, 25° west. The *Salinas* was assigned the position of last ship in the first—port, or southern—column; both outboard-stern stations were considered dangerous, for there was no ship to serve as a shield on one side, there were usually no escorts astern, and the chance of straggling caused by the failure of ships ahead was increased. Thus, tankers were not generally assigned to either "windy corner," but were usually crowded into the middle of the convoy.* However, the convoy commodore of ON 28, in the SS *Manchester Citizen,* did not wish to waste time or cause confusion among the often precariously organized merchant ships by rearranging stations to accommodate the newcomers. On the bridge of the *Salinas,* skipper Lieutenant Commander Harley F. Cope, a salty officer with a wry and ready sense of humor, bit down on his cigar stub and unhappily ordered "Old Sal" to the portside windy corner.

As the British escorts departed, the convoy steamed south at about 25° west in order to keep to the east of the tracks of two eastbound

*There was, of course, no assuredly safe position; one ship of SC 48 was hit and sunk although in the middle of the convoy; the two torpedoes that struck her passed through five columns of ships on the port side!

convoys, HX 156 and SC 51; it would turn southwest at 51° north. The *Sampson* was out ahead, *DuPont* off the port bow, *MacLeish* the port flank, and *Bernadou* and *Lea* off the starboard column. For several days the passage was quiet, but on the morning of the 27th, the *MacLeish* tracked two streaks in the water to port back to their source; the destroyermen thought they were torpedo wakes, but the *MacLeish* searched the vicinity and could not pick up a contact.

That afternoon, a patrolling U-boat sighted smoke and thin masts against the sky over the dark line of the horizon and sent off a contact report on ON 28. The submarine ranged ahead of the convoy, then submerged for an attack approach.

First the *Sampson*, then the *DuPont* picked up a sonar contact on the approaching U-boat and at 1510, *DuPont* attacked with a pattern of depth charges, but to no avail. The destroyer searched for half an hour, but could not regain contact and returned to the convoy. The submarine surfaced and began to stalk ON 28 anew, running ahead of the convoy far out on the port flank, then submerged again to try an approach from off the port bow. But the *DuPont*'s sonar man detected the U-boat, reporting propeller noises dead ahead; the destroyer surged forward and attacked with six depth charges, blasting up towers of white water. When the sea settled, there was a thick smear of oil on the surface and the sharp smell of diesel oil in the air; but despite the hopes of the destroyermen, the U-boat was unhurt. That evening, the convoy made a slight course change to the south, and the shadowing U-boat did not pick it up, losing her chance to strike.

The next day was quiet, but on the morning of the 29th, the submarine was back; the *Sampson*, *DuPont*, and *Lea* all stalked a contact, first ahead and then to starboard, off and on for several hours. Lieutenant Commander E.M. Waldron, the *DuPont*'s aggressive commander, believed in hitting hard and once he attacked with a pattern of twelve depth charges, which was both good and bad technique; it greatly increased the usually slim chance of damaging the submarine, but it used up depth charges too quickly. The contacts persuaded everyone that the U-boats were massing for a night surface attack. The trailing submarine twice sent out position reports on the convoy. And on the *Salinas*, Lieutenant Commander Cope wrote in the Night Order Book that an attack was imminent; he wanted his watchstanders alert.

With a battle developing, the escort commander wanted to disperse the faster convoy vessels, those capable of at least 12 knots, to take them out of danger and make it easier to defend the remainder; he requested permission to detach about a dozen ships. But naval communications were not yet organized to handle the increased traffic necessitated by wartime operations; there were communications delays, and permission was not received until after dark, which was too late for safe and orderly sorting out and reorganization of ships.

With the crews alert for trouble, at 1705, six minutes before sunset, *MacLeish* lookouts saw a dark object in the blue-gray twilight five miles distant; the old destroyer bucked, surging ahead and to port at 25 knots. After a long chase, the U-boat, or night shadow, disappeared. The *MacLeish* and *Sampson* searched the area of the last sighting, popping glowing star shells into the night sky, but did not find the enemy. Slowly, the long, tense night wore on without an attack, despite a shiny hunter's moon. But the *U-106*, thwarted thus far by the alert destroyers, did not give up; her skipper, Kapitänleutnant Rasch, decided to strike farther astern. She closed the convoy from the south. At about 0430, the bright moon went down, and the sea blackened; and, in the *Salinas*, Lieutenant Commander Cope felt that the danger was past. At about 0500, the *U-106* approached the rear of the port column of the convoy, lined up an attack on the stubby naval tanker, and fired a spread of torpedoes at her. At 0508, a torpedo exploded against the port side of the *Salinas*. The tanker shook violently and listed to port, seawater rushing into the hole in her side. Two minutes later, a second "fish" exploded against the ship, underneath the port wing of the bridge.

After the first hit, Lieutenant Commander Ashton B. Smith, Exec of the *Salinas*, was at the voice tube, trying to find out if the fireroom was still operating; the second explosion knocked him back against a stanchion, dazing him and injuring his back, but he remembered to run to the port wing and pull the release cords, letting CO_2 hiss into the tanks to keep the residue of oil and aviation gasoline from catching fire. Back in Iceland, Cope and Smith had discussed the possibility of being torpedoed, agreeing that the *Salinas* might survive one hit, but never two. Therefore, Smith now ordered the engineers up from below; they did not want to leave, arguing that they could still save the ship. Smith, with no time for debate, had the Abandon Ship signal sounded, and the engineers grudgingly secured stations and came topside.

On deck, things looked bad, worse than they were. The tops of the fuel tanks had been blasted off by the shock of the explosions, and geysers of oil streamed into the air, cascading down onto the men at their battle stations. "However," Lieutenant Commander Cope remembered, "we were not very much concerned about our appearance at that time." Lieutenant L.J. Modave fired a series of Very flares to summon help. The crew moved gingerly over the oily sludge to the boats. The sailors were quiet, and the skipper noted with satisfaction that everyone seemed calm; indeed, it appeared to be a routine lifeboat drill. Many of the gunners were still at their guns, despite the order to abandon ship.

"Old Sal" was not ready to die. After servicing the vessels at Iceland, she had little flammable liquid swishing in her belly, and good luck and the prompt action of Lieutenant Commander Smith prevented the dregs and fumes from igniting. The tanker, in ballast, rode light in the water, and the tons of seawater gurgling into the holes in her side were in a sense merely a different and less volatile form of her usual liquid cargo. To the "amazement" of her men, the *Salinas* settled down in the water, just as she always did when fully laden, but she showed no signs of sinking; by 0515, she had even stopped settling. If the seawater could be shut out and repairs effected, she might yet be saved. Lieutenant Commander Cope told Smith, "That fellow'll probably come around to take a look to see why in the hell we haven't sunk. Sound General Quarters, please. I think 'Old Sal' is going to stay afloat for a while—I hope." And the guns were fully manned again.

Lieutenant Ted Jermann, unlike most reservists, was no youngster; he had been a chief in the First World War and Assistant Engineering Officer in the liner *Manhattan* before being recalled to active duty. When asked to furnish an inspection party to go below and assess damage, Jermann went himself, taking his two leading chiefs, Francis H. McIntyre and Rual S. Wilson. Below, the three engineers worked to secure valves on ruptured lines and checked bulkheads; they found that the bulkheads were holding. In the blackness, they could hear the gurgling of onrushing water a few feet away. Jermann was clawing with a wrench at an overhead valve in the boiler room when a dull explosion sounded from above; the wrench tore out of his hand, clanging to the deck. The ship would never be saved like this, he thought; he needed more men. He had to get the skipper to risk more men below.

Topside, the dark sea was empty, the convoy and its escorts having passed on. The men stood by the guns and boats and peered into the night, helplessly watching the black sea for the shiny white streaks of more torpedoes. "We felt very much alone and deserted of friends," Cope remembered. The crew broke out the largest set of colors aboard and ran the flag up the halyards in a gesture of hope and defiance. Division officers conducted musters to determine casualties and perhaps also to provide activity as therapy for worried minds.

Meanwhile, the *U-106* returned to kill the cripple, approaching on the surface, astern and to starboard of the *Salinas*. The tanker was bobbing on the ocean swell, and from the U-boat, it looked as if she were under way. It was this small error of judgment on the part of Kapitänleutnant Rasch that saved the *Salinas* and her men.

At about 0526, the talker at the *Salinas'* stern 4-inch gun reported to the bridge, "Submarine on surface on starboard quarter!" The gunners were hot to shoot, but Cope, reasoning coolly but wrongly, refused to let them; since the torpedo hits were on the port side, he thought that the "target" to starboard might be one of the American destroyers coming back to help. He and the men on the bridge went to the starboard wing to have a look. "Suddenly two white slender ribbons started stretching out in the water toward us. . . . I had the feeling of a man facing a firing squad and watching the bullets coming toward him in slow motion," Cope reported. He said, "Open fire on the submarine!"

Two torpedoes ran past, a little ahead of the tanker's bow, the nearest perhaps 11 yards away. On the bridge, "there was an audible exuding of breaths" as "the white streaks went past our bow . . . and the forward part of the *Salinas* did not disintegrate." Rasch, giving the tanker credit for some headway, had "led" his target a shade too much. The bright track of a third torpedo passed astern of "Old Sal," as close as had the two forward. The *U-106*, deck awash, ran back across the tanker's stern, from starboard to port. And at 0532, the *Salinas'* Number Four gun fired once, a dull, red flame in the dark. The sailors heard "a sound of tearing, ripping steel" and thought that they had hit the submarine's conning tower. The men aft cheered, glad to hit back. It was not likely that the *Salinas'* inexperienced gunners had hit a small, moving target at night with a single shot; perhaps they were lucky, and the projectile had bounced off the water and struck the U-boat a glancing blow on the side of the bridge. But there was no explosion and the submarine was not damaged. After a single shot, the U-boat disappeared into the darkness.

Cope and his officers were sure that it would submerge and finish off the *Salinas*.

It was at this dismal juncture in the fight that Lieutenant Jermann reached the bridge and asked for help below. He reported that the damage to lines, pumps, boiler fronts, and other gear could be repaired and that it looked as if the bulkheads would continue to hold back the water in the flooded compartments; he said he could have the ship under way in three hours. Cope replied that, with the U-boat near and ready to attack again, he could not order anyone below, but that he would let volunteers go down. Jermann asked his engineers, and they all volunteered; so he led his band of brave men into the blackness below.

Most of the crew waited quietly by the boats; gunners and lookouts were at battle stations. Suddenly, the talker at the stern gun reported, "Submarine on surface on starboard quarter! Request permission to open fire." Cope looked with his binoculars at the dim smear approaching from starboard; again, he thought it was a destroyer. He told the bridge talker: "Number 4 gun . . . is *not* to fire without specific orders from the Captain. Acknowledge." The talker repeated the message into his phone. The gunners pleaded for a chance to shoot. The talker said to Cope, "Acknowledged, Captain. But they're sure it's a sub." Cope thought that the dark blur on the graying horizon was larger than a submarine; but everyone else was just as certain that it was a U-boat. Someone said, "Let's get im, Captain." Another added, "Let's shoot the bastard, sir." Cope asked his signalman to challenge the vessel. The shutters of the signal blinker clacked. But there was no response from the vessel. The men on the bridge again remonstrated with Cope to give the order to commence firing. Cope told the signalman, "Challenge him once more, Eakin. If he doesn't answer this time, we'll give hime the works. He rates it." But the approaching ship flashed the correct response to the challenge; it was the *DuPont*, brought to the scene by the *Salinas'* flares. The four-stacker neared, and across the curling water the tanker's men heard the greeting, "Hello, there, *Salinas!*" The sailors of "Old Sal" cheered. Cope told Waldron that he had no casualties on board and that he intended to make for the nearest port, St. John's, Newfoundland, some 700 miles west. The *DuPont* patrolled around the tanker.

Meanwhile, the U-boat was below, reloading torpedo tubes. Rasch believed that he had hit the tanker during his second attack and that she must be going down. But the *DuPont* ruined the *U-106*'s repose.

The destroyer quickly picked up a sonar contact, and in about fifteen minutes, made three brief attacks, releasing eight depth charges. As the *DuPont* finished her last attack and then swung back toward the frothy, white circles of the impact area to try to regain contact, the *U-106* struck back, firing a spread of torpedoes at her. But the *Du-Pont* was a little too quick. She regained contact rapidly and rushed in for another attack with a haste not anticipated by the U-boat; the white tracks of the torpedoes passed astern. Seeking revenge, the destroyer released a pattern of a dozen depth charges, blowing clouds of water skyward; soon the destroyermen observed thick, black oil on the surface, and Waldron thought he had drawn the blood of his tenacious adversary at last.

But the *U-106* was still hale and full of fight. At 0912, the destroyermen sighted a periscope in the water on the port quarter; the *DuPont* investigated but did not attack, for she was low on depth charges. Then, at 0923, the *Salinas'* men saw a periscope off the port beam. That was too much, and the *DuPont* rushed over and dropped three depth charges. The *Salinas* "shook considerably" from nearby blasts, and Ted Jermann and his engineers wondered if the old bulkheads which held out the ocean but few feet away could take the added stress.

Jermann's men shored up buckled bulkheads, mended broken lines and damaged equipment, and repaired boilers; then they straightened deck plating and toted wood for the boiler. Chief Electrician's Mate Albert W. Brown seemed ubiquitous and tireless; he worked almost ceaselessly through the next four days and nights to improve the *Salinas'* chances. Much of the damage, such as a deformed keel, ruptured main cargo and bunker tanks, ripped-out side and bottom plating, and fractured bulkheads was too extensive for shipboard repair. Nevertheless, in a little under five hours after her first wound, the *Salinas* was ready to get under way. The *DuPont*, with only four depth charges left, was ordered back to the convoy, replaced by the *Lea*. At 0955, the *Salinas* got under way, and making one-third speed, began the long journey home.

Meanwhile, up ahead, the convoy was encountering new tribulations. Another submarine, probably the *U-67*, was stalking it. The *Bernadou* attacked a contact at 0837. Then, 14 minutes later, the lookouts on "Bernie" saw a submarine on the surface, seven miles to the south. The old destroyer ran toward the enemy at 25 knots, but the German lookouts sighted her steaming after them, white pompadours of water brushed up by her bow, smoke coiling from her funnels. The U-boat began to dive. *Bernadou* fired a lone shell which made a white splash in the blue water as the U-boat slid safely under. The destroyer picked up a sonar contact and attacked twice with nine depth charges, but too hastily decided to return to the convoy, which was short of escorts because of the *Salinas'* plight, leaving behind a lost opportunity. During the day, the *Bernadou* carried out other attacks. At dusk, the faster convoy vessels were dispersed.

Help was on the way. The cutter *Campbell* and fleet tug *Cherokee* were sent out to aid the *Salinas* and *Lea*. And the *Leary*, *Babbitt*, and *Schenck*, just arrived at Argentia after the long passage west with ON 26, then the *Buck* and *Ludlow*, standing by to take out an HX convoy, were sent to augment the escort of ON 28.

In the *Salinas*, the repair work went on. *Lea* attacked a sonar contact. The day was hard and long, but the night "was a hellish one. The seas came up, we rolled considerably, and no one of course knew whether the next roll would break us in half." Then, shortly after midnight, the engine stopped; all the fuel oil had seeped out of the cracked bunker tanks. For two hours, the ship remained stopped in the quiet darkness, as tense sailors waited while the engineers rigged a line to the diesel tanks amidships; at 0241, the *Salinas* got under way again, running on diesel oil.

The next night, October 31st, the *Campbell* joined the *Lea* in protecting "Old Sal," a most welcome Halloween present for the tanker sailors. The *Cherokee* was late, because while north of the *Salinas*, she sensed that she was being shadowed by a U-boat, so she continued eastward in order not to lead the submarine to the hobbled tanker. She joined the *Salinas* and her escorts on the morning of 2 November; as she had no depth charges or sonar gear, and thus little but her gall to add to the escort, she was placed astern. All four ships reached St. John's safely the next day.

Lieutenant Commander Cope said of his crew: "The conduct of the personnel during the entire period was exemplary."

Meanwhile, the escorts of ON 28, joined by three four-stackers from Argentia, were still fighting to protect the convoy. At twilight on the 31st, the *Leary* moved out and drove off an approaching U-boat with a depth-charge attack. Unable to close the convoy, the submarine swung out and fired a long-range torpedo spread at the merchant ships. The *DuPont* sighted the approaching wakes and·

veered to avoid them. She hunted back down the tracks, looking for
her assailant, but the U-boat had gone. The seas rose. A seaman in
the *Buck*, which with the *Ludlow* was speeding to the fray, sustained
fractured ribs when knocked down by high seas; the two new destroyers joined the escort at 2135. During the night, five of the destroyers attacked sonar contacts, probably water turbulence and
wakes, for the U-boats, outlasted, were abandoning the hunt for ON
28. The next night, the *DuPont* and *Bernadou*, low on fuel, departed
for Argentia. En route, the *DuPont* picked up a sonar contact, and
hard-fighting Lieutenant Commander Waldron expended his fifty-
ninth and last depth charge on it. The remaining merchantmen of
ON 28 were dispersed south of Argentia on the 3rd after a harrowing
but safe trip.[4]

Because the U-boats were unable to mount a determined night
surface attack against it, ON 28 was spared the fate of SC 48. The
submarines were few and were not handled aggressively; they never
reached the propitious position at the propitious moment. For this,
the American destroyers deserved credit: alertness and aggressiveness
saved lives even when the knowledge and technology of how to kill
were lacking. The *Salinas*' men, like the *Kearny*'s, worked with coolness and fortitude in desperate circumstances to save their ship.

The ships of the Atlantic Fleet proved hard to die, and the *Salinas*
incident revealed that even green crews of second-line ships were
willing and able. Atlantic sailors were overcoming their inexperience
and buck fever and learning to do their jobs with the poise of
professionals. Yet, as Admiral King with dour wisdom insisted, his
Fleet still retained too much of its innocence;[5] for it had been lucky
at war, and but a few of its men and none of its ships had perished.
In a few hours, this would change, and the Fleet's lighthearted sailors
would become sadder and harder men.

25.

"Did You Have a Friend on the Good Reuben James?"

THE FOUR-STACKER WAS OLDER THAN many of her men, the decks under her ladders worn from twenty-one years of service; her crew kidded that the pumps were held together with baling wire and started by a hard rap with a wrench. Old-fashioned hand straps on a trolley, "lizards," hung above her main deck; her venerable 4-inch guns "looked strange" to visitors from new ships who were used to modern 5-inchers and elaborate fire-control devices. Once, when a leak developed in her fuel-oil cofferdam, dripping down into the crew's quarters, it was plugged with a mixture of putty, aluminum powder, and various unidentified ingredients thought to possess sealing properties; but part of the leak could not be plugged, so a rubber tube was set up to drain into a bucket and then emptied back into the tanks every few hours. As a sailor off a new destroyer said, "It took ingenuity to keep that old ship going. . . ."

But the *Reuben James* had a good skipper. Lieutenant Commander Heywood L. Edwards was one of the ablest and brightest young officers in the Navy; an excellent student and athlete at the Academy, he had ample destroyer experience and "knew the cans from the keels up." Tex Edwards ran a hustling, efficient ship with firmness and decision, yet the atmosphere on board was relaxed; if a man could not serve with Tex Edwards the odds were that he was no damn good. Her crew was proud of old "Rube," despite her infirmities; perhaps they sensed that these made them better sailors. They pur-

293

chased a large radio-phonograph and $100 worth of records out of the ship's welfare fund, setting up speakers in various parts of the ship. On the forward bulkhead of the destroyer's small wardroom hung a polished scimitar; Boatswain's Mate Reuben James was believed to have taken it from a North African corsair in a hand-to-hand melee during the Barbary Wars almost 140 years before.

"Rube" had been to Iceland many times since the summer, including trips as part of Indigo II—the *Wasp* convoy—and Task Force 15; her escort group brought ON 20 westward. Her crew knew that they were at war: the escort missions were hard and tense; there was little shore leave. As Gunner's Mate Walt Sorenson, two years younger than his ship, wrote to his sister, ". . . I think we will make another trip to Iceland before we go to the Navy Yards. I sure hope I can come home on leave even if it is only for a few days. . . . We sure don't get much time in anymore. . . ."[1]

Sorenson was right. In mid-October, the *Reuben James* went back to Argentia with modern destroyers *Benson, Niblack,* and *Hilary P. Jones* and four-stacker *Tarbell,* prepared to take out HX 156. Sailors back from Iceland told of the *Kearny* and SC 48, of "tankers loaded with high-test aeroplane gas, lighting the lurid scene like great torches. . . ."

The ships left Argentia on the night of the 23rd, the brown hills of Newfoundland quickly receding astern. It was quiet on the darkened destroyers: "The dim shapes of the officers with their binoculars peering through the small round ports of the wheelhouse. Men with headphones. The dark loom of the watch on the bridge wings."

It was cold and foggy on the morning of the 24th; an icy spray blew up off the sea. At about 0900, with the wet fog lifting, the forty-three gray, rolling ships of HX 156 were sighted, steaming in seven columns. The ships carried petroleum products, steel, grain, sulphur, phosphates, sugar, rum, general cargo, and mail. As the American destroyers ranged down the flanks of the convoy, the Canadian destroyer *Annapolis* blinked a signal: "Thanks. Bon Voyage. Good luck." Lieutenant Commander Durgin in the *Niblack* disliked the use of the foreign phrase; he had not forgiven the French for their quick collapse in 1940.

The American escorts were disposed in strange array. The *Hilary P. Jones* was stationed on the port bow of the convoy, *Benson* on the starboard bow; *Reuben James* was on the port flank and *Tarbell* the starboard flank. The innovation was placing *Niblack* astern. Traditionally, the favorite submarine attack positions were off the bows of a convoy,* but as these were also the best defended areas, the U-boats were showing a tendency to strike where the escort was weakest, at one of the stern corners, usually on the side away from the moon. To guard against this, Lieutenant Commander Durgin had suggested to Captain Robert B. Carney of Admiral Bristol's staff that the *Niblack* be stationed astern on this trip; and Carney had agreed to the experiment. Unfortunately, such a disposition negated the already small value of the *Niblack's* new search-radar rig, a highly primitive device. Early radar rigs did not rotate, which meant that the ship had to be turned when it was necessary to focus the radar in any direction but dead ahead or dead astern; and it was not possible to tell whether a contact that appeared on the scope was ahead or astern until the ship moved forward awhile—if the blip grew bigger, the contact was ahead, if it grew smaller it was astern. Also, the equipment broke down often, partly because it had teething troubles, partly because radiomen were inexperienced. Veteran captains at first distrusted its reliability and efficacy. Now, the *Niblack's* stern position rendered her radar almost useless, as it would not be able to scan the waters ahead of the convoy, but would for the most part sweep waters that the ships were already passing through.

At the outset, the convoy was diverted from a northeasterly to a mainly easterly route because of congestion on the original track. The early days out were quiet. Some of the old merchant ships made too much smoke, dark smudges over the horizon to attract the notice of prowling U-boats. At dusk each night, the *Niblack* made a twenty-mile sweep astern to make sure that the convoy was not being shadowed; the escorts maintained night stations from 2,000 to 3,000 yards off the outboard columns, with the *Niblack* usually about 4,000 yards astern. Some of the destroyers vigorously patrolled station, thus increasing their defensive coverage and making of themselves more difficult targets; the *Hilary P. Jones* automatically did so, for she was from Destroyer Squadron 7, whose screening instructions mandated it. Yet, despite the obvious desirability of the practice, not all escort commanders would or could require it. This was partly because there was a lack of consensus as to a standardized body of

---

*The bow attack position spread out before a U-boat's torpedo tubes the largest mass of targets, moving *toward* the attacking submarine, and thus increased the possibility of torpedoes that missed their original targets passing on to strike other ships.

ASW doctrine in the inexperienced Atlantic Fleet, partly because of a lack of decisiveness in older leaders and task group commanders, but mostly because there were pressing technical limitations. Many of the ships, especially the four-stackers, could not always patrol station because they could not afford the increased fuel consumption and still be able to stick with their convoys during voyages protracted by enemy action, bad weather, or route diversions. Harsh reality compromised sound theory, and because it did, on this trip men lost their lives.

On the night of the 25th, the *Hilary P. Jones* attacked a contact, fish or wakes. On the 27th, the convoy was diverted to swing south of the U-boats pursuing ON 28. That day, a gale blew up. The sea "smothered" the forecastles of the destroyers in bright white water, and the ships plunged and rolled. A wind of 65 knots lashed across "forty-foot black, ugly moving hills of heaving water." The *Niblack* registered a roll of forty-eight degrees; sometimes her propellers rose out of the water. Sailors standing gun watches huddled in sodden misery behind splinter shields; men slid and faltered when they moved about, and bruises and cuts were common; loose gear floated from smashed lockers. Water was everywhere, and everyone seemed wet. In wardrooms, metal poles extending from deck to overhead to which the arms of chairs could be fixed—"monkey cages"—were set up. But the storm was not without compensation. As Lieutenant Commander Durgin said, "No subs up today."

But the U-boat skippers knew that submerged they would find no convoys. So the submarines, too, shuddered into the churning crests of violent sea. German lookouts, too, were drenched by waves and blinded by spray; seas crashing over conning towers left the men dangling, breathless and gagging, from safety straps over the icy, wild ocean. The clothing of the Germans, too, was always wet and heavy. The submariners' hands were red and cut, their necks scraped bloody by frozen jacket collars, their bones prey to aches and rheumatism from constant chill and damp; they, too, cursed stubborn captains who held them to what seemed futile duty. But the U-boats stayed up.

The storm raged on. At 1340 on the 27th, seas smashed the after port bulwark of the *Hilary P. Jones*. Lieutenant (JG) C.D. Sooy struggled to secure the damaged bulwark, but onrushing waves swept him overboard. It was impossible to lower a boat, so life buoys were flung over the side and rafts were cut loose; the line-throwing gun shot a rope into the maelstrom of gray-green sea. But Lieutenant Sooy, stunned, sank out of sight. Then Ensign J.C. Houghton went into the water. He swam to Sooy, holding him up, trying to tie the line around him; but he could not do so with waves pouring over them and the sea tugging at them. So, holding on to Sooy, Houghton pulled himself through the icy water toward the stopped, lurching destroyer. The *Hilary P. Jones* was swaying over about forty-five degrees, but Boatswain's Mate 2/C A.T. Mann and Ensign W.R. Lilliott climbed out on a cargo net draped over the steep side of the pitching, rolling destroyer and tried to reach Houghton. On the bridge, Lieutenant Commander Sherman R. Clark feared that four men might die in an attempt to save one.

As the four sailors clung, and grabbed, and struggled along the cargo net, a high, heavy wave burst against the side of the destroyer, tearing Lieutenant Sooy out of the parlous grasp of those who fought so hard to save him. Mann and Lilliott, clutching to the cargo net, managed to cling to Houghton before he, too, was carried away; they dragged him back on deck to be treated for shock and exhaustion. The destroyer rolled down over the body of the man in the water. Clark ordered his men to clear the deck. Weighted by a grim sense of defeat, the men of the *Hilary P. Jones* quit the soaking deck. The storm gradually abated. The destroyers suffered minor damage topside, but Lieutenant Sooy was the only man to die.

On the night of the 28th, near 30° west, the ships turned north at last. The next day, the *Hilary P. Jones* and *Reuben James* attacked brief sonar contacts, probably water turbulence. In a sweep astern, the *Niblack* found a straggling tanker and gave her the convoy's position; by steaming at $10\frac{1}{4}$ knots, the tanker was able to rejoin the convoy before nightfall. On the 30th, the destroyermen learned of the torpedoing of the *Salinas*, about three days' steaming to the west. Shore-based direction-finders, monitoring the transmissions of U-boats made garrulous by Doenitz's coordinated tactics, indicated the presence of submarines in the vicinity of HX 156. Consequently, the American escorts were asked to remain with the convoy an extra day, until the afternoon of 1 November, to give the British time to reinforce with destroyers their eastern ocean escort of small ships. The 30th passed slowly, as the destroyers continued their prosaic work. The same tanker straggled again because she had engine trouble, and the *Niblack* searched for two hours to the southwest before locating her and giving her the convoy's position and course.

Because of the reports of U-boats in the area, there were many calls to general quarters during the day. A slightly overcast night sky descended over the darkling, rippled sea, and in a few hours it was Halloween.

At 0256, lookouts on the conning tower of the *U-552* sighted the dark bulk of ships in the distance, and Kapitänleutnant Erich Topp ordered the submarine after the convoy. The *U-552* stalked HX 156 for 2½ hours, closing from off the port quarter. The *Niblack* was not actively patrolling station, and her radar did not detect the presence of the submarine. But the *U-552*'s approach took too long; then Topp discovered a four-funnel destroyer steaming off the windy corner of the convoy. The German skipper decided that first light was probably too near to allow him to maneuver wide of the escort and make a new attack approach; rather than be too ambitious and perhaps sink nothing, it was better to make certain of at least one target, and what better compensation for the frustrations of the grim war in the Atlantic than to sink an enemy escort vessel. Kapitänleutnant Topp decided to attack the destroyer.* Then he ordered another contact report on the convoy sent out.

Far across the water, on the distant starboard flank of HX 156, the *Tarbell*'s men suddenly picked up a direction-finder bearing on a transmission very close by. The signals were in short bursts; the destroyermen thought they might be numbers and dashes, and when they plotted the RDF bearing, they found that the transmissions were coming from the vicinity of the port side of the convoy. When he learned of the *Tarbell*'s find, the escort CO, Commander Richard E. "Possum" Webb, ordered the *Reuben James* to run down the RDF bearing. But vigilance was belated.

Old "Rube," not patrolling station, was steaming at about 9 knots 2,000 yards off the port beam of the last ship in the port column of the convoy. Tex Edwards, on the bridge "almost constantly" during the passage, was weary from lack of sleep and the steady effort of keeping his body "braced against the rolling of the ship." When he received the message from Commander Webb, he ordered increased speed and a turn to port.

From the *U-552*, the superstructure and stacks of the destroyer were starkly black against the slowly graying sky. At about 0532,

---

*Topp, like most submariners in heat of action, was not restrained by standing instructions to avoid combat with escorts that might be American.

Courtesy: Paul W. Hatch

The USS *Reuben James*. This photograph was taken on 21 August 1941, about two months before the "Rube" was lost.

the *U-552*, 1,000 yards off the port beam of the destroyer, fired a spread of two torpedoes. The *Reuben James* was starting to swing around to port, puffs of black smoke wafting back from her stacks, when the first German torpedo hit. The torpedo smashed into her port side, a little forward of her Number One funnel, below the bridge,* then exploded, ripping a large gash in her side. Water poured in, breaking lines and smashing bulkheads, and the *Reuben James* rocked and shuddered. The blast must have ignited the forward magazine,† for then a huge explosion occurred. "With a terrific roar, a column of orange flame" seared the paling sky, then subsided, "leaving a great black pall of smoke licked by moving tongues of orange. All the ship forward of number 4 stack . . . disappeared."

The explosion broke the spine of the *Reuben James*, and she cleaved in two. Up forward, a chief who was moving up the ladder to the bridge was blown clear of the ship, and Quartermaster Bill Appleton was blown from the helm through the top of the wheelhouse, which "opened up like the petals of a flower," over the fiery bridge and into the sea. Everyone else in the forward part of the ship, including Tex Edwards, young Craig Spowers, and every other officer, was killed almost immediately by the blast, fire, and onrushing sea. The forward part of the ship sank in a sibilant haze of smoke and steam.

The men aft had more chance. Seaman Dan Del Grosso was asleep in his bunk when the force of the explosion flung him to the deck; bent lockers were on their sides and bunks and mattresses were criss-crossed in a tangled shambles in the narrow passageway. He grabbed at his life jacket, but it was pinned under a twisted beam, so he left it and struggled through the wreckage up to the main deck. Topside, flames burned across metal surfaces, feeding on paint; ruptured fuel tanks spewed thick, black oil into the water. The stern was settling. Del Grosso did not have to dive overboard; he merely stepped off the deck into the sea.

Chief Bill Bergstresser led his seven men through the fire, smoke, and debris below up to the fantail, where surviving sailors huddled

*The *Kearny* was hit in almost exactly the same spot on the other side; but the *Kearny* was new, had plates five-eighths of an inch thick made of hard alloy steel, and a split engineering plant, while the *Reuben James* was weakened by the accumulated stress of 21 years at sea, was less well compartmentalized, and had plates three-eighths of an inch thick made of softer rolled steel.

†Topp thought that the explosion was perhaps caused by his second torpedo striking amidships, which is certainly a possibility, but it seems a little more likely, based on the limited available evidence, that the second torpedo passed astern when the destroyer started to swing to port.

in stunned, disorganized groups, waiting for the stern to settle and the fires to drive them into the water. The orange flames crackled and hissed, blazing high around the single remaining stack, and thick spirals of smoke blew aft. Some sailors were cutting loose rafts and heaving them into the sea. A machinist's mate took off his shoes and stuck his toes down into the water; he said it was cold. As the flames rushed aft and the fantail sank, men reluctantly half-slid, half-jumped into the slimy water. Last to go were the wounded and burned, who knew that they would have little hope in the water; finally, as the heat grew too intense, they gamely helped each other off the black and slippery deck into the sea.

Fireman Bob Carr swam to a balsa raft about seventy feet from the ship and joined a group of men clinging to its sides. The sailors were black with oil and shivering from the cold; some were choking and gagging, vomiting oil and salt water.

Seaman Del Grosso could not understand why he was not cold as he swam through the icy water; he thought the oil must somehow have warmed it. He did not realize that he was too numb to feel the cold. He reached a raft and tried to haul himself up onto it, but his oily body kept slipping back into the water; then someone grabbed him and he pulled himself aboard. Most of the men around him were vomiting black oil.

Some men did not make it to the rafts; they suffocated in the oil, or died of their wounds and burns, and a few drowned. The bodies of the dead bobbed inertly on the black swells.

It was quiet on the water. The survivors watched from on and around their rafts as the sea gurgled raucously over the stern section of their ship. Then from inside the destroyer came the screams of badly wounded or dazed men who had not been noticed amid the tangle of wreckage below and were now drowning as the stern sank. Soon it was quiet again.

As the stern went under and the exhausted men on the rafts struggled with fatigue and fear to attain initiative and give direction and coherence to the thus-far random efforts of survival, suddenly several of the destroyer's ready depth charges exploded, and the sea erupted in a huge, shuddering blast. Kapitänleutnant Topp reported, "Wreck atomized by powerful detonation of her own depth charges." The blast flipped rafts into the air and ripped and crushed the bodies of swimmers; jagged slivers of steel and debris whirred through the chill air, splashing in the water. As Fireman Carr remembered, "there was a blinding flash. It felt like I was swimming. Then I realized I couldn't feel any water under me. I turned head-down. I was about 25 feet above the water." Men still clinging to rafts were dazed; covered with sticky, slippery oil, they found it difficult to climb back on board or even to maintain their hold. Sailors in the water were bleeding from mouths, noses, ears; it was getting harder to tell the living from the dead. Sometimes a man holding onto the side of a raft lost his grip and slid under. It was still dark and hard to see when a man drowned, and the survivors, sick, stunned, and exhausted, lacked the strength to swim after the splashing sounds.

On one of the rafts, the sailors saw a long, dark shadow slide past on the water. "It's the goddamn sub surfacing," someone said. "Lay low, everybody," another voice warned. But as the vessel rushed by, they recognized it as a destroyer. They stood on the raft and shouted, but the raft was tilted by their sudden, anxious movements and spun by the wake of the passing ship; fortunately, it did not capsize. But the *Hilary P. Jones* passed on into the darkness.

After the explosion to port, Commander Webb cautiously ordered the *Hilary P. Jones* to make a sonar sweep of the area, screening the *Niblack*, which would rescue survivors; the *Benson* and *Tarbell* remained with the convoy. Soon the *Niblack's* men saw two rafts in the water with sailors clinging to their sides; beyond the rafts, the heads of men propped up by life jackets bobbed in the dusky water. The air was "filled with the sickly stench of fuel oil" and the sea was "flat and silvery under its thick coating." The men in the oily water looked like "black shiny seals"; sounds drifted upward from them, "cursing, praying, and hoarse shouts for help." The *Niblack* cautiously backed amongst the survivors, her sailors flinging lines overboard and rigging cargo nets over the side.

The men holding onto the nearest raft seemed in good shape. They chanted, "We are the *Reuben James'* men!" over and over, as they were drilled to do, so their voices would carry across the water. "But the bobbing blobs of isolated men" were "more pitiful. They're blown up and choking with oil and water, they are like small animals caught in molasses. We are now in a black circle of water, surrounded by a vast silver ring of oil slick. The men to port are drifting toward us and the hove lines are slipping through their greasy, oily hands. Soon many eager hands are grasping our cargo net, but our ship's upward roll breaks their weak and slippery hold." Most of the survivors were too weak, dazed, and oily to make it into the rafts, much less up a cargo net hung over the steep side of a rolling destroyer, so sixteen of *Niblack*'s sailors went down into the lead raft to help survivors out of the water and up the nets and ladders; several chiefs clung to the nets and tried to fasten lines around men in the water. The first man to board the *Niblack* was vomiting black oil. In the sea near the bow, an isolated man, half-blinded by oil and water, spluttered loud curses of frustration. Someone flung him a line and he was towed amidships to the nets and ladders. Off to starboard was "the obscure mass of another loaded raft," and a man on it lit his cigarette lighter and waved it in the darkness. But the raft drifted to leeward, out of range of the lines. The *Niblack*'s men shouted through the megaphones, "Hang on! We'll get you!"

The oil, darkness, and above all, the dazed, exhausted, and sometimes hysterical condition of the survivors protracted the rescue work. It took thirty-eight minutes to bring fifteen men onto the *Niblack*. A dull, red glow began to burn behind the line of the horizon. Lieutenant Commander Durgin went to the wing of the bridge and shouted, "Get those men aboard!"

By 0708, the grim task was nearly done. Then the sonar man reported a contact dead astern, and the wheelhouse phone buzzed; the *Hilary P. Jones* had detected it, too. There were still three men in the water. One, floating limply, was dead; another was unconscious, possibly dead; the third was semi-conscious, but obviously alive. Durgin did what he did not want but had to do. He ordered his men back on board; the engine room telegraph was snapped to full ahead. The *Niblack* lurched forward. The bodies astern bobbed in the swirling wake. The *Hilary P. Jones* ranged in and dropped a pattern of depth charges, "the white rising columns of water tinged with blood color in the dawning."

The destroyers steamed after the convoy. The *Niblack* smelled of oil. Two ensigns who had been down in the raft handling survivors were still, five hours later, naked, "their eyes, hair, and ears . . . plastered with oil in spite of . . . scrubbing." Most of the survivors were dazed by shock and weariness; some were bleeding internally, others were badly burned, and many were hysterical. The *Niblack* saved thirty-five men and the *Hilary P. Jones* ten. About one hundred men died on and in the water around the old *Reuben James* on that bitter Halloween morning.

Even while the rescue work went on, the *Benson* and *Tarbell*, left alone too long with the convoy, attacked sonar contacts. And to the northeast, U-boats were organizing for a fresh attack. HMS *Camelia*, one of five corvettes on the way to meet HX 156, encountered two submarines on the surface, taking them under fire; but both U-boats quickly submerged and escaped. The corvettes joined the American destroyers at 1426.

That night, the moon gleamed intermittently on the dark, rolling water. At 2110, the *Niblack*'s gunnery officer, at the gun director above the bridge, reported a U-boat to port. Three destroyers fired bursts of star shell, but the sighting was on a corvette which had roamed a little off station. The destroyermen were jumpy. Most slept with their clothes on; at mess, some speculated about the best means of abandoning ship if their destroyer were torpedoed. Lieutenant Commander Durgin did not allow men on the *Niblack*'s deck without life jackets on. The night passed without battle.

On the morning of the 1st, British destroyers arrived to take over the convoy. Even as the American destroyers started north with two vessels, one of which was the combat cargo ship USS *Alchiba*, HMS *Buxton* was driving off a U-boat astern of HX 156. And in the next few days, other U-boats approached the convoy, but they never succeeded in striking, and all the merchant ships, including three stragglers, made it safely to port.

En route to Iceland, the American destroyers picked up several sonar contacts. On the morning of the 2nd, the *Niblack*'s sailors remembered the *Reuben James*: when they were called to general quarters, they set a ship's record for speed. Then, at 0718, the *Benson*'s men saw a torpedo wake pass directly beneath the ship. Both the *Benson* and *Niblack* struck back with depth charges. A *Niblack* pattern brought up a gusher of black water and some oil and floating cork. The destroyermen thought they had damaged the U-boat and they waited for the submarine to surface. The *Niblack*'s men were poised to ram, wanting to slice the U-boat in two and pay the Nazis back for dead men on their minds. But if the contact was a U-boat, it was not badly hurt and crept safely away.

On the morning of the 3rd, the destroyermen saw "a great mountain rising straight out of the sea, shaped like a sperm whale's tooth." The coastline was "a great bleak jagged contour of mountains topped by a volcanic cone two thousand feet high and covered with snow." The two convoy ships went into Reykjavik Harbor, where the *Alchiba*, hampered by rising seas and a very green crew, was slowly unloaded. The destroyers steamed on toward Valley Forge: "Up the amazing corridor of Hvalfjördur, carpeted with dark green water and walled by sheer chocolate-colored precipices capped with a strangely white icing of snow. Now and then the walls fall away in gentler curves of dull greens and browns, giving way to black-violet mountains with their heads immersed in white icy clouds. The scale is so vast that one is convinced that the scattered houses and church yonder are tiny scale toys built by the Icelanders for their children."

The destroyers waited sadly at the boom gate as some British destroyers in mottled camouflage paint led out a small group of gray merchant ships. Then the American warships proceeded, on past the *Kearny*, riding well up in the water despite the ragged wound in her side, and anchored. In the *Niblack* and *Hilary P. Jones*, they called the roll of the survivors of the *Reuben James*. The *Niblack*'s sailors carefully lowered three men on stretchers, swathed in dark woolen Navy blankets, over the side, down into a motor whaleboat. The rest of the surviving sailors off the "Rube," wearing clothes given them by *Niblack*'s men, went down to the gig unaided, quietly. In the boat, the sailors sat "hooded in blankets"; some shouted words of goodbye and thanks to the men at the *Niblack*'s rail. A sleety snow was falling. The boat started and quickly chugged out of sight into the snow-blurred dark. And so the four destroyers reached Iceland, mourning one of their tribe.[2]

The nation took the grim news of the loss of the *Reuben James* calmly. One of the President's advisers felt that this was because Americans

always have considered the men in their regular armed forces—Navy, Army, and most of all, Marine Corps—as rugged mercenaries who signed up voluntarily, as do policemen and firemen, for hazardous service; it was, of course, tough luck when any of them were killed in line of duty in a Central American revolution, or on an accidently sunk submarine or on a deliberately sunk gunboat, like the *Panay*, but it was still all in the day's work. There was little or no self-identification of the normal American civilian with the professional American soldier or sailor. In the case of the drafted men, however, the attitude was entirely different. They were "our boys" who must be kept out of harm's way at all costs. Since there were no drafted men in the Navy . . . there was no great popular indignation . . . for the attacks. . . .[3]

Or, as mordant Harry Hopkins once put it, politicians thought that only ground troops had mothers!

The Navy was at war in the Atlantic, but many in the nation still doubted the necessity for sacrifice. As Admiral Stark wrote to a friend: "Events are moving rapidly toward a real showdown. . . . The Navy is already in the war of the Atlantic, but the country doesn't seem to realize it. Apathy, to the point of open opposition, is evident in a considerable section of the press. . . . Whether the country knows it or not, *we are at war.*"[4]

Yet, as the Pacific commander had earlier warned:

> To back into a war, unsupported or only half-heartedly supported by public opinion, is to court losing it. A left-handed, vacillating approach . . . is totally destructive of that determination and firmness of national character without which we cannot succeed. The situation demands that our people be fully informed of the issues involved, the means necessary and available, and the consequences of success or failure. When we go in we must go . . . to the full extent of our resources. To tell our people anything else is to perpetrate a base deception which can only be reflected in lackadaisical and half-hearted prosecution. [5]

But the President and his people were still unwilling to tolerate unpleasant truths; neither sought to use the losses in the ocean battle to sound a more strident trumpet. As Ickes lamented to his diary, "apparently the President is going to wait—God knows for how long or what."[6] But if neither President nor people wished to declare war on cold, realistic grounds of national security, both encouraged Congress to revise the neutrality laws to permit American merchant ships to travel in convoys to the United Kingdom; the losses attendant upon such a step must surely have resulted in a declaration of war by the spring of 1942. In the meantime, the ambivalence of President and people would continue: they would make war, but they would not declare it.

At first, some Axis leaders feared that the sinking of the *Reuben James* might provoke war, but were soon reassured. The Fuehrer felt that the incident showed the United States had not yet made enough progress in rearmament to risk full-scale war; he was sufficiently relieved to finally sanction U-boat operations off Newfoundland. But the measure of escalation was not destined to help Admiral Doenitz win his Tonnage War; the thick fogs off Newfoundland protected merchantmen from the prowling U-boats.[7]

In the Atlantic Fleet, most men were saddened and angered by the loss of the *Reuben James.*[8]

But hard-bitten Ernie King, sparse of praise, wrote Admiral Stark, "I suggest that we go slow in the matter of making 'heroes' out of these people who have, after all, done the jobs they are trained to do. The earlier incidents loom large by contrast with peacetime conditions, but can be expected to become commonplace incidents as we get further along."⁹

Young Ensign Donald H. Dorris heard the news aboard the *Vincennes* in Boston Harbor and thought, "I would like to get transferred to a destroyer. Not much action for cruisers. FDR needs to make up his mind what we are to do."¹⁰

Ensign Tom McWhorter of the destroyer *Sterett* thought it a crude joke when an officer asked, "Have you heard that the *Reuben James* was sunk?" When told that the abysmal news was true, he blurted out the first words that entered his mind: "But that's impossible. Craig is the First Lieutenant of the *Reuben James*. He wouldn't let her sink!" To McWhorter, it was bitter and "so ironical that my closest friend . . . should have been killed as a result of enemy action even before war was declared." He remembered Craig Spowers standing at the gangway of his four-stacker in Casco Bay, capless, a Lucky hanging from his mouth, saying good night, and he thought of the talks they had had of the inevitability of war and Craig once saying, "The only true sign of patriotism is sincere service!" Ensign Tom McWhorter thought it time that the rest of the country started to think that way.¹¹

Lieutenant Commander Sam Dealey, Tex Edwards' former Exec on the "Rube," was on the bridge of the *S-20* off Portland when his radioman, obviously upset, came up the conning-tower ladder and tightly said that he had intercepted a message saying that the *Reuben James* had been sunk by a sub off Iceland. With deliberate calm masking horror and rage, Dealey thanked the sailor and asked him to report any further news. Until that moment, Sam Dealey, like most naval officers, had striven to maintain a correct, professional attitude toward the war, despite anti-Nazi sentiments; he expressed a common attitude by saying that he was "anti-everything except the USA." Now Sam Dealey hurt to kill Nazis.¹²

And so the war that neither the United States nor Germany wanted to declare but neither could afford to terminate continued. As one writer said, "There was now neither armistice nor declared war; but the bodies of US boys were at the bottom of the Atlantic."¹³

And outside the Navy, people went about their daily business, little changed by the deaths of Tex Edwards, Craig Spowers, and Walt Sorenson, who never made it back to the wheatfields of Nebraska, and their shipmates. For no one asked them to remember old *Reuben James.*

And in the Atlantic, the destroyers still went to sea, and the convoys continued to run.

26.

The
Halifax Express

On 1 November, the *Charles F. Hughes, Gleaves, Lansdale, Madison,* and *Simpson,* with a brood of seven merchant vessels, and aided by two Mariners of Patrol Squadron 73, searched the waters south of Iceland for the forty-one ships of ON 30, delayed by bad weather and rough seas. It became necessary to change the Momp several times in order to facilitate a rendezvous. At 0330 on the 2nd, three Mariners took off from the dark waters of Skerjafjordhur to help. Delayed by darkness and fog, they did not reach the American destroyers until 0815. At 0945, in thickening fog, the fliers sighted the squat, gray shapes and white wakes of the Allied ships on the green-gray water below. The patrol planes guided the two groups of ships to the latest rendezvous, at about 57°-18′ north, 28° west, and at 1219, the destroyers assumed responsibility for ON 30 and led the convoy on to westward.

Meanwhile, the PBMs struggled back north through the mist, flying on instruments. The planes became separated as they droned through the wooly, gray fog. After eleven hours in the air, two of the Mariners landed safely on the water back at base; the third, flown by Ensign C.M. Thornquist, did not return. Low visibility precluded an air search for the missing plane and a land search of the shoreline was unsuccessful. The fliers tried to hope that the plane was somewhere out on the water, waiting out the fog; they did not like to think about the lack of radio transmissions from the missing aircraft. It was a cheerless night at Skerjafjordhur.

309

The next morning, an Army P-40 spotted the wreckage of a PBM glittering on a hillside east of Reykjavik. Ensign Thornquist and all eleven of his men were dead. The price of the 75 minutes spent over ON 30 was twelve lives, one for every 6¼ minutes. The fliers could only hope that the destroyermen made the best use of time so dearly bought.

The convoy steamed southwest in early good fortune. Then on the 5th, the *Gleaves* attacked a sonar contact off to port with a good, deep pattern of seven depth charges; but the target was a whale. The next day, lookouts on the *Madison* glimpsed a dark shape submerging off her port bow; minutes later, the destroyer picked up sonar contact on an object moving aft. The *Madison* swung to port to keep the contact ahead, then attacked uncertainly with a deep pattern of two depth charges. After the explosions, the destroyer again swung around to port to search on the reverse course of the last sound bearing, the usual practice when attempting to regain contact. In several minutes, the *Madison* did regain contact and attacked with a deep pattern of five depth charges, but no debris was carried to the shifting surface by the blasts, and she rejoined the convoy. Late the next afternoon, a *Lansdale* lookout sighted a submerging object to starboard. The *Charles F. Hughes* joined the *Lansdale* for a combined search of the area; the two destroyers picked up a sonar contact and made three quick attacks, dropping seventeen depth charges. But despite firm, metallic echoes, there was no U-boat present. The mystery of the tenacious object in pursuit of the convoy was solved shortly afterwards when *Madison's* men sighted a bleeding whale.

Thick fog and intermittent rain squalls helped give the ships of ON 30 a safe passage; the convoy was dispersed off Argentia on the 9th.[1]

The convoys continued to run.

Between 1 November and 7 December, the escort groups of Support Force took fourteen convoys across the North Atlantic, seven each way, riding shotgun for approximately 550 ships.

Ready for their second round trip, the modern destroyers *Ericsson* and *Eberle* and four-stackers *Dallas*, *Ellis*, and *Upshur*, escorting the U.S. Navy oiler *Rapidan*, joined the forty-one merchant vessels of HX 157 off Argentia on the forenoon of the 30th. Two of the merchantmen, unable to maintain 9+ knots, had already been forced to turn back. The convoy vessels carried petroleum products, steel, scrap metal, iron ore, sulphur, nitrates, sugar, refrigerated goods, and general cargo. HMCS *Annapolis* flung the convoy orders over to the *Dallas* by throwing gun, and the Americans assumed control of HX 157. Early out, the weather was good, and Canadian Hudson patrol bombers watched over the ships in daylight until they passed beyond range on the evening of the 2nd of November. The convoy was diverted onto a westerly route to keep it clear of some U-boats known to be stalking HX 156; it did not swing to the northeast until reaching 56°-40' north, then it steamed still farther north, to 60° north, before running east to the Momp.

The news of the loss of *Reuben James* kept the destroyers alert and perhaps jittery. On the morning of 1 November, the *Ericsson* made two brief attacks on an uncertain contact to port, wasting six depth charges. Then the *Dallas* and *Ellis* hunted a good contact most of the same morning, working over the vicinity with thirty-nine depth charges in a search of rare and excellent tenacity. The good hunt of the four-stackers left the *Eberle* alone to defend the entire starboard side of the convoy, and she did not have long to wait for trouble.

Detecting a sonar contact to starboard, she ranged over and struck with a deep pattern of seven depth charges, bringing oil to the surface. Inspired by the hint of damage, the *Eberle* searched for about 45 minutes, but was unable to regain contact. When she returned to the convoy, she discovered the four-stackers still absent astern. The entire starboard side of the convoy had been bereft of escorts for nearly an hour! But the tenacious escorts had flushed a U-boat, though they failed to hurt it. Soon the U-boat surfaced to resume pursuit and send out a contact report on the convoy. In the afternoon, the *Ericsson* investigated a sighting report off her port quarter, but found nothing. There were several alarms in the next few days, as the skittish destroyers attacked several contacts, fish or water turbulence; but fog off the Newfoundland coast prevented the alerted U-boats from finding HX 157. At night, the destroyers, not yet warned by the *Kearny*'s fate, still patrolled too close to the convoy, within 2,000 yards.

Strong easterly winds and rising seas added to the route diversion and prolonged the voyage. A heavy rainstorm and high seas on the 7th resulted in many stragglers, and the convoy was much reduced that afternoon when the American destroyers turned it over to British escorts at about 60° north, 22°-30' west; the U.S. warships took the

Rapidan and three Icelandic steamers north. All the merchant ships of HX 157, including the stragglers, reached port safely. The American destroyers, low on fuel because of their protracted passage and energetic defense of the convoy, reached Valley Forge on the 9th, weary but aware of having put in a good week's work.[2]

The *Roe* and four-stackers *Truxtun, Bainbridge, Sturtevant,* and *Overton* went back to sea prematurely to escort ON 31, switching assignments with the Canadian escort group led by the *Restigouche* ("Rustyguts") and the *St. Croix,* which had gone out to strengthen another group. Rain and rising seas delayed the convoy, and the American destroyers, abetted by PBMs, searched the wind-lashed sea an extra day before accomplishing the rendezvous on the afternoon of 4 November and adding their burden of five vessels from Iceland to the twenty-seven ships of the convoy.

The weather continued bad, and the ships pitched and yawed in high, rolling seas. A sailor on one of the merchantmen was washed overboard, but was recovered; one of the *Roe's* men was injured by a closing hatch cover, and there were the usual minor cuts and bruises and burns from spilled coffee. The trip was long and enervating, but not dangerous, and the convoy was safely dispersed off Argentia on the 15th.[3]

Because of the loss of the *Reuben James* and the increased activity of U-boats off Newfoundland, the new ships *Buck, Swanson,* and *Ludlow* and four-stackers *Cole* and *McCormick* were lent the modern destroyer *Woolsey* for the first part of the passage with the next eastbound convoy. On the morning of the 5th of November, en route to meet HX 158, the *Ludlow* and *McCormick,* after working over a sonar contact, remained behind for an hour to keep the U-boat down, then caught up with the other escorts. A thick fog billowed over the water, and the destroyers, using up precious fuel, searched restlessly south and east of Argentia for the convoy. Then, at night, *Cole's* men sighted a periscope-like object in the water off her port bow, and the four-stacker attacked with nine depth charges to no avail; a short while later, the periscope reappeared briefly, but vanished before the *Cole* could attack. When the destroyers found the convoy late on the afternoon of the 6th, the *Cole* was already so low on fuel that she was forced to return to Argentia. Because of numerous contacts, the *Wilkes* was sent to join the escort for a few days. When old *Greer* arrived to replace the *Cole* she had a fire in her galley, then her stern 4-inch gun was fired by mistake. Thus far, all the omens were bad.

The escorts and forty merchant vessels steamed northeast on a calm, rippled sea at 9 knots through drifting dunes of gray fog. The *Buck*, out ahead, detected a sonar contact to port and went after it; off the port bow of the convoy, the *McCormick* picked up the same contact. At 1829, the *Buck* was in the midst of an attack when *McCormick* slid out of the curling mist only 200 yards away. The four-stacker could not swerve away for fear of passing over *Buck's* depth charges. Her skipper, Lieutenant E.J. Sullivan, yelled "Back emergency full!"; *McCormick* shuddered and slowed, narrowly averting a disaster. Later, in fog and darkness, the *Swanson* was missing from the escort screen for five hours, and the *Woolsey*, five miles out on the starboard beam to surprise massing U-boats, was out of contact with the convoy all night. The escort commander reported that such incidents "forcibly demonstrated" the need for radar.

The night of 6/7 November was long and menacing. The *McCormick* struck at a sonar contact off her port bow; "Lucky Lud" made two attacks on a contact off her starboard quarter; and the distant *Woolsey* joined the thunder with a brief attack. At 2251, the *Buck*, patrolling station, began a turn to port when lookouts called out the shiny crease of a torpedo wake sliding through the black water off her port quarter. The streak passed astern, *Buck's* sudden turn her salvation. The angry destroyer steamed back down the track, but was unable to develop a contact. Soon the *Ludlow* and *McCormick* were again blasting at firm contacts with patterns of depth charges. But it was a profitless night for the destroyers.

In the next two days, the fog intensified and the ships became dark blurs in the soggy mist; the U-boats did not find HX 158. Then winds and seas rose, and by the 11th, a full gale was raging. Much of the time, the dipping, swaying merchant vessels were invisible in the wind-lashed rain. The *Buck* recorded a roll of 52 degrees; "Lucky Lu !" for once belied her nickname and took superficial damage topside. When a merchant sailor was injured in a fall, the *Buck* was lowering a whaleboat to send help, but the destroyer rolled suddenly, and the boat slammed against the davits, ripping a hole in its side;

Chief Pharmacist's Mate W.W. Brown went across the stormy water in one of the freighter's boats. As the weather ameliorated, the destroyers began the tedious labor of rounding up stragglers. On the afternoon of the 13th, the ships reached the rendezvous with the British escort at about 59°-40' north, 27° west, some twenty hours late; only four of the straggling merchant vessels were still missing. All the convoy ships reached the United Kingdom safely, including the stragglers, one after a voyage of more than three weeks. The American destroyers took three Iceland-bound vessels north, arriving on the night of the 14th. It was another long, wearying trip.[4]

The *Edison* was ordered to replace the *Reuben James* in escort group 4.1.3. Methodical Lieutenant Commander Murdaugh talked to other destroyermen at Boston about conditions in the Atlantic; they warned him about bad weather. The Navy's winter clothing was well designed, warm, and tight-fitting to keep out icy wind and water, but it was not yet generally available. Consequently, Murdaugh's men made the rounds of stores that sold fishermen's supplies on the Boston waterfront and purchased warm clothing; heavy sheepskin-lined coats were most popular amongst the crew. Ship's funds were lent to men too broke to finance the clothing, and the officers also supplied loans. The Red Cross was asked for wool, so that the crew's women could knit sweaters and long johns, but the request was refused. The women bought their own wool. (The next winter, with the nation fully at war, it became fashionable for private charities to assist service personnel, and the destroyer then received a large box of Red Cross sweaters; but as the ship was in Oran and the North African sun was warm, the skipper "could not give away the sweaters.") Murdaugh also had two cases of Old Crow brought aboard at Boston; shots would be alloted drenched and tired men coming off watch. Fresh bread and pastries made by Murdaugh's restaurant-trained cooks added to the general sense of contentment aboard the newcomer. *Edison's* greenhorns were going off to war first cabin.

But the new escort group, a swift one with four new ships and only one four-stacker, got off to an unpromising start. The *Benson's* skipper fractured his leg in an accident ashore, and was replaced by his Exec, Lieutenant C.V. Hawk. Then the *Niblack*, while searching off Reykjavik for a tardy Icelandic cargo ship, collided in stormy seas with a Norwegian freighter; she lost an anchor and had a hole

The USS *Vulcan* working on the damaged *Kearny*

punched in her side. The destroyer rushed back to Valley Forge, where the *Vulcan* replated the gash, and she rejoined the escorts at sea. The *Benson, Niblack, Hilary P. Jones, Edison,* and *Tarbell*, shepherding the naval cargo ship *Algorab* and an Icelandic steamer, spent almost three days searching in a storm for the convoy. ON 34 was first delayed, then scattered, by a wild, raging gale; at least one merchant ship was damaged and a dozen were missing. HMS *Vanoc* and seven corvettes struggled to round up ships, while the American destroyers edged south into mountainous seas, searching and waiting, suffering damage to bulwarks, stanchions, and lockers. The rendezvous was not accomplished until the afternoon of the 12th, at about 55°-24' north, 25°-19' west. Arrangements had been made for two Canadian corvettes to accompany the American ships for a time to help them conserve fuel for the obviously long passage ahead, but both corvettes were damaged in the storm and forced to return to base.

The American destroyers and thirty-six merchant ships steamed west and south. The *Edison*, new at the work, attacked a contact on the 13th of November, water turbulence. The storm raged on. From the *Buck*, the *Algorab* was the only ship visible. An attempt was made on the 15th to refuel the four-stacker *Tarbell* from a British tanker in the convoy, but first the tow lines parted, then the fuel hose developed a leak. The intelligent improvisation was thwarted, and the *Tarbell* was forced to depart for Argentia. The weather improved. The destroyers carried out several attacks on sonar contacts, wakes and turbulence. But late on the 17th, another gale blew down on the ships, the wind reaching force 11. High seas rushed over drenched bows, snow and sleet swept out of a black sky, reducing visibility. At each dawn, there were fewer ships present; on the 20th, twenty-two ships remained. The next day, the vessels steamed into a dense fog southeast of Cape Race and, with scattering inevitable, it was decided to disperse the convoy at about 46°-18' north, 52°-40' west. All the ships of ON 34, including the sundry stragglers, made port safely. The U.S. destroyers steamed to Argentia, glad to be done with an arduous two-week passage.[5]

On the morning of 10 November, the new destroyers *Plunkett* and *Livermore*, four-stackers *Decatur, Cole,* and *Badger*, and Coast Guard cutter *Campbell* found the thirty-three ships of HX 159 after a search of several hours through chill, gauzy fog. The destroyers and merchant ships steamed a westerly, then northerly, route. The escorts, commanded by Captain Alan Kirk, patrolled 5,000-6,000 yards out from the convoy as visibility allowed, harbinger of improved technique learned at cost. In the fog and darkness, one merchant vessel became separated and returned to Halifax. The merchant masters of HX 159 handled their ships well, executing course changes with "very little disorder"; but station-keeping was "ragged," and the starboard ships were "seldom in column and never at proper distance." As usual, the convoy vessels made excessive smoke. The *Plunkett*'s radar rig was the inefficient, immobile, old type, and although the *Decatur* had a better model, hasty installation and inexperience led to frequent breakdowns. Thus, it was difficult for the escorts to keep station at night. Rough seas made the sonar gear "valueless and ineffective" much of the time; in stormy weather, "ships could not hear their own propellers let alone those of . . . ships of the convoy, or submarines." The task of the sonar men was complicated by schools of big fish which seemed to follow the ships. The *Decatur* attacked a false contact. The *Plunkett*'s officer of the deck reported a torpedo wake and ordered a sharp turn before realizing that it was the track of a large fish. One of the lookouts on the "Charlie P" sighted a "torpedo" wake crossing beneath the ship from port to starboard, then reversing course and retracing its track!

Two days later, the *Badger*, unfortunate *Kearny*'s replacement, and the *Decatur* attacked firm contacts. Late the next day, the *Decatur*'s listening gear picked up high-speed propeller noises of unusual clarity; Lieutenant Commander J.C. Sowell on the bridge could hear them. Off to port, a surfaced U-boat was turning to close the convoy. The *Decatur* swung out to attack, and the U-boat submerged; the propeller noises abruptly stopped. Below the surface the U-boat swung to starboard, keeping inside the destroyer's turning circle, and maneuvered to throw out "knuckles" of water turbulence, so that the sonar men above would echo-range on her wake instead of her hull. The submarine was off the *Decatur*'s port bow, and Sowell took his ship in for an attack. The destroyer released five depth charges, but they exploded far wide of and behind the U-boat. John Schmidt brought the *Badger* over to help and the four-stacker soon picked up a contact, probably on *Decatur*'s wake, and attacked it without result. Unable to regain contact, the destroyers rejoined the convoy.

Again, rain, hail, and snow blurred the sea and sky, and the wild, black-green ocean rolled at the ships. On the 15th, the *Badger* twice jarred to emergency slowdowns to avoid ramming the suddenly glimpsed *Livermore*; sailors sustained minor injuries from skidding on wet decks and from hatches slamming shut. And, as usual, in the destroyers:

> The days ground you with dull and unvarying cruelty. The watches on the bridge struck as inexorably as the bells of a clock. Half your life you spent on the bridge; no night passed but that the hard hand on your shoulder and the malevolent light in your face jerked you from sleep made troubled and uneasy by the tossing of that steel shell that encased you and with whose destiny yours was so irrevocably welded. And the clanging call of the general alarm rasped you to battle stations, night and day, from sleep and from meals, always with the same emptyhandedness of failure in the end. . . . you sought an enemy as shadowy and untouchable as Nemesis.[6]

The ships were late to the Momp, but miraculously, only one vessel straggled. The British eastern ocean escort was also late, and the two groups of ships groped toward each other in hazy, but less violent weather. The British escorts used the radio too frequently for the ease of Captain Kirk, who acidly noted, "The radio discipline of British-Canadian Escort Units is very lax . . . apparently radio silence is unknown to them." But the war-wise British understood what the Americans had yet to learn, that sometimes speedy communications are preferable to completely secure, but slower communications.

On the morning of the 19th, at about 62° north, 22°-30' west, HMS *Rockingham* and four corvettes and five trawlers took charge of the convoy. All the ships of HX 159, including the lonely straggler, reached port safely. The American destroyers went north to Iceland with the store ship USS *Yukon* and four U.S.-flag merchantmen.

The introduction of the "Treasury"-class Coast Guard cutter *Campbell* to ocean-escort duty was a success. Although the sturdy ship was not as versatile or potent as a destroyer, she stood up to the stormy seas and was very economical of fuel, consuming only 51,000 pounds as compared to the 65,000-72,000 pounds used up by the larger escorts.

Captain Kirk sounded an old lament, requesting more modern destroyers for the Support Force; he pointed out that the need to conserve fuel limited the speed and the activity of the four-stackers, warning, "At low speeds, these ships, in effect, were as vulnerable as the convoy. . . ." But most of all, Kirk worried about the lack of efficient radar in face of the enemy's bold surface tactics at night; "Escorts without Radar are not properly equipped for war service. . . . If the enemy can see in the dark, our ships are like blind men.

. . . The escorts are then entirely on the defensive, and are not able to conduct aggressive, offensive operations against the enemy." And so the Atlantic sailors learned as they fought.[7]

Storms damaged ships and altered escort schedules. Hence, after only four days in, the *Ericsson* and *Eberle* and four-stackers *Dallas*, *Ellis*, and *Upshur* drew an odd-numbered convoy. They left Iceland on the 13th with naval auxiliaries *Almaack* and *Tarazed* and an Icelandic cargo ship. The next morning, one of *Ericsson's* men, Seaman 3/C F.J. Carozza, was stricken with appendicitis and it was decided to transfer him to the better facilities of *Tarazed* for treatment. During the transfer, the *Eberle* screened the two ships and a bulky Mariner cruised in the gray sky overhead.

Suddenly, the *Eberle* picked up a sonar contact ahead, a U-boat trailing the main force. Lieutenant Commander E.R. Gardner swung the *Eberle* through the gray swells after the submarine. The U-boat turned to port as the destroyer closed to 700 yards, then, at high speed, veered sharply to starboard, creating crinkly ripples of underwater turbulence. The *Eberle's* sonar man lost the hull of the U-boat amidst the wakes and knuckles of water, and the destroyer turned to starboard and commenced another search. It took her about twenty minutes to regain contact; the submarine was some 1,000 yards off her port beam. As the *Eberle* swung over and lunged in for an attack, the U-boat, invulnerable to sonar detection as the destroyer neared, hooked around on an opposite heading. The *Eberle* steamed on along the U-boat's last-known heading, dropping five depth charges from her racks and looping two abeam from her Y-gun in a fine, deep pattern. But the "ash cans" fell wide of and behind the U-boat, and the rumbling, boiling explosions brought no debris to the surface. Aided by the low-flying Mariner, the *Eberle* tenaciously searched for four hours more, but the U-boat escaped.

The ships reached the Momp the next day, but the convoy was delayed and scattered by a storm. After using up fourteen hours' worth of fuel while fitfully searching and waiting in the vicinity of the rendezvous, the American ships met the escort and merchant vessels of ON 35 at about 60°-15' north, 22° west, on the morning of 15 November; thirteen ships were already missing from the convoy. The American destroyers and the Canadian corvette *Sherbrooke*, which was attached to the U.S. escort for several days because the delayed rendezvous and stormy seas portended a long, fuel-consuming passage, led the twenty-six merchant ships on a west by southwest heading.

The merchant vessels of ON 35 were poor at station-keeping and deficient in virtually every aspect of convoy discipline. Many of them made excessive smoke in daytime and kept lights on at night in bad weather to avoid collision. Captain M.Y. Cohen, the escort commander, thought it a wretched rabble of the sea. Then on the 16th, the ships were struck by gale-force winds, snow squalls, and high, churning seas. Although there were many stragglers, some as far as 30-40 miles astern, the convoy commodore made no attempt to close up or reorganize the ships during lulls in the storm. Finding it difficult to maintain steerageway at the low speed that the laboring smaller and slower ships could manage in the storm, the large, high-speed vessels maintained speed and moved ahead, further stringing out the disordered convoy. As the storm continued, ON 35 grew more disorganized; and as the merchant vessels became more scattered and strung out, they imperiled their own safety, for the escorts could defend fewer of them.

The ships pitched and rolled in the turbulent ocean. *Dallas'* deck log recorded: "Average period of ship's roll over a period of twenty-five rolls noted to be 9.2 seconds; minimum period 7.8 seconds; maximum period 10.2 seconds. Maximum roll 30." On the night of the 18th/19th, a course change to the southwest to take the ships clear of a suspected U-boat concentration southeast of Greenland brought about further chaos in the muddled convoy, and more ships straggled. Still more ships became separated in the mist and squalls off the east coast of Newfoundland. By the morning of the 27th, only seven of the merchant ships were with the escort, and one of the destroyers was missing. The *Ellis*, wandering alone through the storms with her sonar gear broken and a hospital case aboard, was given permission to head for Argentia. The remnant of the convoy was dispersed off Newfoundland on the 27th. All the merchantmen reached port safely. The destroyers, after a trying two-week trip, had a short journey home.[8]

On the morning of the 17th, after an easterly search through rising seas in cold, windy weather, modern destroyers *Mayo* and *Nicholson* and four-stackers *Babbitt*, *Leary*, and *Schenck* met the sixty-one vessels of HX 160 off Argentia. The escort commander, Captain "Sol"

Phillips, elected to place his four-stackers ahead and off the bows and his two new ships off the quarters to get wider coverage of the flanks and stern. Steaming on a northerly route, the merchantmen maintained station well and their signalling was good, but as visibility deteriorated, many sought to keep at least stern lights on at night; the busy escorts challenged sixteen light violations in one night. The convoy steamed into snow squalls on the 19th, and several of the destroyermen received minor bruises and burns from falls and spilled coffee as the seas became stormier.

In the afternoon of the 19th, the *Leary* entered the history books when her radarman picked up a blip on his scope and called out a U-boat off her starboard bow. It was recorded as the first American radar contact on a hostile vessel. But it may have been only a whale. The object submerged, and was picked up on the sonar gear, and *Leary* attacked with a shallow-set pattern of five depth charges, but without result. On the morning of the 20th, the *Nicholson* attacked a contact off her port quarter, also to no avail; then her green men reported a periscope astern, but the *Mayo* investigated and found nothing.

After a two-day lull in the weather, another storm struck on the night of the 22nd. As they pitched and rolled, the destroyers took minor damage topside. The new destroyers, suffering the growing pains of youth, sustained cracked side-plating, and the *Nicholson* developed a leak which flooded her sound room. Captain Phillips, worried about the fuel situation of the four-stackers, tried to arrange a more westerly Momp, but the British escorts, too, were delayed by the gale and behind schedule. The *Babbitt* was sent ahead in the storm to scout for the British but, by dark on the 25th, the two escort groups still had not met. Phillips resolved to wait until 1000 the next morning, then detach the other escorts to Iceland and, in the *Mayo*, keep on with the convoy. However, the Redcoats arrived early the following morning, and after several hours of sorting out and re-forming the milling, rolling ships, the British took command of the convoy, and the American destroyers steamed north with five merchantmen.

The stormy seas thrashed the ships with increasing fury, ripping away bulwarks, smashing boats, denting lockers, and sweeping ladders, hoses, and loose gear over the side. The *Mayo* reported leaks and slightly buckled decks: the *Babbitt* sustained buckled and warped bulkheads and doors, dished-in plating, and broken antennae. The destroyermen were cold and always damp, but as the *Babbitt*'s skipper said, "Curiously, no one was sick at sea. No colds, no illness. We were uncomfortable, often wet, but never sick." Seasickness was not treated with preventive medicine; a man either got over it, as "almost everyone" did, or he could not remain a destroyerman.

On the night of the 27th, as the ships labored on toward Iceland, the *Babbitt* picked up a radar contact about 1,000 yards astern and to port. The four-stacker swung around and headed back toward the contact; the blip disappeared from the radarscope, but the sonar gear returned a solid, metallic echo as the object submerged. The *Babbitt* attacked with five depth charges, the explosions making white, fried-egg patterns on the black sea; she then searched for half an hour, but could not regain contact. The destroyers reached Iceland late on the 28th, weary from another protracted voyage.

In his report, Captain Phillips sounded a familiar lament; he urged more training for the crews. In his opinion, the radar and sonar operators required work in better weather and milder seas to improve their technique and conning and attack personnel needed work at the British attack-teacher machine being installed at Casco Bay. The escort crews were not sufficiently well practiced to detect and counter, almost instinctively, the agile maneuvers of U-boats in attack and evasion. Gunnery training was also needed; the *Mayo*'s men had not fired their guns in seven long months. As Phillips noted: "If adequate training periods are not scheduled it is useless to assume that the escorts are proficient in the use of the equipment provided."[9] But the shortage of destroyers still had Admiral Bristol robbing Peter to pay Paul, and the exigencies of war subverted requirements of training. Captain Phillips needed time; but Admiral Bristol had none to give.

The ships of ON 37 were delayed and scattered by storms that developed into a gale, and the Momp was changed three times even before the American escorts, the *Buck*, *Swanson*, *Ludlow*, *Greer*, and *McCormick*, left Valley Forge on the morning of the 21st. The destroyers reached the rendezvous the following morning, but found no convoy vessels atop the heaving gray rollers. Assisted by two PBYs, they searched eastward and, at noon, sighted wisps of smoke coiling above the horizon, then the dark silhouettes of ships. At 1311, the American escorts assumed from HMS *Watchman* responsibility for the convoy; only thirty-five vessels were present, as six had already turned back, four were missing, and one was straggling about

15 miles astern. The convoy vessels steamed southwest at less than 6 knots; the destroyermen knew that they were in for another lengthy passage.

On the 23rd, a gale struck. Force 10 winds howled across black-green seas, driving high ridges of water at the bucking, rolling ships. Sometimes the merchant vessels, lightly laden or in ballast, hung over the crests of tall rollers, their propellers spinning out of the water. Although they showed too many lights at night, convoy discipline was otherwise good, but it was not proof against the storm. By dawn on the 24th, the destroyers counted only sixteen ships in sight; after dark, only nine ships were present. The next night, the *Swanson* and *Greer* nearly collided in the stormy blackness off the starboard side of the convoy. The newer destroyers took more topside punishment than the four-stackers, whose men, out of grim necessity, were more adept at securing ship for heavy weather. By the 26th, only three ships were with the dispersed escorts. The *Greer* temporarily fell behind when the seas carried away the cover of her after hatch, flooding the steering engine room; the *McCormick* stood by her sister ship. In the wild gray seas the escorts worked doggedly to round up stragglers and, by the 28th, the *Swanson* had four merchantmen in her care, the *McCormick* three, the *Buck* between six and ten, and the *Greer*, ordered to Argentia because of lack of fuel, one. The convoy was formally dispersed on the 30th, south of Argentia; all its ships made port safely. The weary escorts headed for the barn.[10]

On the 23rd of November, the *Roe* and *Woolsey* and the four-stackers *Bernadou*, *DuPont*, *MacLeish*, and *Lea* steamed in company with the naval tanker *Sapelo* to meet HX 161 south of Argentia. The merchant ships and their Canadian escort were delayed by fog and rising seas, and a new rendezvous was set, farther south, for that afternoon. To make the rendezvous on time, the destroyers had to turn up 15 knots, so the slow *Sapelo* was sent back to Argentia to await the next convoy. Dashing south, the destroyers located the convoy, whose forty-six vessels carried petroleum products, grain, refrigerated goods, and general cargo. The convoy steamed an easterly course along 44° north to avoid the confusion of weather-beaten stragglers building up to the north. Seas were so high and visibility was so low that even on the first night out there were stragglers.

At 0320 on the morning of the 24th, the *DuPont* was steaming through damp, gauzy fog when her lookouts sighted a merchant ship dead ahead at 200 yards. Her skipper ordered the engineers to back emergency full and, as the destroyer responded, the merchant vessel passed ahead. But the destroyermen were granted no time to relish the reprieve. Abruptly, broad on the *DuPont*'s port bow, the Norwegian freighter *Thorshovdi* loomed out of the mist, looking huge at close range. As the destroyer edged back, the freighter slid to port in an attempt to pass ahead, but there was not time, and the *Thorshovdi* rammed into *DuPont*'s port bow. The destroyer's stem was demolished to the keel, her plating was split at frame 8, and two forward compartments were wrecked. Her men promptly shored up the forward bulkheads, but her mangled bow would not stand the stress of a winter crossing, and she was detached to Boston. Doubtless, the prospect of liberty mitigated the misfortune in the eyes of her crew, especially as there were no casualties in the accident, but the loss was a severe one for the Support Force to bear; the *DuPont* would not take out a convoy again for two months. Although the *Thorshovdi* was not gravely hurt, she straggled from the convoy as a result of collision damage, but made it safely to the United Kingdom.

For the destroyers and convoy, the days were foggy, cold, and rainy. The ships were pelted by dark squalls of hail and snow, and sailors stood their watches in damp misery. A watchstander in the *Lea* suffered a sharp scalp wound when he was flung into a gun shield by a sudden deep roll; a *Woolsey* sailor fractured one of his fingers when turned out of his hammock. The high waves, gray-green in the day, silver-black at night, rolled ever higher, the horizon swayed, and sea and sky were the same slaty color.

Destroyermen learned to stand with feet braced apart, arching their bodies with the rolling of the ship, and they got used to the elevator-like dropping sensation in the stomach when the ship fell; they learned to climb icy, swaying ladders in the night without seeing the rungs. The seasick ones tried to eat so that they would have something in their stomachs to throw up and thus avoid the painful, bile-tasting dry heaves. One skipper was seasick in rough weather during most of his first year in a destroyer in the Atlantic and, in another destroyer, soaked officers coming off watch could always count on "Somebody's Rocking My Dream-Boat" being on the wardroom record player. Such simple tasks as eating, sleeping, and moving about, normally performed in a relaxed manner, required intense effort and became work. Duty became hard work. Men could not move fast, nor could they do things that required two hands; one hand was always needed for holding on. The investment of concentration in simple tasks wearied men mentally and dulled their reactions, and shorthanded crews meant extra tasks and tired watchstanders; yet their lives depended on alertness. Vigilance was the prerequisite of survival. Officers checked out sonar and radar operators to make sure that they were not reading comic books or otherwise "doping off." Watchstanders tried to frighten each other into alertness with tales of U-boat packs nearby. Sometimes a man on watch escaped the tedium, fatigue, cold, and ubiquitous stinging spray by falling asleep, thus failing his shipmates. Destroyermen might battle shore patrols for each other, lie, falsify ship's records for each other, and risk their lives in combat for each other, but they would rarely forgive such betrayal as sleeping on watch. When an officer saw a sailor with a black eye, or chipped teeth, or facial lacerations, he knew that crewmen had reminded the man of his responsibilities in an unofficial but nonetheless effective manner. And as with the men, so with the ships. The destroyers, too, lost efficiency, as the pounding seas limited their speed and ability to turn quickly; they grew sluggish and handled sloppily.

By 2 December, the men and ships of HX 161 were weary and strained. And then the storm intensified into a full southerly gale. Rushing bursts of white water crushed in the starboard side of the *Lea's* bridge structure and smashed a window of her pilot house; three of her men were injured in falls, a raft was damaged, and loose gear was swept overboard. Taking similar punishment, the old *Bernadou*, low on fuel, developed engine trouble and was ordered to Iceland. Staggering alone through a snow squall and thrashing seas, she made it safely to Valley Forge.

On the *Lea*, during the afternoon of the 2nd, Storekeeper 2/C W.H. Kast was moving along the port side when a high wave lunged in and knocked him, smothering in the cold froth, into the gray sea. The destroyer searched for half an hour, but did not find her lost man. Then, pounding seas washed Seaman 2/C Percy Meadows overboard from the *Roe* and he was drowned.

On the morning of the 3rd, the ships reached the Momp, and there were only eight stragglers. Eastbound ships tended to straggle less than those that were westbound because they were faster and more heavily laden.* Because the British escorts were delayed, the *Lea* and *MacLeish*, short of fuel, were ordered to Iceland with an Icelandic cargo ship; they made it by the 5th. The *Roe* and *Woolsey* stayed with the convoy, scouting a little eastward and waiting for the Redcoats. The ten British escorts rose into sight atop high, distant waves on the afternoon of the 3rd at about 57°-24′ north, 18°-33′ west. The American destroyers came a long way with HX 161; the United Kingdom was as close as Iceland.

But the trip was not over. En route to Iceland, waves struck the *Roe*'s Number Two torpedo mount, causing the torpedo firing pin to fire by percussion. The torpedo came out of its tube, bounced off the after deckhouse, and hit Electrician's Mate Alfred H. Buck, crushing and amputating his foot. For five minutes, the "fish" rolled menacingly along the starboard side of the *Roe*'s fantail before tumbling over the side. Chief Warren Walsh improvised a tourniquet and strapped it to Buck's foot to check the bleeding, while Pharmacist's Mate 3/C Frank Mullen struggled aft to help; but the rushing seas pounded the corpsman to the deck, fracturing his left arm and leg, and he had to be taken below to his own sick bay. Pharmacist's Mate 1/C J.E. McDaniel and Lieutenant (JG) E.J. Cohen, the medical officer, made it to the stern and did what they could for Buck. The *Roe* sustained a small hole in her main deck, which was plugged with caulking cotton, and only a minor leak resulted. After thirteen days at sea in violent weather, the *Roe* and *Woolsey* reached Iceland on the 5th.

At Valley Forge, the destroyers rested fitfully to prepare for another trip; two of their men had died this time out and others were badly hurt. The ships were battered and the men exhausted, but they brought thirty-nine ships, including a straggler from SC 56, nearly all the way across the Atlantic. Being young and tough, the destroyermen were resilient; in a few days, they would be ready for sea again. It was well that this was so, for there was always more work to be done.[11]

Weary destroyermen found scant rest in Iceland. Liberties in dreary Reykjavik were rare, and anyway there was not much to do ashore; Scotch whisky cost $30 a fifth. In their free time, the sailors argued

---

*The Americans escorted the faster eastbound convoys, the HX series, while the Canadians escorted the slower SC convoys; but the westbound ON convoys were a mixture of fast and slow ships and thus slower than the HX convoys.

with each other about women, sports, naval tactics, politics, and religion. They read, too, mostly mysteries and westerns in tattered paperbacks, magazines, and comic books. Some played touch football or went mountain climbing. They stood deck watches and gun watches on the ships in Valley Forge as the Northern Lights sparkled in the night sky and the mist eddied over the craggy lava mountains. "There was a saddening effect in the way the wind never stopped blowing, and in having to listen to its sad moaning hour after hour. . . ."

The Icelanders were aloof, and most officers visited Reykjavik only on mandatory business, such as convoy conferences:

> Usually we would arrive from Hvalfjördhur in the forenoon, and the group of captains from the merchant ships and the escorting destroyers would arrive at the conference room singly or in small groups. When all were assembled, the briefing officer, a Commander in the Royal Canadian Navy, would enter on a cloud of Scotch, and start his talk: "Gentlemen, you have all been in convoy before. I don't have to tell you how important it is to keep closed up, don't make smoke, don't show any lights at night, etc." Afterward we would wander the streets of the town, and finally wind up at the Officer's Club. This was a cold, bare, high-ceilinged room on the main drag, decorated in rose and bilious green, and peopled by naval officers, Army personnel, and a sprinkling of civilians, sitting at little, round tables and staring at their drinks. After a round at the table where most of my officers could be found, I'd walk down to the sloping quay and take the motor whaleboat back to the welcome warmth and cheer of my ship's wardroom. There were no contacts with the civilian population. On the street they would pass us rapidly, without a glance in our direction. I remember the extraordinary fairness of the women's skin and hair.[12]

There was an enlisted men's club in town, but it was just as cheerless as that of the officers. Later, the sailors set up some good clubs in Nissen huts up at Valley Forge. The officers sometimes dined at the Hotel Borg, self-styled "Palace of the North." The younger ones danced with Icelandic girls, who arrived with the music at nine o'clock. "They will not sit with you nor allow you to sit at their table. About half of them speak English—nice, blonde, rosy-cheeked girls. The first date is to go to their homes to be approved by their parents." One of the "characters" of the shore establishment was "The Wicked Priest," a tough Father who could outdrink most of the destroyermen.

Occasionally, the Americans visited British ships in the anchorage for drinks or to use the Royal Navy's attack teachers; they reciprocated by inviting the food-short British to the U.S. ships for dinner.

Captain R.M. Blackman, skipper of the repair ship HMS *Blenheim*, was an especially gracious host to the American destroyermen. He constructed ship models as a hobby, and about this time he was working on his masterpiece, a remarkably precise replica of a paddle-wheel gunboat, circa 1845. Some of the Americans, like the *Badger's* sailors, learned "to be most fond of the British and have a hearty respect for their ability as sea fighters."

At Valley Forge, the holding ground was poor and storms blew down from the ice cap through the aisle-like fjords. The sailors found little relaxation there as they worked to keep their ships off the rocks. Few were sorry to leave Iceland. "When at last we sailed away, no Reykjavik townsfolk came down to the shore to see us off. For . . . days, they had been looking through us as though we were not there. In all that time, they had seemed to be saying to themselves that some day all this would pass, the war would end, the strangers would go away, and then they could be alone again, alone with their storms and their lights and their constant, moaning wind."

But a handful of men were reluctant to leave. They were men who had made one trip too many, men who were afraid to go out again. They were youngsters who lacked the stamina for destroyer duty, who never got over their seasickness, and old men spoiled by easy years of peacetime duty in calm seas and fair weather. They were afraid of submarines, and heard the cold-steel pinging of the sonar gear in their sleep; or they were afraid of the sea, and worried that their ship would not come up again after her next deep roll; or they were afraid of making decisions in a profession in which the cost of error was human life; or they were afraid of failure; or they were just afraid. There was the skipper of one of the new destroyers. He began to drink heavily and, one night, wrecked the room of a British liaison officer. The Englishman complained to the American authorities. The skipper persuaded one of his ensigns to pose as a British officer and telephone the American shore commander, saying that the matter had been settled amicably. "This stupid stratagem was discovered in due course. The skipper was relieved of his command, and subsequently his resignation was accepted 'for the good of the service,' and his ensign had his commission revoked. When the going gets tough, it takes only a little time to weed out the unfit, but sometimes peacetime operations are not sufficiently tough."

Few gave in to the fear. Most willingly set a westerly course toward Skaggi Point and embarked upon the long voyage home.[13]

No rest for the weary — an Atlantic Fleet destroyer at "Valley Forge"

It was snowy and windy when the *Plunkett, Livermore, Decatur, Badger, Cole,* and cutter *Campbell* took four ships, including the naval auxiliaries *Hamul* and *Rapidan,* south toward a rendezvous with the thirty-nine ships of ON 39. In the meantime, the convoy was hit by two storms and became badly scattered, causing the Momp to be changed several times. The two groups of vessels groped for each other on a stormy ocean. The need for security and a "blind spot" south of Iceland made communications difficult. Changes of Momp and difficulty in finding the convoy caused the American destroyers to spend an extra two days at sea. On 28 November, with the help of a Mariner, the *Livermore* and *Decatur,* searching ahead, found the convoy. Since darkness was near, Captain Kirk, the escort commander, decided to postpone the rendezvous until morning light. However, during the night, the convoy failed to pick up a route change although the escorts did, with the result that in the morning the U.S. destroyers were 12-15 miles astern of the merchant ships. Finally, on the afternoon of the 29th, at about 61°-18′ north, 24°-12′ west, the American escorts assumed responsibility for the convoy, which was a mess already; many of the ships had returned to port or were straggling, and two were en route to Reykjavik, victims of collision damage. The twenty-two vessels were woefully strung out, "several ships being as much as one mile in advance of the main body."

The destroyers plowed into the stormy seas, trying to chivvy the merchantmen into more compact array. A vessel that was too far out ahead refused to drop back when ordered to do so by Captain Kirk in the *Plunkett,* her master arguing truthfully that his ship did not steer well in rough seas at the low convoy speed; Kirk shunted the vessel to a position off the port flank so that her maneuvers would not endanger the escorts or other ships in the low visibility. Then as the convoy steamed southwest, the weather worsened, developing into the massive gale of 1/2 December.

Fearful of collision, the ships showed running lights in the stormy darkness; masters maintained great intervals between one another, stringing out the convoy so as to "almost guarantee success of a submarine attack. . . ." Desperate masters of struggling, laboring vessels ignored the orders of the convoy commodore in order to ease the burden on their own ships. The empty or lightly ballasted vessels rode well up in the water; handling sloppily, they were difficult to keep on station. Ships tilted their sterns up out of the water as they bucked and rolled across foamy slopes, propellers churning in air, engines racing.

Heavy seas bashed the four-stackers hard. The *Cole's* deck log read: ". . . vessel pitching deeply and rolling heavily. . . . mountainous seas. . . ." In the *Badger*, sailors worked to correct engine trouble, caused by water seeping into fuel lines, and struggled to repair cracked plating. Said John Schmidt, "Whenever we arrived in port, we had contrived a sort of miracle of seamanship unknown to the gold platers in their brand new ships." But the new ships took hard blows, too. One watch on the *Plunkett* could not be relieved for twelve hours because "passage of personnel . . . topside could not be safely effected." "Charlie P" recorded a roll of 52 degrees. All the escorts had hoses, gas drums, lifelines, ladders, lockers, and loose gear swept overboard, and boats and rafts damaged; the crews took minor cuts, bruises, and burns. But no serious damage or grave injuries occurred.

Each morning, the gray sky revealed fewer ships present. The *Plunkett's* radar equipment functioned only "spasmodically" and the *Decatur's* set "failed completely," making it harder than ever to locate strayed merchant vessels. One merchantman, the *R.J. Cullen*, lost a propeller in the storm and waited behind forlornly with the *Livermore* and *Campbell* for a British destroyer and tug to come out and help her off to Iceland. ON 39 gradually disintegrated in the gale, and by the 3rd of December, the four destroyers guarded the *Hamul*, *Rapidan*, and only six merchant ships. The *Plunkett* ranged a hundred miles astern, looking for a U.S.-flag freighter that had come from Iceland with the American destroyers, but did not find her. On the 4th, the *Cole* and *Badger*, short of fuel, were detached; the *Decatur*, newest of the Navy's four-stackers, hung on doggedly. Then the *Rapidan* broke down, and the *Plunkett* held her hand. Finally, at 1900 on the 4th, the remnant of the convoy was dispersed at about 53°-34' north, 39°-30' west; all the merchant ships, including the towed *Cullen*, reached port safely. The *Decatur* still had the pep to drop depth charges on a sonar contact, probably water turbulence, en route to Argentia.[14]

The *Red Wing* was a minecraft built in 1917; she had sowed mines in World War I and, between wars, served humbly as a tug. During her conversion, her watertight bulkheads aft were ripped out to make room for a salvage hold. In the fall of 1941, she was in port having machine guns installed, and virtually crewless. Almost all her officers were green; her Exec, a lawyer, was recently commissioned. Only the skipper and chief engineer had been to sea before, although one leading chief had experience in civilian tugs. Nevertheless, because of the constant possibility of damage from Atlantic storms or enemy action, or from grounding due to the poor holding ground at Hval-fjördhur, the Support Force needed a tug in Iceland. The *Red Wing's* orders were hastily cut. She received three days' notice of the mission. Most of her crew were recruits who reported in a body the day before the ship was to sail. The skipper lined them up on deck and asked all engineering ratings who had experience with reciprocating engines to fall out: no one did. He then left the ship, walked across the dock, and soon returned with a sailor in skivvy shirt and dungarees who showed the engineers how to get up steam. Rated as a harbor salvage tug, the *Red Wing* was not entitled to oceanic charts, so the Hydrographic Office refused to give her charts of the waters around Iceland; the captain had to purchase a portfolio of maps. On Thanksgiving Day, while getting under way, the *Red Wing* rammed the dock. Despite that inelegant start, her crew brought the tug safely to Argentia.

On the night of 28 November, the *Red Wing* joined the fleet tanker *Sapelo* under the wing of the *Charles F. Hughes, Wilkes, Madison, Lansdale,* and four-stacker *Sturtevant* heading out to join HX 162. She was not the only green auxiliary present. Her problems were those of most naval auxiliaries in a time of rapid expansion; priority as to trained personnel and forceful, dynamic leaders usually went of necessity to warships, which were also hard pressed for experienced men. The ships were still forming up when the *Sapelo* proved the point by running into the *Lansdale*, punching a one-foot hole in the destroyer's side plating along her port quarter near the waterline. The destroyermen made repairs en route.

On the morning of the 29th, the American ships joined the thirty-nine vessels of HX 162, which carried petroleum products, steel and scrap, trucks, cotton, grain, sugar, refrigerated goods, and general cargo. The ships started through a snowstorm on a northeasterly track; the seas rose. And then, on 1 December, the great gale began. The days were short and sunless, sea and sky swayed interchangeably, and mountainous seas tumbled over the dipping, sliding ships. A roller ripped open a hatch on the *Madison*, flooding her steering engine room; the *Lansdale* lost two depth charges washed overboard. The SS *Pleiades*, bound for Iceland with several American diplomats, was forced to turn back when her deck cargo shifted and her engine faltered; four other damaged merchantmen turned back. By the night of the 2nd, there no longer was a convoy; ships were scattered randomly alone and in little groups in the vicinity of the convoy's track.

The *Red Wing* pushed her bow into the high, gray rollers, water cascading down her decks toward her stern. Water seeped below and, because the tug did not have watertight integrity, accumulated in the area of the salvage dump. "As she shook and groaned under a big sea, her stern quivered like a bowl of jello." Her crew was too green to realize that the old harbor craft, miscast in a wild winter gale in the North Atlantic, was in trouble; they bailed green water out of her for most of the passage and assumed that it was that way on all ships, that it was merely a routine part of "going to sea!" Then, as salt water seeped through oil vents, the tug began to stall frequently. The crew drained the water out of the oil, and the *Red Wing* surged ahead at top speed of 11 knots to catch up with the convoy. She maintained station for a time, then fell behind again as more water leaked into the fuel. Occasionally, her rudder jammed, making her steam in eccentric circles, reminding the men on nearby ships of "a puppy dog chasing its tail." But *Red Wing* hung on.

The storm abated a little on the 3rd, and the destroyermen counted four merchant vessels still with them. The escorts spent much of the next three days roaming astern and wide of the track, rounding up stragglers. All the destroyers sustained minor damage: short circuits caused by flooding, ruptured degaussing cables, bulwarks and loose gear swept away, and smashed boats. Then on the afternoon of the 6th, the *Red Wing*'s youngsters reported a U-boat near; and the tug inopportunely broke down again. The *Sturtevant* hied back to ride shotgun while her men worked at the fuel lines once again.

By the morning of the 7th, the destroyers had rounded up twenty-three ships and turned them over to the care of HMS *Vanoc* and four other escorts at about 58°-42' north, 22°-30' west. With ample fuel, the British ships cruised the area of the Momp and brought in eight more stragglers; two merchantmen fell in with ships from SC 57, so only one vessel of the convoy steamed alone to Britain.

The American destroyers arrived at Hvalfjördhur with the *Sapelo* and *Red Wing* on the 9th. The British station ship was forced to maneuver frantically in order to bring the eccentric-steaming *Red Wing* to heel. Finally, the tug and her inexperienced crew, their rugged ocean initiation over, steamed in to join the company of tough ships and resolute men at Valley Forge.[15]

There was little rest for the weary at Valley Forge. On the 29th of November, a storm blew up, and a mail boat from the cruiser *Wichita* was swamped. The *Babbitt's* men got a boat over the side in eight minutes and rescued the drenched postman off "The Witch" and all but two sacks of mail. The same day, the *Mayo*, while maneuvering to moor at a buoy, slammed her bow into the side of a merchant tanker. As ever, the destroyermen were not sad to depart Iceland. The *Mayo*, *Nicholson*, and four-stackers *Babbitt*, *Leary*, and *Schenck* left with a U.S.-flag merchantman to meet ON 41. As the ships ran through the stormy waters south-southwest of Reykjavik, the old *Leary* fell back with a jammed rudder; she stopped, then started, limping along at 5 knots, then stopped again. With the *Nicholson* standing by, her men soon cleared the rudder, the trouble having been caused by a wrench wedged under the crankshaft of the steering engine; whether it was an accident caused by carelessness, or the deliberate act of a frightened man reluctant to go out again, was impossible to tell. But the *Leary's* troubles were not over. The seas rose, and later in the afternoon, a big roller broke over her forecastle, shattering the glass in a dozen windows on her bridge, cracking the forecastle deck in three places, bending seven stanchions, damaging the training shaft on her Number One gun, and washing a ready box of 3-inch shells over the side. Two men were slightly injured, cut by shattered glass. The crew set to work shoring up the weakened stanchions.

Meanwhile, ON 41 was in difficulty. It was a slow convoy, making about 5½ knots. Two of its destroyers were low on fuel and were forced to leave on the 3rd; but four corvettes brought the merchantmen to the Momp, at about 60°-15' north, 23°-30' west, on the morning of the 4th, and remarkably, twenty-eight of the original thirty vessels were still present. Nevertheless, the delay, slow speed, and the misfortune to the *Leary* all portended a fuel crisis for the American destroyers. For the first two days, with the *Nicholson* remaining astern with beset *Leary*, the convoy was guarded by but three escorts. The gray, rolling ships steamed grimly on to westward.

The *Babbitt* had an efficient radar set, and in the late afternoon, her skipper and OOD would "identify the ships in company visually and by radar pip, then note the appearance of these pips so the ships could be identified by them alone after it was dark." But in a storm, no precaution helped; that night, wild seas scattered the merchantmen. At 0140 on the 5th, the *Babbitt* picked up a radar contact, but

A North Atlantic convoy, December 1941

it disappeared from the scope when the destroyer turned after it; it may have been a strayed convoy vessel. Later, she attacked a sonar contact, but it was most likely water turbulence. The four-stacker was aggressive on this trip; her skipper, Lieutenant Commander V. C. Havard, had only had the ship a month and he wanted to mark his administration the right way—by getting a U-boat.

On the 6th, the seas began to moderate, and the *Nicholson* and *Leary* joined up with the convoy. The destroyers set to work rounding up numerous stragglers. On the 9th, the *Mayo* and aggressive *Babbitt* attacked a sonar contact, probably a wake or fish, with fifteen depth charges, but then searched the area for only ten minutes before re-joining the convoy; any contact worth a barrage of fifteen depth charges was worth more than a ten-minute search, or any contact so faint or mushy as to warrant so cursory a search did not merit fifteen depth charges. The destroyermen were still learning.

On the morning of the 10th, the seas were running high again. The four-stackers were low on fuel and the *Schenck* and *Leary* had leaky tanks, so all three of them were detached to Argentia. En route, the *Babbitt*, not willing to miss any chance to get a sub, worked over a sonar contact, making several attacks and dropping fourteen depth charges, but without result.

The *Mayo*, also vexed by leaking fuel tanks, and the *Nicholson*, deprived of sonar gear by the flooding of her sound room in the escort of HX 160, remained with the convoy. The winds increased to force 7, brushing up tall, white-crested rollers. The merchant ships moved so slowly that the vessels of Canadian-escorted ON 42 caught up to them and for a time five Canadian corvettes reinforced the thin and hobbled American escort. When the Canadians went on the next day, they left HMCS *Leftbridge* behind to help. Finally, on the evening of the 14th, the convoy, still east of Cape Race, was dispersed, and the two destroyers headed for the barn, ready for calm waters and still bunks after twelve days that had seemed like more at sea.[16]

The *Edison* was in port when a young radioman showed Lieutenant Commander Murdaugh a notice he had picked up in a Boston bar; it was in the form of a letter, purportedly a product of the America First Committee and bearing a facsimile signature of Charles Lindbergh; its distribution was at the expense of the special budget of the German Embassy in Washington. The missive attacked the naval war in the Atlantic, stating that it was not America's war, and urged crews to desert. Furthermore, some of the bartenders, waiters, and prostitutes who worked East Coast waterfront dives were paid to get destroyermen to lay over long enough to miss their ships or to go AWOL.

Sailors by dint of their profession were not isolationists. While not always fond of the British or desirous of entering the war, they knew what was going on in the Atlantic and understood the need to stop the Nazis. In August of 1941, when the House of Representatives passed by a single vote an act to continue conscription, opponents of the draft "were criticized bitterly by even the most poorly informed seaman" amongst the destroyermen. Yet, at the same time, the sailors felt a sense of alienation from the nation as a result of their duties; they had the feeling that the country was not backing them, that the risks they took in the Atlantic went unknown and unappreciated. Sometimes their sacrifices and hardships elicited the jeers of bitter countrymen; in Boston, there was more than one bar-room altercation between destroyermen in from a tough westbound run and Irish anglophobes.

Inevitably, the Navy—and the nation—paid a price for the undeclared war. A handful of men gave in, some out of fear, others out of self-pity. Most of the few who sought to avoid battle were hard cases who needed scant rationalization, who wanted a little too much to remain in warm bars and cozy beds and not again endure misery and fear at sea, and who cared too little for the added burdens that they thus imposed on better men. They worked out a technique for defection: since a man was not deemed a deserter until he had been absent without leave for more than thirty days, a sailor might jump ship, enjoy himself until his money had nearly gone, then hitchhike to California and turn himself in before thirty days had elapsed. He would spend time in the brig, then be reassigned to a Pacific Fleet ship, thus avoiding the rigors and perils of combat duty in the Atlantic. There were even rumors of ships missing sailings because of the desertion of a few key men.[17]

The defections were few and, except as indicative of the ambivalence of the nation, unimportant; the reason why they received disproportionate notice amongst the Atlantic sailors was the chronic shortage of personnel. The Atlantic ships were undermanned. But, at last, the President was ready to take action to meet the fleet's long-felt need for more men. Admiral Stark was afraid that wartime operations in the Atlantic and the advent of prosperity would diminish volunteer enlistments; indeed, he feared that the loss of the *Reuben James* alone "set recruiting back about 15 percent." So, in November, the President grudgingly authorized the use of draftees in the Navy. As Admiral Stark wrote, "The President in giving final approval said he just hated to do it; but sentiment is just getting out of my system. . . ."[18]

Yet, in the meantime, the manpower shortage caused hardships; for shorthanded crews were prey to fatigue. The *Edison* once went out on an escort mission with a crew of ninety-eight! Once, before a mission, Lieutenant Commander Murdaugh called Captain Tom Hickey, an old Academy friend and personnel officer for Atlantic Fleet destroyers, to plead for more men. Hickey was a tough destroyerman who hated his desk and wanted to get back to sea duty; but he was good at his job because, like his boss, Ernie King, he knew how to say no, a talent that kept him lashed to his desk. He told his friend, No! Murdaugh persisted, and finally Hickey offered to empty out the Norfolk brig for the *Edison*; Murdaugh could have the best of the jailbirds. Murdaugh was in no position to cavil, and things worked out well; he drew no skulkers or brig rats, just men who had enjoyed a liberty a little too spectacularly or missed a ship by chance, and he was glad to have them and they were glad to be needed.[19]

Another developing personnel problem was whether to keep the reservists together in organized units, where possible, or split them up as a matter of policy. Hickey and his staff were of the opinion that cliques were bad for discipline and fostered inefficiency; experience showed that both service and sailor did better when a man was changed from civilian to combat sailor by the shock of total immersion, rather than by letting him get wet a little at a time. But local pride, translated into political pressure, demanded that units retain their integrity. Then, late in the year 1941, a reserve unit of hard urban youngsters pillaged the hold of a store ship en route to Iceland, breaking into cases of cigarettes and whiskey. The unit was promptly split up, and thereafter, personnel officers discreetly made it policy to break up reserve units.[20]

On 5 December, the *Edison* was short-handed when she went out again; along with the *Hilary P. Jones, Benson, Niblack,* and old *Tarbell*, she met the forty-four merchant ships of HX 163 south of Newfoundland. The convoy steamed northeast in temperate weather. One merchant vessel suffered engine trouble and had to return to port. On the 6th, a dense, sodden fog shrouded the ships and the *Benson's* men, testing their new radar equipment, were delighted to discover that they could find stragglers easily on the radar screen despite the fog. On the 8th, there were numerous sonar contacts; the sailors had heard the news of Pearl Harbor and were edgy. The *Tarbell* worked over one contact with sixteen depth charges, and the *Benson* and *Niblack* carried out more modest attacks.

On the 11th, the seas rose and skies darkened. The merchant ships turned on running lights whenever making course changes and some tried to keep at least a stern light on all night. The destroyers were kept busy roving after offenders and getting the lights put out, but it was a frustrating task and they never managed to quash the practice entirely. With stormy seas lengthening the passage, the *Tarbell* was detached on the 12th. That night, at 2240, the *Benson* picked up a radar contact off her port beam; it soon disappeared from the scope, replaced by a sonar contact. The destroyer sheered off through the mist to search when, suddenly, the *Niblack* slid out of the haze on her port bow. Lieutenant Commander Clifford A. Fines ordered "all astern full" and a collision was averted, but the near-crash exemplified the limitations of the early radar equipment and lent plausibility to the reluctance of veteran skippers to put full trust in it.

The storm intensified on the 13th. High seas smashed down at the rolling ships and drenched men; visibility was less than 500 yards in the mist and rain. The *Edison* became separated from the convoy and after searching for it until the 15th, proceeded alone to Iceland. The *Hilary P. Jones*, also lost, searched in the vicinity of the Momp. The *Buck* and *Niblack* were still together with about sixteen merchant ships. Finally, despite the danger of collision and dispersion, the vessels were forced to heave to, remaining huddled against the blows of sea and sky for thirty-two hours. The *Benson* had to go to the aid of the SS *Nidardal*, which was reported to be storm-damaged and sinking, about 145 miles south. She searched all day on the 16th, then, failing to find the merchant ship, proceeded to Iceland. The Canadian corvette *Pictou* came upon the survivors of the *Nidardal* and picked them up. The *Buck*, too, soon lost the other ships in the storm, and more merchantmen straggled.

On the 15th, PatRon 73 planes searched in the fog and rain, trying to bring the remnant of the convoy and the British eastern ocean escort together, but the fliers could not locate any ships in the "soup." In the afternoon at about 58°-28' north, 22°-52' west, British corvettes *Dahlia* and *Arabis* reached the lonely *Niblack* and the thirteen merchant ships still with her. Then the *Hilary P. Jones* turned up, and the four escorts steamed on until the American destroyers were relieved later in the afternoon by the rest of the British-Canadian escorts. Protected from harm by the storm, the scattered merchantmen of HX 163 reached port safely. The American destroyers were reunited at Valley Forge.[21]

Convoy ON 43 looked unlucky from the start. It was scattered by storms west of Scotland, and followed for the better part of two days by U-boats, while ahead, two more submarines were waiting near 60° north, between 25° west and 30° west, astride its route. When the *Woolsey, Roe, Bernadou, Lea,* and *MacLeish,* escorting a Panamanian freighter, arrived at the Momp south of Iceland on 11 December and met the British corvette HMS *Hibiscus,* waiting with a soaked, gray brood of but four rolling ships out of an original family of twenty-three, it seemed certain that, this time, the American warships would have to fight their way across.

The rest of the day, destroyers searched thirty miles along either side of the convoy's track, but they found no more ships. Thus, there was an escort for each merchantman as the ten vessels staggered westward together through high, churning slopes of sea. The storm continued, and on the 15th, at about 54° north, near 40° west, the small convoy was formally dispersed. Seven of the vessels of ON 43 had turned back, but the rest, sheltered as well as hindered by the storm, made it to port safely.

As the destroyers headed toward Argentia through the high, rough seas, they were forced to slow to 7 knots to ease the pounding stress on the four-stackers. The seas smashed the bridge windows on the *Lea*; that was the only significant damage sustained in a voyage undertaken under so many harbingers of gloom.[22] And so another routine trip on the Iceland run had been completed.

Thus ended the first three months of the war of the U.S. Atlantic Fleet. The Support Force brought the merchant ships toward Britain in safety, but although some of its men and one of its ships were slain by the enemy and the sea, the Atlantic sailors brought back no scalps as signs of their prowess. They worked hard and they fought hard, but they waged their grim war in loneliness and frustration. As a *Decatur* gunner remembered long after: "Nor had we ever seen the Enemy. We had steamed . . . miles hunting Them, we had bloodied Them and They us, and we had never seen Them. There seemed no real victory and no real defeat. If either had won anything, we had, because the convoy had made it."[23]

And adversity bred in the sailors of the Atlantic Fleet a sense of hard and gallant tasks done in obscurity, at its peevish worst a form of self-pity, at its best a special pride in themselves, all the stronger because they did not have to share it with anyone else. They were alone; the nation was at peace, and they were at war. They were alone—except for each other. And that is what they fought for until the nation was prepared to give them something better. They fought alone, out of pride and duty, and for each other. It was the only battle cry they had, but one. For the Atlantic Fleet was first to fight.

The Atlantic fleet found no glory in its ocean, but its men owed their dead a worthy epitaph; and so, for the men in the *Reuben James* and the *Kearny,* and the destroyermen drowned in winter storms, and the fliers whose seaplane exploded in rolling tumbleweeds of flame in the hills not far from Reykjavik after another mission in the fog, they came to think one thing worth remembering: the Atlantic Fleet was first to fight.

27.

Turpentine and Red Roses: Sun-Tanned Atlantic Sailors

AND IN THE SOUTH ATLANTIC, other Atlantic sailors waged a very different kind of war.

Jonas Ingram and his men began the South Atlantic Patrol in late April 1941, when the light cruisers *Memphis* and *Cincinnati* hied out of Newport. Their first sweep was uneventful save that, southwest of the Cape Verdes, one of their float planes sighted a heavily armed, flagless merchant ship; the cruisers gave chase, but were too distant to catch her. When the ships reached the replenishment port of Recife, Brazil, Admiral Ingram went ashore to look over facilities and establish working relationships with various local officials, civilian and military. He found the Brazilian leaders "polite enough, but uncommunicative."

President Vargas was aware that he would need American help in defending Brazil's vulnerable northeast coast, but he also respected the success of German arms; he cooperated with the Americans in small matters, but temporized over large ones. When the Brazilians did cooperate, they appeased the Germans by claiming that they were merely giving in before U.S. threats of occupation or of economic reprisal. As Ingram noted, Brazil "wants to end up on the winning side and is not prepared to gamble."[1]

The Americans found Brazilian Army officers aloof and suspicious, as a result, in some cases, of nationalism, and, in others, of pro-Nazi sentiment. Naval officers were friendly, because they were less insular

343

and had greater hopes of getting equipment and weaponry from the United States. Civilian officials, reflecting the uncertainty of their superiors, moved slowly and cautiously, demonstrating what, to the energetic Americans, seemed "the typical 'mañana' attitude."

Ingram found the harbor at Recife small, but adequate; fuel would have to be brought in in naval tankers, and the local diet of beans, fish, rice, and fruit would have to be supplemented for American sailors. It would be best to have a tender stationed in Brazilian waters, but such decisions awaited the judgment of President Vargas. Ingram realized that, with her poverty and lack of efficient transportation and communications, Brazil could be of little direct help in the war, but her geographic position was pivotal and her cooperation with the United States could have a crucial psychological impact on other Latin American states. He was aware that the Brazilians, seeing the mostly uninvited advent of the Americans as a blow to their national pride, tended to resent it; hence, he sought to have them think of American warships as representatives of Brazil as much as of the United States. He was sincere when he told Vargas that he considered himself "not merely an accredited agent of a friendly power," but someone who knew and liked Brazil and was concerned for her best interests. More important, Ingram worked to inculcate the same attitude in his command, urging his officers to learn Portuguese and cultivate courtly manners, reminding them that Recife had an established culture long before the Puritans ventured into the Massachusetts wilderness. Brazilians were invited to the ships, hopefully to share in the Americans' pride in them. The gregarious and demonstrative Ingram made friends easily as he visited schools, clubs, and homes, and he was careful to avoid politics. There was little friction between the Brazilians and sailors on liberty. The Brazilians were cheerful, friendly, and polite; the sailors were gregarious and spent money freely, particularly on the cheap and excellently crafted alligator luggage fashioned by local artisans. The Brazilians had a deep sense of personal and national dignity which discouraged crass familiarity. Once, in late July 1941, when a rumor circulated in Bahia that sailors off the *Omaha*, *Somers*, and *Laramie* were insulting women, a vexed crowd began to gather, but Brazilian police and American shore patrols straightened out the misunderstanding and prevented trouble.[2]

Ingram's men saw a lot of ocean in but few months. For example, between the end of April and the end of August, the South Atlantic force's four old light cruisers—the *Memphis, Cincinnati, Milwaukee,* and *Omaha*—and four new, long-range destroyers—the *Davis, Warrington, Somers,* and *Jouett*—made twenty-six patrol sweeps along the triangle Trinidad - Cape Verdes - Brazil, steaming 81,282 miles. At sea, the easy monotony of a warm sun and an endless vista of blue-green ocean was rarely broken by alarms. In late September, the *Davis* and *Warrington* made a depth-charge attack on a periscope-like object that suddenly appeared in the water near the *Memphis* and they hunted unsuccessfully for a U-boat that had torpedoed a U.S.-flag tanker 500 miles off the Brazilian coast.

In October, another U.S.-flag freighter, the SS *Acadia,* was scheduled to sail for Lagos, Nigeria, with technicians and material for the building of PanAmerican Airways ferry fields in Africa, but the merchant sailors refused to sail in the eastern half of the ocean under British escort, feeling that there would be less risk of attack if they were guarded by ships of a neutral nation. So the *Memphis, Davis,* and *Jouett* did the honors for the jittery merchantmen, who soon received a firmer skipper.

In the late fall, several attacks were made on dubious sonar contacts, and the *Cincinnati's* men swore that, off the Azores, a U-boat had fired a torpedo at their old cruiser, but no drama or tragedy attended the humble pursuits of the South Atlantic command. Since the weather was fine, the seas calm, and the missions less than urgent, Ingram's ships got in more training than did vessels on combat missions in the North Atlantic. They had little contact with the rest of the fleet and few men were transferred or replaced. Consequently, Ingram's crews were able to develop a cohesiveness not found in other commands. Ingram wrote: "The training obtained during the patrol is excellent. The sea habit is developed and the casual attitude is dissipated . . . especially in close proximity to reported sinkings. The psychological effect of being required to maintain constant vigilance is excellent." But the ships, away from the main currents of battle, did not get much useful training in antisubmarine warfare.

Ingram's ships carried orders requiring that, in the event of an encounter with major German warships, they try to trail them until planes and more ships could assist in giving battle. If surprised by German vessels more powerful than themselves, Ingram's patrol ships would be able only to essay a desperate, close-range torpedo attack; more likely, they would be wrecked by enemy fire before they could close to effective torpedo range. If a minor enemy force or a single enemy ship were encountered, Ingram was authorized to engage the Germans.

In the fall, when four new destroyers were added to the South Atlantic squadron, Ingram was able to deploy four task groups, each composed of one old cruiser and two new destroyers. And there was progress ashore. PanAmerican Airways built facilities for aircraft at eight key sites along Brazil's northeast coast and, in November, President Vargas authorized their use by the Americans. In the first days of December, a chief storekeeper arrived in Recife and rented large warehouses near the docks; to tend the warships, the *Patoka* arrived at Recife, while the *Thrush* went to Belém and the *Clemson* to Natal.[3] And, best of all, a novel event added zest to the prosaic steaming of Jonas Ingram and his tanned and merry men.

On the gray, drizzly morning of 4 November the *Omaha* and her destroyers were on patrol when they received radio reports of a ship sunk and another attacked by a German raider in the vicinity of 3° north, 22° west. The American officers were skeptical, believing correctly that a U-boat rather than a surface raider must have made the attacks. Float planes from the *Omaha* searched all day in overcast and intermittent rain, but found no sign of either victims or assailant on the sea below. When the *Memphis*, en route from Lagos, arrived on the scene to take over the search, the *Omaha* and *Somers*, running low on fuel, steamed back toward Recife, their crews disappointed at having chased another phantom across the lonely southern seas.

On the morning of the 6th, at 0506, sixteen minutes after morning general quarters, lookouts on the American warships sighted a darkened vessel not far away; their position was about 00°-40' north, 28°-04' west, some 660 miles north-northeast of Recife. Captain Theodore E. Chandler in the *Omaha* ordered a course change to investigate the unidentified freighter. At 25 knots, the cruiser and destroyer closed the ship. The *Omaha* directed her to give her international call by searchlight signal; the *Somers* ranged ahead, taking station off the freighter's bow, ready to deliver a torpedo attack, should she turn out to be a German merchant cruiser prepared to fight. The stranger did not respond to the *Omaha*'s signals.

The darkened freighter flew an American flag and had U.S. flags painted under her bridge, on both sides; the words "Willmoto Philadelphia" were painted on her stern, and she flew KIGF flags from her signal halliards. The *Omaha* ordered her to heave to. Captain Chandler inquired by megaphone, "Why don't you answer signals?" There was no response. Chandler tried again. The dark ship remained mute. Finally, a voice from across the water identified the vessel as the SS *Willmoto*, home port Philadelphia, bound from Capetown to New Orleans with general cargo. That answer, in good English, made sense, but the cruiser sailors were suspicious. Perhaps it was a case of the wish fathering the thought for, after six uneventful months of patrol, Jonas Ingram's men were eager for a fight. Someone insisted that the freighter's sailors did not look like Americans. Officers who consulted *Merchant Ships of the World, 1940* contended that her characteristics did not conform to those given in the reference book. A sailor on the *Somers* said that the freighter had the same general aspect as a German survey ship he had once seen in Miami. Captain Chandler decided to send over a boarding party.

Despite the danger of the ship turning out to be an auxiliary cruiser determined to fight or a blockade-runner set for scuttling, the *Omaha's* men stampeded to volunteer for the boarding party. Lieutenant George E. Carmichael, a cool, reliable sailor, drew the duty of commanding the party, and selected his men, remembering to include in the band Chief Watertender Henry C. Coronado, a tough man in any kind of fight. The eager boarders were issued small arms and, at 0637, went over the side. Captain Chandler reasoned that if the ship were German she might be making for a rendezvous with a U-boat, and ordered two float planes launched to watch for submarines.

The mysterious vessel was indeed German, the blockade-runner *Odenwald*, bound from the Orient to Occupied Europe with a cargo of raw rubber, tires, oats, peanuts, tannic acid, and oils and chemicals; she carried a crew of forty-five. Her skipper, Captain Loers, knew that the *Odenwald* was finished as soon as he sighted the American "battleship." He tried to play out his losing hand with the only technique open to those who draw fate's low cards—bluff. When this failed, he ordered his freighter scuttled. A brace of demolition charges was placed aft, sea-suction valves were opened, and manhole plates aft were removed. But the Germans had delayed too long, and the scuttling parties worked in too great haste and too carelessly.

Lieutenant Carmichael's boat approached the *Odenwald* from the starboard side. The Americans could see the freighter's crew running about on deck, clearly in process of abandoning ship; weighted bags containing codes and orders splashed down into the blue water, sinking quickly. At about 0645, just as the boat reached the side of the German ship, two muted explosions rumbled inside the after part of the vessel. Leaving his men in the boat, Carmichael climbed to the main deck; thick, acrid smoke spiraled up from below. He was unable to make his way through the unfamiliar ship in the haze. Carmichael roamed the deck, .45 in hand, herding Germans back from the rails and lifeboats, thinking that they might be of some use in saving the ship. The first officer told him in a brisk British accent that it was too late, the freighter had already been scuttled. Meanwhile, eager Chief Coronado led the rest of the party up on deck, ready to "shoot the hell" out of any Germans giving Mr. Carmichael trouble.

The smoke seemed to be thinning, so Carmichael and Coronado went below. They rounded up containers, tins, and boxes and lugged them topside for disposal overboard in case they contained inflammables. The ship had a slight list, but there was neither fire nor extensive damage below; some of her after compartments were flooded, but Carmichael thought that they could be isolated without much danger or difficulty. The *Omaha*'s deck was congested with would-be "volunteers who were with difficulty restrained from entering the boats bound for salvage duty"; and soon a contingent of engineers arrived aboard the *Odenwald*, followed by repair and salvage parties.

Machinist's Mate Furman D. Waltrip and his men went below and sealed the watertight doors and closed the sea valves. The Germans had left nuts and bolts for dismantled manhole plates in the after bulkhead of the engine room right on the deck where they had been removed, so it was a simple matter to replace the plates. The pumps were put into operation, and the cargo was shifted to lessen the portside list.

Not being familiar with the German engine-room arrangement and valve nomenclature, the Americans had to trace lines and pipes back to their sources in order to learn how to work the machinery. The German officers refused to help. Finally, one was persuaded at gunpoint to lend a hand, but he was of small use.

Shipfitter 1/C Franklin E. King dived overboard and swam underwater, trying to discover where the holes were in the ship's bottom. An inquisitive shark swam by, and sailors on deck fired weapons in the air to scare it off, "but neither King nor the shark appeared to be frightened," and King went about his work. Carpenter A.L. Alton joined King in the water, but neither swimmer could find the holes. As the list diminished, however, the engineers were able to locate the punctures from inside the ship.

Meanwhile, Captain Chandler was contemplating the legal and logistical implications of his impulsive action. He realized, of course, that a belligerent vessel could legitimately be seized only by the ships of another belligerent power. Yet the freighter was flying the American flag and posing as an American ship and, as such, might rightfully be boarded by an American man-of-war; also, the boarding operation could be construed as an attempt to prevent a vessel in distress from sinking. Chandler was not certain what he should do with the freighter. His warships were low on fuel and Recife was the nearest port, but he did not want to take her there, for fear of involving the Brazilians in the international legal squabble that was sure to develop. He was considering beaching her on St. Paul's Rocks when optimistic reports from his salvage crew persuaded him that he might be able to reach Trinidad.

The cruisermen had the *Odenwald*'s list under control. Shortly after 1800, they got her under way, and soon she was making 9.2 knots; her list was only 2½ degrees, and with her engines functioning, the pumps began to gain on the flooding. The ships proceeded Indian-file, with the *Somers* leading and listening for U-boats, the *Odenwald* in the middle, and the *Omaha* astern, ready to rush up quickly to rescue her salvage crew if the freighter suddenly foundered. The cruiser sailors were disagreeably surprised to notice that the *Odenwald*, painted a light, dirty gray, was much harder to see at night than was the smaller and more distant *Somers*, painted standard U.S. Navy blue-gray.

En route, stringent fuel economies proved necessary. The *Omaha*'s engineers consolidated oil residues in the empty tanks; the *Somers* rigged a sail in the hope of reducing fuel consumption by some five gallons an hour! The ships reached Port of Spain on the 15th, refueled from the USS *Polaris*, then went on to San Juan, arriving on the 17th.

The *Somers*' sail and Carmichael's boarding party lent a nineteenth-century touch to the capture of the *Odenwald*, then Ted Chandler and Jonas Ingram added another. With tongue in cheek, they recalled the days when the Navy patrolled the South Atlantic for clandestine slave-traders, and asserted that the stopping of the *Odenwald* was lawful, for her darkened state and suspicious demeanor raised the possibility that she was engaged in the slave trade. Ted Chandler and his men had brought in a blackbirder![4]

After Pearl Harbor, the war of Jonas Ingram was much the same. Washington thought to send about 150 Marines to protect the plane sites in Brazil from sabotage by pro-Nazi elements; but the Brazilians warned Captain Hodgman and the land-bound sailors in "Bomb Jesus Street" that no armed foreigners would be allowed near Brazilian airfields. It was finally agreed that the Marines could come ashore as "tourists" and perform guard duties, but their arms must be left stacked in crates on board the *Patoka*. Ingram urged that Brazilian troops be used to protect the fields, thinking that the Brazilians "would cheerfully and with great pride" assign men to the duty, but this sensible advice was not taken. Eventually, as the local populace came to take the presence of the Americans for granted, the Marines were permitted to stand sentry duty with rifles.

The air patrols impressed the Brazilians, who grew increasingly enthusiastic about cooperation with the United States. Ingram nurtured this sentiment by insisting that his squadrons file operational reports with Brazilian district commanders. Once, when Recife officials fined a U.S. firm for violation of a local ordinance, the businessmen appealed to Ingram to use his prestige with the Brazilian officials on their behalf; but he refused, stating that he was in Brazil to fight U-boats, not to promote commerce. Admiral Ingram organized a far-reaching and competent network of coast-watchers amongst fishermen of the northeast coast. The natives would not accept remuneration for their work or for hospitality to Americans staying with them. But Ingram, discovering that the natives were anxious to have pictures of their families—a remote dream for poor fishermen— sent service photographers through the jungle to take pictures. It was a small thing, but indicative. Jonas Ingram still ran a happy ship.[5]

Ingram desperately wanted to get a heavy cruiser to back up the venerable light cruisers in his force, but the better ships were needed elsewhere. He managed to wangle a promotion to vice admiral by arguing that he needed more rank to impress the all-chief, few-Indian navies of Latin America: "Rank carries weight and prestige in South America, but Rear Admirals are a dime a dozen in the Brazilian Navy Department alone."[6]

Honest and uncomplicated, Ingram was popular with the Brazilians. President Vargas, distressed at the intensity of inter-service bickering in the Brazilian armed forces, offered to place all three services under the operational control of Admiral Ingram. But the State Department suspected that the offer was bogus, and the President and Frank Knox certainly did not want a simple, direct American sailorman to be enmeshed in the tangled service politics of a Latin state, so the idea was politely rejected. Nevertheless, Ingram took a

lively and helpful interest in the development of the Brazilian services, and when he was not impressed with what he saw he said so:
"The Air Force is an elite organization of excellent social standing
and particularly well uniformed and groomed. They dislike to cover
1200 miles a day in the Force VPs. They would rather drop red roses
and assignation notes from a plane over their gals' homes. It is a
racket, but they may improve with some more material and the
application of plenty of turpentine. . . . Rio is the home of art,
culture, beauty and loving. There are no warriors there and it's no
place for a warrior to go except for recreation leave." As the Brazilians gained in experience and tenacity, Ingram accorded them more
responsibility. Sometimes he permitted Brazilians to command joint
U.S.-Brazilian naval task forces.[7]

War intensified the pace and scope of the South Atlantic patrols.
The ships steamed as far south as the Falkland Islands, and drew
special assignments as well as regular patrol sweeps. By spring, the
South Atlantic warships were averaging twenty-four days at sea each
month. The old cruisers were not comfortable ships to serve in in the
tropics, but the avuncular and enthusiastic Ingram, with a blend of
kindness and "turpentine," kept morale high and instilled an aggressive spirit into his compact, homey fleet.[8]

In the spring, the *Memphis, Cincinnati, Winslow, Somers,* and
Jouett escorted two U.S. Army transports to Ascension Island, where
an Army airfield for ASW and ferry operations was to be built. The
transports were inefficiently loaded, the soldiers had no experience in
moving supplies and equipment ashore, and the weather turned bad.
The operation, which should have been a simple one, dragged on
and taxed everyone's nerves; it became necessary to use ships' boats
and most of the sailors, working on a twenty-four-hour basis, to
unload the ships. The merchant marine crews refused to do overtime
duty, which made for much bitterness and many near fights between
them and the sailors. Ingram took part of his force back west when
the first ship was finally unloaded, leaving Captain Graf of the *Cincinnati* in charge, for he was "a good slave driver, and plenty tough."
The Army built a 6,000-foot runway on the desolate island; it ran
dead into the wind and off a cliff. "A natural catapult," observed
Jonas Ingram, glad to be gone.[9]

In antisubmarine warfare, Ingram's men were aggressive, but woefully green. At first, they thought that they had sunk a U-boat every
time one of their depth charges exploded. In the broad expanse of
water where they operated it was more expeditious to use planes for

scanning the miles of empty ocean, and to use ships for escort work and anti-raider sweeps. So, in 1943, when the U-boats arrived in the South Atlantic, it was the men who flew the Navy Liberators who defeated them in a series of sharp, bloody, air-surface fights. Although Ingram never got the heavy cruiser he longed for, his ships did not sail with an empty bag. In 1943 and 1944, they added more blockade-runners to their sack.*[10] The quiet war of Jonas Ingram was not without its sense of attainment.

In the late summer of 1941, Winston Churchill, needing ships to improve British troop-lift capacity and to carry reinforcements to the East, decided to borrow about twenty cargo ships and a dozen fast transports from the merchant marine and Navy of his good friend, Franklin Roosevelt. The Prime Minister, who possessed a very flexible concept of American neutrality, wanted the ships to be manned by American crews, and he hoped that British troops might board the transports at Halifax or perhaps even New York! In early September, the President considered the request with his naval advisers and decided to provide six transports and six cargo ships for the hard-pressed British. However, the following month, with the Atlantic battle intensifying and Congress considering modification of the neutrality laws, he changed his mind. Reluctant to risk American-manned ships on a British mission in submarine waters or in range of German air power, he told Churchill that he preferred that the British man the dozen ships, which could be loaned to the Royal Navy under the provisions of Lend-Lease; he agreed that, if the British did not have enough men, the ships could be manned by Americans, provided they took a safe route. Churchill accepted use of the ships on the President's terms.

The cargo ships were transferred from the American to the British merchant marine and became the SS *Empire Egret*, SS *Empire Pintail*, SS *Empire Fulmar*, SS *Empire Widgeon*, SS *Empire Peregrine*, and SS *Empire Oriole*.† They were assembled as Convoy CT 5 and, laden

---

*The *Savannah* and *Eberle* ended the career of the *Karin*; the *Cincinnati* and *Milwaukee* forced the scuttling of the *Anneliese Essberger*; the *Somers*, without a sail, put an end to the career of the *Weserland*; and the *Omaha* and *Jouett* finished the *Rio Grande* and *Burgenland*.

†Formerly, the SS *Nightingale*, SS *Howell Lykes*, SS *Hawaiian Shipper*, SS *Exemplar*, SS *China Mail*, and SS *Extavia*.

with general cargo and personnel, were provided an imposing escort of nine modern, long-legged destroyers; for the early part of their passage, they were given a nearby covering task force that included the *Yorktown, New Mexico, Philadelphia, Savannah*, and a squadron of new destroyers. The ships sailed late in October, taking a north-eastern track across the north-central Atlantic, destined for a long passage. The convoy made several route changes to avoid suspected U-boat concentrations. On the 30th, the destroyers detected what seemed like propeller noises and worked over a seemingly firm contact with depth charges. The escorts, new to the sonar conditions of the Atlantic, were restless, and throughout the day they picked up other contacts and carried out more attacks. After a quiet Halloween, on 1 November, direction-finder bearings taken on nearby transmissions indicated that a U-boat had sighted the convoy and was sending out a homing beacon to attract other submarines. Then the weather worsened, and the seas grew high and rough. The American destroyers were required to continue eastward beyond the Momp with the convoy; the British eastern ocean escort force was delayed by the storm. Pounding eastward in thrashing seas, the destroyers grew low on fuel. On 3 November, a destroyer sighted white tracks in the water, perhaps torpedo wakes; but the escorts searched and could not find a U-boat. The Redcoats arrived at last on the 5th, and the American destroyers turned the convoy over to them at 56°-30′ north, 11° west, not far from Londonderry.[11]

At Halifax, between 8 and 10 November, the equivalent of a British division and its gear was loaded aboard the American-manned, U.S. Navy transports *Wakefield, Mt. Vernon, West Point,* * *Leonard Wood, Joseph T. Dickman*, and *Orizaba*. The convoy was designated WS 124, with Captain Donald B. Beary in the *Mt. Vernon* as commodore. Dapper Rear Admiral Arthur B. Cook in the carrier *Ranger* commanded the escort force, Task Force 14.

The carrier, along with cruisers *Quincy* and *Vincennes*, and eight new destroyers, left Casco Bay on the 9th, amidst much speculation as to the task force's mission; the next day, the warships met the transports off Halifax. The transports were organized in a two-column line astern; the port column consisted of the older, cranky ships that were likely to give trouble, while the three former luxury liners made up the starboard column. The *Ranger* and a cruiser steamed 800

---

*Formerly the liners, *Manhattan, Washington,* and *America*.

yards ahead of the transports, with the other heavy cruiser a like distance astern. The destroyer *Wainwright* led the procession, and the *Rhind* brought up the rear. The *Moffett*, *Mayrant*, and *Trippe* patrolled 2,000 yards off the port column, and the *McDougal*, *Rowan*, and *Winslow* were off the starboard column.

The ships steamed south at 14 knots. In good weather the *Ranger* flew combat air patrols and search sweeps, and constantly had four fighters and six scout bombers spotted on the flight deck, armed and ready for launching. On the 12th, the *Joseph T. Dickman* jammed a rudder and ran across the bow of the *Orizaba*, but the latter, handling well for once, managed to swing away smartly, avoiding a collision. For a time, the *Vincennes* dropped behind with the *Rhind*, slowing down and heading into the sea, so that her doctors could perform an appendectomy on a sailor. The ships steamed through Mona Passage on the 15th, the sailors watching the dark shadow of the Puerto Rican coast in the gray distance to port. The *West Point*'s doctors performed an appendectomy on Gunner Samuel Mason, of the 43rd Royal Artillery, compliments of the Lend-Lease Act.

The ships refueled at Port of Spain on the 17th, and some of the crews drew liberty. The cruiser sailors, who had spent much time in Iceland, were impressed with the tropical foliage; in the saloons, they sang heartily, glad to be gone from Reykjavik. The convoy sailed on the 19th, joined by the naval tanker *Cimarron*. Thanksgiving Day was warm and stuffy on the warships; one sailor spoke for everyone when he noted, "Thanksgiving dinner was quite good, but I preferred to be eating it in Kentucky."

Afflicted with engine trouble, the *Leonard Wood* frequently lagged behind with the *Moffett*, forcing the convoy to reduce speed every time she threatened to pass out of sight astern. On the 22nd, one of the carrier planes mistook a dark shadow on the water for a U-boat; the *Wainwright* investigated, but found nothing. When the ships crossed the equator, the pollywogs were ducked and paddled, painted and sheared, and flung into nauseating concoctions—eggs, oysters, and turkey intestines. On the 24th, a *Ranger* plane reported a submarine, but it was only a whale.

The sea was surprisingly rough. It was rougher, thought the cruiser sailors, than they had seen it most of the time they were in the North Atlantic, but the winds were not high and there were no long, rolling swells. Although the ships did not pitch and roll, they sometimes shipped water through open ports, and it was rumored that two men were washed overboard during the trip. As sea conditions permitted,

The USS *Ranger* helping to escort WS 124 toward Capetown, November 1941

the *Cimarron* fueled the destroyers and transports. On the 27th, at 17° south, 20° west, the *Ranger* and her plane-guard destroyers headed back to Trinidad. No one wanted to risk a U.S. carrier in the eastern Atlantic. Captain Charlton E. Battle in the *Quincy* became escort commander, and thereafter the cruisers catapulted their float planes in regular patrols.

The Admiralty reported that four U-boats and the German tender *Python* were operating off the African coast. At 1335 on 28 November, Captain Frederick L. Riefkohl of the *Vincennes* thought he saw a periscope off his port bow; the cruiser turned in an attempt to ram, and then the destroyers searched the area, but could not pick up a sonar contact. The consensus of the cruisermen was that "Fightin' Freddie" had seen a whale or a dolphin. Nevertheless, "Vinnie Maru" launched two float planes armed with depth charges to patrol until dark. But the cruiser was spooked. Shortly after the planes took off, a gunner saw a whale close aboard to port and began screaming, "Submarine! Submarine! Submarine!" It must have reminded some of the veteran chiefs of a Chinese fire drill. Later, a sailor wrote in his diary: "At first after the Captain's sight, we were all watching the water to see where the torpedo might strike and wondering if it might strike under the bridge and blow us off. It was rather an exciting but helpless feeling."[12]

On the 1st of December, one of the *Vincennes'* planes sighted oil slicks on the surface 50 to 70 miles ahead; then planes from the *Quincy* sighted an unidentified vessel 90 miles away. The cruisermen hoped to encounter the *Python*; as one said, "She would be good practice for more formidable game later on." But the German tender, far to the east and south, was sunk that same day by the Royal Navy.

A southeasterly gale developeed on the 6th, and lasted for nearly two days. Even the big cruisers rolled as much as 32 degrees, and the convoy had to reduce speed and alter course to ease the stress on the destroyers. The *Vincennes* lost a damaged float plane over the side when members of a too-large work gang got in each other's way.

On the 8th, the ships learned of the Japanese attack on Pearl Harbor. The sailors could not understand how the Pacific Fleet could have permitted itself to be taken in so dismal a state of unreadiness. They were confident of defeating the Japanese and, in a way, relieved that the tensions and ambiguities of their uncertain war in the Atlantic were over at last. As one young cruiser officer wrote: "There are no

downcast faces on board the *Vincennes* over the prospect of a war
with the Japanese Empire. Many of us would like for the *Vinnie
Maru* to go from Africa to the Pacific on a raiding cruise. That
would really be worth while. . . . It will be good to be fighting a
declared war for a change. . . ."

The long voyage ended when the ships reached Capetown on the
afternoon of 9 December.[13]

Liberty in Capetown was joyful. The sailors were welcomed into
private homes, the girls were pretty and bright, and everyone in the
city seemed to be giving a party—all the time! The people made little
distinction between officers· and enlisted men, and as one cruiser
officer noted, "the men seem definitely to find the best looking girls."

The transports sailed on the morning of the 13th, escorted as far as
Durban by the American destroyers and the British cruiser *Dorset-
shire*. Then they passed into the care of the Royal Navy.*

In mid-December, the two cruisers, six destroyers, and tanker of
Task Force 14 steamed out of Table Bay, leaving Capetown behind.

---

*The six American ships sailed on east of Suez, destined to be caught up in the
chaos of the disintegration of the British and Dutch colonial empires.

The *Mt. Vernon* was sent to Singapore to unload troops who were captured by
the Japanese two months later. The skipper then asked to rejoin his division, but
instead his transport drew a succession of odd jobs from the increasingly desperate
British; they carried a group of rambunctious Australian troops from Suez to
Fremantle and evacuated refugees from the Netherlands East Indies, crossing the
Pacific to San Francisco in March.

The other five transports disembarked British soldiers at Bombay on 27 December. Captain Beary then wanted to return westward, but the British insisted
that he remain. After several weeks, the three older ships were released, but the
West Point and *Wakefield* were ordered to carry 9,778 British soldiers to Singapore. Beary was furious at having wasted time in Bombay while the situation in
Malaya was deteriorating and becoming more dangerous for his ships, when he
might have taken the reinforcements directly to Singapore in the first place.

The two transports sailed eastward, disembarking the troops at Singapore on
29 January 1942. Japanese bombers came over that day and the next, and the
British were able to send up a total of but seven fighters to meet the two raids.
On the 30th, the *West Point* was straddled by a brace of bombs. Then the
Wakefield was hit by a bomb, which penetrated to the sick bay, killing all hands
there. The ships hauled anchor and fled to Batavia, carrying 2,200 refugees. The
busy, pressured British were not always able to provide an adequate escort for
the ships, and Captain Beary became enraged on one occasion when a British
escort vessel took station between two columns of convoy ships, as if using the
auxiliaries as a shield against submarine attack (actually, the British skipper was
probably moving to the middle of the convoy to provide the ships with better
AA coverage).

Despite the long voyages and crowded conditions aboard the transports, the
health of crews and passengers remained good. By spring, Captain Beary and his
weary band were back in the U.S. Navy.

On the *Vincennes*, the sailors were still enjoying memories of their liberty:

> The men are still talking about Cape Town and hoping that we return. That is the first place they have been where a uniform was an introduction to the best people more than the other way around. We have had only one Court Martial from the visit . . . where ordinarily there would have been several. . . . The men did less drinking, etc., there than in any other port. They found that they could get dates with respectable girls and were welcome in nice homes. It was the nearest that they have come to being able to visit their own homes.

After the joys ashore, the sailors were contented men, and they went to sea looking for a fight. A German raider was said to be operating off the African coast, but few men expected to be seeing action soon. As one disappointed cruiserman noted, "We needed to go toward Singapore for that. . . . That is what we are out here for, and that is the reason for my wearing a uniform. Most of the officers are feeling the same way and are glad that finally we are actually fighting in the open. There are always some who do a lot of griping, but it is mainly superficial."[14]

The ships steamed with the cruisers and *Cimarron* in column, two destroyers ahead and two off either beam. Occasionally, the warships spread out in a scouting line to look for submarines or raiders. On the afternoon of the 20th December 1941, an unidentified ship was sighted on the horizon; a rumor circulated that she resembled the German raider reputed to be in the vicinity. The *Quincy* investigated, but all she found was a Greek freighter carrying Lend-Lease planes and tanks to Capetown. The *Vincennes'* men were unhappy because they were afraid Captain Battle would "hog" any action that came for his own *Quincy*.

Christmas trees brought from Africa were put up in the "Vinnie Maru" and the Christmas dinner was sumptuous, but there was not much authentic cheer; the men were a long, long way from home, the weather was warm, and the war news was not good. The *Winslow* chased a suspicious ship, and Captain Battle, in the giving spirit of the season, confounded his critics in the "Vinnie Maru" by letting her join in the chase, but the vessel turned out to be a passenger liner. The destroyers also suffered a false alarm, tracking a whale for a while. The placid routine and disappointments must have dulled the vigilance of lookouts and watchstanders, for that night a merchant ship on an opposite heading passed through the outer screen of destroyers completely unobserved and got within 3,000 yards of the cruisers before the *Mayrant* finally sighted her and illuminated her by searchlight. Captain Riefkohl was not pleased.

The ships reached Trinidad on the 29th, but shore leave there seemed stale and prosaic after Capetown. Task Force 14 steamed back through Mona Passage and on to Norfolk. One of the sailors predicted:

> 1942 will be a war year, as will probably '43, '44, and '45. . . . We have a war to fight and we will win it. If we are backed fully at home, the war may not be so long; otherwise it may drag on for years.[15]

And throughout the Atlantic Fleet, men pondered the tidings of war and hoped for a fortunate fate.

28.

Air Raid
Pearl Harbor

LIKE OTHER AMERICANS, THE MEN of the Atlantic Fleet would always remember how it was when they first got the word, sure that their lives would be very much changed by the events of that first Sunday in December 1941: "Air raid Pearl Harbor X This is not a drill."

At Valley Forge, a cold wind blew through the dark, and the Marines learned the news from people in communications, from hand radios, and from each other. After the first shock, there was "a feeling of general relief." The uncertainty of a twilight peace was over, and the Marines knew that now they would have to be sent to the Pacific. In the weeks ahead, the men of the Sixth Marines, powerless to help old friends and kindred units who were fighting hard, doomed battles at Wake Island and in the Philippines, heard the war news with a sense of guilt and bitterness as they cursed the eerie keening of the Icelandic wind and waited impatiently for sailing orders.[1]

Jonas Ingram was shaving when he got the word. He was worried about his son, Bill, who was serving in the *Oklahoma*. Later, he learned that Ensign Ingram survived his capsized ship to carry on the fight from a gun station on the *Maryland*, where he was reproached for fighting without his cap.[2] In the *Maryland*, new to the war, neatness still counted.

Aboard the *Sterett*, bobbing at anchor in Great Sound, Bermuda, there was little surprise or excitement, a feeling that "the event of war with Japan, long expected by all Navy men, had at last become a reality." Everyone assumed that the damage to the Pacific Fleet would prove light and that the striking force of Japanese carriers would be promptly hunted down and sunk. Only her Chief Engineer was worried, for he had served in the *West Virginia*, the battleship which early reports said had been sunk, and had many friends aboard. But "the news was received in general with a degree of smugness and a firm confidence. . . ."[3]

Aboard the heavy cruiser *Vincennes*, en route to Capetown, the sentiments were a combination of surprise at the unreadiness of the Pacific Fleet, relief that the undeclared war was over, and desire for battle in the Pacific. As one sailor noted in his diary:

> Since I held up my right hand and swore my oath, I have been in the Arctic Ocean, North Atlantic, South Atlantic, Caribbean Sea, Pacific Ocean, and the Indian Ocean. Foreign places and countries visited are Bermuda, Trinidad, Iceland, Newfoundland, Panama, South Africa, Cuba—and I shall include New England, for New England was the strangest of all. . . . I have seen hundred-knot gales with mountainous seas which engulfed a destroyer, and heavy snow in September, and blistering hot days in December. . . . But also there have been cold, damp, terribly exhausting watches, after which I barely had the energy to climb into my bunk, only to jump out before I was hardly sound asleep at the cry over the loudspeakers, "Man Your Battle Stations," followed by the soul-shattering general alarm. But without one the other would not be nearly so pleasant, and I am glad to be where I am, only hoping for a chance to prove my worth to my country.* [4]

On the *Babbitt*, helping to escort ON 41 westward, the sailors were "surprised." They thought that the Japanese would have been wiser to strike in southeast Asia, and avoid attacking American territory. They believed that their own job in the Atlantic would now be an easier one, because they would enjoy full "popular support."[5]

Up ahead in the dark, Captain Thebaud in the *Mayo* was thinking along similar lines, feeling that any small remaining vestiges of apathy and doubt left from the peacetime days had just gone "over the side with a bang."[6]

The *Edison* was taking HX 163 eastward when her crew learned the news. The men on her bridge were stunned into silence until a

---

*Lieutenant Dorris had but eight months to live when he made this diary entry, for the *Vincennes* and the *Quincy*, after months of seeking a surface gunnery action, finally caught up with their destiny in early August. By that time, their luck was all gone, and both cruisers went down without much chance to fight in the Battle of Savo Island.

short, tough youngster from Brooklyn growled, "We'll now give three silent cheers for the bastards who jumped ship to join the Pacific Fleet!" In Lieutenant Commander Murdaugh's opinion, the event was a "tremendous relief" to his men. When they took out a convoy, their eyes automatically searched the nondescript array of merchant vessels, looking for those that bore the flag of their own country, symbolizing that they were not alone in the battle. They had seen too few such flags; now they knew that they would see more. Like others who stood gun watches in the worst of the Atlantic storms and whose ships, even when at anchor in Hvalfjördhur, could commence firing within five minutes, they did not understand why it took the Pacific Fleet ships so long to open effective fire on the attacking Japanese aircraft.[7]

The *Hornet*'s air group got the word on the carrier at Norfolk. One flier wrote home:

> In the period approaching Christmas, it seems bitterly ironical to mouth again the time-worn phrases concerning peace on earth, goodwill to men, with so many millions hard at work figuring out ways to reduce other millions to slavery or death. I find it hard to see the inherent difference between men and the rest of the animal kingdom. Faith lost—all is lost. Let us hope tonight . . . all people throughout this great country have the faith to once again sacrifice for the things we hold essential to life and happiness. Let us defend these principles to the last ounce of blood. But then, above all, retain reason enough to have charity for all and malice toward none. If the world ever goes through this again, mankind is doomed. This time it has to be a better world.* [8]

The men of the Atlantic Fleet reacted to the news of the Japanese attack on Pearl Harbor with surprise, complacence, confidence, anger, dedication, and hope. They felt a sense of relief that the anomalous position of their country and the uncertainty of their own mission would be clarified, and were glad that they would now enjoy the united support of a committed nation. They would do their work as they had before, with dedication and courage, but they would feel better about it. For now they were fighting for something more than each other.

In Washington, the President was "shaken" by the stark news; war was not unexpected, given the state of relations with Japan, but

---

*The letter was written by Ensign Bill "Squire" Evans of Torpedo Squadron 8. Six months later, Ensign Evans and every man in his squadron but one was killed in action at the Battle of Midway.

FDR "did not expect to get hurt" so badly at its outset, and the Japanese attack was a "terrible blow to . . . his faith in the Navy and its ships. . . ." He was unusually somber. Secretary Knox was appalled; he confessed that he felt "something terrible." Secretary Hull was outraged.

But, as in the Fleet, surprise and fury were tempered by relief at the ending of a long agony of doubt and stress. As Secretary Stimson recorded, "When the news first came . . . my first feeling was one of relief that the indecision was over. . . ." And the President, although "serious," seemed to have "a much calmer air" as the tension of undeclared war and its "awful burden of decision" began to ebb at last; someone said, "I think the boss really feels more relief than he has had for weeks."[9]

Meanwhile, the Germans had been alerted to the details of the previously consummated Anglo-American strategic agreements by exposés in the American isolationist press on 4 and 5 December. Wehrmacht staff officers were studying the "Roosevelt war plan" when the Japanese struck at Pearl Harbor.[10]

The Fuehrer, taken "completely by surprise" by the Japanese attack, became charged with optimism, bursting enthusiastically in on several of his generals with the dispatch reporting the news clutched in his hand. To the generals, he seemed enormously relieved. One remembered: "I gained the impression that the Fuehrer felt that the war between Japan and America had suddenly relieved him of a nightmare burden. . . ." And the Naval Staff "joyfully welcomed Japan's entry into the war," the sailors happy at "the filing off of their fetters which Hitler had imposed upon them out of respect for the USA." German leaders dared to hope that Japan would divert American attention and resources to the Pacific, despite the Germany-first decision. The Japanese strike meant that the Atlantic isles and West Africa were temporarily secure from Anglo-American invasion and, with American warships removed to the Pacific, it might be possible for German surface ships again to sortie into the Atlantic. Perhaps best of all, Germany no longer feared diplomatic isolation or suffered under the psychological handicap of confronting a hostile world virtually alone.[11]

But behind the aura of optimism lurked a spirit of resignation, fear, and pessimism. As Ribbentrop realized, the Japanese attack

"brought about what we had wanted to avoid at all costs, war between Germany and America." To one fatalistic naval officer the
dramatic events in the Pacific made little difference, for war between
Germany and America already existed. In spite of his elation, even
the Fuehrer brooded self-pityingly that the United States would
"abandon East Asia for a time in order to crush Italy and Germany
first." Thus, the Germans sensed that the bulk of American power
might yet be directed against Germany and that the blow of Japan
might serve but to unify the American nation.[12]

Curiously faithful in living up to his pledges to friendly nations,
Hitler was ready to join Japan in war on the United States, which he
accepted grimly and fatalistically, feeling that such was already the
reality in the Atlantic. He was aware that that limited naval war
would intensify as American merchant vessels were sent into the eastern Atlantic, and a formal avowal of belligerency could not, therefore, be postponed much longer. It was in Germany's interest to strike
before the Americans were fully ready and while some of their power
had to be diverted to the Pacific. Hence, on 9 December, General Order #14 directed Admiral Doenitz to commence unrestricted submarine warfare against U.S. shipping. Doenitz began to plan Operation
Paukenschlag, U-boat operations off the American coast. And, on 11
December, Hitler formally declared war on the United States, citing
as his reasons the undeclared naval war in the Atlantic and President
Roosevelt's "intention . . . to attack Germany by 1943. . . ."[13]

Meanwhile, the Wehrmacht high command had been working on
the "Roosevelt war plan" to prepare a strategy for Germany and, on
14 December, the planners presented their suggestions to the Fuehrer.
They predicted that the Anglo-Americans would lack the power to
force a landing in Europe until 1943, although they acknowledged
that the amphibious enemy might be able to occupy the Atlantic
islands and North Africa in 1942. Accordingly, they advised Hitler
that if victory in Russia were not won by the end of 1942, Germany
would have to go over to the defensive in the East, in order to
deploy forces against an Anglo-American invasion of the Continent.
They called for a stronger German naval and air effort in the Atlantic to prevent "American forces and munitions" from reaching the
battlefields; a land offensive in North Africa to take Suez and
dominate the Mediterranean; and strengthening of the defenses of the
Atlantic isles, West Africa, Iberia, and France. Basically, these recommendations were similar to the ones that the Naval Staff had been

making for a long time on the necessity for land and air operations to support a worldwide siege of Great Britain. The Fuehrer, incensed at the thought of passing over to the defensive in Russia, dismissed the staff conclusions as "drivelling nonsense."[14] The planners hoped that, with 25 divisions from the East, Germany would be able to drive Allied arms from Africa and then buy the time to turn the Continent into a true Fortress Europa. The Germans would not win World War II, but they might not lose it, either. But it was already too late. German resources were increasingly strained by the relentlessly mounting stresses of a two-front war; the time had gone when intelligent priorities and realistic strategic planning would have endowed Germany's great tactical victories with significant strategic meaning. Once again German planners had cause to rue the fact that the Fuehrer, a hero on land, was a coward at sea.

After the shocking success of the Japanese, nothing seemed impossible, and disquieting rumors were rife in the Atlantic.

The battleship *Texas* sighted a blimp cruising off New England, and the Office of Naval Operations warned that it might be a German mother ship capable of launching airplanes in an attack on the U.S. East Coast! The destroyer *Trippe*, peacefully en route from Norfolk to Newport, was attacked by U.S. Army planes that dropped four bombs, all of which missed—as usual.[15]

Then it was learned that the French cruiser *Barfleur* had sailed from Martinique and, on the basis of that misinformation, the carrier *Wasp*, the light cruisers *Nashville*, *Brooklyn*, and *Savannah*, and the destroyers *Sterett*, *Stack*, *Lang*, and *Wilson* were ordered from Bermuda to the French islands prepared to strike. But the French ships were all still in port.[16]

In response to resurgent fears of a German blow in the Western Hemisphere, contingency plans for preventive seizures of vulnerable points were updated. Operation Rubber called for landings in the Natal-Recife area of Brazil by the First Marine Division and the Army's Ninth Infantry Division, if and when the President directed. Operation Bungalow provided for an assault landing in the French islands by the Ninth Division, and fresh planning was undertaken for a possible landing in the Cape Verdes. However, as it became apparent that the Germans did not have the means to project their ample power into the New World, these plans were discarded and it soon became possible to turn from problems of hemispheric defense to preparations for offensive operations across the Atlantic.[17]

Most of the Atlantic Fleet was destined to feel the hard impact of the Japanese attack.

On the day after Pearl Harbor, the President and Admiral Stark concluded that at the very least the carrier *Yorktown*, three battle-ships, and one squadron of modern destroyers would have to be transferred from the Atlantic to reinforce the battered Pacific Fleet. Later in the week, the President made the sad, painful decision to replace Admiral Stark with a man whose toughness he admired, Admiral Ernest J. King. Some people thought the President was making his old friend the scapegoat for the disaster at Pearl Harbor; but the President believed that, in replacing Stark, he was acting decisively to avoid the problem that had plagued Mr. Lincoln during the Civil War before he found Sam Grant to command his armies— finding a leader worthy of his men. He considered it imperative to shake off the lethargy of peacetime ways and discard habits fit for less cruel times. "Betty" Stark was a man for times of thought and conciliation, for working with Congress and the Bureaus to build a Navy, for shaping future strategy. But Ernie King, a brighter and harder man, was better made for the stern duties and difficult deci-sions of war, and the President wanted him to lead the Navy and carry out the plans shaped by Admiral Stark in the ruthless fight ahead. As the Atlantic sailors said, it was a time for the sons of bitches. And it was no coincidence that the President picked the leader of his Navy from amongst those with experience at war, from the ranks of the Atlantic Fleet.[18]

Admiral Ingersoll, highly intelligent, but remote and lacking in fire and charisma, replaced King as Commander-in-Chief, Atlantic Fleet. But he lost ships to the Pacific, and by the end of December he was left with seventy-six destroyers, most of them four-stackers, and a hundred patrol planes as the backbone of his command. Aside from the Support Force and Jonas Ingram's small fleet, he maintained a little task force of heavy ships at Hvalfjördhur in case German raiders tried to break out into the Atlantic. Most of the heavy cruisers and old battleships were held in reserve in the Argentia-Casco Bay area and at Norfolk. The *Ranger* and her supporting units were at Ber-muda.[19] Ingersoll's first task was to tell his task force commanders what resources they would have to part with and what they could not have.

Admiral Bristol wrote urgently of vital priorities established by the hard test of undeclared war:

> Under present conditions of operation . . . we have been working with seven escort groups. This is a tight schedule and has been maintained with difficulty. It imposes a severe strain on the personnel which will become progressively serious as the winter advances. It also imposes serious strain on the ships. . . . Due to the shortage of destroyers when we started the escort-of-convoy, the size of the group was of necessity set at five. Early experience indicated and subsequent experience has confirmed that five ships are not enough to assure reasonable security for convoys of the size which have to be handled.

He requested more escort groups or at least more ships per group; and he asked that the groups be maintained intact, as free as possible of shifts of vessels and personnel, so that tactical cohesion and unit pride would be increased; finally, he suggested that more time be allotted his destroyers for training and overhaul, for the bad weather that protracted voyages and damaged destroyers also hindered the training of green crews by limiting lay-over time in port.[20] Admiral Bristol's points were cogent and wise; had he gained them, the Support Force would not only have improved its defensive capability, but it would have been able to develop an offensive potential: the Atlantic Fleet would have been able to kill U-boats.

But the Atlantic Fleet's problem had not changed: it still was short of ships and time. As Ingersoll told Admiral Bristol: "I see little hope for much improvement in the general situation regarding escorts for convoys. It may even get worse than it is now. . . . CinCPac asked for four more squadrons of destroyers. . . . With all the foregoing, and three or more months of bad weather ahead of us, with resulting damage to vessels, I see no immediate possibility of improving the situation by increasing the number of escort groups, or number of ships in a group, permanency of groups, increasing length of overhaul, or time for training."[21]

Ingersoll was telling the same thing to Jonas Ingram, who still wanted a heavy cruiser: "I hope we shall not lose any more to the West Coast. We are scraping the bottom now every time we get a job to do, and destroyers will be at a premium for months to come. I don't see any relief until the latter part of the year, when new construction will make itself felt." And Frank Knox told the public: "I'm afraid it is like trying to draw water out of a desert."[22]

Admiral King aboard the Atlantic Fleet's flagship, the USS *Augusta*,
October 1941

Admiral Bristol, knowing it was hopeless, but owing it to his men to try again, told Ingersoll: "The spirit is willing—but they simply have not any physical surplus left to draw on. . . . Unless the ships are ready and the crews refreshed and keen to go, they are of no use to me."[23] It was an old story: the Atlantic Fleet still lacked ships and time.

Not that the Atlantic Fleet lacked work. Most of its destroyers were busy escorting merchant convoys in the western Atlantic; its heavy ships were used to screen troop convoys to Iceland and the United Kingdom and to provide a thin reserve line of defense against raiders. The Atlantic Fleet was fighting the Battle of the Atlantic.

If the tasks of the Atlantic Fleet were vital, they were also largely invisible. And while the fleet was busy in deep water, a few U-boats began a massacre of American coastal shipping. Tankers burned and seamen drowned in fiery water within sight of pleasant beaches until the meager coastal commands organized local convoys and mustered a ragtag array of planes and small escorts to drive the U-boats to the Caribbean by spring. But in the time of slaughter, the public asked, "Where is the Navy?"[24] The Atlantic Fleet was fighting the Battle of the Atlantic.

V:
The Last Convoys

29.
The
Winter War

BETWEEN THE TIME OF PEARL HARBOR and mid-February 1942, while the U-boats, seeking the routes of least resistance, slaughtered many attractive and defenseless targets off the American coast, the warships of Support Force were not idle. They escorted twenty-four convoys, twelve each way, of about 750 ships across the North Atlantic. And the work was done in safety, but not in ease, for weather was the constant foe of the winter war.

On the morning of 10 December 1941, the destroyers *Gleaves*, *Dallas*, *Upshur*, and *Ellis*, and the new "Treasury"-class Coast Guard cutter *Ingham*, escorting Army freighter *Mattole*, searched for hours in squalls southeast of Cape Race before meeting the forty-six merchant vessels of HX 164. The ships took a north-northeast track through snowstorms, clinging together on high, frothy rollers in blurred visibility. The convoy plodded for a week through the gray, stormy seas, but on the night of 18/19 December, when they were a little short of the Momp, many of the merchantmen were scattered by a massive gale; all of them reached Britain safely. The American warships rounded up five Iceland-bound vessels and took them north in driving rain, arriving on the 20th.[1]

On the 14th of December, the *Wilkes*, *Charles F. Hughes*, *Lansdale*, *Madison*, and *Sturtevant*, escorting USS *Alchiba*, were steaming south from Iceland toward a rendezvous with the seventeen vessels of ON 45 when the *Sturtevant*'s sonar man heard a torpedo-like noise in the water to starboard. The four-stacker swung to the right, and the whirring sound passed down along her starboard beam. No one saw the torpedo. The *Sturtevant* searched, gained a sonar contact, and attacked with five depth charges. After losing contact in the din of explosions and the underwater turbulence, the destroyer searched the area and, half an hour later, one of her men sighted what looked like a periscope in the water, but it disappeared before the *Sturtevant* could line up an attack. The destroyers went on toward the rendezvous.

Not until the afternoon of the 16th, after a long search in the vicinity of the Momp, did the American ships come upon HMS *Wanderer*, of the British escort; they were then told that the convoy had already been dispersed because it had been so badly scattered in stormy weather at about 58°-30' north, 18° west. The destroyers started southwest with amply protected *Alchiba*; the next night, three of the escorts were detached. En route, the *Charles F. Hughes* sustained weather damage to her steering gear. The scattered convoy vessels all made it to port safely. The *Wilkes* and *Madison* dispersed their one-ship convoy southeast of Cape Race, then headed for the barn.[2]

The forty-eight vessels of HX 165 carried steel and scrap, petroleum products, alcohol, grain, copra, sugar, and general cargo; the escorts *Buck, Swanson, McCormick, Greer*, and *Herbert* went along to make sure the goods got through. The destroyers met the convoy south of Argentia on the 17th December and began a long, northerly passage. A pharmacist's mate in the *Buck* gave in to fear and had to be treated for hysteria. It was a quiet voyage, and the merchantmen were turned over to the British on Christmas Eve at about 60° west, 24° north. There was but one straggler, the SS *Shantung*, which later caught fire and was abandoned; the rest of the convoy vessels reached port safely. The American destroyers passed Christmas Day peacefully en route north with the Icelandic freighter *Dettifoss*.[3]

On the 19th, the *Benson, Niblack, Edison, Hilary P. Jones*, and *Tarbell* left Iceland with three merchant vessels to meet the twenty-four ships of ON 47. While searching for the convoy on the 21st, the

Edison attacked a sonar contact, then, with no convoy to distract her, hunted for the U-boat for an hour and a half, but failed to regain contact. On the afternoon of the 22nd, several British escorts reached the Momp, but they had no merchant ships with them. The British commander said his ships had been at sea seven days, but that he had not actually seen any of the convoy vessels since the first day out. The American destroyers, abetted by two British destroyers, searched back along the track of the convoy and came upon about twenty merchantmen rolling on the gray-green sea. The American escort took station, and the ships headed west, then southwest. But that night, another intense storm blew up out of the dark sea, and many of the vessels strayed once again. Some of the lost merchant ships showed lights, which permitted one of them, a lonely freighter, to be found by the *Niblack*. Only a few vessels were present on the 23rd, and the convoy was ordered dispersed that night. All the merchant ships reached port safely. Four-stacker *Tarbell* returned to Iceland to refuel before setting forth on the long westward passage. Alone en route to Argentia, she was delayed by an electrical fire and engine trouble, but she made it home at low speed by the end of the month. The *Edison* also suffered engine trouble and made the trip alone. It proved a gimpy passage for the destroyers.[4]

HX 166 was spooked from the start. Its thirty-six ships left Halifax in rain, fog, and snow; outside the harbor, eight of them could not find the others in the mist-blurred grayness and returned to port. The veteran HMCS *Annapolis* was detained by mechanical troubles, and the two other Canadian escorts found it hard to keep the convoy together; confusion was increased when an SC convoy passed nearby, and then some inbound merchantmen, sailing independently because they had been dispersed early, steamed into the midst of the already disorganized collection of ships. On the afternoon of the 23rd of December, the *Plunkett*, *Cole*, and *Badger*, and the cutter *Campbell*, helped by PBYs from Argentia, rounded up twenty-one vessels, while the *Decatur* steamed eastward in company with the tanker USS *Kaweah*. When the planes reported thirty-one other ships milling in the area, Commander "Possum" Webb decided to go on with what he had; in the next three days, seven more ships joined. Stormy weather was encountered during the passage, but no U-boats. The destroyers turned the convoy over to the British on New Year's Eve at about 60°-40′ north, 22°-40′ west. Later, the 8,200-ton freighter SS *Cardita* was torpedoed and sunk by a U-boat. The American destroyers greeted the New Year en route to Iceland with *Kaweah* and four merchantmen.[5]

The *Gleaves, Dallas, Upshur, Ellis*, and *Ingham* left Iceland with two merchantmen on the 23rd, but the twenty-eight vessels of ON 49 were held back by storms, and the U.S. destroyers roved far south looking for them. At last, on the afternoon of the 27th, at about 58°-30′ north, 22°-45′ west, they took over from the British escort. The ships steamed to 25° west, then took a southwesterly route home. It was a quiet passage, there was only one straggler, and the convoy was safely dispersed in a thick fog southeast of Cape Race on 5 January. The slow start made for a long but not harsh voyage.[6]

At daylight on 29 December, the *Mayo, Babbitt, Leary, Schenck*, and *Simpson* searched the waters south of Argentia for some sign of HX 167; faulty navigation caused the convoy to miss the rendezvous. The destroyers searched the dark blue, empty sea through the chill, sunny morning, guided by plain-language messages from HMCS *Annapolis*; the three messages from the Canadians reported widely separated positions. A PBY found the convoy, and the destroyers rushed at 25 knots to overtake it, at high cost in fuel consumption. At 1215, the warships sighted forty-two merchant vessels arrayed in nine columns on the inky, rippled water. Assuming command of the convoy at 1400, they led the merchant vessels north, northeast, and then east across the Atlantic.

On the 30th, an evaporator in the SS *Stonestreet* burst, killing one merchant sailor and seriously injuring three others; the *Simpson* sent her medical officer and a corpsman over to the vessel, which then steamed back to St. John's, watched over by a PBY. The *Leary* attacked a sonar contact off the starboard bow of the convoy, but the attack was futile, for the target—a whale—was already inside the destroyer's turning circle when the attack commenced. Off the port flank of the convoy, the *Schenck* depth-charged a false contact. The *Simpson*, having been hurried out of dry dock, was handicapped by lack of a protective shield on the sonar head beneath her, so her sound equipment did not function at speeds in excess of 5 knots.

On the night of the 30th, white dots of stinging snow lashed across a black sky, heralding a three-day gale. High seas poured over the bucking, rolling ships, and the convoy fell forty hours behind schedule; the Momp was changed three times. But the merchant vessels of this convoy were first-rate, doggedly maintaining proper station in the storm and refusing to give in to the temptation to show lights at night; the ships clung together as they pitched into the foamy gray rollers. On the dark, bucking *Babbitt*, the quartermaster made the first entry of the New Year in the deck log:

> Listen my hearties, and you shall hear
> of our midnight watch, the first of the year
> 'Tis one sixty-seven, HX you may say
> That we are escorting so well on her way
> Stationed to port, 600 yards on her bow
> We're keeping our station though the Lord knows how. . . .
> Oh, the old *Babbitt* . . . on the surface so far
> On top may she float to the end of the war.[7]

On the 3rd as the weather moderated, one of the convoy vessels, the USS *Delta*, refueled the *Babbitt* and *Schenck*, an innovation that promised to add to the endurance and usefulness of the short-legged four-stackers. However, *Leary* could not be fueled before dusk; she was detached to Iceland the next day, and replaced on the 5th by the corvette HMS *Dahlia*. The destroyers turned the convoy over to the rest of the Redcoats on the morning of the 7th at about 60°-30' north, 22°-30' west; there was only one straggler, SS *Beaconoil*, and all the merchantmen reached port safely. The American ships took the *Delta* and five merchantmen toward Iceland. En route, shortly after 2200, the *Mayo* made two abortive attacks on a false contact, the first marred by an error in reporting the range of the target, the second ruined by jammed depth-charge racks. But at 2240, the *Babbitt* did find a U-boat. The four-stacker, steaming off the starboard quarter of the small convoy, picked up a contact 1,500 yards to starboard. She swung right, but as she turned, the surfaced U-boat submerged into the black water. The *Babbitt* surged toward her target, losing contact at 300 yards as her sound cone passed over the submarine; the U-boat curled back toward the destroyer, and the *Babbitt*'s pattern of depth charges exploded astern and to one side of the submarine. The *Mayo* came over to lend a hand, and the two destroyers searched the black sea in the night cold for an hour and a half, but could not regain contact. Then the two destroyers steamed after the rest of their tribe, up ahead on the lonely night sea.[8]

Three small, slow cargo ships left Iceland on 30 December in company with the *Buck, Swanson, McCormick, Greer*, and *Herbert*, but they became separated in the stormy darkness and returned to Reykjavik. Free to run at high speed, the destroyers reached the Momp ahead of schedule and patrolled along 60° north to find the twenty-five merchant ships and escort of ON 51. They led the convoy on a southwesterly track. Less disciplined than those of HX 167, the merchant ships made excessive smoke in daytime and showed lights at night. The *Buck*'s medical officer performed an emergency appendectomy on one of her sailors on the wardroom table.

The weather became stormy again and, on the 7th, a gale developed. Winds reached force 8, lashing undulant crests of icy, foamy water at the rolling ships. By the 9th, six merchant vessels were missing. The *Greer* and *Herbert*, in need of fuel, were detached to Argentia. Old *McCormick* tried to hang on with the two new ships. The destroyers doggedly smashed their bows into the rushing seas, plunging and swaying, but by noon on the 11th, only three merchant vessels were still with them; they dispersed their charges at dusk, southeast of Cape Race. All the convoy vessels managed to reach port safely. The *Swanson* headed north for Argentia, but the lucky *Buck* and *McCormick* steamed for Boston to refit.[9]

Escort missions grew harder for, as bad weather increased, the Argentia-based PBYs were able to spend less time over departing convoys; and progressively fewer modern destroyers were available for the escort groups. In January, the fliers spent 43.8 hours patrolling over convoys; they were successful in finding the ships only about half the times assigned. And with new destroyers needed in the Pacific and to escort heavy ships and troop convoys, more and more four-stackers were pressed into service on the North Atlantic shuttle.

On the 4th, the *Woolsey* and the four-stackers, *Bainbridge, Truxtun, Broome*, and *Dickerson*, met the thirty-three vessels of HX 168 south of Argentia. It was the *Dickerson*'s first escort mission, and the other four-stackers' first trip since early fall. Air cover was scheduled on the 4th and 5th, but the PBYs of Patrol Squadron 82 were stopped both days by storms. A U-boat was reported off Cape Race, so the convoy was diverted in a hook to the north, steaming to 52° north before heading northeast. On the 6th, the *Bainbridge* attacked a false sonar contact and a periscope-like object in the water with eight depth charges.

A dense, clammy fog settled down over the sea and, on the morning of the 7th, two merchant ships collided in the murky darkness; damaged and leaking, they were both forced to turn back. A Canadian corvette helped one ship in, but the other, invisible in the thick mist, limped alone back to St. John's. Soon an intense gale blew up, scattering many of the ships and, on the 9th, vessels of westbound ON 52 passed through the remnant of HX 168 and added to the disarray. As the gale intensified, the merchant ships dispersed without orders, each trying to ride out the storm at its best speed and safest heading. Force 9 seas and force 10 winds—"The numbers don't go higher," noted one weary destroyerman in his ship's log—thrashed and shrieked at the ships; by the 10th, the convoy consisted of three merchantmen and the *Woolsey*. The next day, the destroyer passed two of the merchant vessels into the hands of the British escort led by HMS *Wanderer* and took the third toward Iceland.

Most of the merchantmen were scattered over a wide area between 57°-30′ north and 59°-20′ north and 24°-20′ west and 26° west, and not all of them were lucky. Despite mist and stormy seas, *U-43* found the 5,246-ton Swedish freighter SS *Yngaren* at 0400 on the 12th and torpedoed her. She sank rapidly, and only two of her forty men survived. The other merchant vessels reached port safely. The scattered American destroyers reached Valley Forge with but minor damage topside and only cuts and bruises to harm their men.[10]

The *Plunkett, Decatur, Badger, Cole*, and *Campbell* left Iceland with the tanker USS *Sapelo*, the Army freighter *Mattole*, and four merchant vessels on the night of 6 January 1942 bound for a rendezvous with ON 53; but the thirty-one vessels of the convoy and their escort were delayed by storms, and it was not until the morning of the 10th, at 59° north, 22° west, that the American destroyers met and assumed responsibility for the merchantmen. A long, hard passage was certain.

On the 11th, a gale struck; wind velocity reached force 10. High dunes of water rolled down on the vessels, which pitched and swerved in the churning ocean. The *Plunkett* and *Campbell* were battered topside, but the four-stackers suffered most. The *Badger* lost a boat over the side, then as she plunged and rolled, there was a sharp, cracking sound and her mainmast snapped at the level of the bridge, crashing onto the deck forward; even the ship's bell was twisted loose by the wild winds and seas and flung into the water. The *Cole* lost three ready ammunition lockers and ninety-six rounds of 3-inch washed overboard, sustained cracks and seams in her side plating forward, and the splinter shield on her Number One gun was buckled. So quickly and so sharply did she roll that at times it seemed she might capsize; she registered a port roll of 68 degrees. One of her watch officers wrote repetitively: "vessel pitching deeply and heavily, rolling quickly and laboring greatly. . . . laboring greatly. . . . rolling quickly and heavily. . . . Vessel pitching deeply and heavily, rolling quickly and heavily, and laboring greatly." But the old *Cole* endured and survived.

On the 13th, the *Badger* struggled off toward Argentia for emergency repairs; the next day, the *Cole* was detached because she was low on fuel. The other escorts searched in vain for their scattered flock and, by the 18th, were left with but three ships. Then the *Decatur* was detached to take the SS *Northern Sword* to St. John's; the freighter had sustained serious storm damage and her holds were flooded. The *Plunkett* and *Campbell* persevered with the *Sapelo* and *Mattole*. Finally, the two-ship convoy was dispersed south of Argentia at dusk on the 19th.

The scattered merchantmen of ON 53 were all right until they neared the coast of North America and encountered U-boats engaged in Operation Paukenschlag. Then the SS *Empire Wildebeeste* was torpedoed near 60° west while en route to the U.S. East Coast. The SS *Vassilios A. Palemis* was torpedoed and sunk south of Newfoundland, only twelve of her thirty-three crewmen surviving. Southeast of Cape Race, the SS *Icarion* was torpedoed and sunk, almost half her crew perishing. The SS *Hallfried* was sunk off the U.S. coast, and the SS *Silveray* was torpedoed as she approached Halifax. The toll was three ships sunk, two damaged; the remaining vessels of the convoy reached port safely, although some of them were the worse for storm damage. All the American destroyers suffered extensive storm damage and required repairs in Boston; but no destroyermen died.[11]

The *Campbell* almost evened the score for the torpedoed merchant ships. Steaming alone southeast of Halifax on the afternoon of the

22nd, en route to Boston, the Coast Guardsmen sighted a surfaced U-boat stalking a British freighter. The cutter made a cautious approach, and the U-boat submerged before she had time to attempt a shot. After she had searched the vicinity for an hour and a quarter, her lookouts saw the U-boat on the surface, about seven miles away, moving east. She pursued the submarine but, in a few minutes, the German lookouts sighted her rocking into the swells astern and dived. The *Campbell's* gunners fired four rounds from their forward gun, but the shells whistled over the blue water and exploded in white splashes wide of the submerging U-boat. The cutter searched for two and three-quarter hours, but did not pick up a sonar contact; at 1710, she abandoned the hunt.

At 1900, a red glow lit up the black sky over the horizon. The U-boats had claimed another ship, a tanker, judging by the look of the sky. The cutter searched cautiously toward the reddened sky, echo-ranging for submarines. The sea was empty and still. Three and a half hours passed. Suddenly her sonar man called out a U-boat nearby; then the men on deck saw her. The U-boat was only 500 yards away, low in the black water, her deck awash with shiny white foam. At the same time, the Germans saw the *Campbell* and quickly submerged; the Coast Guardsmen did not get a chance to swing their guns and open fire. The *Campbell* charged in and dropped six depth charges at 100- and 150-foot settings, blowing up gushers of white water. A few minutes after the detonations, the *Campbell* regained contact and dropped six more depth charges set alternately at 150 and 250 feet. The cutter then swung away and fired a star shell. A pale white-yellow sheen flickered over the black swells. The exploding depth charges flung up humps of bright water. Then a submarine broached the dark surface, rose to about fifteen feet, and subsided; some of the Coast Guardsmen said they saw her roll over and sink. A film of oil shone on the eerily lit water. Then, instead of waiting until daylight, the *Campbell,* too sure of her kill, went off in search of the source of the fire in the sky. The submarine—perhaps the *U-130*—was hurt and leaking oil, but she was not slain. As she escaped, she left a moving stain of oil on the surface, marking her for death in the daytime. But by daylight the *Campbell* was far away. Soon she came upon a blazing Norwegian tanker, her bow almost perpendicular in an ocean of flames. Because the *Campbell* was inexperienced, the tanker went unavenged.[12]

On the morning of the 10th, the *Wilkes* and *Madison,* the old *Sturtevant,* and two novices, the four-stackers *Roper* and *Jacob Jones,* met the forty-one vessels of HX 169 south of Argentia. Because there were U-boats off Cape Race, the *Annapolis* and three Canadian corvettes of the western local escort remained with the convoy until dusk on the 11th, and the *Ellis* joined from Argentia for a similar stint; a strong air patrol watched over the ships one day during a brief period of good weather.

In the heavy layer of fog that hung over the sea on the 10th, two of the merchant ships collided and returned to port damaged; another turned back because her lifeboats were not in seaworthy condition. Late on the 10th, lookouts on the *Sturtevant*, whose skipper had only been on board for thirteen days, reported a green light approaching through tendrils of mist. The destroyer sounded a long blast on her whistle and swung to starboard but, at 2250, she and a merchant ship struck together at the bows, bounced apart, then hit side to side. Fortunately, the blow was glancing, instead of dead-on, and damage was minor; both ships were able to stay with the convoy.

The commander of the escort, Commander Walter W. Webb, was thinking positively; with ten escorts for two days, it seemed that he had a "golden opportunity" to kill a U-boat. But, wisely, the convoy was diverted from swinging onto a direct northeast course and advised to hook along close to the Newfoundland shore until well north of Cape Race. Consequently, Webb's aspiring hunter-killer group encountered no U-boats, which was perhaps good luck considering the fog and the lack of experience of his destroyermen. But on the 11th, despite the mist, a straggler, the SS *Africander*, was torpedoed, but not sunk, somewhere out in the blurred grayness.

As the seas began to rise and grow stormy, the *Sturtevant's* luck continued bad. One of her chiefs warned a seaman to put on his life jacket, but the sailor refused. Barely fifteen minutes later, the seaman was swept overboard while needlessly going aft to fetch water for cooking. The destroyer searched for an hour, but did not recover his body. Intermittent snow squalls swirled out of leaden skies, and white-crested rollers surged at the pitching, swaying ships. The sailors sustained cuts and bruises from falls and from slamming into bulkheads. Many of the merchant vessels straggled in the black nights, some rounded up by the rolling destroyers in the cold, pale light of dawn. By the 16th, the *Jacob Jones* and eighteen merchant vessels were missing; after searching in vain for the other ships, the *Jacob Jones* proceeded alone to Iceland through the gale. When the remaining destroyers and merchant vessels reached the Momp at about 60°-30' north, 22°-40' west, only three British escorts were present. In order to better protect the remnant of the convoy and because his ships, low on fuel, needed to avoid the punishing trip north to Iceland, Commander Webb was given permission to take his destroyers on to Londonderry.

Thus, on the 21st, two weeks before the formal commissioning of Naval Operating Base, Londonderry, Commander Webb's weary destroyers unexpectedly opened the ball in Northern Ireland. Irish cities and towns seemed to the American sailors small and excessively quiet, and the dour Presbyterian tradition discouraged merriment. Rain often wept from gray skies. But the pubs were warm and cozy and the people, in contrast to the stiff and sullen Icelanders, were gregarious and hospitable; and the pretty Irish countryside seemed like the green, green grass of home to tired sailors used to the gnarled, shrubless tundra of Iceland.[13]

A gale was blowing wildly when the *Mayo, Babbitt, Leary, Schenck,* and *Simpson* departed Iceland on the night of 11/12 January 1942 in company with the U.S.-flag freighter SS *Omaha*. After a few miles, the merchant master refused to continue the voyage; he brought his freighter back to Reykjavik to await better weather. Such instances increased the contempt of the destroyermen for merchant sailors. Ashore, the merchant crews had plenty of money and whiskey, and talked tough, but they sometimes missed important sailings; at sea, they seemed to do as they pleased, beyond the discipline and suasion of lethargic masters, and were little use in a crisis. There were many brave men in the merchant marine—the toughest of destroyermen did not doubt the courage of the men who sailed in tankers—but somehow the bravery of individuals did not suffice to endow the civilian service with a hardy tone, a spirit of endurance and sacrifice; lack of discipline and wartime training and a hangover of attitudes and practices from the bitter labor strife of the 1930s marred the efficiency and reputation of the merchant marine.

The destroyers, steaming through snow squalls and stormy seas, reached the Momp on the 14th to find no ships in sight on the steeply rolling crests of the sea; the twenty-seven merchant ships and six escorts of ON 55 had been delayed and then scattered by the gale.

Meanwhile, at about 58°-30′ north, 20° west, not far from the Momp, despite the storm, two stragglers, the SS *Empire Surf* and SS *Chepo*, were discovered by a tenacious U-boat, torpedoed, and sunk. The American destroyers searched all day, encountering strayed merchantmen, but could not find the British escorts; then radio contact was established and a new rendezvous arranged. The gale intensified during the night, as the rolling ships of both escort groups ranged through the stormy blackness, trying to round up stragglers.

At about 0400 on the 15th, the *Mayo* was forced to alter course to mitigate the pounding of the sea and permit men relieved from watch to go aft safely. Engulfed by hills of shiny black water, the destroyer continued to search, her radar set functioning. Suddenly, at 0420, a darkened vessel loomed ahead; it was the British destroyer HMS *Douglas*. Unable to swing away in time, the *Mayo* rammed her in the port side, punching a hole in her plating and causing flooding. The British ship would have to go to Iceland; worse, the escort commander, Sol Phillips, having none of his four-stackers nearby, was forced to use the *Mayo*, his best ship, to screen the damaged British destroyer on her trip north.

On the 15th, the *Leary* collected eight merchant vessels, and the other escorts rounded up a dozen more; thus, as the swaying destroyers led the convoy west, then southwest, there were but five stragglers. But on the night of the 16th, the gale intensified anew; force 10 winds lashed at the heaving black ocean and the dripping, deeply rolling four-stackers. Finally, with only eleven merchantmen still present, the escort commander ordered the ships to heave to. This last resort merely resulted in more scattering. The destroyers spent the 17th fruitlessly trying to round up strays, but steaming was laborious in the wild storm; the drenched four-stackers grew sluggish in the pounding seas. On the 18th, the *Babbitt* and *Leary* were detached to St. John's in need of fuel; the *Schenck* departed for Argentia the next day.

On the 20th, the *Mayo*, returning from Iceland, met the *Simpson*, lonely, but still grimly escorting a single freighter, the SS *Lockenby*. The two destroyers joined in a search to the east and west of the southwesterly convoy track, but enjoyed no luck; the thrashing gray seas limited the speed and, thus, the range of the search. The next day, the destroyers were ordered to give up their attempt to reassemble the convoy; they released their single ship at about 53° north, 36° west. Of the myriad stragglers, only the two long lost were harmed by the U-boats on their lonely passage. The *Mayo* and *Simpson* steamed for the warmth of Boston.[14]

The escort of HX 170 began grimly. The *Niblack* was en route from Casco Bay to Argentia on the 11th of January when a Norwegian freighter suddenly groped out of billowing morning fog, bearing down on her. The destroyer edged to port, and the cargo ship, running at slow speed, struck her side a glancing blow. The destroyermen shored up the frames in one of her forward compartments, and the *Niblack* was fit to continue her mission.

A newcomer to escort work was a third trim "Treasury"-class Coast Guard cutter, the *Alexander Hamilton*, introduced to service because the *Campbell* and *Ingham* had fared well on the Iceland run.

All day on the 15th, the *Niblack*, the old *Tarbell* and *Overton*, and the virgin *Alexander Hamilton* searched southwest of Argentia through a blur of dank, musty fog for HX 170. Fog kept the helpful PBYs moored on the green water at Argentia, and the destroyers searched without luck. That night the *Niblack's* radar detected ships approaching and, at 1927, her lookouts discerned dark smudges in the mist. Two vessels having turned back for repairs, the convoy consisted of twenty-nine ships. The *Ellis* and *Greer* and the small cutter *St. Augustine* joined the escort for two days to help it through dangerous coastal waters.

The fog burned off the water the next day, and the PBYs were able to provide nearly nine welcome hours of air cover for the ships. The convoy steamed close to the shoreline to avoid U-boats prowling off Cape Race, then turned northeast. On the afternoon of the 16th, the *Tarbell* hunted a sonar contact for an hour, attacking with fourteen depth charges, but she returned to the convoy without a kill. On the 19th, at nearly 55° north, the ships made a sharp course change to the northeast to shorten the voyage and to avoid approaching westbound convoy ON 57; two nights later, they were directed to swing abruptly to the southeast to avoid a U-boat that was operating south of Reykjavik.

The ships reached the Momp on the 22nd, but found no British escort. The *Tarbell*, low on fuel, was sent north with two Iceland-bound vessels, while the other escorts rolled on rising seas, awaiting the tardy Redcoats. That night a massive gale struck the ships. Force 10 winds soughed across white-fringed, black waves, and the convoy

was forced to heave to. Pitching and rolling, the vessels clung together and managed to avoid colliding with each other, always a
danger when hove-to.

On the 24th, the *Overton* was detached because she was low on
fuel. In the afternoon, the British escorts, led by HMS *Chelsea*,
arrived to take command of HX 170, which miraculously was still
intact. All the merchant ships reached port safely, but one of the
escorts was slain on the way to Iceland.

After leaving HX 170, the *Alexander Hamilton* was unexpectedly
assigned to tow the store ship USS *Yukon*, which had broken down
in the storm while en route from Iceland to join ON 57; the new
destroyer *Gwin* was sent down from Hvalfjördhur to screen the towing
operation. Despite squally weather and stormy seas, the cutter pulled
the lamed auxiliary through the pounding ocean, and by midday on
the 29th, the ships were only ten miles off Reykjavik. Then the
British tug *Frisky* arrived to take over the tow. By 1315, the ships
were only eight miles off Skaggi Light: the *Frisky* was towing the
Yukon, the *Gwin* was ahead and to starboard, and the *Alexander
Hamilton* was about 4,000 yards off the store ship's port bow; the
cutter was running up to 15 knots after parting the tow.

Meanwhile, the *U-132*, on patrol southwest of Reykjavik, had
been attracted by the accumulation of vessels off Skaggi Point. She
made a submerged approach from starboard and fired a spread of
four torpedoes at the clustered ships; the *Yukon*, the largest ship,
was her main target. But Kapitänleutnant Vogelsang must not have
realized that the *Yukon* was under tow, for, in plotting his torpedo
run, he credited her with greater headway than she was making.

The *Gwin*, used to serving with heavy warships in fast task forces,
had not had the opportunity to gain much aptitude in antisubmarine
warfare, and did not pick up the approach of the *U-132*. One of the
German torpedoes passed 250 yards astern of the *Yukon*, and two
others passed harmlessly between the store ship and the tug; but one
"fish" missed the *Yukon* and hit the cutter. Suddenly, the starboard
side of the *Alexander Hamilton* exploded in a billow of gray-black
smoke and streaks of jagged orange flame as the torpedo penetrated
her plates near the bulkhead between the fireroom and the engine
room. Seven of the "black gang" were killed immediately, and the
blast burst the deck of the compartment above, dropping sailors
down into a steam-clouded cauldron of hissing, boiling water.

On board the mangled cutter, there was no panic despite the green-
ness of the crew. Leaders and officers steadied the jittery and or-

ganized the work of escape and rescue. Men calmly made their way topside through wreckage and darkness; sailors, some burned, struggled to open jammed steel doors in order to free themselves. Topside, the Coast Guardsmen discovered that the explosion had destroyed three of their seven lifeboats, so some of the able-bodied had to remain with the sinking cutter for an hour; luckily, the bulkheads below held against the icy flood, and there was ample time to remove all of the crew. In the water, high, churning waves capsized some of the lifeboats; struggling sailors clung to their sides. Assisted by an Icelandic fishing trawler, the *Gwin* rescued many of the Coast Guardsmen. Of the unlucky cutter's 213 men, only 26 died.

The loss of a ship so close to shore mortified the command at the Naval Operating Base, Iceland, and ten American and four British destroyers were ordered down from Hvalfjördhur to hunt the *U-132*. Late that night, the *Sterett* and *Stack* detected a firm sonar contact 21 miles off Skaggi Light, and worked over the area for four hours, the muted thumping of their depth charges lingering in the cold, silent night, but they failed to kill the *U-132* and avenge the loss of the *Alexander Hamilton*.

The *Frisky* finally towed the fortunate *Yukon* into port to be repaired by the *Vulcan* in time to sail in a February convoy. The tug then went out again to try to retrieve the flooded, battered *Alexander Hamilton*, but the towline parted in rising seas, and darkness soon forced abandonment of the salvage operation. That night, high winds and a swift current drove the wallowing cutter northwest. At last, on the afternoon of the 30th, the *Frisky*, screened by two destroyers, made a towline fast and began to drag the grievously damaged cutter toward Reykjavik. Working with an inert ship was hard, and progress was excruciatingly slow; by late afternoon, the vessels were still twenty miles off Skaggi Light. Then, abruptly, the cutter slumped in a 50-degree list to starboard. The tow parted and, in five minutes, the *Alexander Hamilton* capsized and sank. Less lucky than her sister ships, the *Alexander Hamilton* did not survive her maiden mission on the Iceland run.[15]

On the night of 19/20 January 1942, the *Woolsey*, *Bainbridge*, *Truxtun*, *Broome*, and *Dickerson* left Iceland in company with the *Yukon*, the *Kaweah*, and three U.S.-flag merchantmen, including the reluctant *Omaha*, bound for a Momp at 56°-40' north, 22° west; meeting points were being arranged farther south because of winter weather and U-boats patrolling off Reykjavik. Meanwhile, the thirty-four merchant ships of ON 57 were scattered by a storm shortly after leaving Liverpool, and the convoy had to be re-formed off the coast of Scotland; the delay suggested a long wait at the Momp for the American destroyers and a protracted passage, so the Canadian corvette *Kenogami* and the Free French corvette *Aconit* were sent to join the Americans.

As force 8 winds rolled rough seas over the bows of the plunging ships and squalls of hail and snow blurred the gray sky and ocean, the woes of the destroyers increased. One of the merchant ships, the *Oneida*, developed a dangerous list when her ballast shifted in the storm, and she was escorted back to Reykjavik by the *Aconit*. The *Kenogami*, with a case of acute appendicitis on board, was forced to depart hurriedly. And then the *Yukon* suffered her engine breakdown. At last, on the 24th, seventeen rolling merchant vessels of ON 57 appeared, dark forms against leaden sea and sky. As the escorts and ships from Iceland formed up with the convoy, the vessels of HX 170 arrived, too. Fortunately, the milling ships managed to avoid any collisions, and Captain M.Y. Cohen in *Woolsey* soon led his diminished brood on to westward.

That night, an intense gale struck; force 10 winds, with gusts up to force 12, lashed furiously at the heaving, billowing sea and pitching, rolling ships. The convoy became scattered. Although the four-stackers had not steamed very far from the Momp, they were already running low on fuel. The *Dickerson*, damaged topside by the wild storm and short of fuel, was detached to St. John's. The thirsty *Bainbridge* tried to refuel from the *Kaweah*, but the churning seas parted the fuel lines. Doggedly, the destroyers plowed into the steep waves. By dark on the 29th, the *Woolsey* and *Bainbridge* had but four merchant ships with them; and thirty-two miles away, the *Truxtun* and *Broome* guarded another hardy quartet.

On the 30th, the *Bainbridge* and even the modern *Woolsey* tried to fuel from the rolling tanker, but the lines parted each time, torn loose by the high, white-laced waves. The next day, the *Woolsey* tried again, but the lines could not be maintained. Desperate for oil, the *Bainbridge* kept trying. Her sailors would make fast the towlines, then secure the fuel lines and hoses; the destroyer would suck in several thousand gallons of black oil before the towline was ripped away, and then the fuel lines would have to be cast off. Three times the *Bainbridge* rigged for fueling, and three times the lines parted, but in the brief intervals of pumping, the four-stacker imbibed sufficient fuel to keep her going with the remnant of the convoy.

Finally, the gale abated, the destroyers were able to refuel from the handy *Kaweah*, a marked improvement in escort technique which added precious range to the destroyers. The escorts rounded up a few more stragglers, and the ships steamed west under gray skies, passing well south of Newfoundland, the destroyers detaching vessels according to their destination; the last merchantmen were dispersed on 7 February. The weary destroyers, nearly three weeks at sea with ON 57, took the *Kaweah* and the ammunition ship USS *Nitro* on to Casco Bay and thence to an earned rest in Boston.[16]

On the 22nd, another diminished escort consisting of the *Gleaves*, *Dallas*, *Upshur*, and *Ingham* led the old destroyer tender *Melville*, which had served four-stackers at Londonderry in World War I and was now sailing east to take up her old job in a new war, to the rendezvous with the forty-three merchant vessels of HX 171 southeast of Cape Race. Escort groups were getting smaller, their numbers lessened by winter storm damage. The destroyers and cutter, joined by the *Cole* for the coastal passage, took the convoy northeast. The white-foamed seas ran swift and high, but the skies were mostly clear, and PBYs watched over the ships for twelve hours on the first two days out. The convoy turned east at 44° west and took a southerly track to the Momp. On the 27th, a sailor in the *Dallas* received twenty-five days' extra duty for throwing garbage over the side; ships' trash could help alert U-boat skippers to determine traffic patterns.

The American escorts reached the Momp, between 53° north and 54° north, less but one straggler, and she fell in with SC 65. Because the British escorts were delayed, the Americans were directed to remain with the convoy an extra day. Then, having come so far east, they were permitted to go on to Londonderry with the *Melville*, instead of making the long trip north to Hvalfjördhur. And so the escort of HX 171, an easy voyage, ended on a happy note for the destroyermen.[17]

The forty-four ships of ON 59 were delayed by squalls, stormy seas, and route changes made to avoid concentrations of U-boats.

Escort arrangements for the convoy were complicated. On the 25th, the *Wilkes* and *Madison* left Londonderry to steam for the Momp; the escort force was missing one ship because on the day before sailing, the *Roper* dragged anchor in the River Foyle and was damaged in a collision with a British freighter. Meanwhile, the *Jacob Jones* brought three merchant vessels south from Reykjavik to the Momp. But she soon received news of the delay to the convoy and, not having enough fuel to wait several days at the Momp, she proceeded independently through stormy weather with her three merchantmen, two of which straggled. The destroyer released the remaining vessel off Cape Race.

On the 29th of January, the *Wilkes* and *Madison* met the convoy at about 54°-35′ north, 21°-30′ west; short-legged *Sturtevant* sailed two days later than the new destroyers in order to conserve fuel, joining the escort on 3 February. Many merchant ships had already scattered in the bad weather, so that the convoy numbered only thirty vessels when the American escorts assumed command of it. The passage west was squally, but peaceful. In the *Wilkes*, a sailor sustained a fractured ankle while trying to secure loose gear on the quarterdeck in a storm. The *Wilkes* and *Sturtevant* dispersed Halifax-bound ships on the 5th at about 46° north, 57° west. The *Madison*, with only a day's fuel in her bunkers, and the *Jacob Jones*, down from Argentia, took the U.S.-bound vessels south, dispersing them on the 6th at 41°-30′ north, 52°-53′ west. All the stragglers of ON 59 reached port safely. This was the last crossing for the old *Jacob Jones*. Young, energetic Lieutenant Commander Hugh Black offered his four-stacker for service against the U-boats ravaging shipping off the East Coast. And on the last day of February, off the Delaware Capes, the *U-578* torpedoed the *Jacob Jones* in a night surface attack. The four-stacker broke in half, and Black and most of his men died before they had a chance to fight.[18]

Three merchantmen of HX 172 dropped out early, unable to maintain stated speed, and were reassigned to a Sydney convoy. The remaining fifty-four vessels of the convoy were met southeast of Cape Race on the 28th by the *Buck*, *Swanson*, *DuPont*, *McCormick*, and *Herbert*. The ships started on a northeasterly track in cold, misty weather, and the PBYs were missing the first day out. But the fliers were overhead earning their money on the 29th, and one of the seaplanes signalled a lifeboat nearby. The *Swanson* investigated and picked up thirteen men and one fortunate canine, survivors from the Norwegian cargo ship *Ringstad*, torpedoed five days before. The weary seamen reported two other boats were missing, and said that the submarine had given them the course to nearest land. For needed practice, the *Swanson's* gunners fired eight rounds of 5-inch and several hundred rounds of machine-gun slugs at the bobbing boat, but did it little damage; the old *McCormick's* men showed the gold-plater gunners, with their elaborate fire-control equipment, the right way to shoot by putting several shells into the boat.

The convoy vessels made excessive smoke, but their station-keeping, signalling, and darkening-ship arrangements were fine, and the destroyers had little trouble on their account. On the 1st, the *McCormick* attacked a sonar contact astern with eleven depth charges; the attack was made on the wakes of stragglers which the *Herbert* was rounding up. But it was not a wake that the *DuPont* attacked that night. The four-stacker's radar set picked up a blip at 2,100 yards, then her lookouts sighted briefly the blur of a U-boat low in the water, deck awash; suddenly, the submarine disappeared. The *DuPont* rushed in and dropped a dozen depth charges, but the explosions did not hurt the U-boat. After a fruitless search of only thirty minutes, the destroyer rejoined the convoy.

On the 3rd, the merchant sailors held gun drill and proved that weapons in the hands of the untrained were more dangerous to their users than to the enemy; one man was hit by random machine-gun fire and two were badly hurt when an antiaircraft shell exploded prematurely. Out of such incidents arose the naval armed guard units, trained gun crews assigned to merchant vessels. The destroyers sent a doctor and some medics to the merchantmen. The *Buck* sent the corpsman who had suffered an emotional breakdown in December during the escort of HX 165; he had climbed back onto the wild horse.

All through the night of 3/4 February, the *Swanson's* men were picking up RDF bearings at close range, as if a U-boat were tracking the convoy and sending out frequent position reports. The ships changed course, and the U-boat never found them. The merchant vessels, less one straggler, were turned over to the British on the 4th; all the vessels reached port safely. The destroyers steamed on to Iceland.[19]

With the *Alexander Hamilton* gone, the *Niblack, Tarbell,* and *Overton* left Valley Forge on the 30th of January, weak in numbers, but fortunate that their convoy was small. They met the twenty-one ships of ON 61 on the afternoon of the 1st at about 57°-55' north, 24°-30' west, took over from the British escort group led by HMS *Keppel,* then headed on to westward. The next day, the destroyers picked up strong RDF bearings, and the *Niblack* and *Overton,* attempting to compensate in more aggressive tactics for lack of numbers, made a high-speed search of the vicinity, but found nothing. On the morning of the 3rd, the *Niblack* investigated another RDF bearing, but found nothing. The U-boats seemed near; but they did not find the convoy.

At first, the weather was hazy, and the choppy green sea was serried by whitecaps; then the mist thickened, high winds blew up, and rain and snow dripped out of dusky skies onto rising seas. Despite the stormy weather, the convoy vessels maintained station well; but too many of the masters tried to keep at least a stern light on at night in the low visibility, and the destroyers were kept busy running down light violations—sometimes it took a half hour of shouted argument through megaphones, including threats of shooting, to force masters to turn out lights. However, bad weather helped to hide the ships from prowling U-boats.

On the evening of the 8th, the *Overton* attacked a sonar contact that turned out to be a drifting buoy. Then the ships learned of the sinking of the Free French corvette *Alysse* by the *U-644* nearby. But they encountered no U-boats, and the vessels of ON 61 were peacefully dispersed in two sections far south of Newfoundland on the 9th and 10th. After dispersal, the *Niblack* and *Tarbell* hunted through eddying fog for two hours, searching out a sonar contact, but did not find the U-boat.[20]

HX 173 was troubled at the outset. One of the ships could not find the convoy in the fog off Halifax and returned to port. Early on the morning of 2 February, a U-boat torpedoed the 8,096-ton Dutch tanker *Corilla;* the ship did not catch fire and was able to limp back to port. The Canadian escorts could not find the U-boat. There were thirty-one vessels in the convoy when the *Nicholson, Edison, Bernadou,* and *Lea* joined it south of Argentia on the 3rd. A thin, cold sleet drizzled out of an overcast sky, and thick coils of fog twisted over the green water; soon big, soggy flakes of snow began to fall. Early on the morning of the 4th, in low visibility, a small Russian tanker was demolished in a collision with a freighter; the *Lea* rescued the thirty-nine men and two women of the Russian crew, but on the water there was a widespread stain of black oil from the wrecked tanker, a lure for alert U-boats. The next day, the *Bernadou* investigated a red distress flare that burst in the gray sky ahead, and picked up ten survivors from a Belgian freighter; the seamen were haggard and exhausted after two weeks in an open boat.

"Bernie" attacked a dubious sonar contact on the 6th; the *Nicholson* depth-charged a stronger one on the 7th. The seas were not violent, but visibility was still poor, and the destroyers had to round up stragglers each morning. The five British escorts, led by HMS *Watchman*, joined on the night of the 9th, assuming command the following morning; there was only one straggler.

The weather grew stormier as the U.S. destroyers steamed north for Iceland with two naval auxiliaries and two merchant vessels. In the storm, the *Lea* nearly collided with the store ship USS *Mizar*, and the *Nicholson* became separated from the other ships, but they were all safely moored in Valley Forge by Lincoln's Birthday.[21]

On the night of 4/5 February, the *Gleaves*, *Dallas*, *Upshur*, *Roper*, recovered from her recent collision, and *Ingham* said goodbye to Londonderry and steamed down the grimy River Foyle, heading out to sea to earn their money once again. Throughout the afternoon of the 5th, the warships picked up a persistent submarine contact, as if a U-boat were trying to trail them to their convoy. They attacked the contact seven times, releasing thirty depth charges. They did not hurt the U-boat, but they did keep her down.

The American warships met the thirty merchant vessels of ON 63 at about 55°-15' north, 22° west, on the morning of the 7th. Shortly afterwards, at 1122, as they were steaming southwest, a lookout in the *Upshur* sighted a submarine on the surface only two miles away. The four-stacker swung around, working up to 20 knots, but the German lookouts saw her turning, and the U-boat slid under the sea. The *Upshur* and *Ingham* searched the vicinity for over two hours, dropping fifteen depth charges, but did not pick up a firm contact.

Soon, the U-boat, determined not to lose the convoy before dark, came up again. Back on station only a few moments, the *Upshur* once again sighted her bold adversary on the surface, 8,000 yards distant. She swung around and steamed after the submarine at flank speed, hoping to get within killing range before being discovered; but three minutes later, the U-boat started to submerge. The *Upshur* fired two rounds from her forward gun, the shots splashing in the water well wide of the canted gray conning tower, and the U-boat was once again safely under water. The *Gleaves* came back to assist the *Upshur* in the search, but the U-boat was too good, and neither destroyer picked up a sonar contact, although they hunted for an hour and a half. The next day, the *Upshur* and *Gleaves* attacked sonar contacts near the convoy. They did not kill the U-boat, but they drove it off. And the rest of the passage was quiet. There were no stragglers, and the *Gleaves* dispersed the merchant vessels in safety on the morning of the 13th at 42° north, 55° west. Then the destroyers and the *Ingham* steamed north through a snowstorm toward Argentia.[22]

HX 174 was disrupted by a dense fog off Halifax. One of its thirty-one vessels failed to sail, one returned to port after groping alone in the thick fog outside the harbor, one was damaged in a collision in the fog and went back to port, and seven were straggling, lost in the murky grayness. Thus, the *Plunkett, Badger, Babbitt, Schenck,* and cutter *Campbell* met a small, scattered convoy south of Argentia on the 9th of February.

Squat black shapes in the eddying mist, the ships steamed eastward. The *Schenck* attacked two sonar contacts on the 12th, and on the 15th, the *Badger* stood by a disabled merchant ship while her crew effected repairs. The British were a day late to the Momp, so the *Schenck* and *Babbitt* took two merchantmen on to Iceland, and the other escorts waited with the convoy for the Redcoats. The British warships arrived on the 17th. The fog protected both convoy vessels and stragglers of HX 174, and none was waylaid by U-boats. The American escorts steamed north to the sparse cheer of Valley Forge.[23]

The *Buck, Swanson, DuPont, McCormick,* and *Herbert* met the forty-two vessels of ON 65 far southwest of Reykjavik, at 58° north, on the afternoon of Lincoln's Birthday; the convoy was as important as it was large, for it included twenty-nine tankers. As the ships steamed southwest in drizzly rain and musty fog, several of them

The USS *Gleaves* in the ice-strewn waters of the North Atlantic

strayed in the low visibility. Gray-green seas rose, and ships without cargo or adequate ballast rolled and labored desperately. The storm intensified, lasting the length of the passage.

On the 19th, southeast of Cape Race, with a fierce, icy wind soughing like a distant locomotive and black rollers engulfing the ships in bursts of shiny, white water, a depth charge broke loose from a locker in the *Swanson* and rolled around her deck. Sailors came up from below, and in a brief, dangerous tussle, secured the heavy cylinder; one torpedoman was badly injured by the "ash can." The storm scattered most of the merchant vessels and hurt the escorts. Old *McCormick* was a mess. The wind snapped away her mast, her radio, radar, her Talk-Between-Ships (TBS) antennae were destroyed, her searchlight and searchlight platform were wrecked, and the wiring to most of her battle circuits was put out. The four-stacker reeled alone and lost in the storm, but she limped home to Argentia. The remnant of the convoy was dispersed far southwest of Argentia, at about 43°-50′ north, 47°-45′ west; one of the merchant vessels, the SS *Egda* was torpedoed and seriously damaged off Halifax, but the rest of them made it to port safely. The weary, weather-damaged U.S. destroyers headed gratefully for the barn.[24]

HX 175 numbered twenty-seven ships when the *Mayo, Decatur, Leary,* and *Simpson* met it southwest of Argentia on the 15th. The weather soon grew stormy and, on the 17th, the *Simpson* lost a man overboard; the sailor, held up in the water by his life jacket, was soon sighted by his shipmates and rescued. One of the *Mayo's* men became so seasick that he had to be admitted to sick bay, a rare occurrence in the destroyers, and her skipper had to be treated for bruises.

On the morning of the 23rd, the destroyers and convoy were met at the Momp, 56°-05′ north, 22°-30′ west, by an understrength escort of three British corvettes; the rest of the British force had gone to assist SC 67, which had lost a tanker torpedoed and a corvette, HMCS *Spikenard,* sunk with all hands save eight men. Thus, it was requested that the American ships remain with HX 175 up to their "prudent limit of endurance." Sol Phillips decided to send the *Decatur* and *Leary* on to Iceland with two Icelandic freighters and retain the *Mayo* and *Simpson* with the corvettes and merchantmen. So the passage eastward continued.

On the 24th, two of the *Mayo's* men became involved in a bitter fight, product of the pervasive tension of escort duty, and the lack of privacy and enforced personal contacts in small ships on prolonged runs with too little time in port. One of the men was slashed in the knee with a knife. Later, a lookout on the *Mayo* sighted what appeared to be the dark shape of a conning tower against the sea and sky, about ten miles distant; the destroyer searched the vicinity but found nothing. The merchant crews of HX 175 were disciplined and able seafarers, and there was only one straggler from the convoy, all of whose ships reached port safely; they helped to make a long passage an easy one for their escorts. The *Decatur* and *Leary* reached Iceland on the 25th; the luckier *Mayo* and *Simpson* made it to Londonderry the same day.[25]

Thus far, the ocean more than the U-boats had been the most formidable foe of the winter war. The fierce storms pounded and damaged the ships, draining them of precious fuel; drenched and exhausted the crews, draining them of the energy and alertness vital to survival; protracted the voyages; strung out the convoys; enhanced and yet also mitigated the menace of the U-boats, which the destroyermen did not have the technology and experience to kill. But no merchant ship had been lost to U-boats while in the company of American destroyers since the black night in mid-October when the *Kearny* had been torpedoed. Hoping to continue the trend of good luck, the *Nicholson*, *Edison*, *Bernadou*, and *Lea* left Iceland on 16 February, bound for the rendezvous with ON 67 and, unknowingly, for the most violent of the Support Force's battles.

30.

"Skipper, She Was Close Enough to Throw Spuds At!"

EN ROUTE TO MEET THE CONVOY the weather was stormy and, on the 18th of February 1942, one of the *Edison*'s men had his leg broken when he was struck down by a wave while on watch. The destroyers found ON 67 on the 19th, a day late due to the storm; the convoy consisted of about 40 motley vessels arrayed in eight straggly columns. The escorts, under the command of Commander Albert C. Murdaugh in the *Edison*, took station, the *Edison* 4,000 yards off the starboard bow of the convoy, the *Nicholson* a like distance off the port bow; the *Lea* was 4,000 yards off the starboard quarter, abreast the last vessel in the last column by day, moving up off the center of the column by night; the *Bernadou* patrolled in the same way on the port flank. Canadian corvette *Algoma*, working her way back to St. John's, after having gone all the way to Londonderry with an eastbound convoy, was assigned the stern position.

An innovation in the convoy was the presence of SS *Toward*, a rescue ship fitted out with high-frequency direction-finder equipment, with people and spaces to care properly for several hundred survivors, and with a lot of special rescue gear, including a large dip net for scooping burned or exhausted men out of the water as quickly and painlessly as possible.

Although several of the escorts were equipped with radar, poor design, frequent mechanical breakdown, and inexperienced personnel hampered the efficiency of the equipment; only the *Nicholson*'s set functioned with any consistency during the passage.

399

The ships steamed southwest, then south-southwest, at about 8½ knots, the destroyers patrolling station at 12½ knots. There was fog early in the voyage, but it dissipated, and visibility became good. The days were cold and gray, and the ships rocked across rippled green swells; the merchantmen puffed curves of black smoke against the blue-gray sky.

At noon on the 21st, the *Edison* attacked a sonar contact off the bow with a pattern of five depth charges, blowing tall peaks of white water skyward, but the contact was false, probably fish. There were a half-dozen U-boats patrolling within striking range of ON 67, and two were very close. Yet the Germans had not sighted the convoy. At about 1730, a U-boat far astern and to starboard sent out a routine check-in message to Admiral Doenitz's headquarters. The *Toward* picked up the transmission on her HF/DF equipment, and the *Lea* was sent out to investigate. But the *Lea*'s radar set was not working, and the four-stacker searched desultorily for about an hour without sighting the U-boat and then returned to her station. Soon darkness set in, and the *Lea* and *Bernadou* moved up to their night stations, leaving the last ships in the two outermost columns vulnerable. And it was here, at one of the "windy corners," that the first men of ON 67 died.

The ships were at about 49° north, 38° west, and George Washington's Birthday was only a minute old when lookouts on the conning tower of the *U-155* sighted ships astern and to starboard in the moonlit area between the blackness of sea and sky. The Germans made out "about seven steamers" and three "old destroyers." Kapitänleutnant Adolph Piening, a capable and determined officer, decided to attack the vessels at the rear of the port column, where the escort was weak. The *U-155* worked stealthily toward the placid ships, taking three hours to approach.

At about 0215, the *Bernadou* picked up a brief, mushy sonar contact. The four-stacker swung to port to track it, but after three minutes the contact faded. It was probably on the wakes of the merchant ships ahead, but had it been sharper and clearer, "Bernie" would have spent more time tracking it and might have encountered the *U-155*.

As the submarine approached, Piening selected his targets, intending to fire as the *U-155* closed. At three minutes past 0300, Piening ordered a shot at a 7,000-ton tanker, but his torpedomen could not fire in time. The *U-155* continued to close in and, at a range of 1,000 meters, a torpedo hissed out of her #1 tube, aimed at a tanker. Closing to 600 meters, she fired another "fish" at a small tanker next in line. Then the *U-155* turned sharply away.

The first German torpedo exploded against the side of the 7,984-ton British tanker *Adellan*, lifting the ship in the water; a high bolt of bright orange flame streaked at the night sky, and the blazing tanker began to settle. Piening's second torpedo struck the 1,800-ton Norwegian freighter *Sama* near her engine spaces. The ship jolted up at the impact of the explosion, then began to settle; almost immediately, she was under water astern as far as her mainmast. Then there followed a loud explosion inside the ship as her boiler exploded. The *Sama* was finished.

Some of the merchant vessels were shooting red and yellow flares to signify an attack. The *Nicholson*, vainly trying to illuminate the invisible foe, fired clusters of star shells, casting a yellow-white shine on the dark sea forward. Astern, the black water glowed red-orange with the reflection of the burning tanker. The *U-155* remained coolly on the surface, about 300 meters from the sinking *Sama*.

Suddenly, the *Bernadou's* dark bulk loomed in the night; the destroyer was coming back at high speed toward the windy corner. She was headed straight at the *U-155*, and Piening shouted for a crash dive. The watchstanders scrambled down the conning-tower hatch, and the U-boat's bow churned foamy water as it angled for the safety of the dark, cold depths.

But the *Bernadou* was blind. The destroyermen never saw the *U-155's* small, gray silhouette against the black backdrop of the night sea and sky. And the crisp, noisy wakes of the merchant vessels made it impossible to pick up a sonar contact when the submarine submerged. "Bernie" swept on astern in angry, futile search. And a few minutes later, below, Piening and his men heard the muted rumble of exploding depth charges come from far away.

While the *Bernadou* hunted vainly, the *Nicholson* picked up 19 survivors from the *Sama*, and *Toward* found one; *Algoma* rescued 11 lucky men off the unlucky tanker. The work of rescue was not easy. It was difficult to see men in the black water and hard to haul them aboard; thus, *Nicholson's* men suggested that life jackets should be fitted with lights and lines to facilitate rescue.

Meanwhile, the convoy vessels steamed slowly on. And at 0355, the *U-155* surfaced to resume the chase. The sea was dark and empty and seemed suddenly very still. Piening ran wide around the track of the convoy, hoping to sweep ahead during daylight and be in position for another night surface attack. He stalked the convoy for over 6½ hours. Once, at 1042, the *Edison*, sweeping out from her station, headed toward the U-boat. The German lookouts were slow to pick up the gray destroyer's sudden approach against the gray-blue backdrop of sky and sea, and again Piening had to hurriedly order an emergency dive. The *U-155* slid beneath the choppy swells. But the *Edison*'s men never saw the submarine whose shadowing they had disrupted. *U-155* remained submerged for a time, then surfaced to renew the hunt. But Piening was no longer alone.

Kapitänleutnant Ulrich Borcherdt's *U-587* and Kapitänleutnant Wilhelm Zahn's *U-69* had also discovered and were tracking the convoy. Soon tough, daring Kapitänleutnant Krech brought his *U-558* to the scene, exchanging messages with Piening. En route were the *U-158* of capable Kapitänleutnant Erwin Rostin and the *U-162* of green, cautious Kapitänleutnant Jürgen Wattenberg. It was a mixed pack of wolves that was gathering to tear at ON 67. Krech was excellent, and Piening and Rostin were good; but Borcherdt was unlucky, Zahn too methodical, and Wattenberg too inexperienced. The attrition of war had cost the German Navy some of its best skippers, and some of the rest lacked the aggressive, kinetic, opportunistic temperament necessary to success in the unstable, rapidly shifting tactical circumstances of submarine warfare. Neither Borcherdt, nor Zahn, nor Wattenberg would be able to carry out a successful approach and attack on the convoy. Not all the wolves were valiant.

The afternoon of the 22nd grew dim, and rain squalls screened the convoy from the gathering U-boats by day and through the night. But the skies cleared on the 23rd, and at 1210, the *Edison* worked over a sonar contact off the starboard column with a pattern of five depth charges; the blasts brought no debris to the surface. The *Edison* patrolled the area, but could not regain contact amid the din and water turbulence created by the passing merchant ships. Grimly, the *Edison* searched for an hour and three-quarters, until the thin masts of the convoy vessels dropped below the black line of the horizon, but she could not find the U-boat. Her attack may have been made on a wake, or perhaps it drove off the *U-587* or the *U-69*.

Commander Murdaugh was certain the U-boats were near, organizing for a wolfpack attack after dark. So, in the afternoon, he sent the *Bernadou* and *Lea* to sweep out to the limit of visibility—15 miles abeam and 10 astern—to try to drive the U-boats under so they would not be able to pick up the convoy's night course change; he was trying to buy some time for ON 67.

The *Lea*, her radar working, searched to starboard and astern, but found nothing. The *Bernadou* was steaming a dozen miles out from the port side of the convoy when, at 1617, she picked up a sonar contact which quickly faded. Lieutenant Commander Robert E. Braddy, distrusting the contact, attacked with only two depth charges. But a few minutes later, "Bernie" regained contact, and Braddy drove her in hard, attacking with eight depth charges. Fountains of white water hissed upward from the blasts and, when the sea calmed, there were several filmy patches of oil on the surface. Braddy thought his attack might have damaged the U-boat, but it had not; he might have attacked *U-587*, *U-69*, or a large fish. The *Bernadou* discovered nothing of menace on the rest of her sweep and soon rejoined the convoy. But she might have kept a U-boat at bay.

As dark drifted in on the ships, the convoy executed a course change to the southwest, at about a 45-degree angle to its previous south-southwest heading; the vessels were at about 44° north, 42° west, far southeast of Cape Race. Murdaugh hoped that the U-boats would lose ON 67 in the darkness and continue tracking the convoy on its old heading. The stratagem had worked many times in the past, but this time it did not; for there were too many U-boats after ON 67. It was quiet on the escorts as the sailors watched the dark night sea and waited for battle.

Kapitänleutnant Krech was first to find ON 67. At 2120, the lookouts on the *U-558* sighted the convoy ahead. Krech's approach took two hours. Three times the submarine attempted to close to effective attack range, but each time the *Bernadou*, sweeping astern on a leg of her patrol, appeared and forced the submarine to turn away. The *Bernadou*'s men never saw the U-boat whose approach they were disrupting.

Then a sudden thunder squall developed, and Krech's men lost sight of ON 67; but when the brief storm ended, visibility was better than it had been all night, and the lookouts saw white lights in the distance, at about 44°-30' north, 42°-30' west. Two merchant ships, fearful of collision, had shown lights in a storm once too often. The *U-558* closed the port side of the convoy to 1,000 meters, keeping well astern of the *Bernadou*. At 0045, the U-boat fired two torpedoes at the 5,578-ton Norwegian tanker *Inverarder*. An explosion ensued, and a geyser of water rose up from the side of the vessel, which flashed a red distress light from her mast. The ship went down slowly by the bow, and her forty-two men had ample time to launch her boats and row to safety; the *Toward*, screened by the *Bernadou*, picked up the survivors. *U-558* retired into the darkness without being seen by any of the escorts. *Inverarder*'s stern angled up out of the black water, rudder and propeller in the air, as she sank.

Krech's boat dropped astern and then crossed over to the other side of the convoy, reloading her #1 and #2 tubes and sending out another contact report. The *U-158* arrived in the area, but could not see any ships; so Kapitänleutnant Rostin asked Krech to send out a beacon signal to guide him to the convoy. Meanwhile, Kapitän-leutnant Wattenberg's *U-162* had made contact with ON 67. But Wattenberg, with the caution of inexperience, was striving for a per-fect textbook approach, and lacked the confidence to press a night surface attack in moonlight; and so he failed to achieve anything.

But by 0230, the persistent Krech was ready to strike anew. His *U-558* approached the convoy, about 2,500 meters off the starboard column, astern of the patrolling *Edison*; Krech ordered a spread of four torpedoes as his boat closed. Suddenly, a blue light flashed from the destroyer, only 600 meters away, and the *Edison* commenced to swing around in a sweep of her sector. Krech, fearing that he had been sighted and reluctant to break off his attack approach, ordered one of the stern tubes fired at the pesky destroyer. But the set-up was hasty, the target angle difficult, and the destroyer in the process of turning; the torpedo missed. *U-558* was compelled to retreat out into the darkness. But the *Edison*'s men never saw the U-boat whose strike they had deterred; and they never knew that they had been attacked.

\ Krech soon brought his boat back into another attack approach, lining up a tanker and a freighter for his four forward tubes; and, at about 0255, the *U-558* began firing her "fish." Two torpedoes struck the 9,432-ton Norwegian tanker *Eidanger*, blowing up a high cascade of water from the side of the ship; the tanker was mortally hurt. But Krech fired the second brace of torpedoes while swinging his boat away, and both missed.

Upon hearing explosions, the merchant ships began to fire red flares. The *Edison*, *Nicholson*, and *Bernadou* shot star shells into the black sky, illuminating the fringes of the dark sea with a pale film of artificial light. In anger and frustration, the *Edison* and *Lea* ranged down the starboard side of the convoy, seeking the invisible U-boat, which had fled astern.

Krech and his watchstanders saw the two destroyers hunting fruitlessly beneath clouds tinted yellow. After about 5 minutes, the light faded, and the blind destroyers zig-zagged back to their stations. In the *U-558*, the Germans strained to hoist spare torpedoes through narrow, cluttered passageways and manhandle them into the forward tubes. Krech urged his men to hurry; he hoped to strike again before dawn.

Meanwhile, guided by Krech's beacon, the *U-158* reached the vicinity; but her lookouts still saw no ships on the dark night sea. Rostin decided to submerge and use his listening gear; and soon the U-boat picked up the sound of ships. She surfaced, and her bridge watch soon saw the flares and star shells that followed Krech's attack. By 0425, the men on the *U-158* discerned the shadows of three vessels ahead; one was a large tanker, another a corvette, and the third perhaps a small freighter. Rostin realized he had come upon some stragglers and decided to sink the tanker before seeking the rest of the convoy.

Rostin brought his boat in from starboard and fired two torpedoes from his forward tubes at about 600 meters. At least one "fish" hit the 8,032-ton British tanker *Empire Celt* forward; and "several bull's eyes" glowed "like lightning" along the side of the vessel, internal fires showing through ports. The tanker, flashing a red distress light, slumped down by the bow. Rostin debated a second attack, but decided that another approach would take too long and "be a waste of time"; he gave orders to continue the pursuit of ON 67. "I want to reach the convoy before daybreak," he told his men. "It can't be far away." He was right.

At 0535, Rostin's lookouts observed dark smudges of smoke against the graying sky. The *U-158* approached from astern along the port side of the convoy. Suddenly, Rostin's men were surprised by the rumble of explosions, and the watchstanders saw two tall spouts of water erupt on the far side of ON 67. Kapitänleutnant Krech, a tartar this night, had brought the *U-558* back into the fight.

Krech's men had rediscovered the convoy astern and to port, five miles away, at 0514. Only three of the forward tubes had been reloaded but, with dawn approaching, Krech could wait no longer. The *U-558* closed the starboard side of the convoy and at 0550 fired three torpedoes at two 5,000-ton freighters and a large tanker.

The first torpedo struck the 8,009-ton British tanker *Anadara*. The tanker shuddered and limped on, trailing smoke, but she was ready to die. Krech's second torpedo exploded in the side of the 9,550-ton

British tanker *Finnanger*, a little abaft her bridge. A "column of fire" streaked from the doomed ship. The third torpedo hit the 4,365-ton British freighter *White Crest* amidships, and the smoking vessel soon went down. Then the *U-558* swung away, retreating to load her #4 tube, but keeping the convoy in sight. Neither the *Edison* nor the *Lea* sighted the U-boat.

The *Bernadou*, on the opposite side of the convoy, fired 11 rounds of star shell, but she saw nothing in the sallow light. But the *U-158* was there. Rostin, however, was hesitating in his target selection; in looking for the biggest game, he was wasting precious time, for it was fast growing light. Closing at high speed, the *U-158* made an attack approach on a 4,000-ton tanker, but then Rostin shifted targets. "It gets brighter and brighter," her quartermaster nervously noted in the U-boat's deck log. At 0635, fifteen minutes before full dawn, the *U-158* fired two torpedoes at a large tanker from medium range. One shot hit the 8,146-ton British tanker *Diloma*, but not in a vital spot; shaken and smoky, the hurt vessel plodded on. Rostin then attempted to run through the merchant ships to the opposite side of the convoy to take advantage of a better attack backdrop of low clouds, but the *U-158* was seen and forced to crash dive. As the merchantmen passed overhead, Rostin took his boat astern, running deep. The merchant ships made a din in the water, complicating the sonar search of the escorts. Soon Rostin's men heard the distant rumble of harmless depth charges.

While Rostin escaped, the *Algoma*, rushing back to look after the *Diloma*, unwittingly passed near the *U-558* and forced Krech's boat to crash dive. So, both active U-boats were down, where they could do little harm.

The *U-158* soon surfaced to continue her pursuit of the convoy. However, as Rostin's boat approached, the *Bernadou* ranged out in a sweep of her sector and , although the destroyermen did not see the submarine, they drove her under again.

The *U-558* also surfaced, but short of torpedoes and with daylight arrived, Krech did not press on with his usual fury. Soon the *U-558* came upon the abandoned, drifting *Eidanger*, holed amidships and well down by the bow. Krech fired a torpedo from a stern tube at the maimed vessel. It struck forward, the explosion breaking the tanker apart amidships, and the foreship drifted away. Krech then decided to give his gunners some needed shooting practice. The Germans fired 48 rounds of high-explosive shells at the aftersection of the derelict, scoring one hit at the waterline. Finally, 15 rounds of incendiary shells set ablaze the hulk of the tanker, twice killed by the U-boats.

Meanwhile, up ahead, the *U-158* surfaced again, shaking green and white water off her bridge and deck like an uncomfortably wet hound, and relocated the convoy. But the tenacious *Bernadou*, making another sweep of her sector, approached and unknowingly drove Rostin's boat out beyond visual range.

In the *Edison*, Commander Murdaugh was a worried man, singing a worried song. He requested permission either to execute a radical shift of course or to disperse the convoy, but the still peacetime-oriented naval communications system was congested as usual and it took nearly seven hours for an affirmative response to arrive. In the meantime, he decided that the only safety lay in more aggressive tactics.

The convoy and its escorts were vulnerable because of the invisibility of the enemy. At night it was virtually impossible to detect visually the small, gray U-boats, used on the surface like oceangoing motor torpedo boats, even at close range. The U-boats, able to see their bulkier foes first, enjoyed the combat initiative. They were free to strike first or evade at will, while the harried escorts were forced to react defensively. The good shepherds of the Atlantic were gallant but, in the absence of reliable radar, they were blind and thus helpless.

Murdaugh resolved to leave the merchant ships with scant protection and use his destroyers offensively, sending them far out from the convoy to drive off the pursuing U-boats, disrupting the enemy's searches and the momentum of his attacks. Such tactics were contrary to established practice, which stressed close protection of the convoy, but he was convinced that the destroyers had to take the initiative away from the U-boats if the rest of the merchantmen were to survive another night.

In the afternoon, the *Toward* picked up U-boat transmissions from ahead and to port; so the *Nicholson* was sent out to investigate. At 1323, the destroyer was steaming 15 miles out from the convoy when her men sighted a U-boat on the surface, about five miles distant. The *Nicholson* headed after the submarine, fearing to open fire lest she forfeit surprise. Then at 1339, the destroyermen spotted another U-boat on the surface off to port. The U-boats were probably Rostin's *U-158* and either Borcherdt's or Piening's boat. Lieutenant Commander John Keating kept the *Nicholson* after his first target, but before he could close to good firing range, the German lookouts sighted the approaching bulk of the destroyer against the horizon, and both submarines "pulled the plug" and went down.

Methodically pinging and listening, the *Nicholson* searched the area. At about 1430, she passed almost directly over the *U-158*, and Rostin's men waited grimly for the crash of depth charges. But the *Nicholson*'s sonar man did not pick up the U-boat, and the destroyer passed on. Then Keating ordered his ship slowed to steerageway. The quiet destroyer arched slowly on the swells, listening for the enemy below. It was a dangerous ploy with two U-boats nearby, but Keating was willing to take the risk. The U-boats had killed too much.

At 1550, with all quiet above, Rostin carelessly took the *U-158* up. The submarine broached the surface, and her watchstanders scrambled up onto the wet bridge. The lookouts were stunned to sight the *Nicholson*, 1,500 meters away, waiting, a patient cat crouched at a mousehole. The Germans scurried down the conning-tower hatch as her general quarters claxon rasped and Rostin shouted for a crash dive. But the *Nicholson*'s men had not seen the *U-158*.

The destroyermen had gambled by showing their ship in dangerous waters, and won; because they were blind, they never knew of their triumph. But the *Nicholson* persisted, getting under way again, searching and pinging, then stopping to listen again. Keating continued the hunt until 1744, then broke it off to return to the convoy. The *Nicholson*'s pluck deserved a better end than another empty bag, but because her skills did not match her courage, her luck was bad.

Meanwhile, at about 1515, the *Toward* had picked up a U-boat transmission astern and to starboard, and Murdaugh sent the *Lea* out to hunt. At 1707, 20 miles off the starboard flank of ON 67, the *Lea*'s men saw a U-boat on the surface at long range. The destroyer chased the submarine for half an hour before the Germans spotted her and took their boat under. The *Lea* prowled the area, picked up a sonar contact, and, at 1746, attacked with eight depth charges; but the blasts of white water carried no debris to the surface. Although the *Lea* twice regained sonar contact, each time the contact quickly faded. Patiently, she continued searching.

The U-boat skipper, probably Krech, decided to make good his escape on the surface, but he was impatient and, thus, careless. At 1813, the submarine broached only 800 yards off the starboard quarter of the American destroyer. The *Lea* had nearly a minute in

A U.S. destroyer in the North Atlantic

which to slay the U-boat but, surprised, she took too long to swing her stern gun to bear, and the submarine disappeared once more in a long, white crease of bubbly sea. The *Lea* charged in and attacked with a pattern of nine depth charges, blasting high pillars of shiny water out of the darkling sea. The destroyer resumed the search, regained sonar contact, and at 1847 attacked with five more depth charges. The destroyermen believed that they had slain, or at least badly hurt, the submarine. At 1900, the *Lea* departed to rejoin the convoy; but her attacks had hardly shaken up the U-boat.

Yet the hard work of the *Nicholson* and the *Lea* was not without purpose. If they lacked the eyes and expertise to kill the wolves, they were able to keep them at bay. And soon it was the *Edison*'s turn.

After her traumatic encounter with the *Nicholson*, the *U-158* was running submerged. All was quiet on the surface and, at about 1817, Rostin decided to take his boat up again to chase the convoy at high speed; but again he was careless. The *U-158* broached, and her lookouts cracked the hatch and went to their watch stations. Suddenly, they saw a destroyer, stopped and listening, less than 2,000 meters away. Rostin ordered a crash dive. The destroyer was the *Edison*, stalking a sonar contact; but her men failed to see *U-158*.

Rostin, thinking the same persistent destroyer was still after his boat, decided to carry out a submerged attack. But at periscope depth, the U-boat was sluggish and stern-heavy, possibly because of the torpedoes remaining aft, and could not be held in trim long enough to line up a good shot. Thus, unseeing *Edison* was preserved from unknown danger for the second time in the fight around ON 67.

At about 1900, the convoy made a sharp 68-degree turn to the northwest. But the *U-158*, ahead and to starboard, was still too close to be evaded. Rostin's boat surfaced and approached for another attack.

At 2008, the *Edison*'s sonar man picked up a contact off the starboard bow. The *Edison* swung over to investigate, but Rostin's lookouts saw her in the turn; and in the pale moonlight a lookout on the destroyer saw the U-boat submerging. The *Edison* surged in and dropped a pattern of depth charges set at medium depth; the blasts brought no sign of damage to the surface. The *Edison* resumed her search and twice more regained contact; she attacked with deeper patterns of depth charges, blasting mounds of white water up out of the churning sea. But the explosions were not near enough to hurt the *U-158*.

The *Edison* continued to search and listen, search and listen. At irregular intervals, she dropped small patterns of depth charges on fickle contacts; if Murdaugh could not sink the U-boat, he was determined to keep her down. Rostin's men felt the shudder of the detonations, but they did not worry much, for the blasts were "all not very near." The *Edison* spent four hours and twenty-four depth charges in hunting the U-boat; she did not kill *U-158*, but she prevented Rostin from attacking the convoy. The long, night fight seemed a standoff.

At 0205 on the 25th, as the *Edison* was steaming back toward the convoy, her lookouts sighted the tenacious U-boat on the surface, only 300 yards abeam. She swung over in a hard, tight right turn to try to ram the U-boat as she began to dive; but the *U-158* got under too quickly. In plaintive frustration, the destroyer's Exec told Murdaugh, "Skipper, she was close enough to throw spuds at!"

But the *Edison* was unable to pick up a sonar contact, and the elusive *U-158* escaped again. The destroyer dropped a single depth charge as a gesture of both deterrence and frustration; while darkness lasted, she patrolled between the convoy and the U-boat's point of submergence. But Commander Murdaugh need not have worried longer. His tenacity had at last exhausted the ample fight in *U-158*. There were no more contacts that night. The pink glow of dawn meant that men and ships had survived another night of blindness and were a few miles closer to safety.

On the 25th, the *Bernadou* ran down a couple of RDF bearings and attacked a sonar contact with seven depth charges, perhaps Zahn's boat, or Wattenberg's, or perhaps fish; but the fight was finished. Admiral Doenitz ordered his U-boats to break off the hunt for ON 67, for they were not in contact and were low on torpedoes and too far west.

The weather grew stormy on the 26th, and several merchantmen straggled. The Coast Guard cutter *Spencer* arrived to augment the escort. Most of the convoy was safely dispersed that night, but eight vessels went on to Halifax with the weary escorts, who needed to refuel after a grueling passage.

Of the two cripples of ON 67, only one survived. *Diloma* made it to Halifax. *Empire Celt* had limped off toward St. John's soon after being hit, and a tug and a trawler were sent out to assist the hurt tanker in to port. She hung on for 385 miles of her long, painful journey, but on the morning of the 26th, only 35 miles from St.

John's, the weakened tanker broke in half in rising seas, bringing the toll of ships lost from the convoy to eight, including six precious tankers. The tug and trawler rescued 31 of the *Empire Celt*'s men, but six others drifted off in a lifeboat and were not found. They were the last men to die from ON 67, whose escorts, despite fighting with bravery and cunning, were defeated by lack of the eyes to see at night.[1]

And as a lingering reminder of the lost opportunities in the fight in the vicinity of ON 67, the *Edison* carried a box of hand grenades on her bridge. The precaution sometimes drew derisive comments from other destroyermen, but *Edison*'s men laughed last when, late in 1943, word came in of a melee at close quarters between the four-stacker *Borie* and the *U-405*, fought briefly at the last with small arms, knives, and the wardroom crockery. Although not a sophisticated form of missilry nor an ASW weapon approved by the Bureau of Ordnance, the grenades cheered *Edison*'s men. It was, after all, better than throwing spuds.[2]

31.

Saying Good-bye to It All

IRONICALLY, THE BRITISH AND CANADIANS, who had for so long "frankly and eagerly looked forward" to American entry into the war, soon found it a mixed blessing. The Atlantic Fleet was required to transfer modern destroyers and heavy ships to the Pacific, to provide escorts for troop convoys, and to use precious ships to protect routine movements in U.S. coastal waters. By February 1942, the Support Force had diminished to less than twenty destroyers. The British had changing commitments east of Gibraltar and the Canadians were vexed by problems of maintenance and by too rapid expansion. As the base facilities at Londonderry became ready for use, Admiral King decided to shift convoy routes south in order to lessen stress on ships and men and to allow American destroyermen to improve their proficiency by using the Royal Navy's ASW training equipment at Londonderry. But shortages of ships and the fluid strategic situation made for delays in setting up the "Newfie-to-Derry" run, and all three navies sometimes found it difficult to make good on their promises of paper ships. The new plans mandated that escort groups would be integrated under British direction, because the British were to contribute the greatest number of ships to the escort pool. Admiral King was amenable to the change, despite his mistrust of the British, because he felt that "the present system of divided control is wasteful of our resources."

Under the new system, a Western Local Escort Group of British, Canadian, and several Free French escorts would take the convoys

413

from Halifax to 45° west, a distance of about 700 miles; then a Mid-Ocean Escort Group from a pool of fifteen destroyers and fifty-two corvettes of the Royal Navy, twelve destroyers and forty-nine corvettes of the Royal Canadian Navy, and fifteen American destroyers would take the convoys from 45° west to 22° west, about 500 miles from Londonderry; finally, an Eastern Local Escort Group of British destroyers, corvettes, and trawlers would bring the convoys from 22° west to dispersal areas off Scotland; an Iceland Group of five American four-stackers would provide a shuttle escort service to and from 22° west for ships going to and coming from Iceland.[1]

In the spring, the American-escorted HX and SC convoys encountered little woe; the U-boats were operating in less dangerous, more profitable areas. Most escort groups consisted of one or two U.S. destroyers and three or four Canadian corvettes.

For example, the *Benson* and *Broome*, and the Canadian corvettes *Alberni, Collingwood,* and *Hepatica* made a routine passage at the end of February with the twenty-four ships of HX 176. The weather was snowy and foggy. At 0400 on the 26th, one of the corvettes sighted a U-boat attempting to close the convoy and tried to ram her, but the submarine quickly dived; the escort then made an unsuccessful depth-charge attack. Later in the day, strong head winds developed into a stiff gale, and although the storm prolonged the voyage, it helped shield the convoy from U-boats.[2]

HX 178 was hampered by bad luck and the mechanical breakdowns of the vessels of its western ocean escort. A freighter straggled in dense fog off Halifax and was torpedoed and sunk by a U-boat. The Canadian destroyer *Witherington* was slowed by boiler trouble and the new Canadian minesweeper *Drummondville* proved not yet fit for war service in the North Atlantic. The mid-ocean escort, consisting of the destroyer *Gleaves*, the cutter *Spencer*, and the Canadian corvettes *Bittersweet, Chilliwack, Shediac,* and *Algoma* joined and took the twenty-two merchant vessels eastward through foggy and stormy weather; no U-boats found the ships.[3]

In mid-March, the destroyers *Buck* and *Bristol*, accompanied by the British corvettes *Kingcup, Loosestrife,* and *Dianella*, and the Free French corvette *Roselys*, started eastward with the twenty-two vessels of HX 179; soon, one merchantman returned to port for engine repairs and another straggled. The weather grew stormy, and one of the *Loosestrife's* officers was killed when he sustained a fractured skull in a fall caused by rising seas. Later, the *Buck* expended twenty-one depth charges in two attacks on a firm sonar contact; then the *Bristol* and *Roselys* carried out a well-executed coordinated attack on another good contact, but the escorts carried another empty bag into Londonderry.[4]

On the evening of 7 April, the *Simpson* missed an opportunity. She was escorting two ships from HX 182 to Londonderry when she picked up a sonar contact. The *Simpson* surged in to attack, but when her sonar beam passed over the submarine, the U-boat swung to port. She released eight depth charges, but the U-boat was far abeam of the explosions. Her skipper then rejoined the two cargo ships, not wishing to leave them unprotected; he failed to press his attack or even to keep the U-boat down until complete darkness settled in. When Admiral King learned of the shoddy performance, he was furious.[5]

The westbound convoys were also normally quiet during the spring. For example, at the end of February, the *Plunkett*, the cutter *Campbell*, two British destroyers, and two corvettes took the thirty ships of ON 69 westward through intermittent rain squalls in an uneventful passage. One of the merchant vessels survived the long ocean passage only to be sunk by two torpedoes from a U-boat while en route to Baltimore.[6]

In mid-March, the *Benson*, *Broome*, *MacLeish*, *Alberni*, and *Collingwood* took the twelve vessels of ON 75 westward through storms and high seas. The destroyers sustained cracked deck-plating and assorted storm damage requiring thirteen days in the yard. St. Patrick's Day was unkind to the destroyers, whose war paint included no green. At 1350, the *Broome*'s sonar man thought he heard two torpedoes passing near the ship and, at 1629, the *MacLeish* had to dodge a wake that might have been another torpedo; but neither ship was able to pick up a sonar contact. The rest of the voyage was not disturbed by any leprechauns.[7]

It was during the escort of ON 77 that the Support Force had its last good chance to destroy a U-boat. The *Niblack*, the *Ingham*, and five corvettes were protecting twenty-eight merchantmen when, suddenly, in the early minutes of 25 March, the British tanker *Imperial Transport* was torpedoed twice in her port side. The tanker, in ballast, did not explode; she floated for a long time, and the Canadian corvette *Mayflower* and the French corvette *Aconit* were able to rescue her entire crew of fifty-one. In the blackness, the *Niblack* ranged astern down the port side of the convoy, but could not find the U-boat. The night and morning passed uneventfully but, at 1500, the *Niblack's* men sighted a U-boat moving at high speed on the surface, about ten miles out from the port side of the convoy. The destroyer swung off in pursuit, soon turning up 25 knots. The U-boat skipper was sending off a contact report and he determinedly kept his boat on the surface until 1523, when the destroyer was 11,000 yards away. Then the U-boat submerged in a long, white streak of bright water.

Underwater, the U-boat maneuvered to keep her wake between her hull and the destroyer. Not properly sweeping the target with his sound beam, the *Niblack's* sonar man took his bearings on the U-boat's wake. As the destroyer churned closer, her sound beam passed above the target, and the U-boat then turned in a half-circle to port, running on an opposite heading to and abeam of the *Niblack*. The destroyer released four depth charges at too-long intervals of eighty yards; the first "ash can" exploded about 100 yards off the port quarter of the U-boat and the rest of the pattern fell well astern of her.

The *Niblack* searched anew and, after half an hour, regained sonar contact at a range of 500 yards. She commenced her attack run, and when her sound beam passed over the target, the U-boat again swung to port. The destroyer released ten depth charges, but they exploded well astern and abeam of the U-boat.

At the end of her attack run, the *Niblack* turned back on an opposite heading and in four minutes regained contact. When the U-boat was ahead and to starboard, about 500 yards away, she fired a torpedo at the ship. The *Niblack's* sonar man heard the "fish" coming, and the destroyer turned sharply to starboard to avoid it, losing the contact.

The *Niblack* resumed her search. At 1704 and again at 1742, she dropped single depth charges to worry the Germans. Then, at 1748, she regained sonar contact at 1,300 yards and headed in for another attack. The U-boat again swung away to port to present her wake to the destroyer, then curled around the wake on a heading opposite and parallel to the *Niblack*; once again, the *Niblack's* depth charges exploded astern and to one side of the U-boat.

After searching briefly again, at 1805, the *Niblack* dropped a pattern of depth charges as a parting gesture, and then steamed back to the convoy. She kept the U-boat down long enough to spare the merchantmen from attack, but imperfect sonar and attack technique robbed her of her chance to kill.[8]

By late April, all the American destroyers had gone from escort duty in the North Atlantic, posted to other duty. Only a few Coast Guard cutters and Navy patrol craft remained to fight beside the doughty Canadian and British escorts and other stray friends in the Battle of the Atlantic. The work of the Support Force was done.

With his command drained of ships for other duties and the burden of escort operations passing to the British and Canadians, Admiral Bristol felt that his situation was increasingly "anomalous": "We maintain the same coach for the team and they're trying to keep the same team together without a coach." He calculated that his ships had brought more than 2,000 vessels safely across the Atlantic, while losing only eight of them to U-boats. The Force's first kills of U-boats came in March 1942. They belonged to the PBY fliers of Patrol Squadron 82 at Argentia, and were scored against two of the Pauken-schlag boats: Ensign Bill Tepuni blasted the *U-656* south of Cape Race, and Chief Don Mason killed the *U-503* off the Grand Banks. In April, the Support Force was disbanded.

Admiral Bristol and his staff hated the thought of departing the destroyer tender *Prairie* for a shore billet in some "stone frigate" in Boston. But before they left Argentia, on 20 April, Admiral Bristol, a kind and competent man who had for too long held a job beyond the abilities of his forces, suffered a heart attack on board his flagship and died.[9]

The little battles of the Support Force illustrated the state of anti-submarine warfare in the U.S. Atlantic Fleet in six months' experience at war.

The major difficulty was a technical one: lack of reliable radar to counter the aggressive night surface attacks of an invisible enemy. As long as U-boats were able to sight escorts before being sighted themselves, the combat initiative remained in their hands. The good shepherds were blind.

Another grievous problem was the lack of modern destroyers, which led to flawed organization: to balance long-range gold-platers against short-legged four-stackers, divisions had to be split up to form mixed escort groups. The result was lack of coordination amongst the escorts caused by unfamiliarity, varying doctrines, and different ship aptitudes and needs. As strategic necessity required escorts to be shifted to other duties, the turnover in the escort groups added to the lack of coordination and retarded the growth of a strong sense of unit pride; men had pride in their squadron or their division, but not in the escort group to which they happened to be attached. Most men realized that escort groups needed to be made permanent, in order to afford the destroyers coordinated training and experience, but lack of ships made that impossible. The British, with the German surface fleet inactive (unlike the U.S. Navy's foe in the Pacific), were able to invest more intensively in the antisubmarine effort; and their escort groups were more stable, much to the benefit of both charisma and technique. Many naval officers were coming to realize the need for centralized direction of the antisubmarine warfare effort. As one destroyerman said, "Doenitz acts, we confer!"[10]

Tactics lacked tenacity and aggressiveness because of a too-great desire to afford convoy vessels impeccable protection; the Atlantic Fleet was fighting defensively. After the *Simpson*'s lost opportunity in April, Admiral King angrily wrote: "Dogging a sure submarine contact over a long period of time may now be considered a principle in anti-submarine warfare. Nothing should be allowed to discourage its application. . . . The convoy . . . should not be allowed to . . . curtail the persistent dogging while there is a reasonable possibility of a sure kill." As Captain W.D. Baker told Commanders Murdaugh and Keating, "You've got to go out and run them down." And the *Escort of Convoy Bulletin* warned emphatically: "*The offensive spirit must prevail.*" The cardinal virtue of tenacity was at last acknowledged: "Experience and theoretical calculation have shown such a small probability of inflicting lethal damage upon a submerged submarine with a single depth charge attack that the problem of repeated attacks becomes of primary importance." Increasingly, destroyermen concurred in the need for more aggressive and tenacious tactics, partly because it was thought that Commander Murdaugh's dynamic tactics in the escort of ON 67 had saved his convoy from appalling slaughter.[11]

War operations had taught the Atlantic destroyermen to patrol well out from the convoy, in order to keep submarines beyond good firing range, and to patrol station actively, in order to lessen gaps in the escort screen and enhance their chances of detecting approaching U-boats; crews learned the worth of radar and how to refuel short-legged ships from convoy tankers amid stormy seas. But because of inexperience search-and-attack techniques remained deficient in execution and consistency. The Support Force did not encounter many U-boats in its six months at war and, therefore, did not have much opportunity to learn from and correct its errors; in a trial-and-error endeavor, the fewer the trials, the higher the percentage of error. Technique and doctrine evolved out of experience, not out of theory, but experience differed and bad habits evolved as well as good ones. One destroyerman said, "I would instruct my men at sea, but I had no idea what . . . the other ships were doing. Six weeks might pass without comparing notes. . . ." And a pilot confirmed: "antisubmarine operations were a hit-or-miss proposition, with no established doctrine. Each activity controlling aircraft had its own set of instructions. . . ." To gather, collate, and evaluate the experience upon which doctrine had to be built, the Anti-Submarine Warfare Unit was set up in Boston in February under the dynamic Captain Baker, auguring better days ahead for the Atlantic sailors.[12]

It was found that, there being no body of standard search-and-attack procedures, small but costly mistakes were made in the excitement of combat; for example, a sonar man might fail to sweep the target with his sound beam, echo-ranging on the target's wake instead of its hull, or, in relaying information to the bridge, he might omit a small but vital detail of the target's behavior. As the Support Force accumulated experience in its education in violence, it became possible to identify common errors and establish fixed techniques and uniform procedures. Sonar operators were trained to report in a prescribed manner, in order to lessen the chance of errors of omission; they were relentlessly trained to take both bow and stern bearings on targets and to play the sound beam back and forth across the target, in order to make certain that they were echo-ranging on the U-boat's hull and not her wake and to guard against the U-boat passing suddenly beyond the range of the beam with an unexpected burst of speed. The duties of the key attack personnel—sound officer, plotting officer, conning officer, etc.—were precisely defined, in order to avoid ambiguity and confusion. Depth-charge settings were prescribed for various tactical situations, in order to lessen the frequency with which depth charges were set too deep or too shallow; crews were trained to ready depth charges for faster dropping and to space them better. Specific methods of searching for a lost contact were prescribed. The box, or rectangular, search pattern was favored over the almost instinctive tendency to circle back; turning around was more direct and faster, but it could foul the sonar gear by making an extra wake. Ships were enjoined always to turn toward the direction of the target's last movement to avoid masking that movement with their own wake.[13]

The harsh demands of combat served, as Admiral King promised, to weed out lax or unfit officers who "in spite of their previous good peacetime records were not the seamen or leaders likely to inspire . . . the offensive killer spirit in their crews." In 1942, "some few" of the Atlantic Fleet's destroyers were "excellent"; "many" were "acceptable"; and some were below standard due to inexperience.[14] But the Atlantic Fleet's day was coming.

The advent of radar and ASW doctrines rooted deeply in hard-bought experience soon reestablished the destroyer's innate superiority over the U-boat; submarines were vulnerable because they had to approach very near convoy vessels if they were to do them harm, and because of the excessive communications upon which their coordinated "wolfpack" tactics depended. Before long, the good shepherds, their sight improved and their technique refined, would fall murderously upon any wolf that approached their flock. And, once again, blood would stain the North Atlantic; but it would be the thick, black blood of the gray wolves. The Support Force had gone, but the best of its men had shaped a legacy of courage and dedication in lonely battles on a stormy ocean to bequeath to their better favored successors, whose victory would thus be partly theirs.

Antisubmarine warfare was not the only significant task of the Atlantic Fleet in the first winter and spring of war. Another major duty was the escort of troop convoys.

In mid-December, Task Force 19 was organized from the old battleship *Arkansas*, the light cruiser *Nashville*, and the destroyers *Ericsson*, *Eberle*, *Livermore*, *Ludlow*, *Hamilton*, and *Palmer*; its mission was to protect convoy CT-16, transport *Chateau Thierry* and three British transports carrying U.S. and Canadian troops to Iceland. The ships left Halifax on the 16th. Steaming at moderate speeds, they were less vulnerable to submarine attack than were the slow, ponderous merchant convoys, and the passage was uneventful. The convoy and its escort arrived in Iceland on the 23rd.

On Christmas Day, with the *Ingraham* replacing the *Palmer* and the *Kearny* added—the latter able to make 25 knots despite a patch over the hole in her side, Task Force 19 brought the *Chateau Thierry* and the store ship *Tarazed* west. In the next few days, there were a few dubious sonar contacts, most of them made by the *Ingraham*, which was learning the escort trade, but nothing developed and, in keeping with the spirit of the season, the ships enjoyed a peaceful return trip.

Happy to be going home at last, the *Kearny*'s men opened the New Year with a glad entry in the deck log:

> Enroute from bleak Iceland we'll
>   never get lost on
> This ocean while heading for famous
>   old Boston.

The *Kearny* steamed into Boston, still carrying the remains of her dead in her dank, mangled fireroom. She would be back in combat by April.

The *Ludlow*'s men hoped that in the new year "Lucky Lud" would live up to her nickname:

> You have your blackout, show no lights
>   And since five March in forty one
> To convoy escort, Atlantic run
>   You've traveled a lot for a little girl
> From training cruise to war's mad whirl
>   You've felt the treat of Guantanamo's heat
> And the chilling blast of Iceland's sleet
>   And known to you is Argentia's mist
> So too is Scollay on your list
>   And so tonight near your first year end
> The Captain and crew a greeting send
>   With brimming hearts and a little cheer
> We join to wish you, **A HAPPY NEW YEAR**.[15]

In mid-January 1942, Task Force 15, the old battleship *Texas*, the heavy cruiser *Quincy*, and Destroyer Division 16, left New York with the transports *Chateau Thierry* and *Munargo* and HMS *Strathaird* carrying the first U.S. Army troops to the United Kingdom. Everyone was aware that the Germans would relish sinking the transports, in order to make good Hitler's frequent but hollow boast that the U-boats and Luftwaffe would make it impossible for the Americans to send an expeditionary force to Europe; so, as a *Sterett* sailor said, "We took maximum precautions with that outfit. . . ." The *Wasp* accompanied the convoy on its few first few days out to protect it with her aircraft. Stormy weather was encountered on the 18th, but otherwise the passage was uneventful, proving anticlimactic to the keyed-up sailors.

When the ships reached the Momp on the 23rd, the British escort force was not yet there; arriving in the afternoon, it consisted of two venerable four-stackers, which surprised the American sailors, who anticipated a more formidable force. The American warships took the *Munargo* on to Iceland, while the British destroyers took the *Chateau Thierry* and the *Strathaird* to Northern Ireland.

On the gray Monday morning of 26 January, the transports anchored in Belfast Loch and began disembarking 3,900 troops of the U.S. Thirty-Fourth Infantry Division. The riflemen, in battle dress, destined for violent appointments in North African groves and on cold, Italian hills, were ferried across the slaty water toward gaily decorated Dufferin Dock in lighters bearing gentle names, *Royal Daffodil, Canterbury, Princess Maud, Maid of Orleans*. The band of the Royal Ulster Rifles played the "Star-Spangled Banner," speeches were made by numerous dignitaries, and refreshments were served to a happy crowd, both stirred and entertained. Officials scrambled to greet the "first American," but both they and the public relations men were confounded. The lead column of soldiers came ashore at a minor pier; the man met at the main dock and dubbed the "first American" by the journalists and politicians was actually about the 501st man to land!

The use of ships and the diversion of Army troops for the build-up in Britain meant that the impatient Marines had to remain in Iceland a little longer. The soldiers carried in the *Munargo* relieved only the 3rd Battalion of the Sixth Marines. Task Force 15 left Iceland on the 31st and brought the *Munargo* and her glad Marines home.[16]

In February, a huge troop convoy was organized to take Army troops to the United Kingdom and bring the rest of the Marines back from Iceland. The convoy, AT-12, consisted of thirteen ships, carrying 14,688 men. Naval transports *Fuller, Barnett, George F. Elliott, Neville*, Army transport *American Legion*, and the SS *Duchess of Atholl* carried 8,493 soldiers bound for Belfast along with 1,153 sailors to activate the Naval Operating Base, Londonderry; the naval auxiliaries *Betelgeuse, Alhena*, and *Almaack* carried the soldiers' heavy equipment. Also, the naval transports *McCawley*, *Heywood*, and *Munargo*, and the SS *Borinquen* carried 5,042 green Army troops destined to relieve the Marines in their "certain cold place." War having been declared, draftees and reservists could be sent beyond the Western Hemisphere without political complications, and General Marshall thus did not have to spare veteran troops for Iceland. The fleet oiler *Chemung* and the store ship *Polaris* rounded out the big convoy.

To defend the host, Rear Admiral H. Kent Hewitt was given Task Force 32: the old battleship *New York*, the light cruiser *Philadelphia*, and the destroyers *Rhind*, *Rowan*, *Mayrant*, *Roe*, *Trippe*, *Hilary P. Jones*, *Ludlow*, *Charles F. Hughes*, *Lansdale*, and *Ingraham*.

The escort force steamed down from Casco Bay and met the convoy off New York on the 19th. The *Chemung* promptly earned her keep by fueling four of the destroyers. The ships went on to Halifax, delayed by the *American Legion*, which suffered from chronic engine trouble; the escorts topped off with fuel, and the cranky transport was left behind in Halifax. A track below 50° north was followed for most of the passage, in order to avoid the worst of the North Altantic weather; the days were cold and foggy. There were several sonar contacts, but the convoy's 13-knot speed kept it out of harm's way. In the darkness on the 27th, the *Trippe* struck the starboard side of the *Charles F. Hughes* a glancing blow, causing minor damage. The only casualty that occurred was in the *Hilary P. Jones* when a gunner injured a seaman in a fist fight. On the 27th, at 52°-35' north, 25° west, the large Belfast section of the convoy was transferred to the care of five British destroyers, while the American warships and the rest of the convoy vessels steamed for Iceland.

At 1010 on 8 March, General Marston officially closed down Headquarters, First Marine Brigade, and boarded "Wacky Mac." The Marines and their gear were loaded on the four transports and, on the 14th, the task force, joined by the *Quincy*, sailed from Valley Forge. At noon on the 17th, at 53°-30' north, 25° west, they met the two escorts and seven ships of the Belfast group, carrying 3,000 men of the Royal Air Force and some U.S. Army men, for the return trip westward.

Despite a southerly route and fast convoy vessels, the modern destroyers, vigorously patrolling station and making protective sweeps, had to be refueled by the cruisers several times; it was no wonder that the old four-stackers, which had escorted slow convoys

in northern waters, had so often run low on fuel. On the 19th, a
Philadelphia float plane discovered a damaged merchant ship not far
away from the convoy; the vessel was down by her stern and a third
of her length forward had been amputated by a torpedo, but her
watertight bulkheads held and she still floated. The *Roe* was sent to
protect her until a tug and other escorts arrived. On the 20th, a
corpse, buoyed up in the water by its life jacket, drifted by the
Charles F. Hughes, a grim reminder to the destroyermen of why they
were there. The *Rowan* and *Rhind* attacked dubious sonar contacts,
wakes or turbulence, the same day. On the 21st, the *Betelgeuse*
broke down, and the *Hilary P. Jones* stood by her while her crew
fixed the trouble and got under way again. The rest of the passage
was uneventful, and the ships reached New York on 25 March.

The Marines enjoyed a memorable liberty, then went back to a
changed Corps of callow youngsters, whose help they would need if
they were to avenge dead friends and bitter defeats in their distant
western ocean. Some went south to New River to help train and lead
crack outfits in the First Division, soon to ship out for Guadalcanal;
most went on to westward, to Camp Elliott, to shape the hard Second
Division, destined to make a legend on part of an island called
Tarawa. The Polar Bear Marines were home at last.[17]

Some of the troop convoys were smaller and less glamorous. On
14 March, off Halifax, the *Swanson* and *Nicholson* met the transports
SS *Empress of Canada* and SS *Orbita*, which were carrying 4,000-5,000
British and Canadian troops. The ships were protected by aircraft
the first four days out. Both destroyers attacked sonar contacts,
perhaps large fish; three *Swanson* men were burned as a result of a
faulty firing circuit at their K-gun. Depth-charge attacks were made,
but were abbreviated by the need to watch over the troopships,
which led the escort commander to report that even small troop
convoys should be escorted by more than two destroyers. The transports handled well, kept station easily, and showed no lights. It was
an easy passage for destroyermen used to the eccentricities of the
large, slow merchant convoys. The warships entered Greenock Bay
on 22 March.

Five days later, the two destroyers left to meet the SS *Banfora* and
SS *Rangitiki*, carrying 5,000 British and Canadians west. On the
30th, the *Banfora*'s rudder jammed. British seamen, intending to signal that the ship was out of control, mistakenly flashed one red

A modern destroyer bucks into Atlantic rollers

light—the signal that the ship had been torpedoed—instead of two!
The error "caused some consternation" aboard the destroyers. The
next day, the *Rangitiki* took her turn and also broke down. The
passage was made at 14 knots and for the most part in stormy
weather, so there was little to fear from U-boats. The destroyers
brought their charges safely to Halifax on 6 April.[18]

In April, Task Force 37, the *Philadelphia, Ericsson, Eberle, Livermore,* hale *Kearny,* and old *Cole* and *Bernadou* led the troop transports of AT-14, *Orizaba, Munargo,* SS *Borinquen,* SS *Banfora,* and
SS *Warwick Castle* eastward toward the United Kingdom and Iceland
in another milk run.[19]

No soldiers were lost from the troop convoys brought across the
ocean by the ships of the Atlantic Fleet. And the Fuehrer discovered
that his assumption about the demise of Mahan's doctrines was premature.

In the spring, the Atlantic Fleet was reduced to a size little larger
than the old Atlantic Squadron.

Several new ships were shaking down. The *Hornet* spent thirty-
five days working in the Gulf of Mexico, and her skipper reported:
"We have had a very fruitful and productive cruise, and I can assure
you that this ship is ready for war at any time, any place." Accordingly, the carrier was assigned to carry Army B-25 medium
bombers for Lieutenant Colonel James H. Doolittle's raid on Tokyo.
The *Washington* and *North Carolina,* the Navy's newest battleships,
were working hard on gunnery in the Gulf under the stern direction
of Rear Admiral John W. Wilcox, who, impressed by the *Bismarck's*
quick destruction of HMS *Hood,* stressed "early hitting as never
before," with good results.[20]

After steaming thousands of miles but seeing no action, the sailors
of the veteran ships were restless. A man in the *Vincennes* noted: "I
want to go to sea again. . . . This is really a joke sitting here in Long
Island Sound, with half the A.A. battery manned and picket boats
circling the ship. Someday we may see some action, but by that time
we shall be stale, at this rate."[21]

Ernie King also thought it time for the heavy ships to fight, and
when the British, concerned lest German surface ships sortie into the

Atlantic and wishing to send more ships east of Suez, asked the U.S. Navy to base a task force at Scapa Flow, King complied. He decided to send the *Washington* to the United Kingdom, holding the *North Carolina* back in the western Atlantic to support Admiral Ingersoll's depleted units protecting the Casco Bay-Argentia and Bermuda approaches. On 15 March, King ordered Task Force 39 organized. A powerful squadron, it consisted of the *Wasp, Washington, Wichita, Tuscaloosa, Wainwright, Plunkett, Madison, Sterett, Lang,* and *Wilson.* He gave the command to Admiral Wilcox, a "hard-bitten old sundowner," who he hoped would show the British an efficient outfit.[22]

The ships steamed out of Casco Bay into a rough and choppy sea, but the weather was not stormy. Dipping into the troughs, the *Wasp* shipped some green water on her high flight deck, and the *Washington* took bursts of white water across her main deck, but, to the *Sterett's* men, the Atlantic was reasonably calm for March.

One day out, a sailor on the battleship saw a man go over the side. He gave the alarm, but curling whitecaps made it difficult to see the splashing of a man struggling in the water, and the lost sailor could not be sighted. A muster was held to determine who was missing, but all hands were present. Everyone relaxed, thinking that the report was erroneous and that no one had been washed overboard after all. Someone was sent to inform Admiral Wilcox of the event, but the admiral was not in his cabin and could not be found on deck. At last it was realized that the man missing overboard was Admiral Wilcox! The *Wasp* launched two scout bombers to search the choppy sea. Neither plane sighted a body, but one of them suffered a mechanical failure and crashed, killing both pilot and radioman.

There was some feeling that Wilcox, a stern disciplinarian, might have been murdered! But he was a poor sailor, intimidated by the sea, and on previous occasions had expressed fear of falling overboard. Nevertheless, he did not like to stay in his cabin or on the bridge for long periods, preferring to prowl the decks on improvised inspections. He must have been making one of his impromptu tours when he was swept overboard. Task Force 39 had lost three men on its first full day at sea, a grim omen of futility.[23]

The rest of the passage was uneventful and, on 3 April, the American warships were led through fog into the wide bay of Scapa Flow by HMS *Edinburgh.* Thereafter, they trained with British ships so that they might function in battle as a fully integrated part of the

Home Fleet. The destroyermen practiced antisubmarine operations with British submarines and attended ASW teaching sessions. The British were glad to have the Americans with them, the Lyness Officers' Mess going so far to cement Anglo-American relations as to put ice in the drinks. The Americans consumed much Scotch, but took a while getting used to the British beer, which one destroyerman described as "putrid—an ungodly swill that tasted and looked like spunkwater." Rear Admiral Giffen, who had inherited command after the death of Wilcox, reported to Admiral Ingersoll: "I am really proud. . . . Men clear eyed and trying so hard, officers on their toes and all trying like hell to show the Home Fleet how—and I think and know we are. At least the Admiralty now is furnishing paint to their ships. Maybe we looked too good."[24]

In April and May, the *Wasp* carried needed fighter planes to besieged Malta in two dramatic missions, and the American sailors felt that "we had at last done something that had a direct bearing on the course of the war." The U.S. ships continued to train intensively, but saw no combat. Nevertheless, as the first American heavy warships to reach Britain, they received much favorable publicity, which perhaps impressed too much "Ike" Giffen and his men, who were cocky and looking for a fight. But in distant Brazil, shrewd old Jonas Ingram summed up the future of Task Force 39 in a mordant comment to Ingersoll: "I note by the press that Ike over in Scapa Flow says he commands the fighting part of the American Navy. All the Huns have to do is tie the *Tirpitz* up to a tree in Norway and allow all her crew to go on extended leave; she will still contain most all the British Navy, likewise Ike's force."[25]

After weeks of desultory steaming as part of a distant covering force screening convoys to northern Russia from surface attack, the heavy ships nearly got a chance to fight. On Independence Day, the *Wainwright* joined convoy PQ-17 long enough to refuel and became caught up in a fierce sea-air battle with German aircraft. She impressed the British with her heavy and accurate antiaircraft fire and her willingness to steam to the stations under heaviest attack. Meanwhile, it was rumored that the *Tirpitz*, the *Admiral Scheer*, and eight German destroyers were coming out from Norway to hunt down the convoy.

The Anglo-American distant covering force led by HMS *Duke of York* included a carrier, two battleships, seven cruisers, and about twenty destroyers and corvettes; the *Washington*, *Wichita*, *Tusca-*

loosa, and four U.S. destroyers were part of the force. The crews wanted to try to cut off the retreat of the German ships and thus force the prudent enemy into decisive battle at last; but the Admiralty was unwilling to risk the warships within range of German land-based aircraft, and the force was ordered to withdraw, to the bitter disappointment of the men in the ships. But the German ships were not seeking a fight and very quickly returned to port; however, the convoy was ravaged by planes and U-boats and massacred.

Perhaps, in general, the British were too conscious of the threat to their sea communications posed by the *Tirpitz* and the few remaining German surface ships, and allowed the enemy to chain too much of the Royal Navy to sterile defense posts, vainly watching and waiting. Perhaps the Admiralty should have relied more on the RAF to keep German ships out of the Atlantic and spared more powerful ships for use in the Pacific, where the need for them in 1942 was desperate.

The Americans transferred the *Wasp* to the Pacific and, in the summer, Admiral King decided to send the *Washington* to the hardpressed Pacific Fleet. King's decision was founded on strategic necessity, but there were those who believed it was influenced by anger at the British for their failure to fight more aggressively in the Atlantic, particularly northwest of Norway on the grim 4th of July 1942.[26]

And so Task Force 39 never found its coveted surface battle.

For the men left in Iceland, the winter was long and misspent.

The seaplanes were hampered by wretched weather, and they flew a steadily declining number of hours as the winter intensified.* And many of the flight hours were logged on aborted missions. Wisely, the British abandoned seaplane operations in October, relying on land-based Hudsons to provide fitful watch over the waters south of Iceland. At Skerjafjordhur, ice and frozen spray on the planes, high winds, and choppy water interfered with maintenance as well as with operations, and rain and fog often rendered missions meaningless when flown. Then, on 5 January, succor was brought to the weary and frustrated fliers: the tender *Albemarle* came in with five precious PBY-5A amphibians to base at Reykjavik Aerodrome and replace the battered seaplanes. High winds and heavy rains delayed the transfer

---

*Between mid-September and the end of January, they flew the following total hours each week: 49½; 90; 137½; 92; 124; 89; 59; 97½; 32; 41; 23; 11; 29; 51; 35; 15; 39; 0; 15.

ashore of the amphibians. Between the 11th and 14th, the storm intensified and, by the 15th, it had become the worst hurricane Iceland had seen in seventeen years. The wind lashed the island at 90-95 knots, with gusts above 100 knots. A Nissen hut was blown sixty feet in the air before crashing down on the RAF runway; six RAF Whitleys were secured to 6,000-pound concrete blocks, but the wind drove the planes along the runway! In Valley Forge, the American transport *Stratford* lost both her anchors in the maelstrom and was beached, in order to prevent her from endangering other storm-driven ships.

At Skerjafjordhur, the seaplanes bobbed and slithered in the gray water. One of them, strung tautly at the end of its mooring lines, was raised up by the gale winds and rising water and flipped upside down. With rain and high waves constantly smashing over their bows, all eleven of the moored PBYs and Mariners filled with water and sank. One manned plane was isolated in a nearby fjord; the sea was too wild for it to take off or for the base to send over a boat to remove its crew. So Lieutenant (JG) D.W. Hundley started its engines and headed the seaplane into the fierce wind; for nine hours he and his men kept the nose turned into the gale. Twice, an entire wingtip dipped under water, but each time the flying boat righted itself. The fliers, huddled in lonely misery, ran their little one-cylinder engine bilge pump continuously to drain the plane of water. Both seaplane and damp crew survived the storm.

Captain Daniel V. Gallery, tough and droll commander of the air station, was enraged by the seaplane losses. In his opinion, the aircraft at the main anchorage should have been saved in the same manner as was Hundley's plane "had crews been aboard, bailing them out and keeping the engines turning over. . . ." The fliers argued that the winds constantly shifted, making it impossible to keep the planes headed into them at all times and that, thus, extensive damage to the aircraft would be inevitable; they insisted that leaving crews aboard during the hurricane might well have resulted in heavy loss of life, as well as of material. After the memorable blow, the *Albemarle* left Iceland with most of the seaplane crews. Like everyone else who served on the bleak island, the fliers departed gladly, but they were dogged by a vague sense of defeat.

The amphibians that lingered in Iceland were excellent long-range reconnaissance aircraft, but they were miscast in their new role. At 140 knots, the PBY-5As did not have the speed or agility to make the

Seaplanes wrecked in the great gale of January 1942

most of short breaks in the inclement weather and swoop in on
offensive ASW strikes, especially since they often had to fly into
strong headwinds. Heavy bombers, such as the B-24 Liberators, could
carry twice as many depth charges, could travel twice as fast, and
were tougher combat planes, so when the airfield at Keflavik that
could handle them was completed, they took up most of the burden
of ASW flights from Iceland; they used airborne radar to find and
destroy U-boats in the "black pit" of the mid-North Atlantic.[27]

The sailors left in Iceland grew edgy. The endless succession of
dismal, gray days was depressing, and the best efforts of the men
seemed devoid of significant purpose. In the tender *Belknap*, which
had been in Iceland since September, the men complained of late
mail and lack of fresh foods and recreation; they resented having to
stay on to fuel heavy ships, an awkward and laborious procedure
for an aircraft tender, even after the seaplanes had departed. Although
the *Belknap* was undermanned, her men were often shifted to work
ashore. Complaints and problems concerned minor matters, but they
took deep root because the men could not see positive accomplish-
ments derive from their small sacrifices and hard work. The crew
began to feel sorry for itself. The *Belknap*'s deck log entry for 1
January 1942 read:

> No other ships present we wait alone
> The New Year's Day—and orders home!

As other ships came and went and the *Belknap* remained, morale
drooped lower. Then Admiral Bristol, perhaps vexed by the whining
undertone of reports from the aviation units in Iceland, ordered an
inspection. The inspecting officer rated the general appearance of the
Naval Operating Base poor and stated that the *Belknap* was in a
sorry, substandard condition. The fliers insisted that they always
had a greater percentage of their seaplanes ready to fly than did the
Army and RAF, who used sheltered land-based planes. One out-
spoken flight officer wrote of the inspection: "Balls! This comment
on *Belknap* results from personal politics and jealousies."[28]

Nevertheless, an unhappy situation was developing in the tender.
There was an increasing number of courts-martial and captain's masts;
wardroom arguments shifted from refighting the Civil War to bitter
and personal ones between the regular officers and the reservists. In
mid-March, matters reached a critical point when a machinist's mate

slashed another sailor's wrist with a knife and had to be taken ashore under armed guard for observation.

That incident and the advent of spring and better weather, symbolic of rebirth, made the crew begin to pull together once again and shed their self-pity. The men were young and resilient, and morale "greatly improved." In May 1942, the USS *Belknap* at last received sailing orders and steamed out past Skaggi Light to return to the United States, her men perhaps a little burdened by a gray, chill guilt.[29]

Frustration and quiet triumph marked the first six months of the war of the Atlantic Fleet.

The men in the heavy ships did not find their surface gunnery battle, although they ventured all the way to Capetown and Scapa Flow in search of it.

The Marines felt a sense of waste and guilt as they lingered in the North Atlantic powerless to prove their theories of amphibious warfare or to bring succor to old friends and familiar places in the Pacific.

The fliers and those who sustained them found discouragement in futile missions through northern storms and mists and the wet, numbed fatigue of working on ice-glazed planes.

The destroyermen won a muted victory, for their convoys made it safely across the ocean. But they were unable to pay back the U-boats for their losses, especially that of the *Reuben James*, and this made it hard for them to appreciate their victory.

On 9 June 1942, the *Sterett*, one of the last of the Atlantic ships to pass on to westward, moved through the Panama Canal and steamed into the Pacific. She rolled gently on slow Pacific swells, and the men

> thought back over the long days and nights in the Atlantic when there was no respite from violent rolling and pitching; when 35-degree rolls were commonplace (and once even 48 degrees); of green water, freezing cold, beating against the bridge and spraying in sheets high over the director platform; of balancing our plates on our legs as we tried to eat in the wardroom while hanging on by our legs; of the struggle it was to try to stay in our bunks at night, let alone getting some sleep; of the U-boat alarms in the middle of the night that sent us running to our battle stations as we fastened up our life jackets—with a subconscious thought of that cold, black water. We were glad to be back in the Pacific where the real Naval war was—but also where you could see what you were fighting,

and where the water was warm enough that a man would have a fighting chance of survival if his ship was shot out from under him. [30]

In the Pacific, the *Sterett*'s men fought a tangible enemy. The dark Solomons nights were filled with blood and terror, but in the orange-red shards of fire burning on the black water, the sailors knew that they were making their foes pay dearly for the boredom, the fear, and the suffering that they endured as the common lot of men at war; in the Pacific, the bluejackets would find the exhilaration of victory and the certain knowledge that their dead were avenged and their sacrifices honored.

In the Atlantic, the crews fought an invisible foe, were denied the thrill of victory and the certainty that their hardships were meaningful, and there seemed, despite ample courage and dedication, a weary emptiness, a vague, gray sense of failure. But the Atlantic Fleet did its job, for the convoys made it safely home.

The Atlantic Fleet did its job. But it had no time for glory.

32.

A Cold, Black Shore

IN THE WINTER OF 1941-1942, the ocean was the foe that most tested the endurance and skill of the Atlantic Fleet; in February 1942, it brought tragedy to the Fleet when two of its ships were lost against a desolate shore.

The destroyer *Wilkes* and the supply ship *Pollux* left Portland at 1630 on 15 February, bound for Argentia on a routine milk run. They were joined by four-stacker *Truxtun* at about 0800 the next morning. The passage was uneventful until the late afternoon of the 17th, when snow began to fall, lasting all through the night. The sea was stormy and, in the stinging spray and blur of the snowfall, visibility was poor. The ships zigzagged through the wet darkness, the *Pollux* steaming in the middle of the formation, the *Truxtun* off her port bow, the *Wilkes* off her starboard bow. By 2000, the *Pollux* could not be seen from the *Truxtun*; the destroyer maintained station by picking up on her sound gear the propeller noises of the supply ship. Gradually, the snow turned to a soggy sleet, and the seas began to moderate.

Steaming at 12 knots and taking soundings, the ships edged along the southern coast of Newfoundland, groping in the blurred darkness for the entrance to Placentia Bay. Visibility was only about 200 yards, and attempts to pick up radio bearings on Cape Race and Sable Island were unsatisfactory. With visibility that low and the ships near the coast, the *Pollux*'s skipper wanted to cease zigzagging,

435

but he could not signal his recommendation to the *Wilkes* because she was only intermittently visible and he either feared to use his radio because there might be U-boats nearby or he did not have a TBS system on board.

By shortly after 0400 on the 18th, the ships were just off the southwest tip of Ferryland Point, only two miles from the channel to Placentia Bay; they were slightly off course, but the soundings revealed deep water beneath them, and there seemed no cause for worry. All three vessels were maintaining strong watches. Typically, on the *Pollux*, the navigator was on the bridge with a duty officer on each wing; there were two men in the sky lookout stations, two others in the crow's nest, and the men of the forward gun crew were also serving as lookouts. It was 0410; ahead, less than a football field's length away, was a black shoreline of wet rocks and high, steep cliffs. Over the hum of engines and other shipboard noises, no one heard the sound of the silver-black surf spilling its cold froth against those shadowy rocks and, in the sleety darkness, the lookouts did not see the dark loom of the cliffs.

Suddenly, the navigator on *Truxtun*'s bridge, Lieutenant Arthur L. Newman, and the officer of the deck on the port wing called out a warning of a dark object about 75 yards ahead. Lieutenant Newman ordered full-right rudder, hoping to turn his ship seaward. The destroyer started to swing to starboard, then, with a sliding, grinding shudder, ran aground onto a submerged ledge of rock. She was pinioned on a starboard-jutting spur of the underwater reef. Lieutenant Commander Ralph Hickox ordered most of his men up on deck with life jackets on. Then he sought to back the *Truxtun* down off the projecting finger of shoal, but the wind swung her stern to port and her stern grounded on the main part of the rocky shelf. The destroyermen tried to contact the *Wilkes*, but she did not hear them; then they began to signal with the searchlight. Meanwhile, the punctured destroyer was shipping water in her after engine room, and her "D" tanks holed, black fuel oil gushed and gurgled into the churning gray-green sea. The *Truxtun* began to list.

At 0414, two of the *Pollux*'s officers and her gunners up forward reported lights ahead; these were the *Truxtun*'s searchlight signals. Then her lookouts saw a curved promontory off her starboard bow. Her skipper returned from the chartroom and ordered full speed astern and hard-right rudder, intending to swing the *Pollux* out to sea. But at 0417, she ran hard aground, skidding jarringly along a submerged reef. Her bottom forward was ripped by the shoals, flooding her #1, #2, and #3 holds. Her forward fuel tanks were ruptured, and thick streams of oil spewed out onto the water. No attempt was made to back the *Pollux* down off the rock; she was flooding so rapidly that, if refloated, she would have quickly sunk. At 0420, with his ship already listing by the bow, the commanding officer ordered full speed ahead to drive the *Pollux* more firmly aground to prevent her rapid sinking. Below, the bulkhead of her forward engine room was containing the flood of icy water, and the ship did not seem in extreme danger.

Meanwhile, the *Wilkes*, although holed in her bottom by a small rock, was not pinned fast and limped seaward through the shoals to stand by in deeper water, anxious to help, but impotent to do so without sharing the fate of her companions.

The *Truxtun* and *Pollux* were aground in a small, rock-strewn cove on the southwest corner of Ferryland Point. Deep water ran right up to the sheer faces of bony cliffs, 100 to 200 feet high. Underneath the cliffs, there were two slender wedges of beach, one on the eastern side of the cove, near the *Pollux*, where the promontory jutted out to sea, the other across on the western shoreline, near the *Truxtun*. Both of these narrow refuges would be submerged at high tide.

It was apparent that neither boats nor rafts could be controlled in the wild surf of the cove and no ship could enter, for fear of running aground. No help could come from the water. Forlornly, the *Wilkes* floated several life rafts toward the *Pollux*, but they could not be retrieved in the swirling, gray sea. The *Pollux* signalled the destroyer to relay a message that immediate assistance was needed from land.

The gray dawn was cold and cheerless. On board the grounded vessels, records and money were collected for safekeeping, and blankets, clothing, provisions, and emergency medical stores were carried topside. Heavy seas pounded at the stationary ships pinned to their rocky anvils; the danger of sinking faded before the greater menace of being broken up by the relentless pounding.

The sea steadily slammed the *Truxtun's* damaged port side against the shoal; the ship lurched and pounded, listing to port. Her crew lowered the motor whaleboat to try the dangerous sixty-yard run to the small beach off their port beam, but the seas pounded the boat against the destroyer's side, crushing it into fragments. Gradually, jarringly, the entire port side of the *Truxtun's* hull was smashed in by the churning seas. Her after keel plates were buckling from the pounding; water flooded her after engine room, which had to be abandoned, along with her after quarters and fireroom.

Meanwhile, the *Pollux* was also breaking up. Several large, jagged cracks appeared in her main deck forward, and it seemed to her men "only a matter of time" before the forward section of the ship would snap off at frame 67, between the #2 and #3 holds. Most of the men were ordered aft.

After losing their whaleboat, the *Truxtun's* men began to plan more carefully. All the 3-inch manila line and wire cable on board was run out on the forecastle and tied together to make a lifeline long enough to reach the small beach to port. Then, Boatswain's Mate 1/C Harry M. Egner and Seaman 2/C Jim Fax went over the side into a raft and, paddling furiously in the swirling surf, reached the beach, where they made the long line fast. Two more rafts, each carrying about six men, were launched into the churning water, the sailors paddling and pulling themselves and the rafts along the line to the beach, where Seaman Edward Bergeron climbed the cliff and went for help. Several men manned the rafts again, hoping to pull them back through the wild surf to the destroyer to rescue more of the crew, but the line became tangled and had to be parted. Fearful of the flimsy-looking rafts, the *Truxtun's* men lowered the sturdier gig but, pounded by the sea into the ship and onto the shoals, the boat was quickly smashed and sunk.

Across the cove, some of the *Pollux's* men, using lines, tried to swim through the maelstrom to the small beach beneath the promontory off the starboard bow, but no one made it. Finally, Lieutenant Russ Garnaus and four men boarded the motor whaleboat and started for the shore; bouncing and skittering on the heaving crests of foamy water, nearly capsizing several times, the boat made it to the beach, where the men fastened a line. But it proved impossible to use the line to ferry rafts back and forth between ship and beach because the forward section of the *Pollux* had been weakened and there were shards of steel and wooden wreckage in the water that would have punctured the rafts. The *Pollux's* sailors then rigged out the forward 10-ton cargo boom with a volunteer perched precariously on it out over the turbulent water, but the boom was not long enough to reach the promontory. The ship steadily listed to starboard, and cargo nets were flung over her port side. When her list reached about 25 degrees, and it appeared that she would soon capsize, her skipper gave those men who wanted to try and reach shore by swimming or by clinging to pieces of floating wreckage permission to go over the side. About ninety men elected to go into the water. But with the bulkhead of the forward engine room still holding, the ship abruptly ceased listing, and the captain forbade any more men to enter the water.

Ashore, Seaman Bergeron struggled two miles across the bleak, snowy countryside and came upon a mining camp, where he was offered help for his shipmates.

In the cove, the old *Truxtun* was breaking in half at her after engine room. Suddenly, she began to arch to starboard in a list even steeper than that of the *Pollux*. The line on her forecastle could no longer be worked; men clustered cheerlessly near the forecastle, on the bridge, on the well deck, at the galley deckhouse. Water was flooding the forward engine room and the firerooms "at a great rate"; the boilers and generators were secured, the machinery spaces abandoned. Lieutenant Commander Hickox realized his ship was doomed but, as his surviving officers remembered, he sought to avert panic by remaining calm and not displaying "the least anxiety or fear." At last accepting the desperation of their plight, about nine men decided to chance the surf and managed to paddle two more rafts to the beach; most of the crew chose to remain on the capsizing destroyer as long as possible rather than risk the heaving, icy water and the sharp, green-black rocks of the cove. Finally, on the sharply canted bridge of the foundering destroyer, Hickox ordered the word passed that all who wanted to risk swimming to the beach had permission to do so. Some men went over the side; most did not. By noon, the *Truxtun* lay on her side; her smashed after part was broken off. The men still on her side moved their hands and stamped their feet to try to keep warm. The seas continued to pound the wreck into the rocks. Waves and the lurching of the ship swept sailors off the side and into the swirling water; those who remained flung ammunition boxes into the maelstrom to assist the men who had been driven off. The ship began to break apart anew, this time at her #3 funnel. The blows of the sea pushed and jolted men off the side of the hull until only three remained. The *Truxtun* broke into a third section.

By afternoon, about a hundred men from the mining camp appeared on the cliffs above and began to help the few spent and oil-covered men on the little shelf of beach near the destroyer to climb to the top. There was nothing they could do for the two hundred men of the *Truxtun* and *Pollux* who were in the water.

The *Truxtun's* sailors, although lacking vigorous leadership and reluctant to leave the illusory safety of their ship until the last extremity, were brave men. As one of them recalled: "The conduct of officers and crew could not have been surpassed. . . . There was no panic or hysteria and all orders were carried out promptly and enthusiastically. The spirit of the men was exceptionally high up until the time the ship actually turned on its side and the seas began washing them off, but even then they showed no fear and seemed calmly resigned to fight their way in until the very end." But as so often for the Atlantic sailors, courage was not enough. Most of the swimmers died.

The nearest land was only 60 yards away, but the powerful tide pushed the men in the water straight in toward the high, sheer cliffs, despite their increasingly arm-weary attempts to swim toward the beach. So steep were the cliffs that the enervated swimmers could not gain a handhold and pull themselves up to safety; the water was too deep to give them sufficient leverage to push themselves up. The strong backwash soon swept most of those who managed to reach the cliffs back out to sea.

The water was paralyzingly cold and thick with oil. The numbed sailors quickly became exhausted from trying to swim in the "tar-like" coating; blinded by oil, retching and sputtering, they struggled with decreasing vigor in the rough seas. The bodies of both the living and the drowned were flung repeatedly against the rocks and bloodied and bruised until sucked away, torn and crushed. Most of the destroyermen died in the water, some, like Ensign H.W. Taylor, while deliberately swimming back out into deeper water to try to help shipmates in worse condition. A few of the strongest swimmers, choking, exhausted, and slimy with oil, came near enough to the little beach to be pulled ashore through the blasting surf by rescue teams of earlier survivors.

The *Pollux's* swimmers were luckier. The tide swept them in nearer the small beach off the supply ship's bow, and perhaps more than 20 percent of them reached the shore. Storekeeper 3/C Alfred Dupoy scaled the cliff, then jumped down to a narrow, rocky projection that jutted into the sea not far from his ship. Sailors from the *Pollux* tried to reach Dupoy with a heaving line but, the line-throwing gun having been lost in the flooded armory, they had to throw by hand and the line fell short. Then, using light cord with a weight on the end, they managed to reach Dupoy with a thin line. Dupoy fastened the cord, and a sailor, dangling above the icy, white-laced waves, swung over from the ship, bringing a much stronger line. A bosun's chair was then rigged from the ship to the ledge of rock—just in time. For, at last, the sturdy bulkhead of the forward engine room collapsed and the ship began to flood aft and to list more sharply to starboard. In an hour and a half, all the men still aboard the *Pollux* were brought to shore in the bosun's chair.

The survivors, many of them spent and bruised, huddled in wet, chilled misery on three narrow patches of sand and rock—Dupoy's ledge, the beach under the promontory reached by the swimmers from the *Pollux*; and the beach across the cove reached by a few of the *Truxtun*'s men. The incoming tide would soon sweep across the narrow wedges of land.

At about 1430, a dory that the local men had lugged overland from the town of St. Lawrence rescued the three numb men still clinging to the *Truxtun*'s side. Newfoundlanders and American sailors from the base at Argentia, who later joined the rescue, worked to drag the survivors off the ledges of beach and shoal and up the almost vertical cliffs. The sailors were hauled up, one at a time, by lines secured to their waists. Dangling from lines along the sides of the cliffs, the civilian rescuers kept the ropes around the sailors from fouling and prevented them from snagging on sharp outcroppings of rock. The dory was almost swamped as it worked along the beaches, the local men dragging the last of the live swimmers from the frothy surf.

Heavy seas lashed against the shore. On Dupoy's ledge, several men disappeared, washed soundlessly off the rocky shelf by pounding waves to perish in the black, icy water unnoted by their dazed and weary shipmates. One of the first survivors to reach the cliff top, Lieutenant Jim Boundy, of the *Pollux*, was everywhere at once as he worked tirelessly to haul men to safety. Once, when he saw that some of the weary able-bodied were lingering too long near the warmth of a small, bright fire, he prodded them back to the edge of the cliffs to help drag up and care for their shipmates. Everyone remembered a tough chief off the minesweeper *Brant* who went down to the diminishing beach and remained there for four hours as the black sea advanced, securing lines about men too stunned or weak to save themselves. Alone in the rising water, he worked until everyone had been lifted to safety.

Despite high winds and bitter cold, the people of the nearby towns of Lawn and St. Lawrence turned out to assist. They helped remove the sailors to the mining camp, where the oil was washed from their bodies and their injuries were treated. In the morning, the able-bodied walked the four miles into St. Lawrence; the others were carried there on horse-drawn sleds. There was no local hospital, so the serious cases were boarded in private homes. As one sailor said: "The people were poor but they outfitted survivors with blankets, warm clothes, boots, fed them, cleaned them up as best they could and turned them in in their own beds. None would even listen to offers to pay for food and clothing expended." The seafaring Newfoundlanders knew what it was to lose ships and men to the wild winter ocean.

Only forty-two of the *Truxtun*'s men lived through the last ordeal of their old destroyer. There were a hundred and thirty-two survivors from the luckier *Pollux*. Approximately two hundred and twelve men died, until then the Atlantic Fleet's largest single casualty list of the war. High seas prevented the recovery of all but a few bodies; exposure and the battering they took amongst the rocks made only perhaps a half-dozen of these identifiable. Lieutenant Commander Hickox was identified by his Academy class ring. Many of the bodies had no identification tags, and the loose and improper way in which their life jackets were tied indicated a need for stricter life-saving drills, as did the reluctance of the crews to take to the rafts and too passive leadership in organizing the men for escape, harsh legacies of inexperience.

Dreadful weather conditions off Newfoundland, the fallibility of human judgment and technology, and inexperience created the tragedy. Had navigation and communication between ships been better, radar more advanced, and had the uncertain shore been approached more cautiously, it might have been averted; more training might have mitigated it. Its legacy was improved vigilance, for it was a grim reminder that, in the North Atlantic, danger lurked, even in well-traveled courses; and complacency was the predecessor of grief.

The Navy requested appropriations for a hospital for the people of Lawn and St. Lawrence, but labor and materials being in short supply, it could not be built until after the war. And then, the flag that flew over the hospital site as construction went on was the one that had flown atop the USS *Truxtun* on the last day of her eventful life.[1]

And so, fittingly, it was the cold, gray ocean, and not the enemy below, that brought a parting agony and frustration to the fleet and men who bore its name.

33.

Phoenix

AND SO THE ATLANTIC FLEET found no glory in its cold, rough ocean, as it fought a phantom foe in lonely battles on stormy seas to shape a legacy of knowledge and pride for better-favored successors.

Monotonous steaming and the nebulous contacts of escort and antisubmarine warfare operations brought out such unglamorous, plodding qualities as steadiness, endurance, tenacity, the product of endless, grim, grinding routine. The public would never deem the prosaic Atlantic operations inspiring and decisive, as were the great carrier battles and fierce torpedo-gunnery clashes of the Pacific War; nor, in truth, did the sailors, who preferred the more dangerous, but also more exciting and prestigious, Pacific duty. Nevertheless, the men of the U.S. Atlantic Fleet, Mr. Roosevelt's Navy, were, of all Americans, the first to fight in World War II; and despite U-boats and the stormy winter ocean, the ships of the Atlantic Fleet won a quiet and vital triumph. They brought the convoys through and, in Mr. Roosevelt's phrase, delivered the goods.

During and immediately after the undeclared war, the men and ships of the Atlantic Fleet brought about 2,500 vessels and thousands of ground troops across the ocean in safety; only eight vessels and no soldiers were lost while in their care. They lost four of their own ships and about 375 of their men to the U-boats and the sea, the cost of their education at war.

In the years that followed, the Atlantic Fleet steamed in triumph in the waters of the enemy. It brought the Army into battle until no landing ground on the shores of Fortress Europa was safe from its amphibious task forces. Its hunter-killer antisubmarine task groups stalked the U-boats until no patrol area was safe from its gray warships and blue-gray planes. The Atlantic Fleet's ships and planes destroyed 115 U-boats at the cost of 1 escort carrier, 6 destroyers, 4 destroyer-escorts, and 5 cutters.

The tale of how this was done is another, a different, and a better-known story. That it was done attests to the skill, dedication, and courage of the men who remained in the Atlantic after the summer of 1942. Tough and astute sailors with experience at war, they taught and led a willing band of newcomers to forge a fighting fleet and, at last, to shape proud legends out of the muted battles and endless patrols of their cold, gray ocean. It was they who endured long enough to learn how to prevail and thus avenge those who died in the grim time of learning.

And so, in much more than a ballad, the men of the Atlantic Fleet remembered the old *Reuben James*, whose sailors never knew of the victory at sea by a fleet that never heard the tunes of glory.

Abbreviations

AdminHist	Administrative History
AFLant	Air Force, Atlantic Fleet
AR	Action Report
ASW	Antisubmarine Warfare
AtRon	Atlantic Squadron
BB	Battleship
BatDiv	Battleship Division
BatFor	Battle Force
C	Commander
CincLant	Commander-in-Chief, Atlantic Fleet
CINCUS	Commander-in-Chief, U.S. Fleet
CNO	Chief of Naval Operations
CO	Commanding Officer
COA	Classified Operational Archives
Com	Commander
ComAtRon	Commander, Atlantic Squadron
CruDiv	Cruiser Division
DD	Destroyer
DesDiv	Destroyer Division
DesFlot	Destroyer Flotilla
DesLant	Destroyers, Atlantic Fleet
DesRon	Destroyer Squadron
DGFP	*Documents on German Foreign Policy*
DirFltTrng	Director of Fleet Training
Flex	Fleet Landing Exercise

FMD	Fleet Maintenance Division
HX	Halifax Convoy
Lant	Atlantic Fleet
LC	Library of Congress
Momp	Mid-Ocean Meeting Point
NA	National Archives
NDL	Navy Department Library
NOB	Naval Operating Base
ON	Westbound Convoy
OpTrngLant	Operational Training Command, Atlantic
OpHist	Operational History
PatFor	Patrol Force
PatRon	Patrol Bomber Squadron
PBY	Catalina Patrol Bomber
PHA	*Pearl Harbor Attack* Hearings
PhibLant	Amphibious Force, Atlantic Fleet
PhibLantTrng	Amphibious Training Command, Atlantic
SC	Sydney Convoy
ScoFor	Scouting Force
SOPA	Senior Officer Present Afloat
SouLantFor	South Atlantic Force
SubDiv	Submarine Division
SupFor	Support Force
TF	Task Force
TG	Task Group
TU	Task Unit
TransDiv	Transport Division
TrngDtchmt	Training Detachment
USNavForEur	U.S. Naval Forces, Europe
USNIP	*U.S. Naval Institute Proceedings*

Notes

PROLOGUE
The President Defines the Problem
1. Harold L. Ickes, *The Secret Diary of Harold L. Ickes*, II, *The Inside Struggle, 1936-1939*, 274-279 and *passim*; John M. Blum, *From the Morgenthau Diaries*, I, *Years of Crisis, 1928-1938, 488-498* and *passim*.

2. Capt. Tracy Kittredge, USNR, "United States-British Naval Cooperation, 1940-1945," MS, 37-39, Appendix, 18, and *passim*, COA; US 79th Cong, *Hearings . . . Pearl Harbor Attack*, Pt. 9, 16, *Passim*; Ladislas Farago, *The Tenth Fleet*, 135-137 and *passim*; Samuel Eliot Morison, *History of U.S. Naval Operations in World War II*, I, *The Battle of the Atlantic, Sept. 1939-May 1943, 206-207* and *passim*; Int, RearAdm. Henry C. Fitz, USN, (Ret.), 14 July 1965; Letter, Capt. V.C. Havard, USN, (Ret.), June 1964; L. Pratt, "The Anglo-American Naval Conversations of January 1938, *International Affairs*, Oct. 1971.

PART I — EARLY DAYS IN THE ATLANTIC
Bending the Pencil
1. Annl Rpt, SecNav, 1939-1941, COA; Int, RearAdm. Thomas J. Hickey, USN (Ret.), 19 July 1965; Kendall Banning, *The Fleet Today*, 27, 33, and *passim*; Lt. James Kirkpatrick, USN, "Promotion for Enlisted Men," *USNIP*, Jan. 1932, 15; Capt. George F. Cottle, (MC) USN, "The Turn-over of Personnel," *USNIP*, March 1939, 379-382; Cdr. George C. Dyer, USN, "Promotion Systems — Past, Present, and Future," *USNIP*, Feb. 1940.

2. Ltrs. RearAdm. Sherman R. Clark, USN (Ret.), June-Aug. 1964.

3. Clark Ltrs; Kirkpatrick; Cottle; Dyer; Gen. Curtis E. LeMay, USAF (Ret.), with Mackinley Kantor, *Mission With LeMay*, 76-77.

4. Clark Ltrs; LtCdr. Joel Newsom, USN, "Results Vs Training," *USNIP*, Jan. 1939; RearAdm. Bryson Bruce, USN (Ret.), "Natural Competition," *USNIP*, Aug. 1948, 1367-1371.

5. Clark Ltrs.

6. ComDDsBatFor to DirFltTrng, 9 Feb.1938, Records of the Fleet Training Div., NA, RG 38, Box 216; Clark Ltrs; Annl Rpt, SecNav, 1938-1940, COA; Lt. Franklin G. Percival, USN (Ret.), "Peace-Time Artificiality," *USNIP*, Dec. 1934; Cdr. C.S. Arthur, USN, "A Real Solution for the Paperwork Quandary," *USNIP*, Oct. 1947, 1185-1190; Capt. Walter Strohbehn, USN, "Should We Train Ships or Men?" *USNIP*, July 1950; Newsom; Dyer; Cottle.

7. Newsom, 21.

8. ComDDsBatFor to ComDesFlot 2, 17 Aug. 1938, ComDesRon 3 to DirFltTrng, 25 Feb. 1938, ComDDsBatFor to DirFltTrng, 3 Apr. 1939, NA, RG 38, Boxes 216, 219, 244.

9. ComBBsBatFor to DirFltTrng, 13 Nov. 1937, NA, RG 38, Box 219; ComCruisersScoFor to DirFltTrng, 19 July 1938, NA, RG 38, Box 216.

10. ComCruisersScoFor to DirFltTrng, 20 July 1938, NA, RG 38, Box 217.

11. ComBBsBatFor to DirFltTrng, 24 Mar. 1938, NA, RG 38, Box 216.

12. ComDDsBatFor to CINCUS, 25 Feb. 1938, ComDDsBatFor to CNO, 1 Mar. 1938, NA, RG 38, Boxes 217, 219; Memo, CNO to ComAtRon, 24 June 1941, Records of the Atlantic Squadron, NA, RG 313, Box 4; FltAdm. William F. Halsey, USN (Ret.), and J. Bryan III, *Admiral Halsey's Story*, 46.

13. ComDDsBatFor to CINCUS, 25 Feb. 1938, NA, RG 38, Box 217.

14. Cdr. Ralph C. Parker, USN, "An Analysis of the Air Menace," *USNIP*, May 1932; LtCdr. Russell M. Ihrig, USN, "A Pass Defense for the Battle Line," *USNIP*, Aug. 1937; LtCdr. Logan C. Ramsey, USN, "Aerial Attacks on Fleets at Anchor," *USNIP*, Aug. 1937; *infra*, "A Mirror to War: Fleet Problem XX."

15. Parker, 649-662.

16. ChiefBuAir to CNO, 31 July 1940, NA, RG 313, Box 2; ComAircraft to ComAtRon, 15 June 1940, ComBatFor to CINCUS, July 1940, Cinc-Lant File, Folder A4-1/VA, COA; *supra*, Note 14.

17. ComDesRon 2 to DirFltTrng, 9 Mar. 1938, ComCruisersBatFor to Dir-FltTrng, 7 July 1938, CINCUS to CNO, 15 Oct. 1938, NA, RG 38, Box 218, ComDesFlot 1 to DirFltTrng, 12 Mar. 1939, NA, RG 38, Box 243; LtCdr. Buford Rowland, USN, and Lt. William Boyd, USNR, *U.S. Navy Bureau of Ordnance in World War II*, 219-259.

18. ComAircraftBatFor to DirFltTrng, 12 July 1938, NA, RG 38, Box 217.

19. Memo, CNO to ComAtRon, 24 June 1941, NA, RG 313, Box 4.

20. ComAircraftBatFor to DirFltTrng, 28 June 1938, NA, RG 38, Box 217; ChiefBuAir to CNO, "Analysis of Aircraft Carrier Operations," July 1940, #4001, CNO File, Folder A4-3A, COA.

21. LtCdr. A.B. Vosseller, USN, "The Patrol Plane and the Future," *USNIP*, Nov. 1940.

22. Cdr. David D. Lewis, USN, *The Fight for the Sea*; W.J. Holmes, *Undersea Victory*; ViceAdm. Kurt Assmann, GN (Ret.), *Deutsche Seestrategie in Zwei Weltkriegen*; Capt. Stephen W. Roskill, RN, *The War at Sea, 1939-1945*, I, *The Defensive*; Morison, I; Farago; Roskill, *A Merchant Fleet in War, 1939-1945, The Navy at War, 1939-1945*.

23. Fitz Int; Clark Ltrs; Narrative of Exercise 5, FP XX Folder 1, NA, RG 38, Box 76; "Escort of Convoy Bulletin," 1941, CNO File, Folder A4-3/FF, COA; ASW Critiques, Tenth Fleet Files, COA; "Preparation for Convoy Duty," "Instructions for ASW, Surface Craft," 1941-1942, Tenth Fleet Files, Cabinet 2, COA; Farago; Holmes; Lewis; Morison, I.

24. Gen1Bd to SecNav, 23 May, 22 Oct. 1940, Memos, DirFltTrng to DirFMD, 1939-1940, Records of the Fleet Maintenance Div., Carton 373, Folders 1, 3, COA; various Serials, Records of the General Board, 1938-1940, COA; FltAdm. Ernest J. King, USN (Ret.), *Fleet Admiral King*, 298-300, 446-448; Lt. J. Lodeman, USN, "A New Type for the Navy," *USNIP*, June 1932; Lewis; Roskill, I; Farago, Ch VI; Morison, I.

25. CTG 24.7 to ComUSNavForEur, 26 Nov. 1942, "ASW—Strategical Analysis," Tenth Fleet Files, Cabinet 4, Drawer 2, Item 20, COA; "The Tactical Parameters in Underseas Warfare," Tenth Fleet Files, Cabinet 2, COA; CNO to ComDDsBatFor, 29 Dec. 1941, CNO File, Folder A16-3(17), COA; LtCdr. Leonard Doughty, USN, "The Effect of Depth Charges on Submarines," *USNIP*, Mar. 1935; Cdr. William A. Read, USN, "Anti-Submarine Measures, Old and New," *USNIP*, May 1941; John M. Ide, "Sonar, Secret Weapon of the Sea," *USNIP*, Apr. 1947; Maurice Prendergast, "Sonar and Asdic, Anti-Submarine Sisters," *USNIP*, Aug. 1948; Rowland, 131-155; Lewis; Farago.

26. ComDesFlot 1 to DirFltTrng, 29 Jan. 1938, NA, RG 38, Box 221; *infra*, Note 30.

27. CINCUS to CNO, 3 Feb. 1938, ComDDsBatFor to DirFltTrng, 18 July 1938, NA, RG 38, Box 221; DirNavComm to DirFltTrng, 2 July 1940, CincLant File, Folder A5-2, COA; CNO to CINCUS, 15 Oct. 1940, FMD, Carton 374, Folder 16, COA; Fitz Int; Farago.

28. ComDesDiv 21 to CNO, 9 Mar. 1938, NA, RG 38, Box 221.

29. CINCUS to CNO, 3 Feb. 1938, ComDesDiv 21 to CNO, 9 Mar. 1938, ComDDsBatFor to DirFltTrng, 18 July 1938, NA, RG 38, Box 221.

30. ComDDsBatFor to DirFltTrng, 18 July 1938, NA, RG 38, Box 221.

31. ComDDsBatFor to CNO, 22 June 1939, NA, RG 38, Box 247.

32. ComSubDiv 11 to DirFltTrng, 28 Mar. 1941, NA, RG 313, Box 3.

33. ComDesRon 3 to DirFltTrng, 9 Jan. 1940, NA, RG 38, Box 282.

34. Int, RearAdm. Albert C. Murdaugh, USN (Ret.), 26 July 1965.

35. Ltr, Capt. Francis Craven, USN (Ret.), 27 May 1965; Clark Ltrs; Fitz Int; Murdaugh Int; Franklin G. Percival, "Future Naval War," *USNIP*, Dec. 1940; Lt. (JG) Waldo Chamberlain, USNR, "The Tradition of the Offensive in the United States Navy," *USNIP*, Oct. 1941; Holden A. Evans, "Our Muscle-Bound Navy," *Collier's*, 11 June 1938.

36. Newsom, 20.

37. Clark Ltrs.

38. AtRon Courts-martial File, NA, RG 313, Box 25.

39. Ltr. RearAdm. John W. Schmidt, USN (Ret.), 13 June 1965; Hickey Int; Murdaugh Int; Havard Ltr; Clark Ltrs.

A Destroyer for Sadie Hawkins Day

1. Lt. Richard W. Leopold, USNR, "Fleet Organization, 1919-1941," MS, 1-28, COA; "AdminHist, CincLant," MS, 3-11, NDL; Cdr. John D. Alden, USN, *Flush Decks and Four Pipes*, 19; Norman Padelford, "An Atlantic Naval Policy for the United States," *USNIP*, Feb. 1940.

2. Annl Rpts, ComTrngDtchmt, and ComScoFor, 1937-1938, NA, RG 80, 313, Boxes 40, 8; Rpt, Flex 4, Gen. Walter Short, USA, and Umpire Rpts, Flex 4, NA, RG 38, Box 230; "Summarized Results of Shore Bombardment Practices," NA, RG 313, Box 4; "AdminHist, ComPhibLant-Trng," MS, NDL; Gen. Holland M. Smith, USMC (Ret.) and Percy Finch, *Coral and Brass*, 48-85 and *passim*; Hickey Int; Jeter A. Isely and Philip A. Crowl, *The U.S. Marines and Amphibious Warfare*; Cdr. I.E. McMillan, USN, "Gunfire Support Lessons Learned in World War II," *USNIP*, Aug. 1948.

3. Lt. Frederick M. Curran, USNR, "A Naval Reservist's Impressions of a Shakedown Cruise," *USNIP*, Apr. 1939; Jon Atwater, "Deep Sea Collegians," *Current History*, Apr. 1941; Cdr. W.B. Porter, USN, "The Development of a Destroyer Watch Officer," *USNIP* June 1946, 775-778; Schmidt Ltr; Clark Ltrs.

4. "AdminHist, CincLant," MS, 11, NDL; various Memos, SecNav File, 1937-1940, NA, RG 80; Adm. William D. Leahy MS, 1937, LC; Memo, CO USS *Leary*, 10 July 1939, CO USS *Bernadou* to CNO, 17 July 1940, NA, RG 313, Box 2; Deck Log, USS *Texas*, Apr.-May 1939, NA, RG 45.

5. ComAtRon to CINCUS, 7 June 1938, 22 June 1939, NA, RG 313, Box 8; Annl Rpt, ScoFor, June 1937, NA, RG 80, Box 40.

6. CO USS *Arkansas* to BuConRep, 2 March 1939, NA, RG 313, Box 30.

7. ComAtRon to CINCUS, 7 June 1938, 22 June 1939, Annl Rpt, ComTrngDtchmt, 7 June 1938, Annl Rpts, ComAtRon, 1939-1940, Annl Rpt, CINCUS, 1940, NA, RG 313, Box 8; Annl Rpt, ComScoFor, June 1937, NA, RG 80, Box 40; Memo, TrngDtchmt, 14 Mar. 1938, June 1937, NA,

RG 80, Box 40; Memo, TrngDtchmt, 14 Mar. 1938, NA, RG 38, Box 230.

8. Farago, 52-53 and *passim*; Havard Ltr; Fitz Int; Hickey Int; *supra*, Note 7.

9. ComAtRon to CINCUS, 22 June 1939, NA, RG 313, Box 8; *supra* Note 7.

10. Cong. O'Toole to SecNav, and various Memos and Ltrs, 1938, File NY3/L9-3, Memo, Capt. Ingersoll, WPD, 21 Feb. 1938, F.E. Turin to N.R. Hamilton, n.d., File NN1/FF(380106)Y, NA, RG 80; CNO to Cong. Wallgren, 7 June 1939, FMD, Carton 360, Folder 4, COA.

11. Kittredge MS, 42-64, 148-189, and *passim*, COA; Louis Morton, "Germany First: The Basic Concept of Allied Strategy in World War II," OCMH, *Command Decisions*; Maurice Matloff and Edwin M. Snell, *Strategic Planning for Coalition Warfare, 1941-1942*; Mark S. Watson, *Chief of Staff: Prewar Plans and Preparations*.

12. Leahy Papers, MS, 1938, LC; "AdminHist, CincLant," MS, 16-17, NDL.

13. Leahy Papers, MS, 1938, LC; "AdminHist, CincLant," MS, 18-19, NDL; *Morgenthau Diaries*, I, 515-522.

14. "AdminHist, CincLant," MS, 16-19, NDL; ComAtRon to CINCUS, 22 June 1939, NA, RG 313, Box 8.

15. "AdminHist, CincLant," MS, 18-19, NDL.

16. "AdminHist, CincLant," MS, 18-20, NDL; Hickey Int.

A Mirror to War: Fleet Problem XX

1. Typescript MS, "Fleet Problem XX," Records of CINCUS, NA, RG 313, Box 85; various Rpts and Critiques, CO USS *Babbitt* to CINCUS, 28 Feb. 1939, ComSubDiv 15 to CINCUS, 12 Mar. 1939, ComWhiteFor, 15 Mar. 1939, ComAircraftScoFor to CINCUS, 15 Mar. 1939, ComBlack-Flt to CINCUS, 28 Mar. 1939, CO USS *Cushing*, n.d., NA, RG 313, Boxes 85, 86; USFlt OpOrder 13-38, 4 Nov. 1938, NA, RG 313, Box 24; CNO Memo, "Summary and Comments of proposed draft of FP XX," NA, RG 38, Box 258.

2. AtRon Memo, Flex 5-FP XX, 8 Apr. 1939, NA, RG 38, Box 258; Isely, Ch. I; Smith, 48-85; "AdminHist, ComPhibLantTrng," MS, NDL.

3. ComBlackFlt to CINCUS, 28 Mar. 1939, NA, RG 313, Box 86.

4. *Supra*, Note 3.

5. *Supra*, Note 3; Philip Goodhart, *Fifty Ships that Saved the World*, 98 and *passim*.

6. CO USS *Babbitt* to CINCUS, 28 Feb. 1939, NA, RG 313, Box 86.

7. AtRon Memo, Flex 5-FP XX, 8 Apr. 1939, NA, RG 38, Box 258.

8. *Supra*, Note 7.

9. "AdminHist, CincLant," MS, 26-29, NDL; ComAtRon to CINCUS, 22 June 1939, NA, RG 313, Box 8.

Germany: Ships and Strategy

1. Saul Friedlander, *Hitler et Les Etats-Unis, 1939-1941*, Ch. I-II; James V. Compton, *The Swastika and the Eagle*; William E. Dodd and Martha Dodd, *Ambassador Dodd's Diary, 1933-1938*; William Russell, *Berlin Embassy*; Paul Seabury, *The Wilhelmstrasse*.

2. Amb. Dieckhoff to FM, 7 Dec. 1937, Amb. Dieckhoff to StSec, 22 Mar. 1938, *DGFP*, I, 653-656, 696-698, and *passim*.

3. War Diary, German Naval Staff, Sept.-Dec. 1939, COA; ONI, "Fuehrer Conferences on Matters Dealing with the German Navy," 23 Feb. 1940; GrAdm. Erich Raeder, GN (Ret.), *My Life*, 285, 346-347, and *passim*; F.H. Hinsley, *Hitler's Strategy*, 31-59 and *passim*; Hans L. Trefousse, *Germany and American Neutrality, 1939-1941*, 25-42, 83-89; Friedlander, Ch. I-II; Joachim von Ribbentrop, *Memoirs*.

4. OKW Memo, "Intensification of the Sea War," Sept. 1939, C-100, IMT, *Nazi Conspiracy and Aggression*, I, A, 845.

5. Chargé Thomsen to FM, 12 Sept. 1939, GerEmbUS to FM, 1 Oct., 1 Dec. 1939, *DGFP*, VIII, 51, 179-180, 470-471; Hinsley, 131, 141, 169-175, and *passim*.

6. H.R. Trevor-Roper, *Hitler's Secret Conversations, 1941-1944*, Intro; Carl-Axel Gemzell, *Raeder, Hitler und Skandinavien, Der Kampf für Einen Maritimen Operationsplan*; Walter Ansel, *Hitler and the Middle Sea*, Ch. XXIV and *passim*; Raymond Cartier, *Hitler et Ses Généraux*: Helmuth Greiner, *Die Oberste Wehrmachtfuhrung, 1939-1943*; Anthony Martienssen, *Hitler and His Admirals*; Herman Rauschning, *Hitler Speaks*; Alan Bullock, *Hitler*; Adolf Hitler, *Mein Kampf*; Otto Dietrich, *12 Jahre Mit Hitler*; Ernst von Weizsächer, *Memoirs*; Felix Gilbert, *Hitler Directs His War*; Esmonde M. Robertson, *Hitler's Pre-War Policy and Military Plans, 1933-1939*; Paul Schmidt, *Hitler's Interpreter*; Gen. Franz Halder, GA (Ret.), *Hitler als Feldherr*; Gen. Walter Warlimont, GA (Ret.), *Inside Hitler's Headquarters*; GrAdm. Karl Doenitz, GN (Ret.), *Memoirs, Ten Years and Twenty Days*; ViceAdm. Friedrich Ruge, FGN, *Der Seekrieg*; Hinsley, 1-9, 40-42, 52-56, 88-89, 161-169, and *passim*; Raeder; Stefan Possony, "Decision Without Battle," *USNIP*, June 1946; Edward L. Barker, "German Naval Aviation," *USNIP*, July 1950.

7. Herbert Rosinski, "German Theories of Sea Warfare," "Strategy and Propaganda in German Naval Thought," *Brassey's 1940*, 88-101, *Brassey's 1945*, 125-142; Correlli Barnett, "Sailor With a Flawed Cutlass," *The Swordbearers*, 176-195; ViceAdm. Wolfgang Wegener, GN, *Die See-Strategie des Weltkrieges*, 3-17, Ch. III, and *passim*; Adm. Reinhard Scheer, IGN (Ret.), *Germany's High Seas Fleet in the World War*; Assmann, 19-65 and *passim*; Raeder, 44-86 and *passim*; Gemzell; Capt. G. von Koblinski, IGN (Ret.), "The German Navy," *USNIP*, June 1933; LtCdr. J.W. Jamison, USN, "German Naval Strategy of the World War," *USNIP*, Jan. 1939; Waldo Chamberlain, "German Naval Strategy in 1914," *USNIP*, Sept. 1940.

8. ONI Ints, ViceAdm. Kurt Assmann, GN, "Aspects of the German Naval War," "Relations Between the Supreme Command of the German Armed Forces and the Naval War Staff," 1945, COA; Fritz E. Giese, *Die Deutsche Marine, 1920-1945*, 4-30; Gemzell, 28-115, 285-286, and *passim*; Assmann, 116-136 and *passim*; Raeder, 106-265; Martienssen, 3-11; Hinsley, 7-9; Wegener; Doenitz; William A. Weidersheim, "Factors in the Growth of the Reichsmarine, 1919-1939," *USNIP*, Apr. 1941.

9. Edward P. Von der Porten, "German Naval Strategy in the Second World War," MS, NDL; Assmann ONI Ints, COA; Raeder, 270-286; Doenitz, 37-50; Martienssen, 11-15; Gemzell; Assmann.

10. ONI Int, GrAdm. Karl Doenitz, GN, "Essay on the War at Sea," 1945, COA; Assmann ONI Ints, COA; Von der Porten MS, NDL; Doenitz, 18-50 and *passim*; KptzS Karl Doenitz, GN, *Die U-Bootswaffe*; Farago, 24-41, 125-127, 247-251; Martienssen, 4-7; Raeder; Hans Herlin, *Verdammter Atlantik*; C.H. Spilman, "The German Submarine War," *USNIP*, June 1947.

11. Jochen Brennecke, *The Hunters and the Hunted*, 10-12.

12. "Fuehrer Conf," 3 Sept. 1939, "Reflections of C-in-C, Navy, On the Outbreak of War."

PART II—THE NEUTRALITY PATROL
The Long, Bad Days Ahead

1. ComAtRon to CINCUS, 22 June 1939, NA, RG 313, Box 8.

2. Blum, *Morgenthau Diaries*, II, *Years of Urgency, 1938-1941*, 90-91.

3. "AdminHist, CincLant," MS, 30-34, NDL; Goodhart, 98-100 and *passim*; Llewellyn Woodward, *British Foreign Policy in the Second World War*, 39, 83n, and *passim*.

4. "AdminHist, CincLant," MS, 36-41, NDL; RearAdm. Julius A. Furer, USN, *Administration of the Navy Department in World War II*, 184.

5. ComDesRon 10 to ComAtRon, 7 Sept. 1939, DesRon 10 "Status of Armament," 19 Sept. 1939, NA, RG 313, Box 15; AtRon Memo, 24 Oct. 1939, FMD, Carton 371, Folder 7, COA.

6. PatFor Memo, 10 Oct. 1939, NA, RG 313, Box 15.

7. ComDesRon 10 Memo, 25 Oct. 1939, NA, RG 313, Box 14.

8. CNO to ComAtRon, 23 Sept. 1939, NA, RG 313, Box 15.

9. *Supra*, Note 8; Havard Ltr; Hickey Int; RearAdm. John D. Hayes, USN (Ret.), Int, 28 July 1964.

10. ComDesRon 10 Memo, 25 Oct. 1939, NA, RG 313, Box 14; Lt. Frederick Funke to ComAtRon, 19 Sept. 1939, NA, RG 313, Box 15.

11. ComDesRon 31 to ComAtRon, Dec. 1939, ComAtRon to CNO, 16 Jan. 1940, CincLant File, Folder A4-1(2), COA.

12. ComDesRon 30 to CINCUS, 8 Dec. 1939, NA, RG 313, Box 2; CO USS *Ellis* to CNO, 20 Nov. 1939, NA, RG 38, Box 167.

13. Memo, Recommissioned DDs, n.d., FMD, Carton 365, Folder 10, COA.

14. ComAtRon to CNO, 27 Sept. 1939, NA, RG 313, Box 15.

15. *Supra*, Note 14.

16. CNO-Capt. Denfeld Tlphne Convstn, 19 Oct. 1939, NA, RG 313, Box 15; Capt. Denfeld to CNO, 24 Oct. 1939, FMD, Carton 372, Folder 7, COA; PatRon 52 OpOrder 1-40, 3 Aug. 1940, NA, RG 313, Box 23.

17. AtRon Memo, 24 Mar. 1940, FMD, Carton 372, Folder 9, COA; Pat-Wing 5 to C/S AtRon, 6 Nov., 8 Dec. 1939, NA, RG 313, Box 8; various Memos, FMD, Cartons 371, 372, 376, COA, NA, RG 313, Boxes 15, 23; various Deck Logs, AtRon DDs, Sept.-Dec. 1939, NA, RG 45.

18. Ltr, Capt. Francis Craven, USN (Ret.), 24 June 1965; Fitz Int; Hickey Int; Morison, I, 39-42; Frederic Sondern, "Admiral Stark, Ambassador Extraordinary," *Reader's Digest*, Oct. 1944, 41-45; Farago, 90; Maurice Matloff, "Mr. Roosevelt's Three Wars: FDR as War Leader," *The Harmon Memorial Lectures in Military History, #6*; M. Matloff, "Franklin Delano Roosevelt as War Leader," Harry Coles, *Total War and Cold War*, 47-57; William R. Emerson, "FDR," Ernest R. May, *The Ultimate Decision*, 135-153; Kent R. Greenfield, *American Strategy in World War II*, 50-51, 76-79, and *passim*.

19. "AdminHist, CincLant," MS, 46-51, NDL; CNO Memo, Oct. 1939, NA, RG 313, Box 15.

20. "AdminHist, CincLant," MS, 42, NDL.

21. ComAtRon Memo, 15 May 1940, AtRon OpOrder 3-40, West Gulf Patrol, 12 Apr. 1940, FMD, Carton 365, Folders 4, 10, various Memos, FMD, Cartons 365, 372, 375, 376, COA, NA, RG 313, Boxes 8, 15, 23.

22. Hickey Int; Fitz Int; Havard Ltr; Gen. Smith, 68-69.

23. ComAtRon to TG COs, 19 Oct., 27 Nov., 14 Dec., 1940; NA, RG 313, Box 8; BrigGen. R.E. Rowell, USMC, Attache' Rpt, 9 Feb. 1940; AlNav Dsptchs, AtRon Memos, FMD, Cartons 365, 371, Folders 7, 9, 372, 375, Folder 1, COA; USS *Tuscaloosa* Memo, 20 Nov. 1939, NA, RG 313, Box 8, Memos, Boxes 8, 15, 23; David Irving, *The Rise and Fall of the Luftwaffe*, 54.

24. CO USS *Borie*, Narrative of Events, 3-9 Oct. 1939, ComCruDiv 7 to ComAtRon, 19 Oct. 1939, NA, RG 313, Box 2.

25. CO USS *Twiggs* to ONI, 26 Dec. 1939, NA, RG 313, Box 15; G.H. Gill, *The Royal Australian Navy, 1939-1942*, 132.

26. Woodward, 83n; Winston S. Churchill, *The Second World War*, I, *The Gathering Storm*, 513-514, 529, and *passim*.

27. ONI Memo, 16 Dec. 1940, NA, RG 313, Box 15; Von der Porten MS, 59, NDL; Jochen Brennecke, *Schwarze Schiffe Weite See, Die Geheimnisvollen Fahrten Deutsche Blockadebrecher*.

28. Ickes, *Diary*, II, 709; Brennecke, 71-94, 115.

29. ONI Memo, 16 Dec. 1940, NA, RG 313, Box 15; AlNav Msges, Memos, FMD, Carton 375, Folders 1-7, Carton 376, Folders 7, 8, COA;

Msge, OpNav to ComAtRon, 20 Oct. 1939, NA, RG 313, Box 2, Memos, Boxes 2, 8, 15, 23; Brennecke, 63-67, 71, 91, 173, Epilogue, and *passim*; Friedlander, 65.

30. ComDesRon 2 to ComPatFor, 23 Nov. 1940, NA, RG 313, Box 23; CNO Memo, Oct. 1939, NA, RG 313, Box 15.

31. Ltr, RearAdm. Paul F. Dugan, USN (Ret.), 11 Aug. 1965; Deck Log, USS *Tuscaloosa*, 19 Dec. 1939, NA, RG 45; "AdminHist, CincLant," MS, 54-56, NDL; *Columbus* File, FMD, Carton 375, Folder 2, COA; Brennecke, 162-170; *Time*, 1 Jan. 1940, 22, 27.

32. Msge, CNO to USS *Tuscaloosa*, 20 Dec. 1939, FMD, Carton 375, Folder 2, COA; *Time*, 1 Jan. 1940.

33. CO USS *Philip* to CO 7th NavDist, 21 Dec. 1939, NA, RG 313, Box 8; Msges, FMD, Carton 375, Folder 2, COA; Friedlander, 67.

34. ComDesRon 2 to ComPatFor, 23 Nov. 1940, NA, RG 313, Box 15, Memos, Rpts, Boxes 8, 15, 23; AtRon Memo, 24 Mar. 1940, FMD, Carton 371, Folder 9, Memos, Msges, Carton 375, Folders 1-7, Carton 376, Folders 7-8, COA.

35. ComDesRon 10 to C/S AtRon, 28 Mar. 1940, NA, RG 313, Box 1.

36. ComDesRon 10 Memo, 25 Oct. 1939, NA, RG 313, Box 14; ComDDs-AtRon to DirFltTrng, 27 Aug. 1940, ComAtRon to DirFltTrng, 25 July 1940, Rpt, CO USS *Breckinridge* to DirFltTrng, 8 Aug. 1940, NA, RG 38, Boxes 269, 275; Schmidt Ltr; Clark Ltrs.

37. Ltr, RearAdm. John W. Schmidt, USN (Ret.), 15 May 1965.

38. *Supra*, Note 37.

39. Schmidt Ltrs; Clark Ltrs; Havard Ltr; Hickey Int; Murdaugh Int; Cdr. W.B. Porter, USN, "The Development of a Destroyer Watch Officer," *USNIP*, June 1946, 775-778.

40. ComDesRon 31 to ComPatFor, 22 Nov. 1940, NA, RG 313, Box 1.

41. *Supra*, Note 40.

42. ComDDsPatFor to ComPatFor, 14 Dec. 1940, NA, RG 313, Box 1.

43. ComDesRon 31 to ComPatFor, 22 Nov. 1940, ComDDsPatFor to ComPatFor, 14 Dec. 1940, NA, RG 313, Box 1; AtRon Memo, 4 June 1940, CincLant File, COA.

44. ComPatWing to ComAtRon, 6 June 1941, CincLant File, Folder A4-1/VA, COA.

45. ViceAdm. Charles A. Lockwood, USN (Ret.) and Col. Hans C. Adamson, USAF (Ret.), *Through Hell and Deep Water*, 85.

46. BritNavAttaché to CNO, 24 Nov. 1939, FMD, Carton 367, Folder 10, COA.

47. Rpt, Bd of Investigation, USS *Ranger*, 17 Jan. 1940, NA, RG 313, Box 25; ComAircraft to ComAtRon, 15 June 1941, CincLant File, Folder A4-1/VA, COA.

48. Adm. Lockwood, 82.

49. ComTransAtRon to ChiefBuNav, 31 Oct. 1940, NA, RG 313, Box 28.

50. File, Bd of Investigation, Grounding of USS *Yarnall*, 5 Jan. 1940, NA, RG 313, Box 15.

51. "AdminHist, CincLant," MS, iii-iv, 1, 6-11, 30-34, and *passim*, NDL; Kittredge MS, 6-10, 13, and *passim*, COA; Robert J. Quinlan, "The United States Fleet: Diplomacy, Strategy, and the Allocation of Ships, 1940-1941," in Harold Stein, *American Civil-Military Decisions*, 155-190; William L. Neumann, "Franklin Delano Roosevelt: Disciple of Admiral Mahan," *USNIP*, July 1952; Frances Perkins, *The Roosevelt I Knew*, 4-5, 33, 97-99, 163-164, and *passim*; Louis W. Koenig, *The Presidency and the Crisis*, 43 and *passim*; ViceAdm. Ross T. McIntire, USN (Ret.), with George Creel, *White House Physician*, 82-83, 118, and *passim*; William E. Livezey, *Mahan on Sea Power*, *passim*; William E. Rigdon with James Derieux, *White House Sailor*, *passim*; Matloff; Emerson; Greenfield.

52. Farago, 42-43; "AdminHist, CincLant," MS, 46-50, NDL.

53. War Diary, German Naval Staff, Sept.-Dec. 1939, COA; Trefousse, 25-52, 83-89, and *passim*; Friedlander, Ch. I-III; Raeder, 167, 346-347, and *passim*; Hinsley, 55-59 and *passim*; Ruge, 128-129 and *passim*; Martienssen; Doenitz; David D. Mercer, "Experiences of A Naval Port Director, 1939-1945," *USNIP*, Feb. 1950.

54. Kittredge MS, 13, 76-78, 193, 207-209, and *passim*, COA; Quinlan, 178; Matloff; Emerson; Perkins; Farago.

55. War Diary, German Naval Staff, 15 Sept., 7 Nov. 1939, COA.

A Blue Flag at Ivigtut

1. Goodhart, 27.

2. Kittredge MS, 158-164, COA.

3. CO USS *Quincy* to CNO, 20 June 1940, CNO File, Folder A4-5(1)EF73, COA; "AdminHist CincLant," MS, 68-70, NDL.

4. "AdminHist, CincLant," MS, 68-70, NDL.

5. Memos, Duggan to Welles, Welles to FDR, 31 May, 1 June 1940, *ForRelsofUS, 1940*, V, 1147-1155.

6. Adm. Stark to FDR, 2 June 1940, *ForRelsofUS, 1940*, V, 1155-1156.

7. Welles to FDR, 3 June, 19 July 1940, *ForRelsofUS, 1940*, V, 1157, 1165; "AdminHist, CincLant," MS, 68-70, NDL.

8. CNO, DivPanAmAffs, "Reports of Bilateral Staff Conversations, 1940-1942," NA, RG 38, Box 1; *ForRelsofUS, 1940*, V, 167-170 and *passim*.

9. "AdminHist, CincLant," MS, 72-74, NDL; Morison, I, 30-32; Havard Ltr; Hayes Int; Schmidt Ltrs.

10. "AdminHist, ComGreenlandPat," MS, 2-7, "AdminHist, CincLant." MS, 129-133, NDL; USCG, "The Coast Guard at War, Greenland Patrol," 2-8; Brennecke, 34; William L. Langer and S. Everett Gleason, I, *The Challenge to Isolation, 1937-1940*, 429-433, 683-687; Capt. R.T. Merrill, USCG, "The Role of the Coast Guard Within the Navy,"

USNIP, Aug. 1946; Earl P. Hanson, "Should We Buy Greenland?" *Harper's*, May 1940.

11. "AdminHist, ComGreenlandPat," MS, 6-20, "AdminHist, CincLant," MS, 129-134, NDL; USCG, "Greenland Patrol," 8-10; Deck Logs, USCGC *Duane*, USCGC *Northland*, USCGC *Campbell*, May-Dec. 1940, NA, RG 26; LtCdr. Charles Moran, USNR, "From Greenland's Icy Mountains," *USNIP*, Sept. 1940; Walter Davenport, "Defense on Ice," *Collier's*, 12 Apr. 1941.

12. Kittredge MS, 81, 94-107, 120-147, 168-176, 302-310, and *passim*; Watson, 114 and *passim*; Matloff and Snell, 12-15 and *passim*; Stetson Conn and Byron Fairchild, *The Framework of Hemisphere Defense*, I, *USA in WWII*, *WestHem*, 37-39 and *passim*; Forrest C. Pogue, *George C. Marshall*, II, *Ordeal and Hope, 1939-1942*, Ch. III-IV; L. Morton, *passim*.

13. *Supra*, Note 12; L. Morton, 20.

14. Kittredge MS, 13, 64-71, 108-119, 168-176, 191-192, 207-214, 245-261, 302-304, and *passim*, COA.

15. Kittredge MS, 186-188, 212-242, 384-399, 472-474, and *passim*, COA; Rpts, USNavAttache'London, Spring 1940-Spring 1941, CNO and CincLant Files, Folders A8-2, COA; "AdminHist, ComUSNavForEur," MS, 1-16 and *passim*, NDL; ViceAdm. Charles A. Lockwood, USN (Ret.), *Down to the Sea in Subs*, *passim*; Matloff and Snell, 28-31; Ltr, ViceAdm. Bernard L. Austin, USN, 18 Aug. 1965.

16. Kittredge MS, *Supra*, Notes 14, 15.

17. *USinWorldAffairs, 1940*, 83-113; *Hearings*, House-Senate Naval Affairs Committees, 73rd Cong, 3rd Sess, 1940, *passim*; William D. Puleston, "Strategy With a One-Ocean Navy," *Atlantic*, Dec. 1940; John T. Flynn, "Can Hitler Invade America?" Hanson Baldwin, "The Naval Defense of America," and "If England Falls — *What of The British Fleet?*" *Reader's Digest*, Apr., June, Aug., 1941.

18. *DocsonAmForRels, July 1939-June 1940*, 56-65.

19. FDR to Mrs. J. Borden Harriman, 9 Jan. 1940, FDR, *Personal Letters*, III, Pt 2, 986.

20. "AdminHist, CincLant," MS, 68-72, NDL; CNO, DivPanAmAffs, Staff Conversations, NA, RG 38, Box 1.

21. Goodhart, 42-43, 86-92, and *passim*; Churchill, *Second World War*, II, *Their Finest Hour*, 22-25, 142-143; Ickes, *Diary*, III, *The Lowering Clouds, 1939-1941*, 186; Robert E. Sherwood, *Roosevelt and Hopkins*, I, 213-214; Conn and Fairchild, I, 51-62.

22. Ickes, *Diary*, III, 199-200.

23. Churchill, *Second World War*, III, *The Grand Alliance*, 145-146, 188-189, 399-407; Goodhart, 37-38; Woodward, 80.

24. "AdminHist, ComUSNavForEur," MS, *passim*, NDL; Rpts, USNavAttache'London, Summer 1940, CNO and CincLant Files, Folders A8-2, COA; Kittredge MS, 191, 222, and *passim*, COA.

25. Ickes, *Diary*, III, 233-234; Memo, FDR to Knox, 22 July 1940, FDR, *Letters*, III, Pt 2, 1050-1051.

26. Ickes, *Diary*, III, 283; Captain Dudley W. Knox, USN, "Some Naval Aspects of the War Debt Question," *USNIP*, May 1932; Goodhart, 100, 147.

27. Ickes, *Diary*, III, 283, 291-294; *Morgenthau Diaries*, II, 177-182; Churchill, III, 399-415; Goodhart, 158-177; Memo, Cabinet Meeting of 2 Aug. 1940, FDR, *Letters*, III, Pt 2, 1050-1051; *DocsonAmForRels*, July 1940-June 1941, 207-214; Woodward, 80-89; Eugene C. Gerhart, *America's Advocate: Robert H. Jackson*, 214-220; Conn and Fairchild, I, 51-62.

28. Kittredge MS, 190-206 and *passim*, COA; Hicket Int; Hayes Int; Fitz Int; War Diary, USNavAttachéBerlin, 3 Sept. 1940, CNO, Naval Attachés' Rpts, ONI, NA, RG 38, Box 1.

29. War Diary, USNavAttachéBerlin, 3 Sept. 1940, CNO, Naval Attachés' Rpts, ONI, NA, RG 38, Box 1.

30. Goodhart, 159-160, 180-191; *Supra*, Note 27.

Ceremonies Appropriate to a Neutral Nation

1. "AdminHist, ComDesLant," MS, 1-6, NDL; ComDesLant Memo, 7 Sept. 1940, FMD, Carton 373, Folder 4, COA; AtRon Memo, 4 June 1940, CincLant File, COA; Hickey Int.

2. ComDDsPatFor to CNO, 13 Dec. 1940, "Final Rpt on Transfer . . . " NA, RG 313, Box 2; "AdminHist, ComDesLant," MS, 6-14; Hickey Int; Cdr. Walter Karig, USNR, *Battle Report*, II, *The Atlantic War*, 15; *New York Times*, 5-7 Sept. 1940.

3. AdminHist, ComDesLant," MS, 7-14, NDL.

4. ComDDsPatFor to CNO, 13 Dec. 1940, NA, RG 313, Box 2.

5. ComDDsPatFor to CNO, 13 Dec. 1940, NA, RG 313, Box 2; ComDes-Lant Memo, 7 Sept. 1940, Memos, Rpts, FMD, Carton 373, Folder 4, COA; AR, ComDesDiv 62, 20 June 1941, Serial 65, COA; Hickey Int; Craven Ltrs; Hayes Int; Fitz Int; Karig, II, 15-24; John Fernald, *Destroyer from America*, 3-38 and *passim*; Cdr. Alden, 21-25; Farago, 159; Goodhart, 193-214; Daniel S. Greenberg, "U.S. Destroyers for British Bases — Fifty Old Ships Go to War," *USNIP*, Nov. 1962; Cdr. Donald I. Thomas, USN, "The Four-Stackers," *USNIP*, July 1950; Ens. Howard Kay, USN, "The Fifty Old Maids Come Through," *USNIP*, Sept. 1950.

6. ComPatForDDs to CNO, 13 Dec. 1940, NA, RG 313, Box 2; Fernald; Goodhart; *Supra*, Note 5.

7. Greenberg, 70-83; Goodhart, 239-231; Cdr. Alden, 23-26 and *passim*.

8. Rpt of Bd of Experts on Naval and Air Bases . . . " FMD, Carton 367, Folder 1, COA; "AdminHist, CincLant," MS, 78-79, 90-97, "AdminHist, ComCaribbean," MS, *passim*, NDL; BuYds & Docks, *Building the Navy's Bases in World War II, passim*; Watson, 477-485; LtCdr. Ephraim

R. McLean, USN, "The Caribbean — An American Lake," *USNIP*, July 1941; Lawrence and Sylvia Martin, "Outpost #2: The West Indies, Our New Stake in the Caribbean," *Harper's*, Mar. 1941.

9. "AdminHist, CincLant," MS, 78-79, 90-97, and *passim*, NDL.

10. "AdminHist, ComNOBBermuda," MS, 1-13, "AdminHist, ComCaribbean," MS, *passim* NDL; Goodhart, 218-226 and *passim*.

11. "AdminHist, ComNOBBermuda," MS, 1-13 and *passim*, NDL.

12. *Supra*, Note 10; *infra*, Note 13.

13. *ForRelsofUS, 1941*, II 63-82 and *passim*; Woodward, 88; Goodhart, 218-226; John G. Winant, *Letters from Grosvenor Square*, 35-37.

14. War Diary, NOB Bermuda, COA; "AdminHist, ComNOBBermuda," MS, 15-75 and *passim*, "AdminHist, ComCaribbean," MS, 191-193 and *passim*, NDL; BuYds & Docks, *Building the Navy's Bases . . .*, *passim*; Stetson Conn, Rose C. Engelman, Byron Fairchild, *Guarding the United States and its Outposts*, II, *USA in WWII*, *WestHem*, Ch. XIV-XV.

The German Response

1. GerEmbJapan to FM, 10 Sept. 1940, Hitler to Mussolini, 17 Sept. 1940, *DGFP*, XI, 57-58, 104, and *passim*; "Fuehrer Conf," 6 Sept. 1940; Theo Sommer, *Deutschland und Japan*, 208-212, 452-456, and *passim*; Cartier 44; Hinsley, 181; Friedlander, 120-132 and *passim*; FldMrshl. Wilhelm Keitel, GA (Ret.), *Memoirs*, 93-94, 120-122; von Ribbentrop, 142, 150, and *passim*; Gen. Franz Halder, GA, *Kriegestagebuch*, II, 110 and *passim*; William A. Shirer, *Berlin Diary*, 532-537; Galeazzo Ciano, *Diary*, 288; Trefousse, 65-74, 139; John W. Masland, "Japanese-German Naval Cooperation in World War II," *USNIP*, June 1948.

2. OpsEvaluationGroup Rpt #51, "Antisubmarine Warfare in World War II," 1-15, 85, and *passim*, COA; CTG 24.7 to ComUSNavForEur, 26 Nov. 1942, "ASW — Strategical Analysis," Tenth Fleet File, Cabinet 4, Drawer 2, Item 20, COA; War Diary, German Naval Staff, Sept. 1939-Dec. 1940, COA; Von der Porten MS, *passim*, NDL; Assmann ONI Ints, Doenitz, ONI Int, COA; OKW, *Kriegestagebuch*, I, 62E, 73E and *passim*; Doenitz *Memoirs*, 99-117; Herlin, *passim*; Farago, Ch. III; William K. Hancock and M.M. Gowing, *British War Economy*, 209 and *passim*; J.M.A. Gwyer, *Grand Strategy*, III, Part 1, 9 and *passim*; Roskill I, 82-134, 343-365; Harald Busch, *U-Boats at War*, Ch. II; Wolfgang Frank, *Enemy Submarine*, *passim*, and *The Sea Wolves*, 50-95; Cdr. Lewis, Ch. VII-VIII and *passim*; Terence Robertson, *Night Raider of the Atlantic*, *passim*; Heinz Schaeffer, *U-Boat 977*, *passim*; Wolfgang Ott, *Sharks and Little Fishes*, *passim*; Frgtnkptn Werner Hartmann, GN, *Feind Im Fadenkreuz*, *passim*; Kvtnkptn Wolfgang Lueth, GN, and Kptnlt Klaus Korth, GN, *Boot Greift Wieder An!*, *passim*.

3. "Fuehrer Conf," 6, 26 Sept. 1940; War Diary, German Naval Staff, Sept.-Nov. 1940, COA; Von der Porten MS, 118-127 and *passim*, NDL; Ansel, Ch. I-IV; Raeder, 332-339; Gemzell, 223-224 and *passim*; Hinsley,

95-106, esp 97-98; Martienssen, 83-85; Greiner, 152-171.

4. "Fuehrer Conf," 14 Nov. 1940; Von der Porten MS, 118-127, 146-148, and *passim*, NDL; OKW, *Kriegestagebuch*, I, 179; Halder, *Kriegestagebuch*, II, 177-178, 196; Greiner, 152-171; Hinsley, 112-116, 120-122, 126; Martienssen, 94-96, 116-118; Ansel, Ch. I-IV; Friedlander, 154-163; Raeder; Ruge.

5. Hitler to Franco, 17 Sept. 1940, *DGFP*, XI, 93-98.

6. Hitler to Franco, 18 Sept. 1940, Memo, Hitler-Franco Hendaye Meeting, 23 Oct. 1940, FM Memo, n.d., 19 or 20 Nov. 1940, War Diary, Wehrmacht Operations Staff, 8, 10 Dec. 1940, *DGFP*, XI, 106-108, 371-376, 619-623, 816-817; Halder, *Kriegestagebuch*, II, 163; Friedlander, 185-186; Ian Colvin, *Master Spy*, 149.

7. Memo, Montoire Meeting, 24 Oct. 1940, GerEmbFrance to Fm, 1 Nov. 1940, Minute, ChiefDeptNatDef, Wehrmacht OpsStaff, 12 Dec. 1940, *DGFP*, XI, 385-392, 449-451, 860-863; William L. Langer, *Our Vichy Gamble*, 93-96; Friedlander, 186-193.

8. "Fuehrer Conf," 23 Feb., 6 Sept., 14 Nov., 1940; War Diary, German Naval Staff, Sept.-Dec. 1940, COA; Assmann ONI Ints, Doenitz ONI Int, COA; Raeder; Doenitz; Hinsley; Martienssen; Friedlander, Ch. III-IV; Compton, *passim*; ViceAdm. Kurt Assmann, GN (Ret.), "Why U-Boat Warfare Failed," *Foreign Affairs*, July 1950.

9. War Diary, German Naval Staff, June-Sept., Dec., 1940, COA; Halder, *Kriegestagebuch*, II, 49; Ansel, Ch. IV; Hinsley, 89-95, 107-142, esp 131-132; Telford Taylor, *Hitler's Secret Book*, xxiv; Trevor-Roper, Intro; Raeder; Martienssen; Greiner.

A Passage to India

1. "AdminHist, CincLant," MS, 92-93, NDL; Langer, 96-105; CNO to USNavObsvrMartinique, 21 Aug. 1940, CNO File, Folder EF28, COA; Frank Gervasi, "Our Designs on Martinique," *Collier's*, 11 Jan. 1941.

2. ComAtRon to CNO, "Estimate of Situation for Seizure of India I and II," 13 Aug. 1940, ComAtRon to CNO, 31 Oct. 1940, AtRon Plan for Seizure of Martinique, CNO File, Folder A16-3(12), ComAtRon to CNO, 21 Oct. 1940, ComAtRon OpPlan, 2 Nov. 1940, CincLant File, COA; CNO to CincLant, 15 Feb. 1941, FMD, Carton 372, Folder 4, COA; Conn and Fairchild, I, 84-88 and *passim*.

3. "AdminHist, CincLant," MS, 92-93 and *passim*, NDL; Morison, I, 32; Langer, 103-104.

4. Memo, BrigGen. L.T. Gerow, USA, to C/S, USA, 24 Jan. 1941, CNO File, Folder EF, COA.

5. "AdminHist, ComSouLantFor," MS, 3-9 and *passim*, NDL; Schmidt Ltrs; Craven Ltrs.

6. Michael G. Kammen, "Operational History of the Flying Boat, Open-Sea and Seadrome Aspects, Atlantic Theatre, World War II," MS, BuNav Weapons, 78-130, COA; PatFor OpOrder 9-40, 9 Nov. 1940,

FMD, Carton 371, Folder 9, Dsptch, CNO to CincLant, 6 Apr. 1941, FMD, Carton 372, Folder 10, COA.

Plan Dog: Admiral Stark and the "Germany First" Decision

1. FM Memo, 22 Sept. 1940, *DGFP*, XI, 150-152.

2. Kittredge MS, 308-314 and *passim*, COA; Matloff and Snell, 25-27; L. Morton, *passim*; Conn and Fairchild, I, 106-107.

3. Kittredge MS, "Plan Dog," Appendix A, COA; Adm. Stark Testimony, Ltrs, Adm. Stark to Adm. Richardson, 12 Nov. 1940, *PHA*, Pts 5, 16, Pt 14, 971; Watson, 119-123; L. Morton, *passim*; Conn and Fairchild, I, 90-92.

4. Kittredge MS, 247-260, 271-292, 295-296, 309, 315-321, 332-333, 347, 435, and *passim*, COA.

A Memento of a Ghostly Chase

1. "AdminHist, ComDesLant," MS, 26-27, NDL; Murdaugh Int; ChiefBu-Nav to ComAtRon, 4 Sept. 1940, FMD, Carton 373, Folder 4, COA.

2. "AdminHist, ComDesLant," MS, 33, NDL; Adm. Stark to Adm. Kimmel, 10 Feb. 1941, Adm. Nimitz to Adm. Kimmel, 3 Mar. 1941, *PHA*, Pt 5, 2100-2102, Pt 16, 2153-2155; "AdminHist, ComOpTrng-Lant," MS, *passim*, NDL; Memo, FDR to SecNav, 23 Dec. 1940, FDR, *Letters*, III, Pt 2, 1088-1089.

3. WestGulfPat OpOrder 1-40, 10 Nov. 1940, CNO File, Folder A4-3(5), Memos, Dsptchs, Msges, FMD, Carton 375, Folders 6, 7, COA; War Diary, German Naval Staff, Nov. 1940, COA; Brennecke, 204-229.

4. Narrative, USS *Plunkett*, 15-16 Nov. 1940, CO USS *McCormick* to ComDesDiv 63, 20 Nov. 1940, CNO File, Folder A4-3(5), COA; Deck Logs, USS *Plunkett*, USS *McCormick*, USS *Broome*, USS *Simpson*, Nov. 1940, NA, RG 45.

5. War Diary, German Naval Staff, 1 Dec. 1940, COA.

6. Trefousse, 41.

7. Deck Log, USS *Sturtevant*, 8 Dec. 1940, NA, RG 45; Memos, Dsptchs, Msges, FMD, Carton 371, Folder 9, Carton 375, Folder 7, COA.

8. Deck Log, USS *McCormick*, 11 Dec. 1940, NA, RG 45; Memos, Dsptchs, Msges, FMD, Carton 371, Folder 9, Carton 375, Folder 7, COA.

PART III — THE ATLANTIC FLEET
Gentlemen from the Pacific

1. "Fuehrer Conf," 4 Feb. 1941; Ribbentrop to Molotov, 12 Nov. 1940, Dieckhoff Memo, 9 Jan. 1941, various Hitler-Ribbentrop Meetings with European diplomats, Winter 1940-1941, *DGFP*, XI, 1061-1063 and *passim*; Halder, *Kriegestagebuch*, II, 225, Friedlander, 148-157; Ernst Kris, *German Radio Propaganda*, 225-229.

2. Conn and Fairchild, I, 104; Watson, 124-125; Kittredge MS, 435, COA.

3. Adm. King, *passim*; Farago, 82-95 and *passim*; Morison, I, 51n, 114-116; Robert McCormick, "King of the Navy," *Collier's*, 16 Jan. 1943; Gen. Smith, 76-80; Hickey Int; Fitz Int; Schmidt Ltrs; Clark Ltrs; Craven Ltrs; FltAdm. Andrew B. Cunningham, RN (Ret.), *A Sailor's Odyssey*, 466 and *passim*.

4. Adm. Stark to Adm. Kimmel, 13 Jan. 1941, *PHA*, Pt 16, 2144-2145; Adm. King, 308.

5. Adm. King, 311-316; Farago, 82-85, 90.

6. LtCdr. Thomas McWhorter, USN, "Stand and Fight: The Story of a Destroyer in Battle," MS, 1-5, NDL.

7. Adm. Stark to Adm. Kimmel, 13 Jan. 1941, *PHA*, Pt 16, 2144-2145.

8. Murdaugh Int.

9. Kittredge MS, 245-333, *passim*, COA; Watson, 367-382.

10. Kittredge MS, 325-380 and *passim*, COA; "ABC-1" Rpt, 27 Mar. 1941, *PHA*, Pt 15, 1487-1542; Watson, 367-382; Birkenhead, *Life of Lord Halifax*, 521; Langer and Gleason, II, *The Undeclared War, 1940-1941*, 285-289.

11. Farago, 98-101, 159, and *passim*; Cunningham, 471; Rpts, USNav-AttacheLondon, Fall 1940-Spring 1941, CincLant File, Folder A8-2, COA.

12. Kittredge MS, 373-375, COA.

13. "AdminHist, CTF 24," MS, 5-7, NDL; Kittredge MS, 390-391, COA; Conn and Fairchild, I, 104.

14. Fitz Int; Craven Ltrs; Clark Ltrs; "AdminHist, CTF 24," MS, 9-11, "AdminHist, CincLant," MS, 114, NDL; Farago, 97-98, 137-141; Morison, I, 51-53, 85-86; Donald Macintyre, *U-Boat Killer*, 63-68.

15. "AdminHist, ComUSNavForEur," MS, 14-20, 43-59, NDL; Kittredge MS, 393-397, COA; John W. Blake, *Northern Ireland in the Second World War*, 255-298, 335, 397, and *passim*; Morison, I, 53-54.

16. "AdminHist, CincLant," MS, 124-128, NDL; Kittredge MS, 375-381, COA.

17. "AdminHist, ComDesLant," MS, 28-29, 34, NDL; CNO Memo, 24 June 1941, NA, RG 313, Box 4; ComDesRon 31 to DirFltTrng, 22 Jan. 1941, NA, RG 313, Box 6.

18. DDsSupFor OpPlans 2-41 - 11-41, 5, 8, 15, 16, 21, 22, 25 Apr., 9, 22 May 1941, CincLant File, COA; ComSubsLant to SubsLant, 26 May 1941, NA, RG 313, Box 5.

19. Adm. Lockwood and Adamson, 88-90.

20. "AdminHist, ComSouLantFor," MS, 3-15, "AdminHist, CincLant," MS, 242-248, NDL; Fitz Int; Craven Ltrs; Fletcher Pratt, "The South Atlantic—A Diplomatic Campaign," *USNIP*, June 1948; Morison, X, *The Atlantic Battle Won*, xv-xvii, 208; Farago, 190-191 and *passim*.

21. CincLant to Atlantic Fleet, 24 Mar. 1941, Tenth Fleet Files, Cabinet 1, Drawer 5, and CincLant File, COA.

An Order With No Teeth

1. Henry L. Stimson and McGeorge Bundy, *On Active Service in Peace and War*, 367-368; *Morgenthau Diaries*, II, 193; Goodhart, 242-243; Walter Lippmann, "The Atlantic and America," *Life*, 7 Apr. 1941, 86.

2. Ickes, *Diary*, III, 466, 470, 485.

3. Matloff and Snell, 52; Conn and Fairchild, I, 93, 101-104; Stimson, 366-371; Ickes, *Diary*, III, 388-499 and *passim*; *Morgenthau Diaries*, II, 175, 193, 253, and *passim*.

4. OEG Rpt#51, 8-16, Kittredge MS, 406-407, COA; CTG 24.7 to Com-USNavForEur, 26 Nov. 1942, Tenth Fleet Files, Cabinet 4, Drawer 2, Item 20, COA; Roskill, I, 343-344, 362-364, 451-482, and *passim*; Hancock and Gowing, 205; Gwyer, III, Pt 2, 9; Busch, 37-38, 176; Doenitz, 127-182; Ruge, 155-162; RearAdm. W.S. Chalmers, RN (Ret.), *Max Horton and the Western Approaches*, *passim*; William Diebold, "The Wartime Use of Shipping," *Foreign Affairs*, July 1941; Macintyre; Frank, *Sea Wolves*; T. Robertson.

5. Adm. Stark to Adm. Kimmel, 4 Apr. 1941, *PHA*, Pt 16, 2160-2163; Kittredge MS, 406-407, COA; CTG 24.7 to ComUSNavForEur, 26 Nov. 1942, Tenth Fleet Files, Cabinet 4, Drawer 2, Item 20, COA.

6. Kittredge MS, 411-428, COA; "AdminHist, CincLant," MS, 141-143, NDL; Stimson, 368-371; *Morgenthau Diaries*, II, 251; Ickes, *Diary*, III, 483; Sherwood, I, 356.

7. Kittredge MS, 411-416, 425-428, 435, and *passim*, COA; "AdminHist, CincLant," MS, 141-145, NDL; Conn and Fairchild, I, 105-110; Watson, 387-391.

8. Adm. Stark to Adm. Kimmel, 19 Apr. 1941, *PHA*, Pt 16, 2163-2165.

9. Kittredge MS, 425-435, COA; "AdminHist, ComNOBIceland," MS, 8-9, NDL; Stimson, 370-371; Roskill, I; Morison, I, X.

10. Ickes, *Diary*, III, 510-513; *Morgenthau Diaries*, II, 253; Kittredge MS, 441, COA.

11. Ickes, *Diary*, III, 520-523.

12. Stimson, 371; Ickes, *Diary*, III, 523.

13. Stimson, 371.

The Germans: Reckoning With Mahan

1. "Fuehrer Conf," 4 Feb. 1941; War Diary, German Naval Staff, Feb.-Apr. 1941, COA; Ansel, Ch. VI-VII, XXIV-XXV; Greiner, 376-379; Hinsley, 140, 176-184; Friedlander, 178-185; von Ribbentrop, 210.

2. OKW Directive #24, 5 Mar. 1941, *DGFP*, XII, 219.

3. Amb Ott (Tokyo) to FM, 31 Jan. 1941, FM Memo, 23 Feb. 1941, FM to Ott, 24 Feb. 1941, Ott to FM, 27 Feb. 1941, FM Memos, 31 Mar. 1, 4 Apr. 1941, Ott to FM, 5, 11, 15 May 1941, *DGFP*, XI, 1231-1233, XII, 139-151, 154-155, 386-394, 405-409, 453-458, 714-715, 755, 777-780, 820-822; F.W. Deakin and G.R. Storry, *The Case of Richard Sorge*, 223-224;

Langer and Gleason, II, 311-318, 345-354, 471-484; Friedlander, 194-199, 228-241; Hinsley, 176-184; Greiner, 374-385; Trefousse, 91-101; Raeder, 364.

4. Kt.Adm. von Gadow, GN, "Der See- und Handelskrieg," *Deutschland im Kampf*, Apr.-Nov. 1941, esp June, Aug., Nov., 1941; War Diary, German Naval Staff, Mar.-Aug. 1941, COA; Von der Porten MS, 148-152 and *passim*, NDL; Ansel, Ch. XXIV; Hinsley, 194-198, 210-212; Martienssen, 116-118; Assmann, 206; Eugene Stanley, "The Myth of the Continents," *Foreign Affairs*, Apr. 1941; Adolf Halfeld, *USA, Greift in die Welt*, 439-444 and *passim*.

5. FM Memo, 28 Apr. 1941, OKH Memo, 30 Apr. 1941, *DGFP*, XII, 664-666; "Feuhrer Conf," 6 June 1941; Langer, Ch. IV; Langer and Gleason, II, 494-496, 761-767; Greiner, 152-171; Ansel; Warlimont; Hinsley; Raeder.

6. OKH Directive, Plan Isabella, 7 May 1941, *DGFP*, XII, 731-733.

7. FM Memo, 11 May 1941, The Paris Protocols, 27-28 May 1941, *DGFP*, XII, 755-763, 892-900; Langer, Ch. IV; Langer and Gleason, II, 497-510, 761-786; Friedlander, 202-203.

8. FM Memo, 2 June 1941, *DGFP*, XII, 940-952; Langer and Gleason, II, 761-767; Langer, Ch. IV.

9. Langer, 157-160; Friedlander, 202-203; Greiner, 152-171; Hinsley, 112-122, 126; Martienssen, 116-118 and *passim*.

10. Cartier, 246; Possony, 762.

11. Draft, Fuehrer Directive #32, "Preparations for the Time After Barbarossa," 11 June 1941, *DGFP*, XII, 1012-1016; Ansel, Ch. XXIV-XXV; Greiner, 390-392.

12. "Fuehrer Conf," 4 Feb., 18 Mar., 20 Apr., 1941; War Diary, German Naval Staff, Mar.-Apr. 1941, COA; Ritter Memo, 14 Mar. 1941, OKW Memo, 25 Mar. 1941, *DGFP*, XII, 295-296, 363; Doenitz, 183-194; Raeder, 346-347; Busch, 41-44; Friedlander, 187-190, 208-217; Ruge, 128-129; Trefousse, 144.

13. War Diary, USNavAttachéBerlin, 17 Mar. 1941, ONI, NA, RG 38, Box 1.

14. War Diary, German Naval Staff, Mar.-Apr. 1941, esp 18-25 Mar., 20-30 Apr., COA; "Fuehrer Conf," 18 Mar., 20 Apr. 1941; Memo, FM PolDept, 12 Apr. 1941, *DGFP*, XII, 529-530; Doenitz, 183-191; Raeder.

Bread and Butter for Ernie King

1. "AdminHist, CincLant," MS, 159, NDL; FDR to Stimson and Knox, 26 Apr. 1941, FDR, *Letters*, III, Pt 2, 1147.

2. CNO to C/S, USA, 22 May 1941, CNO File, Folder A16-3(10), COA.

3. CincLant OpOrders, May 1941, CincLant File, COA; Memo, AdjGen

William Dick, USA, 10 Feb. 1941, CNO File, Folder A16-3(10), COA; "AdminHist, CincLant," MS, 159-161, NDL; Conn and Fairchild, I, 109.

4. Kittredge MS, 436-439, COA; "AdminHist, CincLant," MS, 160-161, "AdminHist, ComPhibLantTrng," MS, *passim*, NDL; Adm. Stark to Adm. Kimmel, 24 May 1941, *PHA*, Pt 16, 2168-2169; Conn and Fairchild, I, 106-108, 118-120; Ickes, *Diary*, III, 502-503; Robert D. Heinl, *Soldiers of the Sea*, 311; Roskill, I, 380.

5. Estimate of Situation, "Seizure of the Azores," 1 May 1941, CNO File, Folder A16-3, COA.

6. CincLant to CNO, 23 May 1941, CNO File, Folder A16-3, COA; Conn and Fairchild, I, 117-121.

7. CNO Memo, 28 July 1941, CG PhibLant to CincLant, 27 Aug. 1941, C/S PhibLant to CG PhibLant, 4 Oct. 1941, CNO File, Folder A16-3, COA; "AdminHist, Com AFLant," MS, *passim*, NDL; various Rpts, CincLant File, Folder A4-1/VA, COA.

8. Min Huene (Port) to FM, 17, 23 Mar., 20 Apr. 1941, *DGFP*, XII, 300-302, 343-344, 589-590; Halder, *Kriegestagebuch*, II, 177-178; OKW, *Kriegestagebuch*, I, 404; Langer and Gleason, II, 366-371, 514-519, 587-589.

9. Demaree Bess, "American Strategy Pains Portugal," *Saturday Evening Post*, 30 Aug. 1941, 18.

10. C/S PhibLant to CG PhibLant, 4 Oct. 1941, CNO File, Folder A16-3(17), COA; Halder, *Kriegestagebuch*, II, Summer-Fall 1941, *passim*.

11. Langer and Gleason, II, 587-589, 669-670; Morison, X.

12. CNO Memos, OpOrders, Apr.-May 1941, Serials 037312/06538, CNO File, Folder A4-1, COA.

13. CNO OpOrder 12-41, Apr. 1941, CNO File, Folder A4-1, COA; Deck Log, USS *McDougal*, Apr.-May 1941, NA, RG 45; Pat Frank and Joseph D. Harrington, *Rendezvous at Midway*, 29.

14. LtCdr. McWhorter MS, 7-8, NDL; Deck Log, USS *Mississippi*, May-June 1941, NA, RG 45.

15. Craven Ltrs; Deck Log, USS *New Mexico*, May-June 1941, NA, RG 45.

16. Deck Log, USS *Idaho*, May-June 1941, NA, RG 45.

17. CincLant OpOrders, T/Os, Feb.-Oct. 1941, CincLant File, COA.

18. CincLant to CNO, OpOrder TF 1, 2 May 1941, CincLant File, COA; OEG Rpt #51, War Diary, German Naval Staff, May-Aug. 1941, COA; Adm. Stark to Adm. Kimmel, 24 May 1941, *PHA*, Pt 16, 2168-2169; Morison, I; Roskill, I; Doenitz.

19. CincLant to CNO, OpOrder TF 1, 2 May 1941, CincLant File, COA; "Fuehrer Conf," 22 May, 24 June 1941; War Diary, German Naval Staff, May-June 1941, COA; Havard Ltr.

20. War Diary, German Naval Staff, June 1941, COA; Deck Log, USS *Texas*, June 1941, NA, RG 45; Farago, 43; Doenitz, 189-190.

21. "Fuehrer Conf," 22 May 1941; Trefousse, 114-119; Friedlander, 208-217; Hinsley, 169-175; Martienssen, 116-118.

22. "Fuehrer Conf," 24 June 1941; War Diary, German Naval Staff, June 1941, COA; Doenitz, 189-190; Hinsley, 171-173; Farago, 43; Friedlander, Ch. VI; Trefousse; Martienssen.

23. Deck Log, USS *Mississippi*, 3 July 1941, NA, RG 45; War Diary, German Naval Staff, July 1941, COA; *DocsonAmForRels*, IV, 16-22.

24. CTF 2 to CNO, "Surface Patrol Tasks, 26 Apr.-20 Aug.," 9 Sept. 1941, TF 2 OpPl 5-41, 22 July 1941, Adm. Turner Memo, 30 Sept. 1941, CNO File, Folder A4-3, COA; Deck Logs, USS *Ranger*, USS *Tuscaloosa*, USS *Eberle*, USS *Livermore*, USS *McDougal*, USS *Kearny*, Apr.-Oct. 1941, NA, RG 45.

25. LtCdr. Robert John Esslinger, USN, "Narrative," COA; Havard Ltr.

26. LtCdr. McWhorter MS, 18-19, NDL.

27. Murdaugh Int.

28. "AdminHist, ComGreenlandPat," MS, 20-23, NDL; USCG, "Greenland Patrol," 2-6; Irving, 158.

29. "AdminHist, ComGreenlandPat," MS, 32, 36-40, NDL; "OpHist, Flying Boats," MS, 13, COA; Deck Logs, USS *Belknap*, USS *Truxtun*, USS *Broome*, 12 May-19 June 1941, NA, RG 45; CNO to CincLant, 8 May 1941, Dsptch, ComPatWingSupFor to CNO, 8 June 1941, FMD, Carton 367, Folder 1, COA.

30. "AdminHist, ComGreenlandPat," MS, 21-22, 25-28, 33, NDL; USCG, "Greenland Patrol," 16-20, 34-36; Deck Log, USS *Reuben James*, June 1941, NA, RG 45.

31. "AdminHist, ComGreenlandPat," MS, 30-38 and *passim*, NDL; USCG, "Greenland Patrol," 8-12 and *passim*; Deck Logs, USCGC *Northland*, USCGC *North Star*, May-Oct. 1941, NA, RG 26.

32. Cdt USCG Memo, 11 Dec. 1940, USCG File 610, NA, RG 26.

33. "OpHist, Flying Boats," MS, 21-40, COA.

34. Farago, 83.

When the "Nazis" Invaded the New World

1. "OpHist, Flying Boats," MS, 9-12, 17-18, COA; "AdminHist, CTF 24," MS, 4, 32, NDL; Murdaugh Int; H.V. Morton, *Atlantic Meeting*, 93, 110, 120-126; Macintyre, *U-Boat Killer, passim*.

2. ComPatWingSupFor to ComSupFor, 27 May 1941, CNO File, Folder A4-1, COA; "AdminHist, CTF 24," MS, 5-11, NDL.

3. "Fuehrer Conf," 22 May 1941; War Diary, German Naval Staff, May 1941, COA; Raeder, 351-359; Ruge, 166-173; Ludovic Kennedy, *Pursuit, The Chase and Sinking of the Battleship "Bismarck"*; Roskill, I, 395-417;

Von der Porten MS, 130-137 and *passim*, NDL; Capt. Russell Grenfell, RN, *The "Bismarck" Episode*; C.D. Bekker, *Defeat at Sea*, Ch. III.

4. ComPatWingSupFor to ComSupFor, 27 May 1941, Memo, SecSt Hull to Adm. Stark, Rpt of Consul at Halifax, CNO File, Folder A4-1, COA; "OpHist, Flying Boats," MS, 15-16, COA.

5. Dsptch, CTG 4.2, 24 May 1941, FMD, Carton 373, Folder 4, COA; Conf Int, June 1965.

6. "AdminHist, ComGreenlandPat," MS, 28-30, NDL; USCG, "Greenland Patrol," 26-32; Deck Log, USCGC *Northland*, May 1941, NA, RG 26; Kennedy, 116-119; Roskill, I, 395-417; Joseph Schull, *The Far Distant Ships, An Official Account of Canadian Naval Operations in the Second World War*.

7. GtBritAirMin, *Coastal Command*, 13-15; Kennedy, 147, 152-154, 162-163, 183; Karig, II, 33; Roskill, I, 411.

8. Ickes, *Diary*, III, 528.

9. Sherwood, I, 360-362; Samuel I. Rosenman, *Working with Roosevelt*, 283.

The First Shot: The *Niblack* Incident

1. Kittredge MS, 427, COA; "AdminHist, CTF 24," MS 33-35, NDL.

2. ComDesDiv 13 to ComSupFor, 17 May 1941, ComSupFor to CincLant, 17 May 1941, CNO File, Folder A16-3, COA; Ltr, RearAdm. E.R. Durgin, USN (Ret.), 18 June 1965; Deck Log, USS *Niblack*, Apr. 1941, NA, RG 45; "AdminHist, CTF 24," MS, 5-11 and *passim*, NDL; Cdr. Lewis, 158.

3. ComSupFor to CincLant, 17 May 1941, CNO File, Folder A16-3, COA; Durgin Ltr; Deck Log, USS *Niblack*, Apr. 1941, NA, RG 45.

4. War Diary, German Naval Staff, Apr.-July 1941, COA; German Records and U-Boat Logs, Mr. Harry Rilley, COA; CincLant to CNO, 17 May 1941, CNO File, Folder A16-3, COA; Durgin Ltr.

5. Ickes, *Diary*, III, 539-540; Langer and Gleason, II, 520-521.

6. "Rpt, Comm on Naval Affairs . . . 29 July 1941," *DocsonAmForRels*, IV, 88-93.

7. Durgin Ltr; Hayes Int.

8. AR, ComDesDiv 62, 20-21 June 1941, Serials 65, 66, COA.

A Certain Cold Place

1. Ickes, *Diary*, III, 536; Conn and Fairchild, I, Ch V.

2. Adm. Stark to Adm. Kimmel, 24 May 1941, *PHA*, Pt 16, 2168-2169.

3. Kittredge MS, 474-478, COA; Conn, Engelman, Fairchild, II, 395, 459-460, 466-481; Watson, 487-490; Conn and Fairchild, I, 121-129 and *passim*; Langer and Gleason, II, 522-524; "AdminHist, ComNOBIceland," MS, 9 and *passim*, NDL; USMC, *History of U.S. Marine Corps Operations in World War II, I, Pearl Harbor to Guadalcanal*, 38.

4. Conn, Engelman, Fairchild, II, 466-481, 505-506; Kittredge MS, 474-483, COA; Watson, 487-490.

5. Kittredge MS, 479-481, COA.

6. John L. Zimmerman, "The First Marine Brigade (Provisional), Iceland, 1941-1942," 5-6; Maj. M.L. Brown, USMCR, "The United States Marines in Iceland, 1941-1942," passim; Heinl, 311; USMC, I, 37-38; Morison, I, 75.

7. Kittredge MS, 480-483 and passim, COA; Conn, Engelman, Fairchild, II, 466-481; Watson, 487-490.

8. Amy E. Jensen, Iceland, 11-36, 41-44, 56-62 and passim; Donald E. Nuechterlein, Iceland, Reluctant Ally, 1-8; "AdminHist, ComNOB-Iceland," MS, 1-5, NDL.

9. Jensen, 31-318, 320-321; Nuechterlein, 20-26; Morison, I, 74; Roskill, I, 345; "AdminHist, CincLant," MS, 129-131, NDL; "Fuehrer Conf," 20 June 1940.

10. PM Jonasson to FDR, FDR to PM Jonasson, 1 July 1941, DocsonAmFor-Rels, IV, 454-457; Welles Memo, 22 June 1941, BritEmb to StDept, 27 June 1941, ForRelsofUS, 1941, II, 779-782; Ger Chargé Denmark to FM, 17 July 1941, DGFP, XIII, 161-162; Nuechterlein, 27-33.

11. Zimmerman, 6-9; Brown, 3; USMC, I, 38-39; Heinl, 311; "AdminHist, CincLant," MS, 161-165, NDL; Kittredge MS, 479-483, COA; First Marine Brigade OpOrder 1-41, 4 July 1941, CincLant File, Folder A4-3, COA; Time, 21 July 1941, 30.

12. AR, ComTransDiv 2, 22 July 1941, Serial 0100, COA; Deck Logs, USS Charles F. Hughes, USS Plunkett, USS Niblack, USS Gleaves, USS Lea, USS Ellis, USS Bernadou, USS Upshur, USS Buck, USS Lansdale, 22 June-7 July 1941, NA, RG 45; Karig, II, 52-54; Zimmerman, 8-9; Brown, 4; Heinl, 311-312; Morison, I, 74-77.

13. "AdminHist, ComNOBIceland," MS, 15, NDL; War Diary, German Naval Staff, July 1941, COA; Halder, Kriegestagebuch, II, 442-443; Walter Schellenberg, Memoirs, 236.

14. ARs, ComTransDiv 2, 19, 22 July 1941, Serials 098, 0100, COA; Deck Logs, USS Charles F. Hughes, USS Plunkett, USS Niblack, USS Gleaves, USS Lea, USS Ellis, USS Bernadou, USS Upshur, USS Buck, USS Lansdale, 8-22 July 1941, NA, RG 45; "AdminHist, ComNOBIceland," MS, 16-17, NDL; Zimmerman, 10; Brown, 5; Karig, II, 54.

15. Stimson, 372-374; Ickes, Diary, III, 571; SecNav Knox to Mrs Knox, 13 July 1941, Knox Papers, MS, LC; Langer and Gleason, II, 576-578; DocsonAmForRels, IV, 457-458.

16. War Diary, German Naval Staff, 8, 10, 16-18, 20 July 1941, COA; "Fuehrer Conf," 10 July 1941; Etzdorf Memo, 16 July 1941, DGFP, XIII, 102n; Von der Porten MS, 150, NDL; Martienssen, 116-117; Hinsley, 169-175; Trefousse, 116-119; Friedlander, 252-257.

17. Kittredge MS, 545-551, COA; "AdminHist, ComNOBIceland," MS, 27-

29, NDL; CincLant OpPlan 5-41, 15 July 1941, CincLant File, COA; Deck Logs, USS *Tarbell*, USS *DuPont*, July 1941, NA, RG 45.

18. Memo, "Arrival of the 33rd Pursuit Squadron," Fall 1941, CNO File, Folder A16-3(10), COA; Lt. (JG) Donald Hugh Dorris, USN, *A Log of the "Vincennes,"* 81-86; Deck Logs, USS *Wasp*, USS *Overton*, USS *Bainbridge*, USS *Sturtevant*, USS *Niblack*, USS *Hilary P. Jones*, July-Aug. 1941, NA, RG 45; War Diary, German Naval Staff, 12 Sept. 1941, COA; "AdminHist, ComNOBIceland," MS, 27-29, "AdminHist, CincLant," MS, 176-177, NDL; Conn, Engelman, Fairchild, II, 483-484.

19. Zimmerman, 10-15; Brown, 5-7; USMC, I, 41-45; Heinl, 312; Karig, II, 56-58; Conn, Engelman, Fairchild, II, 498-507; Nuechterlein, 34-36; Schmidt Ltrs; Havard Ltr; John Hunt, "U.S. Occupation of Iceland, 1941-1946," PhD Disstn, Georgetown U, 1966; 1stMarBrig OpOrder 1-41, 4 July 1941, CincLant File, Folder A4-3, COA.

20. Zimmerman, 13-16 and *passim*; Brown, 7, 11.

21. ComPatRon 74 to ComPatWing 7, 20 Aug., 2 Sept. 1941, CincLant File, Folder A4-3/VF2, DirFltTrng to CNO, 23 Jan. 1941, CincLant File, Folder A4-1/VA, Rpts, Fall-Winter 1941, CincLant, CNO Files, Folders A4-1, A4-3, COA; "OpHist, Flying Boats," MS, 19-20, 41-45 and *passim*, COA; "AdminHist, ComAFLant," MS, 6-8, 35, and *passim*, "AdminHist, ComNOBIceland," MS, 29-30, NDL; Conn, Engelman, Fairchild, II, 504-507.

22. "AdminHist, CincLant," MS, 212-213, NDL; Deck Log, USS *New Mexico*, Aug. 1941, NA, RG 45.

A Goodly Company

1. Adm. Stark to Capt. Cooke, 31 July 1941, *PHA*, Pt 16, 2175-2177; Kittredge MS, 473-474, 493, 540-546, and *passim*, COA; Conn and Fairchild, I, 128-129.

2. Farago, 52, 67-71 and *passim*, OEG Rpt #51, 8-16 and *passim*, COA; "AdminHist, CTF 24," MS, *passim*, NDL; Macintyre, *Naval War*, 108-121; Roskill, I, 343-344, 451-471; Martienssen, 118; Morison, I, *passim*; Doenitz, *passim*; Jurgen Rohwer, *Die U-Boot-Erfolge der Achsenmachte 1939-1945*, *passim*, William V. Pratt, "Warfare in the Atlantic," *Foreign Affairs*, July 1941; Fletcher Pratt, "The U-Boats Are Coming," *Saturday Evening Post*, 6 Dec. 1941.

3. FM Memo, n.d., prob 23 May 1941, Amb. Ritter Memo, 9 June 1941, *DGFP*, XII, 854-861, 987-988; Trefousse, 89-90; Friedlander, 193; Hinsley, 169-175, esp 173.

4. Ickes, *Diary*, III, 50; Langer and Gleason, II, 578; Kittredge MS, 540-551, COA; "AdminHist, CincLant," MS, 174-176, NDL; Adm. Stark Test, Ltrs, *PHA*, Pts 5, 16, *passim*.

5. "AdminHist, CincLant," MS, 182-187, NDL; Kittredge MS, 540-551, COA; CincLant OpOrders 5-41, 6-41, 15, 19 July 1941, CincLant File, COA; Conn and Fairchild, I, 128-132.

6. Kittredge MS, 545-555, COA; Conn and Fairchild, I, 130-132.

7. FM to Amb. Ott, 28 June 1941, Amb. Ott to FM, 14, 17 July 1941, *DGFP*, XIII, 40-41, 131-134, 158-160; War Diary, German Naval Staff, June 1941, COA; Deakin and Storry, 231; Langer and Gleason, II, Ch. XX; Hinsley, 185-188; Friedlander, 264-276; von Ribbentrop, 159.

8. Ickes, *Diary*, III, 567.

9. Adm. Stark to Capt. Cooke, 31 July 1941, *PHA*, Pt 16, 2175-2177; Kittredge MS, 552, COA; "AdminHist, CIncLant," MS, 143, NDL.

10. Ickes, *Diary*, III, 574.

11. Kittredge MS, 493, 498-510, COA.

12. Kittredge MS, 545-555, COA; Langer and Gleason, II, Ch. XX; Conn and Fairchild, I, 132-333.

13. FDR Memo, Argentia Conf, 23 Aug 1941, James Roosevelt and Sidney Shalett, *Affectionately, FDR*, 334-338; "AdminHist, CincLant," MS, 194-195, NDL; Deck Logs, USS *Augusta*, USS *McDougal*, USS *Madison*, Aug. 1941, NA, RG 45.

14. H.V. Morton, 8, 26-27, 33, 42-43, 50-57, 62-70, 80-85, 89-107, 110, 120, 125-126, 137-140; Sherwood, I, Ch. XVI; Karig, II, 60-64; Churchill, III, 428-430; Morison, I, 69-71; Maj. Russell P. Strange, USAF, "The Atlantic Conference, The First Roosevelt-Churchill Meeting," *USNIP*, Apr. 1953; Theodore A. Wilson, *The First Summit, passim*; FDR to King George VI, 11 Aug. 1941, FDR, *Letters*, III, Pt 2, 1198.

15. Kittredge MS, 482-483, 562-564, COA; H.V. Morton, 144-150 and *passim*; Watson, 400-410; Matloff and Snell, 53-58; Conn and Fairchild, I, 133; Langer and Gleason, II, Ch. XXI.

16. Kittredge MS, 553-588, COA; Sherwood, I, Ch. XVI; Langer and Gleason, II, Ch. XXI; Welles-Cadogan Memo, 9 Aug. 1941, FDR-Churchill Memo, n.d., *ForRelsofUS, 1941*, I, 345-363.

17. Kittredge MS, 553-588, COA; Watson, 401-409; Wilson, Ch. VII, 291-292 and *passim*; Sherwood, I, Ch. XVI; Morison, I, 54-56, 69-71; Matloff and Snell, 53-58; Churchill, III, 441-449; Langer and Gleason, II, Ch. XXI.

18. H.V. Morton, 144-150, 155-160; Churchill, III, 447-449.

19. Friedlander, 260-264; Compton, *passim*.

20. H.V. Morton, 160-168; Zimmerman, 14; Sherwood, I, 443; Churchill, III, 449-450; "AdminHist, CincLant," MS, 204, NDL.

New Man on an Old Ship: the *Greer* Incident

1. AR, DesDiv 61, and Encs, 9 Sept. 1941, ComDesDiv 61 to CincLant, 9 Sept. 1941, Serial 003, COA; German Records and U-Boat Logs, Mr. Harry Rilley, War Diary, German Naval Staff, Sept. 1941, COA; Deck Log, USS *Greer*, Sept. 1941, NA, RG 45; Cdr. Lewis, 161-165; *Marine Rundschau*, III, 1962; Farago, 43-44.

2. AR, DesDiv 61, 9 Sept. 1941, COA; "AdminHist, CincLant," MS, 220-221, NDL.

3. *DocsonAmForRels*, IV, 16-22, 93-99.

4. Kittredge MS, 589-595, COA; Sherwood, I, 449;451; Ickes, *Diary*, III, 608; Langer and Gleason, II, 746-748; Theodore Roscoe, *History of U.S. Destroyer Operations in World War II*, 34.

5. Churchill, III, 517.

6. "Fuehrer Conf," 17 Sept. 1941; War Diary, German Naval Staff, Sept. 1941, COA; OEG Rpt #51, 17-18, COA; Doenitz, 175-178, 183-184, 191-193; Raeder, 285, 346-347, 351-352; Ruge, 128-129, 228-233; Friedlander, 279-283; Hinsley, 169-175; Martienssen, 117-118; Trefousse, 120; Roskill, I, 473-475.

7. War Diary, USS *Belknap*, 14 Sept. 1941, COA.

8. Lt. Dorris, *Log*, 89-90.

9. "AdminHist, CTF 24," MS, 80-81, NDL.

Buck Fever

1. "AdminHist, ComGreenlandPat," MS, 39-44, "AdminHist, CincLant," MS, 223-227, NDL; USCG, "Greenland Patrol," 164-168; Deck Logs, USCGC *Northland*, USCGC *North Star*, Sept. 1941, NA, RG 26; Reg Ingraham, *First Fleet*, 17-22.

2. Conn, Engelman, Fairchild, II, 466-481, 484-494.

3. AR, ComTransDiv 3, 7 Oct. 1941, Serial 0126, CO USS *Truxtun*, to CincLant, 6 Oct. 1941, ComDesRon 31 to CincLant, 18 Oct. 1941, Cinc-Lant File, Folder A16-3, COA; Rpt, PD 3rdNavDist, 25 Sept. 1941, FMD, Carton 372, Folder 4, COA; War Diary, German Naval Staff, Sept. 1941, COA; var Rpts, Tenth Fleet Files, COA; Deck Logs, USS *Idaho*, USS *Truxtun*, USS *Bainbridge*, USS *MacLeish*, USS *Overton*, USS *Reuben James*, USS *Benson*, USS *Niblack*, USS *Hilary P. Jones*, Sept. 1941, NA, RG 45; Lt. Dorris, *Log*, 88-90; LtCdr. McWhorter MS, 15, NDL; Roscoe, 31-32; Conn, Engelman, Fairchild, II, 495-498.

4. Adm. Stark to Adm. Hart, 22 Sept. 1941, *PHA*, Pt 16, 2209-2211.

5. *Supra*, Note 3.

6. AR, ComTransDiv 3, 7 Oct. 1941, Serial 0126, LtCol. William E. Riley, USMC, Rpt on Indigo III, 15 Oct. 1941, COA; Memo, AdjGen, USA, 3 Nov. 1941, CNO File, Folder A16-3(10), Voyage Rpt, USS *Alcyone*, 14 Oct. 1941, CNO File, Folder A4-3/AKss, COA; Conn, Engelman, Fairchild, II, 495-498.

7. War Diary, NOB Iceland, COA; "AdminHist, ComNOBIceland," MS, 41-50, NDL; Memo, AdjGen, USA, 3 Nov. 1941, CincLant to CNO, 28 Aug., 2 Oct., 1941, CNO File, Folders A16-3(10)-A16-3(17), COA; Schmidt Ltrs; Lt. Dorris, *Log, passim*; Zimmerman, 10-15; Brown, 9-11; Morison, I, 77; USMC, I, 41-45; Heinl, 312; Conn, Engelman, Fairchild, II, 498-507; Karig, II, 54-56 and *passim*; Nuechterlein, 34-36 and *passim*; Jensen, 322-325 and *passim*.

8. AR, ComTransDiv 3, 7 Oct. 1941, Serial 0126, COA; Deck Logs, USS *Idaho*, USS *Truxtun*, USS *Bainbridge*, USS *MacLeish*, USS *Overton*, USS *Reuben James*, USS *Benson*, USS *Niblack*, USS *Hilary P. Jones*, 25 Sept.-3 Oct. 1941, NA, RG 45; Wirt Williams, *The Enemy*, 73 and *passim*.

9. "AdminHist, CincLant," MS, 213-217, NDL.

10. "AdminHist, CincLant," MS, 213-217, NDL; Deck Logs, USS *Wasp*, USS *Mississippi*, USS *Vulcan*, Sept. 1941, NA, RG 45; War Diary, German Naval Staff, 26 Sept. 1941, COA.

11. Lt. Dorris, *Log*, 90-96; Havard Ltr; Schmidt Ltrs; "AdminHist, CincLant," MS, 251-252 and *passim*, NDL; Deck Log, USS *Idaho*, Nov.-Dec. 1941, NA, RG 45.

12. Lt. Dorris, *Log*, 97-99; Deck Log, USS *Wasp*, Oct. 1941, NA, RG 45; "AdminHist, CincLant," MS, 213-217, 251-252 and *passim*, NDL.

13. Lt. Dorris, *Log*, 100.

14. War Diary, USS *Belknap*, 30 Sept. 1941, COA.

15. Lt. Dorris, *Log*, 92-93.

16. "AdminHist, CTF 24," MS, 61-78, "AdminHist, CincLant," MS, 183, 213, "AdminHist, ComNOBIceland," MS, 35, NDL; "History of Convoy and Routing," MS, Tenth Fleet Files, COA; OEG Rpt #51, COA; AR, ComDesDiv 62, 20 June 1941, Serial 65, COA; CTG 24.7 to ComUSNav-ForEur, 26 Nov. 1942, Tenth Fleet Files, Cabinet 4, Drawer 2, Item 20, "Preparation for Convoy Duty," "Protection of Convoys," "Naval Shipping Control in Time of War," var Memos, Tenth Fleet Files, Cabinet 2, COA; Kittredge MS, 554, COA; ONI Rpts, 1941, A8 File, NA, RG 313, Box 24; Fitz Int; ViceAdm. Peter Gretton, RN, *Convoy Escort Commander*, *passim*; D.A. Rayner, *Escort*, *passim*; Morison, I, X, *passim*; Cdr. Lewis, *passim*; Farago, *passim*.

17. "AdminHist, CTF 24," MS, 74-75, "AdminHist, ComNOBIceland," MS, 35, NDL; Deck Logs, USS *Mayo*, USS *Plunkett*, 10 Aug.-4 Sept. 1941, NA, RG 45.

18. "AdminHist, CTF 24," MS, 70-71, "AdminHist, CincLant," MS, 290, NDL; Deck Logs, USS *Bernadou*, USS *Lea*, USS *Cole*, USS *Ellis*, USS *Lansdale*, USS *Gleaves*, USS *Charles F. Hughes*, USS *Madison*, Aug.-Sept. 1941, NA, RG 45.

19. COs USS *Tarbell*, USS *McCormick*, USS *McDougal* to ComDesDiv 17, 14, 16, 18 Oct. 1941, CNO File, Folder A16-3, COA; Deck Logs, USS *McDougal*, USS *Tarbell*, USS *McCormick*, Sept. 1941, NA, RG 45.

20. "AdminHist, CincLant," MS, 221, NDL; Schull, 79-86; Roskill, I, 467-470; Churchill, III, 517; CO USS *Gleaves* to ComBatDiv 3, 19 Sept. 1941, CNO File, Folder A16-3, COA; Deck Logs, USS *Gleaves*, USS *Madison*, USS *Lansdale*, USS *Charles F. Hughes*, USS *Overton*, USS *Truxtun*, USS *Bainbridge*, USS *Reuben James*, 15-23 Sept. 1941, NA, RG 45; War Diary, German Naval Staff, Sept. 1941, COA.

21. Adm. Stark to Adm. Hart, 22 Sept. 1941, *PHA*, Pt 16, 2209-2211.

22. CTG 24.7 to ComUSNavForEur, 26 Nov 1942, Tenth Fleet Files, Cabinet 4, Drawer 2, Item 20, "Instructions for ASW, Surface Craft, 1942," Tenth Fleet Files, Cabinet 2, Drawer 2, COA; "Escort of Convoy Bulletin," 3, 10, 27 Nov., 18, 31 Dec. 1941, CNO File, Folder A4-3/FF13, Tenth Fleet Files, COA; Fitz Int; Farago, *passim*.

2<del>.</del>. CNO Memo, 19 Sept 1941, CincLant File, Folder A5/BB, CincLant Rpt, 1941, COA; Schmidt Ltrs; Clark Ltrs; Murdaugh Int; Hickey Int; Havard Ltrs; Craven Ltrs; Fitz Int; Ltr, ViceAdm. Hewlett Thebaud, USN (Ret.), 8 July 1965; LtCdr. McWhorter, MS, *passim*, NDL; Lt. Dorris, *Log*, *passim*; Cdr. Lewis, *passim*; Farago, *passim*.

PART IV—WAR

Admiral Bristol Runs the Milk

1. AR, TU 4.1.1, 1 Oct. 1941, Serial 002299, CNO Rpt, 9 Dec. 1941, Serial 01203816, COA; HX 150 Folder, Tenth Fleet Files, COA; Deck Logs, USS *Ericsson*, USS *Eberle*, USS *Dallas*, USS *Upshur*, USS *Ellis*, 16-26 Sept. 1941, NA, RG 45; Morison, I, 86-88; Farago, 132-133.

2. ON 18 Folder, Tenth Fleet Files, COA; Deck Logs, USS *Gleaves*, USS *Madison*, USS *Lansdale*, USS *Charles F. Hughes*, 23 Sept.-3 Oct. 1941, NA, RG 45.

3. HX 151 Folder, Tenth Fleet Files, COA; Deck Logs, USS *Plunkett*, USS *Kearny*, USS *Livermore*, USS *Decatur*, USS *Greer*, 23 Sept.-3 Oct. 1941, NA, RG 45.

4. ON 20 Folder, Tenth Fleet Files, COA; Deck Logs, USS *Hilary P. Jones*, USS *Niblack*, USS *Benson*, 29 Sept.-9 Oct. 1941, NA, RG 45.

5. HX 152 Folder, Tenth Fleet Files, COA; Deck Logs, USS *Mayo*, USS *Babbitt*, USS *Leary*, USS *Schenck*, USS *Broome*, USS *Salinas*, 29 Sept.-9 Oct. 1941, NA, RG 45; Cdr. Harley F. Cope, USN, *Serpent of the Seas*, 98-103; "AdminHist, CTF 24," MS, 86, NDL.

6. ON 22 Folder, Tenth Fleet Files, COA; Deck Logs, USS *Ericsson*, USS *Eberle*, USS *Dallas*, USS *Ellis*, USS *Upshur*, 6-15 Oct. 1941, NA, RG 45; "AdminHist, CTF 24," MS, 87, NDL.

7. HX 153 Folder, Tenth Fleet Files, COA; Deck Logs, USS *Bernadou*, USS *DuPont*, USS *Lea*, USS *MacLeish*, 6-16 Oct. 1941, NA, RG 45.

8. ON 24 Folder, Tenth Fleet Files, COA; Deck Logs, USS *Plunkett*, USS *Livermore*, USS *Kearny*, USS *Decatur*, USS *Greer*, 11-16 Oct. 1941, NA, RG 45; Gilbert N. Tucker, *The Naval Service of Canada, passim*; Schull, *passim*; Cdr. Lewis, 208, Ch. XIII; Fitz Int; Farago, *passim*; Alan Easton, *50 North, An Atlantic Battleground*, 15, 23, 29, 40, 44, 52, and *passim*; Macintyre, *U-Boat Killer*, *passim*; Morison, I, X, *passim*; War Diary, German Naval Staff, Oct. 1941, COA.

Sailors off the *Kearny*

1. AR. USS *Kearny* and Enclosures, 20 Oct. 1941, AR, USS *Livermore*, 18 Oct. 1941, AR, PatRon 73, 23 Oct. 1941, AR, CTU 4.1.5, 8 Jan. 1942, Serial 001, COA; Cdr. Robert John Esslinger, USN, "Narrative, Rpts, Cdr. John S. Roberts, USN, CO USS *Vulcan*, SOPA Iceland, Oct.-Nov. 1941, COA; Deck Logs, USS *Kearny*, USS *Plunkett*, USS *Livermore*, USS *Decatur*, USS *Greer*, 11-19 Oct. 1941, USS *Vulcan*, Oct.-Dec. 1941, NA, RG 45; Thebaud Ltr; War Diary, German Naval Staff, Oct. 1941, German Records and U-Boat Logs, Mr. Harry Rilley, COA; *Time*, 27

Oct., 10 Nov., 1941, 28-29, 25; Cdr. Lewis, 166-169; Easton, 62-88; Karig, II, 71-76; Morison, I, 92-93; Schull, 87.

2. OEG Rpt #51, 15, 24, 83, and *passim*, COA; War Diary, German Naval Staff, Sept.-Dec. 1941, COA; OKW, *Kriegestagebuch*, I, 62E; Doenitz, 107, 135, 175-178, and *passim*; Roskill, I, 453-482, 473-475, and *passim*.

3. FDR, *Public Papers and Addresses*, X, 438-444; *DocsonAmForRels*, IV, 27-32.

4. Easton, 91.

5. Sherwood, I, 462; *New Republic*, 21 July 1941, 72-73.

6. Sherwood, I, 462-463.

7. Chargé Thomsen to FM, 17 Oct. 1941, *DGFP*, XIII, 652-653.

8. War Diary, German Naval Staff, 18-20 Oct. 1941, COA; Trefousse, 112, 121; Friedlander, 279-283.

9. LtCdr. McWhorter MS, 19, NDL; Schmidt Ltrs.

10. Lt. Dorris, *Log*, 101-102.

11. Adm. King, 345-346.

12. Sherwood, I, 332-333; Quinlan, 178; Emerson, 142; Watson, 360-366; Walter Lippmann, "The Case for a Smaller Army," *Reader's Digest*, Nov. 1941; Ross Collins, "Do We Need A Mass Army?" *Reader's Digest*, June 1941.

13. Adm. Stark to SecSt Hull, 8 Oct. 1941, *PHA*, Pt 16, 2216-2218; Kittredge MS, 598-600, COA.

"Old Sal" at the Windy Corner

1. HX 154 Folder, Tenth Fleet Files, COA; CO USS *Gleaves* to CTU 4.1.2, CO USS *Charles F. Hughes* to CTU 4.1.2, 21 Oct. 1941, COA; Rpts, USS *Algorab*, 25 Oct. 1941, CNO File, Folders A4-3, A16-3, COA; Deck Logs, USS *Charles F. Hughes*, USS *Gleaves*, USS *Lansdale*, USS *Madison*, 12-21 Oct. 1941, NA, RG 45.

2. ON 26 Folder, Tenth Fleet Files, COA; Deck Logs, USS *Mayo*, USS *Babbitt*, USS *Badger*, USS *Leary*, USS *Schenck*, USS *Broome*, 18-30 Oct. 1941, NA, RG 45; Schmidt Ltrs.

3. HX 155 Folder, Tenth Fleet Files, COA; Deck Logs, USS *Roe*, USS *Bainbridge*, USS *Overton*, USS *Truxtun*, USS *Sturtevant*, 18-27 Oct. 1941, NA, RG 45.

4. ON 28 Folder, Tenth Fleet Files, COA; AR, USS *Salinas*, 4 Nov. 1941, AR, USS *Lea*, 3 Nov. 1941, COA; German Records and U-Boat Logs, Mr. Harry Rilley, War Diary, German Naval Staff, Oct.-Nov. 1941, COA; Deck Logs, USS *Salinas*, USS *DuPont*, USS *Bernadou*, USS *Lea*, USS *MacLeish*, USS *Leary*, USS *Babbitt*, USS *Schenck*, USS *Buck*, USS *Ludlow*, 23 Oct.-3 Nov. 1941, NA, RG 45; Cdr. Cope, 103-119; Karig, II, 77-79; "AdminHist, CincLant," MS, 239, NDL.

5. Adm. King, 346.

"Did You Have a Friend on the Good *Reuben James?*"

1. LtCdr. McWhorter, MS, 9-11, NDL; Hickey Int; Adm. Lockwood and Adamson, 72-73, 82-89; Karig, II, 80-81; *Time*, 10 Nov. 1941, 24.

2. HX 156 Folder, Tenth Fleet Files, COA; AR, TU 4.1.3 and Enclosures, 3 Nov. 1941, Serial 23, CTU 4.1.3 to CTF 4, 26 Nov. 1941, CNO File, Folder A16-3, Rpt, USS *Alchiba*, 30 Dec. 1941, CNO File, Folder A4-3/AK22, COA; German Records and U-Boat Logs, Mr. Harry Rilley, War Diary, German Naval Staff, Oct.-Nov. 1941, COA; Deck Logs, USS *Niblack*, USS *Hilary P. Jones*, USS *Benson*, USS *Tarbell*, 23 Oct.-3 Nov. 1941, NA, RG 45, Clark Ltrs; Ltr, Capt. R.E. Webb, USN (Ret.), 18 May 1965; Ltr, Rear Adm. E.R. Durgin, USN (Ret.), 25 June 1965; LtCdr. Griffith B. Coale, USNR, *North Atlantic Patrol*, 10-38; Cdr. Lewis, 171-174; Karig, II, 80-82; Morison, I, 94; Gilbert Cant, *America's Navy in World War II*, 38-39; Harald Busch, *U-Boot auf Feindfahrt*, *passim*; Frank, *SW*, *passim*; Busch, *UBaW*, *passim*; Ott; Herlin; Hartmann.

3. Sherwood, I, 462, 464.

4. Adm. Stark to Adm. Hart, 7 Nov. 1941, *PHA*, Pt 16, 2121.

5. Adm. Kimmel Memo, 26 May 1941, *PHA*, Pt 16, 2233-2238.

6. Ickes, *Diary*, III, 650.

7. War Diary, German Naval Staff, Nov. 1941, COA; "Fuehrer Conf," 13 Nov. 1941; Ciano, 391; Doenitz, 183-193, 204, and *passim*; Ruge, 228-233; Friedlander, 251, 257-259.

8. Havard Ltr.

9. Adm. King, 346.

10. Lt. Dorris, *Log*, 105.

11. LtCdr. McWhorter, MS, 19-20, NDL.

12. Adm. Lockwood and Adamson, 90-91.

13. *Time*, 17 Nov. 1941, 13.

The Halifax Express

1. ON 30 Folder, Tenth Fleet Files, COA; AR, TU 4.1.2, 12 Nov. 1941, Serial 0-97, AR, TF 4, 3 Dec. 1941, Serial 0601, AR, PatRon 73, 6 Nov. 1941, COA; Deck Logs, USS *Charles F. Hughes*, USS *Gleaves*, USS *Madison*, USS *Lansdale*, 30 Oct.-9 Nov. 1941, NA, RG 45.

2. HX 157 Folder, Tenth Fleet Files, COA; AR, USS *Eberle*, 10 Nov. 1941, Serial S-1, Memo, CTU 4.1.1, Dec. 1941, CNO File, Folder A16-3, COA; Deck Logs, USS *Ericsson*, USS *Eberle*, USS *Dallas*, USS *Ellis*, USS *Upshur*, 29 Oct.-9 Nov. 1941, NA, RG 45; Doenitz, 178.

3. ON 31 Folder, Tenth Fleet Files, COA; AR, PatRon 73, 8 Nov. 1941, COA; Deck Logs, USS *Roe*, USS *Truxtun*, USS *Bainbridge*, USS *Sturtevant*, USS *Overton*, 2-15 Nov. 1941, NA, RG 45.

4. HX 158 Folder, Tenth Fleet Files, COA; CTU 4.1.8 to ComSupFor, 18 Nov. 1941, CincLant File, Folder A16-3, COA; Deck Logs, USS *Buck*,

USS *Ludlow*, USS *Swanson*, USS *McCormick*, USS *Cole*, USS *Greer*, USS *Woolsey*, USS *Wilkes*, 2-15 Nov. 1941, NA, RG 45.

5. ON 34 Folder, Tenth Fleet Files, COA; Murdaugh Int; Deck Logs, USS *Benson*, USS *Niblack*, USS *Hilary P. Jones*, USS *Edison*, USS *Tarbell*, 9-22 Nov. 1941, NA, RG 45.

6. Williams, 136, 150.

7. HX 159 Folder, Tenth Fleet Files, COA; CTU 4.1.4 to CTF 4, 24 Nov. 1941, CincLant File, Folder A16-3, COA; Deck Logs, USS *Plunkett*, USS *Livermore*, USS *Decatur*, USS *Cole*, USS *Badger*, USS *Yukon*, 8-20 Nov. 1941, NA, RG 45.

8. ON 35 Folder, Tenth Fleet Files, COA; CTU 4.1.1 to CTF 4, CO USS *Eberle* to CTU 4.1.1, Nov. 1941, CincLant File, Folder A4-3, COA; Deck Logs, USS *Ericsson*, USS *Eberle*, USS *Dallas*, USS *Ellis*, USS *Upshur*, 13-27 Nov. 1941, NA, RG 45.

9. HX 160 Folder, Tenth Fleet Files, COA; AR, CTU 4.1.5, n.d., COA; Havard Ltr; Deck Logs, USS *Mayo*, USS *Nicholson*, USS *Babbitt*, USS *Leary*, USS *Schenck*, 16-29 Nov. 1941, NA, RG 45.

10. ON 37 Folder, Tenth Fleet Files, COA; CTU 4.1.8 to CTF 4, Dec. 1941, CincLant File, Folder A4-3, COA; Deck Logs, USS *Buck*, USS *Swanson*, USS *Ludlow*, USS *Greer*, USS *McCormick*, 21-30 Nov. 1941, NA, RG 45.

11. HX 161 Folder, Tenth Fleet Files, COA; Havard Ltr; Schmidt Ltrs; Fitz Int; Deck Logs, USS *Roe*, USS *Woolsey*, USS *Bernadou*, USS *DuPont*, USS *MacLeish*, USS *Lea*, 22 Nov.-5 Dec. 1941, NA, RG 45; Williams, 70-74, 92-100; QM 2/C James Boyd, USCGR, "Lookout," *Atlantic*, July 1941, 113-119; LtCdr. William Exton, USN, *He's In the Destroyers Now*, 46-50, 87-175.

12. Schmidt Ltrs.

13. Schmidt Ltrs; Havard Ltr; Fitz Int; Lt. Dorris, *Log*, 90-92, and *passim*; William G. Schofield, *Eastward the Convoys*, 143-147, and *passim*.

14. ON 39 Folder, Tenth Fleet Files, COA; CTU 4.1.4 to CTF 4, 8 Dec. 1941, CincLant File, Folder A4-3, COA; Schmidt Ltrs; Deck Logs, USS *Plunkett*, USS *Livermore*, USS *Decatur*, USS *Cole*, USS *Badger*, 26 Nov.-9 Dec. 1941, NA, RG 45.

15. HX 152 Folder, Tenth Fleet Files, COA; AR, TU 4.1.2, 23 Dec. 1941, Serial S-105, COA; Deck Logs, USS *Charles F. Hughes*, USS *Wilkes*, USS *Madison*, USS *Lansdale*, USS *Sturtevant*, 28 Nov.-13 Dec. 1941, NA, RG 45; Cdr. F.M. Curran, USN, "Tales of North Atlantic Gales," *USNIP*, Nov. 1944, 1357-1361.

16. ON 41 Folder, Tenth Fleet Files, COA; Havard Ltr; Deck Logs, USS *Mayo*, USS *Nicholson*, USS *Babbitt*, USS *Leary*, USS *Schenck*, 29 Nov.-14 Dec. 1941, NA, RG 45.

17. Murdaugh Int; LtCdr. McWhorter, MS, 12, NDL; Morison, I, 95-98.

18. Adm. Stark to Adm. Kimmel, 25 Nov. 1941, *PHA*, Pt 16, 2101.

19. Murdaugh Int; Hickey Int.

20. Hickey Int.

21. HX 163 Folder, Tenth Fleet Files, COA; AR, CO PatRon 73, 21 Dec. 1941, COA; Deck Logs, USS *Benson*, USS *Niblack*, USS *Edison*, USS *Hilary P. Jones*, USS *Tarbell*, 4-19 Dec. 1941, NA, RG 45.

22. ON 43 Folder, Tenth Fleet Files, COA; Deck Logs, USS *Roe*, USS *Woolsey*, USS *Bernadou*, USS *Lea*, USS *MacLeish*, Dec. 1941, NA, RG 45.

23. Williams, 234.

Turpentine and Red Roses: Sun-Tanned Atlantic Sailors

1. AR, TF 3, 23 May 1941, Serial 004, COA; "AdminHist, ComSouLantFor," MS, 3-17, NDL; Pratt, 691-696; GerEmbBrazil to FM, 6 Nov. 1941, *DGFP*, XIII, 743-744.

2. ARs, TF 3, 23 May, 4 Sept. 1941, CTF 3 to CincLant, 4 Sept. 1941, CTF 3 to CNO, 11 Nov., 20 Dec., 1941, CincLant File, CNO File, Folders A16-3, A4-3, COA; "AdminHist, ComSouLantFor," MS, 17-23, NDL; "AdminHist, CincLant," MS, 320-321, NDL; Pratt, 692-693.

3. AR, TF 3, 4 Sept. 1941, CTF 3 to CincLant, 4 Sept. 1941, CTF 3 to CNO, 11 Nov., 20 Dec., 1941, CincLant File, CNO File, Folders A16-3, A4-3, COA; "AdminHist, ComSouLantFor," MS, 17-23, NDL; Pratt, 692-694; TF 3 Genl Tactical Doct 1-41, 23 June 1941, CincLant File, Folder A16-3, COA; Dsptch, CNO to CincLant, 15 Nov. 1941, FMD, Carton 374, Folder 3, COA; "AdminHist, CincLant," MS, 318, NDL.

4. AR, TG 3.6, 12 Nov. 1941, CTG 3.6 to CNO, 21 Nov. 1941, and *Odenwald* Rpts, CincLant File, Folder A16-3, COA; "AdminHist, ComSouLantFor," MS, 24-30, NDL; Brennecke, 261-262.

5. CTF 3 to CNO, 20 Dec. 1941, CNO File, Folder A4-3, COA; "AdminHist, ComSouLantFor," MS, 34-36, NDL; Pratt, 693-696.

6. "AdminHist, CincLant," MS, 318, NDL.

7. "AdminHist, CincLant," MS, 318-322, NDL; Pratt, 693-696.

8. Fitz Int; "AdminHist, CincLant," MS, 325-333, NDL; Morison, X, 208-228, and *passim*.

9. "AdminHist, ComSouLantFor," MS, 46-47, NDL; "AdminHist, CincLant," MS, 312-314, NDL.

10. Morison, X, 208-228; Fitz Int; Brennecke, 327, 343, 381, 396, and *passim*.

11. Sherwood, I, 454-455; Churchill, III, 491-493; CT 5 Folder, Tenth Fleet Files, COA.

12. Lt. Dorris, *Log*, *infra*, Note 13.

13. ARs, TF 14, TransDiv 19, 28 Dec. 1941, Serial 016, ARs, USS *West Point*, 10 Jan. 1942, Serial 01, 15 Feb. 1942, Serial 06, 22 Apr. 1942, Serial 012, COA; CNO to ComTransDiv 19, 26 Sept. 1941, CincLant OpOrder 1-41, 1 Nov. 1941, CincLant File, Folder A4-3, COA; Lt. Dorris, *Log*, 107-132; Deck Logs, USS *Ranger*, USS *McDougal*, USS *Wakefield*, USS *West Point*, Nov.-Dec. 1941, NA, RG 45; Morison, I, 109-113.

14. Lt. Dorris, *Log*, 140-144.

15. Lt. Dorris, *Log*, 132-154; ARs, TF 14, TransDiv 19, 28 Dec. 1941, Serial 016, ARs, USS *West Point*, 10 Jan. 1942, Serial 01, 15 Feb. 1942, Serial 06, 22 Apr. 1942, Serial 012, COA; Deck Logs, USS *McDougal*, Dec. 1941, USS *West Point*, USS *Wakefield*, Nov. 1941-Apr. 1942, NA, RG 45; Morison, I, 112-113.

Air Raid Pearl Harbor

1. Zimmerman, 15-16; USMC, I, 45-46; Brown, 11.

2. "AdminHist, CincLant," MS, 272, NDL; Walter Lord, *Day of Infamy*, 130.

3. LtCdr. McWhorter, MS, 22, NDL.

4. Lt. Dorris, *Log*, 124-132, 140-144.

5. Havard Ltr.

6. Thebaud Ltr.

7. Murdaugh Int.

8. Alexander T. Griffin, *A Ship to Remember*, 37-38.

9. Perkins, 379-380; Stimson, 393; Ickes, *Diary*, III, 662-663; John M. Blum, *Roosevelt and Morgenthau*, 425.

10. Capt. Tracy B. Kittredge, USNR (Ret.), "A Military Danger: The Revelation of Secret Strategic Plans," *USNIP*, July 1965.

11. War Diary, German Naval Staff, Dec. 1941, COA; Keitel, 162; Halder, *Kriegestagebuch*, III, 329, 353, and *passim*; Assmann, 161; Raeder, 363-364; Hinsley, 189, 194; Martienssen, 119; Friedlander, 271; Trefousse, 137-147.

12. Assmann ONI Ints, COA; Friedlander, 291-296; Trefousse, 148-153; Martienssen, 119-120; Hinsley, 189, 194; von Ribbentrop, 159; Raeder, 363-364; Ruge, 128-129 and *passim*.

13. "Fuehrer Conf," 12 Dec. 1941; War Diary, German Naval Staff, Dec. 1941, Assmann ONI Ints, COA; Doenitz, 195-224; *DocsonAmForRels*, IV, 618-623; Farago; Hinsley; Martienssen; Trefousse.

14. Kittredge, 730-743.

15. "AdminHist, CincLant," MS, 254-255, NDL.

16. "AdminHist, CincLant," MS, 255-257, NDL; LtCdr. McWhorter, MS, 24-25, NDL; CTF 3 to CNO, 20 Dec. 1941, CNO File, Folder A4-3, COA.

17. "AdminHist, ComPhibLantTrng," MS, Ch. II, 26, Ch. III, 4-14, 22, 29-33, Ch. IV, 13, and *passim*, NDL; Langer, Ch. V-VIII; Matloff and Snell; Watson.

18. Hickey Int; Craven Ltrs; Farago, 82-83, 85, 90-95; Sherwood, I, 201-202 and *passim*; Adm. King, 349-358; Morison, I, *passim*; Adm. Furer, *passim*.

19. "AdminHist, CincLant," MS, 260-261, 268-273, NDL; Havard Ltr; Fitz Int; Hickey Int; Farago, 135-137; Morison, I, 206-207 and *passim*, X, *passim*.

20. "AdminHist, CTF 24," MS, NDL, *infra*, Note 23.

21. "AdminHist, CTF 24," MS, NDL, *infra*, Note 23.

22. "AdminHist, CincLant," MS, NDL, *infra*, Note 23.

23. "AdminHist, CincLant," MS, 260-273, 278-281, "AdminHist CTF 24," MS, 101-119, NDL.

24. "AdminHist, CincLant," MS, 270-271, NDL; Farago, Ch. IV-XIV; Morison, I, *passim*.

PART V—THE LAST CONVOYS
The Winter War

1. HX 164 Folder, Tenth Fleet Files, COA; AR, PatRon 73, 21 Dec. 1941, COA; Deck Logs, USS *Gleaves*, USS *Dallas*, USS *Ellis*, USS *Upshur*, Dec. 1941, NA, RG 45.

2. ON 45 Folder, Tenth Fleet Files, COA; Deck Logs, USS *Wilkes*, USS *Charles F. Hughes*, USS *Lansdale*, USS *Madison*, USS *Sturtevant*, Dec. 1941, NA, RG 45.

3. HX 165 Folder, Tenth Fleet Files, COA; AR, PatRon 73, 28 Dec. 1941; Deck Logs, USS *Buck*, USS *Swanson*, USS *Greer*, USS *McCormick*, Dec. 1941, NA, RG 45.

4. ON 47 Folder, Tenth Fleet Files, COA; Deck Logs, USS *Benson*, USS *Niblack*, USS *Hilary P. Jones*, USS *Edison*, USS *Tarbell*, Dec. 1941, NA, RG 45.

5. HX 166 Folder, Tenth Fleet Files, COA; Deck Logs, USS *Plunkett*, USS *Decatur*, USS *Badger*, USS *Cole*, Dec. 1941-Jan. 1942, NA, RG 45.

6. ON 49 Folder, Tenth Fleet Files, COA; Deck Logs, USS *Gleaves*, USS *Dallas*, USS *Upshur*, USS *Ellis*, Dec. 1941-Jan. 1942, NA, RG 45.

7. Deck Log, USS *Babbitt*, 1 Jan. 1942, NA, RG 45.

8. HX 167 Folder, Tenth Fleet Files, COA; AR, CTU 4.1.5, 8 Jan. 1942, Serial 001, COA; Deck Logs, USS *Mayo*, USS *Babbitt*, USS *Leary*, USS *Schenck*, Dec. 1941-Jan. 1942, NA, RG 45.

9. ON 51 Folder, Tenth Fleet Files, COA; Deck Logs, USS *Buck*, USS *Swanson*, USS *McCormick*, USS *Greer*, Dec. 1941-Jan. 1942, NA, RG 45.

10. HX 168 Folder, Tenth Fleet Files, COA; AR, CTU 4.3.5, 1 Feb. 1942, AR, VP 82, Jan. 1942, COA; Deck Logs, USS *Woolsey*, USS *Bainbridge*, USS *Broome*, Dec. 1941-Jan. 1942, NA, RG 45.

11. ON 53 Folder, Tenth Fleet Files, COA; Schmidt Ltrs; Deck Logs, USS *Plunkett*, USS *Decatur*, USS *Badger*, USS *Cole*, Jan. 1942, NA, RG 45.

12. AR, USCGC *Campbell*, 24 Jan. 1942, COA; War Diary, German Naval Staff, Jan. 1942, COA.

13. HX 169 Folder, Tenth Fleet Files, COA; AR, CTU 4.3.5, 1 Feb. 1942, AR, VP 82, Jan. 1942, COA; Deck Logs, USS *Wilkes*, USS *Madison*, USS *Sturtevant*, Jan. 1942, NA, RG 45; "AdminHist, ComUSNavForEur," MS, *passim*, NDL; Blake, 255-298, 335, and *passim*; Morison, I, 53-54, 119.

14. ON 55 Folder, Tenth Fleet Files, COA; AR, CTU 4.1.5, 15 Jan. 1942, Serial 002, COA; Cdt NOBIceland to CNO, 22 Jan. 1942, Tenth Fleet Files, Cabinet 2, Drawer 4, COA; Havard Ltr; Deck Logs, USS *Mayo*, USS *Babbitt*, USS *Leary*, USS *Schenck*, Jan. 1942, NA, RG 45.

15. HX 170 Folder, Tenth Fleet Files, COA; AR, DesRon 11, 31 Jan. 1942, Serial 07, AR, CTU 4.3.5, 1 Feb. 1942, AR, VP 82, Jan. 1942, War Diary, US NOB Iceland, Jan. 1942, COA; USCG, "The Sinking of the *Hamilton*," COA; War Diary, German Naval Staff, Jan.-Feb. 1942, COA; Deck Logs, USS *Niblack*, USS *Tarbell*, USS *Overton*, USS *Ellis*, USS *Greer*, USS *Yukon*, Jan. 1942, NA, RG 45.

16. ON 57 Folder, Tenth Fleet Files, COA; Cdt NOBIceland to CNO, 22 Jan. 1942, Tenth Fleet Files, Cabinet 2, Drawer 4, COA; Deck Logs, USS *Woolsey*, USS *Bainbridge*, USS *Broome*, USS *Yukon*, Jan.-Feb. 1942, NA, RG 45.

17. HX 171 Folder, Tenth Fleet Files, COA; AR, CTU 4.3.5, 1 Feb. 1942, AR, VP 82, Jan. 1942, COA; Deck Logs, USS *Gleaves*, USS *Dallas*, USS *Cole*, USS *Upshur*, Jan.-Feb. 1942, NA, RG 45.

18. ON 59 Folder, Tenth Fleet Files, COA, Deck Logs, USS *Wilkes*, USS *Madison*, USS *Sturtevant*, Jan.-Feb. 1942, NA, RG 45.

19. HX 172 Folder, Tenth Fleet Files, COA; AR, CTU 4.1.8, 8 Feb. 1942, Serial 005, AR, VP 82, Jan. 1942, COA; Deck Logs, USS *Buck*, USS *Swanson*, USS *DuPont*, USS *McCormick*, Jan.-Feb. 1942, NA, RG 45.

20. ON 61 Folder, Tenth Fleet Files, COA; AR, CTU 4.1.3, 12 Feb. 1942, Serial 5, COA; Deck Logs, USS *Niblack*, USS *Tarbell*, USS *Overton*, Jan.-Feb. 1942, NA, RG 45.

21. HX 173 Folder, Tenth Fleet Files, COA; Deck Logs, USS *Nicholson*, USS *Edison*, USS *Bernadou*, USS *Lea*, Feb. 1942, NA, RG 45.

22. ON 63 Folder, Tenth Fleet Files, COA; Deck Logs, USS *Gleaves*, USS *Dallas*, USS *Upshur*, Feb. 1942, NA, RG 45.

23. HX 174 Folder, Tenth Fleet Files, COA; Deck Logs, USS *Plunkett*, USS *Badger*, USS *Babbitt*, USS *Schenck*, Feb. 1942, NA, RG 45.

24. ON 65 Folder, Tenth Fleet Files, COA; Deck Logs, USS *Swanson*, USS *Buck*, USS *DuPont*, USS *McCormick*, Feb. 1942, NA, RG 45.

25. HX 175 Folder, Tenth Fleet Files, COA; Deck Logs, USS *Mayo*, USS *Decatur*, USS *Leary*, Feb. 1942, NA, RG 45.

"Skipper, She Was Close Enough to Throw Spuds At!"

1. ON 67 Folder, Tenth Fleet Files, COA; Murdaugh Int; German Records and U-Boat Logs, Mr. Harry Rilley, War Diary, German Naval Staff, Feb.-Mar. 1942, COA; Deck Logs, USS *Edison*, USS *Nicholson*, USS *Bernadou*, USS *Lea*, Feb. 1942, NA, RG 45; Rohwer, 80-81.

2. Murdaugh Int.

Saying Good-Bye to it All

1. "AdminHist, CincLant," MS, 277-281, 284-286, 290-295, "AdminHist, CTF 24," MS, 101-119, NDL; SupFor OpPl 2-42, 20 Feb. 1942, CincLant

File, Minutes, Ottawa Conf on Escort Problems, 23-24 July 1942, Tenth Fleet Files, Cabinet 2, Drawer 2, COA; Fitz Int; Schull, 97-101.

2. HX 176 Folder, Tenth Fleet Files, COA; Deck Logs, USS *Benson*, USS *Broome*, Feb.-Mar. 1942, NA, RG 45.

3. HX 178 Folder, Tenth Fleet Files, COA: Deck Log, USS *Gleaves*, Mar. 1942, NA, RG 45.

4. HX 179, Tenth Fleet Files, COA; AR, USS *Bristol*, 23 Mar. 1942, Serial 001, COA; Deck Log, USS *Buck*, Mar. 1942, NA, RG 45.

5. AR, CTU 24.1.4 and Enclosures, 13 Apr. 1942, AR, CTU 21.6.1, 25 Mar. 1942, Serials 014, 0012, COA.

6. ON 69 Folder, Tenth Fleet Files, COA; Deck Log, USS *Plunkett*, Feb.-Mar. 1942, NA, RG 45.

7. ON 75 Folder, Tenth Fleet Files, COA; Deck Logs, USS *Benson*, USS *Broome*, USS *MacLeish*, Mar. 1942, NA, RG 45.

8. AR, USS *Niblack*, 9 Apr. 1942, COA; Deck Log, USS *Niblack*, Mar. 1942, NA, RG 45.

9. War Diary, TF 24, Mar.-May 1942, COA; "AdminHist, CTF 24," MS, 115-116, 120, 129, "AdminHist, CincLant," MS, 295, NDL; Morison, I, 122-125, 304, 317-345; Macintyre, *U-Boat Killer*, 55-67; Farago, 68-69; Cdr. Lewis, 187-188.

10. CTG 24.7 to ComUSNavForEur, 26 Nov. 1942, Tenth Fleet Files, Cabinet 4, Drawer 2, COA; Farago, Ch. VI, XII; Morison, I, X, *passim*.

11. AR, CTU 21.6.1 and Enclosures, 25 Mar. 1942, Serial 0012, COA; "Escort of Convoy Bulletin," 3, 10, 27 Nov., 18, 31 Dec., 1941, CNO File, Folder A4-3/FF13, COA; "Instructions for ASW . . . 1942," Tenth Fleet Files, Cabinet 2, Drawer 2, var Memos, Tenth Fleet Files, Cabinets 2, 4, COA; Morison, I, 122, X, 21-25, 32-54.

12. "AdminHist, CincLant," MS, 308, 460, "AdminHist, ComAFLant," MS, 45, NDL; Fitz Int; Cdr. Lewis, 184-185; Adm. King, 449-451; *supra*, Notes 10, 11.

13. *Supra*, Notes 10, 11, 12; "AdminHist, ComOpTrngLant," MS, Ch. I, XXVIII, NDL.

14. CTG 24.7 to ComUSNavForEur, 26 Nov. 1942, Tenth Fleet Files, Cabinet 4, Drawer 2, COA; Schmidt Ltrs; Fitz Int.

15. Deck Logs, USS *Eberle*, USS *Ludlow*, USS *Ericsson*, USS *Kearny*, Dec. 1941-Jan. 1942, NA, RG 45.

16. War Diary, USS *Texas*, Jan.-Mar. 1942, COA; LtCdr. McWhorter, MS, 26-27, NDL; "AdminHist, ComUSNavForEur," MS, 14-20, 43-59, NDL; Blake, 255-266, 271-273, 291-293, 298; Zimmerman, 16; USMC, I, 45-46.

17. TA 12 Folder, Tenth Fleet Files, COA; AR, CincLant, 5 Apr. 1942, Serial 00162, COA; Deck Logs, USS *Charles F. Hughes*, USS *Hilary P. Jones*, USS *Ludlow*, USS *Roe*, USS *Lansdale*, Feb.-Mar. 1942, NA, RG 45; Zimmerman, 16; Brown, 12; USMC, I, 46; Conn, Engelman, Fairchild, II, 523-527; RearAdm. H.D. Cooke, USN (Ret.), "The Atlantic Convoys," *USNIP*, Aug. 1950.

18. CT 12 Folder, Tenth Fleet Files, COA; ARs, CTU 21.6.1, 25 Mar., 7 Apr., 1942, Serials 0012, 0014, COA; Deck Logs, USS *Swanson*, USS *Nicholson*, Mar.-Apr. 1942, NA, RG 45.

19. AT 14 Folder, Tenth Fleet Files, COA; War Diary, USS *Cole*, Apr. 1942, COA; Deck Logs, USS *Ericsson*, USS *Eberle*, USS *Livermore*, USS *Kearny*, USS *Bernadou*, USS *Cole*, Apr. 1942, NA, RG 45.

20. "AdminHist, CincLant," MS, 259-261, 268, NDL.

21. Lt. Dorris, *Log*, 160.

22. "AdminHist, CincLant," MS, 334-339, NDL.

23. LtCdr. McWhorter, MS, 32-35, NDL; "AdminHist, CincLant," MS, 338-339, NDL; Deck Logs, USS *Plunkett*, USS *Madison*, Mar.-Apr. 1942, NA, RG 45; Morison, I, 168.

24. LtCdr. McWhorter, MS, 36-40, NDL; "AdminHist, CincLant," MS, 342, NDL.

25. LtCdr. McWhorter, MS, 40-45, NDL; "AdminHist, CincLant," MS, 342, NDL.

26. "AdminHist, CincLant," MS, 345, NDL; Morison, I, 167-186; Hickey Int; Fitz Int.

27. "OpHist, Flying Boats," MS, 56-75, COA; "AdminHist, ComNOB-Iceland," MS, 51-53, "AdminHist, ComAFLant," MS, 35, NDL.

28. War Diary, USS *Belknap*, "OpHist, Flying Boats," *supra*, Note 27, *infra*, Note 29.

29. War Diary, USS *Belknap*, Jan.-Apr. 1942, COA; Deck Log, USS *Belknap*, Jan.-May 1942, NA, RG 45; "OpHist, Flying Boats," MS, 58, COA.

30. LtCdr. McWhorter, MS, 45-46, NDL.

A Cold, Black Shore

1. AR, USS *Truxtun*, 20 Feb. 1942, AR, USS *Pollux*, 20 Feb. 1942, AR, USS *Wilkes*, 19 Feb. 1942, AR, SOPA Argentia, 16 Mar. 1942, COA; "AdminHist, CTF 24," MS, 119-120, NDL.

Bibliography

UNPUBLISHED ORIGINAL SOURCES

1. CLASSIFIED OPERATIONAL ARCHIVES, Navy Yard, Washington, D.C.

Records of the Commander in Chief, United States Atlantic Fleet
Records of the Chief of Naval Operations
Records of Support Force, Atlantic Fleet
Records of the Fleet Maintenance Division
Records of the Convoy and Routing Section, OpNav, Tenth Fleet
German Naval Records
Records of the General Board of the Navy
War Diaries, and Ship and Station Records
   USS *Belknap*
   Patrol Squadron 73
   U.S. Naval Operating Base, Bermuda
   U.S. Naval Operating Base, Iceland
   U.S. Naval Operating Base, Londonderry
   USS *Texas*
   USS *Cole*
   USS *DuPont*
   U.S. Naval Operating Base and Air Station, Argentia
   Destroyer Squadron 7

Kriegstagebuch, Seekriegsleitung, War Diary, German Naval Staff

Separate Serials

Originator	Serial	Date
Com., Patrol 2	— , 142	10/3/39, 10/16/39
Com., New England Patrol	146, 156	10/25/39, 11/17/39

485

Originator	Serial	Date
Com., DesDiv 62	65,66	6/20/41, 6/21/41
TF 3	004	5/23/41
Com., BatDiv 3	0449	—
Com., TransDiv 2	098, 0100	7/19/41, 7/23/41
TF 3	0018	9/4/41
Com., DesDiv 61	—	9/9/41
Com., TransDiv 3	0126	10/7/41
LtCol. Wm E. Riley USMC	—	10/15/41
Livermore	046	10/18/41
PatRon 73	—	10/23/41
CTU 4.1.1	002	10/30/41
Lea, CTU 4.1.3	— , 023	11/3/41, 11/3/41
Cdr. J.R. Roberts	—	11/4/41
PatRon 73	— , —	11/6/41, 11/8/41
Salinas	C-91	11/7/41
Eberle	S-1	11/10/41
CTU 4.1.2	097	11/12/41
CTG 3.6	—	11/12/41
Eberle	S-2	11/27/41
CTU 4.1.5	—	—
CTF 4	0601	12/3/41
CNO	01203816	12/9/41
PatRon 73	—	12/14/41
TF 3	0029	12/20/41
Gleaves	027	12/21/41
CTU 4.1.2	S-105	12/23/41
Livermore	432	12/25/41
CTF 14	016	12/28/41
Jacob Jones	S-001	1/5/42
CTU 4.1.5	001, 002	1/8/42, 1/15/42
Campbell	—	1/24/42
Com., DesRon 11	07	1/31/42
Com., DesRon 7	004	1/31/42
SOPA Argentia	081	2/2/42
CTU 4.1.8	005	2/8/42
CTU 4.1.3	5	2/12/42
CincLant	0069	2/16/42
Wilkes	—	2/19/42
Pollux	—	2/20/42
Truxtun	—	2/20/42
CTU 24.6.2	S-11, S-12	3/9/42, 3/11/42
CTU 24.6.4	09	3/16/42
Bristol	001	3/23/42
CTU 21.6.1	0012	3/25/42
CTU 24.6.4	05	3/31/42

Originator	Serial	Date
CTU 24.6.5	004	3/31/42
CincLant	00162	4/5/42
CTU 21.6.1	0014	4/7/42
Niblack	—	4/9/42
CTU 24.1.4	014	4/13/42
CTU 24.6.3	012	4/15/42
CTU 24.6.4	013	4/15/42

Manuscripts
    Annual Reports: Secretary of the Navy, 1937-1941.
                   Chief of Naval Operations, 1939-1940.
                   Commander in Chief, U.S. Fleet, 1939-1940.
                   Atlantic Squadron, 1939-1940.
                   U.S. Atlantic Fleet, 1940-1941.
    Capt. Tracy Kittredge, USNR, "United States-British Naval Cooperation, 1940-1945."
    Bureau of Naval Weapons, Michael G. Kammen, "Operational History of the Flying Boat, Open-Sea and Seadrome Aspects, Altantic Theatre, World War II," 1960.
    Operations Evaluation Group Report #51, Charles M. Sternhill and Alan M. Thorndike, "Antisubmarine Warfare in World War II," 1946.
    Lt. Richard W. Leopold, USNR, "Fleet Organization, 1919-1941," 1945.
    USCG, "Sinking of the *Hamilton*."
    Cdr. Robert John Esslinger, "Narrative."
    ONI Interviews: Vice Admiral Kurt Assmann, "Aspects of the German Naval War" and "Relations Between the Supreme Command of the German Armed Forces and the Naval War Staff."
               Grand Admiral Karl Doenitz, "Essay on the War at Sea."
    "History of Convoy and Routing," Tenth Fleet.

(I would like to acknowledge the efficiency and kindness of the COA personnel, especially Mrs. Mildred Mayeux and Mr. Harry Rilley.)

2. NAVAL RECORDS, NATIONAL ARCHIVES, Washington, D.C.
    Records of the Commander in Chief, U.S. Fleet, Record Group 313.
    Records of the Atlantic Squadron and Patrol Force, Record Group 313.
    Records of the Fleet Training Division, Record Group 38.
    Naval Attaché Reports, Record Group 38.
    Records of the Secretary of the Navy, Record Group 80.
    CNO Division of Pan American Affairs, Record Group 38.
    Records of the U.S. Coast Guard, Treasury Department Branch, Record Group 26.

Correspondence, Commander Battle Force, Record Group 313.

Ships' Deck Logs, Record Group 45.
   U.S. Aircraft Carriers: *Ranger, Wasp*
   U.S. Cruisers: *Augusta, Omaha, Memphis, Tuscaloosa, Vincennes*
   U.S. Battleships: *Arkansas, Idaho, Mississippi, New Mexico, Texas*
   U.S. Auxiliaries: *Albemarle, Belknap, Denebola, Salinas, Vulcan, Wakefield, West Point, Yukon*
   U.S. Destroyers: *Babbitt, Badger, Bainbridge, Benson, Bernadou, Borie, Broome, Buck, Cole, Dallas, Decatur, DuPont, Eberle, Edison, Ellis, Ericsson, Gleaves, Greer, Herbert, Charles F. Hughes, Reuben James, Hilary P. Jones, Jacob Jones, Kearny, Lansdale, Lea, Leary, Livermore, Ludlow, MacLeish, Madison, Mayo, McCormick, McDougal, Niblack, Nicholson, Overton, Plunkett, Roe, Sampson, Schenck, Simpson, Somers, Sturtevant, Swanson, Tarbell, Truxtun, Upshur, Wilkes, Woolsey.*

Ships' Deck Logs, Record Group 26
   U.S. Coast Guard Cutters: *Campbell, Cayuga, Duane, Modoc, Northland, North Star, Raritan*

3. NAVY DEPARTMENT LIBRARY, "Main Navy," Washington, D.C.
   Manuscripts
      "Administrative History, Commander in Chief, Atlantic Fleet."
      "Administrative History, Commander, Destroyers, Atlantic Fleet."
      "Administrative History, Commander, Task Force 24."
      "Administrative History, Commander, Greenland Patrol."
      "Administrative History, Commander, South Atlantic Force."
      "Administrative History, Commander, Naval Operating Base, Iceland."
      "Administrative History, Commander, Naval Operating Base, Bermuda."
      "Administrative History, US Naval Forces, Europe."
      "Administrative History, Caribbean Commands."
      "Administrative History, Caribbean Sea Frontier."
      "Administrative History, Amphibious Training Command, Atlantic Fleet."
      "Administrative History, Commander, Service Force, Atlantic Fleet."
      "Administrative History, Commander, Air Force, Atlantic Fleet."
      "Administrative History, Commander, Fleet Operational Training Command."
      ONI, "Fuehrer Conferences on Matters Dealing with the German Navy."

LtCdr. Thomas McWhorter, "Stand and Fight: The Story of a Destroyer in Battle."

Edward P. Von der Porten, "German Naval Strategy in the Second World War," 1962.

Bureau of Supplies and Accounts, "Special Report on Operations and Organization of the German Naval Supply System During World War II."

Bureau of Ships, "An Administrative History of the Bureau of Ships During World War II."

4. LIBRARY OF CONGRESS, Washington, D.C.

Frank Knox Papers
William D. Leahy Papers

5. LETTERS FROM AND INTERVIEWS WITH ATLANTIC FLEET PERSONNEL

History cannot be written exclusively from official records, and the following officers provided many illuminating tales of the Atlantic sailors and ships during the period of this study. So if this work has the "feel" of "the way it really was" in the Atlantic, it is partly because of these men who were junior officers in 1941.*

Vice Admiral Bernard L. Austin
Rear Admiral Sherman R. Clark
Captain Francis S. Craven
Rear Admiral Paul F. Dugan
Rear Admiral Edward R. Durgin
Rear Admiral Henry C. Fitz
Captain V.C. Havard
Rear Admiral John D. Hayes
Rear Admiral Thomas J. Hickey
Rear Admiral Albert C. Murdaugh
Rear Admiral John W. Schmidt
Vice Admiral Hewlett Thebaud
Captain Richard E. Webb

PUBLISHED PRIMARY AND SECONDARY SOURCES
BOOKS

Alden, John D. *Flush Decks and Four Pipes*. Annapolis: U.S. Naval Institute 1965.

Ansel, Walter. *Hitler and the Middle Sea*. Durham: Duke University Press, 1972.

Arnold, H.H., *Global Mission*. New York: Harper, 1949.

Assmann, Kurt. *Deutsche Seestrategie in Zwei Weltkriegen*. Heidelberg: Kurt Vowinckel, 1957.

*All ranks are U.S. Navy (Retired)

Auphan, Paul, and Mordal, Jacques. *The French Navy in World War II*. Annapolis: U.S. Naval Institute, 1959.

Ballantine, S. Duncan. *US Naval Logistics in the Second World War*. Princeton: Princeton University Press, 1947.

Banning, Kendall. *The Fleet Today*. New York: Funk & Wagnalls, 1940.

Beasley, Norman. *Frank Knox, American*. Garden City: Doubleday, 1936.

Bekker, C.D. *Defeat at Sea, The Struggle and Eventual Destruction of the German Navy, 1939-1945*. New York: Ballantine, 1956.

Berker, Friedrich. *Die Amerikanische Neutralitat Im Krieg, 1939-1941*. Leipzig: Essener Verlags Anstalt, 1943.

Blake, John W. *Northern Ireland in the Second World War*. Belfast: Her Majesty's Stationery Office, 1956.

Blum, John M. *From the Morgenthau Diaries*, vols. 1-2. Boston: Houghton Mifflin, 1959-1965.

——————————. *Roosevelt and Morgenthau*. Boston: Houghton Mifflin, 1970.

Bowen, Harold G. *Ships, Machinery, and Mossbacks, The Autobiography of a Naval Engineer*. Princeton: Princeton University Press, 1954.

Bragadin, Marc' Antonio. *The Italian Navy in World War II*: Annapolis: U.S. Naval Institute, 1957.

Brennecke, Jochen. *The Hunters and the Hunted*. New York: Norton, 1957.

——————————. *Schwarze Schiffe Weite See, Die Geheimnisvollen Fahrten deutsche Blockadebrecher*. Hamburg: Gerhard Stalling, 1958.

Bulkley, Robert J. *At Close Quarters, PT Boats in the United States Navy*. Washington, D.C.: Naval History Division, 1962.

Bullock, Alan. *Hitler*. New York: Bantam, 1953.

Burns, James M. *Roosevelt: The Lion and the Fox*. New York: Harcourt, Brace, 1956.

Busch, Fritz O. *Die Deutsch Kriegsmarine Im Kampf*. Berlin: Tannen, 1943.

Busch, Harald. *U-Boat Auf Feindfahrt, Bilberichte vom Einsatz im Atlantik*. Frankfurt: C. Bertelsmann Guetersloh, 1942.

——————————. *U-Boats at War*. New York: Ballantine, 1955.

Cameron, Ian. *Wings of the Navy, The Story of the Fleet Air Arm in World War II*. London: Hodder & Stoughton, 1962.

Cant, Gilbert. *America's Navy in World War II*. New York: John Day, 1943.

Carter, Worrall R., and Duvall, Elmer E. *Ships, Salvage, and Sinews of War, the Story of Fleet Logistics Afloat in Atlantic and Mediterranean Waters During World War II*. Washington, D.C.: Government Printing Office, 1954.

Cartier, Raymond. *Hitler et ses Généraux*. Paris: Librairie Arthéme Fayard, 1962.

Chalmers, W.S. *Max Horton and the Western Approaches*. London: Hodder & Stoughton, 1954.

——————————————. *Full Cycle, The Biography of Sir Bertram Home Ramsay*. London: Hodder & Stoughton, 1959.

Charles, Roland W. *Troopships of World War II*. Washington, D.C.: The Army Transportation Association, 1947.

Churchill, Winston S. *The Second World War*, Vols. 1-3. Boston: Houghton Mifflin, 1948-1950.

Ciano, Galeazzo. *Ciano's Diary*. London: Heinemann, 1947.

Coale, Griffith B. *North Altantic Patrol*. New York: Farrar & Rinehart, 1942.

Colvin, Ian. *Master Spy, The Incredible Story of Admiral Wilhelm Canaris . . .*, New York: McGraw-Hill, 1951.

Compton, James V. *The Swastika and the Eagle, Hitler, the United States, and the Origins of World War II*. Boston: Houghton Mifflin, 1967.

Conn, Stetson, and Fairchild, Byron. *The Framework of Hemisphere Defense* in *US Army in World War II* Series, *The Western Hemisphere*, I. Washington, D.C.: Office of Chief of Military History, 1960.

Conn, Stetson, Engelman, Rose C., and Fairchild, Byron. *Guarding the United States and its Outposts*, in *US Army in World War II* Series, *The Western Hemisphere*, II, Washington, D.C.: Office of Chief of Military History, 1964.

Connery, Robert H. *The Navy and the Industrial Mobilization in World War Two*. Princeton: Princeton University Press, 1951.

Cope, Harley F. *Serpent of the Seas, the Submarine*. New York: Funk & Wagnalls, 1942.

Craig, Gordon A., and Gilbert, Felix, eds. *The Diplomats, 1919-1939*, II, *The Thirties*. New York: Atheneum, 1953.

Craven, Wesley F. and Cate, James L. *The Army Air Forces in World War II*, I, *Plans and Early Operations*. Chicago: University of Chicago Press, 1948.

Cunningham, Andrew B. *A Sailor's Odyssey*. London: Hutchinson, 1951.

Davis, George T. *A Navy Second to None, The Development of Modern American Naval Policy*. New York: Harcourt, Brace, 1940.

Deakin, F.W., and Storry, G.R. *The Case of Richard Sorge*. New York: Harper, 1966.

Dieckhoff, Hans Heinrich. *Zur Vorgesschichte des Rooseveltkrieges*. Berlin: Junker & Duennhaupt, 1943.

Dietrich, Otto. *12 Jahre Mit Hitler*. Munich: Gunter Olzog, 1955.

Dodd, William E., and Dodd, Martha. *Ambassador Dodd's Diary, 1933-1938*. New York: Harcourt, Brace, 1941.

Doenitz, Karl. *Die U-Bootswaffe*. Berlin: E.S. Mittler & Sohn, 1939.

——————————————. *Memoirs, Ten Years and Twenty Days*, London: Weidenfeld & Nicolson, 1959.

Dorris, Donald Hugh. *A Log of the "Vincennes."* Louisville: Standard Printing Co., 1947.

Easton, Alan. *50 North, An Atlantic Battleground.* London: Eyre & Spottiswoode, 1963.

Exton, William. *He's In the Destroyers Now.* New York: Robert M. McBride, 1944.

Farago, Ladislos. *The Tenth Fleet.* New York: Obolensky, 1962.

Fernald, John. *Destroyer From America.* New York: Macmillian, 1942.

Frank, Pat, and Harrington, Joseph D. *Rendezvous at Midway, USS "Yorktown" and the Japanese Carrier Fleet.* New York: John Day, 1967.

Frank, Wolfgang. *Enemy Submarine, The Story of Gunther Prien, Captain of U47.* London: William Kimber, 1954.

——————————. *The Sea Wolves.* New York: Ballantine, 1955.

Friedlander, Saul. *Hitler et Les Etats-Unis, 1939-1941.* Geneva: Librairie Droz, 1963.

Furer, Julius A. *Administration of the Navy Department In World War II.* Washington, D.C.: Government Printing Office, 1959.

Gallery, Daniel V. *Clear the Decks!* New York: William Morrow, 1951.

Gemzell, Carl-Axel. *Raeder, Hitler und Skandinavien, Der Kampf für Einen Maritimen Operationsplan.* Lund: CWK Gleerup, 1965.

Gerhart, Eugene C. *America's Advocate: Robert H. Jackson.* Indianapolis: Bobbs-Merrill, 1958.

German Foreign Office. *Roosevelts Weg In Den Krieg, Geheimdokumente zur Kriegspolitik des Praesidenten der Vereinigten Staaten.* Berlin: n.p., 1943.

Giese, Fritz E. *Die Deutsche Marine, 1920-1945.* Frankfurt am Main: Bernard & Graefe, 1956.

Gilbert, Felix. *Hitler Directs His War.* New York: Oxford University Press, 1950.

Gill, Hermon G. *Royal Australian Navy, 1939-1942,* in *Australia in the War of 1939-1945* Series, Series 2 (Navy). Canberra: Australian War Memorial, 1957.

Goebbels, Joseph. *The Goebbels Diaries, 1942-1943.* Garden City: Double-day, 1948.

Goodhart, Philip. *Fifty Ships that Saved the World, The Foundation of the Anglo-American Alliance.* Garden City: Doubleday, 1965.

Grassmuck, George L. *Sectional Biases in Congress on Foreign Policy.* Johns Hopkins University Studies in Historical and Political Science, Series LXVIII, No. 3. Baltimore: John Hopkins Press, 1951.

Great Britain, Air Ministry. *Coastal Command.* New York: Macmillan, 1943.

Greenfield, Kent R. *American Strategy in World War II: A Reconsideration.* Baltimore: Johns Hopkins Press, 1963.

Greiner, Helmuth. *Die Oberste Wehrmachtfuhrung, 1939-1943.* Wiesbaden: Limes, 1951.

Grenfell, Russell. *The "Bismarck" Episode.* New York: Macmillan, 1949.

Gretton, Peter. *Convoy Escort Commander.* London: Cassell, 1964.

Griffin, Alexander T. *A Ship to Remember, The Saga of the "Hornet."* New York: Howell, Soskin, 1943.

Gwyer, J.M.A. *Grand Strategy,* III, Part I. London: Her Majesty's Stationery Office, 1964.

Halder, Franz. *Hitler als Feldherr.* Munich: Muenchener Dom-Verlag, 1949.

——————————. *Kriegestagebuch,* Vols. 1-3. Stuttgart: W. Kohlhammer, 1962-1964.

Halfeld, Adolf. *USA, Greift in die Welt.* Hamburg: Broschek, 1941.

Halifax, Earl of Birkenhead. *The Life of Lord Halifax.* London: Hamish Hamilton, 1965.

Hall, H. Duncan. *North American Supply.* London: Her Majesty's Stationery Office, 1955.

Halsey, William F. and Bryan, J., III. *Admiral Halsey's Story.* New York: McGraw-Hill, 1947.

Hancock, William K., and Gowing, M.M. *British War Economy.* London: His Majesty's Stationery Office, 1949.

Harris, Brayton. *The Age of the Battleship, 1890-1922.* New York: Franklin Watts, 1965.

Hartmann, Werner. *Feind Im Fadenkreuz, U-Boot auf Jagd im Atlantik.* Berlin: Die Heimbucherei, 1942.

Hase, Georg von. *Die Kriegsmarine im Kampf um den Atlantik.* Leipzig: Hase & Koehler, 1942.

Hedin, Sven. *Sven Hedin's German Diary, 1935-1942.* Dublin: Euphorion, 1951.

Heinl, Robert D. *Soldiers of the Sea, The United States Marine Corps, 1775-1962.* Annapolis: U.S. Naval Institute, 1962.

Herlin, Hans. *Verdammter Atlantik, Schicksale deutsche U-Boot-Fahrer.* Hamburg: Nannen, 1959.

Hinsley, F.H. *Hitler's Strategy.* Cambridge: Cambridge University Press, 1951.

Hitler, Adolf. *Mein Kampf.* Boston: Houghton Mifflin, 1925.

——————————. *Hitler's Secret Book.* New York: Grove Press, 1961.

——————————. Hermann Rausching, ed. *Hitler Speaks.* London: Butterworth, 1940.

——————————. Gordon Prange, ed. *Hitler's Words.* New York: American Council on Public Affairs, 1944.

_____. H.R. Trevor-Roper, ed. *Hitler's Secret Conversations, 1941-1944*. New York: Farrar, Strauss & Young, 1953.

Holmes, W.J. *Undersea Victory, The Influence of Submarine Operations on the War in the Pacific*. Garden City: Doubleday, 1966.

Hubatsch, Walther. *Der Admiralstaab und Due Obersten Marinebehörden in Deutschland, 1848-1945*. Frankfurt am Main: Bernard & Graefe, 1958.

Hull, Cordell. *The Memoirs of Cordell Hull*. 2 vols. New York: Macmillan, 1948.

Ickes, Harold L. *The Secret Diary of Harold L. Ickes*. Vols. 2-3. New York: Simon and Schuster, 1953-1954.

Ingraham, Reg. *First Fleet, The Story of the US Coast Guard at War*. Indianapolis: Bobbs-Merrill, 1944.

International Military Tribunal, Nuremberg. *Nazi Conspiracy and Aggression* and *Trial of Major War Criminals*. 14 vols. Washington, D.C.: Government Printing Office, 1946-1948.

Irving, David. *The Rise and Fall of the Luftwaffe*. Boston: Little, Brown. 1973.

Isely, Jeter A. and Crowl, Philip A. *The U.S. Marines and Amphibious Warfare*. Princeton: Princeton University Press, 1951.

Jensen, Amy E. *Iceland: Old-New Republic*. New York: Exposition Press, 1954.

Jones, Ken and Kelly, Hubert. *Admiral Arleigh [31-Knot] Burke, The Story of A Fighting Sailor*. Philadelphia: Chilton, 1962.

Jones, S. Shepard, and Myers, Denys P. (and Goodrich, Leland M., Vol. IV). *Documents on American Foriegn Relations*, I-IV, (1938-1941). Boston: World Peace Foundation, 1939-1942.

Kaden, Kapitänleutnant. *Auf Uboot jagd gegen England*. Leipzig: Hase & Koehler, 1942.

Karig, Walter. *Battle Report, I, The Atlantic War*. New York: Rinehart, 1946.

Keitel, Wilhelm. *The Memoirs of Field-Marshal Keitel*. New York: Stein & Day, 1965.

Kemp, P.K. *Key to Victory, The Triumph of British Sea Power in World War II*. Boston: Little, Brown, 1957.

Kennedy, Ludovic. *Pursuit, The Chase and Sinking of the Bismarck*. New York: Viking, 1974.

King, Ernest J., and Whitehill, Walter M. *Fleet Admiral King, A Naval Record*. New York: Norton, 1952.

Knox, Collie. *Atlantic Battle*. London: Methuen, 1941.

Koenig, Louis W. *The Presidency and the Crisis, Powers of the Office from the Invasion of Poland to Pearl Harbor*. New York: King's Crown Press, 1944.

Kris, Ernst, et al. *German Radio Propoganda*. New York: Oxford University Press, 1944.

Langer, William L. *Our Vichy Gamble*. New York: Norton, 1947.

Langer, William L., and Gleason, S. Everett. *The Challenge to Isolation, 1937-1940*. New York: Harper, 1952.

——————. *The Undeclared War, 1940-1941*. New York: Harper, 1953.

Leahy, William D. *I Was There*. New York: McGraw-Hill, 1950.

LeMay, Curtis E., with Kantor, MacKinley. *Mission With LeMay*. Garden City: Doubleday, 1965.

Leverkuehn, Paul. *German Military Intelligence*. New York: Praeger, 1954.

Lewis, David D. *The Fight For the Sea, The Past, Present, and Future of Submarine Warfare in the Atlantic*. Cleveland: World, 1961.

Livezey, William E. *Mahan on Sea Power*. Norman: University of Oklahoma Press, 1947.

Lockwood, Charles A., and Adamson, Hans C. *Through Hell and Deep Water*. New York: Greenberg, 1956.

Lockwood, Charles A. *Down to the Sea in Subs*. New York: Norton, 1967.

Lott, Arnold S. *Most Dangerous Sea, A History of Mine Warfare, And an Account of US Navy Mine Warfare Operations in World War II and Korea*. Annapolis: U.S. Naval Institute, 1959.

Ludecke, Kurt G.W. *I Knew Hitler*, New York: Scribner's, 1937.

Lueth, Wolfgang, and Korth, Klaus. *Boot Greift Weider an!* Berlin: Erich Klinghammer, 1943.

Macintyre, Donald. *The Naval War Against Hitler*. New York: Scribner's, 1971.

——————. *U-Boat Killer*. London: Weidenfeld & Nicolson, 1956.

——————. *The Battle of the Atlantic*. New York: Macmillan, 1961.

McIntire, Ross T., with Creel, George. *White House Physician*. New York: G.P. Putnam's, 1946.

Manvell, Roger, and Fraenkel, Heinrich. *Goering*. New York: Simon and Schuster, 1962.

Martienssen, Anthony. *Hitler and His Admirals*. New York: E.P. Dutton, 1949.

Matloff, Maurice, and Snell, Edwin M. *Strategic Planning for Coalition Warfare, 1941-1942*, in *US Army in World War II* Series, *The War Department*. Washington, D.C.: Office of Chief of Military History, 1953.

Mauch, Kurt. *Amerika und der Krieg*. Leipzig: Nationale Verlagsgesellschaft, W. Conrad, 1941.

Morison, Elting E. *Admiral Sims and the Modern American Navy*. Boston: Houghton Mifflin, 1942.

_____. *Turmoil and Tradition: A Study of the Life and Times of Henry L. Stimson*. Boston: Houghton Mifflin, 1960.

Morison, Samuel Eliot. *History of United States Naval Operations in World War II*, I, *The Battle of the Atlantic, Sept. 1939-May 1943*. Boston: Little, Brown, 1947.

_____. *History of United States Naval Operations in World War II*, X, *The Atlantic Battle Won, May 1943-May 1945*. Boston: Little, Brown, 1956.

_____. *The Two-Ocean War*. Boston: Little, Brown, 1963.

Morton, H.V. *Atlantic Meeting*, New York: Dodd, Mead, 1943.

Nuechterlein, Donald E. *Iceland, Reluctant Ally*. Ithaca: Cornell University Press, 1961.

Oberkommando der Wehrmacht, *Kriegestagebuch*, I and II. Frankfurt: Bernard & Graefe, 1965.

Ott, Wolfgang. *Sharks and Little Fishes*. New York: Dell, 1957.

Perkins, Frances. *The Roosevelt I Knew*. New York: Viking, 1946.

Pogue, Forrest C. *George C. Marshall, Ordeal and Hope, 1939-1942*. New York: Viking, 1966.

Potter, E.B. et al. *The United States and World Sea Power*. Englewood Cliffs: Prentice-Hall, 1955.

Pratt, Julius W. *Cordell Hull*. I, *1933-1944*. New York: Cooper Square, 1964.

Randall, Thomas H. *Halifax, Warden of the North*. Garden City: Doubleday, 1965.

Raeder, Erich. *Der Kreuzerkrieg*, 2 vols. Berlin: E.S. Mittler & Sohn, 1921.

_____. *My Life*. Annapolis: U.S. Naval Institute, 1960.

_____. *Struggle For the Sea*. London: William Kimber, 1959.

Rayner, D.A. *Escort, The Battle of the Atlantic*. London: William Kimber, 1955.

Ribbentrop, Joachim von. *The Ribbentrop Memoirs*. London: Weidenfeld & Nicolson, 1953.

Riesenberg, Felix. *Sea War, The Story of the US Merchant Marine in World War II*. New York: Rinehart, 1963.

Rigdon, William M., with Derieux, James. *White House Sailor*. Garden City: Doubleday, 1962.

Robertson, Esmonde M. *Hitler's Pre-War Policy and Military Plans, 1933-1939*. London: Longmans, Green, 1963.

Robertson, Terence. *Night Raider of the Atlantic, The Saga of the German Submarine "The Golden Horseshoe," and Her Daring Commander Otto Kretschmer*. New York: E.P. Dutton, 1956.

Rogge, Heinrich. *Die Neutralen und Deutschland*. Berlin: Junker und Duennhaupt, 1940.

Rohwer, Jurgen. *Die U-Boot-Erfolge der Achsenmachte 1939-1945*. Munich: Lehmann, 1968.

Roosevelt, Franklin D. *The Public Papers and Addresses of Franklin D. Roosevelt*, Vols. 7-10. New York, Macmillan, 1941-1950.

——————————. *FDR, His Personal Letters*, III.   New York: Duell, Sloan, & Pearce, 1950.

Roosevelt, James, and Shalett, Sidney. *Affectionately, FDR, A Son's Story of A Lonely Man*. New York: Harcourt, Brace, 1959.

Roscoe, Theodore. *History of United States Destroyer Operations in World War II*. Annapolis: U.S. Naval Institute, 1953.

Rosenman, Samuel I. *Working With Roosevelt*. New York: Harper, 1952.

Roskill, Stephen W. *The War at Sea, 1939-1945*, I, *The Defensive*. London: Her Majesty's Stationery Office, 1954.

——————————. *The Secret Capture*. London: Collins, 1959.

——————————. *The Navy at War, 1939-1945*. London: Collins, 1960.

——————————. *A Merchant Fleet In War, 1939-1945*. London: Collins, 1962.

Ruge, Freidrich. *Der Seekrieg, The German Navy's Story*. Annapolis: U.S. Naval Institute, 1957.

Russell, William. *Berlin Embassy*. New York: E.P. Dutton, 1941.

Schaeffer, Heinz. *U-Boat 977*. New York: Norton, 1952.

Scheer, Reinhard. *Germany's High Seas Fleet in the World War*, London: Cassell, 1920.

Schellenberg, Walter. *The Schellenberg Memoirs*. London: Andre Deutsch, 1956.

Schmidt, Paul. *Hitler's Interpreter*. New York: Macmillan, 1950.

Schofield, William G. *Eastward the Convoys*. Chicago: Rand McNally 1965.

Schull, Joseph. *The Far Distant Ships, An Official Account of Canadian Naval Operations in the Second World War*. Ottawa: Department of National Defense, QPCS, 1961.

Seabury, Paul. *The Wilhelmstrasse, A Study of German Diplomats under the Nazi Regime*. Berkeley: University of California Press, 1954.

Seibert, Theodor. *Das Americanische Ratsel, Die Kriegspolitik der USA unter Roosevelt*. Berlin: Zentralverlag der NSDAP, 1941.

Shafter, Richard A. *Destroyers in Action*. New York: Cornell Maritime Press, 1945.

Shepardson, Whitney H., and Scroggs, William O. *The United States in World Affairs*, 3 vols. (1938-1940). New York: Council on Foreign Relations, Harper, 1939-1941.

Sherwood, Robert E. *Roosevelt and Hopkins.* 2 vols. New York: Bantam, 1948-1950.

Shirer, William A. *Berlin Diary, The Journal of a Foreign Correspondent,* 1934-1941. New York: Knopf, 1941.

Smith, Holland M., and Finch, Percy. *Coral and Brass.* New York: Scribner's, 1948.

Sommer, Theo. *Deutschland und Japan Zwischen den Machten, 1935-1940.* Tübingen: JCB Mohr, 1962.

Stimson, Henry L., and Bundy, McGeorge. *On Active Service in Peace and War.* New York: Harper, 1947.

Taylor, Theodore. *The Magnificent Mitscher.* New York: Norton, 1954.

Thomas, Charles W. *Ice Is Where You Find It.* Indianapolis: Bobbs-Merrill, 1951.

Trefousse, Hans L. *Germany and American Neutrality, 1939-1941.* New York: Bookman Associates, 1951.

Tucker, Gilbert N. *The Naval Service of Canada, Its Official History,* 2 vols. Ottawa: Minister of National Defense, 1952.

Tuleja, Thaddeus V. *Twilight of the Sea Gods.* New York: Norton, 1958.

_____. *Statesmen and Admirals.* New York: Norton, 1963.

Tully, Grace. *FDR, My Boss.* New York: Scribner's, 1949.

Turnbull, Archibald, and Lord, Clifford L. *History of United States Naval Aviation.* New Haven: Yale University Press, 1949.

U.S. Coast Guard, *The Coast Guard at War, Greenland Patrol.* Washington, D.C. n.p., n.d.

U.S. Congress, House and Senate Naval Affairs Committees, *Hearings,* 75th-77th Cong., 1938-1941. Washington, D.C.: Government Printing Office, 1939-1942.

U.S. Congress, *Hearings before the Joint Committee on the Investigation of the Pearl Harbor Attack,* 39 vols. Washington D.C.: Government Printing Office, 1946.

U.S. Department of State, *Documents on German Foreign Policy, 1918-1945,* Series D (1937-1945) 13 vols. Washington, D.C.: Government Printing Office, 1949-1964.

U.S. Department of State, *Foreign Relations of the United States,* (1938-1941). Washington, D.C.: Government Printing Office, 1955-1963.

U.S. Marine Corps, Frank O. Hough, Major Verle E. Ludwig, USMC, and Henry I. Shaw, *Pearl Harbor to Guadacanal, History of U.S. Marine Corps Operations in World War II,* Vol. I. Washington, D.C.: Historical Branch, G-3, HQ, U.S. Marine Corps, 1958.

U.S. Marine Corps, M.L. Brown, *The United States Marines in Iceland, 1941-1942.* U.S. Marine Corps Historical Reference Series, #34, Historical Branch, G-3, HQ, U.S. Marine Corps, 1961.

U.S. Navy, Bureau of Ordnance, Buford Rowland and William B. Boyd, *U.S. Navy Bureau of Ordnance in World War II*. Washington, D.C.: Bureau of Ordnance, Navy Department, 1953.

U.S. Navy, Bureau of Ships, L.S. Howeth, *History of Communications-Electronics in the United States Navy*. Bureau of Ships and Office of Naval History, 1963.

U.S. Navy, Bureau of Yards and Docks, *Building the Navy's Bases in World War II, History of the Bureau of Yards and Docks and the Civil Engineer Corps, 1940-1946*, Vol. I, Washington, D.C.: Government Printing Office, 1947.

Vandegrift, A.A., and Asprey, Robert B. *Once A Marine, The Memoirs of General A.A. Vandegrift*. New York: Norton, 1964.

Vandenberg, Arthur H. *The Private Papers of Senator Vandenberg*, Boston: Houghton Mifflin, 1952.

Vulliez, Albert, and Mordal, Jacques. *Battleship "Scharnhorst."* Fair Lawn, N.J.: Essential Books, 1958.

Warlimont, Walter. *Inside Hitler's Headquarters, 1939-1945.* London: Weidenfeld & Nicolson, 1964.

Watson, Mark S. *Chief of Staff: Prewar Plans and Preparations*, in *US Army in World War II* Series, *The War Department*. Washington, D.C.: Historical Division, Department of the Army, 1950.

Wegener, Wolfgang. *Die Seestrategie des Weltkrieges*. Berlin: E.S. Mittler und Sohn, 1929.

Weigert, Hans W. *Generals and Geographers, The Twilight of Geopolitics*. New York: Oxford University Press, 1942.

Weizsäcker, Ernst von. *Memoirs of Ernst von Weizsacker*. Chicago: Regnery, 1951.

Wertenbaker, Thomas J. *Norfolk, Historic Southern Port*. Durham: Duke University Press, 1962.

Wescott, Allen, et al. *American Sea Power Since 1775*. Philadelphia: Lippincott, 1947.

Williams, Wirt. *The Enemy*. New York: Signet, 1951.

Willoughby, Malcolm F. *The US Coast Guard in World War II*. Annapolis: U.S. Naval Institute, 1957.

Wilson, Theodore A. *The First Summit*. Boston: Houghton Mifflin, 1959.

Winant, John G. *Letter from Grosvenor Square*. Boston: Houghton Mifflin, 1947.

Wirsing, Giselher. *Der Masslose Kontinent, Roosevelts Kampf un die Weltherrschaft*. Jena: Diederichs, 1942.

Woodward, David. *The "Tirpitz" and the Battle for the North Atlantic*. New York: Norton, 1953.

Woodward, Sir Llewellyn. *British Foreign Policy in the Second World War.* London: Her Majesty's Stationery Office, 1962.

Zimmerman, John L. *The First Marine Brigade (Provisional), Iceland, 1941-1942.* Washington, D.C.: U.S. Marine Corps, 1946.

ARTICLES

Arthur, C.S. "A Real Solution to the Paperwork Quandary," *USNIP,* October 1947.

Assmann, Kurt. "Why U-Boat Warfare Failed." *Foreign Affairs,* July 1950.

Atwater, Jon. "Deep Sea Collegians." *Current History,* April 1941.

Baldwin, Hanson. "The Naval Defense of America." *Harper's Magazine,* April 1941.

——————. "If England Falls—*What of the British Fleet?*" *Reader's Digest,* August 1941.

Barker, Edward L. "German Naval Aviation." *USNIP,* July 1950.

Barnett, Correlli. "Sailor With a Flawed Cutlass." in *The Swordbearers, Supreme Command in the First World War.* New York: Morrow, 1964.

Bess, Demaree. "American Strategy Pains Portugal." *Saturday Evening Post,* 30 August 1941.

Boyd, James. "Lookout." *Atlantic,* July 1944.

Bruce, Bryson. "Natural Competition." *USNIP,* August 1948.

Chamberlain, Waldo. "German Naval Strategy in 1914." *USNIP,* September 1940.

——————. "The Tradition of the Offensive in the United States Navy." *USNIP,* October 1941.

Collins, Ross A. "Do We Need a Mass Army." *Reader's Digest,* June 1941.

Cooke, H.D. "The Atlantic Convoys." *USNIP,* August 1950.

Cottle, George F. "The Turnover of Personnel." *USNIP,* March 1939.

Curran, F.M. "Tales of North Atlantic Gales." *USNIP,* November 1944.

Curran, M. "A Naval Reservist's Impressions of a Shakedown Cruise." *USNIP,* April 1939.

Davenport, Walter. "Defense on Ice." *Collier's,* 12 April 1941.

Deac, Wilfred P. "America's Undeclared Naval War." *USNIP,* October 1961.

Diebold, William. "The Wartime Use of Shipping." *Foreign Affairs,* July 1941.

Doughty, Leonard. "The Effect of Depth Charges on Submarines." *USNIP,* March 1935.

Dyer, George C. "Promotion Systems—Past, Present, and Future." *USNIP,* February 1940.

Emerson, William R. "FDR," in May, Ernest R. *The Ultimate Decision, The President as Commander in Chief.* New York: Braziller, 1960.

Evans, Holden A. "Our Muscle-Bound Navy." *Collier's*, 11 June 1938.

Farnum, Grace C. "Claude Augustus Swanson." in *Dictionary of American Biography*, Vol. 22, Supplement II. New York: Scribners, 1958.

Flynn, John T. "Can Hitler Invade America." *Reader's Digest*, April 1941.

Gervasi, Frank. "Our Designs on Martinique." *Collier's*, 11 January 1941.

Greenberg, Daniel S. "US Destroyers for British Bases." *USNIP*, November 1962.

Hanson, Earl P. "Should We Buy Greenland." *Harper's Magazine*, May 1940.

Heinl, R.D. "What Happened to the Royal Marines." *USNIP*, February 1949.

Ide, John M. "Sonar, Secret Weapon of the Sea." *USNIP*, April 1947.

Ihrig, Russell M. "A Pass Defense for the Battle Line." *USNIP*, August 1937.

Jamison, J.W. "German Naval Strategy of the World War." *USNIP*, January 1939.

Kay, Howard N. "The Fifty Old Maids Come Through." *USNIP*, September 1950.

Kirkpatrick, James. "Promotion for Enlisted Men." *USNIP*, January 1932.

Kittredge, Tracy B. "A Military Danger: The Revelation of Secret Strategic Plans." *USNIP*, July 1955.

Knox, Dudley W. "Some Naval Aspects of the War Debt Question." *USNIP*, May 1932.

Koblinski, G. von. "The German Navy." *USNIP*, June 1933.

Lippmann, Walter. "The Atlantic and America." *Life*, 7 April 1941.

_____. "The Case for a Smaller Army." *Reader's Digest*, November 1941.

Lodeman, J.V. "A New Type for the Navy," *USNIP*, June 1932.

McCormick, Robert. "King of the Navy." *Collier's*, 16 January 1943.

McLean, Ephraim R. "The Caribbean—An American Lake." *USNIP*, July 1941.

McMillan, I.E. "Gunfire Support Lessons Learned in World War II." *USNIP*, August 1948.

Martin, Lawrence and Sylvia. "Outpost No. 2: The West Indies, Our New Stake in the Caribbean." *Harper's Magazine*, March 1941.

Masland, John W. "Japanese-German Naval Collaboration in World War II." *USNIP*, February 1949.

Matloff, Maurice. "Mr. Roosevelt's Three Wars: FDR as War Leader." *The Harmon Memorial Lectures in Military History*, #6, Colorado Springs, US Air Force Academy, 1964.

Mercer, David D. "Experiences of a Naval Port Director, 1939-1945." *USNIP*, February 1950.

Merrill, R.T. "The Role of the Coast Guard Within the Navy." *USNIP*, August 1946.

Moran, Charles. "From Greenland's Icy Mountains." *USNIP*, September 1940.

Morison, Elting E. "Naval Administration in the United States." *USNIP*, October 1946.

Morton, Louis. "Germany First: The Basic Concept of Allied Strategy in World War II." Office Chief of Military History, *Command Decisions*. New York: Harcourt, Brace, 1959.

Neumann, William L. "Franklin Delano Roosevelt: A Disciple of Admiral Mahan." *USNIP*, July 1952.

Newsom, Joel. "Results versus Training." *USNIP*, January, 1939.

Padelford, Norman J. "An Atlantic Naval Policy for the United States." *USNIP*, September 1940.

Parker, Ralph C. "An Analysis of the Air Menace." *USNIP*, May 1932.

Percival, Franklin G. "Peace-Time Artificiality." *USNIP*, July 1934.

_____. "Future Naval War." *USNIP*, December 1940.

_____. "What This War Means to the US Navy." *USNIP*, December 1941.

Porter, W.B. "The Development of a Destroyer Watch Officer." *USNIP*, June 1946.

Possony, Stefan. "Decision Without Battle." *USNIP*, June 1946.

Pratt, Fletcher. "The U-Boats are Coming." *Saturday Evening Post*, 6 December 1941.

_____. "The South Atlantic—A Diplomatic Campaign." *USNIP*, June 1948.

Pratt, L. "The Anglo-American Naval Conversations of January 1938." *International Affairs*, October 1971.

Pratt, William V. "Our Naval Policy." *USNIP*, July 1932.

_____. "Warfare in the Atlantic." *Foreign Affairs*, July 1941.

Prendergast, Maurice. "Sonar and Asdic, Anti-Submarine Sisters." *USNIP*, August 1948.

Puleston, William D. "Strategy With a One-Ocean Navy." *Atlantic*, December 1940.

Quinlan, Robert J. "The United States Fleet: Diplomacy, Strategy and the Allocation of Ships, 1940-1941." Harold Stein, *American Civil-Military Decisions*. Birmingham: University of Alabama Press, 1963.

Read, William A. "Anti-Submarine Measures Old and New." *USNIP*, May 1941.

Rosinski, Herbert. "German Theories of Sea Warfare." *Brassey's Naval Annual*, 1940.

_____. "Strategy and Propaganda in German Naval Thought." *Brassey's Naval Annual*, 1945.

Roskill, Stephen W. "Copros Not Convoy: Counter-Attack and Destroy." *USNIP*, October 1956.

Sondern, Frederic. "The Navy: The Silent Service." *Current History*, April 1941.

——————————. "Admiral Stark, Ambassador Extraordinary." *Reader's Digest*, October 1944.

Spilman, C.H. "The German Submarine War." *USNIP*, June 1947.

Stange, Russell P. "Atlantic Conference, The First Roosevelt-Churchill Meeting." *USNIP*, April 1953.

Stanley, Eugene. "The Myth of the Continents." *Foreign Affairs*, April 1941.

Stratton, Roy O. "Germany's Secret Naval Supply Service." *USNIP*, October 1953.

Strohbehn, Walter W. "Should We Train Ships or Men?" *USNIP*, July 1950.

Thomas, Donald T. "The Four-Stackers." *USNIP*, July 1950.

Vosseller, A.B. "The Patrol Plane and the Future." *USNIP*, November 1940.

Votaw, Homer C. "The Brazilian Navy in World War II." *USNIP*, May 1950.

Wiedersheim, William A. "Factors in the Growth of the Reichsmarine, 1919-1939." *USNIP*, March 1948.

Willingham, S.D. "Modern Submarines versus Major Warships." *USNIP*, April 1941.

(The process of preparing a book for publication is an arduous one, beyond the skill and patience of any individual. No author could share this task with better people than those at the Naval Institute Press. I am particularly indebted to Mr. Thomas F. Epley, Editorial Director, for his advocacy of the book and his determination to make it a first-rate production; to Mary Veronica ("Ron") Amoss, the most thorough and nicest editor any author ever had; and to Frank Uhlig, Jr., for his vast knowledge of the U.S. Navy and its ways and his sharp, dry wit. In preparing the book for publication, these people have become more than "my publisher"; they have become my friends.)

Index

505